FAMILIES
IN A
GLOBAL
CONTEXT

FAMILIES IN A GLOBAL CONTEXT

EDITED BY

CHARLES B. HENNON
STEPHAN M. WILSON

Routledge
Taylor & Francis Group

www.routledgementalhealth.com

Routledge
Taylor & Francis Group
270 Madison Avenue
New York, NY 10016

Routledge
Taylor & Francis Group
2 Park Square
Milton Park, Abingdon
Oxon OX14 4RN

© 2008 by Taylor & Francis Group, LLC
Routledge is an imprint of Taylor & Francis Group, an Informa business

Printed in the United States of America on acid-free paper
10 9 8 7 6 5 4 3 2 1

International Standard Book Number-13: 978-0-7890-2708-5 (Softcover) 978-0-7890-2707-8 (Hardcover)

Library of Congress Cataloging-in-Publication Data

Families in a global context / Charles B. Hennon, Stephan M. Wilson.
    p. cm.
  Includes bibliographical references.
  ISBN: 978-0-7890-2707-8 (hard : alk. paper)
  ISBN: 978-0-7890-2708-5 (soft : alk. paper)
  1. Family—Cross-cultural studies. I. Hennon, Charles B. II. Wilson, Stephan M.

HQ515.F3444 2007
306.8509—dc22   2007039822

Visit the Taylor & Francis Web site at
http://www.taylorandfrancis.com

and the Routledge Web site at
http://www.routledge.com

To my family and good friends everywhere,
especially Bruno, Astrid, James, Pete, Stephan,
Wendy, Sarah, Janice, and Tina.
And above all, my daughter Kelsey.

Chuck

I dedicate this book to particular families: Boniface Lele, Wilson and Jane Rose Njue and their families, Alice and Sampson Ondigi and their children, Lucy, Paul, Esther, Tabby, and their family, Kulela wa Mutia, Kamene and Rose, to my closest friends and colleagues at Kenyatta University, and a myriad of others in Kenya; to Huang Ren Song and her family, to Baomei and her family, and to Wenzhen, Jinren, and Huamin and their extended families as well as to colleagues at Zhejiang Shuren, Nanjing Normal, and Nanjing Medical universities in China. I also dedicate this book to my own family—to my wife Kathleen and to our children Amos, Amelia, and Joy who have shared so much of our shared life journeys so far with me as I have encountered and learned from families across cultures.

CONTENTS

MIDDLE EAST: FAMILY LIFE IN TURKEY AND IRAN

ASIA AND OCEANIA: FAMILY LIFE IN INDIA, CHINA, THE PHILIPPINES, AND AUSTRALIA

Chapter 12. Family and Tradition in Modern India 295
Duleep C. Deosthale
Charles B. Hennon

Chapter 13. Chinese Family—Developments and Changes 325
Aimin Wang

Chapter 14. The Family in the Philippines 353
Belen T. G. Medina

EMERGING TRENDS

ABOUT THE EDITORS

Charles B. Hennon is Professor, Department of Family Studies and Social Work, and Associate Director, Center for Human Development, Learning, and Technology at Miami University. Educated at Geneva College and Case-Western Reserve University he was previously Professor of Child and Family Studies, the University of Wisconsin–Madison and is the founding Editor of the *Journal of Family and Economic Issues.* He has been a Visiting Scholar at the John. E. Dolibois European Center, Grand Duchy de Luxembourg as well as at several universities in Brazil and Europe. His scholarly interests include Mexican American families, family supports and interventions, at home employment, religious influences on family functioning, and rural families worldwide. Dr. Hennon is a certified family life educator and is the author of numerous articles, book chapters, and books including co-author of *Family-Centered Policies & Practices: International Implications.*

Stephan M. Wilson is Dean of the College of Human Environmental Sciences and Professor of Human Development and Family Science at Oklahoma State University. His most recent position was Associate Dean for Academic Affairs in the College of Health and Human Sciences and a Professor of Human Development and Family Studies at the University of Nevada, Reno. His PhD and MS are from the University of Tennessee, Knoxville. He was previously a Professor of Family Studies at the University of Kentucky and a Fulbright Visiting Professor at Kenyatta University. Dr. Wilson also lived in Kenya for three years (1976-1978 and 2000-2001) and has done work in China. He has over ninety publications including a recently co-edited volume with Gary W. Peterson and Suzanne K. Steinmetz on *Parent-Youth Relations: Cultural and Cross Cultural Perspectives* (2005). He has served on the Editorial Board for *Family Relations* and for *Marriage and*

Family Review and serves as an occasional reviewer for other journals particularly related to family, culture, and adolescent scholarship. In particular, his scholarship has focused on Chinese, Appalachian, and Kenyan families. He is a certified family life educator. He is a Fellow of the National Council on Family Relations and winner of the Jan Trost Award for lifetime contributions to cross-cultural family scholarship.

CONTRIBUTORS

Maria Lúcia M. Afonso is a psychologist and has a doctorate in education. Retired from Federal University of Minas Gerais (1978-2003), she is a visiting professor at Federal University of São João del Rei, Brazil. Her research interests are related to family, gender relations, group dynamics, and psychosocial intervention. Recent publications focus on group dynamics, family relations, gender, and socialization; books include *Oficinas em dinâmicas de grupo: um método de intervenção psicossocial* (Group dynamic workshops as a method for social action) and *Psicologia Social e Direitos Humanos* (Social psychology and human rights). She has been a consultant for public policies regarding families and communities.

Akbar Aghajanian is Professor of Sociology at Fayetteville State University, a constituent institution of the University of North Carolina. His undergraduate education was at Shiraz University while his graduate work in sociology and demography was completed at Duke University. He has published extensively on families in Iran, and is a noted expert in this area. Articles have appeared in journals such as *International Journal of Sociology of the Family, Journal of Divorce and Remarriage,* and *Demography.* His current research is on evaluation of family planning in Iran.

Sandra Betts is Lecturer in sociology at the University of Wales, Bangor. She received her degree in sociology at the University of London and also studied at the University of Durham. Research interests include gender and the sociology of childhood and the family. In addition to her many other publications, she has edited two books about women in Wales: *Our Daughter's Land: Past and Present* and *Our Sisters' Land: The Changing Identities of Women in Wales.*

Teresa Diaz Canals is Assistant Professor in the Department of Sociology, Faculty of Philosophy and History, University of Havana, Cuba. She is a specialist on ethics and is developing research on morals and families in Cuba and has delivered lectures in several countries such as Argentina, Puerto Rico, Spain, Honduras, and Germany. A recent book is *Ver claro en lo oscuro /El laberinto poético del civismo en Cuba/* (Clearly seeing in the darkness / Poetical labyrinth of civic-mindnedness in Cuba).

Murat Çemrek is in the Department of International Relations at Selcuk University, Konya, Turkey. He received his PhD in political science from Bilkent University and taught in Kyrgyzstan. He has completed postdoctoral research on the relations between Turkey and the European Union (EU) in the Collegium Budapest, Hungary. His publications have appeared in *Euro Agenda*, *Turkish Studies*, and *Tezkir* among others.

Dilek Cindoglu received her PhD from State University of New York at Buffalo. She is Assistant Professor in the Department of Political Science, Bilkent University and serves as assistant chair. She is a sociologist working on gender and work, power, health, and sexuality issues in contemporary Turkey and in the Middle East. She was a visiting fellow at the Center for Gender and Sexuality at New York University, senior fellow at St. Antony's College in Oxford, and an Honorary Fellow and Fulbright scholar at Women's Studies Research Center of University of Wisconsin at Madison, and Visiting Fulbright Specialist at Miami University. The author of around twenty publications, her work has appeared in *Women's Studies International Forum*, *International Journal of Manpower*, and *Journal of Biosocial Science*.

Graham Day is Senior Lecturer in Sociology and Head of School in the School of Social Sciences, University of Wales, Bangor. He was educated at the University of Oxford (MA and PhD). He is joint editor of the journal *Contemporary Wales* and has published widely on the sociology of Wales, community and rural sociology, and economic and social restructuring. Recent books include *Civil Society in Wales: Policy, Politics and People,* and *Making Sense of Wales: A Sociological Perspective.*

Duleep C. Deosthale received his PhD from the University of California, Los Angeles. He also earned masters degrees from Indiana State

University and Jawaharlal Nehru University, a Diploma from University of Barcelona, and a BA from Jawaharlal Nehru University. He has been active in international education for over fifteen years. Presently he is Associate Professor and Assistant Dean for international education at Marist College. Previously, he held the position of Director, Center for International Programs, University of Alabama at Birmingham. He was a visiting professor in Germany. Research interests include film and sexuality, and gypsy families. Among other duties, in his current position he helps international students, especially from India, understand and adjust to American culture. His goal is to identify new models and approaches to internationalizing all aspects of education.

Rosario Esteinou is a Research Professor in the Research and Higher Studies in Social Anthropology Center in Mexico City. Her interests are related to family and kinship. Recent publications have focused on parenting, changes in structure and family relations, history of the family, family roles, new tendencies in family formation, and family policy in Mexico. Dr. Esteinou is the author of numerous articles, books, research reports from different perspectives including anthropology, sociology, demography, and history. Her latest book is *Fortalezas y desafíos de las familias en dos contextos: Estados Unidos de América y México* (Strengths and challenges of families in two contexts: The United States of America and Mexico).

Ana Vera Estrada is a Researcher at the Center for Research about Cuban Culture "Juan Marinell" and Adjunct Professor at University of Havana, Cuba. She earned her PhD at Charles University (Czech Republic). Her recent research interests have been family history, oral history, and oral traditions. She recently prepared a report on this topic for UNESCO. Dr. Estrada has been an invited lecturer at several universities and research institutions in Cuba, Spain, Mexico, United Kingdom, Argentina, Chile, Czech Republic, Dominican Republic, and Barbados. The director of a Permanent Seminar about Family and member of the Group on Family and Childhood of the Social Science Latin American Council, she has been invited to international forums and conferences and has organized lectures and conferences on family in Havana. She was a panel member at the 2006 International Forum, Workshops and Seminars on Population and Migration sponsored by UNESCO at Universidad Nacional de Córdoba, Argentina and has published several reports, articles, and book chapters.

Bruno Hildenbrand completed his studies in sociology, political sciences and psychology at the University of Constance. He is currently Professor at the Institute of Sociology, Friedrich Schiller University of Jena. His previous positions include those he held at the Psychiatric Centre of the Philipps University of Marburg, at Johann Wolfgang Goethe University of Frankfort, and at Berufsakademie, Villingen-Schwenningen. He is also a lecturer and supervisor at the Training Institute for Systemic Therapy and Consultation in Meilen (Zuerich), Switzerland. Regarded as one of the leading qualitative researchers in family sociology, he is former editor of the journal *System Familie* and an Advisory Editor for the journal, *Family Process*. He was co-editor for the special issue Farm Family Responses to Changing Agricultural Conditions: The Actors' Point of View (*Journal of Comparative Family Studies*). A recent book is *Fallrekonstruktive Familienforschung. Anleitungen für die Praxis* (Case reconstruction in family research. Guidance for practice).

Belen T. G. Medina has been with the Sociology Faculty of the University of the Philippines for fifty years. She obtained her BA (cum laude) and MA from the same university, after which she took postgraduate studies at Cornell University as a Fulbright/Smith Mundt scholar. She trained in the Sociology of Development at Delhi University as an UNESCO Fellow and obtained a Certificate in Social Research for Developing Societies (with Merit) at the University of London. With a Ford/Rockefeller grant, she was a visitor at various universities in the United States. She is the recognized expert on the Filipino family and has published many articles and books on this topic. Her book, *The Filipino Family,* now in its second edition, is a widely used university textbook. Professor Medina is an elected life member of the Phi Kappa Phi International Honor Society and the Pi Gamma Mu International Honor Society in Social Science.

Lucy W. Ngige is a Senior Lecturer and Chair of the Department of Family and Consumer Sciences at Kenyatta University in Nairobi, Kenya. She holds a PhD and an MA in Family and Child Ecology from Michigan State University and a BEd from the University of Nairobi. She is a consultant for the Centre for African Family Studies and the African Union (AU) on a continental plan of action for the family in Africa. Dr. Ngige has traveled widely in Africa, Europe, and North America as a visiting scholar and researcher. She has done work for the UN that deals with families and children of the Sudan and related to street children in Nairobi. Dr. Ngige's work on family influences on adolescent social competence and her qualitative work describing African marriage is groundbreaking in East Africa. Her general area of research is marriage and family relationships from a multicultural perspective.

Alice N. Ondigi is a Lecturer in the Department of Family and Consumer Sciences at Kenyatta University in Nairobi, Kenya. She holds a PhD from Kenyatta University and an MEd and BEd from the University of Minnesota. She is a family life educator and has a special research interest in the role of families in human development across the lifespan. The author of seven publications, Dr. Ondigi is conducting a study of competency among Kenya adolescents. She has offered consultancies on HIV/AIDS in the workplace, homeless families, and caregiving.

Rossella Palomba is Head of the Department on Social Behaviour and Policies at the National Institute for Population Research and Social Policies, in Rome. Her main fields of interest include the analysis of changes in family structure and behavior, women's roles within families and society, new lifestyles, and policy implications of demographic trends. She is coordinating a European project on social and family policies. Dr. Palomba is the author of numerous research reports, articles, and books concerning family life, demography, and society such as the two-volume *Population, Family and Welfare.*

Livia Popescu is a Professor in the Social Work Department, Babes-Bolyai University, Cluj-Napoca, Romania. She received her PhD at Babes-Bolyai University. She received a Fulbright fellowship and was in residence at the University of North Carolina at Chapel Hill. More recently, she has been a visiting researcher at Yale. Her primary research projects and publications are on poverty, family policies, and related gender issues. Due to her expertise in these areas, Dr. Popescu has been an invited participant in many international forums, conferences, and research projects. Some of her work has appeared in *Communist and Post-Communist Studies* as well as *Social Work and Globalization.*

Maria Roth is a Professor and Head of the Social Work Department, Babes-Bolyai University, Cluj-Napoca, Romania, where she also earned her PhD in psychology. She is an international member of the Oxford Centre for Research into Parenting and Children. With a Fulbright fellowship she conducted research at the University of North Carolina at Chapel Hill. Child protection, especially abused and disadvantaged children, is her main research domain. A respected expert on children and social policy in Romania, Dr. Roth is frequently invited to participate in international conferences and workshops and to contribute to scholarly publications. Recent books include *Theory and Practice in Social Work* and *Protectia copilului - dileme, conceptii si metode* (Child protection: Dilemmas, concepts and methods). She has published in many journals including *Social Work in Europe* and *Journal of Family and Economic Issues.*

Sule Toktas is Assistant Professor, Isik University, Turkey. She studies minorities, gender, and international migration. Her articles have appeared in journals such as *International Migration, Women's Studies International Forum, European Journal of Women Studies, Minerva,* and *Muslim World* and is co-author of *Yurtdışından Gelenlerin Nicelik ve Niteliklerinin Tespitinde Sorunlar* (Immigration to Turkey: Problems of data collection and evaluation systems). She received her PhD from Bilkent University and has an MS from Middle East Technical University.

Jan Trost is Professor Emeritus of Sociology, Uppsala University, Sweden. He has been a visiting professor at many schools including University of Minnesota, Indiana University, University of North Carolina at Greensboro, University of Leuven (Belgium), and Hebrew University(Israel). He is the author of numerous journal articles and book chapters in several languages; representative books include *Särbo–ett par, två* hushåll (Living Apart Together [LAT] relationships—one couple, two households) and *Familjen i Sverige* (Family in Sweden). His current research deals with conceptualizations of family and also with LAT relationships. He is Honorary President of the Committee on Family Research. His reputation as an international scholar has resulted in the annual Jan Trost Award for Outstanding Contributions to Comparative Family Studies by the National Council on Family Relations.

Tom Spencer-Walters received a BA (with Honors) from the University of Sierra Leone and two MA degrees and a PhD from the

University of Washington. He is Professor and Chair of Pan-African Studies and Coordinator of the African Studies Program at California State University, Northridge. Previously, he was Coordinator of International Programs at CSUN and Resident Director of the California State University International Program at the University of Zimbabwe. The author of a number of books and other publications (e.g., *Shared Visions* and *Memory and Indigenous Knowledge Systems: Africa and the African Diaspora*), his research interests include family dynamics in Africa and the Caribbean and the relationship between orality and literacy. He recently held a Fulbright position at the University of Fort Hare (South Africa) where he conducted examinations of orality, literacy, and voice as collective memory. This research was noted as helping to contribute to the literacy needs of adult learners locally and globally. Professor Spencer-Walters has participated in forums on the conflict in Sierra Leone and currently serves as Executive Consultant for the Freetown Overseas League, Inc.

David de Vaus is Professor of Sociology, and Head of the School of Social Sciences at La Trobe University, Melbourne. He formerly was Head of Research and Senior Principal Research Fellow at the Australian Institute of Family Studies. He is well known as an expert on family life in Australia and is the author of many research reports, journal articles, book chapters, and a number of books, including *Letting Go: Relationships Between Adults and Parents* and *Diversity and Change in Australian Families.*

Aimin Wang is an Associate Professor at Miami University, Oxford, Ohio. He has a BS and MS from Peking University in Beijing, China, and a PhD in child development from the University of Nebraska–Lincoln. On the faculty of Peking University for seven years and a visiting professor at the University of Nebraska-Lincoln, after completing his PhD he joined Miami University. He has authored several book chapters and books in China, such as *JiaTing XiLi* (Family psychology). He also has published over 20 articles and many book chapters, in both China and the United States, in the areas of children's social development and cross-cultural studies.

Gizem Zencirci is a PhD candidate in the Department of Political Science, Bilkent University. She holds an MA and a BA from the same department. Her general research areas involve theories of nationalism, the politics of the subject, ideology, state-building, and the public sphere, as well as issues of gender, sexuality, and urban studies. Papers have been presented at conferences such as Secularism, Religious Nationalism, and the Public Sphere in Comparative Perspective.

Susan Ziehl is Associate Professor in the Department of Sociology and Industrial Sociology, Rhodes University, Grahamstown, South Africa. Previously she spent two years at the University of Neuchatel, Switzerland. She received graduate degrees from the University of Stellenbosch and Rhodes University. Her many publications show that her research interests include feminism and modern reproductive technology (particularly surrogacy), family law and multiculturalism, single-parent families, and affirmative action and sexual harassment policies. Professor Ziehl is producing some of the leading scholarship on family life in South Africa, a relatively new focus of scientific study in her country. Her published work includes articles in *African Socio-logical Review, Society in Transition,* and *Social Work,* plus the book *Population Studies.* She was a Chief Research Specialist at the Child, Youth and Family Development Unit of the Human Sciences Research Council in Cape Town.

Chapter 1

Families in Global Context: Understanding Diversity Through Comparative Analysis

Charles B. Hennon
Stephan M. Wilson

From Africa to Asia, the chapters in this book explore the rich variety of family life in seventeen countries. This book exposes readers to in-depth information about a range of family dynamics in each country and demonstrates the diversity in family structures and functioning around the world, apparent not only across nations, but also within. The reader can learn both about specific facets of family life as components of the larger family system, and about family life contextualized within a specific socioeconomic, political, and religious milieu. Using the UN Human Development Index (United Nations Development Programme, 2006), eight nations can be classified as having High Human Development, seven as having Medium Human Development, and two as having Low Human Development.[1]

There are several important features of this book. First, the contributors write about family life in their own natal societies using, to the extent possible, information published in their countries and languages. This approach allows for within cultural understanding. By synthesizing this information, using a comparative analysis approach, readers can gain insights and understanding about families across societies. This allows for cross-cultural or cross-national understanding.

The Series Editor, Suzanne K. Steinmetz, wishes to acknowledge Sean Ascani for editorial assistance.

An "insider's view" (i.e., emic) of family life in each country allows for in-depth understanding of the complexity of family life. This book is thus different from a book written with an "outsider's view" (i.e., etic) by people having less understanding of the culture and societal organization. While all contributors synthesize research and demographic data, they also offer narrative explanations and interpretations. Each contributor interprets his or her country's family life based on a lived experience with an insider's authentic understanding.

Second, all chapters follow a common outline and provide comprehensive information about a broad range of issues typical of family life. Each chapter contains roughly the same type of information. The format allows for a comparative and analytical review of families from different countries. This is to help the reader integrate information into a coherent and meaningful whole. There are, of course, variations among the chapters, as in some cases less information is available. For example, Sierra Leone has been racked for years by war, and there is little social science research to draw upon. In South Africa, Kenya, and Cuba the family as an object of scientific study is in an embryonic state.

Third, the contributors give background information about their countries and the place of families within this broader context. This is to help the reader to have some sense of important historical, political, and religious influences, the economic situation, and other conditions within which families operate. Several contributors write about the influences of industrialization, urbanization, globalization, and Westernization as well as the adoption of information, mass media, and other technology. For example, the chapter on family life in Romania gives extensive information about the transition to a post-Communist society and the concomitant changes in the economy and other aspects of life. Likewise, the chapter on Germany points out the consequences reunification has had on the society and the differences still found between former East and West Germany. Cuban families cannot be understood without an appreciation of living in a socialist state. One cannot understand the twenty-first century Chinese family without some appreciation of the thousands of years of history and its influence on contemporary family life in the world's most populous country. In Turkey, Mexico, and South Africa there have been policies to increase both "modernization" and resiliency in traditional patterns. These countervailing forces give opportunities to, and place challenges before, today's families. The chapter on German family life presents a case study of one family's attempt to balance the demands of modernization and traditionalism.

ORGANIZATION OF THE BOOK
AND OF THE CHAPTERS

This chapter offers an introduction to the book and why it is impor- tant to consider families more globally. Chapters 2 through 18 are organized according to geographic regions (family life in Europe, Africa, Middle East, Asia and Oceania, and Latin America), explore family life in individual societies, and generally observe a standard outline (described in following text). In addition to offering some of our own conclusions and observations, Chapter 19 raises questions about intersections and unique patterns across these seventeen countries and explores some possible crosscutting themes of global families. The editors invite readers to carry out analyses and to forecast likely emerging patterns.

Introduction and overview. Each chapter begins by describing the "typical" types of family patterns within the country's social organization and culture. Important social, economic, political, and other trends are mentioned. Major ethnic, religious, or other subcultures are noted especially as they display marriage and family patterns that differ from the more typical ones. This introduction identifies the family pattern that will be the focus for the analysis in the chapter, that is, the one(s) best describing family life in this country. Demographic and other data are provided, as well as narrative descriptions. A subsection on the family in context gives important information about what might make family life unique in this particular country.

Couple formation and marital dynamics. An analysis of mate selection patterns and customs with an emphasis on the dynamics of couple formation is found here. Included are parental or other kin influence on (or arrangement of) marriages, norms and laws influencing couples, average age at first marriage, cohabitation before marriage, and sexual norms and behaviors. Typical marital roles and dynamics are noted, including issues like love and mate choice, sexuality, and dissolution of relationships. Some chapters present information concerning marriage types, some others report what makes marriages successful. While

typical patterns are described, diversity within the country is explored.
In some cases, wedding customs are explained.

Families and children. Each chapter reviews the place and role of
children and parenting in families. Average family size, birth intervals,
abortion, gender preferences, differences in socialization between boys
and girls, and parenting styles and practices are typically noted. Fertility trends are highlighted. Child-care programs and policies and other
supports for families are discussed. Many contributors discuss the value
of children to parents and to society.

Families and gender. Socialization for gender roles is explained.
Differences in education, employment, and other opportunities are
summarized. Power distribution and employment-family issues are
explained, as are division of labor (household, including employment and food production/preparing), family roles, and sexuality.
A powerful organizing factor in every society, contributors explain
what makes gender important in their countries and why. Trends toward more egalitarian roles are often noted, as are important laws
and social policy.

Families and stress. Major stressors affecting families, in regard to
coping, and adaptation are noted. Careful analyses of one or a few of
these are provided. The emphasis is on survival and resiliency in the
face of adversity, rather than family deficits. Family supports and services are noted as appropriate.

Families and aging. Life expectancy, the proportion of the population considered elderly, and other such facts are typically presented.
This section considers aging within a family context. Family caregiving and how this might differ by gender, social class, and ethnicity
is given special attention. The role of the elderly within families and
society is discussed.

Other family situations. Contributors discuss family patterns that
diverge from the more typical pattern being described. Topics include
remarriages, adoptive families, and extended households, impact of
HIV/AIDS or other major health threats on families, impact of poverty
on families, or some analysis of a common pattern among an ethnic,
religious, or other minority group.

Concluding comments. The chapters conclude with some insightful
remarks about the current state of affairs surrounding families, and
thoughts about what the future might bring.

While all chapters follow a standard outline and contain similar information, they emphasize different topics and have different ways of presenting the information. Occasionally, with the consent of the contributors, additional information, such as current fertility or infant mortality rates, was added. While editing for clarity of expression, an attempt was made not to impact cultural nuances. The reviewing process led to the suggestions for continuity of voice. However, our hope is that we preserved the speakers' own voice to come through thus honoring the richness of cultural expression.

While there is some uniformity of content, there are many examples of rather unique topics. Just a few of the topics covered include

- virginity tests and reconstructive virginity surgery;
- the relationship between bride price and dowry and how these influence mate selection;
- arranging marriages including the use of matchmakers;
- marriage styles, marrying foreigners for economic gain, and keys to successful marriage;
- walking marriages, temporary marriages, gynaegamy, polygyny, and cohabitation;
- divorce rates, laws, "fatherectomy," and correlates of divorce;
- different sets of laws governing the marriages and family life of different religious/ethnic groups within the same country;
- parental leaves, child allowances, and parenting practices including not being allowed to spank children;
- names of children having to be gender specific and laws about surnames;
- adoption, child circulation, fosterage, and flexibility in family units;
- female genital mutilation (i.e., female circumcision);
- domestic violence, honor killings, bride burnings, and the Women's Refuge movement;
- adult children living with their parents;
- caregiving expectations and living arrangements of the elderly, and impacts of policy;
- influences of religion and government policies on family dynamics;
- family hardships related to poverty, war, and social unrest.

LESSONS LEARNED

There are many different ways for families to meet their basic needs as well as to enjoy a certain quality of life. This book does not argue that there are universal or standard ways to solve family problems. With globalization, Westernization, and the movement toward a "global village," there is some convergence of family life patterns (e.g., marrying for love or more egalitarian gender roles). However, there are still important differences across and within societies, sometimes remarkably so. While there are important lessons to be learned about how different families nurture their members, select their mates, manage their stress, and otherwise function, the contributors represented here do not attempt to suggest the one best answer. Rather, the emphasis is on the diversity of lifestyles and family forms found throughout the world.

While there is a discourse about how lessons learned and/or solutions to family dilemmas in one country can be used in other countries, context must be considered (Hennon, Jones, Roth, & Popescu, 1998). Differences in family traditions, religions, cultural values and norms, and typical worldviews about what is right and normal, must be considered for thorough understanding. While indicating how different people often facing relatively similar circumstances attempt different solutions, this book does not suggest that there is a "one size fits all" approach to describing or supporting families.

Another important element to notice is that one cannot necessarily impose policy ideas, concepts, models, or other ideas from one country/ culture to another. Several contributors make this point. The concept of family is different in China or India than in the West. The concept of nuclear family in Mexico differs in important ways from other Western nations. Typical models of the life cycle or families being coresident units do not fit the reality of South Africa. Issues of gender differ widely across the globe, for example, in Iran and Turkey compared with Romania or Brazil. Concepts like stress are not commonly used in India and family stress is relatively unstudied in Italy. Theoretical models of family change used in other societies do not fit the actualities of Italy.

UNDERSTANDING FAMILIES:
CONCEPTUALIZATIONS OF CULTURE AND FAMILY

This book takes the perspective that globally, some aspects of human behavior are more commonly practiced and thus recognizable and understandable. However, culture shapes many behaviors. Culture refers to what a particular collective of people share in common and distinguishes them from other collectives or cultures. Culture encompasses both an abstraction (underlying values and assumptions) and a lived (specific behavior derived from values and assumptions) aspect. One is observable and one is not. Specific behaviors shared by a cultural group are not arbitrary; they are consistent with what the people of that culture value and believe. Without understanding the abstract values and worldviews, behavior is often misunderstood. Understanding the basis of behavior allows for not being surprised, avoiding a cultural faux pas, operating within the context of this culture, and conducting better research. It does not mean one has to like or accept the behavior or the values.

Another dimension of human behavior is the personal. This is how each person or family is unique from each other even within the same culture. Not everyone sharing a culture thinks, values, or acts alike (*Culture Matters,* n.d.). There is a substantial amount of diversity in family life when considered from a global perspective. Understanding the differences among families within countries as well as across countries is becoming more important, both for serious students of the family and for enhancing global literacy. The situations that challenge each family and the strategies each family uses to meet its needs and achieve its goals vary widely. Each family is unique in this way, but within cultures and subcultures, and even across cultures, some more general patterns are observable.

Readers of this book will notice that some societies appear to have a more homogenous family pattern than do others. Even while this might be true, given the space limitations, it is not possible to give equal weight to the within country diversity found in many nations. However, contributors do highlight important differences within their societies. For example, differences among ethnic groups in Kenya and Sierra Leone, blacks and whites in South Africa, and the indigenous peoples compared with more recent immigrants in Australia.[2]

All societies recognize families. However, what is family is often debated. In this book, family is often regarded as an analytical concept or as a socially constructed object (Gubrium & Holstein, 1990). As Gubrium and Holstein (1990, p. 13) stated, "The term 'family' is part of a particular discourse for describing human relations in or out of the household." Family life emerges from commonplace interactions and communications with others. These lead to the understanding of family in terms of relationships acknowledged by the participants as family within a certain cultural context. Even within the more hegemonic forces of a culture indicating what a family "should be," there will be variations. For example, in the United States, a same-sex couple with children does not fit the standard legal and often moral conceptualization of family. Yet, the people in these relationships consider their relationships and interdependencies as being "their family." The same can be true of polygamous families living in the western United States. The practice of gynaegamy among the Kisii in Kenya is another example that is discussed in this book. Distinct from lesbian couples, in this practice an older woman assumes the responsibilities of a "husband and father," adopts the children of the younger woman, and provides for the family. If the younger woman has no children, arrangements are made for a "sperm donor" from among close relatives of the older woman (Wilson, Ngige, & Trollinger, 2003).

Some contributors in this book indicate that the concept of family is a matrix for behavior and social control. It is thus a framework to guide behavior, indicating rights, responsibilities, and obligations. With these ideas in mind, one can come to see that "family" in China does not necessarily mean the same thing as "family" in Sweden or Wales. Each cultural group has expectations for what a family unit is and does. The degree to which a set of family relations comprise a distinct social unit and the range of activities that are carried out by this unit varies from nation to nation, culture to culture, and even family to family.

Culture is not deterministic (Anderson & Sabatelli, 2007; Derné, 1994; Irvine, 1995; Sandstrom, Martin, & Fine, 2003). People pick and choose, innovate, and create ways of living that can then become part of the cultural framework. In this book, culture and societal organization are understood as important influences and traditions for how people actually function in the situational framework of personal lives and family responsibilities. Social groups construct shared expectations about "family" and "not-family" that link notions of dependency, emotional bonding, connectedness, power, distribution of resources, and division of labor.

UNDERSTANDING FAMILIES: APPRECIATING INTRA- AND INTERCULTURAL DIVERSITY IN "BEING FAMILY"

Cherishing and valuing families is important. This leads to concern about and social action on behalf of families and their members. Social action (including policies, programs, education, and so on) can be enhanced and more effective with grounding in solid knowledge. However, studying and understanding families are complex processes. The relationships themselves are complex and intimate, often regarded as private, even sacred (Newman, 1999). Results of studies are presented and integrated in this book as well as other books; readers may benefit from this information. Reflection on diversity, acceptance, and understanding may follow. This method of analysis, dissemination, and learning is important. However, knowledge is not complete and final. The "truth" about families is still unfolding and ever changing.

Families are empirically known entities. That is, besides a concept of family known to people, family units can also be identified empirically. They are real entities, groups within which people act. However, they are also idealized and romanticized. The correspondence between the real (or empirical) world of families and the "ideal type" prescribed by cultural values is often less clear than what textbooks or cultural commentaries (e.g., mass media and religious groups) would perhaps suggest. "When we speak of the character of the family, the structures and functions of the family, we imply a thing, a solid and evident, tangible or intangible object of experience, something of substance and boundaries" (Gubrium & Holstein, 1990, p. 7). Moreover, when information about families is presented, it is often not clearly noted that there can be a distinction between the family as an institution and families as empirical entities. That is, the family as represented in cultural values, expected norms, laws, and the like versus the lived lives of real people. In this handbook, there are aspects of both levels presented.

All families are unique, and no family matches perfectly the model through an amalgamation of divergent research. One should not reify the concept of family or the generalizations about families to the extent that they become "the family" in a particular culture or society. What are real are the everyday lives of billions of people as they are "living and being family." The contributors to this book present an abstraction, derived by integrating research about the realities of families. By considering what is important and given the information available, these contributors "tell a story" concerning what they perceive as "typical families" in their nations. Across cultures (i.e., within and among nations) there are many ways of being family. Not all diversity, all uniqueness, all idiosyncratic variations, can be presented in one book.

UNDERSTANDING FAMILIES:
A COMPARATIVE ANALYSIS PERSPECTIVE

There are several reasons why comparative analysis is helpful for gaining more understanding about family life. Building upon the work of Kenkel (1977), four reasons are presented here.

Comparative analysis can build an appreciation of intercultural family variability and uniformity. Examining other societies provides knowledge and insight concerning the diversity of family organization. Such analysis also helps in sensitizing one to the meaning a certain practice has for the people involved. Examples might include polygamy and monogamy, cohabitation and marriage, staying married or getting divorced, arranged or self-choice marriages, or differential socialization practices for boys and girls. By considering the practice within its cultural context, one can come to have a better understanding of how the practice interweaves with other aspects of family life and how the members of that culture consider it. This intracultural or endemic understanding can then broaden to appreciation of intercultural variability as well as apparent similarities across cultures.

Comparative analysis can enhance objectivity and scholarly understanding. By considering a familiar phenomenon (e.g., mate selection) within an unfamiliar setting, it comes into sharper relief. Objectivity and emotional detachment can be gained through comparative analysis, especially as one employs cultural relativism. Withholding judgment, remaining detached and objective, and considering the place of families or family practices in a culture allows for a sharper analysis. By considering the practice within its cultural context, one can better understand its intended function. Comparing practices across societies, one can appreciate the diversity of ways to meet similar objectives. While subjectivity and personal values still come into play, objectivity can then be used to consider one's own culture as well as other cultures.

Comparative analysis can give a more sensitive appreciation of family patterns within one's own culture. People are often able to be more "objective" about the behavior of other people than about their own behavior. Pervasive and idiosyncratic aspects of one's own society become clearer when contrasted with other societies. By considering a "foreign" practice while making comparative reference to a "familiar" practice, one can start to see the familiar in new, perhaps more objective, ways. For example, the roles of men and women in one's own society can be seen in a new light when one understands the roles of women and men in other societies. How mates are selected, the elderly cared for, or stress managed in one's own society can be juxtaposed with patterns in other societies. Sensitivity to the benefits and shortcomings of the "familiar" and how these relate to other social conditions can be gained. One can perhaps come to better "see" families in her or his more familiar surroundings. Through comparative analysis, what is "natural" and "normal" might be reconsidered as "constructed" and "conventional."

Comparative analysis can motivate people to formulate new questions and hypotheses. For example, when considering social policies and families in a particular country, one might wonder why there are no similar policies in other countries and what would happen if there were. Or, one might be led to wonder how women are controlled sexually and if similar social factors are associated with such control in different societies. This reasoning can lead to hypotheses about what would happen under various conditions of social change to the methods used and the extent of control exercised over women. The same can be said about families dealing with the stress of poverty. Would methods used in South Africa also work in Brazil, China, Germany, or Turkey? The comparative perspective gives a different lens and increases the analytical ability to examine families. Such reasoning might also lead one to ponder if a better society can be engineered.

Yorburg (2002) offers a few additional reasons for a comparative approach. One is determining the importance of genetic factors as opposed to cultural or other factors in determining certain aspects of family life. Such factors might include power distribution, domestic violence, or sexuality. A second reason (similar to what was discussed previously) is learning what is universal and thus presumably essential about family life. Such knowledge can inform debates about whether other organizations can meet basic human needs or in some way substitute for family functioning. A third reason is making judgments about whether families are in some way better or worse off than in the past. This reasoning is based on a type of comparative approach that is historical in nature. A fourth reason is predicting the future. If variation among factors in one society are related to certain outcomes, and similar variations and outcomes are discovered in other societies, then one can predict with more confidence what might happen in an even greater number of societies. As Yorburg (2002, p. 10) argued, "if we compare societies and understand *why* recent trends in family life are happening, we can be more confident about predicting family relationships in the future." Prediction, or perhaps more precisely termed, forecasting, is important; it allows governments and others to better anticipate and plan for the future needs of families and their members.

Several years ago, Sirjamski (1964, p. 34) summarized the rationale for using comparative analysis in family studies.

> The comparative method makes possible a cultural and historical analysis of family organization and institutions in societies. It permits cross-cultural generalizations about families that reveal their universal character in world societies and their particular character in individual societies in the same or different regions or periods. It provides a means to interpret historical changes in families, and to relate these to other social and cultural changes in societies.

Much more recently, Bell and Bell (2000), Adams (2004), Adams and Trost (2005), Ingoldsby and Smith (2005), and Campos (2006), among others, have made similar observations—that a comparative analysis requires theories to explain more, that broader generalizations can be established, and new propositions can be specified to explain discrepant findings from different societies. It is obvious that generalizations about phenomena cannot be made if information about these phenomena is limited to a single culture. However, many of the propositions that are treated as universal explanatory statements and generalizations are based on information obtained in only one society, often the United States or other Western societies. It is questionable if these propositions have "culture free" validity and applicability within other cultures. Systematic comparative analysis is thus vital for gaining better understanding of, and developing explanations about, families. Such information can then be more valid and global.

In many ways, cross-national inconsistencies (i.e., diversity) contribute to increasing knowledge about families. Inconsistencies produce tension for more detailed consideration and explanation. Why are there differences? Why do all societies (or similar societies) not have similar family organizations, or experience similar changes over time in family patterns? Specification in explanations can be better achieved by comparative analysis. That is, some explanations become more generalized and less culture bound while other explanations are seen as endemic to a particular societal context. Consequently, both the goals of universal as well as contextualized understanding can be forwarded via comparative analysis.

As a technique, comparative analysis helps in extending the understanding of what aspects of family life are more universal and which are more particular to a culture. Likewise, comparative analysis can help remove idiosyncratic and ethnocentric blinders that hinder understanding of why family life is organized as it is and what it means to the participants. Readers of this book can come to see that the familiar can be complex and the unfamiliar can be made more understandable, and that while there are some aspects of families that appear to be more universal, there are many aspects that are more particular.

NOTES

1. The Human Development Index is a ranking of 177 nations according to the combined factors of longevity (life expectancy at birth), knowledge (adult literacy rate and school enrollments), and a decent standard of living (based on purchasing power parity). The Index is constructed from currently available indicators. The various Human Development Reports provide a wealth of information about countries separately as well as aggregate data. The Index is an alternative to other development indicators, as it focuses more on the living conditions of real people even

while tapping reports for a variety of specific indicators (e.g., health, technology, fertility, education, and poverty) can help one better understand the context of families within a specific society or comparatively across societies. The Index and Reports are used throughout this book. For more information, see United Nations Development Programme (2006). Family life in the nations with High Human Development covered in this book are (with the 2006 ranking in parentheses): Australia (3), Sweden (5), Italy (17), United Kingdom (Wales) (18), Germany (21), Cuba (50), Mexico (53), and Romania (60 and having recently moved from Medium to High Human development). Those nations with Medium Human Development are: Brazil (69), China (81), The Philippines (84), Turkey (92), Islamic Republic of Iran (96), South Africa (121), and India (126). The nations included with Low Human Development are Kenya (152) and Sierra Leone (176).

2. Using nations as the reference for locating families as "types" and discussing family life only within a specific nation has some drawbacks. The world has been and is still becoming more homogeneous in many regards. The patterns of family life found in a society today are the result of a cultural mélange resulting from centuries of contact with other groups. However, using nations as a focal point helps readers have a sense of location and is a way to identify family life within a society having spatiotemporal boundaries. This is not to imply that these societies are static entities and in all ways dissimilar from each other, or that all families within a society will be mostly similar to each other while having less in common with families within other national boundaries. There are certainly conditions such as laws, social policy, cultural norms, geography, and history that function to provide an extent of homogeneity among families within particular societies. However, there is also heterogeneity of families within societies to keep in mind. Too great an emphasis on "the family" within "a country" might obscure important differences within that society, and some identified difference or diversity in family life across nations could be more apparent than real.

EUROPE:
FAMILY LIFE IN WALES,
SWEDEN, GERMANY, ROMANIA,
AND ITALY

Chapter 2

The Family in Wales:
Change and Transformation

Sandra Betts
Graham Day

INTRODUCTION

The family in Wales achieved notoriety in 1995 when a prominent
government minister, visiting a large public housing district in the capital city, Cardiff, drew attention to the exceptionally high proportion
of local households headed by single mothers (see, for example, "Is
This What John Redwood Meant," 2003). His comments set off a public debate in which many of the social ills and problems of modern
Britain were attributed to the condition of the contemporary family
and its recent transformation from what was assumed as its "traditional" or normal pattern. Subsequently, the family has been at the
center of a number of policy interventions and measures aimed at re-
storing it to its previous stability. Although similar observations
could have been made about comparable areas in many other British
cities, it was no accident that a visit to Wales should have triggered
such a furor. Wales has undergone rapid, and often dislocating, social
change and in many ways its experiences in the course of its transition toward a postindustrial social order typify what has happened in
the rest of the British Isles as well.

Wales is one of the three countries of the island of Great Britain,
situated on the west, facing the Irish Sea. A large part of its geography
consists of rural upland terrain. Modern Wales was formed during the

industrial revolution, when its coal, iron, and steel industries assumed worldwide importance. The bulk of its population at that time gravitated toward the booming South Wales coalfield, where the majority of the current population, of just fewer than three million, continues to live. The expansion of the industrial labor force also attracted many English and Irish migrants, as well as small numbers of people from a variety of other ethnic backgrounds. Many settled in the dock areas servicing the export trade. The larger part of Wales remained, however, a thinly populated and relatively impoverished rural countryside, with a comparatively homogeneous population (Adamson & Jones, 1996). Marked rural-urban contrasts persist to the present day. The old industries, which exercised an enormous power over the formation of characteristic patterns of Welsh life, including the family, declined dramatically from the 1960s onward. They have been largely eclipsed by the rise of the modern service economy, which accounts for 60 percent or more of current employment, and by the development of newer industries such as electronics and engineering (Day, 2002). This economic and social restructuring put Wales at the forefront of the deindustrializing and reindustrializing experiences of the 1980s and led to major disruptions in many local communities. Combined with radical changes in welfare policy aimed at increasing levels of individual responsibility and reducing alleged "dependency," this has resulted in significant adjustments to family composition and organization (cf. Rosser & Harris, 1995).

The national miners' strike of 1984-1985 encapsulated much of this change. A defeat of a trade-union-led struggle to defend an established pattern of working and community relations resulted in the virtual disappearance from Wales of an industry once employing a quarter of a million men (one in every four male Welsh employees). Around this industry had grown a distinctive kind of stable working-class community with a strong social and cultural identity. Newer kinds of work required a different workforce, including greater numbers of female employees, located in new places. Consequently, there is a new economic and social geography in Wales, linked with new patterns of class and gender relations (Day, 2002). Adaptation to these changes required many individuals and families to show considerable flexibility and mobility, both socially and geographically, now frequently asserted as essential values in relation to economic survival and prosperity.

Rural parts of Wales have undergone similar changes. The relative decline of agriculture, and the development in its place of small-scale manufacturing and service activities such as tourism and leisure, has brought about comparable shifts in community structures and in rural lifestyles. These are associated with significant demographic changes linked to urban-rural migration and retirement relocation. These changes have important consequences for family adjustments through the life cycle and for relationships with wider kin (i.e., family members outside the immediate household).

Although varying in details from what has happened elsewhere in Britain, most of these developments are not unique to Wales. Wales has been fully incorporated within the United Kingdom (UK) for centuries, and in almost all respects its legal and governmental system corresponds to that of its dominant neighbor, England. Welsh people have been subject to the same laws, regulations, and policies, and share the same broad social and cultural characteristics as their English counterparts. However, since 1999 there has been significant devolution of powers to implement policy to a new Welsh Assembly in Cardiff, which has taken over some of the executive functions previously administered from the British parliament at Westminster (National Assembly of Wales, n.d.). There are some early signs of policy divergence in key areas, including education and social welfare, which have implications for Welsh families.

Families in Welsh Context

Welsh families closely resemble English and wider British norms. Where Wales differs most noticeably is in the survival, and indeed the recent revival, of the Welsh language spoken by about one-fifth of the population (Day, 2002). Numerically, the majority of Welsh speakers live in the more heavily populated south of the country, but the presence of the language is most marked in the more remote, and relatively rural, areas of the west and north. In some areas it remains the dominant language of the home. The language is connected closely to an awareness of a separate Welsh cultural and national identity. These have been recognized through the gradual development of a set of distinctive political and bureaucratic institutions, as well as in continuing demands for greater autonomy. The language continues to provide the focus for a distinct ethnic and national awareness of Welshness, expressed through a vigorous campaign to preserve and develop the everyday use of Welsh. However, many of the other features that once distinguished Wales from England, such as the importance of nonconformist Protestant religion and an ethos of political radicalism and socialism, are no longer particularly marked. The past century saw a considerable convergence between Wales and the rest of the United Kingdom. At the same time differences have increased within Wales, between areas and between different social groupings, making Wales at present quite a fragmented country and society (Day, 2002; Osmond, 1988).

Given these matters, it is not surprising that Wales has faced major changes in family life over the past thirty years. The picture today is one of considerable family diversity, and uncertainty, surrounding an increasingly differentiated process of family formation, in which few of the supposedly established features of family life and familial ideology have gone unchallenged. Traditional nuclear families, consisting of a married couple residing with dependent children, account now for less than one-quarter of all households (Office of National Statistics [ONS], 2001). For growing numbers of individuals, this represents just one of several possible family types that they will encounter during their lifetimes. Changes in patterns of marriage, cohabitation, divorce, childbearing, and lone parenting have produced new variants of household composition and new styles of family life, in a period of exceptionally rapid, and occasionally disorienting, social change.

COUPLE FORMATION AND MARITAL DYNAMICS

Despite the extensive changes that have been occurring, sometimes producing panic reactions predicting the imminent decline or collapse of the family, officially sanctioned and celebrated marriages remain the foundation of most British families. Marriage is sustained as the normal pattern by a host of social, legal, and economic supports. There are 1.2 million households in Wales, of which 37 percent include a married couple with or without children (ONS, 2001). As is the case throughout the United Kingdom, marriages are contracted monogamously, and at least theoretically, based on free choice and romantic love. Affective individualism is the major influence on marriage and couple formation. The centrality of ideologies of romantic love and individualism is reinforced in a variety of ways, not least through the role of the media including popular magazines and television. Couples are expected to develop mutual affection stemming from personal attraction and compatibility as a basis for contracting marriage relationships. The expectation is that marriage will be rewarding and satisfying for both partners, who, at least in principle, hold equal and independent status in the relationship. In most cases, other family members exert only a limited influence over the choices made by individuals (Rosser & Harris, 1995; Yewlettt, 1996).

Typically, the neo-local residence of a nuclear unit characterizes family formation. The nuclear unit almost invariably forms a separate household although it will maintain connections, to varying degrees, with wider kin. In the recent past, the classic extended family pattern of frequent contact and geographical proximity was well established in many parts of Wales. This pattern was typical in both rural and urban working-class communities (Rees, 1950; Rosser & Harris, 1995). Now it is much weaker owing to greater mobility and spatial spread, and higher levels of household self-sufficiency. A wide range of socially accepted, as well as less approved, variations exist side by side with these more typical characteristics, leading to quite varied family forms within contemporary Wales. Over the next few years the number of married couple households is expected to decline with a corresponding increase in other kinds of households, particularly that of cohabiting couples. The number of people living on their own is projected to grow by over one-third, to around 430,000 in 2016 (Welsh Office, 1999).

Marriage Rates

Despite the strong support given to marriage, both ideologically and institutionally within Welsh life and culture, the annual rate of marriage has been falling since the mid-1970s. The number of marriages solemnized in Wales has fallen from 22,424 in 1971 to 13,024 in 2001 (National Assembly of Wales [NAW], 2003). On the surface this appears to suggest that the institution of marriage is losing its popularity among Welsh people, but a more detailed examination of the figures corrects this impression and reveals important variations between groups. There has been a marked decline in the number of single people getting married. There is also some evidence that a small but rising section of the population appears to be deliberately opting out of marriage as an institution. However, this is compensated for by a significant increase in the number of people who remarry after divorce. The number of marriages involving a divorced male increased from 1,962 in 1971 to 3,648 in 2001. For females, there was a similar increase from 1,884 to 3,622 (NAW, 2003). It is clear that remarriage of both divorced and widowed people accounted for an increasing proportion of total marriages and it now accounts for more than one-quarter of all marriages taking place in Wales. Partly as a consequence, changes have also occurred with respect to age and marriage.

Age at Marriage

Welsh men and women are now marrying later than they did in the late twentieth century (NAW, 2003). Between 1971 and 1990 the average age at marriage for men rose from 26.6 years to 30.3 years; for women, it rose from 24.3 years to 27.8 years (Welsh Office, 1993). During the same period, teenage marriages declined significantly. In 1971, 30 percent of marriages involved girls aged twenty or less, by 1995 this figure had fallen to only 4 percent and in 2001 it stood at only 2 percent (NAW, 2003). However, the proportion of those marrying over the age of forty-five years has remained relatively constant. While these age trends reflect what has been occurring in the United Kingdom as a whole, couples in Wales still tend to marry younger than in the rest of the United Kingdom. The rate of teenage marriage remains higher in Wales than elsewhere in Britain. This probably reflects the rather different class composition of the Welsh population where, despite rapid economic change, the proportion of manual worker households is higher than for Britain as a whole.

Cohabitation

The fall in the rate of marriage in the last twenty-five years accompanies a notable increase in the rate of cohabitation. As part of the sexual revolution since the 1960s, there has been a marked relaxation of the social and moral pressures against couples living together without marriage. Nevertheless, from time to time, churches and some politicians continue to take a stand against people "living in sin." While the trend toward cohabitation is observable in Wales as it is in the rest of the United Kingdom, Wales has the lowest percentage of cohabiting couples of any part of Britain. Traditional social controls might remain stronger in Wales than elsewhere. In the late 1980s, 7 percent of men and 8 percent of women in Wales were cohabiting compared with 13 percent of men and 14 percent of women in Great Britain as a whole (Haskey & Kiernan, 1989). More recent figures (2001) recorded approximately 8 percent of all households to consist of cohabiting couples (ONS, 2001). The majority of couples who cohabit (51 percent) have no children, while 45 percent have dependent children and 4 percent nondependent children only.

Cohabitation seems to be an experimental stage before marriage. Surveys indicate that the majority of young people see cohabitation as a trial marriage (Kiernan & Estaugh, 1993). This indicates a fundamental shift in sexual norms and behaviors that is beginning to be recognized in law as the status of common law partners is revised to confer new rights and obligations.

Divorce

Many regard the increased incidence of divorce as one of the most significant changes in family life over recent decades, and one that has contributed greatly to destabilizing traditional notions of family continuity. Successive changes in the law, by removing concepts of blame and guilt from marital breakdowns, have meant that divorce has become progressively easier to obtain. Divorce rates in the United Kingdom increased sixfold, from a rate of 2.1 per thousand marriages in 1961 to a rate of 12.7 per thousand marriages in 1987 (Office of Population Censuses and Surveys, 1987). Altogether, roughly one-third of all marriages are likely to end in divorce, giving the United Kingdom the highest rate in Europe. Figures for Wales also show an increase in the incidence of divorce in the latter part of the twentieth century, but the divorce rate remains below that for England, again suggesting the relative persistence of traditional social controls.

Figures on divorce petitions filed in Wales reveal a steady increase of 14 percent from 9,070 in 1981 to a peak of 10,750 in 1992. However, numbers of divorce petitions in Wales, as in the United Kingdom as a whole, have recently begun to fall and stand at 8,648 in 2002 (NAW, 2003). This might well be a consequence of declining marriage rates rather than any indication that the institution of marriage is becoming more stable. At the same time, it should be noted that high divorce rates could indicate that the marriage relationship has become more, not less, important, with a greater emphasis being placed upon the quality of the relationship between partners. However, despite the growth of a whole industry of marriage guidance and counseling, there are few clear guidelines as to how to achieve and sustain rewarding and loving relationships in a situation where individuals bring increased expectations to marriage.

The rise in the likelihood of divorce is one reason for the growing numbers of lone-parent families in Wales. A lone-parent family is one in which a conjugal bond either has been severed or was not initiated. Undoubtedly, lone parenting is becoming a more significant, and more accepted feature of family life in Wales. One-parent households make up 11 percent of all households in Wales and one-fifth of all Welsh children live with a lone parent. Women head most lone-parent families (ONS, 2001). The majority of these women (55 percent) are economically inactive and thus dependent upon welfare benefits. This has made them the subject of much debate and controversy in the United Kingdom, as will be explored later in this chapter.

FAMILIES AND CHILDREN

It is a major responsibility of the family to produce, nurture, and socialize the next generation. Families in Britain now tend to be much smaller than they were in the past and the child-rearing phase of family life is shorter and more concentrated, although the time-span during which each child is dependent has increased. Statistics show a steady decline in birthrate since the early 1960s, achieving relative stability during the 1980s and early 1990s. The birthrate per 1,000 women aged fifteen to forty-four has fallen from 85.1 in 1971 to 52.3 in 2002 (NAW, 2003).

Illegitimacy

A much commented upon feature of the period from the 1980s onward is the growing separation between childbearing and marriage.

Today one-half of all births in Wales occur outside of marriage compared with only 7 percent in 1971 (NAW, 2003), although in the majority of instances the names of both parents are registered on the birth certificate. The highest rates of extramarital births occur in the predominantly urban areas of South Wales.

The stigma once attached to illegitimacy has weakened considerably, although concern is still expressed publicly over the number of teenage pregnancies. In fact, the number of girls (under sixteen) conceiving in the United Kingdom fell slightly (from 7,800 to 7,300) between 1991 and 1992, and in 2002 only 9 percent of all births in Wales were to women under the age of twenty (NAW, 2003).

Fertility Trends

The trends in Wales, as in other parts of Britain, are toward the postponement of parenthood and smaller family size. Since the early 1970s, couples have delayed starting their families. Whereas in the late 1980s more than two out of every five births were to a mother less than twenty-five years old, by the late 1990s the figure had fallen to less than one-third. The number of births is now lower than it has been for almost thirty years (NAW, 2002a) and remaining childless is increasingly becoming a deliberate option.

Reasons for the decline in the birthrate are many. They include improved contraception, availability of abortion, the influence of the women's movement, the increased participation of women in the labor market, the prolonged period of childhood dependency, and the lack of adequate and affordable child-care facilities. All of these factors play their part. Good quality and affordable child-care services are crucial for combining paid work and family life and for increasing the opportunities for women. Child care also enables women to respond to the demand from the economy for their greater participation in the workforce especially in taking up the vastly increased proportion of part-time jobs that have come into being in Wales.

Services for Children

The 1989 Children's Act provides the general legal framework for services for children in Britain. Its enactment represents part of a growing, although still patchy, social awareness of the needs of children. More specifically, the legislation defines day-care provision and the duties of local authorities with respect to registering these facilities. Local authorities are required to provide day care for children in need as is appropriate (Welsh Assembly Government, 2007a). Together with the Local Education Authority, they are also obliged to review the general provision of day care within their areas, and keep a register of those who act as child minders or provide day care for children aged less than eight years.[1] There has been a growth of child-care services in Wales throughout the 1990s. Day nurseries look after children below the age of five years for the length of the adult working day. Places in day nurseries have more than trebled since 1991. Playgroups provide sessional care, for a morning or afternoon rather than a whole day, usually for children aged three and four. The number of places with playgroups has decreased by 14 percent from a peak in 1997. The number of places with child minders, who provide services for children less than eight years, have decreased since 1997 by 24 percent. Some of this decrease is likely to be the consequence of reviews of registrations that might have removed child minders who no longer offer their services. Between 1997 and 2001, the number of places in out-of-school clubs has doubled.

Most of the increase in child-care services has been in the private sector rather than in public provision. Public funding for child-care services in the United Kingdom is low compared to many other European countries. In Wales, only 2 out of every 1,000 children under the age of five years has a place in a local authority day nursery and these places are usually reserved for children in need (Statham, Holtermann, & Stone, 1996). Most families requiring child care must either pay for it, or make informal arrangements with relatives and friends. Child care is not cheap. Large-scale studies covering Great Britain have found that women who pay for care of their under fives spent (in 1991) on average around one-quarter of their weekly earnings (Marsh & McKay, 1993). Not surprisingly, surveys of parents' use of day care find that better off families spend more than families with low incomes. The 1991 British Household Panel Survey (reported in Dex, Lissenhurgh, & Taylor, 1994) found that high-paid working women were ten times as likely as the low-paid to use formal child-care services, such as a nanny, nursery, or child minder.

Difficulties with the affordability of child care are one reason why, despite the fact that the employment of mothers in Wales has risen continuously, the labor market position of certain disadvantaged groups has worsened. This is especially so for lone parents who now constitute nearly one-quarter of all families with dependent children. In addition to lack of public provision, there is still little support from employers for child care. What is available is mostly restricted to the public sector (i.e., hospitals, colleges of further and higher education, and government bodies) rather than private companies.

Other Child-Care Issues

Other child-care issues particularly relevant to Wales have to do with rurality and language. Providing child-care services in rural areas, like other family services, poses a particular challenge because small and scattered populations make it harder for group services such as nurseries and out-of-school clubs to be economically viable. Rural incomes are often also low, making it difficult for families to afford child care. Although geographically Wales is a predominantly rural country, more than one-half of the day nurseries operate in urban areas and many of the remainder are based in towns rather than villages. Out-of-school schemes are similarly less likely to operate in rural areas. Child minding is a more practical option for child care in sparsely populated areas, because child minders only need to take care of two or three children to make ends meet. Evidence suggests that almost 70 percent of Welsh child minders work in rural areas (Moss et al., 1995).

An important factor when choosing child care for many Welsh-speaking parents is that the child will be able to use its first language with the child-care provider. Increasing numbers of English-speaking families are also recognizing the benefits to their children of learning Welsh at an early age. Welsh language playgroups (*Ysgolion Meithrin*) offer the most common form of Welsh language preschool experience. These provide sessional rather than all-day care. A survey undertaken by the Thomas Coram Research Unit (Moss et al., 1995) asked child-care providers about the amount of Welsh they used with children in their care. Children were more likely to hear Welsh in a group setting where at least one member of the staff could speak some Welsh, than with a child minder. One-third of day nurseries described themselves as using Welsh "a lot" (defined as running the service mainly through the medium of Welsh, or bilingually) and a further 43 percent used the language "a little" (defined as teaching basic Welsh words and nursery rhymes). The remaining 25 percent were unable to offer any Welsh language experience to the children. Among child minders, despite their predominantly rural location, 14 percent used Welsh a lot and 22 percent a little, with over 60 percent using none (Moss et al., 1995).

FAMILIES AND GENDER

Equality for gender opportunities, both in paid employment and in the home, was the focus of much debate and policy making in the latter half of the twentieth century. Considerable progress has been made and, as in the rest of the United Kingdom, the official ideology in Wales today is one of sexual equality. The incorporation of European Union legislation and policy guidelines into British legislation means that gender equality has been mainstreamed as a policy directive (NAW, 1999; Welsh Assembly Government, 2007b). Formal equality in the public spheres of employment and education has gained legislative backing. The Equal Pay Act and the Sex Discrimination Act both came into effect in 1975, making it illegal to discriminate on the grounds of gender with respect to pay, recruitment, and promotion. The Education Act of 1986 and the Education Reform Act of 1988 sought to establish equal opportunities in schools, partly through the implementation of a standardized national curriculum. Thus, formal sanctions that previously prevented women from straying too far from conventional definitions of gender roles have been lifted. Nowadays, in theory, women are free to enter any area of education and occupation, and have been gaining admission into politics, the clergy, and many other previously male-dominated spheres. However, while progress is apparent, many obstacles remain in the way of complete equalization. These obstacles have much to do with entrenched social and cultural attitudes concerning gender roles that are institutionalized within the structure and ideology of the family in Welsh and British society. The legacy of a history of heavy industry in parts of

Wales has led to accusations that Welsh men are particularly "macho" in their attitudes (Scourfield & Drakeford, 1999).

Employment

As noted in previous text, one major way in which the position of Welsh women has changed significantly in recent decades is in terms of participation in the labor market. Women in Wales have always had relatively low economic activity rates compared with those of women elsewhere in Britain, largely because of the economic importance of heavy industries such as metal manufacturing, mining, and docks. This has been changing with the shift toward lighter manufacturing employment and services. Female economic activity rates in Wales have increased from 37 percent in 1971 to 63 percent in 2003 (Equal Opportunities Commission, 2003). This gradual rise echoes the pattern found more generally in the United Kingdom, although the current figure for Wales still lags behind the U.K. figure of 67 percent. Only Northern Ireland, with a similar history of male-dominated industrial employment, has a female economic activity rate lower than that for Wales. Male economic activity rates declined during the latter part of the twentieth century from 78 percent in 1971 to 72 percent in 1997 (Rees, 1997). More recent figures indicate something of a recovery to 79 percent in 2002 (ONS, 2002a).

There is a further significant aspect of developing employment patterns in Wales, which relates closely to the interaction between women's domestic and employment roles. The labor market shifts described have also brought about the replacement of full-time male employment, often in skilled occupations, with semi-skilled and unskilled work in the service sector, and in assembly work, much of it available on a part-time basis. In 2002, almost one-half of the women employed in Wales had part-time jobs (ONS, 2002a).

There are problems with such statistics. As elsewhere, much of the contribution of women to the economy goes unrecorded. Part-time employment below a certain number of hours a week, or beneath a given pay threshold is not recorded. The extent of home working is very difficult to estimate, and largely involves women. Much caring work undertaken by women, even if it is paid, falls below the qualifying threshold for insurance and taxation and is therefore unlikely to appear in documented statistics. Similarly, women contribute considerably to family businesses, such as farms or corner shops or to the enterprises of their self-employed partners. However, these women are not recognized as being employed in their own right. As self-employment is high and growing among men, especially in rural Wales, there is likely to be significant undercounting of women's contribution to the economy in these areas (Ashton, 1994).

In Wales, as is generally the case in the United Kingdom and Europe, there are distinct patterns of gender segregation in work, both by industry and by occupation. Women tend to be concentrated in service-sector fields (particularly education, welfare, and health), clerical work, sewing, catering, and other personal services. The less-developed financial services sector employs a small (12 percent) but growing number of women. Women in the manufacturing sector are found overwhelmingly in semiskilled manual work, in industries such as engineering, clothing, and food processing. Compared with England, there are relatively few women professionals working in science, engineering, and technology (Rees, 1997).

The current Welsh workforce is quite rigidly divided along gender lines. Men and women work in different industrial sectors, in dissimilar jobs subject to different terms and conditions of employment, and receive unequal amounts of pay. Female employees working full-time earn on average 13 percent less than the average hourly earnings of male full-time employees (ONS, 2002b). Despite its economic renewal, hailed by many as an economic miracle (with advancements in aerospace, bioscience, IT, and optronics with new jobs offering good prospects, Wales is the only region or nation of the United Kingdom to have a bigger percentage increase in private sector employment than public sector since 1999; Welsh Assembly Government, 2007c), Wales continues to be a low-wage economy, and the various forms of work that are allotted to women tend to be among the worst paid. Even so, many families rely upon female wage-earners to make substantial contributions to the household income. This situation differs greatly from earlier dependence upon men earning a "family wage," which tended to underpin notions of male dominance within the home. Changes in access to paid employment, even where the economic returns are low, have important consequences for family life.

Education

One reason for continued gender segregation in the labor market is that women and men tend to pursue different education and training trajectories. Access to learning plays a powerful role in the division of the workforce into male and female areas. Despite developments that have helped to reduce the impact of gender on who ultimately gets what jobs, gender segregation in education and training persists. Schools in Wales have participated in a series of major changes since the mid-1970s that have included the introduction of the national curriculum and Standard Attainment Targets (SATs). More recently, new systems of measuring school performance have given rise to the publication of so-called league tables that rank schools in terms of their relative scores on standardized tests of pupil achievement (Welsh Assembly Government, 2007a). The effects of these reforms on equal opportunities appear mixed. One of the issues receiving the most attention has been that figures now show girls to be achieving similar examination results to boys and actually doing better at some levels (Rees, 1997; Welsh Assembly Government, 2007a). This is not a solely Welsh phenomenon because similar patterns appear elsewhere. Indeed, the issue of underachieving boys is now being identified as a cause for concern in many European Member States.

While the results obtained by girls have improved, there is still a clear gender divide in subject choice, which feeds through into the range of industries and occupations open to women. The gender divide remains operative despite the fact that the national curriculum obliges both girls and boys to study, up to a certain basic level, subjects that have been nontraditional for their gender. Although many initiatives have been introduced to encourage girls to follow studies that are more advanced and into nontraditional areas, for example, science and engineering, for the most part they have been limited in their effects (Rees, 1992). Gender separation by subject continues into post–compulsory education and training. Women are keen consumers of postschool educational opportunities but are more likely to pursue academic rather than vocational training courses. Women constitute the majority of further education students, but are frequently found in evening classes and among self-funded students, rather than as employer-sponsored students on day or block release (time off during working hours, which are longer than day release, such as several days or a week off to attend classes). Two-thirds of students with day-release arrangements are men. Women are less likely to end up with formal qualifications, which are those that are certificated or that result in the award of a specific qualification, as a result of their studies. Consequently, the labor market recognizes and rewards women's knowledge and skills less than men's.

Part of the explanation for the difference in educational orientation and attainment is found in young women's own views of their futures. A study of 500 South Wales schoolgirls described their anticipation of a working life fragmented by child-care responsibilities that inhibited their entry to education and training. Girls expected to undertake part-time employment to accommodate child-care needs. Given that part-time employment is predominantly in unskilled or semiskilled work, girls were not then motivated to pursue qualifications that would bring access to more highly skilled jobs (Pilcher, Delamont, Powell, & Rees, 1989; Pilcher, Delamont, Powell, Rees, & Read, 1990; Rees, 1992). While girls increasingly recognize the importance of being economically independent in adult life and occupying a role in the public world of work, their aspirations and their subject and career choices remain heavily constrained by their perceptions of future family life and responsibilities (Yewlett, 1996).

Family Life

Traditionally, family life in Wales centered on a sexual division of labor with women being responsible for domestic work and child care and men for breadwinning or providing. The wider social relationships of the local community reinforced these lines of separation, in which men and women engaged in distinct activities and made use of different facilities and institutions. The working-class culture of South Wales, in particular, had a notably masculine ethos, much stereotyped in popular and literary depictions in terms of male enthusiasm for rugby football, drinking, and male voice choirs. The matching image was of the "Welsh Mam," a powerful figure within the home and the dominant partner in child rearing and socialization (Adamson & Jones, 1996).

There is little to suggest that any radical shift in the division of domestic labor and caring work is taking place in Wales. Despite women's increased participation in paid work, there is not much evidence of the arrival in Wales of the "new man," ready to share domestic tasks and to shed the conventional masculine image. While men might "help out" more around the house than previously and do occasional work like painting and decorating, household repairs, and car maintenance, the major responsibility for daily domestic chores and for child care remains with women. A study of three generations of Welsh women investigated changes in ideas about who is responsible for various household tasks and who helps in their execution (Pilcher, 1994). A shift was noted in the vocabularies used, from the grandmothers "owning" the domestic work, to the mothers "expecting some help," to the granddaughters (many of whom were not yet living with a partner) expecting housework to be "shared." However, these indications of a change in expectations are not supported by evidence of any alterations in the actual division of labor.

A later survey in the South Wales valleys found that whereas 90 percent of couples were of the opinion that men must share housework equally with women, only 50 percent felt that this "always" happened in their household. Twenty percent said it "never" happened (Adamson & Jones, 1996). Thus, while attitudes suggest that the classic image of a male culture serviced by its women is in decline, practice reveals a rather different picture. Wider U.K. research confirms that while men might be more ready to help, most household tasks are still regarded as the responsibility of women when they join or return to the workforce, and even when women are the sole wage earners (Gershuny et al., 1986; Morris, 1990; Warde & Hetherington, 1993; Wheelock, 1990). This is particularly true for women employed part-time, of whom there are an especially high proportion in Wales, with 46 percent of all female employees working part-time (ONS, 2002b).

So, for some women, domestic and caring responsibilities still form a major barrier to participation in the labor force. For example, 44 percent of noneconomically active women report that it is too difficult for them to combine having a job with looking after children (Chwarae Teg, 2002). In an aging population, care for the elderly is another factor increasingly affecting women's ability to have paid work.

Increasingly, women in Wales are participating in the paid labor market, developing a heightened awareness of the value of education, and seeking for themselves a level of independence that previous generations of Welsh women neither expected nor sought. The female identities of younger Welsh women are no longer grounded so firmly in the domestic sphere. At the same time, real change is slow to come about and there are still clear gender divisions in education, training, and employment, a lack of child-care facilities, and an uneven domestic division of labor. All of these act as barriers to the full and equal participation of women in the Welsh economy and society.

Socialization Practices

The family plays a crucial role in perpetuating barriers to the full and equal participation of women through processes of socialization. In a modern democratic society where it is impossible formally to deny opportunity, the preservation of sexual and gender divisions relies heavily on informal beliefs and sanctions. Likewise, in a society in which obvious discrimination is condemned, and legally sanctioned, the construction of apparently "natural" gender differences helps to preserve the separation of roles and thus the inequalities upon which the economic and social systems might still depend. Thus the socialization of boys and girls, and the ways in which they develop apparently contrasting personalities and roles, is an essential factor in the perpetuation of gender divisions (Betts, 1996).

Sport

An exemplary area of gender-segregated activity in Wales is found in sport. Sport remains a bastion of Welsh (and British) male culture, and cultural forces combine with the structural organization of sports to discourage and even exclude girls at all levels from taking part. Sport in Wales is primarily defined as Rugby and Association Football (soccer), each of which remains largely closed to girls (while recently some girls do participate). Both in the school and in the community there is a lack of sporting provision and encouragement for girls, leading to a gradual disengagement from sport as they approach adolescence. This lack of provision links to cultural and naturalistic assumptions about male and female bodies. Concern with the body is common among young adolescents. However, as boys become motivated to strengthen and expand their bodies in order to gain cultural acceptance and approval, girls move toward a preoccupation with attractiveness and diminishing their bodies (Sutton, Hutson, & Thomas, 1996). Thus cultural stereotypes of masculine and feminine body image, together with the unequal provision for sport in Wales, means that gender becomes the overriding factor explaining the exclusion of girls from sporting activity and coincidentally from a major source of cultural honor and prestige.

FAMILIES AND STRESS

As noted previously in this chapter, issues surrounding the family assumed growing significance in public debates in Britain during the 1990s. Lower rates of marriage, higher rates of divorce, increased cohabitation, rising numbers of lone-parent families and single mothers, changing attitudes toward sexuality and toward unconventional family forms such as gay and lesbian households, and women's increased participation in the labor market, have all been the subject of heated debate. Numerous explanations are suggested for what some take to be the "decline" of the family. Breakdown of traditional moral values, increased unemployment and labor market insecurity, easier divorce and abortion, and women's liberation are among the suggested causes. High rates of truancy, an increase in juvenile crime, and the loss of parental control are seen as among the consequences.

Unemployment and greater levels of flexibility in working patterns undoubtedly place many families in Wales under stress. The importance of work as a source of male identity and status has been a significant cultural value threatened, for many, in the recent economic circumstances. Among reasons provided by young single mothers for preferring to live alone, the lack of male earning power and the problems that arise when men cannot live up to ideals of domestic responsibility, figure prominently (Berthoud, McKay, & Rowlingson, 1999). Experience of family life under stress is not always conducive to couples remaining together.

Domestic Violence

One factor that can produce enormous strain for family members is domestic violence. In a culture placing a high premium on the value of stable family life, there is growing awareness that the family cannot always provide the expected haven of emotional support and mutual affection. In reality, many Welsh women experience violence and abuse from their partners, and children from their parents. Indeed, domestic violence affects thousands of women and children in Wales each year. For example, 7 percent of women aged sixteen to fifty-nine reported being a victim of partner violence (nonsexual) in 2004-2005. This percentage was slightly higher than for all regions of England. Being separated is associated with higher prevalence rates of partner abuse. Women who were in poor health or have a limiting illness or disability are disproportionately more likely to have experienced abuse in the past year. Higher prevalence rates of intimate abuse are associated with relatively lower levels of socioeconomic status. There is no evidence of variations in the prevalence of intimate violence by ethnic background (Finney, 2006). Women are most likely to suffer violence within the family, at the hands of their closest and most intimate male relatives, rather than in the public domain (Elliot, 1996).

In the past, women who experienced violence in the home often felt that they were the rare exception to normality, and that this was somehow their own fault. They therefore kept it hidden, leaving the myth of the happy family unchallenged. It was not until the advent of the feminist movement (in the 1960s and 1970s) that domestic violence become known and its existence publicly acknowledged. In Wales, as in the rest of Britain, the Women's Refuge movement has focused attention on the issue and sought to provide support for women and children experiencing domestic violence. Refuges offer sanctuary to women and children desperately in need of a respite from a life of beatings and bullying. The first Welsh refuge was established in Cardiff in 1975, run on a voluntary basis in premises supplied by the local housing authority (a tier of government responsible for public services in its area) (Cardiff Women's Aid, 1990). Members of Welsh Women's Aid, who set up the refuge, operated it as a support group for women using the refuge and as a point of contact for women seeking help. There was no resident warden or paid refuge worker.[2]

In more recent years refuge development has expanded rapidly, using the standard U.K. benchmark figure for refuge provision (one family per 10,000 population). Welsh Women's Aid has grown from a cluster of pioneering "grass roots" Women's Aid groups of the 1970s to a leading national provider of services, to victims of domestic abuse, delivered through its thirty-one local Women's Aid groups. In addition to providing refuge accommodation, these groups have diversified into outreach and resettlement services and specialist support for identified groups such as young women (sixteen to twenty-four years) and ethnic minority groups. The development and rapid increase in Women's Aid information centers around Wales now provides an easy and safe access point for those who need information or more informal contact with Women's Aid.

The refuge movement is a clear example of women's survival and resilience in the face of adversity. Despite the fact that they are sometimes depicted as threatening the "traditional" family and invading its privacy, there is strong local support for refuge groups within their communities. If the traditional family is based upon male authority and a man's right to exercise this authority over other members of his household in any way he sees fit, then the existence of refuges that enable women and children to escape this domination certainly challenges the family. The existence of refuges for women and children experiencing or threatened with violence is one way of empowering Welsh women and beginning to redress the power balance within families that for so long favored men (Charles, 1991).

FAMILIES AND AGING

As in other western European countries, life expectancy in Wales has steadily increased, and there are larger numbers of older people alive today than ever before. The rural and coastal districts of Wales have also been highly attractive in recent years to people of retirement age, migrating in from England. At present, Wales has a higher proportion of elderly people than any other region of the United Kingdom. The proportion of people in Wales over the age of seventy-five is four times greater than it was in 1931 (mid-2001 population estimate). As a consequence, the 1990s and the early years of the twenty-first century have witnessed an increasing concern with social policy issues concerning the provision of services for, and care of, the elderly. The majority of the elderly in Wales are women, who constitute two-thirds of those aged sixty-five or over, and three-quarters of those aged eighty-five or more. At the age of sixty, life expectancy for women is twenty years, compared with fifteen for men (NAW, 2002b).

Gender issues compound the effects of ageism to reinforce the low status of the elderly in society. Perhaps paradoxically, older people today probably experience lower status and less power than in previous generations. In a society undergoing constant change, the accumulated knowledge of older people often seems to the young no longer a valuable store of wisdom, but simply behind the times. Therefore, the elderly come to constitute a social problem, a dependent group that needs to be dealt with and catered for.

Social Policy and Caregiving

The 1990 Community Care Act was designed to promote a better-planned and more integrated range of needs-led social services, which would enable service users to exercise greater choice. It was influenced, among other things, by a concern for the needs of the elderly as well as by the heavy and mounting social security obligations being incurred toward them. Under the legislation, funds hitherto administered by the central government Department of Social Security were transferred to the control of local authorities as care providers. There was an underlying ideological ambition to introduce market forces into the sphere of social care, in order to increase choice, competition, and value for money. The Act urged that local Social Service Departments should become assessors, purchasers, and enablers of services. At the same time, it was proposed that the direct provision of services by local authorities should be minimized in favor of encouraging the use of domiciliary services (i.e., provided in the person's own home) and residential services (provided in a nursing or retirement home/hostel) from the commercial, charitable, and voluntary sectors. This was less strictly mandated in Wales than in England. The overall aim was to reduce the proportions of elderly people in institutional care and to maintain them, wherever possible, in their own homes—hence the term community care. Implicit in this reasoning was the assumption that noninstitutional care would be less costly.

Certainly, the elderly are major consumers of intensive care packages, including residential and nursing home care, and 45 percent of all local authority expenditure on personal social services is devoted to the elderly. In 1995, about 75 percent of people over the age of eighty and living in the community were not prepared to discuss the possibility of admission to residential care. The other one-quarter recognized that it was a possibility but preferred to postpone any decision for as long as possible or hoped that "it would not come to that" (Wenger & Robinson, 1996). For most, maintaining their independence means remaining in their own homes.

Residential care, the only other option available for many, is increasingly located in the private sector. By 2001, 70 percent of available beds for elderly people were in the private and voluntary sector. Places in local authority residential care homes declined from 7,119 in 1990 to 4,534 in 2001. Places in independent (private and voluntary) homes rose in the same period from 8,619 to 10,703 (NAW, 2003). This has led to the circulation of horror stories about the quality of care, the standards of monitoring, and incidences of abuse occurring in private residential homes. Contrary to the intentions of the 1990 Act, the number of residential beds for the elderly in Wales has not declined and there has been no increase in domiciliary services. This failure has been particularly noticeable in the more rural areas. The absence of growth in domiciliary provision means that many older people have no real choice; despite their desire to remain at home, the support services are not available to make this possible.

Social Support Networks

Among those elderly people who do remain in the community, the lack of adequately funded public domiciliary services leads to a reliance on family and community support. Research in rural Wales has identified the existence of various types of support networks (Wenger, 1994). These are defined according to the availability and proximity of family, and the level of involvement with kin, friends, neighbors, and the wider community. Presence or absence of local kin is a key variable, and migration is shown to play a major part in network formation, whether it is the migration of the elderly persons themselves, or the migration decisions of relatives, friends, and neighbors. Inevitably, in circumstances of economic change, where some places offer poor employment prospects, and when critical social policies are geared to the mobility of labor, support networks can be easily undermined as members choose to leave an area.

The most common type of network is the locally integrated support network, mostly found in the larger villages and small towns (Wenger, 1994). Such networks include close relationships with local family, friends, and neighbors who are usually based on long-term residence and active community involvement in church and voluntary organizations in the present or recent past. These provide a supportive milieu in which network members have long-term knowledge of each other's lives. Expectations of mutual aid are part of a modus vivendi deeply enmeshed with family, friends, and neighbors in an ethos of generalized reciprocity. The local family-dependent type of support network in which relatives meet all support needs can be found in all types of communities, but is particularly common in rural areas with scattered settlement patterns.

A typical example of this is a situation where a widowed mother lives with or very near to a married daughter. In this context, the daughter tends to assume growing responsibility for the care of the mother as the dependencies of age increase. Sisters and daughters-in-law might also play a part in providing support. The local self-contained support network is a minority type associated with low population density and restricted opportunities for social contact in earlier phases of life. Elderly people with this type of network tend to adopt a household-focused lifestyle, relying primarily on self-help and crisis intervention from neighbors. In this case, relationships with relatives are distant or infrequent.

The wider community-focused support network is a common middle-class adaptation associated with migration, particularly retirement migration. Family members are geographically distant and support comes from local friends and associates. Membership in local voluntary groups is a common strategy for meeting people and making friends in the new community. The private restricted support network, again typically associated with the absence of local kin, arises where older people have few friends nearby and a low level of community contacts or involvement. In these situations, they must rely on self-help or formal social services. Those with private restricted support networks tend to be a more heterogeneous group than older people who have other types of support networks. A high proportion has never married and/or been caregivers for parents (Wenger, 1994).

OTHER FAMILY SITUATIONS

As has already been noted, Wales is characterized by a growing diversity of family types. Cohabiting couple families, stepfamilies, gay and lesbian families, and lone-parent families increasingly challenge the traditional nuclear family based on legal marriage. While all of these alternative family forms are viewed as a problem by some, and by others as a sign of moral decay and decline, it is the latter form—lone-parent families and in particular single mothers—that have been the focus of most concern.

Lone Parents and Problem Families

The "problem" of the single mother exploded into one of the nastiest of family policy issues during the 1990s. Government attitudes hardened as lone parents came to be regarded not as victims with special needs for financial and social support, but as irresponsible and, in the case of unmarried mothers, manipulative people supposedly willing, for example, to have a baby in order to gain access to housing provided by the public authorities. Unmarried mothers became prime targets partly because they constituted the fastest growing category putting pressure on the public purse. In 1990, 13.8 thousand families in Wales were in receipt of family credit.[3] By 1999, this had risen to 23.1 thousand. The largest group of these families is one-parent families headed by women. This is also the group likely to be most responsive to a harsher benefit climate. There was a strong view that the payment of high rates of welfare benefit encouraged young women to become pregnant, and that cutting off benefit would reduce the level of single parenthood.

These attitudes formed part of a broader New Right attack on the so-called dependency culture, which was fought on both economic and moral grounds. Moral decline was seen as bringing about economic decline. The argument presented was that the welfare state had displaced the role of the family as the main provider of welfare—children no longer needed to look after their elderly parents, parents could not control their children, and fathers abandoned their families. Likewise, without proper role models in the nuclear family, teenage boys become delinquent "yobs," and teenage girls become unmarried mothers (Dennis & Erdos, 1992). It was argued that when the State, and not the family, becomes the first port of call in times of trouble, the result is increased public expenditure and a growing tax burden that is a disincentive to industriousness. Increased expenditure is incurred directly by family "breakdown" because of rising numbers of benefit claims, and indirectly as the result of the perceived link between lone parenthood, crime, and other social problems.

Single parenthood is seen as morally damaging and is discouraged. According to New Right thought, the logical solution was to replace state support to families and individuals with assistance from within the family itself. The hope was that withdrawing outside support would pressure families to look after their own. There were several policy examples of this, including the withdrawal of income support for sixteen to eighteen year olds; the Criminal Justice Bill 1994, which introduced parental responsibility for a child's misdemeanors; and the Child Support Act 1990. In the latter parental responsibility was realigned along biological lines and the boundaries of state intervention expanded. Lone mothers receiving Income Support, Family Credit, or Disabled Worker's Allowance are now compelled to authorize the secretary of state to take action to recover maintenance from the absent father, regardless of the father's current circumstances.

Developments in family policy in the early 1990s illustrate the dilemmas and confusions of the boundary line between the public and private worlds of the family. In these terms, if the family works as expected, it can be left alone. If it "fails," leaving women and children vulnerable, then the State must step in. To do so, however, raises what economists would call a problem of moral hazard. Too much cushioning by the State eases pressures to take responsibility, and family breakdown can increase. Too little state supervision and care, and individuals are left vulnerable to dysfunctional family relationships. The Conservative Government was in the midst of trying to sort out this tangle when it was voted out of office in 1997. Under the leadership of Tony Blair, the new Labour Government made family policy one of its earliest priorities. In November 1998 it issued a consultative paper, Supporting Families, which tried to avoid excessive and politically risky moralizing while advocating measures to strengthen marriage and the family. It included the suggested creation of a National Family and Parenting Institute to provide expertise and guidance on the "proper" regulation of family life.

CONCLUDING COMMENTS

As noted during the course of this chapter, considerable recent public anxiety and debate in Wales, and throughout Britain, has been directed at the alleged fragmentation of the family and the associated breakdown of established patterns of domestic and family life (Dennis & Erdos, 1992; Phillips, 1996). Explicitly or implicitly, issues to do with the role and character of the contemporary family have been at the center of policy discussions having to do with the reconstitution of the welfare system, the perceived problem of law and order, and the various moral panics that have arisen around parenting, the discipline of children, child abuse, and the responsibilities of men and women toward one another and within the home.

Despite its rejection of many of the ideological principles and policy tenets of the previous long-lived Conservative political regime, the "New Labour" governments (from 1997 on) have kept many of the same policy orientations toward families. Indeed, one of the first debates they faced had to do with its proposals to reduce the level of welfare benefits paid to single parents, in line with the intentions of the preceding administration. The general thrust of the "welfare to work" policies the government has pursued have continued to impact in numerous ways upon the organization and conduct of family life. For example, by transferring state support from those who are viewed as welfare-dependent to those who are employed, effectively the government has been shifting control of income away from women, who still have primary responsibility for the home and family, back toward men, who often continue to be seen as the primary wage earners. In the realm of law and order, measures like the imposition of curfews on disorderly young people and the introduction of antisocial behavior orders (ASBOs) continue to treat the family as the natural sphere of order, control, and social discipline. Likewise, parents (usually mothers) whose children are truant from school have been threatened with legal penalties, including imprisonment, to make them take their responsibilities more seriously.

The creation of the National Assembly for Wales has allowed some limited room for maneuver toward a distinctive Welsh social policy, including family-oriented measures. One significant development has been the appointment in 2001 of a Children's Commissioner for

Wales, following the outcome of a particularly serious investigation of past child abuse in care homes in North Wales. This followed a 1999 policy initiative called Children First, which aimed to "transform services for children in need and their families thereby enabling those children to lead fuller, more successful lives as adults" (NAW, 2001, p. 1). Such innovations put Wales ahead of England, and when the English parliament belatedly began to catch up with Welsh developments, there was some argument as to whether or not the Welsh model ought to be followed. Despite these limited signs of an emergent independent policy dimension, the new political conditions in Wales are not likely to produce major variations between the direction of development taken by Welsh families and that followed by families across the English border. The basic social and economic forces shaping the family are too powerful for such limited constitutional and administrative change to have much effect. Many of the changes described in this chapter have to be seen rather as the unavoidable outcome of the predominant social importance that a broadly liberal-democratic society attaches to individual choice and responsibility, and to the equalization of rights among different categories of persons, including especially men and women. These aims and values make the conduct of family life a matter for continual negotiation between its members. It is anticipated that they will continue to generate novel, and sometimes challenging, family forms, and to pose difficult questions about the boundaries between the public and private spheres, and the limits to collective intervention and control. Consequently, the family is likely to remain close to the heart of political and media concerns, as different interests seek to encourage or obstruct particular sorts of family.

At the same time, the majority of people in Wales continue to place great importance upon the significance of stable family life, and the role of marriage, or at least long-term commitment between partners, and the proper care and upbringing of children. Amidst all the changes, and the apparent experience of upheaval and disruption, there are still important and well-established continuities in the ideals and practice of family life, which ensure that the family remains a vital and basic social institution within the organization of Welsh society.

NOTES

1. Child minders are people who do not work within a child-care center but look after a small number of children in their own homes, or in the children's home.

2. A warden is a supervisor, someone who runs, manages, or looks after/is responsible for the day-to-day operation of a refuge or other facility such as a student hall or dormitory.

3. Family credit and income support are means tested forms of welfare payment based on level of family or personal income and are designed to raise income above poverty thresholds. In October 1999 Family Credit was replaced by Working Families Tax Credit.

Chapter 3

Diversity of Families in Sweden

Jan Trost

INTRODUCTION

The Kingdom of Sweden is by tradition a homogenous society despite several centuries of immigration.[1] For example, during the sixteenth century, Sweden "imported" skilled workers for the mining and iron industries. They came mainly from the Belgium area. For a couple of decades after World War II, Sweden imported skilled and semiskilled workers from countries such as Finland, Poland, and Greece. The immigrants, however, were rapidly assimilated and soon became Swedes. A new historical trend emerged during the last decade or so when rapid assimilation of immigrants from very different societies, Vietnam and Iran, for example, occurred.

There are no significant minorities in the country. The sole minority consists of the Saami (previously called Lapps) living in the northern part of the country and numbering about 10,000 out of Sweden's nine million inhabitants. Foreign-born of first-generation immigrants include Danes, Norwegians, Finns, Yugoslavs, Greeks, and Turks. Christianity, in the form of Lutheranism, is the prevalent religion (almost 90 percent of the population) and there are a few other denominations (e.g., Roman Catholic, Muslim, and Jewish) (World Factbook, 2006).

Sweden has a high standard of living under a capitalist system (especially of high-tech capitalism) interwoven with substantial welfare benefits. Peace and neutrality have aided this for all of the twentieth century. Additional factors for the strong economy are a modern distribution system, excellent internal and international communication systems, and a skilled labor force. Around 90 percent of industrial output is from privately owned firms. Agriculture accounts for only 2 percent of gross domestic product and 2 percent of employment (World Factbook, 2006).

Families in Swedish Context

The dominant family pattern is the nuclear family. Almost all children are born into a household where both parents live and ideologically the parents/spouses are to live together until one of them dies. However, social reality is different; there are many divorces and separations. More than one-third of all households are one-person households and about 40 percent of the population lives in households with four or more inhabitants (Trost, 1993).

Politicians and the owners of factories realized at the beginning of the 1960s that workers need not be imported from other countries. Sweden had a pool of potential workers—that is, housewives. This realization occurred as the renewed sex-role debate began. These movements made housewives (i.e., traditionally defined as a social institution during the previous half century), disappeared as an institution around 1970. Housewives were encouraged to seek employment and schooling with the aid of various subsidies.

Now, almost all men and women are part of the labor force. However, about one-half of the women are gainfully employed half-time or less while most men are employed full-time (Trost, 1993). The childcare system for children older than about one year of age is well established in most municipalities at a subsidized cost dependent upon the parents' financial situations.

Parents have the right to a parental leave of absence for up to one year with almost full payment. Parents can distribute this leave as preferred until the child is eight years old. However, the father has to take at least one month's leave or the parents lose that month. The rational is to encourage fathers to be more actively involved with their children, for the sake of both the fathers and the children.

For over a half century Swedish society has been characterized by its social welfare approach, as in many European societies. Schools and universities are free of charge; no one pays much for health care; and pension plans are funded to a certain level by government. Direct and indirect taxes are high by international standards. Inhabitants in return receive many benefits and therefore do not require much private insurance, except for housing, cars, and the like.

It can be said either that all Swedes live on social welfare, or that no one does. The expression "to live on welfare," does not have the same meaning in Sweden as it does in countries such as the United States. Welfare or social welfare are not pejorative terms. The welfare system consists of many benefits and programs for people in financial or other troublesome situations.

By international standards families in Sweden enjoy a good life. The United Nations Human Development Index ranks Sweden at number five in the world. As just indicated, there are many social support programs and health care is universal and modern. Average life expectancy in Sweden is among the highest in the world at 78.3 years for men and 82.9 for women (2006 estimate). Infant mortality is low (2.76 per 1,000 live births) as is the death rate (10.31 per 1,000 population). Literacy rates stand at around 99 percent for both men and women. Per capita income is high. Only about 6 percent of the population lives below the official poverty line. Unemployment rates are relatively low (6 percent in 2006); only about 1 percent can be considered long-term unemployed. Inflation is very low and the economy is strong. Sweden is a member of the European Union (Statistiska Centralbyrån, 2003; UNDP, 2006; World Factbook, 2006).

COUPLE FORMATION AND MARITAL DYNAMICS

After World War II, the marriage rate increased and in 1965 it was higher than ever before. However, after 1966, the rate for first marriages and remarriages steadily decreased, dropping. by about one-half within less than a decade and has continued to decrease but at a slower pace (Statistiska Centralbyrån, 2003). As the marriage rate decreased, the cohabitation rate increased. The loss in the number of marriages was more than equaled by the increase in the number of cohabitations. These changes have occurred in most Western societies, but they started earliest and are the most extreme in Sweden (Trost, 1979). Before the middle of the 1960s, there were few cohabiting couples and there was no term for the phenomenon. After a decade of decreasing marriage and increasing cohabitation rates, cohabitation became a social institution. Cohabitation has not replaced marriage, but is an institution alongside marriage (Trost, 1981).

Before these changes occurred, four elements were closely connected in time: the marriage ceremony; moving in together; having sexual intercourse together; and having the first child about a year later (Trost, 1979, 1995). With some exemptions, the marriage ceremony and the moving in together occurred at the same time, that is, the same day. This seems to have been true for all Western societies. To start having sex together was normatively prescribed. While the ideal norm prescribed chastity before marriage, almost all couples had sex before they married. One indicator of this is that around the year 1960, one-third of all brides were pregnant at the time of their weddings (97 percent of the weddings were with a religious ceremony) (Statistiska Centralbyrån, 1968). The fourth element, having a child, was connected to the others in a double way. Preferably and normatively, children should not be born to unmarried mothers, but should come soon after the wedding.

These four elements lost their normative power when cohabitation became a social institution and they are no longer connected to each other in the pattern of the past. In some countries, for example Belgium, there is still a connection between having a child and being married. In Sweden, more than one-half of all children born and about two-thirds of all first born children are born to a mothers who are not married (Statistiska Centralbyrån, 2003). In Belgium, only about one out of seven children are born to a woman who is not married (Trost, 1993).

In many countries today, when the two in a couple are in love, they move in together if possible. They might move in together after a thought out decision, or one person just increasingly stays over night until the couple realizes that they are cohabiting. Frequently, others look upon cohabitation as premarital. That is a misperception. Many couples can be classified as postmarital (if one or both are divorced) or postcohabiting. Few couples decide to cohabit and then to marry. They just move in together. For a majority, marriage is a reality in the end.

Within the context of these trends in decreasing marriage rates and increasing cohabitation, something happened to bring about a spike in the marriage rate in 1989. January through October was typical. About the same number of marriages occurred as in previous years and as in the following years. In November, the rate doubled. About

2,000 couples could be expected to be married, but 4,000 couples married. In December, the rate was thirty-two times higher than in the previous and following years. While 2,000 couples could be expected to marry, 64,000 did so (Statistiska Centralbyrån, 2003).

The rules about widows' pensions changed January 1, 1990; those who were married before this date were partially covered when widowed. The amount is, however, low and with many restrictions. In September and October the mass media reported that there were long lines of couples at registries to get married. This was not so when reported but the message became a self-fulfilling prophecy. This can partly be understood by the fact that there existed a large pool of couples ready to marry when "time is ripe," as many say. The mass media's reports, as well as the marriages of friends and others, were cues for a large number of couples to marry.

Weddings

Within the traditional system, which ended around 1970, the parents of the bride alone or together with the groom's parents organized the wedding, including the ceremony and the party. The party was preferably grand with many guests invited if the parents could afford to do so. Mainly, the parents invited their close relatives and friends. Restrictions were applied for friends of the bride and groom with only some of their very close friends being invited. For the most part, the party was for the parents to show that their daughter and son married.

This system has changed. Now, many marriages are remarriages for at least one of the spouses and large numbers of grooms and brides are of mature age, meaning in their thirties and forties, and financially independent. Most organize and pay for their weddings themselves and decide whom to invite. The wedding is theirs and not their parents'. The median age at marriage for women in 2002 was 31.5 years and for men 34.3 years. In 1960, the corresponding ages were 23.3 and 26.4. The median age for first marriages in 2002 was 29.9 for women and 32.2 for men. In 1960, the figures were 22.8 and 25.7 (Statistiska Centralbyrån, 2003).

Younger couples often want the same, a marriage of their own, and they organize the wedding in cooperation with their parents (of whom many are themselves divorced and with new spouses or partners) who are to pay for the wedding. The invitations are often restricted to a few relatives and many friends of the couple, with restrictions on the number of friends of the parents. As a father said at his daughter's wedding party: "We four parents gladly pay for this party which the bride and the groom have organized, and we are happy we were invited, too."

The decision of when to marry has also changed. In the traditional system the decision of when to marry was closely connected to such events as the finishing of an education and having a good job, or having found an apartment (at that time most Swedes lived in rented or co-op flats; now more live in houses of their own), or the bride being pregnant. It is important to stress that pregnancies rarely made forced marriages. Rather, pregnancy gave a cue for a decision of when to marry. Soon wanting a child was another cue for the couple marrying.

The system of today is different. Few couples in Sweden who co-habit decide to marry when they want a child. Likewise, housing, a good job, or being in a good financial situation are no longer cues for marrying. The cues vary widely and the ideas of "when the time is ripe" are often invisible. For example, the contributor knows a couple who had decided to marry to celebrate the day they had begun cohabiting five years ago. However, some months before that date, the bride-to-be learned that she was pregnant. She did not want to marry when pregnant because she wanted to be able to take an active part in the party. The couple simply decided to postpone the marriage until the seventh anniversary of their cohabitation.

The historically low marriage rates during the last three decades have resulted in a large number of cohabitants, with many intending to marry sometime in the future. It can be argued that the previous marital ceremony and party were a rite of passage—after which the two changed statuses, started living together, could openly share a bedroom, and were expected to soon have a baby. Now, the marital ceremony and party make a *confirmation rite*—confirming that the two are a couple. As they have been living together, many have a child or children. This means that there are few real changes because of the marriage. Slightly cynically, it can be stated that the sole differences are that the couple has to divorce if they want the relationship to end, and there will be financial impacts when they divorce or when one of them dies that differ from the case if they were cohabiting without being married. In general, during cohabitation and marriage there are no discerning differences. However, at separation/divorce, there are clearer rules for those divorcing than for those separating from co-habitation. Divorcing couples share all assets equally (unless they have a marital contract stating otherwise). Ex-cohabitants share only what is bought for their common use during the cohabitation. The financially well-off benefit from cohabitation while the less well-off benefit from marriage when separating or divorcing. Inheritance rights also differ; cohabitants do not inherit from a deceased partner.

For some, the idea of a confirmation rite is not fully adequate. The contributor of this chapter has interviewed couples who held the idea that in the long run one should be married. They decided to marry because they had been invited to so many marriages of friends that they felt a push to have a big party themselves. This means to marry.

Remarriages, Recohabitations, and Stepfamilies

With the high dissolution rate among couples and with remarriages and recohabitations, many stepfamilies are formed. That is, a parent marries or cohabits with a person who is not the biological parent of the same child. The extent of these stepfamily households is not known, but an indicator of their increasing amount is the remarriage rate. In 1900, 10 percent of all marriages were remarriages in which one (or both) partner was remarrying. In 1950, the figure was 19 percent and in 1998, as many as 30 percent of all those marrying were couples where at least one of the spouses was previously married (Historisk statistik för Sverige, 1969; Statistiska Centralbyrån, 2003). How many of those who marry are separated from a previous cohabitation? No data are available, but an educated guess would be, many.

Traditionally, one could only speak about remarriages. Now, re-cohabitation has to be considered. Many of those living in a marriage are living in a remarriage, and even more of those cohabiting, are re-cohabiting. In a remarriage, at least one of the spouses has to be previously married. The other spouse might have cohabited with someone other than the present spouse before starting a cohabitation with him or her, in what later became a (re)marriage.

Dissolution of Relationships

The number of divorces is known, but not how many cohabiting couples separate. There are some estimates, but they are not fully valid.

Many of those cohabiting separate after months or years, and quite a few marry. Some cohabiting dyads are eventually dissolved by the death of one of the partners. However, no valid data exist on these patterns.

When speaking about separation among cohabiting couples, one has to consider the nature or structure of the phenomenon of cohabitation. On one side, it can be claimed that they live under marriage-like conditions. On the other side, cohabitation is not a homogenous category. Some couples start to cohabit very early in their relationships, some even from the first day they know each other. Some start later. Some cohabiting relationships should be compared to the going-steady period (or even the courtship period) in the traditional mate selection and marriage system, while others start as late as during what was the engagement period.

Two hundred years ago, marriages tended to be dissolved through the death of one of the spouses when the other was still young and had minor children. The mortality rate decreased rapidly during the nineteenth century and continued to do so during the twentieth century. This means that there was not a great demand for divorce until about a 100 years ago. For example, in the period 1881-1890, there were thirty divorces per 100,000 existing marriages. In 1950, there were 500 (Historisk statistik för Sverige, 1969). Now, few marriages with minor children are dissolved by the death of one of the spouses/parents, but divorce and separation dissolve many.

In a sense, there are few bad marriages or cohabiting relationships. Divorces were uncommon a hundred years ago. Now they are common. Bad relationships end while the better ones continue. Today it is no shame to divorce or to have divorced parents or children. This does not mean that the divorces and separations are easy matters for the people involved. On the contrary, almost all individuals divorcing, as well as their children, and to some extent relatives and friends, find the dissolution of the relationship difficult and hurtful.

Since 1916, the law has permitted divorces based on no-fault as well as fault principles. In 1975, a new divorce law allowed divorce without stating grounds. Before 1975, the spouse wanting a divorce had to accuse the other spouse of some misbehavior like adultery, or to claim that the marriage broke up. Since 1975, the one who wants a divorce just says so.

During the first half of the twentieth century the divorce rate increased and then remained stable until 1966, when the rate started increasing again (Statistiska Centralbyrån, 2003). However, during the last thirty years or so the rates reported are not valid. This is because with the decrease in marriage rates, many of the current marriages are long-term and are much less divorce prone than newer marriages.

As the divorce rates are somewhat misleading, following marriage cohorts is enlightening. Of those who married in 1956, about 25 percent had divorced after thirty-five years. Those who married five years later were at the same level of divorce after twenty years of marriage, and those marrying in 1981 were at that level after only twelve years. Recently, the increase in divorce rates seems to have disappeared, at least there have not been any remarkable increases among those who married in 1976 and later. However, those marrying in 1991 reached 20 percent divorced after only seven years of marriage (Statistiska Centralbyrån, 2000). One problem with cohort data is that one has to wait many years to discover what happens to a cohort. Current trends are thus hard to predict.

FAMILIES AND CHILDREN

At the end of the 1920s and the beginning of the 1930s, the birthrate in Sweden as well as in many other Western countries was decreasing and reached low levels. Genetics as well as eugenics were popular subjects in several countries at that time. In Sweden, governmental committees suggested ways to increase the birthrate so that immigrants would not replace the "Swedish race." There was also concern about "cleanliness" to the effect that "lower quality" persons should not have children.

In order to increase the birthrate it was suggested that the state should give each mother a certain amount of money (as a child alimony) until the child was sixteen years old. This has been in effect since 1947. Households with many members and a sparse financial situation could receive housing subsidies, in effect from 1945. These are just a couple of examples of pronatality as promoted by the Swedish parliament. However, the birthrates started to increase at the end of the 1930s and a decrease started in 1948 (Historisk statistik för Sverige, 1969; Statistiska Centralbyrån, 2000, 2003).

Cleanliness of the population (i.e., eugenically correct) was addressed by a law requiring that some persons should be sterilized if they were, for example, schizophrenics or morons. In 1938, the parliament passed an abortion law, not to provide women with solutions to unwanted pregnancies, but to make sure that cleanliness would be upheld. Since 1939, a woman can have an abortion if raped (rapists could give negative genes to the child), in case of incest, and if she or the father of the fetus had genetically inheritable negative traits. A fourth ground was severe medical problems that could harm the pregnant woman or the child.

More recently, the fertility rate has decreased and was at a Total Fertility Rate (TFR) of 1.6 children per woman in 1983. In the beginning of the 1980s, a calculation was undertaken of what would happen with the birthrates, building upon the fact that Swedish women, on average, wanted 2.4-2.5 children during their lifetime (Trost, 1990). As almost no woman has more children than she wants given the availability of modern contraceptive techniques and with access to free abortions, the TFR would never exceed that value for more than a short time. Additional considerations were that few women want to have a child when in a bad relationship or without a husband/ cohabitant, the high divorce and separation rates, and estimates of sterility and the risk for sterility increasing with age. The conclusion was reached that the TFR would increase and reach a maximum of about 2.1 in 1990/1991 and then decrease again. That is exactly what happened.

A further decrease was expected for some years and in 1999, the TFR reached a record low level of 1.5. Predictions were that there would be an increase again after 2000 to about 2.1, unless the value system changed dramatically. The current (2006) fertility rate is estimated at 1.7 children born per woman and the birthrate is 10.27 births per 1,000 population. The current population growth rate is about 0.16 percent but is expected to become a negative 0.02 percent in the next few years. If this happens, the prediction is that by the year 2015, Sweden's population will decline by about 200,000. A consequence will be that the proportion of the population below the age of fifteen will be further reduced (to about 16 percent) while the proportion older than age sixty-five will increase to around 21 percent (Trost, 1990; UNDP, 2006; World Factbook, 2006).

Abortion

The legal abortion rate increased during the 1960s and the beginning of the 1970s and has since remained stable. Since 1975, Sweden has had a law giving women the right to an abortion until the end of the eighteenth week of gestation. About 95 percent of the abortions take place before the end of the twelfth week (Statistiska Centralbyrån, 1995a). The increase in the abortion rate was not due to legal changes, but changes in decision-making practices. The discussion here is about legal abortions. Today there are no illegal abortions, but four decades ago there were many. For obvious reasons, no one knows how many. However, there is no evidence that abortions have been used as "delayed" contraception as may have been the case in other European countries.

In the past many Swedish teenagers had children. Currently in Sweden, few do. With intensified and compulsory sex education in schools, the teenage pregnancy rate has dropped considerably. For example, the abortion rate for seventeen-year-olds is about twenty per 1,000 girls of that age. Almost all pregnancies among teenagers are aborted and few babies are born. In 1995, only 0.4 percent of all children born were to a girl aged seventeen or younger. For the category of fifteen to nineteen year-old children, the age-specific fertility rate for the same year was 0.0086 compared with 0.1257 (the mode) for the twenty-five to twenty-nine-year-old category (Statistiska Centralbyrån, 2000). Teenagers who were Swedish citizens had an age-specific fertility rate of 0.0069, while non-Swedish teenage citizens living in Sweden had a rate of 0.0331. Immigrants have a somewhat higher birthrate than others, but traditionally the rates have paralleled each other.

Child Rearing Ideology

In some countries, one can speak about a child rearing ideology. However, it is hard to demonstrate a real ideology for child rearing in Sweden. However, child rearing values are related to Swedish democracy. Sweden is one of the oldest democracies in the world. The first parliament was held in the city of Arboga in 1435, but even before that, the inhabitants elected their kings. The idea of democracy is connected to more than elections and parliaments; it has to do with the rights of humans to be treated with respect. For example, Sweden never had slaves. There has been a long tradition of freedom for everyone including for children. The idea of treating children as human beings thus has a long tradition.

The second influence on child rearing is related to the first. For a long time teachers and others have been forbidden to spank children. During the 1970s, Swedes debated if parents could be allowed to spank their children. The debate resulted in a law prohibiting parents from spanking their children. This law prohibits not only physical, but also emotional or mental, "spanking" or abuse. One peculiarity with this law is that there are no sanctions connected to the prohibition. If a parent spanks a child, no authorities could interfere. If the spanking is classified as child abuse, other laws with sanctions apply. While there are no exact legal definitions of the terms spanking and abuse, in Swedish there are clear differences between the meanings of the terms. In any case, severe spanking is abuse.

The democratic background is important to understanding the new law and what happened. There is no tradition of spanking in Sweden as there is in some other European countries (even if some of the Ingmar Bergman movies might give an impression of the opposite). People agreed, and still do, with not correcting their children either physically or with harsh mental punishment. Teachers spoke often about the law, and still do so. Children are aware that their parents are not allowed to spank them. If they did, what would their neighbors say or believe about them? Immigrant parents who come from cultures where spanking is not only permitted but also prescribed, soon learn from their children that in Sweden spanking is a criminal behavior (i.e., against the law). Even worse, it is defined as a disgusting behavior.

DeLey (1986) compared American and Swedish students' attitude toward parents spanking their children. The results showed that 90 percent of the Americans had been spanked, compared to 60 percent of the Swedes. Similarly, 60 percent of the Americans indicated that parents should spank their children, while only 20 percent of the Swedes agreed.

FAMILIES AND GENDER

Equity between women and men is a major issue in Sweden just as it is in many other Western countries. This is true on a macro- as well as a microlevel; that is, in society more generally as well as in intimate relationships. The ideology is that women and men should work for equality in their homes, in the relationship between spouses as well as in child rearing. One can see quite a few fathers taking their children to day-care centers and picking them up. Fathers are in the playgrounds with their children. Still, most of the care and responsibility remains with the mothers. Similarly, couples share a lot of the household work; but still more common to find wives taking responsibility for making sure that dishes are washed, that the home is vacuum cleaned, and that the clothes are washed, to mention some examples. Christensen (1982) wrote about the woman's new burden, meaning that she has the responsibility to make sure that her husband/cohabitant behaves according to the rules of equity. If he does not, it is her fault; she is to be blamed. Andenæs (1989) said about the same; that equity in reality is the task of the woman. If she fails at this task, she should not let others see that she fails. Therefore, many women pretend that their husbands/ cohabitees behave according to the ideology. In this way, women mask their lack of capacity for making their male partners stick to the rules of equity.

Ideological Code

Gender equity is an issue where political unanimity has been demonstrated for decades. Nevertheless, to some extent in Sweden as well as in so many other countries, this is close to what is called lip service. In the socialization of small children at home and in the child care organized by municipalities or other organizations, gender equity is certainly an issue. However, the ideological code of men as the standard against which women are compared is prevalent and active (Smith, 1993). To illustrate, boys can be more active and aggressive than girls, and boys receive more attention. This is the case throughout society even though strong attempts are made to ensure equity in all aspects of life, including socialization and training. For example, schoolbooks and other socialization mechanisms are scrutinized carefully so that they do not contain biased information or give messages contrary to the gender equity ideology. Real social life, however, cannot be controlled in the same way, and it is in life that the ideological code acts.

The standards for men and women, for boys and girls, are set although society tries to act in a contrary manner.

Although there have been many changes, traditional views on selecting an occupation or profession still survive. There are examples of changes (e.g., previously almost all students at law and medical schools were males, but now the majority is females). At the same time, almost all nurses are still females. One can say that some of the traditional male occupational areas have changed so more females are included, but the traditional female areas have remained as they were.

There are important differences in the incomes or salaries of men and women. Men have, on average, salaries more than 18 percent higher than those drawn by women (Statistiska Centralbyrån, 1995b). These differences are partly due to many women working part-time, especially those with minor children. Few men work part-time, even those with small children. There is still a difference in salaries in favor of men when occupation and work time are held constant. This difference is small in most occupational areas, varying from almost no difference up to more than 20 percent difference (Statistiska Centralbyrån, 1990-1991).[2] More important, however, is that when a male-dominated area turns into a female-dominated one, the salaries do not have a tendency to increase as much as for male areas. Salaries seem to adhere to the ideological code.

Largely, women are mothers and fathers are men. Or as an eight-year-old girl said, "Men are so lazy—they only work" (Åberg, 1996). She added that when men/fathers come home from their jobs they just sit down, read the newspapers, and watch the TV. Women/mothers, when they come home, prepare food, clean up, and do other household tasks. However, quite a few fathers (and mothers, the ideological code, again) bring their children to day care and/or pick them up in the afternoon. Fathers are seen with baby strollers nowadays, which one would not have seen a few decades ago.

Gender and Parental Leaves

The legal rule about parental leave (of which the father, if he exists, has to take one month or the parents lose it) is also aimed at reaching the goal of gender equity. Most fathers use their right to a month with almost full payment. However, according to many informal sources, what happens is not the same as when mothers take a leave of absence. Most of these fathers take care of their children, but they do not take the same responsibility as mothers in preparing food, cleaning dishes, cleaning the home, or washing clothes. Fathers often say they are babysitters—mothers never say the same about themselves.

While most fathers take at least some leave of absence to care for their children, the number varies. The more education and the higher the occupational position, the more leave of absence fathers take. At the same time, the more one's workmates would suffer from taking leave of absence, the fewer the number of fathers who take leave. Fathers employed by the government take more leave than fathers employed by private companies. There are no good recent data, but older data show that the smaller the work place, the fewer the number of fathers who use their right to take a leave of absence (Trost, 1983).

Gender differentiation still exists in Sweden despite the long tradition toward democracy and gender equity. A great deal more is to be done. However, one should recognize the various means employed for reaching the ideal—a society where gender is not a differentiating categorization.

FAMILIES AND STRESS

Given the current social, political, and economic conditions, families in Sweden do not face the magnitude of stressors sometimes found in other nations. In a sense, Swedish families face many of the same stressors found in any Western, industrialized society. There are a few issues discussed in this chapter that indicate some distinctive areas of stress. These are the dissolution of relationships, the responsibility placed on women for ensuring an equal division of household labor, and immigrant families perhaps finding assimilation difficult.

Dissolution of Relationships

While the divorce rate is high and stigma is not an issue, and many cohabitation relationships end, the breakup of intimate relationships are typically stressful. As in other societies, whenever people have been involved in a close personal relationship, the ending can be hard not only for the intimate partners, but also for their children. As noted in previous text, many children are born to cohabiting couples. These children, as well as those whose parents divorce, can experience loss and other negative feelings and consequences. To some extent, relatives and friends will also find the dissolution of the relationship difficult and hurtful.

Cohabitation breakups are less institutionalized and harder perhaps in some ways but easier perhaps in other ways. It could be quicker, but not having a definite end date as a legal divorce might make it more ambiguous. One major difference between ending a marriage and cohabitation is the clearly institutionalized means for divorcing. Ending cohabitation is less defined by social and legal rules. There are also differences in financial impacts. When divorcing, unless there is a marital contract stating otherwise, couples share all assets equally. There are thus clear guidelines and a person who brought fewer assets to the marriage can benefit financially from divorce. This can lead to concerns about fairness but helps maintain a more equal standard of living postmarriage. Cohabitants who are ending their relationships share only what they have acquired for their common use during cohabitation. Consequently, people who were/are less financially well-off will not benefit to the same extent financially when cohabitation ends compared with the situation if they had been married. A less equal postcohabitation standard of living could result, perhaps in more financial difficulties for some people.

The "New Burden" on Women

As noted in previous text, couples share in completing household work and child care. Compared with some other cultures, the stress of women being almost totally responsible for the upkeep of the home and the raising of children is relatively absent in Sweden. Women do not suffer in this regard as has been noted in many other nations. However, women still are more responsible for ensuring that household tasks are completed. While he might help, she is often responsible for making sure the domestic chores are completed.

The new burden for women is the responsibility of ensuring that their husbands or cohabitant partners act in accordance with the cultural rules of equity. It is considered her fault if he does not. If the inequality is known, she could be criticized for not being able to maintain, on the microlevel, the cultural expectations for gender equality. If equity is in reality the task of the woman, this is obviously not fair or equal. The necessity for women to monitor men to ensure that gender equality and a fair division of household labor are maintained can be stressful. If a woman fails at this task, she understands that the blame is hers. It is her responsibly, her burden. Consequently, if she does not succeed at maintaining the desired equality, she will likely keep this a secret. The result is women pretending that their mates behave according to the gender equality ideology to mask their inability to ensure that their partners stick to this ideology. In many situations then, stress can result—from striving to achieve equality (the emotional work, the negotiations, and the conflicts), from the worry of trying to adhere to a cultural norm, and from the shame that can result from failure.

Immigration and Assimilation

The homogeneous nature of Sweden was described in the Introduction to this chapter. There are few minorities in the common sense of the word. The country is mainly Swedish and Lutheran. In the past, immigrants typically came from societies similar to Sweden, and quickly assimilated to become Swedes. More recently, families have been migrating from regions dissimilar to Sweden, bringing different customs, family patterns, and religions. Some of these families might find social life difficult for various reasons.

There are few other families from the same cultural background for one thing. Fewer natural support systems are available. Another reason is that Swedish culture is rather hegemonic and less multicultural in orientation. While Swedes are tolerant and respectful of human rights, families from climates and cultures quite different from Scandinavia could discover that maintaining a distinctive cultural identity is problematic. Quick assimilation might also prove difficult given the distinctive differences in values, norms, and religion.

These newer immigrant families could find that living in a homogeneous society is stressful in ways not found in more multiethnic, multicultural societies. This is not to say these families are unwelcome or that they will fail, only that the assimilation process might prove more difficult than anticipated for former immigrants and be a more stressful experience for these families. As indicated in the Introduction, with more immigration from diverse cultures, the historically rapid assimilation might be a thing of the past. If so, future immigrants might experience less stress at the same time that some Swedish families experience the stress of a changing society.

FAMILIES AND AGING

Prenatal and infant mortality rates are low in Sweden. The infant mortality rate is 2.76 and the under-five mortality rate is 4 per 1,000 live births. Maternal mortality ratio (1990-2004) was 4 per 100,000 live births with the adjusted ratio being 2 for the year 2000. Life expectancy for males as well as for females in Sweden is among the highest in the world. One hundred years ago life expectancy at birth was 52.7 years for men and 55.3 for women. Now, the life expectancy is 78.3 years for men and 82.9 for women with an overall average life expectancy of 80.5. Among the 2000-2005 cohort, 86 percent of males and 92 percent of females are expected to survive to age 65. A great proportion of the population is of an advanced age; 17 percent are sixty-five years of age or older. After age sixty-five, the sex ratio is 0.77 males for each female. With the low birthrates during some decades and the probable low birthrate in the years to come, the aging of the population is inevitable (Historisk statistik för Sverige, 1969; Statistiska Centralbyrån, 2000; UNDP, 2006).

As is true elsewhere, a few more boys than girls are born; in Sweden, 6 percent more boys are born. Under age fifteen years, the ratio is 1.05 males to females. With the low mortality rate, the gender ratio changes from a surplus of males to a surplus of women at about age fifty-seven. At age sixty-five, retirement age, there are 11 percent more women than men, while at age eighty there are 52 percent more women than men (Statistiska Centralbyrån, 1996).

These figures mean that most minor children have both maternal and paternal grandparents who are still alive. It also means that quite a few minor children have great-grandparents and that many middle-aged persons have parents who are alive and have adult children and grandchildren. However, there has never been a tradition of extended families in Sweden and there are no tendencies visible for any change in that direction, if extended family means persons of more than two generations living in the same household.

Families and Housing

One can look at social reality in these respects from society's point of view, such as using a demographic perspective with the household as the unit of analysis. In such a case, the term household could substitute for family, which seems to be a better term from this perspective. However, if looking from an individual or small group perspective, the view is different. Many persons have family members who are not restricted to the same household as the person herself or himself. For example, when asked about who are the members of her family, a child might include one or several grandparents and a great-grandparent. Her answer includes not only the household where she lives but also a number of other households or parts of other households. These households might be in the same geographical area, or distributed over a large area, perhaps on more than one continent. From the perspective of a seventy-five-year-old, his or her family might consist of members from various households. For example, from households of the person's children and grandchildren as well as from his or her own household (Levin & Trost, 1992).

The census shows that 40 percent of all households in Sweden are one-person households, 31 percent are two-person households, 12 percent have three persons, and 17 percent of the households have four or more members (Statistiska Centralbyrån, 1992). Historically, these figures show a strong trend toward smaller households, as is the case in all Western countries.

Given the number of one-person households, the conclusion is often drawn that many persons are living alone and lonely. This is, however, a misinterpretation. Using proportions of the population, rather than proportions of households, just under 18 percent of the inhabitants of Sweden live in a one-person household. The rest of the population is distributed as follows: 28 percent live in a two-person household, 16 percent in a three-person household, and 38 percent live in households with four or more members (Statistiska Centralbyrån, 1992).

Second and very important, a person is not lonely just because he or she lives in a one-person household. Loneliness has little to do with the housing situation. Some people are lonely even when living with others, and many people living alone have lots of friends and relatives with whom they frequently interact. While many of the one-person households are those of elderly people and while many of the elderly live in institutions or similar arrangements, evidence shows that few of the elderly are lonely (Tornstam, 1994). Most old people have children or grandchildren who visit, who call over the telephone, who communicate by e-mail, and the like (Tornstam, 1994). Furthermore, there are many self-organized associations for retired people, and groups organize dancing parties, card parties, and the like.

Caregiving

Unlike some other cultures, there is no tradition of the younger generation taking care of the older generation in Sweden. During earlier periods when there was high mortality, there were few elderly requiring care. Sweden started its process of industrialization late compared with most of the Western world. This means that in the middle of the nineteenth century, the majority of the population was still in agriculture, mainly farming and forestry combined. Most of these farmers were peasants, meaning they were family-farming households with no or almost no people employed at the small farm.

When the oldest son had found a wife and married, he would customarily take over the farm from the parents (the father and the mother if both were alive). The tradition was that the son and his wife would buy the farm. A contract was usually written to the effect that a small house or a cottage, a small garden, and a certain amount of cut wood for cooking and heating, and a certain amount of grain per year were given to the parent(s). The son and his wife made up one household and the parents made another. The households were independent of each other except for what the contract stated. This meant that the parents were *satta på undantag,* "put on exemption," in direct translation.

If the elderly were poor, often the case with male and female servants, they were assigned a bed in the poorhouse of the village (together with mentally and physically disabled poor persons). This tradition of society taking care of the poor, aged, and disabled still exists. A great share of the welfare state builds upon this tradition of collective caring for those in need.

OTHER FAMILY SITUATIONS

A dyadic relationship that had not been visualized until recently is named with an acronym for Living Apart Together (LAT). A LAT relationship consists of two persons who define themselves as a married-like couple, but who are living in two separate households (other people might also live in the households). They are likewise considered a couple by their closer social network. The two can be married to each other, or not. These dyads could not have existed before the changes (discussed earlier in this chapter) in the marital and cohabitational structure, for the simple reason that previously, such couples would not have been visible. The four elements mentioned in previous text (the marriage ceremony, moving in together, having sexual intercourse together, and having the first child about a year later) with their normative structure would not have permitted LAT relationships.

In the mid-1990s, about 2 percent of the Swedish population aged eighteen to seventy-four were living in LAT relationships: approximately 60,000 couples or 120,000 persons (Levin & Trost, 1999). A poll conducted in the beginning of 2000 showed an increase to more than 125,000 couples, 250,000 persons, or more than 4 percent of the population. Most of these persons live in Sweden but some have their LAT partners in other countries. Examples of such couples include those not wanting to move in together due to minor children living at home, or those being unable to obtain employment close enough to live together.

The phenomenon of LAT relationships appears on the increase with, for example, high divorce and separation rates, high geographical mobility, and increasing occupational specialization. It might be assumed or presumed that LAT relationships would be found only among the economically well-off. This thinking is based on it being more expensive to live in two households than in one and the long-distance LAT relationships including travel and telephone costs. However, quite a few LAT couples are not so well-off financially. In most cases when a LAT relationship is formed, the two already have their housing and are adapted to the costs. The new relationship thus does not necessarily mean any extra expenses unless the two people involved live far away from each other.

CONCLUDING COMMENTS

For the near future of Sweden, as well as for the rest of the Western world, family life deals with marriage, LAT relationships, and cohabitation. Other aspects of family will probably continue as they have during the last few years. There is no observable reason for any remarkable changes in the number of divorces, separations, children born, mortality, child rearing, or relations between women and men.

However, the number of marriages will remain at a low level in the entire Western world and more countries will experience sudden increases in the number of marriages as happened in Sweden the last month of 1989. With a considerable "pool" of cohabiting couples, where quite a few see marriage as something to occur in the future, booms can easily occur.

LAT relationships will likely increase as one of the alternatives for couples, the others being marriage and cohabitation. LAT relationships could not reasonably have become a social institution without the institution of nonmarital cohabitation. Before cohabitation became common, marriage was the sole institution. With Swedish society's acceptance of cohabitation came an understanding that couples did not have to marry in order to live together with the expectation that they will also have a sexual relationship. Now couples do not even have to live together while still being a couple. Most LAT relationships now are made up of two people who are not married. However, it is possible that with the social acceptance of these relationships more married and cohabiting couples will separate in order not to divorce or end their relationships. Couples can save a relationship by not living together and thus maintain a relationship in which they do not have to be irritated, as easily happens in the long run with couples living together.

NOTES

1. Sweden has a constitutional monarchy form of government and has been independent since 1523. It is located in northern Europe (Scandinavia) between Finland and Norway. In comparative geographic terms, it is about the same size as the State

of California, United States. Over 80 percent of the population is urban (United Nations Development Programme [UNDP], 2006; World Factbook, 2006).

2. Sweden ranks second on the United Nations' Gender Empowerment Measure. Women hold 45 percent of seats in parliament, make up about 50 percent of professional and technical workers, and the estimated ratio of female to male earned income is .81 (UNDP, 2006).

Chapter 4

Diversity in Families: Germany

Bruno Hildenbrand

INTRODUCTION

A presentation of family life in Germany must consider the re-unification (in 1990) of the two German states (Federal Republic of Germany and the German Democratic Republic). Separated for forty years because of World War II, each had different political systems as well as varying legal regulations on families. Prior to 1990, the Federal Republic of Germany (FRG, West Germany) declared that the goal of family policy was to emphasize the independence of the family, to regard it as an institution particularly worthy of protection, and "to create an appropriate basis on which families are able to shape their lives according to their own ideas" (Bundesministerium für Familie und Senioren [BFS], 1994, p. iv). In the German Democratic Republic (GDR, East Germany) the distinction between State and family was vaguer. In particular, the State claimed a greater say in child rearing and took on far-reaching family tasks (Meyer, 1996). Due to this policy, the extremes between familial cohesion and disintegration were more distinct in the former GDR. Differences as well as similarities between family lifestyles in East and West Germany are discussed throughout this chapter. Since reunification, West German family law and political ideas about family apply throughout Germany. Germany is a federal republic of sixteen states with a population of about eighty-two million, of which 88 percent live in urban areas. In the Human Development Index, Germany ranks twentieth and is one of western Europe's richest and most populous nations (United Nations Development Programme [UNDP], 2005).

Families in German Context—Recent Changes in Family Patterns

The models of the ideal family and family reality were largely homogenous until about thirty years ago. Both are rooted in a Christian Occidental paradigm that is the traditional belief of most of the German population. There is some marginal influence from traditional family types brought to Germany through work migration from south and southeast Europe.

Some people claim that a dramatic change in family types is under way. Social scientists have even asked whether the family as an institution could survive. There are various explanations for the alteration of family types in Germany. First, people are marrying at an older age. In 1960, the average age at first marriage for men was 25.4 years and women 23.4. In 1990, men's age at first marriage averaged 28.5 years and women 26.1 (BFS, 1994). In 2002, men at first marriage averaged 31.8 years and women 28.8 (Statistisches Bundesamt, 2004a). The importance of life partnerships without marriage has also been increasing. Cohabiting couples and single parents make up a sizable minority of the population.

The differences in family composition between East and West Germany can be attributed to GDR's family policy that aimed to keep families in the regime's grip. Long-standing, stable marital relationships were an impediment to this goal. In East Germany, up to now, the tendency has been to raise children in households of unmarried partners or lone parents. This was present in West Germany, however in a less marked way. A comparison is shown in Table 4.1.

Divorce rates have been increasing. In 1970 in FRG, there were 15.9 divorces for every 100 marriages and in 1994, 37 divorces for every 100 marriages, while in GRD the rates were 21 in 1970 and 19 in 1994. Since 1997, the increase in divorce has been leveling off in West Germany, whereas in East Germany the divorce rate has been rising. In 2000, the divorce rate in East Germany was 32.3 and in West Germany it was 38.5. For East and West Germany together, it was 37.3. At the same time, remarriage rates have been declining, to just

TABLE 4.1. Family Status of Mothers of Children Under Eighteen (Percentage).

	West		East	
Family Status	**1991**	**2000**	**1991**	**1996**
Married	88.6	86.1	81.2	74.9
Single	2.5	3.0	6.3	8.9
Married, living apart	1.6	2.3	0.6	2.4
Divorced	4.6	5.2	8.8	9.3
Widowed	1.1	1.1	1.0	1.4

Source: Engstler (1999); Engstler & Menning (2003).

over sixty remarriages per 100 divorces in West Germany and seventy-one in East Germany (Engstler & Menning, 2003). Surveys in 1991 and 1998 showed that East Germans (70 percent) valued living together as a family more so than did Restrada West Germans (60 percent) (Informationszentrum Sozialwissenschaften, 2000).

Some social scientists interpret these figures as a crisis of the family (Beck & Beck-Gernsheim, 1990). Others interpret the current developments to characterize the normal status of the family; the 1960s—the "golden age of the family"—are an exceptional case. At that time, more than 90 percent of any adult age group was married (Burkart & Kohli, 1992). Apart from this, the legal form of marriage is said to be undergoing a crisis and many unmarried couples are cohabiting. Survey findings show Germans highly appreciate and value family, parenthood, and partnership (Burkart & Kohli, 1992).

What does family life in Germany mean today? Judging by the picture of the family conveyed by advertising and commercials, the typical family consists of father, mother, one son, and one daughter who is two years younger. This family lives in its own house on the outskirts of the city. The male head, the breadwinner, works full time and his wife works part-time. This "normal family" can be found in Germany, especially in smaller cities in rural areas, where approximately 40 percent of the population lives. Housing and employment helps in explaining this rural lifestyle. In rural areas, around 70 percent of families live in houses they own, higher than the national average of 49 percent

(Bertram, Bayer, & Bauereiß, 1993). In addition, the employment rate in rural areas is higher than it is in areas of industrial concentration.

There is also a difference in family concepts between rural and urban areas. Burkart and Kohli (1992) suggested that German people would have to deal with a pluralization of family forms in the future. This will develop into a polarization of two opposed lifestyles: family-oriented lifestyle in rural areas and individualized lifestyle in urban forms, a legally married couple with children remains dominant, constituting over 80 percent of all families (Engstler & Menning, 2003; Nave-Herz, 1994).

Family patterns reflect racial and ethnic diversity. In 2003, Germany had about 7.3 million foreigners—almost 9 percent of Germany's population (Statistisches Bundesamt, 2004a). Most of these immigrants come for jobs, the majority from other European countries or Turkey. "Coloured" migrants (e.g., from Asia or Africa) make up a small part of the population (Statistisches Bundesamt, 2004a). However, a minority of natives feel disturbed by the immigration of people who, because of their racial difference, appear "outlandish." This resentment can find its expression in criminal xenophobic actions, predominantly among the youth in East Germany. The ethnic makeup is German, 92 percent, Turkish, 2 percent, others, 6 percent (e.g., Serbo-Croatian, Italian, Russian, Greek, Polish, or Spanish) (World Factbook, 2005).

Migrant workers and their families, on average, experience worse conditions of working and living than do Germans; they receive lower wages mostly because they do unskilled or semiskilled work. Likewise, migrant worker families experience worse housing conditions and have fewer educational opportunities (Bauereiß, Bayer, & Bien, 1997).

Religion (often related to ethnic background) also influences family life. In 1992, 88 percent of those interviewed in West Germany and 33 percent in East Germany said they belonged to a religious group. This difference is due to the previous Communist antireligious ideology, which has had its effects even after reunification. The inquiry about people's belief in God, in contrast to their being on the church register, reveals a further secular development. In West Germany, 67 percent of the interviewed declared themselves religious and in East Germany 25 percent. This secular development can be seen when compared with other countries (e.g., United States of America and

Poland where 6 percent do not believe in God and in Ireland 14 percent: Terwey, 1993).

Germans are about equally divided between Roman Catholic (34 percent) and Protestant (34 percent), while around 28 percent are unaffiliated or other. About three million (4 percent) Muslims form the largest non-Christian group (World Factbook, 2005). Most of them are Turkish migrant worker families. The characteristics of Muslim practices (e.g., building mosques, a muezzin who calls the faithful to prayer, ritual slaughtering) create problems of understanding for native Germans. Likewise, many Muslims do not understand the secular habits of the German society.

There are about two million Turks within Germany (Statistisches Bundesamt, 2004a). Turkist culture has notions of women and family that produce differences in the everyday life of these inhabitants. The children of Turkish families, many of whom are born in Germany, sometimes refuse to accept their parents' traditional, Islam-oriented (e.g., ideas about mate selection, sexuality, and family) lifestyle. This can result in deep, unsolvable conflicts within the family. Generally, these conflicts are private, hidden from the public. They sometimes find expression, however, in spectacular acts of violence against family members.

COUPLE FORMATION AND MARITAL DYNAMICS

There were two traditional reasons that people decided to marry: the desire to have a stable love life and the young person's wish to leave the parental home (Burkart & Kohli, 1992). These reasons are no longer of much importance. Both needs can be satisfied by sharing a flat or a house with other people (which is common among students), cohabitation, or being single. Nonmarital partnerships, in particular, form a "new way of life during young age or post adolescent life span" (Nave-Herz, 1994, p. 8). Thus, as mentioned, the average marriage age has risen.

Nowadays, couples often decide to marry when the woman becomes pregnant. Sociologists tend to interpret this as the partners' mutual love ranking behind the couple's orientation toward the child (Herlth, Brunner, Tyrell, & Kriz, 1994). It is a special case when couples deliberately decide against having children (Schneewind, 1997). This might be due to the partnership ranking higher than having children and that personal freedom, leisure time, as well as career, take priority, or the couple's insight that they might be unable to take responsibility for children.

A couple valuing its own relationship less than its relationship with their children often leads to problems. These range from the situation encountered when children begin to leave home and the couple faces redefining its relationship (Welter-Enderlin, 1992) to the situation where the parents divorce and the child becomes "the last remaining indissoluble, unexchangeable primary relationship" for the mother (only about 10 percent of males raise children as a single father after divorce) (Beck, 1986, p. 193; Engstler & Menning, 2003). When interpreting such findings, the most favored explanations stress the disintegration of family relations and, at the same time, the progression of individualized interests (Burkart, 1993). A more distinguished picture is offered by Burkart and Kohli (1992), who elaborate four types of marriage and family relations.

Marriages of the Heart. In rural and working class milieus one finds "marriages of the heart," where the couple loves each other, cares about the relationship, and wants to create a family. Roles attributed to husband and wife largely follow traditional patterns (i.e., he works full time, she stays at home, takes care of the children, and is in charge of the emotional well-being of the family). Unfaithfulness signals failure of the marriage and leads to divorce.

Marriage Based on Partnership. In milieus of technological rationality, chiefly found in large cities and urban agglomerations, "marriage based on partnership" is widespread. The conjugal partners are typically employed professionals. They are usually affluent enough to employ household services and child-care support, while in rural and working class milieus, employed women mostly bear a double burden from household and job. The difficulties in balancing employment and parenthood can result in the decision either to postpone or to avoid having children. Once the couple has children, motherhood is less important than professional career. The child is cared for either by relatives, in public child-care centers, or by both parents.

Individualized Partnerships. "Individualized partnership" couples are represented by the marriage between individualized professionals.

Typically living in an urban milieu, the life courses of the partners are largely compatible, with both placing more value on their careers than on establishing a family with children. Consequently, childlessness is quite common, and this kind of partnership faces the risk of breakup. Separation can be due to unfaithfulness or to a deep alienation from each other conditioned by a professional career, for instance.

The Temporary Pair of Lovers. Found mostly in big cities with universities, the "temporary pair of lovers" holds the traditional values of community and solidarity together with postmodern values of individualism. The institution of marriage is viewed with skepticism, but these people tend to be more willing to have children than the individualized professionals. Division of labor is more or less nonexistent, especially against the background that having a secure occupational position is not the primary goal. It is the man's duty to induce changes for a redefinition of gender roles. The relationship is relatively unrestricted. Jealousy in the case of unfaithfulness has to be justified. People in these relationships are ready to compromise. If love comes to an end, their relationship comes to an end. Yet, the parents usually stay in touch with their children and the former partner.

Divorce

The frequency of divorce has risen drastically since the mid-1960s. More recently the increase has slowed and there are signs of stabilization in the divorce rate at a relatively high level. If the divorce rate remains constant, it is expected that one-third of marriages will eventually end in divorce. The highest rate of divorce is for marriages of five to seven years duration. In 1996, the average duration of a marriage ending in divorce was twelve years. By fifteen years, one-third of marriages have been terminated by divorce. Marrying young appears to be a high-risk factor in explaining marital disruption. Having their parents divorce before reaching the age of twenty affects about 16 percent of the children in Germany (Engstler & Menning, 2003). Before 1989 (the end of the Communist period), the risk of divorce was much higher in East than in West Germany. Divorce rates in East Germany dropped but have risen since 1991. The divorce rate is still lower than the relatively high levels of the 1980s (Engstler, 1999).

FAMILIES AND CHILDREN

The German law about naming children states that first names must clearly be definable by their gender, and they must not offend moral standards. First names can be chosen from all languages. Since 1994, a law about last names has been in force. If the parents bear a single last name, which can be either the husband's or the wife's name, the child also bears this name. If the parents have no single last name, the child can be given either the mother's or the father's name. This choice is valid for all the family's children. Children can have the hyphenated last name of their mother or father if it is "genuine," that is, a name inherited by one of the parents.

Currently the birthrate is 8.6 births per 1,000 population and the infant mortality rate is 4.23 deaths per 1,000 live births. The less than five mortality rate is 5 per 1,000 live births while the maternal mortality rate is 5 per 100,000 live births. The population growth rate is estimated at 0.2 percent (UNDP, 2005). In 2000, the fertility rate in Germany was 1.36 children born per woman (Engstler & Menning, 2003). This is below the population replacement rate for the nation. In 2000, 72 percent of all children were growing up as an only child or with one sibling (Engstler & Menning, 2003). Thus, German children during their first few years primarily deal with adults and do not grow up together with other children. This also applies to families in East Germany since reunification.

Child-Care Centers

In the days of the GDR, the majority of children aged one to three years were looked after in public day nurseries or child-care centers. This was because the percentage of employed women was very high (more than 90 percent). In 1989, day nurseries and child-care centers were available for 82 percent of these children. In West Germany, such options were available for only 2 percent of children aged one to three years (Weber, 1996). After German reunification, many of the public nurseries and child-care centers in the former GDR closed down because the institutions in charge (e.g., firms, collective combines, and municipal authorities) could no longer afford the expenditure necessary for maintaining these facilities. Furthermore, the demand for day nurseries and child-care centers dropped dramatically due to high unemployment among women. Many women also welcomed the opportunity to look after their children themselves. In the meantime, it has become law that children aged three years and over can claim a place in a nursery school. This means that enough places must be available to meet the demand (i.e., a supply quota of 100 percent is required). In 1986, the de facto supply quota fluctuated between 30 percent and more than 100 percent in West Germany. Thus, in some areas there were many more places than there were children who claimed them. This can be attributed to the different financial means of the individual federal states, as well as to the different traditions and emphases in the fields of education and social policy (Bertram et al., 1993).

Comparing two federal states should help in understanding the situation. Both Baden-Württemberg and Bavaria are wealthy states. In Baden-Württemberg, the number of child-care places in 1986 ranged from 95 to 128 per 100 children aged three to five years, depending on the region. In Bavaria, the number of child-care places in 1986 ranged from twenty-nine to sixty-three per 100 children, depending on the region. These differences have their roots in: traditional values that prefer educating children in families; churches or municipal authorities providing child care as a result of these traditional values; and low demand for child-care places because of low rates of employment among women, especially in rural areas (Bertram et al., 1993). By 1994, the proportion had changed. Baden-Württemberg had 1,079 child-care places available per 1,000 children, whereas Bavaria had 880 per 1,000 children (Bauereiß et al., 1997).

In contrast, in the former GDR, about 95 percent of all children aged three to six years attended a nursery school in 1989 (Schmidt, 1996). The remaining 5 percent were cared for in their families, although they could have claimed a place in a nursery school. It is generally assumed that before unification, a quantitative lack of public child care in West Germany corresponded to a qualitative lack of public child care in East Germany (Schmidt, 1996). "The GDR would have been forced to face the challenge to improve educational work, to enhance work productivity and consequently to reduce working hours as well as to reevaluate bringing up children in the family; similarly, the former FRG would have been urged to increase the rate of child-care places" (Klemm, Böttcher, & Weegen, 1992, p. 46).

Child Rearing

The fewer children parents have, the closer the relationship between parents and their children will be, and the more significant the parental educational style turns out to be. Social scientists agree that there has been a change in the last thirty years in Germany. Before, traditional goals in child rearing—such as honesty, tidiness, and obedience—set the tone. Today, parents aim at teaching their children autonomy. In accordance with this development, physically punishing children has lost its significance. A survey showed that 90 percent of parents when asked whether they beat their children denied that they did (Nave-Herz, 1994).

Child-oriented upbringing, facilitated by the small families that parents have, leads to a situation where the process of child rearing is increasingly a matter of negotiation between parents and children. This process starts in early childhood and usually reaches its peak in the period of adolescence. In harmony with this observation, most teenagers answer in surveys that they have a good relationship with their parents (Nave-Herz, 1994). One can assume that this type of upbringing of children is more widespread in the middle and upper classes because it demands hardwork on the part of the parents. If so, this should be the case with more than 70 percent of the population (Geißler, 1996).

Social Policy and Families

In this section, policies concerning different types of financial supports, child welfare and youth programs, and abortion regulations are discussed. The State protects the independence of the family (Article 6 of Constitutional Law). However, the German Federal Government finds in its *5th Family Report of 1994* that the task conferred by the Constitutional Law is "not sufficiently completed" (BFS, 1994, p. 319).

Financial support is one of the governmental measures for families. Thus, the government has planned to reduce the economic disadvantages of parents with children compared with couples without children, by means of compensating for family duties. Such measures include the nontaxation of alimony (*Alimente*) paid by mothers or fathers (up to the subsistence level for a child), as well as the granting of family subventions or subsidies that vary according to the parents' income and the number of children. Family subventions include children's allowance (in 2004, €154 [Euro] for the first three children each per month, for further children €179 each; about US$186 and US$216), housing benefit, tuition aid, educational grants, child-rearing support, and maternity/paternity leave. In Germany, every child receives a children's allowance (*Kindergeld*) from the government. The *Kindergeld* starts with birth and ends at age eighteen, or when university or other education is concluded (at age twenty-eight at the latest). In addition, the parents receive a yearly tax credit, the amount depending upon the income earned.

Families receive further financial support from retirement insurance. People living on social benefits receive health insurance by local authorities. Workers and their employers contribute to retirement insurance that is obligatory for all employees. Their employers pay an equivalent amount each month. The contributions are withdrawn from wages or salary and transferred directly to the retirement insurance providers, which are two insurance companies. It is from these transfers that the current retirement pensions are paid. The person's old-age pension is calculated from the amount contributed to the retirement insurance, from the number of years employed, and partially on the basis of how wages increased over the years. Women who can claim old-age pensions get a three-year employment bonus for each child born and thus enhance their claims for retirement payments. Another income transfer from the State is social assistant benefits. Social assistant benefits are either payments for living costs (for those families whose monthly income is under a defined subsistence level) or support in certain situations such as for people with handicaps or illness (BFS, 1994).

The well-being of the child and the rights of parents plays a central role in the sphere of child welfare and youth programs. These programs offer institutional, partially institutional, and community services to children and juveniles. Partially institutional and community services receive priority. Private institutions are preferred when the State does not have a legal task to perform. Legal tasks are designed "to intervene in the legal sphere of persons who hold parental responsibility for a child or of minors, or to propose judicial interventions of this kind according to the law" (Fieseler & Herborth, 1989, p. 63). Legal tasks would include statutory guardianship and investigating whether parents appropriately care for their children.

Wherever private agencies offer help for children and youth, they receive considerable support from the State. In 1990, West Germany had over 50,000 institutions or agencies for child and youth welfare services (figures beyond 1990 cannot be given due to a dramatic shift in the youth welfare system since reunification). Of these, about 15,000 were owned and administered by the State, about 35,000 belonged to nonprofit organizations, and about 1,000 were profit-oriented enterprises (Landwehr & Wolff, 1993). Governmental and nonprofit organizations carry out the major part of youth welfare. The number of non-state institutions is larger (a ratio of 70:30); this ratio, however, is simply the reverse concerning the staff employed (35:65). This means that 35 percent work for non-state agencies while 65 percent work for state agencies.

New abortion regulations came about after reunification because the law in the GDR was not consistent with the regulations in the FRG. An abortion can be obtained legally without risk of prosecution within the first three months of pregnancy on condition that the woman has consulted an approved counseling agency (Section 218a Criminal Code). The aim of the counseling session is to determine whether there are reasons for an abortion with impunity, and to look for alternatives to abortion. The law states that reasons for terminating pregnancy are approved if, taking into consideration the present and future living conditions of the pregnant woman, the abortion is indicated from a medical point of view in order to avert danger to the woman's life or the threat of a grave impairment of the pregnant woman's physical or mental health, provided that this risk for the woman cannot be averted in a different way reasonable for the woman. This regulation is in practice, yet it is controversial. For instance, the Catholic Church has not made a decision whether the church-administered family advice centers should go on counseling pregnant women if this means that the women are entitled to legal abortions by virtue of the information she gets from the advice center after being counseled.

FAMILIES AND GENDER

Gender issues in families do not mean the visible biological sex, but rather the culturally coined gender. In English, there is a distinction between sex and gender, but there is no such distinction in German

(Heinze, Nadai, Fischer, & Ummel, 1997). It is common among German social scientists to emphasize gender-related social inequalities (Geißler, 1996). However, factual gender-related inequalities have decreased while people's awareness of these has increased.

There are differences in gender status between the former FRG and the former GDR. In the GDR, the issue of equal status for women was practiced as "patriarchal authoritarian liberation from the top" by means of political indoctrination and setting economic conditions. In the former FRG, by comparison, this emancipation process proceeded as "democratic public liberation from the bottom" pushed by the women's liberation movement (Geißler, 1996, p. 275; Gerhard, 1995).

An analysis of the educational system shows that young men and women have equal opportunities in their educational careers. The number of women admitted to universities exceeds the number of men. However, marked differences exist in vocational training that continues on the job. This is true for both the payment received and the prospects of working one's way up. Consequently, the models of occupational careers used by politicians and the general population are mostly oriented to men's life course. This means full-time and continuous employment over their careers. However, women are often expected (by their spouses, families, neighbors, politicians, employers, etc.) to follow traditional patterns of family. Women generally adhere to a gender-specific upbringing and education. In professional life, "male" properties such as self-confidence, dominance, power to assert oneself, and toughness are more highly valued than "female" properties such as discretion, emotional, social, and humane strengths.

Another source of differences between the genders can be seen in family structures in which the husband's importance as the single figure of authority has dwindled, which even applies to families where patriarchal patterns have dominated (e.g., in farm families) (Planck, 1964). However, the more power the husband has in his job, the less he needs in the family. Thus, patriarchal relationships prevail in families within the lower classes (Nave-Herz, 1994).

In 2000, the employment rate among women with children was 65 percent in the former FRG and 89 percent in the former GDR, and 70 percent overall (see Engstler & Menning, 2003). In 2002, 39 percent of women with children had part-time employment in the former FRG and 19 percent in the former GDR. These figures raise the question of how the division of labor in families is structured (Statistisches Bundesamt, 2004a). In general, women continue to bear the double burden of household and employment.

Men are more ready to contribute to housework when paid-work hours are at a different time than are the employment hours of their wives. However, Nave-Herz (1994) concluded that traditional patterns of division of labor continue to exist. That is, wives, albeit employed, are in charge of the household. If both partners are at home at the same time, women prefer quickly doing the chores themselves to instructing husbands, thus training them for "learned helplessness."

Fathers tend to participate in child rearing and caring more than, say, thirty years ago. However, from the change in some fathers' behavior, one cannot assume a change in the "father role" as such. The paternal role is closely linked to the part men play in their paid jobs and is influenced by the prevailing differences between men and women in professional life (Nave-Herz, 1994).

The change from a patriarchal to a partnership model of marriage has also brought about a change in people's privacy and sexual relations. Sexual passion, as part of increased privacy, is thus experienced equally by men and women (Welter-Enderlin, 1992). An increasingly open discussion about sexuality and the impact that the student unrest in the 1960s had on removing the taboo from sexuality facilitated this development.

FAMILIES AND STRESS

An abundance of stressors affect families living in a complicated, permanently changing social world. Of these, three are discussed in relation to German families—poverty, violence, and compatibility of family and employment.

Poverty

In Germany, poverty is no longer an issue of how to survive physically. Surviving is secured by governmental help, which can be claimed without time restrictions by every needy citizen. In 1993, about five million people lived on the dole (i.e., received welfare benefits); 73 percent of them were Germans and 27 percent were people from abroad (Bauereiß et al., 1997). In 2000, between 9 percent (West Germany) and 12 percent (East Germany) lived below the poverty line, which is defined as a monthly income less than 50 percent of the average of incomes in Germany (Statistisches Bundesamt, 2004b). Relative poverty, on the other hand, means that persons are excluded from leading a certain way of life. This occurs because they have a lower income than what is considered as the minimal requirement in the member states of the European Union (Geißler, 1996). The subsistence level is defined as 50 percent of the national median income. People with incomes below this are considered relatively poor. Between 1990 and 2000, around 8 percent of the population was below this income level.

The characteristics of persons and households in need include age (younger) of child, migrant family status, number (more) of children, and single-parent status. Figures reveal that the rate of poverty in West and East Germany are about the same. However, East German statistics show that the gap between the poor and the rich has increased in the last few years (Statistisches Bundesamt, 2004b).

Violence

Whether violence in German families has increased remains controversial. "The cases of child abuse statistically registered, almost halved between 1973 and 1982 and since then have held a level of about 1,200 cases a year" (Engfer, 1993, p. 618). There has also developed an enhanced sensitivity to violence against children (Engfer, 1993). Certainly, it can be said that there have been increased ongoing discussions about violence within families.

Engfer (1993) found that 10 percent of the mothers and 8 percent of the fathers surveyed beat their children with objects of various kinds; 13 percent of the partners within couples have used physical force when getting divorced (Nave-Herz, Daum-Jaballah, Hauser, Matthias, & Scheller, 1990). Violence toward parents is reported from families where adult children care for elderly people. Causes for violence often relate to features of the perpetrator's personality and/or drug or alcohol addiction. Variables such as financial distress, job strain, loss of the job, and lack of public or private support for family adds to the previously mentioned conditions (BFS, 1994).

Compatibility of Family and Employment

Recently, certain changes have strongly provoked families into re-structuring their internal relationships. One of the achievements of the modern (European) society is the normal workday (Monday to Friday, eight hours a day) and the normal work contract (collective wage agreement, unlimited and full-time employment). On this basis, the expected amount of work was limited, sufficient time-off was granted, and there was certain security in terms of the near finan-cial future.

The normal workday and normal work contract are subject to two conditions. The first is the gender-specific division of labor with the husband doing the breadwinning and the wife the housework. The second condition is an ongoing economic prosperity. However, the "golden age of the family" with an efficient housewife, loving spouse, and always cheerful mother of two children together with a smart and successful spouse who, in the evening, comes home from work tired, but nevertheless good-tempered, was of short duration. So was the short dream of everlasting prosperity with ceaselessly increasing growth in economic production, income, and consumption (Lutz, 1984). Both phenomena reached their peak in the 1950s-1960s, but the memory is alive and seen in people's expectations to continue the lifestyle of this past period.

Those two conditions no longer exist. Estimates suggest that three-quarters of today's employed people have employment that deviates from the normal amount of work time. Men, to an increasing extent, no longer have the stability associated with continuous employment under normal work contracts. At the same time, women's employment rate is growing, and these women are trying to gain continuity in their employment lives.

In addition to changes in work contracts, employment time has be-come more flexible. Flextime, part-time (particularly for women), and temporary work enable workers to have more control over their sched-ules. The advantages gained, however, are in danger of being lost due to the "just-in-time" concept that employers often follow. The just-in-time concept means that the workers are on call depending on the amount of work to be done by the company. Thus, work time of the employed has become more deregulated. Workers have little influence on how their work time is organized.

Finally, the demands of work (a result of the "Protestant ethic") on one's life have risen along with a change in values. During the period when the normal employment contract and work time were acknowledged, the family was a "counter-world" in which people lived. Today, time spent in employment activities offers the opportunity for self-realization. However, many people still use the image of the old model of normal work time and employment contracts. This mental model defines the standard by which the relation between employment and family life is determined. This is most obvious when examining the relation between employment and family life among women.

As mentioned, women usually try to create continuity in their employment over their life spans. This is why they marry at an older age, give birth to a smaller number of children, interrupt employment contracts less frequently, and often seek part-time work in order to make employment and family more compatible. Although men are afflicted by the current job deregulation, the majority behave as if the division of labor linked with normal employment contract and working hours was still there. That is, the husband is the breadwinner and the wife takes care of the family and the home that represent the haven in a heartless world (Lasch, 1977).

As matters stand today, the employed woman also claims for herself such a soothing "haven." In fact, however, she is now in charge of both spheres of duty. She contributes to the family income (many families could not cope financially without her support) and she makes the family a place where the individual members find recuperation from their struggles with the daily demands from the outside world. The family also sets performance standards. Middle-class children and adolescents have appointment books filled with commitments, such as piano lessons and ballet. These have to be completed with the help of the mother-worker who, as a rule, drives her offspring from place to place in her compact car. Studies show differences in men and women's time budgets. Adding housework to paid employment, women, in contrast to men, work eight hours a week more on average (BFS, 1994).

What does this disproportionate sharing between the traditional family model and the changed reality of family life mean for the whole family and for individual family members? For one thing, increased tensions can be expected. The demands for leading a meaningful life are increasing, as are the requirements for developing a shared lifestyle. In instances where a couple cannot realize these needs together, individual partners are more ready to divorce than they were in times when people had to live under worse conditions, hoping for a better life after death. In positive terms, in the same way that deregulation of employment demands readiness to accept changes, living together as a couple or a family demands creativity and abandoning the old myths of the family as an unquestioned haven in a heartless world.

In addition, children, and in particular adolescents, are strongly influenced by the changes in the world outside the family. They are increasingly torn among worlds with entirely different demands and sets of values (e.g., school, business, peer group, shopping malls, religious groups), and here they need help (Hildenbrand & Lanfranchi, 1996). Children and adolescents do not find the help they need in a family that constitutes the picturesque haven. They sometimes need the family to be a place where they can find confrontation, where they can try out different lifestyles with the risk of failing but without suffering consequences that are too harsh. They need parents who, after coming home from a hard working day, still have enough resources at their disposal to shoulder the burden of contradiction and setting boundaries. Single parents often complain that they are not able to meet their children's expectations, and often reach the verge of exhaustion. Yet, this is also true for women living in "intact" families with fathers staying in the background, dedicating themselves to hobbies or occupational careers, and leaving their wives to solve the conflicts with their children in addition to employment and housework.

FAMILIES AND AGING

Studying family relationships across three generations shows the development of both solidarity and competition. After divorce, single mothers tend to rely more on the financial support from their own parents than they did before, similar to American data (Burkart, 1993). Conversely, Lange and Lauterbach (1997) found that 28 percent of children aged ten to fourteen years live under the same roof as their grandparents (but not necessarily within the same household) or in the close vicinity (not more than a fifteen-minute walk). Of the children in the sample, 52 percent lived in the same community as their grand-parents or within the distance of a one-hour drive. Only 20 percent lived farther than a one-hour drive from where the grandparents lived. In most cases, it is the paternal grandparents whom these children live with or live near to. The traditional norm of the wife moving to her husband's place and living together in his parental home or next-door to it persists.

Spatial closeness tells something about the sheer possibilities for nursing intergenerational bonds, but tells nothing about the quality of these relationships. In this context, Lüscher (1993) stated that there are intense contacts, attachment, and help offers particularly between the first and third generations. Conversely, the younger generation is expected to give support to the older generation should care be neces-sary. It is worth mentioning that the state increasingly interferes in the intergenerational relationships, using especially the law of inheritance and care insurance. Intergenerational relationships usually have the in-herent property that the family members act with solidarity, especially when difficult situations arise, or child care is required.

Care Insurance

The effects of the care insurance are astonishing since being launched in Germany in 1996. Care insurance is a national scheme. Each month it is paid together with income tax. Thus each wage is re-duced by expenditures to social welfare, including retirement pension contribution, unemployment insurance, and care insurance. In the long run, care insurance was meant to get a handle on the cost explosion caused by professional caregiving to old people, by transferring the costs to a collective community of insured. The initiators of this in-surance expected that the high expenditure for professional caregiving to old people and the lower benefits paid to families by the care insur-ance for giving medical care to a family member (between about €200 and €650 [US$240-785], depending on the extent of the care neces-sary) would balance each other. It turned out that the major part of caregiving is indeed performed by family members of an ill or dis-abled person. Consequently, not only was the cost of the care insur-ance different from what was expected because family members cost less than professionals, it revealed how many people are cared for by family members.

This could have been foreseen. Earlier studies showed that 70 percent of people aged sixty-five years and older and physically dependent on daily support from caregivers, received care from family members. Family members care for over 90 percent of older relatives living on their own or in families. It is mostly women who are in charge of caregiving. Daughters give care more frequently than sons (43 percent versus 8 percent), daughters-in-law more frequently than sons-in-law (14 percent versus 0.3 percent), and daughters-in-law give care more frequently than sons (14 percent versus 8 percent) (BFS, 1994). The study led by Schütze and Wagner (1995) throws light on the motivations as to why their children often give older relatives care. Very old parents more frequently live with their children than do younger parents. It appears that care within families is generally preferred to care at professional homes. The younger generation seems to give care to the older generation for ethical reasons, but not if excessive demands on the caregivers arise. Accordingly, support from professionals is expected with intensive nursing (i.e., caregiving) cases. This study also showed, not surprisingly, that the closer the bonds between the old people and their children, the better their emotional relationship. However, older people receive care from their children that seems to be independent of the quality of their relationship; it is the family commitment that counts. This study is especially interesting and substantial because the data were collected in a city (West Berlin) where the social milieu for interrelationships is usually expected to be less intense than in rural areas. The city setting might account for the finding that in serious chronic nursing cases, people seek help from professional nursing schemes. In rural areas, by comparison, people might call on professional nursing less frequently.

OTHER FAMILY SITUATIONS

Adoptive and Stepfamilies

In Germany, more than 20 percent of all marriages remain childless (Schneewind, 1997). The majority of these couples wish to have a child. One-third of these couples have medical causes for childlessness. Adoption is an opportunity to rectify unwished for childlessness. In 2000, 6,373 children were adopted in Germany, representing 41 out of 100,000 minors. For each child available for adoption there are fourteen applicants (Engstler & Menning, 2003; Hoffmann-Riem, 1989).

In 1999, 6 percent of children under eighteen lived in stepfamilies; 10 percent of children in East Germany, which was double the percentage in West Germany. The ratio of stepfather families to stepmother families is approximately 9:1 (East Germany: 94:6). This means that in the majority of divorced families, the children stay with the mother (Engstler & Menning, 2003).

The subject of normalization is an important one for stepfamilies. This can be seen from the word *Eltern,* or "parents," a term that only exists in the plural form in German. Thus, German language reflects an assumption that the task of bringing up children is to be completed in pairs only (Hoffmann-Riem, 1989). The expression "normalization as if" then means that the side-by-side existence of biological as well as social parenthood is not explicitly dealt with in Germany. This is usually underpinned by, for instance, the stepfather being addressed as "father," and the stepmother as "mother." As with the adoptive family, a precarious mode of parenthood complicates the attempt to gain normalization. For instance, the position of a stepparent provides no legal rights in upbringing.

The disadvantage (or the challenge) of stepfamilies is that the family history, lying in the past, is never again reactivated. This can lead to painful experiences for all concerned, and the child is faced with the situation of being torn between the two parents (Krähenbühl, 1986).

Extended Families

The number of extended family households has been dropping. In 1988, in the former FRG, 4 percent of all households were extended, with most occurrences in rural areas. In 1988, in the city of Hamburg, less than 1 percent of households were extended (Peuckert, 1991). Neither the older nor the younger generation sees this type of family life as a desirable lifestyle. Living in one's own household, but close to kin, is considered more appropriate.

The multigenerational households of business families (including farms) are an exception to this rule. In farm families, where several generations often live together under the same roof, generational conflicts can be found in two domains in particular (Bohler & Hildenbrand, 1997). If the son who is about to take over the farm develops innovative business ideas, and his father and predecessor does not accept them, difficulties arise which negatively affect the farmers' everyday life. This is even more true with three generations living under the same roof. In Germany, this model of living together is quite usual on farms, but not necessarily desirable. Another conflict arises if the inheriting son develops, together with his wife, his own idea of a couple's family life that is in accordance with modern ideas but not with the traditional pattern of a farm family. The traditional pattern emphasizes an orientation toward business, and the family has to abide. Modern thinking, in contrast, focuses on the couple's love and the children's well-being (Bohler & Hildenbrand, 1990). The Berger family is an example of this change in farm families (Bohler & Hildenbrand, 1990).

The Berger Family—A Case Study

The Berger family farm is located in the Black Forest area of Germany. The farm suffers geographical disadvantages. Covering an area of 32 hectares, 21 hectares are forestland, and 10 hectares are for grazing and pasture, and the remainder is used for growing potatoes and vegetables. The income of this mountain farm is derived now, and it has been for a long time, from forestry, a dairy herd (ten to twelve cows), and the distilling of fruit brandies. Currently living on the farm is the couple running it, the farmer's mother, and his son and daughter-in-law with their recently born child. This subfamily lives in an adjacent building. All these people consider the farm to be their livelihood. However, they earn extra income from nonagricultural sources. The farmer's son (Uwe) works at a sawmill and Uwe's wife (Sonja) is a doctor's receptionist.

Bergers have lived on and farmed this land for seven generations. The farm lies at the edge of an area where the eldest son, by tradition, inherits the entire farm (known as primogeniture). Social prestige defined by property and the size of the farm typically characterized areas where primogeniture is the rule. This description increases the significance of the Berger farm being the largest in the village. Since the end of the nineteenth century, the people of the village have called the family "Schulzenbauer." This is because the farm owner has for decades been mayor of the village. The Berger family has enjoyed considerable status, and at times the greatest social prestige in this village adhering to traditional agricultural and rural customs.

In view of the farm and family history, it is remarkable that Otto Berger (born in 1929) left the farm in 1952 after a quarrel with his father. This quarrel was occasioned by Otto's declared intention to marry a woman from the neighboring area with different farm inheritance norms. In doing so, some people considered that he would be marrying beneath his station. For years Otto worked in a nearby town for a firm dealing in timber and coal. In 1954, after being promoted to foreman and given a company flat to live in, he married Gerda. In 1966, his father was forced to give up the farm due to illness. Otto took it over because his brothers refused to carry on in farming after modernization attempts had failed.

Uwe Berger (born 1962) is the third and youngest child of Otto and Gerda. He has an elder sister (born 1955) and an elder brother (born in 1957 but killed in a car accident in 1975). The eldest brother trained as a baker, but Uwe decided on agricultural training. He did this on his father's farm, thus paving the way for his future inheritance of the farm. The smooth transition is faced with the problem of Uwe's marriage to Sonja (born in 1961). Sonja comes from the artisan and skilled worker class and has been working for the past ten years in the local town as a doctor's receptionist. Sonja's view of life does not correspond to rural and peasant traditions.

Since the beginning of the 1960s, the basic economic problem of farms has been the structural impossibility of taking part in the agroindustrialization process, especially in the intensification of yields, the extension of production areas, and increase of herd size. This inability results from geographical and economic factors influencing conditions of production. The agroindustrial methods of production often used in the flatlands are of limited suitability when applied to hill farms. As far as possible, the farm adopted technical aids to production. In fact, they did this early in comparison to others in the region. One reason for these adaptations was to compensate for the lack of labor. However, machinery remained a substitution for human labor and not for expansion purposes. The traditional level of production did not change.

The logic behind the actions of the managing farmer, Otto Berger, corresponds to that of the traditional peasant attitude: work and save. However, the following maxim can also be considered valid: as much modernization, production adaptation (concentration of the dairy herd, extensive pasturage instead of cereal growing), and machine technology as possible. On the Berger farm, the management strategy motive is of foremost importance. An economic-rational complex is of significance only to the extent that a certain measure of economic viability must be guaranteed if the farm is to survive. Economic viability is not oriented toward innovative entrepreneurship. With a farm on the edge of viability, like that of the Bergers, innovation consists of continuing a family tradition under circumstances that are economically and socially unfavorable. A particular kind of family history and biography is necessary, as is specific (contingent) sociostructural configurations, to assure that in the long term the family will continue to experience peasant-style farming as a satisfactory and fulfilling way of life in the face of constant threats of economic failure. The most important components of this family's structure include the above-average family status, Otto Berger's partial break with family traditions, his suitable choice of marriage partner for the farm, and the beginning of a new agricultural subvention policy (hill farmer aid program).

Uwe Berger, as heir to the farm, aspires to successful structural transformation on this farm, meaning the transition from a farm providing almost all income for the family to a farm providing only a proportion of the income. For this to happen the personalities behind this larger family, particularly the women, will have to adopt modern patterns.

The marriage of Otto and Gerda Berger (in opposition to the conventions of peasant choice of partner according to status) transformed the old institutional element in the marital relationship. It changed from one based on division of labor into a special relationship based on two personalities closely bound. The choice of Gerda as marriage partner, a woman who did not adhere to the traditional peasant way of thinking, turned out to be fortunate for the farm. It is fortunate because, in contrast to her husband, Gerda was free from traditional constraints and able to move forward the adaptation of the farm to an environment that in many respects was structurally foreign and economically threatening.

This tendency is continued in Uwe's wife Sonja, who, like Gerda, comes from an area where the inheritance rules favor all heirs. On the one hand, the two women, especially in how they run the household and raise the children, have departed from traditional peasant patterns. For example, it is traditional for a new daughter-in-law marrying into a farm family to be obliged, during the first years of marriage, to allow her mother-in-law to run the kitchen. This is especially true concerning cooking. Gerda, in contrast, banished her mother-in-law from the kitchen as soon as the farm had formally been transferred to her husband. After living for twelve years in a town, Gerda was in a powerful position relative to her mother-in-law. This, however, had to be supported by a good relationship with her husband Otto. Today, both Gerda and Sonja cook in their own households according to the amount of work to be done.

On the other hand, both Gerda and Sonja identify with elements of the family into which they have married. However, they criticize, with justification, aspects that are out-of-date and no longer acceptable. The men treat this criticism earnestly because it is made on the basis of family loyalty. However, the adaptation to modern realities is not without tension. The dismantling of tradition and class values, which is at the heart of the threat to the continuation of the family farm, makes social status more dependent on individual achievement. Achievements increasingly are measured according to universalistic criteria.

Thoughts on the Disintegration of the Peasant World: The Case of the Berger Family

The typical peasant world, as it was preserved in many German regions up to the last two decades of the nineteenth century, was characterized by its equilibrium among familial organization, farm management, agricultural policy, and economic factors, as well as by a specific worldview. Families like the Berger family were centers of this balanced universe. One reason that farm families were destined to preserve this framework is because they were interested in maintaining their own status and also the farm-related conditions necessary for the demand for labor. Consequently, it is important to look into the process of disintegration of the traditional peasant world as illustrated by the case of a family that considers the farm to be their livelihood. Furthermore, over the last two generations the tradition of the farm owner's selecting a marriage partner suited to life on the farm has visibly dwindled. The crisis of the farm family and the family business can no longer be solved by means of traditional methods of problem solving alone (work and save). The dependence on the hill farmer aid program at least partly leads to the decline of individual freedom and farm autonomy—of values that used to be high principles. Subsidies and aid can only be accepted on condition they help secure the existence of the farm.

Finally, another instance of the disintegration of the peasant world should be mentioned: socialization in farm families was focused on the male heir to the farm, whereas the female offspring were in a way, neglected. This can be seen in the Berger family. Otto's sisters born before World War II married into farms in the region as the previous generations had done as a rule. Both of Otto's youngest sisters and his daughter Iris did not follow this pattern. One of Otto's sisters as well as his daughter trained as clerks in an industrial firm. Such training cannot be executed by Otto's sons Robert and Uwe, whose labor is urgently needed on the farm and who are destined to be the heirs to the farm. This development has not been restricted to the Berger family, and therefore it is not surprising that Uwe has to choose his marriage partner from circles that surpass his father's spheres of interest. In the context of this tendency toward a lack of socializing young women to be farmers' wives, one can understand the revaluation of the daughter-in-law; she is now a rather seldom and precious "commodity" for farm families. This development helps Sonja Berger to achieve full acceptance from, and satisfying integration into, the farm family although she is not an agricultural expert.

This case study shows how families have been adapting to new conditions. The Bergers are an example of how traditional farms located in structurally disadvantaged areas manage to secure their existence. They do this by adaptation to a modern way of life and family style but without being in a position to control the economic conditions beyond an economical family budgeting.

CONCLUDING COMMENTS

In Germany, changes in the family as an institution have been evident since the 1960s. These changes bear typical properties such as increasing reservations about marriage, equal status of conjugal and nonconjugal cohabitation, and a growing female liberation in educational and occupational fields in particular. Notably, the changes brought about due to female emancipation are of significance. Women's employment has increasingly entered into competition with family life, mainly because the traditional distinction between "mother's role" and "father's role" has not yet disappeared. This means that men have been lagging behind the developmental steps that women have successfully taken in the last few decades. To a growing extent, married women and mothers have managed to emancipate from their families, whereas the men's reverse movement toward taking responsibility in the family has been extremely sluggish. This observation is also true for East Germany despite the high female employment rate there.

Therefore, couples choose to not have children or decide on having only a few. The latter is also linked to the fact that being responsible parents has become a more demanding task. The socialization of children is no longer as "natural" a process as it used to be. Society, in particular schools, expects parents to practice an educational style aimed at responsibility and performance orientation. Parents, in turn, have internalized these expectations.

Living together as a couple and a family has become a source of stress relative to meeting various performance standards. For example, love and security count among the significant criteria of a happy and successful marriage and family. If these standards are not satisfied, then conflict and separation may soon follow.

Taken as a generalization, these assessments would imply that marriage and family in Germany are undergoing a crisis. Yet, some objections must be made here. For one, the previously mentioned findings have to be differentiated according to lifestyles (Burkart & Kohli, 1992). That is, families vary in orientations and lifestyles; there are commonalties yet each is unique. For the other, the observed patterns of solidarity between the generations and among blood relationships do not suggest a diagnosis of crisis. Trends toward individualization, which find their expression in the changing meaning of partnership and education, and trends toward solidarity, are no longer contradictions but are two sides of the same coin. The basis of such a development can be found in a society where traditional commitments have lost their importance and where the reflexivity of social relationships is constantly growing.

Chapter 5

Stress and Coping Among Romanian Families in the Post-Communist Period

Livia Popescu
Maria Roth

INTRODUCTION

The social and economic structures of Romania have been changing since the fall of communism. The post-1989 period has been one of uncertainty and challenge to families as they have adapted traditional practices to new realities. In general, families must cope with many stressors while many social security benefits are diminished. With the elimination of the dictatorship and command economy, families have dealt with the opportunities as well as problems of the new democracy and fledging market economy. It is within this context of social stress and changing social policy that specific family functioning occurs.

Romania is the ninth most populous country in Europe and borders the Black Sea between Ukraine and Bulgaria and borders Hungary and Serbia. The country has a temperate climate with cold snowy winters and sunny summers. The country is slightly smaller than the U.S. state of Oregon. Greek Orthodox Christianity is dominant in Romania; it favors submission of women and has more tolerance of sexual life than does Roman Catholicism (e.g., letting priests marry). However, sexuality is for procreation. Before World War II, Romania was a predominantly agricultural country (80 percent of Romanians lived in rural conditions). As generally accepted in the professional literature (Zamfir, C., 1995a), this corresponded to a predominantly patriarchal family model, where men were the heads of their families. Women were devoted to their husbands, children, and households. The idea of male superiority was typical of traditional rural family values.

Families in Romanian Context

Establishing and living in families is approved and reinforced in Romanian culture. The concept of family includes being happily married and having children, but also being financially secure and having a comfortable home. "Family" also includes prospects for personal development, career growth/further education, satisfying leisure time, health care and other benefits. What Romanians face today can challenge these expectations of family life.

The events of December 1989 (known as the Romanian Revolution) resulted from mass movements that ended the dictatorship of Nicolae Ceausescu. Since then Romania has undergone profound transitions in emerging from forty-four years of Communist domination. The postcommunist period brought hardships and opportunities for families; the changes in values, choices, economic and political structures were perceived by many as stressful.[1] Families' responses to stress are reflected in their adaptation mechanisms, meaning assimilation of change and accommodation to new structures. Families, by definition a traditional institution, struggle to resist change and to incorporate as few transformations as possible. However, the tendency of individuals is adaptation, developing new mechanisms reflecting the novelties of the society. These mechanisms can alter the functioning and roles in traditional Romanian families.

In the Romanian Family Code of Laws (Codul familiei, 1954), family is defined as a group of persons united by marriage or affiliation. Marriage is monogamous, and only between male and female. Modern nuclear families do not live together with their families of origin, and are economically independent. This autonomy does not necessarily strengthen nuclear family solidarity, but weakens the relationships with extended families. There is a complex system of biological and social factors changing the way of life of rural families who move to urban areas. This might result in losing their roots and increasing frustrations, alienation, and tensions in families.

In a larger sense, family corresponds to kinship: all people with common ancestors or some manner of blood relationship are family.

This represents the basis for an important network of reciprocal support, having basis in the traditional social fabric of Romanian villages where relatives participated in the main events of everyone in the family (Costa-Foru, 1945). The notion of kinship is essential for the identity of the Maramures mountain region, at the northern border of Romania (Kligman, 1998a), where traditional life is still very much present. In this region, kinship bonds together people related by blood, social contracts, or rituals.

Physically isolated villages often have few kinship groups. This especially characterizes minority group villages surrounded by Romanian villages. For example, in Kide (a village populated by the minority Hungarian people located 44 kilometers from Cluj) there are only two kinship groups in the village and everyone is related to all the others in some way (Roth, 1997). In Kalotaszeg, another traditional Hungarian village, social scientists have observed since the 1960s that marriages take place between people related by extended family bonds. Couples here give birth to only one child. This demographic regulation of the village permits the preservation of the land and wealth of the family. It also leads to the birth of a disquieting number of children with disabilities (Kesziharmat & Kesziharmat, 1977).

In the Communist period, marriage and family life were "territory" designated to be controlled by the Party. This was exposed in the "scientific" explanation of the family code. Ionescu, Muresan, Costin, and Ursa (1975, p. 67) considered that "in our socialist society the maintenance of marriage ceased to be a strictly personal problem of the spouses. The society cannot be indifferent to the fate of marriage and to family." The main family role was to give birth to children and to raise them in the new social spirit, that is, prepare them to be worthy citizens of the Communist society. The politics of the Communist dictator, N. Ceausescu (ruled 1965-1989), were aimed at resisting the Western urban family type, and for the preservation of traditional Romanian family values. This included a partially successful strengthening of rural-patriarchal values. Economic difficulties influenced the attitudes and perceptions of women, as did the pronatalist politics and the rural-patriarchal mentality of the Ceausescu period (Baban & David, 1995).

Urban nuclear families diminished their social functions during the Communist regime. The educational roles especially, were transferred to society. Women had to return to their employment relatively soon after delivery of a baby (new mothers were granted a maximum of 117 paid days off). Nurseries and kindergartens were offered to families. However, nurseries were notorious for being crowded and for providing low quality child care. Women worked equally with men, which was progress compared with their prewar, dominant housekeeper role. However, this meant more duties in a patriarchal family decision-making model. Women had to work and contribute income because one (husband's) wage was not sufficient. As the roles of women (raise children—the more, the best, according to the dominant Communist ideology—and domestic activities) continued to be performed, women's duties had doubled (Petre, 1997).

The nuclear family, with both parents employed and raising one or two children is typical for the Romanian population and for the largest ethnic minority, the Hungarians (7 percent). The German (0.3 percent) and Jewish (0.04 percent) minorities, with constantly decreasing numbers, are characterized by elderly families with the younger generations emigrating out (Institutul National de Statistica [INS], 2003). Roma (or Gypsy) families formed 2.5 percent of the population in 2002, and represent another type of family with numerous children, living several generations in the same dwelling (Zamfir & Zamfir, 1993). They are the only minority whose numbers are increasing, and the estimation is that their percentage in the population is significantly higher than counted by the 1992 and 2002 census (Guvernul Romaniei & UNICEF, 1997; INS, 2003).

In a national study, respondents indicated that they appreciated their family relationships (United Nations Development Programme [UNDP], 1996c). On a scale from one (very bad) to five (very good), the average scores were 4.15 (for 1994) and 4.19 (in 1995). This reflects the importance of family life. The same study showed there were good relationships with neighbors.

COUPLE FORMATION AND MARITAL DYNAMICS

Romanian family law considers a man and a woman to be married if the office of the mayor recorded the marriage. Marriage is based on free consent and full equality between spouses. Homosexual couples cannot marry in Romania. The minimal age to marry is eighteen for a male and sixteen for a female. For "special reasons," which are not specifically mentioned by the Family Code of Laws (1954), females can marry at fifteen years of age, with the approval of their parents. Before 1990, people in Romania tended to marry at a young age and to have only one marriage during their lifetimes. More recently there have been changes. In 1994-1995, the mean age at first marriage was 25.6 for men and 22.4 for women (Comisia Nationala pentru Statistica & United Nations Development Program [CNS & UNDP], 2000; United Nations, 2000, 2003). In 1998, the averages were 26.4 for men and 23.1 years for women.[2] In 2000, the average age at first marriage for a woman was 23.4. Over 80 percent of all marriages were first marriages (UNDP, 1996c). There was an increase in remarriages during the 1990-1998 period, especially among the divorced (CNS & UNDP, 2000). Marriages last, on average, twenty-two years. This indicates a high level of family stability. The marriage rate (number of marriages per 1,000 population in a year) constantly decreased after 1990, reaching 5.8 in 2001 (INS, 2002). Compared with other European countries, Romania has a relatively high marriage rate (UNDP, 1996c).

Civil weddings most frequently are followed by church weddings. Relatives, friends, and others participate, typically resulting in large wedding parties. Their gifts in money and goods represent an important foundation for the couple. In Romanian villages, brides are considered as leaving the parental home and following the groom to the home provided by his family.

There are regional and ethnic variations in customs. Often best men and maids of honor have important roles not only at weddings, but also during the period of starting the young family. The *nas* or godfathers are sometimes family members, or older friends well-off from a material point of view. It is a position of honor, but also of concrete support. They play a mediator role in the interest of the married couple: they interfere in the quarrels (they are supposed to be fair with both spouses, unlike parents) and facilitate economic changes (Kligman, 1998a). They are the main sponsors of the wedding ceremony, and distribute the gifts to the new couple. As much in the present as in the past, they are chosen according to their social and economic status; that is, for the possibilities of social or financial utility. Romania, as part of the Balkan way of survival, is known for the great importance of family relationships in finding good jobs, obtaining housing, and solving (otherwise time consuming) administration problems. This kind of survival by kin mediation was common before 1989, as part of everyone's life experience.

Cohabitation

There are unmarried cohabiting couples, usually without children. The 2002 census provided the first statistical data about the number of people living in heterosexual cohabitation, which was just less than 4 percent of the total. Most of them had not been married before. Unmarried partners cannot inherit from each other. This means that official marriage offers more economic security for partners. There are no official data about homosexual cohabiting couples.

Divorce

The ability of Romanian families to survive and turn to their own ways can be seen in the adaptation of families to a 1966 law restricting divorce by limiting the possibility and prolonged the period of divorcing; this reduced the divorce rate for several years. However, the law ended in 1975 and the divorce rate immediately increased. The total of registered divorces in the period 1967-1971 (28,497) was not as great as registered in 1965 before the law. Neither was it as high as the average (33,740) for the period 1954-1964 (Muresan, 1996). Of those divorced, two-thirds did not have children. This indicates that raising children, often contributing to the burden of life, was not necessarily creating the major conflict within marriages (Mitrofan, 1989).

There was not much change in the divorce rate between 1989 and 1994. There was even a small decrease between 1990-1993, when the average number of divorces was 32,620. During 1990-1997 the divorce rate varied between 1.29 and 1.74 per 1,000 people, with a peak of 1.7 in 1994 and a low of 1.29 in 1992 (CNS & UNDP, 2000; UNDP, 1998). The rate was 1.5 in 2000 and 1.4 in 2001 (INS, 2002; UNDP, 2001, 2004). In comparison, the period 1986-1989 had a divorce rate between 1.5 and 1.6 (Comisia Nationala pentru Statistica CNS, 1996). In recent years, the divorce rate has remained relatively stable or decreased. Within the perspective of a European context, it is below average (UNDP, 1996c).

A breakdown of divorce statistics by age group since 1992 shows some changes. There appears to be an increasing tendency for early divorce reflecting the new legislation in 1993. This earlier divorce might also be a result of demographic changes in marriage patterns. Another change is that the majority of divorces take place in families with minor children. However, as the number of children in a family increases, the probability of divorce decreases. This might indicate that children are a sort of "glue" for marriages (UNDP, 1996c). If one intends to explain the dynamics of divorce with the amount of societal stress, then it appears that pre- and immediately postrevolution periods are not much different.

A possible factor diminishing stress is the abolition of laws restricting mobility of citizens. Before 1989, members of many families lived separately due to their government controlled jobs. This was true for young married couples, especially university graduates. Employed in different areas, they lived apart several years until finally unified or divorced.

It appears that for Romania it is not a general principle that social stress on family life leads automatically to divorce. Stress might also have an adaptive effect. The dynamics of the divorce rate show that families might have learned to communicate better and to collaborate under new conditions, which solicited their accommodation mechanisms. In Romania, as in the surrounding countries except for Russia, the rate of divorce is almost stable in spite of economic crises (Moroianu-Zlatescu, 1997). A healthy defense mechanism of families could be the explanation: families have to mobilize both their emotional and financial resources to cope with difficulties. Housing, durable goods, and food are more affordable when paid for by more than one person. The fear of losing economic status can impede divorce even for couples with marital distress. This appears to be a constant tendency of the marital behavior today.

Sexuality

Sexuality is a recent field for Romanian researchers. A study of Romanian women's understanding of their sexuality, reproductive behavior, and their life as part of a couple was conducted by a Romanian-American team (Baban & David, 1995). The typical respondent was a woman living in Cluj City, married before 1990, with children, had completed high school, was of rural origin, and had an orthodox religious background. The contributors concluded that sexuality was perceived as a personal stress factor. The initial shame and shyness of the couple's sexual life was followed (for marriages during the Ceausescu period) by the fear of unintentional pregnancy. Lack of contraception and the inability and fear to use it amplified this stress. These conditions led the women to lose their capacity to control their own sexual behavior (Kligman, 1998b).

Though sexuality was risky and therefore avoided, these women considered family life important. Family remains widely valued including maternity only inside of marriage. Accidental pregnancies reinforce the feeling of dependency on the male partner. Abortions are considered mostly from a practical point of view, as solving extant problems, and the ethical considerations are rarely mentioned. Economic struggle erodes communication and emotional life between couples.

Wives want to solve problems in conjunction with their husbands. However, it seems to be a difficult issue to do so without external help. Romanian women have the typical frustrations caused by multiple duties (e.g., profession, child rearing, and housekeeping) (Baban & David, 1995).

After the Revolution, the regulation of reproductive behavior by the State went through important changes. The law that interdicted abortion was abolished on the first day of the new government (installed in December 1989). The use of contraceptives was declared legal a few days later. However, research on a national level with 4,800 women showed that 34 percent declared that the last pregnancy was planned, 12 percent indicated accidental pregnancies, and 51 percent considered the last pregnancy as unwanted (Serbanescu & Morris, 1994). This is important because it shows the difficulties of Romanian families, in a period when contraceptives are legal and accessible, in gaining control over their own sexual lives. Studies reveal that women are generally uninformed about contraception methods and the efforts of family planning services seem to be insufficient (Ascroft, 1998; Sauciuc, 1997).

FAMILIES AND CHILDREN

After 1989 economic transformation led to a significant decrease in job security, the deterioration of the overall standard of living, and the lack of affordable housing. These affected family formation. Along with the lessening of societal and political pressure upon an individual's life, these changes also resulted in a modest, but steady, decrease in the number of marriages (from 8.3 per 1,000 inhabitants in 1990 to 6.1 in 2000). These changes were also associated with an increase in age at first marriage and a dramatic drop in births (Berthin, 2002; CNS & UNDP, 2000; UNDP, 1998). The 1996 estimated birthrate was 10.2 births per 1,000 inhabitants, the lowest recorded in Romania in peacetime. This rate was about 33 percent lower than in 1989 (Berthin, 2002). In 2000 it was 10.5 per 1,000 population and the total fertility rate estimated at 1.3 children per woman (Berthin, 2002; United Nations, 2003). These rates were slightly elevated for 2004 (10.69 and 1.35) and 10.7 and 1.36 for 2005 (World Factbook, 2005). The total fertility rate for the Roma in Romania is 2.6, compared with 1.2 for Romanian and 1.3 for Hungarian women (Mizsei et al., 2003). The decline in the number of births reflects the avoidance or postponement of the birth of a second or subsequent child per family. Only a small number of married couples desire no children, or postpone the birth of a first child (UNDP, 1996c).

Women's reproductive behavior varies with level of education and economic situation. In the 1992 census, the average woman with primary school education had 2.6 children compared with 1.1 for women with higher education. In 1994, 37 percent of births were to economically active women (UNDP, 1996c). About 16 percent of births were to women under twenty years of age (Balasa, Halus, Jula, Vasile, & Marius, 1999), about 4 percent of women fifteen to nineteen years of age give birth each year (International Planned Parenthood, nd), and the average age of first birth for women was 22.8 in 1960, 22.4 in 1990, 22.9 in 1996, and 23.9 in 2001 (INS, 2002). Approximately 26 percent of births were extramarital, or occurring outside formal marriage (United Nations, 2003).

Abortion and Contraception

The wave of abortions after the political change in 1989 is similar to the effect of a previous act of liberalization of abortions in 1958. Then, there were 1.5 abortions per birth, which increased until 1965 to 4 abortions per birth. In the following twenty-three years, Ceausescu led a pro-birth (pronatalist) policy that abolished abortion (with exceptions if women were aged forty-five and for those who already had four children or whose life was endangered by giving birth to a child). Prohibiting abortion led to higher rates of maternal mortality. However, frequent abortions have negative consequences for women's health as well.

One early act of the transitional government was to repeal restrictive abortion legislation, and soon thereafter restrictions on sterilization and the use of contraception (United Nations, 2002).[3] In 1988-1989, the ratio of abortions to live births was about 1:1 (UNDP, 1996c). As a consequence of the legal change, the abortion rate increased while the maternal mortality rate declined. The abortion rate rose from 39 abortions per 1,000 women aged fifteen to forty-four years in 1989, to a rate of 199 in 1990. In 1990 and 1991, there were three or four abortions for each birth; by 1994, the rate decreased to 2.16 abortions per live birth (UNDP, 1996c, 1998).

Since 1993, there has been a decreasing abortion rate (315 abortions per 100,000 births in 1990 to 114 abortions per 100,000 births in 2000). In spite of a campaign of antiabortion education in the late 1990s, by 2000, 59 percent of abortions were to women under thirty years of age (INS, 2003). Abortion remains the main fertility control instrument of women and remains the highest (1.2 in 2002) in Europe (CNS & UNDP, 2000; Muresan, 1996; Sauciuc, 1997; United Nations, 1999, 2002; UNDP, 2004). In part this is due to the increasing price of contraceptive pills and the limited number of family planning services (especially in rural communities).

In 1993, about 14 percent of married women (aged fifteen to forty-four) used modern contraception (United Nations, 2002). The contraception prevalence rate (1995-2003) was estimated at 64 percent (United Nations, 2005); however there is an "almost complete absence of contraceptive practices" among Roma families (Mizsei et al., 2003, p. 27). A 1996 study indicated that 14 percent of Roma women used contraceptive methods while 23 percent said they did not have the necessary knowledge. In traditional Roma families, husbands and mothers-in-law are often opposed to the use of modern contraceptives, and men rarely use condoms. Abortions, then, are a rather universal means for family planning among Roma women.

Although the Romanian Ministry of Health, in cooperation with international organizations, includes the implementation of family planning and sex education programs, their impact on the rural population has been low (Popescu, L., 2003). The government faces the need to educate the population in general and health professionals in particular about contraception.

Maternal Mortality

Due to restrictive reproductive health policies enforced in Romania between 1966 and 1989, including an antiabortion law in 1966, fertility rates increased 47 percent in just two years and maternal mortality reached heights unknown in Europe (Greenwell, 2003; Kligman, 1998b). Owing to the risk women took with illegal abortions (done by themselves, at home without sterilized or specific medical instruments, or done more or frequently less by specialized persons for large sums of money), maternal mortality increased. Accounting for more than 80 percent of maternal deaths between 1980 and 1989, illegal and unsafe abortion was the major cause of maternal mortality. On average, a woman might have undergone at least five illegal abortions by age forty and it has been estimated that approximately 20 percent of women of reproductive age might have become infertile as a result (United Nations, 2002).

The maternal mortality rate increased to such an extent that Romania had, previous to 1989, a rate at least ten times that found among other European countries (Baban & David, 1995). The ratio rose from eighty-five deaths per 100,000 live births in 1965, to 170 in 1983 (United Nations, 2002). In 1990, the rate was 130 deaths per 100,000 live births (UNICEF, 1996a). Other sources indicated an even higher mortality rate for 1989: 170 for 100,000 live births (Guvernul Romaniei & UNICEF, 1997; Sauciuc, 1997). The ratio reported for Romania from 1985 to 2003 was thirty-four (UNDP, 2005). After the 1989 repeal of the antiabortion law, maternal mortality steadily decreased (INS, 2001). It appears that progress is being made.

Fertility and Infant Mortality

The fertility rate in Romania in 2000 was 1.35 and the birthrate was between 10.4 and 10.8 (CNS, 2000; CNS & UNDP, 2000; World

Factbook, 2000). These rates in 1998 were 1.3 and 10.5. Even with a more recent slight increase, the levels are lower than in some western European countries (Norway, France, United Kingdom), but they are closer or higher to those existing in the postcommunist countries (CNS, 2000; CNS & UNDP, 2000; Popescu, 2004; UNICEF, 1996b, 2000a). The gross reproduction rate of 1.2 children per married couple is insufficient for the replacement of generations, leading in the 1990s to a decline in population (UNDP, 1996c).

The infant mortality rate (above 20 per 1,000 live births until 1998, above 18 in 1999 and 2000, 19.4 in 2003, and 26.4 in 2005) is higher than in other European countries except Albania, Moldova, the Russian Federation, and the former Yugoslavian Republic of Macedonia (CNS, 1999b, INS, 2005; World Factbook, 2005). The under-five years mortality rate (per 1,000 live births) was twenty-four in 1998 and twenty-one in 2001 (Balasa et al., 1999; United Nations, 2003). The causes of the high child mortality rate are to be found in problems related to the quality of and the difficulties within the medical system. They are also related to the lower living standards of families who have more children and to the quality of the child welfare system, which has not yet developed effective forms of support for children living in inappropriate or dangerous situations, especially in rural areas (Roth, 2000, 2003; Roth & Bumbulut, 2003).

The Importance of Children and Education

As mentioned in previous text, the traditional Romanian family is male-oriented including parental preference for boys. However, both laws and customs are that both genders equally inherit the wealth of parents (Kligman, 1998a). Traditional Romanian families give much attention to children and offer them help even in their adult life. There is also a disquieting trend; more than 40 percent of the children in Roma households suffer undernourishment, bordering on starvation in many (Mizsei et al., 2003).

Access to education is equal to both genders. Gender differences in the adult literacy rate decreased between 1992 and 2005, but the female literacy rate was still slightly lower than that of men: 98 and 99 percent, respectively (CNS & UNDP, 2000; United Nations, 2003; World Factbook, 2005). These rates do not apply for Roma females, who have a high rate of analphabetism and 89 percent have no educational qualifications (Adamesteanu, 1998). The estimate for adult literacy among the Roma is 72 percent, with about a 35 percent gross enrollment rate in schools (Mizsei et al., 2003).

A similar trend is noticeable for university education. In 1998, the proportion of college-educated persons was higher than in 1992 for both genders. However, the increase was greater among women: 6 percent (four in 1992) of the female population has a university degree and 8 percent of the male population (seven in 1992). Females are enrolled less in the vocational and apprentice schools, but they receive a greater percentage of the diplomas from the secondary schools or lyceums (9-12 grades) (CNS & UNDP, 2000). Overall, a slightly higher proportion of females than males were enrolled in primary through tertiary schools in 2002: 77 percent (67 percent men) in primary schools, 77 percent (73 percent men) in secondary schools, and 44 percent (34 percent men) in tertiary schools (United Nations, 2003; UNDP, 2004).

Families consider the investment they make in the education of their children (e.g., schooling, culture, teaching foreign languages, artistic development, and sport performance) to be effective (Zamfir, 1995a). This investment has been maintained since 1989. This is shown by the significant rise in the number of youngsters enrolled in higher education. The rate of enrollment for university education almost doubled between 1990 (11 percent) and 2000 (21 percent) (Comisia Antisaracie si Promovarea Incluziunii Sociale [CASPIS], 2002; CNS & UNDP, 2000; UNDP, 1998).

There is an opposite tendency also, visible in those segments of the population most affected by poverty. School enrollment dropped by almost 3 percent during 1990-1995, but shows an opposite tendency for primary (grades 1-4) and gymnasium (grades 5-8) levels since. Attendance and performance is lower in rural areas (Jigau, 2002). According to a law adopted in 2003 (nr. 268), compulsory school has extended from eight to ten years. The government acknowledged in the National Anti-Poverty Plan the rising number of dropouts and labored to introduce incentives for school participation (CASPIS, 2002). Child allowance for school children is tied to school attendance (see following text). There are also programs to encourage children in poor families: free transportation and stationeries for specific low-income categories in some remote areas, supported by local governments. For children in primary schools there is a free "bagel and milk" provision. School is not compulsory for those aged fifteen to eighteen if the first eight years have been completed. The percentage of children reaching grade five is 96 (UNICEF, nd). Recent enrollments in primary and gymnasium levels in Romania compares favorably with many Eastern European countries (Berthin, 2002; UNICEF, 2000a). Yet, the rising numbers of school dropouts and street children are matters of concern.

Child-Care Allowances

Child-care allowances are a universal benefit since 1993, when full-time employment in the state sector ceased to be the eligibility criterion. The coverage has been extended to children of farmers, as well as the unemployed, self-employed, and privately employed. These families were excluded in the Communist regime and in the early post-communist years. The child is entitled to the state allowance from the first month up to age sixteen, or eighteen if still enrolled in the school system. The eligibility for school-age children depends upon school attendance. School-aged children receive the allowance based on a check (i.e., voucher) confirmed by school authorities only if the child has attended classes on a regular basis. In 2001, 65 percent of pre-school aged children, 93 percent of primary education aged children, and 80 percent of secondary aged youth were enrolled in school (United Nations, 2003). This, of course, does not mean they attended school regularly and thus the family might not receive the allowance.

This increased coverage has not produced significant improvements in child-care conditions inasmuch as it occurred during a period of constant devaluation of the real allowance benefit. The share of GDP allocated to child-care allowance declined from less than 3 percent (1990) to 0.9 percent (1994), and further deterioration through 1996 reduced it to 0.7 percent. Moreover, the allowances are not adequately protected against inflation, which has led to a dramatic loss of their real value compared with 1989 (UNICEF, 1993; UNDP, 1998; Zamfir, 1995a).

Recognizing the high poverty risk of numerous families, the government introduced in 1997 a new provision called supplementary child allowance. Families with two or more children are eligible. The share of the cash child benefits in the average household income varied according to the number of dependent children from 2 percent (household with one child) to 12 percent (household with four and more children) (INS, 2002). Since 2004, family provisions became increasingly selective with the introduction of two benefits: a "complementary" allowance for low-income families, which will substitute for the universal supplementary allowance, and a new "support" for low-income single-parent families. The amount paid is relative to the number of children, but its increase ceases after the fourth child.

Social Services

Within the strained economic context, many families struggle to overcome barriers to achieving a reasonable standard of living and quality of life. Social services, which could help families, are also severely impacted by the economy. The share of public expenditure allocated to health, education, child care, and other social services is maintained at a low level. In contrast, the so-called economic activities, which represent mainly indirect subsidies for the inefficient state-owned companies, continue to share an important part of the government budget. Social welfare did not seem until now to be the first priority of the Romanian governments. Although the share of GDP allocated to social expenditure slightly increased in the 1990-2002 period compared with 1989, the financial support of the social programs and services reduced in real value due to the decline in GDP. According to 2002 data, the social public expenditure was 20 percent of the GDP, where education, health, and personal social services share less than one-half of the total (UNDP, 2004).

Redistributive Policy

In Romania, the postcommunist state regulations concerning both the distributive and the redistributive policies have had significant differential effects, which contrast with the official pro-egalitarian discourse. Some families are much better off, economically, than other families. The economic resources accumulated legally and illegally during the Communist and postcommunist regimes have allowed some people to buy property and to have other advantages in general. At the same time, positive measures directed to empower disadvantaged groups (e.g., women, youngsters, disabled people, and the Roma) have been absent or ineffective.

Chronologically, the first and major universal social protection consisted of compensations for price increases and for subsidies on essential food products, energy, transportation, and housing. For the majority, and especially for those negatively impacted by the market logic, the protection has proven to be inadequate. In some cases, the benefit was only potential because there was a shortage of some subsidized items. Subsidies for electricity and gasoline resulted in a regressive redistribution. The minority of families having significant electrical domestic equipment (approximately 20 percent of the population) or cars (8 percent) benefited more from the subsidies than the rest of the population. In the case of rent paid for housing, the regressiveness is even more important. Until 2000, the state rents were maintained at the 1989 level (which was the same cost as the price of a pack of cigarettes in 1999) while the rent paid for privately owned dwellings are close to the average monthly earnings of the population.

Social security in Romania depends on a combination of universal benefits (state child-care allowance), insurance-based benefits (pensions, unemployment benefit, health care, and maternity benefit), and means tested safety-net provision (social aid benefit, complementary family allowance, and support family allowance for single-parent families). While social welfare provisions are generally inadequate, families in Romania do benefit. The average contribution of the social transfers to the household monetary (cash) income was 29 percent in 2002, and its share is even more important for the households where pensioners, unemployed, and numerous children are members (UNDP, 2004).

Teachers are not prepared to address the problems of poor and neglected children; they also have little supervised practice and practically no training or theoretical basis for working with children with special needs. There are no social workers in the school system (except within some pilot projects, which are only at the beginning and cannot yet demonstrate their efficacy) and few child psychologists. Recently, more qualified personnel are involved in the mainstreaming of children with special needs and learning disabilities, but there is still a great need for child-centered educational services, especially in the rural areas, which impedes the school progress of a large number of children (Jigau, 2002; Pop & Voicu, 2002).

FAMILIES AND GENDER

Since 1952, there has been equal payment for equal work for women and men, so women have become equal work partners with men. Between the two World Wars, the percentage of women working in agriculture in Romania was 87 percent (Gluvacov, 1975). In the period 1959-1973, the number of employed women (in all sectors) rose 126 percent. In 1975, women were 44 percent of the labor force (Buzatu, 1978).

Division of Labor

Equality at the work place did not mean the same in the division of labor at home. Research on organization of spare time (synthesized by Buzatu, 1978) revealed an average of almost six hours of total housework per day, per family. This total was composed of four hours and twenty-four minutes for women and one hour and twenty-eight minutes for men. Between the ages of sixteen and sixty-five, the older a woman was, the more she worked in the household. The age group sixteen to twenty-five worked 150 minutes a day at housework while the age group fifty-six to sixty-five worked 453 minutes.

Earlier research with young married couples showed that 23 percent reported that they equally divided housework. In another 67 percent of the couples husbands helped wives, while in 10 percent housework was reported to be the duty of women (Roth, 1979). Recent and similar data are not available, but studies support the idea that the traditional division of roles between men and women continues to characterize the majority of families. Yet a trend toward an increased participation of men in domestic activities is also noticeable (CNS & UNDP, 2000).

A 2000 public opinion survey showed that 63 percent of the representative sample believed that domestic activities are "mostly woman's rather than man's duty." Moreover, both women (82 percent) and men (86 percent) respondents agreed that "the man is the head of the family." A similar strong support was declared for other defining elements of the traditional gender representations such as: the role of the breadwinner is mostly the man's; the woman should "follow" her man; and men cannot perform the child-raising role as well as women (Fundatia pentru o societate deschisa, 2000; Popescu, 2003). Under these conditions, chances are that traditional gender roles will not be challenged, at least in the near future. See Mizsei et al. (2003) for information about gender relations within Roma families.

The daily agenda of a homemaker living in a rural area is even fuller than that of an urban wife. A typical profile of a woman living in a village was described by Sandi (1996). It shows that women start their working day at five o'clock in the morning and finish it at eleven o'clock in the evening, in between taking care of children, the animals on the farm, cooking for and serving food for all dependent and adult family members, and working in the fields from spring till fall.

In Romania, the lives of women in the rural areas are even harder than that of those living in the cities, because they lack specialized services. Usually there is more difficulty in getting adequate medical services and professional help for children with special needs. There are also no family planning services (UNDP, 1996c). The situation of men living in rural areas is also more restricted than those in the cities, but they usually have more financial autonomy than women (Sandi, 1996).

Employment and Gender

The employment rate of women varied between 56 and 59 percent in the 1994-1998 period, while for men the figures were higher (71-73 percent) (CNS & UNDP, 2000). In 1992, women represented 42 percent of the working civilian population. In 2002, it was 48 percent (UNDP, 2004). When different occupational statuses are considered, the figures show that women form the majority of the "nonpaid family members" (72 percent), but less than one-half of the paid employees (42 percent), employers (22 percent), and self-employed (35 percent) (UNDP, 2004).

The salary received is another factor showing disparities between men and women. Women receive less pay than their male coworkers for every category of economic activity. The ratio of estimated female to male earned income is 0.58 (United Nations, 2003). Their differences in the salary range from 29 percent (in industry) to 2 percent (in agriculture). Fields such as education, health care, and social services, where women make up the majority of workers, have among the lowest average salaries in the country (CNS & UNDP, 2000).

The serious economic imbalances of the transition period influence women also in their participation in paid labor. The unemployment rate increased from 3 percent in 1991, to between 8 and 11 percent in 1999, and was 7 percent in 2003 (CNS, 1999b; UNDP, 1998; World Factbook, 2000, 2004). The unemployment rate of women exceeded that of men between 1994 and 1998, with a maximum of 4.8 percentage points in 1994. In 2002, female unemployment was lower than the male unemployment. However the average period of unemployment tends to be longer for women (i.e., above eighteen months). For 35 percent of the unemployed women, the duration of unemployment was twenty-four months and more compared with 30 percent of unemployed men (UNDP, 2004).

FAMILIES AND STRESS

As should be clear throughout this chapter, Romanian families are currently experiencing a great deal of challenges and stress.[4] The source of stressful circumstances for families tends to be the prevailing poverty since the transition from a command economy and the Communist system of socioeconomic supports for families, to a demand economy and the relative lack of adequate socioeconomic supports.

In the aftermath of the 1989 Revolution, Romania gained an unfortunate reputation due to some serious social problems produced by economic backwardness and poverty. Abandoned children, the poor quality of medical and social care, and low living standards have been some of the problems affecting family life. Demographic and social indicators indicate that poverty continued to be a serious issue in Romania during the 1990-2000 period and beyond (CASPIS, 2004; CNS & UNDP, 2000; United Nations, 2003; UNDP, 2002, 2005; World Factbook, 2005).

In 1989, an estimated 7 percent of the population was poor. By 1994, the poverty rate ranged, according to the methodology employed, between 22 percent (Tesliuc, Pop, & Panduru, 2003) and 39 percent (UNDP, 2002; Zamfir, 1995b). A second wave of impoverishment began in 1997. By 2000, the poverty rate reached 36 percent (26 for urban population and 48 percent for rural population) (CASPIS, 2004; Tesliuc et al., 2003; UNDP, 2004). This is a significant (21 percent) increase over the 1995 rate. Extreme poverty showed a similar pattern over the same time interval, rising from 9 to 14 percent. Severe poverty was estimated as 14 percent in rural and 4 percent in urban areas (CASPIS, 2004). The economic collapse has been the main source of structural-economic poverty. However, distributional poverty resulting from increasing inequality in the distribution of resources and inadequate social protection has also played a role (UNDP, 2002; World Factbook, 2005). The economic growth led to a reduction of the overall poverty rate after 2001, but the impact on extreme poverty was less. In 2002, the poverty rate was 29 percent and extreme poverty was 11 percent (Tesliuc et al., 2003). It is estimated that 25 percent of the population is below the poverty line (World Factbook, 2005). The risk of becoming poor increases with the number of children, especially with the third child. Two-thirds of families with three and more children are living in poverty (Tesliuc et al., 2003). Their condition worsened despite the overall improvement in the poverty rate (CASPIS, 2002).

The poverty risk of a household is dependent upon the occupational status and educational level of the head of the household, and the number of dependent children in the family. The households most at risk are those headed by unemployed persons, farmers/peasants, and single parents. Among the employed, manual workers are more likely to be poor than are those with nonmanual occupations. Households where the head is self-employed are often poorer than households of those employed otherwise. People with inadequate educational attainment are at risk. Data relating the economic condition to the number of dependents show that larger proportions of families with three or more children are facing poverty than other families (Berthin, 2002; UNDP, 1998). The number of dependent children is a poverty-related factor and the hardship of the transition period has been considerable for children. A 1997 study shows that 50 percent of all children live in the poorest one-third of families (Zamfir, 1997). By age, the highest risk of poverty (based on per adult equivalent consumption) is found among children, especially during the adolescent period, second under the age of seven, and third between seven and fourteen years of age

(Marginean, 2004, Tesliuc et al., 2003; World Bank, 2003). Similarly, mono-parental families are "one deep pocket of poverty," "who represent only 11 percent of the poor, but face 30 to 50 percent higher risk of poverty than the comparator households" (Tesliuc et al., 2003, p. 26). The risk for poverty peaked in 2000 and has diminished since for all ages, but is significantly less for families with three or more children and for those over age sixty-five (Marginean, 2004; World Bank, 2003).

A concentration of the various conditions inducing poverty (lack or low level of education, unskilled labor force, irregular employment, numerous children) materializes among the Roma. Subsequently, the majority of the Roma population lives in poverty, even severe poverty: 63 percent of these families are living below the subsistence minimum and 81 percent below the decent minimum (Zamfir & Zamfir, 1993).

While some families are doing well under the new social order, many are not. A news article indicated that one-third of the population subsists on the equivalent of one U.S. dollar per day (Semo, 2000). During 1989-1995, 59 percent lived on US$4 a day. In 1996-1999, the percentage was twenty-three (Balasa et al., 1999; UNDP, 2005). Romania has experienced difficulties adapting to its new political and economic systems, and families have been affected in dire ways. However, Romanian families are resilient and adaptive. Signs of progress are seen and families are adapting their behaviors (as discussed in previous text) to function to the best extent possible.

FAMILIES AND AGING

The population of Romania is just joining the European pattern of aging. Due to the diminution of the birthrate, the proportion of the aged population is increasing within the total population, especially for females. The number of people over sixty-five years of age has gradually increased since 1990, reaching 14 percent of the total population in 2001. It is expected to reach 15 percent in 2015 (Balasa et al., 1999; United Nations, 2003; UNDP, 1998). This rate is lower in the urban area (9 percent) and higher in the rural area (17 percent) (UNDP, 1998). Women over age sixty form a quarter of the females living in rural areas (CNS & UNDP, 2000). Life expectancy at birth is estimated as 68.1 years for males and 75.3 for females (World Factbook, 2005). Life expectancy is a little higher in urban (71.9) than in rural (70.2) areas.

Elderly grandmothers are usually part-time or full-time caretakers of babies of employed mothers. The "several generations together" family life is rarely present in Romania's modern society, but still grandparents are important in caring for grandchildren. This is because babysitting weighs heavily in the budget of a family, even those in which both adults work.

The Decree Law 60 of 1990 allowed early retirement—for those with the minimum number of service years—for men at age fifty-five and for women, at fifty. These ages were five years earlier then the age limit existing before 1989. Ordinance 50/1990 was a legislative initiative having indirect effects on decreasing the retirement age. This provision allowed many employees to move to other categories, thus enabling them to retire at a lower age (Berthin, 2002).

According to Law 19/2000, the standard age for retirement is now sixty for women and sixty-five for men. Those who contributed to the pension fund at least ten years more than the minimum, which is fifteen years, can retire five years earlier than the mentioned age limit. After being pensioned, healthy men and women try to continue in some kind of paid work. For example, physicians continue with private practice, bookkeepers find work with private enterprises, teachers give private lessons (having a good market, because of the fearful exam system in the schools), fitters and mechanics are always in demand, and so on. Those who cannot continue in their profession turn (or return) to agriculture, especially in recent years after land was returned to families from government ownership. The biggest challenge for the elderly is the increase in the price of medicines that are no longer subsidized. For the majority of products, the price is equal to that in Western countries.

The economic activism of the elderly has a simple explanation. Pensions essentially reduce the income of the family. The majority of the pensioners have no significant savings, as they live on the poor state-given salary, from one month to the next. Generally, the younger generation of the family has few resources to support the pensioner.

Caregiving

When elderly people are ill and need care, the members of their families usually provide the caregiving. Specialized service is solicited mostly in the cases when there are no healthy family members or when family relationships are broken. Each county has homes for elderly who have no family support, but there is always a waiting list. Some civil organizations (e.g., Malthesian Knights, Caritas, Yellow Cross, women's organizations within different churches) recently developed programs to care for the elderly in their homes. A special category of elderly in need of community care are the parents of emigrants, a category much represented in Hungarian and German minorities. Compared with Romanians, with 16 percent of their population over age sixty, the percentage of Hungarians over age sixty is twenty and of Germans is twenty-eight. The Jewish community in Romania (with approximately 9,000 people) is mainly composed of people over sixty years of age. Many are lonely persons, even survivors of the Holocaust. The Jewish community has organized its own homes for the elderly and also home-based social services (Roth, nd). The Roma population has the lowest percentage of elderly (5 percent), because they have the lowest life expectancy (Guvernul Romaniei & UNICEF, 1997).

OTHER FAMILY SITUATIONS

The financial aspects of the new economic life strongly influence the evolution of family dynamics in the postcommunist transition period. As already shown, this has resulted in the decrease of such indicators as nuptiality and fertility rates; however, the divorce rate remains constant. Divorce and mortality are the principal sources of one-parent families. Among single-parent families, four-fifths are female headed (CNS & UNDP, 2000).

The majority family model is that of both parents present, having one or two children. There is also another model of families, those with low fertility control and numerous children. During the 1993-1998 period, the majority of the newborn babies had mothers who had a low or medium level of education. Almost half the women delivering babies within the same years were homemakers (CNS & UNDP, 2000). This is most specific for very poor families and mainly Roma for whom the proportion of children represents 41 percent of their to-tal population (Guvernul Romaniei & UNICEF, 1997). This is easily called a deviant family model because of the increased poverty risk of these families (Guvernul Romaniei & UNICEF, 1997). The deviant family model is usually also defined as one leading to the inability of parents to raise their own children, which results in the abandonment of children in institutions (USAID, 2000).

Orphanages and Other Services for Children

The notorious "orphanages" (Children's Homes) are typical of the kind of inadequate social services discussed earlier in this chapter (Roth, 1999, 2003). The children, both in the past and till today, are typically not orphans, but either abandoned children or children placed in residential care by their parents who are not able to care for them. In both cases, the origin of the situation is the poverty of the family and its inability to fulfill the child's basic needs (Roth, 2000, 2003). In the absence of alternative services, in the first six years of the postcommunist regime, the residential solution for children was main-tained and even reinforced, despite the lack of cost-effectiveness and increasing professional criticism. Success of the reforms in child welfare was and still is hampered by the economic conditions of fam-ilies (Greenwell, 2003).

The analysis done by Greenwell on admission and discharge ar-chives of child-care institutions, with a nationally representative sam-ple, showed that in the period 1997-2000 a comprehensive reform started in this system. This resulted in the improvement of the de-institutionalization process, ranging from 24 to 56 percent more than in the pre-reform period; all the same, the institutionalization ranged only between 27 and 32 percent lower than the pre-reform period (Greenwell, 2003). Until 2000, the most common family destinations for deinstitutionalization were international adoptions and foster place-ments. After 2000, there was a large increase in foster placements and internal adoptions. With the law on adoptions of 2004, international adoption stopped, being admitted only for grandparents living out-side Romania (Law 272/June 2004).

As Greenwell noted, there still persists a negative attitude toward adopting or fostering Roma children, who represent a large (but not documented) part of the abandoned or institutionalized children. The reform of foster care, which offers regular income and recognizes work experience of foster careers, has significantly increased the recruitment of foster parents, whose number doubled in the period 2002-2004 (National Authority for Protection of Rights of Children and Adoption [ANPDCA], 2004, 2005).

CONCLUDING COMMENTS

In 1990, the Romanian population was 23.2 million. In 1994, the population was 22.7 million. The 2002 census indicated 21.7 million. The declining population is due to high mortality and decreasing births, combined with out migration (Berthin, 2002; CNS & UNDP, 2000; INS, 2003; UNDP, 1996b).

For the next thirty to forty years, using as a reference period the years after 1989, scientists conclude there will be zero demographic increase and an aging of the population. It is also hypothesized that there will be a significant reduction in the total number of persons living in Romania. The population is decreasing and it is projected that this tendency will continue with a reduction to twenty million people in 2030 (Muresan, 1996). Changing this population decline cannot be enforced on the population by the pressure of laws, as it had been under the dictatorship of Ceausescu. The decline in population should not be considered a purely educational or moral problem. Families should be offered social support and not limited in their tendency to decide whether they can have children, and how many. There will always be families who under or over estimate their capacities in this regard, a risk that each society must accept. Moreover, each civilized society has to be prepared to intervene in helping children born to parents who are not able to raise them. Romania must consider how it can effectively respond. The maintenance of roughly the same divorce rate after the Revolution as before, demonstrates the adaptive capacity of families in the face of stress. This also verifies the ability of families to maintain their own traditions. In contrast, the decline in population indicates dramatic changes before and after 1989 (INS 2002; Muresan, 1996). Starting with 1992, the natural growth was constantly negative (INS, 2002).

Many areas of life have become impossible or difficult to control by legal regulation since the transformation in the society beginning in 1989. As a result, new forms of regulation have appeared. For example, religious institutions offer firm moral principles for family life and especially regarding the domain of sexuality. Different religious orientations (traditional Orthodox, Catholic, Protestant, and others) are competing for adherents, and youngsters are important targets.

The family and neighborhood social safety nets, which were critical under Communism, became inadequate during the transition to the market economy. Growing unemployment, falling wages and pensions, difficulties in coping with changes, have all caused a surge of poverty which none of the existing provisions have been able to alleviate. Families are suffering and this is creating great stress.

Families hold important possibilities for organizing the way of life of individuals. It has to be consensual, a frame within which mature individuals decide on its extension, its duration, its specific ways of communicating, working, and living. The number of families sharing these values is expected to increase.

Political diversity, fear of unemployment, inflation, the temptation of the many consumer goods found in a free market economy, the competition, are all dimensions of the new quality of social life. These challenges are pressing the accommodation capacities of families. For some families the social burden has lessened, for others it has increased, and future directions are uncertain.

NOTES

1. Romania had a Human Development Index (HDI) ranking of sixty-four (of 177 countries) in 2005, up from seventy-nine in 1997 (UNDP, 2005). A crude attempt was made to determine the HDI for the Gypsy or Roma population in Romania. The Index of 0.570 was well below the index number (in 2000) of 0.775 for Romania as a whole. The Roma HDI would be on par with countries like Zimbabwe and Swaziland. Many Roma in a survey indicated that their life quality has deteriorated since the transition from socialism to capitalism (Mizsei, Slay, Mihailov, O'Higgins, & Ivanov, 2003). For more information on the Roma in Central Europe, see Understanding Roma Bibliography [WWW document] URL www.osi.hu/exhibition/collection.html, or http://dmoz.org/Society/Ethnicity/Romani.

2. Based on 1995 data, in Romania 35 percent of married Roma women wedded when they were sixteen, 17 percent at seventeen to eighteen, and 26 percent between nineteen and twenty-two years of age. Only 8 percent of marriages were after this

age interval. Around 70 percent of Roma between the ages of twenty and twenty-four are married or living with a partner. There is a growing number of "custom law marriages" where the couple is considered by their community and relatives as married, but not by the government and the marriages are not legally binding (Mizsei et al., 2003).

3. See United Nations (2002) for a history of abortion policies in Romania.

4. Of specific concern mentioned in *Human Development Under Transition 1996* (UNDP, 1996a, 1996b) are problems relating to particular groups. The living conditions of large families with small incomes, the economic and social problems of Roma families, and problems related to the number of disorganized families and crimes committed by children and young people, are examples. Likewise, the report considers street children, the employment and social integration of youth, support for families in need, children and young people, individual and social problems of the elderly, and the social integration of the unemployed. Many of these same conditions are discussed in Berthin (2002) and Mizsei et al. (2003).

Chapter 6

Family, Italian-Style

Rossella Palomba

INTRODUCTION

The pluralization of living arrangements and the measurement of their degree of diversity on the basis of the dichotomy between married couples and alternatives to marriage do not seem to be adequate tools for understanding the Italian situation. Although the Italian family remains strongly concentrated and settled in the married couple, changes have occurred. Italy cannot be described superficially by labeling it as a traditional country. Traditional and modern are not absolute terms, but their meaning is relative to the historical and cultural context to which they are related. To be modern in today's Europe does not mean to deny traditional life values and to change family behavior drastically. It might well imply an enlargement of life values and life options, the refusal of institutional morality or morality legislated or imposed by the State, increased freedom of choice, replacement of conformism by an increasing sense of responsibility, and greater tolerance toward alternative life choices and new lifestyles (Cliquet, 1991). A process of integration between modern and traditional behavior and attitudes seems to take place in many European countries.

Family in Italian Context

The Italian family has undoubtedly changed over the past twenty to thirty years, but the extent of the changes that have occurred and the trends of the overall process of change in family patterns are not evident. In fact, the Italian family shows continuity with traditional models and a modest increase in new family behavior, the majority of Italian households are still married couples with children. In 2000, married couples with children constituted 46 percent of all households as compared with 2 percent unmarried cohabitation couples, or 9 percent one-parent families. Only 3 percent of young people were living on their own (Menniti, 2004).

The history of the Italian family is one of continuity and diversity. The dominant family form in Italy has always been that of husband and wife. However, up to the mid-twentieth century it was almost impossible to identify a standard profile of family structure because of the widely differing aspects among the various Italian regions and social classes. Extended and multinuclear families were mainly concentrated in the central-northern rural areas, and nuclear families in the southern rural areas and in urban areas (Barbagli, 1988). With economic development and widespread prosperity, the second half of the twentieth century brought about profound changes in many aspects of Italian social life, including the family and family structures.[1] In particular, there has been a significant trend toward the nuclear family, as in other developed countries, though some specific aspects of Italian family life are being maintained, as this chapter shows in detail.

In any case, there are some types of behavior and principles underlying the foundation of the family that are common to most geographical areas and social backgrounds. These include sexual relationships mainly taking place within marriage; the persistence of highly asymmetrical gender and generational relationships; and marriage that in most cases lasts a lifetime. It is easy to see the direct influence on these principles of the moral teaching and doctrine of the Catholic Church, though this interpretation might be too simplistic. One needs only recall, for example, that at least until 1989, the year of the fall of the Berlin Wall, Italy had Europe's largest Catholic political party— besides hosting the Vatican—as well as the largest Communist party in the West. It is therefore a country full of contradictions, opposing ideologies, and willingness to compromise in order to achieve a balance that would otherwise prove impossible. This is particularly obvious in the area of family changes. Italians implement all the possible strategies in order to maintain links between traditional forms and the changes required for adapting to the time and to the demands of modern life.

Italy was and is a Catholic country. However religion, too, has become an area for compromise and the Italians are above all *"la carte"* Catholics who manage to make lifestyle choices enabling them to comply on the outside with religious rules while adapting these to their needs. Therefore, many of the changes in mentality and values that have prompted changes within the family remain under the level of social visibility. Changes in values and norms in the area of reproduction and marriage came about through the sharp reduction of demographic events (i.e., births and marriages), avoiding nontraditional lifestyles. For example, the number of children per woman has sharply reduced and the total fertility rate is one of the lowest in the world (1.26 in 2002). However, 89 percent of children are born to married couples (Istituto Nazionale di Statistica [ISTAT], 2003). The population growth rate is 0.07 percent and the birthrate is 8.89 per 1,000 population (World Factbook, 2005). Marriage rates have reduced and in the period 1984-2001, first marriage rates declined from 707 to 565 per 1,000 for men and from 688 to 600 for women. Ninety-five percent of all marriages consist of people in their first marital experience (Istituto Ricerche sulla Popolazione [IRP], 1999).

If the dominant family type in Italy has not changed much over time, the life of individuals within families has changed considerably. New relationships have come about between family members. Marriages adhere less to the Catholic aim of procreation, are more egalitarian, and can be legally dissolved since 1970 when divorce was introduced in the Italian legal system.[2]

Family roles have changed. Women are better educated and are joining the labor force in increasing numbers. The number of double-earner households is on the rise for both economic need as well as for women's desire to work (49 percent of young married couples are dual-job families). The children of employed mothers are numerous, making up 43 percent of the population of all children under than fourteen years of age (ISTAT, 1996a). The high rate of unemployment (10 percent in 2000 and estimated at 8.6 in 2003) affects men and especially middle-aged women (IRP, 1999; World Factbook, 2004). All these changes have led to a variety of family types, which differ, from the traditional, asymmetrical family type.

In addition, the relationships between generations have changed from both the quantitative and qualitative points of view. Italian children stay in their parents' home longer. In 2000, 56 percent of children aged eighteen to thirty-four years had never left their parental home as compared with 46 percent in 1990 (ISTAT, 1996a; Menniti, 2004). As a result, the number of married couples with adult children has increased, postponing the empty nest phase.

In synthesis, for the Italians, the family with a capital "F" has always meant the one based on marriage, the form that most couples prefer and practice. Italy is a country focused on marriage, other types of families being in the minority. Instead of a drastic break with the past, the Italian change is a process of renewal from within the family. This change is more difficult to be quantified by means of statistical data, but this does not mean that it is any less relevant or significant. The change has occurred, and it is a matter of describing it in the most appropriate way.

COUPLE FORMATION AND MARITAL DYNAMICS

Young Italians remain with mom and dad until they marry and they prefer to remain children longer than in other countries. Percentages of young unmarried men and women living in the parental home are increasing in all age groups and in both sexes (see Table 6.1). The fact that young adults are employed does not imply that they stop living with their parents. Over 70 percent of employed men and women aged twenty to twenty-four and over 40 percent of employed men and

TABLE 6.1. Still Children by Age and Sex, 1990 and 1998 (Percentage).

Age Group	20-24 Years		25-29 Years		30-34 Years		Total	
	1990	1998	1990	1998	1990	1998	1990	1998
Men	88.4	93.5	50.0	70.7	17.8	29.2	59.1	66.5
Women	70.8	83.1	28.1	45.6	9.6	14.7	44.5	50.9
Total	79.6	88.4	39.0	58.3	13.7	21.9	51.8	58.8

Source: Adapted from Sabbadini (1999).

women aged twenty-five to thirty-four continue to live in the parental home (ISTAT, 1996a).

Children As Long As Possible

Many reasons have been offered to explain the recent trend among youths that is changing the life of both children and parents. Difficult economic conditions, desire to continue education, high levels of familism, less authoritarian relationships inside the family, and new behavior of young women concerning education and employment, are some possible explanations for the fact that Italian young people stay in the parental home longer. Among all the possible motivations, education seems one of the most prevalent. The process of leaving the parents' home and forming a new family is increasingly delayed with the rise in the level of education (Palomba, Menniti, & Caruso, 1997).

The age at first sexual intercourse is also quite high, decreasing for the older cohorts of men and women but increasing in the younger ones. While women born at the end of the 1940s had their first intercourse at age 21.4 years on average, women born at the beginning of the 1960s had sex for the first time at 19.4 years of age. However, women born at the beginning of the 1970s had their first sexual intercourse at an average age of 21.7 years, much like women born in the 1940s. Men show the same trend, passing from 18.8 years on average for those born in the 1940s, to a minimum of 18 years among those born at the beginning of the 1960s, and a moderate increase to 18.7 for those born in the 1970s (De Sandre, Ongaro, Rettaroli, & Salvini, 1997). This recent increase in age before the sexual debut might be due to new sexual behavior as a result of fear of contracting AIDS and to the general postponement of marriage, which still represents for many Italians the start of their sexual life.

Couple Formation and Dissolution

Italians are getting married increasingly later. This is an important feature in a country like Italy where unmarried cohabitation is rare and marital fertility is normative. The average age at marriage is 29.9 for men and about 27.1 for women, rising on an average of 1.5 years for men and 2 years for women over the past decade (Sabbadini, 1999).

The age difference between spouses has also become closer (from a difference of 3.8 years in 1960 to 2.8 in 1991), probably because women are more educated (Menniti, 1997).

The meaning of marriage seems to be changing, giving less importance to the Catholic aim of procreation and the requirement of indissolubility. A survey carried out at the beginning of the 1980s showed that 86 percent of the respondents believed that love was the basis and goal of marriage. Only 33 percent said that besides love, children were also necessary (Palomba, 1987). The survey, repeated in 1997, confirmed the importance of love as the basis of marriage (80 percent of agreement) while more importance was given to the presence of children (60 percent) (Menniti & Palomba, 1997). In this survey, a negative aspect concerning marriage was also highlighted; 42 percent of Italians thought that marriage wears out the relationship. This compares with only 24 percent who believed this in 1983. Thus, the romantic way of conceiving marriage seems to be supported and strengthened by the presence of children who represent a way to overcome the difficulties and limitations of being married.

If marriage is based above all on mutual love and this sentiment is lacking, spouses can be willing to stop living together, especially if there are no children. Sixteen out of 100 first marriages end in a legal separation or a divorce (Menniti & Palomba, 1994). The amount of marital breakdown has remained limited compared with other developed countries (Council of Europe, 1996).

According to the Italian legislation, divorce is granted after a three-year period of legal separation. A hearing before a civil court is required for both separation and divorce. The end of marriage thus involves lengthy, costly procedures. An average of eight months is required to get a legal separation, and ten months for divorce, with longer periods in southern Italy or when alimony is requested (Menniti & Terracina, 1997). Separation and divorce have different meanings to the Italians, as well as having different implications from the legal point of view. Separation is the end to the couple's life together; divorce means the definite end of the marriage and the possibility of remarriage (Menniti & Palomba, 1994). The number of legal separations outnumbers that of divorces. In 2001, separations totaled 75,890 as compared with 40,051 divorces (ISTAT, 2003).

FAMILIES AND CHILDREN

Italian family structure is increasingly simple. Family size has decreased, falling from 3.6 members in 1961, to 3.0 in 1981, and 2.6 in 2000. The percentage of families with six or more members fell from 14 percent of total families in 1961 to only 2 percent in 2000. The presence of one-person households, largely due to the population aging process, increased from 19 percent to 27 percent in the same period (Menniti, 2004).

Toward the One-Child Model

The simplification of the nuclear family structure is due to the reduction in the number of children per woman. Italian fertility began to decline at the beginning of the twentieth century, but in the 1960s and 1970s, the speed of the trend quickened to such a point that Italy today has one of the lowest fertility rates in the world. In 1960, live births numbered 923,000. In 1965 they rose to over one million. Since then, the decline has been continuous. In 2002, only 535,538 live births were registered (ISTA, 2003). The total fertility rate (the number of children the average women is expected to have if present fertility trends continue) is well under the level of replacement at 1.26.

The most recent estimates of fertility for the generation of women born in 1960, give a fertility rate of 1.65 (Menniti, 1997). The fertility rate of women under age thirty has fallen considerably, while the rate for older age groups has been more or less stable. While in 1980 women aged twenty to twenty-four showed the highest fertility rate, the twenty-five to twenty-nine age group replaced them ten years later. The only age group with an increasing fertility rate was found in the thirty to thirty-four-year-old age group (ISTAT, 1993). If rates for the birth of the first child are considered, the postponement of parenthood becomes even more obvious. On average, the first child is no longer born before the mother reaches age twenty-five, but is now born after the mother reaches twenty-eight years of age. In 1981, one-half of the first children were born to mothers under age twenty-four, while in 1991 only 26 percent were born to women of that age group (ISTAT, 1993).

The time between marriage and the birth of the first child has increased. While in 1981 less than two years elapsed between marriage and the birth of the first child, this interval is now 2.5 years. There is a tendency to postpone the birth of the first child even longer when the parents have higher educational or job qualifications. Similar trends can be observed between the birth of the first and second child, with a peak interval period of two to three years (ISTAT, 1993).

The sharp decline in fertility took place because of an increasing use of contraception and was not accompanied by an increase in abortions. In fact, from the beginning of the 1980s, the total fertility rate decreased by 24 percent. At the same time, the abortion rate decreased by 16 percent, declining from 16.9 abortions per thousand women aged fifteen to forty-nine, to 9.4 (IRP, 1999). From surveys carried out by the National Health Institute, it appears that in the majority of cases, abortion is a direct consequence of the failure or wrong use of contraceptive methods (Istituto Superiore Sanità [ISS], 1993).

In Italy, relatively few babies are being born but, notwithstanding this fact, the majority of Italian couples have at least one child. The increase in the number of childless couples, which is the most tangible and evident aspect of the decline in the birthrate in other countries, has not really manifested itself in Italy (Council of Europe, 1996). In 1989, 19 percent of married couples were childless; in 1998 there was a modest increase to 20 percent.

The number of families with at least one child less than eighteen years old is decreasing due to the drop in the fertility rate. From the beginning of the 1980s through the 1990s, these families have decreased from 8.1 million to 7.7 million in absolute values and from 41 percent to 35 percent of the total number of households (ISTAT, 2003). The most common kind of household is, and remains, that of the married couple with children, but the one-child model has become the most common.

Italians and Life Values: Conformist or Not?

It is possible to shed some light on the normative context of fertility and the family by using the result of a recent survey (Palomba, 1995a). First, an extremely favorable attitude toward family and parenthood seems to exist in Italy. The most important values and aspirations in life relate to having children, to raising and educating them well, and to having a family and children with whom to live a happy and harmonious life. Men and women evaluate the effect of the birth of a first or a subsequent child on the fulfillment of life objectives differently and this could result in gender-related life strategies.

Men seem to be more conformist than their wives, because they are more in favor of the two-child family model. Actually, they are probably both unable and unwilling to adapt or change their lifestyle based on procreation choices. For men, having children is an ordinary, standard part of life. For women, this is a choice regarding quality of life, partly linked to the number of children they have. However, what is the significance of children for the Italians?

Italians and Child Value to Parents

Italians think that children bring with them the greatest satisfaction they are likely to experience. Children are the most important means of achieving self-fulfillment and the relationship with one's children is the most enduring bond that Italian parents have (Palomba, 1987, 1995a). The family, children, and the Italian tradition that gives great value to the relationship between generations is still important—even in a period in which the marriage relationship is becoming less stable. Undoubtedly, the Italian family has changed in terms of size, function, and internal roles, but even in the context of this change, the parent/child unit remains a firm point of reference in Italian life.

Today, fewer children are born in Italy but this is without a significant rise in childless marriages or couples. The fall in fertility may thus be better explained by the hypothesis of "too much love for the children," or increasing desires and expectations of Italian parents for their children. This induces parents to make their own child look more like the ideal child smiling from the pages of the glossy magazines.

Italians and Children's Social Value

The social value of the activities carried out by the family in caring for children can be measured primarily according to the opportunity granted to the mother to be absent from her employment for a preestablished number of days of maternity leave on full pay. In Italy, this period is presently fixed at twenty weeks (starting eight weeks before the birth). There is an additional period of parental leave, available by law, paid at 40 percent of normal salary which can last until the child

is one year of age. The father can take this leave if the mother continues to work, but few fathers take advantage of this option because the
salary of the father, in the majority of cases, is higher than that of the
mother. Social security pays the salary of the employee on leave at no
charge to the employer. The maternity and/or parental leave also
applies in cases of adoption.

The presence and quality of day-care centers and kindergartens are
additional indicators of the social context of fertility and families
with children. Day-care centers are attended by 12 percent of Italian
children from birth to three years of age. The number of children who
attend preschool is high and exceeds 90 percent of children aged
three to five years (ISTAT, 1996b). Preschools are run by the State
and are free of charge. Local authorities or municipalities run day-
care centers and parents must pay a means-tested fee.

Finally, child allowance benefits paid by the State vary according
to the overall income of the family and the number of family members. Allowances are paid for children under eighteen years of age.
The amount of the child allowance is small and Italians do not consider this economic policy measure an effective support structure in
bringing up children (Moors & Palomba, 1995). For particularly
needy families or for those in difficulty, like single-parent families
and families in which there is a disabled child, there is an increase in
the child allowance check but the amount remains modest.

FAMILIES AND GENDER

Education has always played a fundamental role from the point of
view of female emancipation and gender roles within the family. Improved educational opportunities for women have generally led to an
increase in the number of women going out to work and to a different
attitude toward the family and motherhood.

Italian Women: Better Educated than Men; Higher Rate of Unemployment

Half the students in Italian high schools are now women and many of
them go to university. In 1950, 31 percent of all newly enrolled students
at Italian universities were women. In 1979, this rose to 38 percent, in

1981 to 45 percent, and in 2001 to 56 percent. In some faculties, the number of women students has doubled and in some subjects, women are clearly in the majority (The Arts—70 percent, Mathematics—68 percent, Biology—61 percent). Even in the highly technical faculties, there are a significant percentage of women students (Engineering—18 percent, Medicine—59 percent). Women graduates and students now outnumber their male counterparts: 56 percent of graduate students are women (ISTAT, 2003).

Nevertheless, it is not always the case that a diploma or a degree is the starting point for finding a more satisfying or fulfilling job. The rate of unemployment is much higher among women than among men, and in the less developed parts of the country, reaching 26 percent (ISTAT, 2003). A better-educated woman can thus have reached the finishing post—the acquisition of a new social role because of her education that might imply a different status within the family.

Highly educated housewives are more common in the south of Italy, a less developed area. This is a model for a potential but unachieved double-income family given the lack of suitable employment and the cultural context of this part of the country. However, the lifestyles of these women are different from those of less well-educated women and they are more aware of the balance of roles within the family.

Time and "Ties"

The results of a national time budget survey can be used to investigate the division of labor in Italian families (Palomba & Sabbadini, 1994). Time spent on the family is a good analytical instrument for looking at gender differences and inequality. Men and women form families; marriage, employment, and children mean less flexibility in how they arrange their time. In Italy as in many other countries, a man's life is ordered by the pace and hours of his employment, while a woman has to make daily compromises to reconcile family, social, and possibly even employment commitments.

The birth of a child means that women have to reorganize their time and dedicate more of it to their families. After the arrival of the first child, the mother has to spend about one hour more than before on family time which is usually taken from her time for basic needs (see Table 6.2). When the second child is born, a further hour for the

TABLE 6.2. How Employed Men and Women Aged Eighteen to Forty-Four Years Old, Living As Part of a Couple or As One-Parent Families, Spend Their Time, by Number of Children (Specific Average Duration and Participation Rate).

Number of Children	Women			Men		
	1	2	3 or More	1	2	3 or More
Activity			**Time**			
Family work[a]	5h12'	6h00'	6h54'	1h48'	1h42'	1h54'
Employment	6h54'	6h30'	5h54'	7h48'	8h08'	8h18'
Basic needs[b]	11h00'	10h48'	10h06'	10h48'	10h48'	10h54'
Leisure time	3h00'	3h00'	3h00'	4h42'	4h12'	4h00'
Activity			**Percent of people doing the activity**			
Family work[a]	100.0	100.0	100.0	73.3	68.5	62.0
Employment	61.7	60.8	56.6	75.1	81.6	81.6
Leisure time	95.6	94.2	94.0	98.4	98.2	98.3

Source: Adapted from Palomba & Sabbadini (1994).

[a]Housework, care of other family members, and shopping.

[b]Sleeping, eating, personal hygiene, etc.

family has to be found. When there is a third child, time spent on the family by the mother increases by yet another hour, even if she goes out to work. And what about men? Comparing mothers' and fathers' time-use shows that the gender role division widens visibly. The amount of time men spend in employment increases as the number of children increases from one to three or more children, while that of the mother steadily decreases. The time women spend in employment stays about the same between zero and one child, but it decreases by about one-half-an-hour a day when she has two children and by an hour if she has three or more children. As far as is possible, employed women try to reduce their hours in paid work in order to cope with new needs at home. Men, on the other hand, work more in order to provide for their family's growing needs (Palomba & Sabbadini, 1994).

Italian men and women get involved in housework in different ways. Men are choosy about what they will offer to do. In general, they do not do the laundry or ironing, and they do not do house cleaning or make the bed. This is true regardless of whether there are children living at home or not. If men are living alone with their wives, they help more with the cooking, setting and clearing the table, and shopping. Men's greatest contribution to family work is in the area of maintenance, which is of an occasional nature, requires a certain degree of skill, and fits better with the stereotyped role of men being better at "technical" and "more difficult" things than women (Palomba & Sabbadini, 1994). Gender roles are clearly and rigidly fixed within the family.

Gender roles are already in evidence in childhood. Different behaviors among girls and boys anticipate future adult roles. For example, more than one-half of the girls aged eleven or over spend about one hour a day on housework. Only about 30 percent of their male peers do any housework at all and when they do, they spend less time on it (about thirty minutes). There is a clear distinction between participation in activities such as cleaning/tidying and in setting the table similar to those described for adults (Palomba & Sabbadini, 1994).

Boys and girls have different participation levels regarding housework; helping the mother in cooking or cleaning starts as a game but then the gap widens. In the six to ten years age group, twice the numbers of girls as boys do housework. In the eleven to thirteen years group, the majority of children doing housework are girls and they spend an hour of their time on it (Palomba & Sabbadini, 1994). These are only the first steps along a long road of differences that becomes more marked as children grow older.

FAMILIES AND STRESS

In a country like Italy with a relatively low number of divorces and separations and an overall "stability" of traditional family forms, literature related to family stressors is very limited. Family stress in general is not a common topic of sociological investigation. However, some observations are possible. Mainly, reasons for family conflict and stress originate in two major areas: treatment and assistance requirements of the disabled in the family (i.e., people who cannot undertake the essential tasks of everyday life) and economic factors, especially adult unemployment. Following is a "demographic" outlook on family conflict and stress.

If There Is a Disabled or Unemployed Person at Home

The reduction of the ability to undertake everyday activities—such as the inability to wash one's face or hands, take a bath or shower, dress and undress, eat and chew without difficulty—is a serious factor affecting 3 percent of the Italian population aged six and older (1,783,000 people) (ISTAT, 1996b). Limits on taking care of one's self often mean confinement to bed or to a chair. In such cases, people need continuous assistance.

Disability does not only regard individuals; all the problems and difficulties arising from the presence of a disabled person are shared, handled, and experienced within the family. There are a low number of disabled persons in institutions or nursing homes, while household members, especially women, bear a heavy load in this respect. A total of 12 percent of Italian households have to deal daily with the problems of the assistance to be provided to a disabled family member. Ten percent of the entire Italian population is directly or indirectly involved in problems due to a decline in self-sufficiency (ISTAT, 1996b). The families react by increasing solidarity and help, integrating the disabled person into the daily life of the family.

When people lose their job, Italian families likewise tend to support and protect the individual in difficulty. In the middle-age group (thirty-five to fifty-four years), 3 percent of Italians have lost their job and in 3 percent of married couples with children, the father aged between thirty-five and fifty-four is unemployed (ISTAT, 1996a). Without the father's income, households manage to face up to the situation by economic support from other households. Brothers, sisters, and elderly parents are an indispensable network providing material and psychological aid (ISTAT, 1996a). The Italian family seems to absorb all the stresses like a sponge, works them out and modifies them, while maintaining a strong sense of unity.

FAMILIES AND AGING

Italy is an aging country with a high percentage of the population being elderly. Nineteen percent of the entire population is over sixty-five years of age (about 4.6 million men and 6.5 million women) and 4 percent are over eighty years of age. Life expectancy at birth is

79.7 years (women = 82.8 and men = 76.8). Retirement from formal work is the norm. Since 1992, the age of retirement has been sixty for women and sixty-five for men in private employment (Franco, 2000). Only 7 percent of old people continue to work in gainful employment and they are usually men rather than women (ISTAT, 1996a; World Factbook, 2005).

A Profile of the Italian Elderly

For the most part, the elderly did not benefit from the boom in education. In fact, the majority of old people have at most an elementary certificate and only 10 percent have a higher diploma or a degree. The lowest levels of education are among women and those aged sixty-five years and over: 83 percent are illiterate or have the elementary certificate as compared with 73 percent of men of the same age. The level of education of the elderly will change rapidly when the cohorts now in their fifties reach the age of sixty-five years (ISTAT, 1996a). Overall, the national literacy rate in Italy is 99 percent (World Factbook, 2005).

Health conditions are the major concern in later life for both the elderly and for policy makers. Disability is more common among women. Women live longer than men but are forced to live with longer periods of ill health: 37 percent of elderly women compared with 28 percent of elderly men need care or support to live in the community (ISTAT, 1996a). The degree of independence falls as age increases. As women predominate as age increases due to their longer life expectancy—more than eighty years at birth as compared with seventy-six years for men; 21.8 more years of life expected as compared with 17.9 for men at sixty years of age—elderly women will need care and assistance to a greater degree than men (ISTAT, 1996a).

The family context in which older people live differs when looked at from a gender point of view. Elderly women are more likely than men to find themselves living in a family situation in which the relationship with their husbands, if they were married, has ended, especially due to death. Older women thus tend to live alone, as part of a one-parent family, or as part of a household made up of other people. Men are more likely to be found in those family situations in which the husband/wife relationship is still present, both with and without grown-up children at home. Basically, the lives of elderly men continue in much the same way as when there were younger, as wives tend to outlive husbands. In contrast, if there is no longer a child at home, older women tend to live alone and, as they get older, they might join their children's or another household (see Table 6.3).

Family networks are strong in Italy. It has been estimated that every month about eight million acts of help and support of different kinds (economic support, caring for children or the elderly, help in everyday life) are exchanged among Italian families, with about 100 million acts of help given every year (ISTAT, 1996a). Families and individuals do not benefit in the same way from the informal network. The amount and direction of support depends on family structure and on the presence of children and/or the elderly. Individuals with problems or disabilities receive more support than do others from both formal and informal networks, with informal networks not being a substitute for the formal one.

In the case of the elderly, 16 percent of elderly households receive care and material assistance for health problems, 14 percent receive help in daily housework, and 20 percent receive help in doing various activities (bureaucracy, health therapy, etc.). Economic support is received in 5 percent of the cases (ISTAT, 1996a).

TABLE 6.3. Household Composition for Men and Women Aged Seventy-Five Plus, Italy.

	Men (%)	Women (%)	Total (%)
Only elderly live in the household			
Lives alone	17.0	45.9	35.2
With spouse only	58.1	18.1	32.8
With relatives only	0.7	5.9	4.2
Elderly person lives with non-elderly adults			
With spouse and children	11.9	2.6	7.3
With adult child	3.3	9.6	7.9
With relatives or nonrelatives only	9.0	17.9	12.6

Source: Adapted from Istituto Nazionale di Statistica, 2000. Family Caregiving and Receiving.

The elderly are actively involved in the family network, contributing when they can and as long as they are in good health; 800,000 elderly people give help and support to other families and households. Their support is mostly directed toward their children's families (32 percent) and their grandchildren (13 percent), but there is also help given by elderly people to nonrelatives (30 percent) (ISTAT, 1996a). Women are more often primary caregivers than men.

The Italian Elderly: Integrated or Isolated?

The topic of social integration of the elderly, including the integration of older people within their families, needs special attention for the management of an aging society. In Italy, from the relational point of view, the elderly seem well integrated into their social context. For example, 69 percent of the elderly have frequent contacts with their children and 79 percent have constant contacts with their grandchildren (ISTAT, 1996a). It is notable that the majority of the elderly live near their children's houses or even in the same building, a condition that favors daily contacts. Contacts and relationships with friends and neighbors are also frequent and only 1 percent of older men and women do not have regular contacts with friends (ISTAT, 1996a).

A survey carried out at the beginning of the 1990s sheds light on the Italians' perception of the elderly and on the value of family solidarity (Bonifazi, Menniti, & Palomba, 1996). Ninety-three percent of Italians believe that it is the duty of the children to care for their elderly parents, and 94 percent believe that "the best thing one can do in life is to help them." Only 11 percent believe that "the elderly should stay with the elderly" while 76 percent disagree with the idea that "elderly parents living with their children represent a burden." Care for the elderly is the responsibility of their children even when the children are themselves parents with young children. Children should take in their elderly parents, if necessary, and only as a last resort should the elderly parents or relatives be placed in institutions for old people. The role of the elderly in the society is recognized by the majority of Italians as positive and, at least on the face of it, Italian society seems to accept, integrate, and respect the elderly generations in a traditional way (Bonifazi et al., 1996).

Solidarity between generations is still strong. There is a positive reaction on the part of the Italian population toward new forms of assistance for the elderly and of support for the families in which the elderly live. Social conflicts arise when the limits of solidarity are reached, because the degree to which solidarity is demanded is considered an infringement to the development of the individual's sense of freedom and equality (Van de Kaa, 1981). A stronger tendency toward self-fulfillment and personal freedom can imply a decreasing solidarity. Italy, in this respect, seems to follow different paths, maintaining intergenerational and family solidarity, integrating the elderly in the social context, and at the same time avoiding conflicts.

OTHER FAMILY SITUATIONS

Generally speaking, marriage leads to the end of residing with parents, and the dissolution of marriage increases the variety of family forms recorded among adults: single-parent families, reconstituted families, nonmarital cohabitation, and adults living alone. Instability of marriage in Italy has led to the formation of "new" types of families. However, the demand for statistical information on these families came only over the past decade, causing a delay in providing proper data sources and limiting comparisons over time.

Single-Parent Families

The number of single-parent families due to marital dissolution (divorce or separation) is stable, increasing slightly from 7.6 percent of all households in 1989 to 8 percent in 1998. The divorce rate in 2000 was 13.7 per 100 marriages, similar to the rate in Ireland, but much below that of Belgium (59.9 per 100) and Britain (50.5) (Povoledo, 2003). After divorce, mothers generally receive custody of children (86 percent with about 4 percent to fathers, less than 1 percent to other relatives). Joint custody is increasing. It is now about 9 percent of custody situations (ISTAT, 2003). The reasons for so few custodial fathers are many and in part are to be found in cultural and social difficulties. Also, there is the psychological difficulty for the mother in giving up her custodial role. There is a deep-rooted conviction in Italian courts that only a mother can invest the necessary time and energy in the job of socializer; only she is able to give the right dose of love and affection. In short, the mother is seen as essential to the balanced growth of her children. Everyone seems convinced of this—mothers, fathers and the judges who rule on the custody of minors (Palomba, 1995b).

As a consequence, the living conditions of single-parent families reflect those of the mother, who in general has lower income than that of the father. The percentage of lone mothers who are in poverty (defined as 50 percent of median net income) is 11 percent—the national average is 10 percent. Fathers have to pay child support until the children are eighteen years old or twenty-five years old if they attend university. The court determines the amount of the monthly check with the aim of guaranteeing the children the same standard of living that they had before separation or divorce. In general, fathers and children tend to remain in the same town and this makes regular contact easier. More than 80 percent of noncustodial fathers visit their children once or more times per week (Barbagli & Saraceno, 1997). Children sleep in their father's home less frequently and 31 percent of children never do.

Reconstituted Families

The phenomenon of reconstituted families resulting from divorce and remarriage is relatively new in Italy; only 4 percent of all households are reconstituted families. In general, men are more likely to remarry than women and women remain single longer. Forty-four percent of men remarry after a divorce compared with 28 percent of women (Menniti, 1997). Among reconstituted families (second marriages or cohabitation after the dissolution of marriage), 58 percent of both partners have children living with them, while in 30 percent of the relationships, only one of the partners has children who live with them (Menniti, 1997).

Living Together Outside Marriage

Current marriage rates indicate that most Italians will marry. A limited number of couples are living together without being married and the number of unmarried cohabiting couples remains stable, around 2 percent of all the households in the last decade. Most men and women who live together expect to marry their current partner in

the future. Premarital cohabitation, considered as a stage in the courtship process, is on the rise, increasing from 2 percent of all marriage
cohorts in the 1960s, to 13 percent of all marriage cohorts in the 1990s.
The length of cohabitation is increasing, generally not exceeding two
years (ISTAT, 2000a).

Unmarried partners have higher education than married partners of
the same age and they are more likely to include university-graduated
partners. Unmarried couples are more likely to reside in metropolitan
areas. Cohabiting women are more frequently employed than are married women (57 percent as compared with 32 percent) (Sabbadini,
1999).

Couples consisting of never-married partners are 30 percent of all
unmarried cohabitation couples. In 39 percent, at least one of the
partners has a previous marriage experience and 32 percent are couples where at least one of the two partners is a widow or widower.
Never-married women living with ever-married men are more common than never-married men cohabiting with ever-married women
(ISTAT, 1996a).

CONCLUDING COMMENTS

The Long-Lasting Family

The existence of full nest families (i.e., children still living at
home—70 percent of twenty-nine-year-old Italian men live with parents and there has been a 7 percent increase in thirty to thirty-four-
year-olds living at home; Italy by Numbers, 2001) at later stages of
the parents' lives shows that children are staying on at home longer,
even after they have reached the threshold of economic independence.
This shows that young people are strongly attached to their family of
origin. Children do stay with their parents and prefer to find their own
way in life within the context of the family, no longer viewed as authoritarian, rather than leaving the family nest in which they have grown
up. This lengthens the period of time in which a complex organization of family life is necessary and encourages fathers and, especially,
mothers to maintain their roles of service providers and caregivers
with a consequent rigidity of family gender roles with mothers considered to be the nurturers and fathers the economic providers.

Italy is still in the stage defined as "the golden age of marriage" (Van de Kaa, 1987). The analysis of available data shows that family forms that are alternatives to the married couple are in the minority. For Italians, there are apparently two main alternatives: living with parents in the original family or living with a spouse, and generally becoming parents. Alternative living arrangements are limited. The increasing instability of marriage has not yet produced substantial changes in Italian household structures. Household structures are more influenced by the changes in fertility and mortality as well as the shrinking of family and household to the nuclear family form. The diversification of family forms can be seen mainly in the final stages of life, when the death of a spouse leads to different choices and family behavior by survivors, especially for women. In general, the elderly are socially integrated. The elderly tend to live on their own, their children giving them help and care.

Family Changes As the Basis for the New Welfare

Today, the welfare state seems headed toward insuring rights and guarantees for individuals as members of a family, rather than to the family as an entity. In Italy, mothers, children, and to a lesser extent, fathers, are objects of political actions that protect and support them in various ways. It is more difficult to find actions directed toward the family even if particular types of family, considered at risk of living in poverty or in difficulty, are helped by the State. Some types of households do not have recognized rights: unmarried cohabitators are households which do not exist for Italian law and stepfamilies, and in general second marriages are penalized with respect to the time-honored married couple because the relationships between stepparents and stepchildren have no legal recognition. The principle of fairness, which exists on an individual level, seems not to apply to the family level. While individuals have equal rights before the State, not all families are protected in the same way. This inequality should be corrected before the law—any and all forms of family in which individuals choose to live freely must have the same rights guaranteed.

In addition, in these years of aggressive free market ideology, the need for economic efficiency has relegated all the social problems under a single "accounting item" with their evaluation in terms of economic costs. Therefore, the scientific debate on new contents and tools for the welfare state aims to bring family policies back into play, including them again in the context of factors like security, equality, and solidarity on which the Italian democracy is based. Social rights, the rights individuals are entitled to in a given society, should become an extension and a logical development of human rights, based on the vital principle of equality between individuals and families. Therefore it is important to define the new rules of eligibility, the services provided under these rights, and the way and amount of time that must elapse before needs turn into rights.

Invisible Changes

Continuity in Italian family forms does not mean that there is no change. This change must be analyzed without attempting to impose the same patterns of change occurring in other countries. The diversified forms of individual and family life in Italy are closely dependent on changes in the timing of vital demographic events, such as marriage and childbearing. They are also dependent on the diversification of family choices and strategies related to a single great event in life: getting married and having children. Owing to this, family changes are not so evident from the statistical point of view, and research with new methods of scientific observation is required. Changes in the collective Italian mentality and values held concerning childbearing and marriage have led to a fall in vital demographic events such as birthrates, rather than to the multiplication of nontraditional events (such as births outside of marriage) and alternative family models.

Italian households will become smaller, and therefore the informal solidarity networks will shrink in the future. However, together with an increasingly smaller traditional family, new forms of family life might also develop. In these new forms the bonds of coresidence (still used, however, in many definitions of households by censuses) will lose importance, while the way in which the various groups of relatives, parents, and children "create and pursue common strategies for increasing or preserving economic, power or prestige resources" will be increasingly relevant in defining family boundaries (Sabbadini, 1995, p. 4). There will be more families which depend on the income of other families (children depending on parents, parents living on the income of their children, siblings who provide each other with economic help, etc.) because of unemployment, and this trend will probably continue in the short-term. More elderly people will live alone. At the same time, the family, despite the physical distance, will support the elderly providing help in case of need, thus acting as a social buffer. In other words, a new type of family could develop in Italy, no longer existing as the center for affection, emotional support, and social relationships. Rather, above all, this type could exist for economic and income support, and as a source of assistance and solidarity.

The traditional approach to intergenerational solidarity that considers the family as a group of individuals who behave as one social actor with a common lifestyle (all having the same interests and levels of consumption) should be reconsidered. All family members—men and women; adults, both the young and the elderly; parents and children—will be increasingly visible in the family scenario as holders of specific needs and different personal demands, which might compete or conflict with each other. It is easy to foresee that neither gender nor cohort differences can be ignored in the future, at both the scientific and political levels. The family will appear in all its complexity as the place of caregiving and care receiving, of solidarity and individualism continuously created and renewed (Palomba & Moors, 1998).

This implies a peculiar status for Italy in the demographic and sociological fields not only in terms of the negative record (such as the fall in the birthrate or the population aging), but also in the capacity to adapt to new social requirements while avoiding a radical break with the past. The tasks of social researchers are therefore more difficult, but also more stimulating.

NOTES

1. Italy has a population of fifty-eight million living in a country slightly larger than the U.S. state of Arizona. There are small clusters of Greek-Italians and Albanian-Italians living in the southern part of the country. In the north, there are German-Italians, French-Italians, and Slovene-Italians. In some small areas French and German are spoken. The economy is diversified industrial with about the same total and per capita output as the United Kingdom and France. The north of Italy has more industrial development and the south is less developed and has more agriculture. There is about 20 percent unemployment in southern Italy. Overall, the 2005 estimated unemployment rate was 7.9 percent. Close to 13 percent of the population

lives below the poverty line, defined as 50 percent of median income. The labor force by occupation is divided as follows: services, 63 percent; industry, 32 percent; and agriculture, 5 percent (United Nations Development Programme, 2005; World Factbook, 2004). In terms of relative development, Italy ranks eighteenth (2003) on the UN Human Development Index. Italy is a member of the European Union and the Euro (monetary) zone.

2. In 1975 the new Family Bill established that spouses have the same rights and duties and they decide together the organization of family life.

AFRICA:
FAMILY LIFE
IN SIERRA LEONE,
SOUTH AFRICA, AND KENYA

Chapter 7

Family Patterns in Sierra Leone

Tom Spencer-Walters

INTRODUCTION

The family in Sierra Leone is pluralistic, a reflection of the varied influences upon its evolution and development. The recorded and oral history of Sierra Leone indicates that family laws, structure, function, size, marital relationships, inheritance, and kinship are influenced by traditional, religious, historical, and socioeconomic considerations. To understand Sierra Leone families, it is important to introduce aspects of the country's history and geography. Sierra Leone occupies nearly 28,000 square miles (slightly smaller than the U.S. state of South Carolina) of coastal areas and mountainous ridges of west Africa. It is bordered by Guinea to the west and north, Liberia to the east and southeast, and the Atlantic Ocean in the south. The population has grown from just over 2 million in 1961 (at independence from Britain), to around 3 million in 1974, to about 4.5 million in the mid-1990s, to 6 million today (World Factbook, 1996, 2006).

It is estimated that before the rebel insurgency that started in the early 1990s and culminated with the military overthrow of the demo- cratically elected government in 1997, about two-thirds of the popula- tion lived in the rural areas. Of those, the largest group was the Mende who live in the south and parts of the east. The second largest ethnic group, the Temne, live in the north and in and around the urban areas of the west. Today, each group represents about 30 percent of the popu- lation (World Factbook, 2006). The other 30-35 percent of the popu- lation lives in the Western Area. This includes communities in and around the capital city, Freetown, founded by British philanthropists in 1787 for the repatriation of formerly enslaved Africans who were languishing in the streets of England, Jamaica, and Nova Scotia (Wyse, 1989). The freed slaves, together with the "Liberated Africans" (who were liberated from slave ships on their way to American and Caribbean plantations), form the nucleus of what today is known as the Krios who contribute to the pluralistic nature of Sierra Leone families. This group embraced Christianity and Western education and served as pioneers for the expansion of Western values into areas of west Africa (Frederiks, 2002).

While the previously mentioned three groups are the focus of this chapter, scattered around the country are other linguistic and social groups whose family forms and functioning are similar to, if not identical with, the families of one or more of the three groups. There are also refugees from Liberia's civil war, and small numbers of Europeans, Lebanese, Pakistanis, and Indians. In terms of religions, there are Muslims (60 percent), those following indigenous beliefs (30 percent), and Christians (10 percent) (World Factbook, 2006; some sources suggest that 60 percent follow indigenous beliefs and 30 percent are Muslim). There are several languages: English (official, with regular use limited to literate minority), Mende (the principal vernacular in the south), Temne (vernacular in the north), and Krio (an English-based Creole spoken by the descendants of freed slaves, a first language for 10 percent of the population understood by 95 percent) (World Factbook, 2006). There are many refugees in surrounding countries.

While economic and social infrastructures are not well developed, Sierra Leone has ample agricultural, fishery, and mineral resources. Social disorders (e.g., eleven-year civil war) have held back economic development. About two-thirds of the working-age population is in subsistence or business agriculture and about half of GDP comes from agriculture. Manufacturing is mainly the processing of raw materials and of some goods for the domestic market (about 30 percent of GDP). Mines had been shut down by civil strife but have been reopening. The mining of diamonds is the major source of hard currency; many have been smuggled out of the country (Dorward, 2001). Developing the economy depends on the peace accord holding and international aid (Hirsch, 2001; World Factbook, 2006).

Ethnic pluralism created certain challenges. However, the greater threats appear in the uneasy truce (among rebel groups, warlords, and youth gangs, both in Sierra Leone and surrounding countries, that have maintained ethnic conflicts, insurgencies, street violence, looting, and refugees in border areas) and various health issues including the rise of AIDS (World Factbook, 2006). In a 1995 survey, an estimated 27 percent of people in a high-risk category in Freetown were HIV-1 positive. Other estimates for 2001 are 16,000 children and around 7 percent of those aged fifteen to forty-nine living with AIDS/HIV. The taking of sex slaves, use of sex as a weapon of war, and the lack of health facilities, products, or education, combined with the HIV/AIDS threat in the west Africa region, give rise to concern about the increasing prevalence of the disease in Sierra Leone (International Planned Parenthood [International], 2002; United Nations Development Programme [UNDP], 2003).

Life expectancy is an indicator of health. At between thirty-four and thirty-eight years (depending on estimate used, with thirty-three for men and thirty-six for women), life expectancy in Sierra Leone is among the lowest in the world (for sub-Saharan Africa, the average is 48.8 years). Such concerns are reflected in the UN Human Development Index rank of 176 out of 177. Until recently, Sierra Leone was ranked lowest (UNDP, 2006; International, 2002).

Families in Sierra Leonean Context

Two types of family patterns predominate. The first, extended family, includes husband, wives, children, grandparents, uncles, aunts, cousins, and other blood relatives. All accept each other as members of one closely knit family. This type is preeminent in the rural areas where it has been practiced for generations (Harrell-Bond, 1975, 1977). The fortunes of the head of household, and consequently the number of wives, determine the size of an extended family. Polygyny is frequently practiced in the rural areas. This marital system is especially popular among the Mende and the Temne (Kamara, 1983; McCulloch, 1964). Such households tend to be larger because of the multiple family units within the extended family structure. The evolution of the polygamous family in Sierra Leone is linked not only to a desire for the preservation of kinship ties, but also to the demands of subsistence farming which depends on the collective efforts of the extended families. The polygamous family, with its elaborate division of labor, has proven to be well suited to the conditions of farming communities (Little, 1967).

The second, the nuclear family, is common among the Krios of the Western Area (Adeokun, 1987). This is because of the Krios' early and sustained contacts with Christianity through missionary and philanthropic activities that date to the late 1700s. Upon their repatriation to Freetown, many, including the Black Poor from England and the Maroons from Jamaica and Nova Scotia, had already been acculturated into the Western monogamous marriage system (Frederiks, 2002). Decades later, the teachings of the church and the spread of formal education reinforced this system. Marriages among the Christian Krios are legitimized only through church and civil weddings; the minister and the judge respectively ensuring that this marital bond precludes the couples from simultaneously contracting any other marriages. For the Christian Krios, there was little resistance to the monogamous system because in their view it conferred prestige and distinction (Adeokun, 1987; Wyse, 1989).

A small group of Krios, the Oku (descendants of Liberated Africans), "determinedly refused to abandon the Islamic faith to which they had been converted during the Fulani jihad of 1804 onwards" (Wyse, 1989, p. 9). They are allowed to practice Muslim-style polygyny making it legitimate for a man to wed up to four wives if he has the resources to treat them all equally and fairly. While the Oku held tightly to their Islamic faith in the face of British resistance to the spread of Islam in west Africa, they share many values with the Christian Krio— the language and ancestral rituals (e.g., Sillah, 1994; Spencer-Walters, 2006). Like their Christian counterparts, the Oku Krios share a zest for formal education "even to the extent of nominally assuming Western names when seeking admission to the missionary schools" (Wyse, 1989, p. 9).

COUPLE FORMATION AND MARITAL DYNAMICS

Aspects of mate selection for each of the three largest ethnic groups are reviewed in the following text, including training for marriage within secret societies and the conditions surrounding female and male circumcision, and aspects of the ceremonies involved. Also reviewed are the types of marriages as well as dissolution of marriage. Marriage is universal and early, with an estimated 90 percent of women aged eighteen years and over having been married (International, 2002). Due to similarities between the Mende and Temne, the review is integrative with differences noted.

Mate Selection

Mate selection patterns in Sierra Leone are part of family life and in some of the rural areas, part of community life. Parents or elders usually allow courtship when the ultimate goal is marriage (Little, 1967). Casual dating until recently was prohibited by the dictates of culture.

Among the Mende and Temne young men and women had to go through a period of rigorous training in "secret societies" before courtship and/or marriage. For the Menda, women cannot enter into any contractual marriage until they have gone through a period of initiation into womanhood conducted by the *Sande* secret society. The *Sande,* popularly known as the *Bondo* or *Bundo,* is an organization run by women who have been through the initiation and are committed to maintaining the strict secrecy of this society (Haviland, 1996; MacCormack, 1975; McCulloch, 1964; Samb, 1986; Sierra Leone Research, nd). Some girls as young as nine or ten participate in this ritual. Done in seclusion in social centers built in the bush (training used to last six months, but presently is often seven or ten days and held four or five times per year) and intended to prepare girls for marriage, it is important that they enter the initiation before puberty.

Within the Mende tradition, an uninitiated girl (*gboa;* meaning small) cannot engage in sexual relations or marry an initiated man. The initiation activities include teaching how to cook, care for a family, acquire social etiquette, understand traditional values, and perform traditional songs and dances. Temne women also go through the *Bondo* secret society (Kamara, 1983). For both the Mende and Temne, female circumcision is central to initiation activities (Haviland, 1996; McCulloch, 1964; "Men's Traditional Culture," 1996; Samb, 1986). As marriage is a transaction between families, the perceived benefits of female circumcision must be made manifest to the male suitor. The suitor sees his marriage fees, as, among other things, an investment in the continuation of bloodline through the impending union.

Perhaps 90 percent of Sierra Leonean women are circumcised (Birth Matters, 2001). Many people believe that circumcision surgically preserves a girl's virginity, increases sexual antipathy, and consequently idealizes her marriage chances (Harrell-Bond, 1977). However, the contentiousness of the issue (often referred to as female genital mutilation [FGM]) is driving a wedge between those seeking to end it and those wanting to preserve it. In Sierra Leone, it is pitting noninitiated women, primarily Krios, against women who have gone through the rites. Some people see FGM as an unwarranted and health-threatening procedure that does more to enrich the coffers of the Paramount Chiefs, who must approve of all circumcision rites in their chiefdoms, than it does to preserve traditional beliefs and practices (Samb, 1986). Carol Bellamy, Director of United Nations Children's Fund (UNICEF), rejects the argument that FGM is closely tied with religion or belief systems. She asserted that, "Mutilation . . . is a tradition designed to preserve virginity, ensure marriageability and control sexuality" and one that only serves to keep "women in their place." (Gberrie, 1997, p. 1). There is resistance to this view. A truculent editorial of the *New Citizen* (a Sierra Leone newspaper) reads (Gberrie, 1997, p. 2): "The Bondo bush is a venue where young girls are taught the social mores related to the society in which they will grow up. . . . The attempt to use external and un-African arguments to destroy a whole culture and beliefs will be firmly resisted." Owing to the international prominence given this issue, it is unlikely to go away any time soon.

The equivalent society for Mende and Temne boys is the *Poro* (or *Poi,* meaning "no end, far behind," that is, the laws of the ancestors) (McCulloch, 1964). Whereas the influence of the Mende *Poro* transcends its ritual and socializing functions to include sworn secrecy and claims of mythical and mystical prowess, the Temne *Poro* focuses on initiation rites as well as nominal political functions. Once the young men are circumcised and trained in folk traditions, dancing, singing, and weaving, they are ready to pick or accept a mate who has been chosen for them by the senior male members of their extended families. Mende boys are expected to glean knowledge that includes respect for age, a deep and uncompromising loyalty to their community, self-discipline, and a collective work ethic. Membership in the *Poro* society takes on great significance. A man's worth is judged by his "badge of honor"; that is, successful completion of *Poro* initiation

(McCulloch, 1964). In matters of courtship, a suitor who has gone through the ritual of initiation, including circumcision, is a more acceptable candidate than one who has not. However, given that most of the published information on the various secret societies is dated and given the changes to the society, it is uncertain how these groups function today (for more information see Ferme, 2001; McCulloch, 1964; Sierra Leone Research, nd).

Mate selection is similar among most ethnic groups. All betrothals involve some material transaction. In some cases among the Mende, this might involve girls as young as five being betrothed to men forty years of age or older. The man must accept the financial responsibilities for the girl's upbringing. She will stay with her paternal family until ready for *Sande* training. The man to whom the girl is betrothed is responsible for the expenses incurred during training. After the training, the family of the man will approach the family of the young woman to seal the union. She can change her mind if she does not like the man, in which case her family would repay the expenses incurred while nurturing the relationship. However, her parents would try to discourage this as it could be costly for them and would shame the family (Kamara, 1983).

If the suitor asks for the hand of the woman after *Sande,* he is still required to pay for her training in addition to the *mboya* (marriage payment). These transactions are contractually binding under customary law (Harrell-Bond, 1975). Over the years, modified patterns of this process have been practiced. Many suitors seek alternatives, as they are unable to meet the financial demands of the training and the *mboya*. An example would be when a man and a woman are allowed to cohabit provided he is willing to assist the woman's parents with their agricultural chores for as long as it takes to make up for the lack of *mboya* (McCulloch, 1964).

Like the Mende, if the Temne mate has been identified at an early age, the young man is required to reimburse her family for the costs incurred during initiation in addition to the contractual cost of marriage. A man's right to his children can be transferred to the woman's father if such contractual costs are not paid. Methods of payment have varied from heads of cattle, to poultry, farm products, crafts, and more recently, hard currency (Kamara, 1983; McCulloch, 1964). The financial obligations of the suitor are strictly enforced regardless of how many wives he might have acquired prior to the current marriage negotiation (Little, 1967).

The overarching drive behind marriages in Africa, including Sierra Leone, is procreation. "The ultimate value is not in self-fulfillment in the act of loving; it is rather the ability to create life through the act of loving" (Dorsey, 1982, p. 84). Sons are primarily the purveyors of patrilineal heritage and are therefore more valued than are girls. When a male suitor pays bride price, he is doing so with the expectation that the new wife will give him not only children, but healthy sons to ensure that the family name is permanently etched in the history of his society. Failure to produce sons can be grounds for securing a new wife, marginalization of the wife in question, and in some cases annulment through customary law (Dorsey, 1982).

Krio couple formation is based on a combination of Western values and African influences (Wyse, 1989). Traditionally, casual dating is discouraged because it goes against Krio Christian beliefs. Based upon the author's personal observations growing up in Krio culture, a girl is not allowed to date until she reaches marriageable age, which in many cases is between nineteen and twenty-one years of age. However, this is relaxed if the families mutually agree that marriage is imminent for the couple. Agreement, a vital element of success for any Krio couple formation, usually comes after lengthy background checks by venerated members from both sides (essentially family historians who can articulate family genealogies, sometimes going back a century). These are checks for any family physiological abnormalities or of blood ties, the presence of which would immediately nullify the relationship. Once their checking is finished, these family representatives consult with other knowledgeable seniors in their community before deciding whether the suitor's family is acceptable. The Krio forbid first or second cousins to marry for cultural and biological reasons (Lisk & Williams, 1995). The same holds for the Temne and the Mende, who believe that if first cousins marry, their offspring will die (Migeod, 1970).

The Krio, in spite of Christianity and Western marital dynamics, have not abandoned African traditions (Wyse, 1989). The collective efforts of the family, even the community, supersede the individual interests of the couple. The family is intricately involved in the selection of a mate, the complex negotiation, the planning of the wedding, and the raising of the children and grandchildren. For example, an elaborate engagement ceremony known in the Krio language as *put stop,* a derivative of the Yoruba (Nigeria) marital tradition, immediately follows the conclusion of courtship. This ceremony, combining aspects of Western influence to what is essentially African festivity, symbolically dramatizes the culmination of the family negotiations for the hand of the *yawo* (bride-to-be) (Spitzer, 1974).

Marriage Types

There are several types of marriages in Sierra Leone (Lisk & Williams, 1995). The Civil Marriage Act of 1910 regularized civil marriage, providing for the legalization of monogamous marriages through registries established in the country. Civil marriages are open to all regardless of religious or cultural orientation. Christian marriage was formalized with the Christian Marriage Act of 1907, legalizing monogamous marriages in the church. The validity of both types of marriages "involve substantive requirements of capacity and consent" (Lisk & Williams, 1995, p. 657). Legal ambiguities surrounding "consent" means adolescents can enter into marriage contracts "so long as the requisite consents are obtained" (p. 657). Requisite consent is the prerogative of the parents if the ones to be married are under the age of twenty-one. Another important proviso of these Acts is that before a civil or church marriage can be validated, all other marriages, including any contracted through customary law, must be rendered null and void. The insistence of the Christian Marriage Act that impending marriages be fully publicized three Sundays before the marriage in the church (or churches) where the couple worships, is indicative of a desire to ensure honesty and expose fraud (Lisk & Williams, 1995).

Customary law permits polygamy. Men can marry as many wives as they can support and are in essence taking over the responsibilities that were once those of the woman's extended family. Her existence is always tied to some male figure(s). In the case of the Temne, marriage payment is made to the woman's father. Marriage in Temne traditional culture is a transaction allowing the woman's father to transfer responsibilities for, and control over, to the husband.

The Mohammedan Marriage Act was passed to formalize Muslim marriages ("Mohammedan Marriage Act," 1988; Tully, 1994). The Act guaranteed polygyny among Muslims, limited to four wives.

Where the Islamic faith is practiced, registrars are appointed and given power to issue Muslim marriage licenses. Muslim Krios are less likely to practice polygyny.

Dissolution of Marriage

Marriage is prized in Sierra Leone and dissolution is frowned upon, if not actively discouraged. Among the Mende, the Temne, and similar ethnic groups, if the wife leaves her husband, her father's family can be liable to return the marriage fees as well as gifts her husband has given the family (Migeod, 1970). The children will remain with their father but can visit their mother. Among the Temne traditional marriages, divorce can be initiated by the husband on grounds of witchcraft, idleness, theft, or slandering the husband. In such cases, the marriage payment is not returned. A wife can also be divorced due to desertion or continued adultery and the marriage payment is returned; if she is with a lover, he is expected to either help with the cost or pay it himself. Impotence or continued infidelities by the husband are reasons for the wife or her family to initiate divorce. Marriage fees repayment depends on the circumstances. Divorce is settled by mutual agreement before the town-chief (McCulloch, 1964).

Spousal death might signal the end of a marriage, although the marriage does not end until after the spiritual cleansing of the widow. Three days after the death of the husband, the ceremony is performed to bring closure to the marital relationship and free the grieving wife for remarriage. A widower goes through a similar ceremony.

For the Krio, dissolution of marriage is mainly through divorce proceedings in a court of law. Grounds include adultery, persistent physical abuse, and rape. An individual whose spouse walks out on the marriage and disappears for seven years can have his or her marriage annulled by the courts. The Krios, especially the women, are reluctant to use these options because of the stigma of divorce (Lisk & Williams, 1995). Divorce is emblematic of failure, a legacy of the British Victorian era when divorce was closely associated with immorality (Wyse, 1989). Divorced women are usually shunned and cannot wear the traditional white wedding gowns in subsequent marriages. However, one positive element in problem marriages in Sierra Leone is that a heavy premium is put on reconciliation, specifically because a failed marriage reflects negatively not only on the couple but the families, and even the community.

FAMILIES AND CHILDREN

In spite of many changes in Sierra Leone, tradition and history influence family size as much as socioeconomic conditions. The estimated birthrate is 45.8 per 1,000 population, and the annual growth rate of the country is 2.3 with the total population expected to grow to 6.9 million by 2015. The estimated total fertility rate is 6.5, about the same today as in the 1970s (UNDP, 2006). Other sources suggest a moderate decline in fertility similar to the pattern found in several other African nations (e.g., Burkina Faso, Gambia, and Senegal). In only a very small number of African countries have the fertility rates fallen to below five or six children per woman. The reason for the decline in fertility is attributed to later age at marriage, education attainment of women, urban residence, and more extensive use of modern contraceptives (Cohen, 1998; International, 2002). Conversely, it is also reported that many men, especially Muslims, hold negative attitudes about family planning. In some regions of the world, fertility rates have increased or stalled after falling as there was a resurgence in Islamic values, increased son preference, and shifts in government policies (Cohen, 1998). The Rebel activities, inadequate materials and infrastructure, and lack of financial resources have affected the implementation of family planning programs (International, 2002).

While good data are not currently available for Sierra Leone (due to the war and economy), information is available for other sub-Saharan nations including many in west Africa. West African cultures and societies share features (Oppong, 1987). Without suggesting that these nations are in all ways similar to Sierra Leone, using this information can help contextualize what information is available for Sierra Leone. In the following sections west African data are used to describe the Sierra Leone context.

Contraceptive Prevalence

Contraceptive prevalence is an important proximate determinant of fertility. The fertility transitions seen in developing countries over the past forty to fifty years have been achieved, largely, by increased use of contraception or abortion (and later age at marriage) (Cohen, 1998; Ross & Frankenberg, 1993). In west Africa, contraceptive prevalence rates (CPRs) are associated with moderate to large declines in fertility. Even in countries with no sign of substantial fertility declines, CPRs in urban areas have increased (Cohen, 1998). CPRs are lowest in Africa where, on average, one in five couples currently uses contraceptives. In west Africa, the rate among married women is 8 percent (Levels and Trends, 1998). Contraceptive prevalence in sub-Saharan Africa is 25 percent or more (in more developed areas of the world, the rate is 30 to 40 percent) (Levels and Trends, 1998). Use of contraceptives for spacing of children, rather than for shaping total family size, is found more so in Africa than elsewhere. Contraceptives are replacing traditional spacing practices such as breastfeeding and postpartum abstinence. Other reasons for wanting better control of spacing are protection of the health of children and preserving the future reproductive capacity of mothers (Cohen, 1998). With less sexual controls and increases in the age at marriage, there is more demand for contraceptive use among younger cohorts (Caldwell, Orubuloye, & Caldwell, 1992; Cohen, 1998).

Available evidence shows a strong, continuing, and expanding need for family planning services. The population of sub-Saharan Africa is expected to double within the next twenty-five years. Even as fertility falls, there are a large number of people entering their childbearing years. If it is true that family planning is a means to the end of protecting and maintaining the capacity to continue childbearing (rather than to limit family size), there is little reason to believe that fertility will fall much below four or five births per woman (Bledsoe, Banja, & Hill, 1998).

Premarital Births

In most societies, sexual intercourse and births are normatively confined to legal marriages. It is within such recognized unions that most births take place. However, in sub-Saharan Africa, knowledge of marriage patterns can be complicated. Numerous forms of union exist and entry into marriage can be a long and ambiguous process. Conjugal relationships also appear to be becoming more fluid (Bledsoe, 1990). Among many cultures in Sierra Leone as elsewhere in Africa, a ceremony and the transfer of bridewealth typically delineate marriage. This bridewealth can be symbolic or of substantial value and span several years. The payment, ceremony, cohabitation of spouses, and consummation of the marriage can occur over several months (and not always in the same order). This ambiguity makes it somewhat difficult to determine what a premarital or marital birth is. However, it is estimated that in Sierra Leone a greater proportion of men and women are becoming sexually active in their mid-teens (International, 2002).

Teenaged Mothers

In some areas of west Africa, the proportion of births to teenaged mothers has fallen. Teen mothers face greater risks of pregnancy-related morbidity and mortality, as well as having premature and low birth weight babies. Lost educational opportunities are also problematic. The mother's age at first birth is a particularly important determinant of completed family size when contraceptive use is infrequent. In general, sub-Saharan African countries have high rates of adolescent fertility; the median age of women at first birth being approximately two years younger than in Asia, Latin America, or North Africa (Cohen, 1998). In Sierra Leone, about 21 percent of fifteen to nineteen-year-old females give birth each year (International, 2002).

While marriage trends in some areas of Africa show a substantial shift toward later age at marriage (with a still relatively young age at marriage), in west Africa no such general trend is apparent (the exceptions being Senegal and Guinea) (Cohen, 1998). The proportion of women marrying before the age of twenty is declining rapidly in many nations, but it is not clear if this is so in Sierra Leone. Currently, it appears that only about 6 percent of women and men marry before the age of twenty. In 1992, the average age at first marriage was 27.6 and 24.3 for men and women, respectively. The average age difference between men and women (3.3 years) is smaller in Sierra Leone than found in many west African nations. Cape Verde is the only west African country with a smaller (2.2) difference in the age at marriage, while Gambia (9.2), Burkina Faso (8.6), and Senegal (8.1) have the highest age differences in the region. The percentage of men ever married in Sierra Leone between the ages of fifteen and nineteen is 6, between twenty and twenty-four is 20, and between the ages of forty-five and forty-nine is 97 percent. For women between the ages of fifteen and nineteen, the percentage ever married is 6, between the ages of twenty and twenty-four is 47, and it is 97 percent for women between the ages of forty-five and forty-nine (United Nations, 2000).

Abortion

Abortion is virtually unknown as a method for lowering fertility rates in traditional communities in Sierra Leone. Procreation is seen as a cultural and civic obligation for families; it preserves and nourishes the community (Dorsey, 1982). However, while abortion is illegal, it is a reality among older schoolgirls and educated women in the urban areas. Procedures range from induced miscarriages, such as by taking concoctions of herbs and roots from herbalists, to surgical removal of a fetus by a licensed doctor (Harrell-Bond, 1975; Unsafe Abortion, 2001). About 25 percent of all abortions are among fifteen to nineteen-year-olds (International, 2002). Part of the rationale for abortion is fear of ostracism within their families and communities, not being able to acquire husbands because of the existence of a child by another man, and the public evidence of having engaged in premarital sex. While women who undergo abortion are regarded as promiscuous, with increased levels of education, this association is waning.

Agrarian Communities

In agrarian communities with patrilineal kin groups, families are large for several reasons. First, family size confers status on the male head of household; having more wives and children denote prosperity in the family and insurance for old age. Second, land given to families by the chief is commensurate with family size; the larger the family the larger the plot (Little, 1967). Third, the physical demands of subsistence farming require larger families. More wives and children mean more farmhands that can translate into economic success. Men prepare the land for the planting of major crops, like rice. Wives and children cultivate vegetable gardens, notably corn, peppers, yams, and cassava under the guidance of the senior wife. However, the husband has full control over the yields from the wives' gardens. Finally, the high incidence of infant mortality in Sierra Leone, especially in the provincial areas, has spurred families to have more children with the hope that more will survive (Campbell, 1994). The introduction of publicly administrated social security systems and the commercialization of agriculture could be having an influence on family forms and dynamics (Schafer, 1997).

The maternal mortality rate in 2000 was 2,000 per 100,000 live births. The infant mortality rate in Sierra Leone is alarmingly high (165 deaths to every 1,000 live births), one of the highest rates in the world, if not the highest (UNDP, 2006). However, some progress is being made, as the rate was 182 in 2001. The under-five mortality rate was 316 per 1,000 live births in 2001 and 283 in 2004, the highest in the world (UNDP, 2003, 2006). There are several reasons for Sierra Leone's very poor showing in the area of infant mortality (Aguayo, Scott, & Ross, 2003). These include diseases (e.g., yellow fever), poverty, nutritional deficiencies, overcrowding in cities, poor health facilities, and endemic childhood diseases. Malnutrition rates are among the highest in the world (50 percent of the population is undernourished and 27 percent of children under age five are underweight; UNDP, 2006) and 46 percent of child mortality is attributable to malnutrition. Without sustained policy and action, malnutrition will likely cause an estimated 74,000 child deaths over five years, 252,000 children could be born with varying degrees of mental retardation, and the monetary value of agricultural productivity will be severely reduced (Aguayo et al., 2003).

Krios and the Professional Class

The desired family size is smaller among the Krios, about four children, which is close to the expected completed family size (Campbell, 1994). A specific reason for this lower desired family size is the nature of their monogamous marriage structure that discourages high fertility rates. For example, the postpartum period for a wife is about two years. The postpartum period is also important to the polygamous husband, but he has the advantage of other wives. The Krios' levels of education and literacy also correlate to small family households. Krios believe the Western pattern of family life is superior to the traditional polygamous system (Harrell-Bond, 1975). Since the 1840s, the Krios dedicated their efforts to acquiring formal education and literacy, partially because they believe a successful man is an educated one. This commitment to education was spuriously fortuitous for the Krios because it coincided with British colonial expansion into west Africa in the early 1800s. The Krios were perfect recruits for the British in their desire to spread formal education, Christianity, and their ancillaries including low fertility rates, monogamous marriages, and modern sector employment among all Sierra Leoneans. The Krio see large families as a hindrance to the prestige acquired with education. Their domination of the professional class is a direct result of their education and literacy rates (Adeokun, 1987). Overall, the literacy rate (those aged fifteen and over who can read and write English, Mende, Temne, or Arabic) was estimated as 35 percent, and for youth, 48 percent in 2004. The rate is higher for men (47 percent) than it is for women (24 percent) (World Factbook, 2006).

Professionals in Sierra Leone are centered in Western Area urban centers including Freetown. Those with postsecondary education migrate in search of white-collar jobs. The fertility rate for provincials drops as they move from rural to urban areas.

Involvement with extended family does not cease with membership in the professional class. Tradition obligates professionals from rural areas to take impoverished members of their extended families into their urban households. Sometimes, young children live in the successful member's home so they can receive formal education. Extramarital affairs of husbands confound the picture further. Many professional husbands maintain several extramarital affairs with women who bear children for them. The children are illegitimate by English law, but for the men, they are an extension of their family. The men assume responsibility for these children (e.g., school fees, clothes, or paying rent). These children will carry their names.

FAMILIES AND GENDER

The majority of ethnic groups in Sierra Leone are patriarchal and the dominance of males in every sector of the society is often taken for granted (Dorsey, 1982). It is through organizations like the *Poro* and the *Sande* societies that children are socialized to understand their roles and functions. They are discouraged from dating until around twenty years of age. When permitted to date before age twenty, they must be chaperoned by an older brother or another responsible male member of the family. Krio girls have the same formal education opportunities as boys. However, they are encouraged to train for such professions as nursing, dressmaking, and elementary and secondary school teaching. Krio parents see these professions as appropriately "feminine." Conversely, boys are expected to study medicine, law, engineering, architecture, and politics. Like the Mende, Temne, and Loko, the Krio socialize their boys to be the heads of their families. Parents' reason for boys majoring in the more "demanding" disciplines is that it prepares them for well-paying jobs that they will need to successfully support a family. This attitude is changing as women assert their rights to make their own disciplinary choices.

Employment

As education becomes more accessible to women, more of them are entering the labor force. Nevertheless, male-dominated attitudes have contributed to a gender-based stratified employment in Sierra Leone. Women are disadvantaged because the skills training received are primarily for low-paying jobs (Lisk & Stevens, 1987). The government, as well as foreign donors, put more money into the more prestigious and male-oriented professions like medicine, engineering, and law. The rationale is that these disciplines are crucial to economic and political independence and thus it is important to prepare the citizenry (men) for the impending changes. Men overwhelmingly dominate management positions that often provide opportunities to make decisions that perpetuate female subordination in modern sector employment.

About 55 percent of women are economically active (UNDP, 2006). For more than three decades, advocates have been agitating for significant shifts in government funding to help (through adult education and scholarships provided by certain organizations and businesses) provide improved access for women to disciplines traditionally set aside for men. Some progress is seen in this regard. For example, wider access to higher education has given women a new voice in the populace, which in turn has maximized their political significance (Hoffer, 1972; UNDP, 2001) (e.g., women hold about 15 percent of seats in Parliament; UNDP, 2006). Women became cabinet ministers, mayors, medical doctors, and high court judges long before the women's movement became an important voice in Africa (Wyse, 1989). There is a long tradition of Mende and Sherbro women's participation in local and regional politics (Hoffer, 1972). Although these communities are essentially patriarchal, women regularly headed several chiefdoms (Lisk & Stevens, 1987; MacCormack, 1975). Madam Ella Koblo Gulama, a chief in the Moyamba District of Sierra Leone in the 1960s and 1970s, is an example. Her influence was so strong that she was swept into national political prominence. Nevertheless, the changes have been slow in coming because traditional perceptions of women in Sierra Leone die hard.

Women's participation has been vibrant in the informal sector of the employment market (Lisk & Stevens, 1987; Oppong, 1987). Women from extended family households and poorly educated women might eke out a living by hawking cooked food, cigarettes, candy, and fruits to businesses and offices in urban areas. Although self-employed, the returns from these entrepreneurial activities are minimal compared to the benefits of jobs held by professional men and women (Amarteifio & Davies, 1995). Furthermore, when the government has intervened in the informal sector, it has provided assistance mainly to activities dominated by men, such as metal work, tailoring, repairing services, and woodwork. Such assistance has not been extended to women petty traders, restaurateurs, or food sellers, for example (Lisk & Stevens, 1987). Nonetheless, the services these women petty traders provide are invaluable, mainly because of the affordability of their products in a country whose economy is so volatile.

The picture is somewhat different in the rural areas. Roles are rigidly prescriptive because of the culture and the agrarian nature of the economy. Women's participation in the labor force is central and crucial to the survival of the extended family (Ferme, 2001; Kamara, 1983; Momsen, 2001). Before the rebel war, many women became successful as vegetable farmers, becoming relatively wealthy, with resulting changes in gender and power roles not accepted by many younger men (Momsen, 2001). In the coastal area, women exclusively process and sell fish. (Men do the fishing; in some cultures it is considered bad luck for women to go deep-sea fishing.) In addition, rural women engage in selling and trading foodstuffs such as vegetables, dried fish, and fruits as well as traditional fabrics and crafts. The money earned supplements, perhaps supersedes, the husband's farming income (Lisk & Stevens, 1987; Momsen, 2001).

The recent war destroyed much of the country's infrastructure and the majority of the population makes a living informally. Women have particularly suffered. Many, having lost their husbands and/or fathers to the fighting, are supporting families. Loans by the Association for Rural Development (ARD) are helping women get into businesses. Getting credit is difficult, especially for women. ARD has been distributing group loans and providing business training to over 1,300 people, of which 80 percent are women ("Women are back in business," 2003).

Household Roles

These income-producing tasks do not exonerate the woman from her domestic obligations. A wife has to cook and take care of her husband's needs. Some rural wives have sisters and other relatives in the extended household who can start the cooking before they get home. Urban educated women are expected to perform the same roles, but because of their earning power, are able to employ maids and cooks. Sometimes husbands insist on only eating food cooked by their wives, in which case the wife has to adjust her schedule to meet this demand (Wyse, 1989).

Food holds an important place in family dynamics. A wife who is upset (e.g., over her husband's infidelity) might refuse to prepare meals. The husband's response is to take his case to his in-laws who then approach his family in search of a resolution. Here again, resolution is a family rather than an individual issue. On the other hand, it increases tension if the husband does not eat the food prepared by his wife. She might fear that he is eating food prepared by his "sweetheart" in an extramarital relationship, or eating at his parents' because he is upset with her. If the husband's behavior continues without family intervention, it can lead to ugly confrontations involving him, his wife, and the third party concerned (Harrell-Bond, 1975).

In rural areas, women do not have property rights. Some women are even denied inheritance of their husbands' property although they can inherit from their fathers' family. Even then, they must proceed through their brothers and uncles to secure inheritance (Lisk & Stevens, 1987). Women must request that their husbands write a will so that they have the legal right to property; if they do not, the property reverts to the husband's family on his death (United Nations Development Programme Sierra Leone [UNDPSL], nd).

Krio women can inherit property but preference is given to sons (especially firstborns). A reason for the preference is that husbands worry that if wives remarried, sons can lose the inheritance that would have gone to preserve and advance their lineage (Spitzer, 1974). Within traditional rural families, if a wife dies before the husband, her family receives only those items she brought to the household when she first married, no matter how much she has contributed to the marriage. Under customary law, all the children belong to the husband and his lineage.

FAMILIES AND STRESS

The recent radical changes that Sierra Leone families have experienced are attributable to a combination of factors. Some of these changes are so drastic that they are tearing families apart. With the possible exception of gender issues, the extended family system had functioned well within agrarian communities. It protected children, nurtured the ideal of family, settled disputes, promoted division of labor as an economic necessity, and kept the community stable and intact. However, with the penetration of the missionary, philanthropic, and entrepreneurial influences of the British during the eighteenth and nineteenth centuries, the economic base began to change. The British wanted raw materials to fuel the industrial revolution so they dictated agricultural commodity preferences. Palm oil, for instance, a staple in the diet of many Sierra Leoneans, was needed to run machines in Britain. The patrilocal structure was slowly being replaced or abandoned for the newly created urban centers of the British. Attitudes toward farming changed and educated youngsters sought white-collar jobs. More recently, the volatility of the political system and the rebel and civil wars have deleteriously affected the stability and structure of families.

Constant Negative Growth

Owing to the lingering political malaise, mismanagement of the economy, and international economic problems, the country's productivity decelerated to the point of constant negative growth. This resulted in the deep devaluation of the nation's currency. Modern sector employment stagnated as the price of basic commodities rose; inflation was around 30 percent in 1999, but only around 1 percent in 2002 (World Factbook, 2000, 2006). An outcome was the rapid deceleration of Sierra Leone to the lowest stratum of the Human Development Index (HDI). Zoeteman (2002), using five levels of sustainability, argued that Sierra Leone is the least sustainable nation in the world. Less than 60 percent of the population has access to safe water and less than 30 percent has adequate sanitation facilities. Less than 50 percent of the population has access to essential drugs and many children are not immunized against measles or tuberculosis. About 50 percent of the population is under nourished and around 30 percent of children are underweight and underheight for their age. The death rate is 20.3 per 1,000 population. Life expectancy at birth was 33.7 years in the mid-1990s and between thirty-four and forty-five years in 2000-2006 (male: 33.1-42.4 years and female: 35.6-48.2 years; sources give different ages). About 44 percent of the population is below the age of fifteen with 3 percent over age sixty-five. The median age of the population is 17.7 years (UNDP, 2005; World Factbook, 2000, 2006). The proportion of the people born between 2000 and 2005 expected to survive to the age of forty is around 50 percent. About 36 percent of females and 31 percent of males born in the 2000-2005 cohort have the probability of surviving to age sixty-five (UNDP, 2006).

Given the current state of affairs, families, particularly urban families whose members could have grown over the years with needy relatives from the rural areas, are finding it difficult to make ends meet. Many people are joining the informal employment sector, thereby raising the level of competitiveness among families engaging in the same trade. Crime has increased with unemployment, forcing families to use extreme measures to protect their lives and property (e.g., extra bars on windows, perimeter walls capped with sharp-edged glass, padlocked gates, and vicious dogs). Around 70 percent of the population lives below the official poverty line. Around 75 percent exist on the equivalent of less than US$2 per day (UNDP, 2006).

Agriculture was hit seriously in the earlier and more recent war. In the past, the British promoted a shift toward formal education; rural families spent their earnings educating their children or sent them to rich relatives in the Western Area. Over time, the agricultural work-force was decimated. Staple foods, such as rice once grown in abundance, now have to be imported. Land is becoming scarce and cash is co-opting all other forms of transaction. The nature of the extended family has changed. Kin groups have disintegrated and cultural cohesiveness has suffered as many people have moved away in search of innovative ways of survival. Women, who had traditionally carried the family through their food production and food sales efforts, have had to do more to keep their families intact (Lisk & Stevens, 1987). A residual benefit from this effort is that women have begun to realize their worth to their families and of their potentialities for at least limited self-actualization. In short, the distinctive and prescriptive roles for women in their families have become at best, ambiguous (Kamara, 1983).

Recently, rural families have been ripped apart by warfare. Beyond the great loss of life and bodily harm affecting large numbers of families, other problems emerged. Many families were displaced (often to refugee camps), children were forced or chose to join in combat, men left their families to fight or search for work in conflict free areas, girls and women were raped or taken into forced labor, and many women were left shouldering the burden of providing for their immediate and extended families. The gender ideology prescribes a disproportionate amount of reproductive and domestic labor to women. This labor was compounded by the destruction of traditional support systems and means of livelihood occurring in conflict zones. Lack of basic services, such as health care, added to the difficulties in caring for dependents (Amowitz et al., 2002; Conciliation Resources, nd; Faulkner, 2001; MacIntyre, Aning, & Addo, 2002).

War

Perhaps the most stressful and destructive element for families in recent times has been the rebel war that started around 1990 that pit the legitimately elected government against disgruntled military and paramilitary elements (Bah, 2000; Conciliation Resources, nd; Geoghegan, 2004; Hirsch, 2001). Villages were burned, their women raped and killed, and their young men conscripted to fight the rebels' battles. Some of these "men" were as young as twelve years old. Schools were disrupted because families were afraid of rebel insurgencies in their area. Agricultural activities came to a standstill as farms were burned and residents were afraid to resume their activities. Many families fled to other areas as well as to other nations; over one-half of the population was displaced. Officially over in 2002, the causes of the eleven-year conflict, according to the UN Development office in Sierra Leone (p. 1), "were rooted in a mix of bad governance, denial of fundamental human rights, economic mismanagement, and social exclusion" (cf. Davies, 2000). The chief sources of economic prosperity were ruthlessly disrupted. Consequently, for example, school enrollment dropped, the maternal mortality rates rose to the highest in the world, and immunization coverage declined by more than 40 percent (UNDPSL, nd).

Families became wholly dependent on government assistance or United Nations food programs. Whole villages and towns were forced into refugee centers. Others who could afford the journey traveled to Freetown to stay with relatives, who themselves were overwhelmed with their over stretched economic responsibilities. Those who could not find relatives and friends eventually ended up homeless in the streets of the capital or in refugee camps scattered throughout the urban area. The influx of people fleeing the rural areas burdened even further an already strained infrastructure in Freetown and the various refugee camps. Water shortage, diseases associated with overcrowding, and violent (including sexual) crimes started to emerge. There was no workable political base to deal with these compounding problems.

The future looked promising when a viable government came to power in 1996. Through United Nations efforts, many rural dwellers were returning home to rebuild farms and families, and the economy was showing signs of revival, when junior military officers overthrew the democratically elected government. These officers then invited the rebels to join them in Freetown, starting another deadly assault against families. Bands of soldiers and rebels begin rampaging homes, terrorizing family members, gang-raping wives in front of husbands, stealing valuables, and forcing families out of their houses and occupying or burning them.

These deplorable acts triggered serious refugee problems, particularly because the professional class was the target. Many families escaped to neighboring countries. The professional class became thoroughly depleted and no one doubts the continued decline of the country without it. Those who stayed lived in constant fear of further attacks. Schools and businesses remained closed as protest to this wanton destruction and brutality. Other stories in the media and reports by nongovernmental organizations (NGOs) and international agencies reiterate the ongoing crisis for families, including finding lost family members (United Nations Office for the Coordination of Humanitarian Affairs, nd; USAID Sierra Leone, 2004b).

Over 260,000 people have returned to Sierra Leone from neighboring countries since 2001. Many were anxious to return home before the repatriation program finished at the end of June 2004 (extended to late July). They received a small travel allowance, food, and other items to help reintegrate (UN High Commissioner for Refugees [UNHCR], 2004a, 2004b, 2004c). In addition, UNHCR is supporting community empowerment projects in the regions worst hit by the war. Sierra Leone's President emphasized their importance for helping families recover (UNHCR, 2004a; USAID Sierra Leone, 2004a, 2004c). These are small-scale schemes both identified and conducted by the community with technical support by the American Refugee Committee and with UNHCR funding. Over ninety projects have begun. Their focus is wide ranging, including skills training (e.g., carpentry, cloth weaving, tailoring, hairdressing, and adult literacy for women), HIV/AIDS awareness, health clinics, and improving schools. The lingering effects of the war can be particularly hard for children (Amnesty International, 2004).

The security and cohesiveness of what was once "the Sierra Leonean family" now lies in ruins, or it is reemerging in alien cultures where the dynamics for cultural survival could well be absent. A country that has always thrived in its zestful hopefulness and gracious civility now looks to the international community to help restore the integrity of its families. Thankfully, the UN agencies and NGOs are doing their best to make this possible. Through their work in the refugee centers, UN agencies and NGOs are helping fragmented families cope with displacement and prepare for a return to normalcy.

FAMILIES AND AGING

In Sierra Leone, one of the primary issues in the socialization of children has been the emphasis on respect for the elders. The reverence for age in this country has cosmological significance. People believe that the older one is, the wiser, and the wiser one is, the closer she or he is to the ancestors. In the rural areas, elders settle disputes, lease prime farmlands, and initiate the young into their culture. Among the Krio, older members of a family have the distinction of performing rituals to the departed and the ancestors (Wyse, 1989). Older people must break the kola nuts before anyone can take a bite. They lead prayers and pour libation to the dead.

A primary reason to have many children in traditional societies is the security it provides parents in old age. Aging is a crucial adjunct of family stability and loyalty. However, with the decrease of life span within the last several decades, many children are being robbed of much needed socialization from the old. Indeed, part of the responsibilities of the children is to continue the tradition of caring for their parents when they start their own families.

This is the case with the Temne. The elderly expect children to work on the farms and to care for them in their old age. It is therefore common for men in their forties or even older in polygamous families to marry teenage girls. The hope is that she will take care of him as he grows old. As women live longer, they get the benefit of the children's care that the men crave. This is one of only a few options for elderly woman in a Temne family, because tradition precludes her from remarrying a younger man. Usually, a son will welcome his elderly father or mother in his house because of the bonding it will create with the grandchildren. This is also true in urban centers. Moreover, an additional reason for wanting their elderly parents with them is to help alleviate the stress of living in the city while providing a sense of family cohesiveness through regular visits of other family members.

Another option for the aging Temne parent is to stay with widowed or single siblings with whom he or she can share companionship and living expenses. However, most Temne expect to live with a son or a daughter and her husband when they grow old. Residence preference reveals an overwhelming wish of the elderly to "move in with whichever child, male or female, could best provide for them, love them the most or was the wealthiest" (Dorjahn, 1989, p. 268).

With age comes respect and prestige (Migeod, 1970). The elderly Temne woman frequently helps with initiation or delivering a child. The elderly Temne man ceases to do heavy manual work on the farm, not because of any physical attrition, but because of the prestige age has now accorded him (Dorjahn, 1989). He now supervises the young ones. Elderly individuals have the freedom to express themselves in any way they want. The gender barriers usually confronting the woman ceases to have meaning when she joins the ranks of the elderly. She can invade spaces traditionally reserved for men and can argue with her husband as well as demand equal rights; and she will get results. This late self-actualization is likely to continue, based on statistical data. Today, 52 percent of the population is fifteen to sixty-four years of age. Of these, women are in the majority at 1.6 million compared with 1.5 million men. As life expectancy for men is lower, more women will outlive men, thereby increasing their stature in the society (World Factbook, 2006). Consequently, aging will become a formidable weapon in leveling gender inequities.

With the changing landscape of the rural areas, where children are seeking Western education and migrating to the urban centers and the mining areas, the fortunes of the elderly appear to be waning. The reverence for age has been downgraded to respectful tolerance, sometimes even ambivalence. More and more Temne families, like most others in the country, must now wrestle with conflicting values brought about by the infusion of Western culture into their traditional structure.

OTHER FAMILY SITUATIONS

Single-Parent Female-Headed Household

This family form is most common among professional women who might have studied abroad, are well educated, independent thinking, and self-confident. They could have difficulty maintaining relationships because they intimidate men, or refuse to accept a subservient role in the relationship. Some have children with men they hope will marry them, and when that is not forthcoming, will take the leadership role of their families. Others can be worried about their "biological clocks" as they search for a suitable marriage partner before it is too late. In any of these cases, the woman will likely not raise the children by herself. Her mother, a close female relative, or a nanny will stay in her house and help with the children. The children will have the benefit of their father's participation in their upbringing although he does not live with them. Men in this society will generally accept responsibility for their children in and out of wedlock.

Divorce and Single-Parent Families

There is also the single-parent family that results from divorce. This family structure is unpopular because divorce is not a desirable alternative in Sierra Leone. The social stigma associated with divorce frequently becomes a motivation for the resolution of marital problems. Reconciliation periods are usually mandated before the court will issue a divorce decree (Lisk & Williams, 1995). After the decree is issued for a civil or Christian marriage, the wife frequently gets custody of the children, sometimes not because of the decree but because of the cultural obligations of the wife to raise the children. In extreme cases involving insanity or other abnormalities of the mother, paternal grandparents or responsible female relatives raise the children. When the wife gets custody, she likely invites members of her extended family to move in with her to help with the children. As a result, the single-family household by divorce is an amorphous one to describe within the context of Sierra Leone.

Cohabitation

Cohabitation out of wedlock is becoming an alternative, but it is usually confined to young college-educated professionals. Those who cohabit can be divided into two groups. The first are those who were raised in an urban area, attended university there, and are now trying to establish independence from their parents. The other group represents the influx of professionals from the provincial areas that do not have accessible relatives in the city. They might decide to live in an apartment with their mate. Cohabitation can also be a temporary arrangement for couples not having the necessary funds to marry straight away, but eventually will. The belief in the institution of marriage in Sierra Leone is very strong.

CONCLUDING COMMENTS

The Sierra Leone family institution has maintained its plurality in spite of a move toward monogamous marriage forms. Religious convictions remain strong, but defenders of customary law practices have fought valiantly against any dilution or elimination of customary law marriages. The present political and economic uncertainties notwithstanding, one can easily predict that this plurality will continue to create vistas of mutual tolerance in Sierra Leone.

The Sierra Leone family institution, as it is unfolding now, is in disarray. The rebel war, the military coup, and the lingering political malaise are making it almost impossible for families to retain their cohesiveness. Child soldiers have killed parents and grandparents and torched their own communities. Concerned parents and other family members dispersed the remaining children to kinfolk in scattered parts of the country. In effect, these children have been growing up with little of the cohesiveness that they used to experience.

The fortunes of families will be retrieved when stability comes to Sierra Leone. That could take decades given the magnitude of the devastation from political turmoil. Rehabilitation will involve rebuilding families through social reconstruction and political and ethnic tolerance. The bitterness, especially between the Mendes and the Temnes who are at opposite ends of the conflict, will have to be eradicated before older family members from both groups can once again focus on the task of proper socialization of the young. The latter, however, will need to be reclaimed and reeducated after their ruthless indoctrination into cold-blooded killing. Nevertheless, as many Sierra Leoneans are wont to say about military coups, "this too will pass."

Chapter 8

Families and Households in South Africa

Susan Ziehl

Writing about families in South Africa presents both challenges and opportunities. The challenges derive from the fact that the family has not enjoyed a high political or more generally public profile— something that is reflected in the relatively underdeveloped state of family sociology in this country. Despite efforts by the Human Sciences Research Council (HSRC), there is no well-documented study of family life in South African society as a whole, even though localized studies of family life have been published in the form of monographs. This situation is compounded in that census data have been inadequate for the identification of household composition patterns due to a problematic definition of the family and the exclusion of certain key areas. On a more positive note, the "political miracle" of 1994 initiated a process of stocktaking and reassessment of almost every sphere of South African society. The practical manifestation of this is the publication of a large number of green papers, white papers, and laws, some of which are informed by information relating to family patterns and/or can be expected to impact on family life (e.g., *White Paper on Population Policy; Recognition of Customary Marriages Act*).[1] This chapter provides a broad overview of family-related issues

The contributor would like to thank Professor V. Møller of the Institute for Social and Economic Research at Rhodes University for her assistance in gaining access to some of the material covered in this chapter, as well as members of the Sociology and Anthropology Departments at Rhodes University for their comments on draft versions.

in South Africa today, drawing on these new policy documents as well as the social scientific research available.

As is well known, South Africa has a history of colonial conquest, intergroup conflict more generally, and an official policy of racial segregation—known, in the period 1948 to 1994 as the policy of apartheid; it differentiated among people of African descent (referred to as black or African), of Indian descent (Asian or Indian), of European descent (white), and those of mixed ancestry (black and white unions) as well as descendants of the indigenous Khoisan people (collectively referred to as "Colored").[2] Against this background, it is somewhat ironic that the African National Congress (ANC) government has decided to retain this racial classification system (see Ziehl, 1995 for more information). It has continued to do so due to the correlation between population group and indicators of socioeconomic status (see Table 8.1), to monitor changes in this regard (Ministry for Welfare and Population Development [MWPD], 1997a), and as a means of implementing affirmative action legislation (see Employment Equity Act of 1998).

The South African economy was built on agriculture and mining (gold and diamonds, in particular). Today these primary sector activities account for only about 10 percent of GDP compared with 25 percent by the secondary sector (manufacturing) and 64 percent by the tertiary (services) sector (South African Institute of Race Relations [SAIRR],

TABLE 8.1. Population Groups, Human Development Index, and Changes in the Proportion of Total Income.

Population Group	Proportion of Population[a]	Human Development Index[b]	Proportion of Total Income[c]	
			1985 (%)	1994 (%)
Black	77%	0.500[d]	32.0	38.5
"Colored"	9%	0.663	8.1	8.9
Indian	3%	0.836	3.6	4.0
White	11%	0.901[e]	56.2	48.6

Source: [a]Statistics South Africa (1999); [b]SAIRR (1997)(figures for 1991); [c]SAIRR (1997); [d]Similar to that for the Maldives, Zimbabwe, and Namibia (SAIRR, 1997, p. 30; SAIRR, 1998, p. 103); [e]Similar to that for New Zealand, Australia, the United States, and Japan (SAIRR, 1997, p. 30; SAIRR, 1998, p. 103).

1999b). The country is about twice the size of the U.S. state of Texas. The majority (57 percent in 2003) of the roughly 46.9 million South Africans live in urban areas (United Nations Development Programme [UNDP], 2005). The literacy rate is 86 percent. Despite relatively high unemployment (estimated at 23 percent in 1997 and 31 percent in 2003) and poverty rate, South Africa is categorized as a medium income country and as having a Human Development Index (HDI) in the middle range (0.717 in 1995, 0.697 for 1998 and at 103rd in the HDI ranking, and 0.658 in 2003 that placed it 120th). Based on the recent HDI estimates South Africa compares well with other African countries and is higher than the average HDI of 0.464 for sub-Saharan Africa. Life expectancy was estimated at 64.4 years in the period 1991-1996 (SAIRR, 1997, 1998, 1999b), 54.7 in 1996, and 48.4 in 2003 (UNDP, 2005). However, owing to excess mortality due to AIDS that can result in lower life expectancy, higher infant mortality, and other changes to the demographic profile than otherwise would be expected, life expectancy at birth has also been estimated as 43.5 for males and 43.1 for females (World Factbook, 2005).

In the spirit of compromise that brought about the "new South Africa," the 1996 constitution identifies eleven official languages. Of these, only three are spoken as mother tongue by more than 10 percent of the population—Zulu (22 percent); Xhosa (18 percent); Afrikaans (15 percent)—followed by North Sotho (10 percent) and English (10 percent) (SAIRR, 1998). About 70 percent of South Africans claim a religious denomination with the African Independent Churches representing the single largest category (22 percent of the population) (SAIRR, 1998). A survey conducted in 1993 among final-year high school students from all the major population groups found that 96 percent belonged to a church and that 75 percent of these attended church more than once a month (Van Zyl Slabbert, Malan, Marais, Olivier, & Riordan, 1994; see also Everatt & Orkin, 1993).

Families in South African Context

The concept of family can be defined in different ways depending on the context and purpose of the user (Ziehl, 1997a). For instance, it can refer to a social institution ("the family"), a set of individuals connected by ties of blood and/or marriage (the question of who is "family"), and a group of individuals connected by blood and/or

marriage that share a place of residence (a family household). The concept of household further has a number of dimensions, referring to
people who eat together, share economic resources, and/or who live
together at any particular point in time. Following are the results of a
survey of South African urban households where households have
been identified by means of coresidence (Steyn, 1995). It is the only
large-scale survey result available based on representative samples
from all the major population groups.

The data in Table 8.2 show the distribution of household structures
at the time of the survey (1988 and 1989) and tell something about
family living. Particularly, the data suggest that South Africans generally follow a domestic life cycle involving nuclear and extended
family living—together these account for just over 70 percent of all
households. The data also suggest that it is rare to live either alone, in
a single-parent family arrangement, or with a spouse only.

There are significant differences by population group. The pattern
described most closely resembles the experiences of black South
Africans among whose rates of extended family living are higher than
the average for the society (45 percent versus 29 percent). Indeed,
when focusing on the number of people in households, it is notewor-
thy that of all the black South Africans covered by this survey, only
0.1 percent were living in single-person households, 1 percent in
couple households, and 8 percent in single-parent households. This

TABLE 8.2. Household Structures in Urban South Africa.

Household Structure	Black	"Colored"	Indian	White	Total
Single person	0.7	2.1	1.1	14.9	6.3
Couple	2.9	5.7	5.4	23.9	11.5
Nuclear	36.9	40.3	55.1	46.3	41.9
Single parent	10.6	11.3	6.3	5.1	8.3
Extended	44.6	37.6	30.5	6.9	28.5
Other	4.4	3.2	1.6	2.9	3.5
Total	100.1	100.2	100.0	100.0	100.0

Source: Adapted from Steyn (1995).

Note: Does not total to 100 due to rounding.

compares with the 32 percent and 53 percent who were part of nuclear and extended family arrangements, respectively (Steyn, 1995).

The survey only included urban areas. One covering the entire country would likely yield even higher rates of extended family arrangements among black South Africans. Siqwana-Ndulo's (1998) research in 1992 on a rural village in the Eastern Cape showed that 13 percent of the households consisted of a parent or parents and children alone and only about 3 percent were single-person households. The rest were different types of extended family households as the term is defined in this chapter (see following text). At the other extreme are white South Africans among whom extended family arrangements are unusual, while living alone or with a spouse only is common. As can be distinguished from Table 8.2, the family patterns of Indian and "Colored" communities fall somewhere between these extremes.

In Table 8.2 the term extended family is used loosely to cover all household arrangements including individuals other than those who make up a nuclear family. For black South Africans, the most common arrangement would be a grandparent or grandparents living with a nuclear family (64 percent of all extended families and 29 percent of all households). There are also instances of a married couple living with a sibling of one of the spouses, a niece or nephew, or another relative. Table 8.3 sets out the distribution of the various extended family arrangements (discovered by Steyn, 1995).

While a pattern of extended family arrangements is difficult to identify within a rural black community (Siqwana-Ndulo, 1998), parent(s),

TABLE 8.3. Types of Extended Family Arrangements, as a Proportion of All Extended Families.

Arrangements	Black	"Colored"	Indian	White
Three generations	64	53	39	18
Nuclear family and relative (two generational)	21	31	48	49
Couple and relative	5	7	7	18
Single parent and relative	9	10	6	16
Total	99	101	100	101

Source: Adapted from Steyn (1996).

Note: Does not total to 100 due to rounding.

child(ren), and grandchild(ren) represent the mode (38 percent) and together with cases where the middle generation is absent (24 percent), constitute the majority (62 percent) of extended families in this village.

Living in extended households is considered in other sections of this chapter. For now, it is sufficient to indicate that extended households are common in South Africa, especially among blacks. Close proximity and relationships with kin characterize South African families.

COUPLE FORMATION AND MARITAL DYNAMICS

In contrast to media presentations of "the family in crisis" and "the flight from marriage," most (52 percent) adult South Africans are or have been married. The 1996 census indicated that in the age category eighteen and above, 43 percent were married, 6 percent were widowed, and 3 percent were divorced. Only 5 percent were living together without being married (contributor's calculation based on Ziehl, 1999). However, there are a number of ways in which these figures are problematic. First, because customary marriages were not recognized by South African civil law at the time of the census (Ziehl, 1997b), some might not have been counted as marriages. About one-third of all marriages are traditional marriages (Budlender, personal communication, December, 1998; Ziehl, 1999). Second, due to African customary marriage being a process rather than an event (see following text), it is often unclear exactly when a customary marriage has been concluded (Simkins, 1986; see also Jones, 1998). For these reasons the marriage rate referred to in previous text and indicated in Table 8.4 is probably an underestimation. The National Youth Survey showed that 87 percent of respondents came from families where the parents had not divorced or separated and that 93 percent of parents were married (Everatt & Orkin, 1994).

These figures present a perhaps surprisingly high level of endorsement for the importance of marriage and "the family." This is reinforced by young people; 92 percent of all respondents (and a higher proportion of black youth) agreed or strongly agreed with the statement, "It is important that families stay together." Likewise,

TABLE 8.4. Marital Status of South Africans Eighteen Years and Older (1996 Census).

Marital Status	Black	"Colored"	Indian	White	Total
Never married	46.9	38.4	24.7	19.3	41.7
Married	38.3	45.2	63.8	64.6	43.2
Living together	6.1	6.2	1.0	2.7	5.4
Widowed	5.2	5.8	6.9	6.9	5.5
Divorced	2.5	3.9	3.2	6.2	3.1
Unspecified	1.0	0.6	0.5	0.4	1.0

Source: Ziehl (1999).

82 percent backed the statement, "it is important to be married before having children" (Everatt & Orkin, 1994, pp. 46-47).

Lobola

Even with the strong endorsement of marriage, nevertheless it is also the case that the propensity to marry is lower among South Africans than is the case in more developed societies. This is because "marriage, in every society, must be afforded" (Simkins, 1986, p. 31). This is particularly relevant in the case of black South Africans not only because of a relatively low per capita income, but also because of the practice of *lobola* (bridewealth). This custom involves the transfer of wealth (traditionally measured in head of cattle) from the family of the groom to the family of the bride. It is symbolic of the value attached to children and their labor and can be seen as compensation for the loss of control over their daughter and her offspring. It is also the means by which children are incorporated into the kin group of the father (Jones, 1998).

The impact of *lobola* on marriage rates is due to it usually involving a lengthy negotiating process between the two families, consequently delaying the marriage. It also affects the increasing rates of nonmarital cohabitation and/or the number of extramarital births. Indeed, in focus group discussions with black youths, parents, and grandparents, *lobola* was seldom *not* mentioned and was frequently cited as the reason for premarital cohabitation and pregnancy (Viljoen, 1994). The extent to which this is a justification after the fact and *lobola* is simply part of a discourse that is seldom put into practice is hard to tell (Jones, 1998).

Legislation of Marriage

As noted, African customary marriages have not been recognized as legal marriages in South Africa. The reason is not the custom of *lobola* (which is sometimes stigmatized as the sale of women), but the fact that they are potentially polygynous (Ziehl, 1997b). Dating back to the colonial era, this prohibition is informed by the idea that Christianity does not permit (simultaneous) polygyny, and is an instance of the imposition of European legal systems and culture on African people (Currie, 1994). The prohibition has not been universal. Rather, since the 1920s there has been a situation of legal dualism—civil marriages governed by civil law and African customary marriages governed by African customary law as provided for in the Black Administration Act of 1927, as well as various laws passed by the homeland authorities.

The coming to power of the ANC has meant not only the incorporation of the former homeland areas into South Africa, but the adoption of a constitution guaranteeing both the right to cultural diversity and gender equality. In the case of recognizing customary marriages, however, these two provisions of the constitution clash. Men are identified as heads of the households; women cannot inherit property, and unlike men, cannot take on an additional spouse(s). The Recognition of Customary Marriages Act (1998) seeks to overcome these difficulties by providing for the recognition and registration of all customary marriages whether polygynous or not. It further stipulates that existing polygynous customary marriages will continue to be governed by African customary law. The decision to not outlaw polygamous marriages was based on the idea that such a ban "would be impossible to enforce and that the practice is waning" (p. 14). However, should a man in an existing (de facto monogamous or polygamous) customary marriage wish to take on an additional wife, the provisions of the Act come into effect. These demand that the man apply to the court for the dissolution of the property system previously applicable to the marriage and the division of assets between the various spouses (existing or future). It further provides for the conversion of an existing monogamous customary marriage into a civil marriage, but not vice versa.

The upshot of this new legislation is that it seeks a uniform system of rules for the governance of all marriages that excludes polygyny but includes *lobola.* To some extent the legislation completes the colonial project of replacing African customary law with Western civil law. The exception is that both African and Christian ways of concluding and celebrating marriage are recognized. In addition, *lobola* agreements will be registered and taken into account when decisions are made concerning the maintenance of children after divorce. It is not clear whether the courts will rule on noncompliance to *lobola* agreements during the marriage.

Residence

Housing and residential arrangements influence many aspects of marriage dynamics. For example, living within an extended household is different for a couple than living in a neo-local residence. Unfortunately, studies have not investigated this in South Africa. Consequently, one is left with only a sense of the residential context and the importance this might have for marriages. Within the section Families and Children, readers are introduced to issues of migrancy, domestic fluidity, and extended household living. While the emphasis is on family dynamics and child rearing, the reader can also imagine the impact that such movement or extended household living can have on marriages.

FAMILIES AND CHILDREN

Children represent an important aspect of South African society, both numerically and in terms of cultural values (MWPD, 1997a). In 1996, 35 percent of the population was under the age of fifteen years compared with 5 percent in the sixty-five years and overage category (Institute for Futures Research, cited in SAIRR, 1998). In 2002, these groups were 33 percent and 4 percent, respectively (UNDP, 2004). Fertility levels have been dropping significantly. For instance, the crude birthrate was estimated at 31.2 per 1,000 population for the period 1985-1990, a drop from the 37.2 estimated for the 1970-1975 period (MWPD, 1997a). The birthrate was estimated as 24.6 in 2000 and 18.4 in 2005 (World Factbook, 2000, 2005). The total fertility rate

(TFR) also declined in the course of the twentieth century. It was predicted to reach the level of 3.3 in the period 2000-2005, significantly
lower than predicted for some other African countries (e.g., Nigeria
4.8 and Mozambique 7.0) as well as for Africa as a whole (5.0); the
predicted TFR is higher than that predicted for developed societies
(e.g., Australia 1.9 and United States 2.1) for the same period (World
Bank, cited in SAIRR, 1997). However, preliminary estimates from
the 1996 census indicated that the TFR for South Africa had already
reached the 3.2 level in 1995, down from 4.2 in 1980 (SAIRR, 1998).
Other estimates place the TFR at 2.24 in 2005 (World Factbook, 2005)
and 2.8 for the period 2000-2005 (UNDP, 2005). The total population
growth rate was 2.1 from 1975-2003 and estimated at 0.2 percent for
2003-2015 (UNDP, 2005).

Small Families Are Happy Families

This decline in fertility has been attributed to the population policy
of the previous government. While having far-reaching aims (such as
socioeconomic development, particularly in the case of women), the
policy was successful mainly in promoting the idea that "small families are happy families" and making contraception available through
family planning clinics (Caldwell & Caldwell, 1993). The contraceptive prevalence rate among married women reached an estimated 60
percent in 1994, increasing by 5 percentage points from 1990 (MWPD,
1997a). UNDP (2005) estimates the contraceptive prevalence rate at
56 percent in 1995-2003. There are also indications that South African
women have developed fairly low fertility aspirations. A survey in the
late 1980s identified 3.3 as the desired number of children for all women
surveyed (MWPD, 1997a). There are, of course, differences in fertility
trends among the various population groups. Among whites, fertility
started declining at the beginning of the twentieth century, reached
below replacement level in the 1970s, and was recently estimated at
1.5 (Caldwell & Caldwell, 1993; MWPD, 1997a). For Asians, the
turning point was the 1940s and the TFR is estimated at 2.2. Fertility
among Black and "Colored" South Africans started to decline after the
1960s and is estimated at 4.3 and 2.3, respectively (MWPD, 1997a).
   In contrast to the general trend toward lower fertility, the birthrate
among teenage black South Africans has been increasing. This per-

ception is gleaned from Sadie's analysis of the 1991 census data in conjunction with the results of the Demographic and Health Survey conducted in 1987 and 1989.

Nonmarital Births

According to the 1995 October Household Survey, 29 percent of women who had given birth at some time in their lives had never married (Budlender, 1998). Marital status was recorded at the time of the survey and it is possible that some of these women would marry later. In the same survey, over 40 percent of children under the age of seven years were living with their mother only, compared with 1 percent who were living with their father only. Again, a caveat is in order because this should not be taken to mean that there is a relatively high level of two-generational single-parent families in South Africa. As indicated earlier, such household structures are quite rare. The more common response to extramarital birth is the absorption of the mother-child dyad into an extended family arrangement, usually involving the mother's mother or her sister (Ziehl, 1994b). Variation by population group in the household location of children can be garnered from Table 8.5.

Legislation of Abortion

One of the most controversial pieces of legislation passed by the new South African government is the Choice on Termination of Pregnancy Act of 1996. Replacing the more restrictive Abortion and

TABLE 8.5. Presence of Biological Parents in Children's Households (Percentage).

	Black	"Colored"	Indian	White	Total
Both	40	53	85	89	45
Father only	2	1	0	0	1
Mother only	46	37	10	7	42
Neither	13	9	4	4	12
Total	101	100	99	100	100

Source: Adapted from Budlender (1998).

Note: Does not total to 100 due to rounding.

Sterilization Act of 1975, it provides for the termination of a pregnancy: (1) within the first trimester upon request of the pregnant woman; (2) between the third and fifth months of pregnancy on condition that a medical practitioner is of the opinion that the continued pregnancy would cause injury to the physical or mental health of the woman, there is "a substantial risk that the fetus would suffer from severe physical or mental abnormality," the pregnancy resulted from rape or incest, or "the continued pregnancy would significantly affect the social or economic circumstances of the woman"; and (3) after five months of pregnancy if in the opinion of two medical practitioners the continued pregnancy "would endanger the woman's life; would result in a severe malformation of the fetus; or would pose a risk of injury to the fetus" (p. 2). The Act further indicates that the State will promote pre- and postabortion counseling, but this is not mandatory.

Between the coming into effect of this Act on February 1, 1997 and August of the same year, 13,000 legal abortions were performed (Reproductive Rights Alliance, cited in SAIRR, 1998). This figure is substantially lower than expected on the basis of previous estimates and is attributed to reluctance on the part of medical practitioners to implement the provisions of the 1996 Act as well as a shortage of medical facilities in rural areas (SAIRR, 1998).

Domestic Fluidity

While the domestic life cycle concept places household structures in dynamic perspective (by drawing attention to the fact that most if not all individuals participate in a number of household structures in the course of a lifetime), the complexity and variability of the actual experience of family life is not done justice to. Qualitative research suggests that under circumstances of abject poverty, political and other forms of violence, as well as migrancy, family life can become unpredictable as individuals move between households to cope with the conditions they face. Parenting practices reflect this unpredictability and coping with uncertainty. Children often live with someone other than their biological parents in various types of fostering arrangements.

Spiegel, Watson, and Wilkinson (1996) provided a number of examples from their study of thirty-seven households in Khayelitsha, one of the black residential areas in Cape Town, as a way of illustrating the idea of domestic fluidity and the "stretching" of domestic units over space. This research draws attention to the often-divergent ways in which migrancy is perceived.

Apart from illustrating the different meanings associated with migrancy (temporary absence to ensure a return to a rural base or consolidation of an urban base), these cases also highlight the tendency to share the parental role among a number of adults, rather than just the biological parents. This idea is shown in a study of the residential mobility of children in a rural settlement in Gazankulu, a previous homeland area in the Northern Province (Van der Waal, 1996). High male migration and female unemployment mark this settlement. In January 1990, 43 of the 212 children in this settlement were part of a fostering arrangement. That is, they were not living with an immediate biological parent. This practice is explained with reference to a number of factors, including divorce. Four of the children in this settlement had been left by their mothers with their fathers' relatives after the parents separated because the payment of bridewealth means that the husband has claim to the children, particularly older ones (see following text). Where remarriage occurs the children are effectively raised by another woman (known as the "younger mother" or *mhanintosongo*) and have to compete (often unsuccessfully) with half-siblings for food, emotional support, and so on. This usually means a struggle over parental rights and competition between the parents while children (sometimes secretly) try to visit their biological mothers. "In extreme cases they had to face threats of witchcraft accusations between parents—a common idiom in which parental competition was expressed" (Van der Waal, 1996, p. 40).

Being left with paternal relatives is the exception rather than the rule. Their maternal grandmothers, other maternal relatives, or their own older sisters were raising most of the foster children in this study. The most common reason was the (biological) mother's inability to provide adequately for her children's material needs. Against this background, the most common practice appears to be an unmarried daughter leaving her child/children with her mother while she works elsewhere. Although the expectation in such an arrangement is that the biological mother will support the child financially, in practice this often means that the principal source of income for the child's sustenance is the grandmother's pension (Van der Waal, 1996). This should not be taken to mean that fostering is a one-sided relationship of dependence of the child on the adult concerned. It is more of an exchange relationship where the child provides labor, assistance, and company in exchange for material subsistence. Girls are usually preferred as foster children because they are more inclined than are boys to make a direct contribution to the maintenance of the household in the form of domestic chores (Van der Waal, 1996).

Education is another factor behind fostering. The education is either in the sense of a mother returning to school after the birth or a child being sent to stay with relatives in an area where schooling facilities are available (Van der Waal, 1996).

The fluidity of domestic units is also seen in a "Colored" community in a "shanty town" in the Western Cape, known as "Die Bos" (Ross, 1996). Here one can observe the mobility of both children and adults between households as well as changing domestic arrangements linked to fuel- and food-sharing practice.

Ross's research shows the roles played by both instrumentality and morality in the formation of households. The first is meeting basic needs for food and shelter, for example, and the second refers to "moral concerns (such as an offer of food and shelter resulting from knowledge of a child's limited alternative resources)" (p. 59).

As the cases in previous text are not from representative samples, it is difficult to know how common these experiences might be. Indeed, Spiegel et al. (1996) were aware of this limitation and indicated that it would be fruitful to complement their ethnographic research with large-scale survey data documenting the life histories of a number of individuals drawn randomly. What data such as these do highlight is that for many South Africans, the actual experience of family life is more complex and variable than some models and theories suggest. Such data also demonstrate the way in which various material, political, and other factors prevent individuals from achieving the family life they desire.

Extended Households

Earlier in this chapter it was explained that many South Africans live in extended household arrangements, a pattern found more among some segments of the population than among others. It might be tempting to explain the apparent direct relationship (presented in Table 8.1) between socioeconomic status and extended family/household structure by reference to material conditions (Allen, 1979; Ziehl, 1994a, 1997a). However, cultural predispositions differentiate these communities. It is more likely that for black South Africans, poor material conditions combine with a cultural emphasis on strong extended family ties to produce relatively high levels of extended family arrangements. The opposite is likely true of white South Africans (Ziehl, 1994a). A study of a representative sample of South African youth (sixteen to thirty years of age) found that 80 percent of black and "Colored" respondents agreed or strongly agreed that young people have a duty to look after their relatives, compared with 56 percent of white youth. The figure for the total sample was 77 percent (Everatt & Orkin, 1994).

Speculation has been forthcoming about family pattern trends in South Africa (cf. Amoateng, 1997). However, there is no research available to support such speculation because data showing the distribution of household structures at one point in time begs the question: "What was the situation like in the past?" However, more than that, claims about convergence or divergence cannot be established based on information about the popularity of the nuclear family per se. The nuclear family represents a relatively large proportion of households in all the (urban) communities studied. What is clear is that South Africans of different cultural and socioeconomic backgrounds follow different domestic life cycles and that the distinction between these lies not in the popularity of nuclear family households, but other household forms (single person, couple, and extended family households).

Two different domestic life cycles are offered in Table 8.6. The first is the arrangement commonly found among white and the second commonly found among black South Africans. Fictitious examples, they are offered by way of illustration rather than claiming to be typical domestic life cycles. Some anthropologists have argued that the domestic life experiences of many black South Africans defies classification or categorization in terms of the domestic life cycle concept, whether based on the nuclear family model or any other model (see Spiegel et al., 1996).

TABLE 8.6. Domestic Life Cycles of Sarah and Thandi.

	Household Structure	**Stage**
Sarah		
1.	Nuclear	When Sarah is born
2.	Single person (or other arrangement such as living with friends)	When Sarah finishes school and lives in a flat on her own
3.	Couple	When Sarah marries and lives with her husband
4.	Nuclear	When Sarah's first child is born
5.	Couple	When Sarah's youngest child leaves home
6.	Single person	When Sarah's husband dies
Thandi		
1.	Extended	When Thandi is born (the household consists of her parents, her siblings, and grandmother)
2.	Nuclear	When Thandi's grandmother dies
3.	Extended	When Thandi's first child is born (she stays on in her parental home)
4.	Extended	When Thandi marries, she moves to her husband's home, which also contains his mother (Thandi has two more children)
5.	Nuclear	When Thandi's mother-in-law dies
6.	Extended	When Thandi's sister-in-law moves into the home
7.	Extended	When Thandi's first grandchild is born

FAMILIES AND GENDER

Like all societies, South Africa bears the marks of patriarchy. This shows in the overrepresentation of men in positions of power in the economy, in politics, and in families. For instance, in 1996, women accounted for less than 18 percent of administrators and managers and only 24 percent of parliamentarians were female (MWPD, 1997a). Conversely, educational enrollment rates are high and roughly similar for boys and girls. Whereas women accounted for 47 percent of university students in 1990, this had risen to 53 percent in 1996 (Badsha & Kotecha, 1994; Budlender, 1998).

There are still significant gender differences in the type of courses followed. Only 21 percent of female students compared with 31 percent of males students at South African universities and *technikons* (which focus on the acquisition of technical/practical skills and vocational training) were enrolled for natural science courses in 1993 (National Commission on Higher Education, 1996). Male students outnumber female students at *technikons* (62 percent versus 38 percent) and in postgraduate enrollments at universities (Badsha & Kotecha, 1994; Budlender, 1998). Consequently, women are less likely to be represented in careers such as engineering and others requiring a high level of technical expertise. For instance, in 1991, less than 2 percent of engineers, 7 percent of architects, and 15 percent of medical practitioners in general practice were women (Martineau, 1998). Women are also concentrated in certain types of occupations like clerical work (20 percent of employed females), service/sales work (12 percent), and unskilled work (38 percent), compared with 8 percent, 12 percent, and 27 percent of employed men, respectively (Budlender, 1998). The general trend for women to be concentrated in sectors and occupations that are low in pay is reflected in black women earning 26 percent and white women earning 60 percent of white male employees' salaries in 1995. Whereas more than 70 percent of men with university degrees were earning over R4,000 (about US$700) per month in 1995, this applied to less than one-half of women graduates (Budlender, 1998).

Changing Gender Roles?

That many households in South Africa are female-headed has not substantially eroded attachment to the idea of men as holders of authority over both women and children.[3] Even in female-headed households in Durban township, "a great deal of energy is invested in trying to approximate the old-fashioned blueprint of male head and breadwinner, subordinate mother and so on" (Campbell, 1990, p. 10). An example is Mrs. D., a fifty-four-year-old woman abandoned by her husband who called upon her eldest daughter's boyfriend and later another daughter's husband to discipline her seventeen-year-old "*tsotsi*" son, Themba (*tsotsi* is a local word for a "layabout," or good for nothing). "At no stage did she, or any member of her social circle, consider the possibility that she as a mother should have any power to discipline Themba" (Campbell, 1990, p. 9). Rather, Mrs. D. spoke as follows of her situation: "without a father a child will boastfully attend any party he likes because he knows very well that his father does not stay at home, and he doesn't take any notice of his mother" (Campbell, 1990, p. 9).

Another example is an abandoned woman who raised her children and was still making an economic contribution to the household. However, she handed the role of "household head" to her son when he started making an economic contribution. "It seems as if many women take the role of household head if they are forced to do so—but as soon as a suitable man is available to fill this role, they stand back graciously and allow him to take over" (Campbell, 1990, p. 9).

Campbell's (1990) main argument is that while there is a growing discrepancy between the traditional ideology of men as breadwinners and women as confined to the roles of nurturer and homemaker, this does not translate into a redefinition of gender roles in practice. Therefore, the challenge to the ideology does not "present any real threat to male power and dominance" (Campbell, 1990, p. 11). Among the reasons offered are that many women do not see themselves as oppressed in gender terms and therefore do not see the need for a reworking of gender roles. Another reason is many men do not see the contradiction between their quest for democracy in the workplace and society at large, and their roles in the family. In this respect, Campbell cited the example of a trade union activist described by his wife and children as "a tyrant." "They (spoke) of his determination to impose his will on every member of the household and his fury when he feels they are being disobedient." He described his situation as follows: "In my family I do not have fear, I just instil [sic] discipline in the way I see fit. My problem is the outside world. It is too big for me to sort out" (Campbell, 1990, p. 15). A study of whites in Grahamstown (Ziehl, 1997a) found a similarly high level of acceptance of traditional gender roles.

White couples also experience a highly segregated sexual division of labor—the majority of domestic tasks being performed by either wives or husbands. However, tasks women perform are greater in number, need to be done more regularly, are more time-consuming, and are more likely to be performed indoors than those undertaken by men. The employment of a domestic worker (which is sometimes seen as a solution to the "problem" of women's overinvolvement in domestic labor and this applies in 80 percent of cases) further reduces men's involvement in housework (Maconachie, 1992).

The maintenance of traditional gender roles in South African families and the concomitant greater involvement of women in child rearing are reflected in the results of a nation-wide study of youth (Everatt & Orkin, 1994). The researchers found that while 85 percent of respondents felt that they knew their mothers well, only 65 percent said this about their fathers. Moreover, while just under three-quarters (71 percent) said they received as much attention from their mothers as they wanted, less than half (48 percent) said this about their fathers. Black youth, more so than others, were more likely to be satisfied with the attention they received from their mothers and dissatisfied with their father's involvement. This can be explained with reference to higher rates of husband-absence among black families.

Research also reveals significant differences in the leisure activities of men and women; men being more likely to play sports (87 percent) than women (33 percent), with black women showing the lowest participation rate (25 percent) (Roberts, 1993). A reason for this difference can be the reduced leisure time available to women given their greater involvement in domestic and child-care tasks compared with men.

FAMILIES AND STRESS

There are many stressors facing South African families: desertion, divorce, child abuse, woman abuse, rape, AIDS, theft, crime in general, and poverty. The focus here is, however, only on the latter. In the late 1990s, 35 percent of South African households (about eighteen million people) were living below the poverty line (MWPD, 1997b). More recently, South Africa's rate of the extent of absolute poverty is 45 percent. This indicates that 3,126,000 households, or more than eighteen million people, are living below the poverty line (set at an income of R353) (UNDP, 2000). Approximately 24 percent of the population lives on the equivalent of US$2 per day (UNDP, 2004). Responses to this state of affairs vary from community-based self-help schemes to reliance on the state for financial assistance. As regards the first, there has been a tradition of rotating credit societies (known locally as *stokvels*) in South Africa.

Stokvels

In 1993, there were 24,000 *stokvels* in the major urban centers with a combined buying power of R80 million (Markinor, cited in SAIRR, 1996). In 1995, between 25 percent and 30 percent of the adult black population belonged to *stokvels* (Japp, cited in SAIRR, 1996). *Stokvels* are voluntary, usually small-scale clubs whose members make a regular financial contribution to a common fund and then receive part of or the entire pool on rotation (Buijs & Atherfold, 1995). In a study of two Eastern Cape townships, an association is shown between membership of *stokvels* and female-headed households. It is particularly women who make use of *stokvels* to stretch their meager resources. "Men, on the other hand, seemed less successful in starting or maintaining savings schemes and this appears to be related to an unwillingness to forego spending available cash." Studies show that, relative to women, men are more likely to spend their income on their personal rather than their families' needs (Buijs & Atherfold, 1995, p. 74).

Apart from encouraging and facilitating savings, *stokvels* provide members with a personal line of credit that can serve as emergency cash or as start-up for entrepreneurial activities (Buijs & Atherfold, 1995). *Stokvels* also perform an important social function in poor South African communities. There are monthly parties at the home of the person whose turn it is to receive "the pool," where contributions are received and fines levied for latecomers and those who speak out of turn, and so on. Moreover, the money thus accumulated is often a means by which members can give expression to the principle of *ubuntu*—the idea that "people are people through people," or the idea of humanity that "recognizes that human relations and human survival are paramount values and that material possessions are seen as the means whereby these values can be achieved" (Wilsworth, cited in Buijs & Atherfold, 1995, p. 75).

Given the popularity of *stokvels,* although the communities studied can objectively be defined as poor, there is little evidence of the fatalism and present-time orientation that Lewis (cited in Buijs & Atherfold, 1995) associated with the culture of poverty. Rather, the popularity of *stokvels* suggests "a determination and resourcefulness" that belie the poverty stricken lives of their members and reflect a "future optimism" (Buijs & Atherfold, 1995, p. 77).

FAMILIES AND AGING

Although the South African population has historically been a young one, there are indications of change. Estimates (for 1995) of the proportion of the population that is sixty-five years and older vary from 4 percent (MWPD, 1997a) to 6 percent (Institute for Futures Research, cited in SAIRR, 1997). More recent estimates place the elderly population at 4 percent, with the probability at birth (2000-2005 cohort) of surviving to age sixty-five at 37 percent for females and 25 percent for males (UNDP, 2004). These are all within the 4 to 7 percent range identified by the United Nations as the mark of a mature population, the intermediary category between a young and an old population structure (Ferreira, Prinsloo, & Gillis, 1992). Given the greater than expected decline in fertility as well as the impact of AIDS, the indications are that the relative size of the "older" age category, as a proportion of the total population, will increase extensively in the future. Estimates suggest the growth of the sixty plus age category in Africa will be 146 percent between the years 2000 and 2025, and that it will double in only seventeen years (Adamchak, 1996). For South Africa the projection is that the percentage of the population over sixty years of age will increase from 7 percent in 1997 to 11 percent in 2025 (Kinsella & Ferreira, 1997). Current life expectancy has been differently estimated (depending upon source), but the UN gives it as 47.7 for the 2000-2005 birth cohort (UNDP, 2004).

The Impact of AIDS

The impact of AIDS will likely be to slow the decline in the total dependency ratio (number of individuals under fifteen and over sixty-four years of age per 100 individuals in the economically active age category). The dependency ratio was estimated at sixty-three in 1997 and was expected to fall to fifty by 2025 (due to the decline in fertility). However, considering AIDS, it is now expected to fall to only fifty-six (Myslik, Freeman, & Slawski, 1997). It will be higher than it would have been due to the loss of life to individuals in the economically active age category. This decline is primarily due to a decrease in the neontic dependency ratio (population under fifteen years of age per 100 of the population aged fifteen to sixty-five years), which is expected to fall from fifty-five to forty-two by 2025. Conversely, the gerontic dependency ratio (population aged sixty-five and above per 100 of the population aged fifteen to sixty-five) is expected to increase from seven in 1997, to thirteen in 2025, and to sixteen in 2045.

Apart from the increase in the relative size of the older age category, there is also likely to be an important increase in the absolute number of elderly South Africans. This is because the population is still growing (albeit slower than before) and due to the maturation process (as the present and much larger under age sixty generation matures). In 1997, there were 2.9 million individuals aged sixty and above and 5.6 million in the fifty years and overage category (Kinsella & Ferreira, 1997, 2004), estimates show 2.2 million aged sixty-five and older, 60 percent being females (World Factbook, 2004). Life expectancy is set to decline substantially due to the impact of AIDS; but this will be because of deaths in the under-thirty age category in which HIV infections are most prevalent (Myslik et al., 1997). The upshot of all of this is that a great deal of pressure will be placed on individuals, families, communities, and the State to provide for the material, social, medical, and other needs of the elderly.

Budgeting for the Elderly

While the budget of the MWPD is small relative to some other Ministries (10 percent of the national and provincial budget and 3 percent of GDP in 1997-1998 compared with 21 percent and 7 percent, respectively in the case of education), it has increased significantly since the beginning of the 1990s (MWPD, 1997b; SAIRR, 1997). The present ministry inherited a system heavily biased in favor of caring for the aged. Indeed, the latter accounted for 61 percent of the total welfare budget that includes social pensions and residential care, in the period 1995-1966 (MWPD, 1997b). Although racial parity in terms of pension payouts had been achieved before 1994 (MWPD, 1997b; Oakley, 1998), there were (and are) substantial differences in terms of the type of assistance received by the elderly of different communities.

For white South Africans, most expenditure was allocated to institutional care (about 7 percent of the total welfare budget) (MWPD, 1997b). In the late 1980s, between 8 and 11 percent of elderly whites were living in homes for the aged (Lawton, cited in Ferreira, Gillis, & Møller, 1989). This compared with 5 percent, 0.9 percent, and 0.6 percent in the case of "Coloreds," Asians, and blacks. The proportion of white elderly in institutional care is also high by the standards of developed societies. Corresponding figures for most European and North American societies are between three and 5 percent, with the Netherlands having the highest rate at 10 percent (Schrage-Dijkstra, 1994).

Relative to other middle-income countries and notwithstanding maladministration and corruption, the social security component of the welfare system is well-developed (MWPD, 1997b; Sagner, 1997; van der Berg, 1998). It accounts for 88 percent of the welfare budget and consists of both a private/occupational retirement scheme and a statutory means-tested pension for the elderly (MWPD, 1997b). The former covers 73 percent of the formally employed and, given the high rate of unemployment, 40 percent of the total labor force (van der Berg, 1998). "Coverage rates" for the state pension are even higher and are near universal with 90 percent of blacks, 85 percent of "Colored," 62 percent of Indians, and 20 percent of whites in the appropriate age category (age sixty for women and sixty-five for men) receiving a state grant. The figure for the total population in the relevant age category is 75-80 percent (van der Berg, 1998).

Pensions are a major source of assistance to poor families (Ardington & Lund, 1995; MWPD, 1997b; Møller & Sotshongaye, 1996; van der Berg, 1998). The MWPD reported that in 1993, 7.7 million South Africans (roughly 20 percent) lived in households receiving a state pension and that each pensioner supported five other individuals (MWPD, 1997b). "Pensioners have become comparatively wealthy members of poor communities making the presence of a pensioner a critical factor in many households' well-being" (Donaldson, quoted in van der Berg, 1998, p. 7). Moreover:

> In rural communities, pension income circulates widely and is crucial in combating poverty and reducing material insecurity. It is probably the most effective social programme in targeting and reaching economically-vulnerable groups. . . . Higher black pension levels to achieve parity have reduced rural poverty substantially. (van der Berg, 1998, p. 7)

Given the aging of the population as well as budget constraints, the MWPD has embarked on a restructuring process. This involves two major decisions concerning the elderly: first to cut back on financial support for those in institutional care; second, to improve private company-based retirement funding. In regard to the first, the white paper on welfare described the existing emphasis on institutional care for elderly whites as "unrealistic" and, at between R11,000 and R22,000 per person per annum, as "unaffordable" (MWPD, 1997b, chapter 8, p. 15). Furthermore it regards the emphasis on government's responsibility for the care of the aged as "inappropriate," claiming "the family is the core support system for the elderly" (chapter 8, p. 16). However, apart from the family being "the baseline of (the new) age management programme," the latter will also be community-based with existing homes for the elderly having "the responsibility to provide essential outreach services in the community" (chapter 8, p. 17) and existing specialized welfare centers providing "one-stop or multi-purpose generic services" (chapter 6, p. 4).

This new policy direction resulted in a R50 million cut in subsidies in 1997 that affected all 800 old age homes previously subsidized by the government. The minister indicated that this was to free resources that will be redirected to social security for families and children, especially those affected by AIDS. In the future, homes for the elderly will cater only for those in need of twenty-four hour frail care and will be limited in terms of capacity to 2 percent of those aged sixty-five years and above. In 1996, this meant the exclusion of some 1.85 million elderly from frail care (SAIRR, 1997; also see Oakley, 1998, for a study of the impact of this new policy on a "Colored" community in the Northern Cape).

The white paper declared that state grants to the elderly would continue to be paid to those who qualify. It also indicated that the government will encourage all people in formal employment to belong to a compulsory retirement scheme, educational programs will be put in place to promote retirement planning, and new schemes will be devised for those in informal employment (SAIRR, 1997).

OTHER FAMILY SITUATIONS

The great diversity of family structures in South African society is illustrated in the first part of this chapter. The family patterns associated with black urban dwellers most closely resembles the statistical norm for the urban part of the society as a whole. As such, the family patterns existing within other communities (whites in particular and to a lesser extent Asian/Indian and "Colored" South Africans) can be seen as deviations from this norm. More particularly, whereas black South Africans are following a family pattern centered on extended family households, this is less true of the "Colored" and Asian communities and not at all true of the white community. In the case of the white community, it is the conventional "Western" family pattern of nuclear family households that predominate. More and better research can help illuminate the causes and consequences of these differences.

CONCLUDING COMMENTS

Within the confines of this chapter, it is not possible to do justice to the complexity and changing nature of family life in South African society. Many important issues are only touched upon or are neglected completely: the impact of migrancy on family life; the movement of children among households; child and woman abuse; the Domestic Violence Act (1998); developments around the legal position of fathers of extramarital children, among others.

Also omitted is any serious treatment of theoretical questions around the factors responsible for the present configuration of family patterns or any future trends that might be expected. These will have to await further research and analysis.

NOTES

1. Green papers refer to documents issued by various government departments for public discussion while white papers are for discussion in parliament.

2. The term "Colored" is placed in quotation marks because it is more controversial than the others are and is less often a self-applied label.

3. This is another area of controversy because there are disputes about what constitutes headship (the person who is the oldest? Earns the most money? Owns the house? Has greatest decision-making power, etc.?) Simkins (1986) quoted figures for the proportion of all households that were female-headed, ranging from 18 percent in metropolitan areas to 59 percent in rural areas for 1980. Buijs and Atherfold (1995) indicated that 29 percent of households on the reef (Witwatersrand) were female-headed in 1985.

Chapter 9

Family Diversity in Kenya

Lucy W. Ngige
Alice N. Ondigi
Stephan M. Wilson

Kenya is the cradle of humankind (Leeder, 2004). In accordance with a long history and opportunities for biological and cultural evolution, family patterns in Kenya are characterized by great diversity of customs surrounding family formation and structure across distinct ethno-linguistic groups. The major contemporary groups include Embu, Kalenjin, Kamba, Kikuyu, Kisii, Luhyia, Luo, Meru, and Mijikenda. Minority groups include nonindigenous immigrants from Europe, Asia, the Middle East, and the rest of the world (Republic of Kenya [Kenya], 2002c; Wilson, Ngige, & Trollinger, 2003). Kenya became independent from the British Government in 1963, but has maintained close ties with her former colonizer. Western influence has had a great impact on family patterns, and in particular the introduction of colonial and postcolonial secular laws that regulate marriage and family life, alongside African customary laws.

Families in Kenyan Context

Various forces have shaped family diversity in Kenya including geographic variability; demographic trends; how social and genetic relations are understood; and recent and historic realities of colonization, modernization, urbanization, and economics. These forces have influenced the ways family form and functions have evolved to meet the changing demands on peoples' lives. Here the focus is on geography and economy, population dynamics, and family context. Diversity of family patterns in Kenya is then highlighted, indicating how important factors relate to common variations in family patterns.

The Republic of Kenya straddles the equator on the eastern coast of Africa. It covers an area of 582,000 square kilometers (an area a little larger than France or twice the size of the U.S. state of Nevada). Kenya has eight provinces and seventy-five administrative districts. The majority (82 percent) of the over thirty million population lives in rural areas. Most of the country is arid or semiarid land that does not support human settlement; about 8 percent of the land is arable. About 80 percent of the people live on 20 percent of the land. Agriculture is the mainstay of Kenya's economy, accounting for 26 percent of GDP and manufacturing for 14 percent. Tea, coffee, tourism, and horticulture are the main foreign exchange earners (Kenya, 2002a, 2002b). The annual per capital income is US$340 and the official unemployment rate is 35 percent (Kenya, 2002i).

Kenya ranks 154th of the 177 UN rated nations with a Human Development Index value of .474 (United Nations Development Programme [UNDP], 2005). This value has dropped from a high of 0.540 in 1990 as has Kenya's rank from medium to low human development category. The infant mortality rate (per 1,000 live births) in 2003 was 79, down from 96. The rate was 95.8 for the poorest 20 percent of the population and 40.2 for the richest 20 percent. The under-five mortality rate was 156 in 1970 and 123 in 2003. Maternal mortality reported for the 1985-2003 period was 590 (per 100,000 live births), but is perhaps 1,000 when adjusted for underreporting. Currently about 40 percent of the population does not have sustainable access to improved water sources, compared with around 55 percent in 1990. Around 20 percent of children under age five are underweight. The proportion of the population undernourished declined from forty-four in 1990-1992, to thirty-three in 2000-2003 (UNDP, 2004, 2005).

The probability of surviving to age sixty-five among those born between 2000 and 2005 is 32 percent for females and 35 percent for males. Life expectancy is just over age forty-seven; half the population is below fifteen years of age (UNDP, 2004, 2005). Since the beginning of the epidemic in 1984, 2.2 million Kenyans have been infected and 1.5 million have developed AIDS. One impact of AIDS in Kenya is a decline in life expectancy. Demographers estimate that without AIDS, the life expectancy at birth would be sixty-five years. However, due to the large number of AIDS deaths, the life expectancy has declined to forty-nine years for females and forty-two years for males (Kenya, 2002f). AIDS has also resulted in higher infant mortality rates, lower population and growth rates, and changes in the distribution of population by age and sex than would otherwise be expected. However, the population of Kenya will continue to increase, though at a lower rate, such that it is expected to reach thirty-six million by 2010 (Kenya, 2002f).

Cultural background is extremely important in understanding families in Kenya. Family is the center of community life. Children are highly valued in both traditional and contemporary families. Women's role in procreation is venerated and valued. Traditionally, the emphasis was on large family size, with an average of eight children. A polygynous husband with a large family was held in high esteem by his community. There was also considerable economic advantage in having many wives and children. However, recent population pressure on the land and increasing costs of raising children has led to smaller families (Kenya, 2002d).

Traditional families are characterized by extended patterns where relatives across several generations live in close proximity. A patriarchal kinship system is dominant, where the eldest male is the head of the extended household. Polygyny is common, still accounting for 16 percent of married Kenyans. With urbanization, this trend is shifting to nuclear families with an average of four children (Kenya, 2002d). Connectedness across the past, present, and future is recognized as a hallmark of what it means to be family. A shared ancestral tie to current and future generations through family lineage is the foundation of family life in most Kenyan subcultures. Familism is highly regarded in traditional and contemporary families (Wilson & Ngige, 2005).

Diversity in Family Patterns

Kenya is a diverse country with varied household structures, kinship systems, and religions, all of which influence and are expressed through family life. For each family pattern, differences exist based on many salient factors. There are forty-three different ethno-linguistic groups in Kenya, and each has its own unique cultural variations of marriage and family patterns (Kenya, 2002b). Notable differences exist between rural and urban families in structure and makeup of household residents. For example, a new family pattern has emerged that can be described as a quasi-extended family composed of a basic nuclear family with selected live-in dependent relatives.

Statutory law often is divergent from African customary law (e.g., definition of marriage as monogamous in contrast to polygamous customary marriages, legitimacy of children based on parents' marital status in contrast to the traditional definition of legitimacy based on the status of bridewealth payment by the husband/father to the wife/mother of the child in question). In addition, the law of inheritance and succession is in conflict with the existing customary practice. For example, among the majority of Kenyan ethnic groups, female children, regardless of age and marital status, do not inherit property from their parents (family-of-origin) or their parents-in-law (family-of-procreation).

Religious affiliations include Christian (70 percent), Islam (6 percent), Hindu (1 percent), and African indigenous religions (23 percent) (Wilson et al., 2003). Diverse expectations for marriage and family life exist across religious group and between religious and secular laws of marriage and divorce. For instance, Christian and Hindu teachings about marriage and divorce recognize monogamous marriages, but not African customary marriages that are potentially polygynous. Yet, these polygynous relationships are legally recognized in Kenya. Islamic marriages are also potentially polygynous, where a man is permitted to marry up to four wives provided he is able to sustain multiple wives and their children. Therefore, both monogamy and polygamy coexist in various Kenyan religious communities' marriages (Kenya, 2002b).

Remarkable differences exist by age group. Older generations are more likely to:

1. perpetuate African customary marriages;
2. promote and protect institutions of the exchange of bridewealth;
3. emphasize familism at the expense of individualism in mate selection;
4. have preference for parent-arranged marriages to self-choice, love marriage;
5. approve of multiple wives and large families;
6. follow the practice of widow inheritance;
7. live in an extended family setting especially in rural areas.

Supporting statistics from the 1999 census indicate that 25 percent of older women were in polygynous marriages compared with 10 percent of younger women (Kenya, 2002e). The converse is true of modern, young, educated, and Westernized couples who prefer

1. self-choice, love marriage to a parent-arranged marriage;
2. a formal marriage ceremony over traditional or customary marriage;
3. monogamy over polygyny;
4. individualism over familism;
5. a small family size to a large family;
6. a nuclear family pattern or quasi-extended family setting over the traditional extended family structure;
7. an urban residence over a rural residence.

The majority of educated, medium, and high socioeconomic Kenyans embrace Western culture, either wholly or partly, with lower fidelity to their ethnic-cultural practices in marriage and family life than was true in previous generations. On the other hand, illiterate (30 percent) and poor Kenyans, about 60 percent of the population, are likely to embrace African customary practices governing marriage and family life. Between these two positions are those whose orientation can be described as the blended African-Western culture. This group is in transition, trying to mesh African and Western culture in regard to marriage and family life. Family divergence therefore exists by sociocultural orientation—whether wholly Western, wholly African, or a blend of African-Western culture with various degrees of affinity to both world views in marriage and family life (Wilson & Ngige, 2005).

Variation in Family Structure

The nuclear family composed of a monogamous couple and their children account for 58 percent, while one parent and his or her children constitute 26 percent of Kenyan families (Kenya, 2003). The nuclear family pattern is common among contemporary educated and young Kenyans, as well as among Hindu, European, and American immigrants and is more typical than the extended family. The classical polygynous extended family consisting of one man, multiple wives, and children (16 percent) is commonly found among indigenous older Kenyans (Kenya, 2003).

The modified extended-nuclear family is characterized by several nuclear families whose members are related by blood, marriage, or adoption living in the same homestead or in close proximity to one another. This family pattern is found in predominantly patriarchal clans among indigenous Kenyans living in rural areas, as well as among Asian families living in urban areas.

The modified nuclear-extended family is a blend of quasi-nuclear families with live-in relatives, or nonrelatives who depend entirely on the nuclear family. In this case, the nonrelatives or fictive kin are considered family members. This pattern cuts across all ethnic groups and is commonly found among educated, well-to-do families living in urban areas, which often face expectations that require them to foster needy relatives.

COUPLE FORMATION AND MARITAL DYNAMICS

There is a diversity of ways to initiate marriages in Kenya, but the prescribed ways are unique and vary among communities and across subcultures. The ways in which couples are matched permeate every aspect of an individual's life and experiences throughout his or her life course (Wilson & Ngige, 2005). Marriage is an ancient African institution and has been subjected to many changes in customs and practices over time. It should be noted that in general, culturally sanctioned (collectivist) practices relate to mate selection, marriage, parenting, and relations with other family members. Ideas about obligations and privileges take precedence over individualistic rights and preferences (Ngige, 1993; Schafer, 1997). This is practically universal among traditional Kenyan communities and the minority Asian immigrant families.

Finding Spouses

For modern educated and Westernized youth, romantic love is a prerequisite to companionship marriage regardless of the type or level of parent influence (Wilson et al., 2003). In traditional Kenyan communities, mate selection was predominantly a parental activity (i.e., parents made choices for their children's marriages). As marriage was a major transition and an alliance between two families, it was important and not left to young adult children to decide (Wilson & Ngige, 2005). Marrying members of the same clan or relatives is highly prohibited among most communities, including the Embu, Kamba, Kikuyu, Kisii, and Meru of Kenya (Abere, 2004, Personal communication; Gathii, 2001; Wilson et al., 2003). Kenyan families engaged in parent-arranged marriages based on similar socioeconomic status, personal character, and family background rather than mutual attraction and love (Wilson et al., 2003). In many traditional communities, a daughter was given in marriage as compensation for a debt among the Kikuyu (Kibathi, 2003, Personal communication), as a substitute for a barren wife among the Luo (Ochola, 2003, Personal communication), or to reduce the stigma of an aged single daughter (spinster) among the Kisii (Ondigi, 2004, Personal communication). Parental mate selection is still common among the Maasai, as demonstrated in child betrothal practices (Sharman, 1979; Siamanda, 2004, Personal communication).

In most communities today, cases of forced marriages occur when a girl becomes pregnant and the lover is reluctant to marry her. The girl's father can demand bridewealth from the offending party's family and force the girl to marry the lover to "cover the disgrace" (Beckwith & Saitoti, 1980; Hollis, 1979; Ruto, 2004, Personal communication). The practice of girl-child marriage is another form of parent-arranged marriage where the girl's consent is taken for granted. Among the Maasai, even today, prepubertal girls are sometimes married off without their consent, to older men who may be their father's or even grandfather's age-mates (Ngasike, 2004, Personal communication; Pulei, 2004, Personal communication).

Divergence in Couples Formation

Monogamous couples coexist with polygynous spouses in Kenya across generations, religious affiliations, socioeconomic classes, and ethnic communities. These include the classical polygyny, where one man has multiple wives; and variations such as sororal polygyny, where two sisters are married to one man. Fraternal polyandry is a form of closeted polyandry often practiced by sterile males, whereby a wife is permitted conjugal rights with her brother-in-law or close male relatives for the purposes of perpetuating the sterile male's line in a discreet manner. Her husband remains the "legally recognized father" of her children for the purposes of legitimacy, inheritance, and succession in the event of his death. Bigamy (multiple wives without the benefit of social or legal recognition), serial monogamy, and cohabitation are also practiced.

Gynaegamy is a marriage contract between two females and is distinct from lesbian couples. There are several reasons for practicing this form of marriage. One is childlessness, where a barren woman, who is desperate and has suffered the turmoil and humiliation resultant from cultural oppression and discrimination for not having children, can opt for gynaegamy as an alternative to conventional marriage. Having a sterile husband is a second reason. This involves a woman whose husband was unable to give her children and now she is past childbearing age, yet she desires to raise children who would be recognized as her own. Another reason centers on inheritance and succession. A childless woman is vulnerable to insecurity and disinheritance in old age if she has no children of her own, and in particular if she has no sons through whom she would inherit her husband's property. A fourth reason is preference for male children. In some communities a widow who has borne girls only may not inherit property from her deceased husband, and therefore desires to raise sons of her own through a secondary marriage. Inheritance chasers are an additional reason. A divorced woman with many children can approach a rich widow to maintain her and her children through gynaegamy.

Gynaegamy is often initiated by a middle-aged woman (major woman). The partner is usually a younger woman (minor woman) who has the characteristics such as reproductive capacity and physical energy the major woman is seeking in a partner. According to the Kisii traditions, the major woman pays bridewealth to the family of the minor woman and the marriage is settled and customarily recognized like all forms of traditional marriages (Abaya, 2004, Personal communication; Abere, 2004, Personal communication; Nyaundi, 2004, Personal communication; Ondigi, 2004, Personal communication). The major woman assumes the responsibilities of a "husband and father," adopts the minor woman's children, and provides for her and her children. If the minor woman has no children, the major woman arranges with a close relative for a "sperm donor" so the minor women can sire children for her. No stigma is attached to this form of marriage; on the contrary, it confers special status to the major woman as a community elder among male elders. This is a common practice among many communities in Kenya, where a childless senior wife (and older in age) contracts a gynaegamous marriage in order to redeem her status of womanhood, empower her to own and inherit her deceased husband's property, and to gain respect from both men and women in her community.

Marital Relationships

Most communities in Kenya prepare women for marriage soon after initiation or the ceremony to mark the rite of passage from childhood to adulthood. It is the responsibility of their mothers-in-law and elderly women of the community to train and teach new brides how to care for their husbands and prepare for pregnancy, childbearing, and child rearing. Likewise, their fathers and community elders train the grooms separately. Sex education and training is disseminated during this period (Abaya, 2004, Personal communication). In traditional communities, information on sexual taboos, such as postpartum sexual abstinence among breastfeeding mothers for periods ranging from four to five years was given during this period of preparation for marriage (Wakomu, 1989, Personal communication). In contemporary society, these sexual taboos have been discarded due to education and changing marital patterns from polygynous to monogamous marriages. Submission and loyalty was expected from wives to their husbands but not vice versa. In some cultures, the first wife was not consulted when her husband married subsequent wives. In others, her consent was a prerequisite to subsequent marital contracts. Nowadays women are striving for equality in marital relationships and prefer monogamous marriages rather than polygynous marriages. When family conflicts arise, the extended family plays a mediating role in resolving such problems (Abere, 2004, Personal communication; Nyaundi, 2004, Personal communication; Wilson et al., 2003).

Sexual Activity in Marriage

In traditional communities, the goal of sexual activity in marriage was procreation. When this was not achieved due to sterility or incompatibility, other provisions were made for the couple to have children. These included a secondary marriage in the form of classical polygyny, sororal polygyny, fraternal polyandry, gynaegamy, bigamy, or cohabitation. Abstinence was practiced as a form of natural child spacing and also as a postpartum cultural norm. Mothers of newborns abstained from sexual activity for periods ranging up to five years. Among the Kikuyu, abstinence was observed from the time of delivery until the child was culturally weaned and named, during a ceremony known as the second birth that marked the rite of passage from infancy, or the first birth, to childhood or the second birth (Ngige, 2004).

Among most traditional communities, if a bride was a virgin, she was highly respected and her mother was awarded a special gift for raising her daughter well (Nyaundi, 2004, Personal communication; Ondigi, 2004, Personal communication). On the contrary, among the Kamba and Maasai a husband expected his bride to have been sexually active in her adolescence and well experienced in meeting her conjugal role as a wife. He did not necessarily expect her initiation to sexual intercourse to be with him upon marriage (Wilson & Ngige, 2005).

Marriage has been regarded as the socially acceptable and legitimate institution for childbearing, child rearing, and perpetuation of family lineage (Wilson & Ngige, 2005; Wilson et al., 2003). A childless couple was not regarded as complete until they bore children of their own or adopted children in a culturally prescribed manner. Diverse alternatives within ethnic groups were available to a childless couple depending on whether it was the wife or husband who was sterile. Among Bantus these included hut polygyny, where wives were nonrelatives, and sororal polygyny where a barren wife approached her younger sister to be a cowife and bear children for her. Among Nilotes such as the Luo, fraternal polyandry (i.e., where a sterile man invited his brother to be a sperm donor and raise offspring for him without other marital obligations) and levirate marriages (i.e., whereby a widow was inherited by her brother-in-law for the purposes of raising children for his dead kin) were common practices (Wilson & Ngige, 2005). While these patterns still exist today in rural and traditional communities, they are not as prevalent in urban and contemporary society (Ochola, 2003, Personal communication).

Dissolution of Marriage

Marriage dissolution was a hard decision among traditional Kenyan communities, especially if children were involved. A wife could be divorced if caught in adultery, practiced sorcery or witchcraft, or if she threatened her husband's life. These were considered in the community as unforgivable crimes against the marriage (Wilson & Ngige, 2005). A wife could separate from her husband if abused by him or in-laws. The wife had alternatives that included running away to her family-of-origin, sending for her parents to come and rescue her, or eloping with her lover if she had been caught in adultery. If her husband was the guilty party and he was still committed to her in marriage, it was his obligation to initiate reconciliation and pay a fine to the elders as a symbol of his repentance and pledge for good conduct as a husband (Gitahi, 2002; Wakomu, 1989, Personal communication). If the woman was the source of the marital problem, her husband would send her back to her parents for further training on how to behave as a wife and all that pertains to wifely duties. Marital conflicts and the subsequent temporal separation usually occurred during the early phase of marital adjustment. However, community elders usually settled serious marital problems (Wilson & Ngige, 2005).

Marital dissolution was discouraged as it was costly and had negative consequences for the larger family. Where unavoidable, the guilty party was considered a failure. A man could lose legitimacy rights over his children and the bridewealth was not recoverable. A woman could lose all properties acquired during the marriage and custody of children could be awarded to her husband. Divorced wives usually ended up raising children single-handedly, living single lives thereafter, or settling for a life as a subsequent wife in a polygynous marriage (Sankan, 1995). Today, divorce, distribution of property, and child custody is determined by a court of law.

FAMILIES AND CHILDREN

The family is the center of Kenyan life and children are regarded as economic assets. A woman with more sons gains supremacy over others and is highly respected in her community (Nyaundi, 2004, Personal communication). Common functions of the family include childbearing and child rearing; nurturant socialization where children learn the norms and values of their society; division of labor and economic cooperation for the common good of the family; and regulation of sexual behavior in and outside of marriage (Leeder, 2004).

Parents are primarily responsible for nurturing their children. However, in an extended family system, there is communal responsibility for socializing the young in that all adults are responsible for the upbringing of all children regardless of biological ties. The young learn appropriate gender roles from men and women (Ominde, 1987; Snell, 1986). Discipline is a collective responsibility, where each senior person guides, counsels, and metes out punishment to any child when justified. These understandings of how the community is responsible for nurture and discipline are still intact though practices are changing as urbanization, distance from extended family, and alternative models of parenting compete with traditions.

Mothers have the primary duty of disciplining their children and, in particular, their daughters. Fathers take the chief responsibility for sons' discipline after their initiation rites into adulthood. During rites of passage from one developmental stage to another, children are prepared to undertake their normative developmental roles (Sankan, 1995). During the initiation into adulthood stage, youth are prepared for marriage and family life in special initiation schools (Kenyatta, 1953; LeVine et al., 1994).

Shift from Large to Small Family Size

The average size of a Kenyan household decreased from 5.0 persons in 1989 to 4.4 persons in 1998. Urban households were, on average, smaller with 3.3 persons compared with rural households with 4.6 persons (Kenya, 2001a). Several factors contribute to this shift such as the increasing age at first marriage, the declining fertility rate, and increased use of modern contraceptives. It is estimated that for the 1995-2002 period, the contraceptive prevalence rate among married women was 39 percent (UNDP, 2004).

According to the Kenya Demographic and Health Survey (Kenya, 1999), fertility preferences continue to change from the desire for large to small family size, with 53 percent of women and 46 percent of men indicating they want no more children. Other women (25 percent) and men (27 percent) indicated desire for delaying birth for two years or longer. If all unwanted births were avoided, the fertility rate would fall from 4.7 to 3.5 children per woman (Kenya, 1999).

The rate of fertility in Kenya has continued to decline from 8.1 children per woman in 1978, to 6.7 in 1989, to 4.7 in the 1990s, to 4.0 today. In most communities in Kenya, rural women expect to have two more children than do urban women. Women with no formal education had an average of 5.8 children compared with 3.5 children for women with secondary education (Kenya, 1999; UNDP, 2004).

Abortion

In Kenya, abortion is illegal; the only exception is when a woman's life is in danger (Kenyaweb, 2003). Thousands of women each year undergo illegal and often harmful procedures to end unwanted pregnancies. Some women attempt to induce abortion with sharp objects or toxic drugs. Others turn to traditional healers, who employ herbs or, sometimes, dangerous substances. Some seek assistance from medical personnel, who provide clandestine abortions though they lack professional skills and equipment. A Ministry of Health report (Kenyaweb, 2003) argues that more than one-third of maternal deaths are from unsafe abortions and a large number of women who arrive in hospital emergency rooms with complications from spontaneous and induced abortion burden understaffed, undersupplied, and overcrowded facilities. Policymakers and health care workers are seeking to reduce this health problem with policies that preserve the reproductive rights of women.

One way to aid Kenyan women, and struggling hospital staff, is through postabortion care, a service linking emergency treatment of abortion complications with family planning counseling and comprehensive reproductive health care (Kenya, 2003; Kenyaweb, 2003). The other strategy is to legalize abortion, a position currently being debated in Kenya.

FAMILIES AND GENDER

Gender, a set of characteristics, roles, and behavior patterns, distinguish women from men socially and culturally. Gender is a social and culture-specific construct that defines the ways in which women and men interact. The concept refers not only to the roles and characteristics of women and men but also to the power relations between them. In most societies women have limited access to income, land, credit, and education, and have limited control over these resources (Loutfi, 2001). This certainly is true within modern Kenya.

Of the population working for pay in 1999, 71 percent were males and 29 percent were females; 58 percent of women compared with 42 percent of men were economically inactive. The implication is that wage employment is still dominated by men both in urban and rural areas and that though there have been efforts to improve gender equity, women still occupy a disadvantaged position socially, economically, and politically inside and outside their families (Kenya, 2002k).

The 1999 population census reported 58 percent of the population had completed primary school, 17 percent had attained a secondary education, and less than 1 percent had completed a tertiary or university level of education. School enrollment is comparable up to about age fourteen. From age fifteen upward, the female dropout rate is higher than the male dropout rate (Kenya, 2002h). When income is limited and school fees are high, many families choose to educate sons rather than daughters. About 70 percent of illiterate persons in Kenya are female. The Kenyan Education Analytical Report indicated that only 26 percent of adult women knew how to read and write. The report further suggested that families have many reasons for not sending girls to school, such as the need to assist with child care, food preparation, and other household production activities (Kenya, 2002i). Girls drop out of school in search of employment to supplement family income or to assist in care giving for younger siblings, elderly, and ailing family members. In other cases, girls are given off in marriage at an early age to fetch bridewealth for their families (Wilson & Ngige, 2005; Wilson et al., 2003).

Studies in Kenya show that underinvestment in women's education limits agricultural productivity, while significant gains result from raising women's physical and human capital (KENGO, 1994). When women and men shared the same educational characteristics and input levels, yields increased by 22 percent for food-crop farmers. Women's primary schooling alone raised yields by 24 percent for maize farmers. Investing in women generates significant benefits for society in the form of lower child mortality, higher educational attainment, better nutritional status, and slower population growth rates (Kenya, 2002d).

Investing in women ensures quality and sustainability of economic growth for the nation (Loutfi, 2001).

Kenyan women make up 75 percent of the agricultural workforce in rural areas. The minority, who are educated, are engaged in service professions such as nursing and teaching. The less educated are involved in small businesses in the informal sector or work as *ayas* (housemaids) for affluent families in urban areas (Ondigi, 2003). According to the National Development Plan, the average monthly income of women is about two-thirds that of men and women hold only about 5 percent of land title deeds (Kenya, 2001b). Yet, women still perform the bulk of household work, and most men do not allocate similar amounts of time to parenting and household production (Ngige, 1995).

Traditionally, males and females, from early childhood, were trained and expected to do different things. Men had been responsible for tending cattle, hunting wild game, and protecting the family from external insecurity. Middle-aged and older men socialized younger men for their roles in society. Men acquired property and had the sole right to distribute it or dispose of when need arose. Women were socialized to take care of household and domestic responsibilities such as child rearing; agricultural production; searching for, collecting, and carrying *kuni* (i.e., firewood); fetching water; food preparation and preservation; and house care (Ngige, 1993; Schafer, 1997; Wilson & Ngige, 2005).

Division of labor is gender derived and women have a triple workload: in the home, earning an income, and participating in community work. Men normally do outdoor work including clearing places for farming, plowing, fencing, cutting trees, or doing businesses. Women are engaged in household chores as well as taking care of children and aging parents. Some have noted that this division of labor has reduced the self-esteem of women, as many perceive themselves as little more than "slaves" in the extended family (Ngige, 1995; Ondigi, 2003).

Women, shouldering the bulk of responsibilities for farm labor and care of the young and the elderly, are often overburdened and have little time to organize resources for any reasonable gain. Women bear and rear children, they are the main users of contraceptives, and therefore the main receptors of family planning programs. They are able to determine both the size and quality of the future stock of human resources in Kenya. Along with their role as homemakers, they are the primary managers and users of a variety of natural resources, especially energy and water. They are responsible for most of Kenya's food crop production and a variety of other farming activities, yet their contribution to national development is not recognized (KENGO, 1994).

Paradoxically, despite the moral thinking that women deserve respect as human beings, violence against women is a serious and more common problem than many in contemporary Kenya would like to believe. Traditional culture permits a man to discipline his wife by physical means, which can translate to spouse abuse and assault in the face of the secular law. Traditionally, a woman could not own property and/or transact any property-related business on her husband' behalf without his consent. Women continue to face both legal and social discrimination in family laws such as marriage, divorce, child custody, inheritance, and succession. Women experience a range of discriminatory practices, limiting their political, socioeconomic, and cultural rights that relegate women to second-class citizenship. In 1997, a Kenyan constitutional amendment introduced specific prohibition of discrimination based on gender. However the practice falls short of legislation to implement international conventions on women's rights as human rights (Ngige, Mburugu, & Nyamu, 2004).

Many argue that the government of Kenya can no longer afford to ignore the role of women in socioeconomic and political development, but ought to invest in women's education, health, and political rights. By directing public resources toward policies and projects that reduce gender inequality, policymakers would not only promote equality but also lay the groundwork for slower population growth, greater labor productivity, higher rates of human capital formation, and stronger economic growth. Ultimately, gender equality will strengthen the family and the capacity of its members to make decisions that benefit themselves, their children and grandchildren, and the broader society.

FAMILIES AND STRESS

As in any society, there are many unique as well as more common stressors for families. Two issues that create stress for many families in Kenya are discussed: HIV/AIDS and poverty.

Families and HIV/AIDS

About 2.2 million Kenyans have been infected with HIV/AIDS; 75 percent of AIDS cases occur in adults between the ages of twenty and forty-five with male and female cases being about equal. The peak ages for AIDS cases are between twenty and forty-five for females and thirty and thirty-four for males. Women in the age groups fifteen to nineteen and twenty to twenty-four years are more than twice as likely to be infected as males in the same age groups. About 10 percent of reported AIDS cases occur in children under five years of age. Most of these cases are due to mother-to-child transmission (National AIDS Control Council, 2001).

The socioeconomic impacts of HIV/AIDS on the family and society are far-reaching as people continue to be infected and die in enormous numbers. One of the worst impacts of AIDS deaths is the increasing number of AIDS orphans. All too often these children lack proper care, provision of basic needs, and above all nurturing socialization by their immediate families.

AIDS will also have a significant impact on population size. AIDS deaths reduce the number of people in the reproductive age group who subsequently produce fewer births. AIDS has impacted the health services sector by increasing the number of people seeking related health services thereby increasing the cost of health care to every country in sub-Saharan Africa. AIDS impoverishes families by decreasing household labor and income and by increasing medical and funeral expenses. The family loses its potential for future income when children drop out of school to take care of their ailing parents and to supplement family incomes. Child labor increases when children as young as ten become full-time caregivers and/or child laborers in place of their sick or dying parents (Kenyaweb, 2003).

Assuming that the decline in fertility is maintained, it is anticipated that fertility will fall to 3.6 births per woman by 2010 and 3.2 by 2020. Given the predetermined impact of HIV/AIDS and its future course, life expectancy at birth will continue to drop from fifty in the late 1990s to forty-six years by 2005, and could continue to fall for the rest of the decade. Given the vigorous efforts directed toward combating the HIV/AIDS pandemic, the prevalence rate is expected to attain a constant level of 13 percent within the next ten years and, thereafter, the rate is expected to decrease to 8 percent by 2020. Taking into account the interplay of fertility, mortality, migration, and the effect of the HIV/AIDS pandemic, the total population of Kenya is expected to increase but more slowly than in the last two decades (Kenya, 2002g).

HIV/AIDS is fundamentally challenging traditional patterns of how families take care of their vulnerable members. Adults with AIDS feel stigmatized or fear for the fate of their children once they are dead because other adult family members are already troubled by a large number of extended family AIDS orphans who collectively exceed the ability to adequately provide for them. AIDS is greatly increasing the population of children who need to be cared for outside traditional extended family settings. AIDS is changing how families care for severely ill or dying family members. The epidemic has challenged Kenyans to establish alternative mechanisms of providing care for infected family members and their closest kin and is challenging the traditional balance of responsibilities and obligations between families and the wider society. Strategic solutions include developing community support mechanisms such as religious-sponsored orphanages; community-based early childhood care and development centers; and children's homes managed by nongovernmental organizations and private individuals. These homes are open to both infected and affected orphans (Akunga, 2004; Kiminyo & Ngige, 2000).

In 2000, there were an estimated 900,000 Kenyan HIV/AIDS orphans (UNICEF, 2001). The same study projected an increase to 1.5 million by 2005. With the HIV/AIDS pandemic and the increased number of AIDS orphans, child care has shifted from the extended family to include institutional residential care (i.e., orphanages). A study by UNICEF in 14 districts found over 80,000 children in institutional care in 1997 (UNICEF, 1998). By 2001, the number had risen to 350,000 children enrolled in 228 institutions. As the burden of orphans continues to rise, institutional resources are overstretched to sustain care at an acceptable standard.

Neither the efforts by extended family to absorb the burden of care for AIDS orphans or the creation of new or expansion of already existing institutions are enough to meet the rising needs. Today, elderly grandmothers and siblings as young as ten are coping with family demands and providing care to the majority of orphans in Kenya

(UNICEF, 2001). The Government of Kenya declared HIV/AIDS a national disaster in 1999, and established a National Aids Control Council to coordinate all matters related to the epidemic. These include prevention and advocacy, treatment, continuum of care and support, mitigation of socioeconomic impacts, monitoring, evaluation and research, and management and coordination of HIV/AIDS programs. The government has set up an HIV/AIDS Support Committee in every constituency to supplement resources for caregiving by extended families (National AIDS Control Council, 2000).

Families and Poverty

Poverty is the inability of an individual or household to afford basic necessities such as food, clothing, housing, health, and education for children (Kenya, 2000). Poverty is categorized into three forms: food, overall, and hardcore poverty. Food poverty refers to those whose expenditure on food is insufficient to meet the Food and Agricultural Organization/World Health Organization (FAO/WHO) recommended daily allowance of 2,250 calories per adult. Overall poverty refers to those families whose expenditures on both food and nonfood items do not meet the recommended minimum requirements. The hardcore poor are those who cannot afford the minimum food-energy requirements even if they devoted their entire incomes to food alone. Those families that fall below the poverty line for food and overall poverty categories lead dehumanizing lives according to universal norms of human dignity. They face starvation and lack even basic shelter (Kenya, 2000). Over one-half of Kenya's population lives below the absolute poverty line, lacking access to opportunities, services, information, health, education, productive assets, and markets for their goods and/or labor. The number below the poverty level increased substantially in the 1990s and into the twenty-first century. It is still on the rise due to inflation, shortfall in agricultural production, and constant climatic issues such as droughts and floods (Kenya, 2000).

There is diversity in poverty levels by gender, education, marital status, age of household head, and household size. On the one hand, the prevalence and intensity of poverty among women is higher in urban (63 percent) than in rural (54 percent) areas. On the other hand, rural males (53 percent) are poorer than their urban (46 percent) counterparts. Overall, women experience higher levels of poverty than men regardless of their marital status. Poverty levels among single women are high in both rural (56 percent) and urban (65 percent) areas compared with men where the figures are 48 percent and 42 percent, respectively (Kenya, 2000, 2002k).

Based on gender and marital status, Kenyan women are more vulnerable to poverty than are men. The reasons include the preference of some cultures for male children, who are also placed at an advantage when allocating resources toward education and employment opportunities (Ngige, 1995). Other cultures promote early marriage of girls in return for wealth in the form of bridewealth (Wilson & Ngige, 2005). Early marriage retards or even arrests girls' education and places them at a disadvantage when competing for gainful employment with men. In later life, many women find themselves dependent on their spouses and have little opportunity to fend for themselves and their children (Kenya, 2000, 2002e).

Lack of education reduces people's ability to find gainful employment and is associated with increased poverty. Household heads with no education have the highest incidence of poverty in both rural (64 percent) and urban (66 percent) areas. The lowest poverty levels are among people with tertiary education comprising 7 percent and 14 percent in rural and urban areas, respectively. As education can make a significant contribution to the reduction of poverty, interventions should use education as a strategy. Education confers skills, knowledge, and attitudes that would be used to increase productivity of poor people's labor (Kenya, 2000, 2002i).

In both rural and urban areas, large households have higher rates of poverty (i.e., below the absolute poverty level) than do smaller households. The dependency ratio in Kenya is very high; for every 100 people in the labor force, there are ninety-two dependents. Differences exist by location or residence as indicated in the figures for the rural dependency ratio of 101 to 100, compared with the urban dependency ratio of 56 to 100 (Kenya, 2000, 2002j).

Poverty when cross-tabulated by age of household heads shows different outcomes for urban and rural areas. In rural areas, poverty increases gradually from 37 percent for the youngest heads (fifteen to twenty-nine years) to 58 percent for the retiring ages of fifty-five and above. This implies that families with younger heads are still small and might have fewer expenses, while older heads with larger families have higher expenditure for basic needs such as food, clothing, shelter, health, and education. The depth of poverty is highest for heads in the age group thirty to forty-four when the younger family members are likely to be fully dependent on their parents (Kenya, 2000).

Among urban dwellers, a peculiar pattern emerges showing an inverse relationship between poverty and age of household head. Young heads in urban areas show the highest incidence of poverty, averaging 58 percent. Poverty gradually decreases to 38 percent as the age of the head increases. This could be explained by the life cycle of urban dwellers where young people migrate to urban areas at about age eighteen in search of jobs, and settle down and start their own families by age twenty-five when they are still poor. As they grow older, they master urban survival strategies, acquire better paying jobs, and have fewer children (than past generations or rural dwellers) who they are able to raise adequately (Kenya, 2000, 2002g).

The Government of Kenya has a threefold strategy for poverty reduction. First is redistribution of resources to empower poor households to produce and earn more in order to be able to fend for themselves, rather than being dependent on relief and handouts. Second is secondary redistribution of resources such as the provision of basic health services, safe clean water, nutrition, education, and extension services to poor households to raise their present and future productive capacities. Third are strategies to break the vicious cycle of poverty, and to expand productive capacities to ensure self-reliance for poor households (Kenya, 2000).

Despite the grim demonstration of poverty in Kenya, poor men and women apply enormous creativity, strength, and dynamism on a daily basis to solve the persistent practical problems of daily living. The poor have assets in terms of their own skills, in their social institutions, in their values and cultures, and in their knowledge of their own environment. Given the necessary support, the poor can be the main actors in, as well as the beneficiaries of, sustainable development (Ndambuki, 2000).

FAMILIES AND AGING

The impact of aging in Africa has not been realized until recently, when the African Union (AU) and HelpAge International produced a framework intended to guide the development of national policies on aging by all African Union members (HelpAge, 2001). The report indicated that new thinking is needed to meet the challenges of an aging world. Above all, there is a need to create ways to link strategies that protect expanding older populations with strategies providing development.

Kenya is faced with an increase in the number of elderly and the effect of industrialization and urbanization on the care of the aged. Kenyan elderly have little personal income and usually live with their children. The census of 1999 indicated that 4 percent of Kenyans were sixty-five years or older, whereas 44 percent were aged below fifteen years, and the remaining 52 percent were people between fifteen and sixty-four years of age (Kenya, 1999). The report indicated that in most African countries including Kenya, the majority of the older generation is illiterate. It is typical for people aged fifty and older to have little or no education and this contributes to high levels of poverty and challenges their ability to care for themselves. However, older people who depend on their adult children are advantaged in that they have better health than those who are left to care for themselves (Ethangatta, 1995).

Older males and females contribute to family development in many roles. Such roles include watching over homesteads while other family members are away, child rearing, and offering advice; contributing to economic development; resolving conflict, provision of health care services, and serving as religious specialists (HelpAge, 2001; Ochola, Wagah, & Omalla, 2000).

Older persons often care for their grandchildren while the parents are out of the homestead in economic pursuits. Older persons often perform tasks such as accompanying children to the hospital. Older women usually take care of grandchildren especially the orphaned. The elderly provide advice to family members on what to do at different stages of life, including what to do when they are away from the homestead.

Older persons often contribute to economic development through their involvement in farming, business, handicraft, trade, and formal employment (e.g., teaching). The performance of domestic chores by women such as cooking, washing, gardening, and looking after livestock often goes on until very late into old age. Whether old or not, women do most of the domestic chores like cooking, washing, gardening, grazing, and caring for domestic animals.

Older persons (within the family and the community) are often called upon to advise and to resolve conflict between parties. Their role as conflict managers is critical in the face of a rapidly changing society. With the advent of multiparty politics, tribal conflicts have taken a political dimension apart from the traditional dimensions of cattle rustling, land conflicts, and conquests. They resolve conflicts between husbands and wives, parents and children, and siblings, and contribute to the resolution of ethnic conflicts (HelpAge, 1999a).

Women play a great role in nursing the sick by preparing meals, cleaning linen, attending to their personal hygiene, caring for members with various disabilities, and perform midwifely duties as traditional birth attendants (Daichman, 1998). In recent years, around 44 percent of births have been attended by skilled health professionals (UNDP, 2004). The role of older persons as caregivers for the vulnerable has become even more important in the face of the recent ravages of HIV/AIDS. Older parents whose children have HIV/AIDS face the multifaceted tragedy of losing the economic support of their children who are infected, economically having to support their children who are infected (and their adult children's families), nursing their children when infection turns to full-blown AIDS, losing their children, and having to care for and support their orphaned grandchildren (HelpAge, 1999b).

With the cost-sharing system introduced in government hospitals in the country, many citizens cannot afford formal health care. The quickest and most affordable form of health care that the majority of the sick can acquire easily is alternative and complementary medicine from traditional healers. Older persons usually carry out the roles of traditional healers, midwives, and those serving as African traditional religious specialists. The elderly serve as traditional healers and also preside over traditional rituals (Daichman, 1998).

In a complementary manner, it is the duty of mature children to care for their aging parents. The eldest son is responsible for his aging father, while the lastborn son cares for his elderly mother. The eldest son is the principal heir of his father's estate and is to assume the role of the household head upon his parents' death. The responsibility of taking care of one's parents is rarely evaded because of natural ties of affection and also the potential sanctions (e.g., a possible curse on the children) should they fail in their obligations. In recent times, the economic well-being of the elderly has begun to deteriorate due to de-emphasis on the extended family network and the tradition of mutual obligation across generations (Wilson & Ngige, 2005).

OTHER FAMILY SITUATIONS

Kenya has a long tradition of diversity in family forms. This chapter has also indicated some recent trends in family life, often influenced by factors such as poverty, an aging population, declining fertility, Westernization, and health. This section notes four emerging family patterns.

Cohabitation is a living arrangement between persons of the opposite sex who engage in an intimate relationship without legal commitment (Kabaria, 2003). In most communities, people who cohabited without any recognized marriage ceremony were believed to have violated the cultural norms (Abere, 2004, Personal communication). A pregnant girl could run away from home (elope) with the man who impregnated her to escape the humiliation and conflict within her family-of-origin. Likewise, a poor man who could not afford bridewealth, could cohabit with a girl and start a family until he has accumulated enough wealth to pay bridewealth and make peace with his in-laws (Abaya, 2004, Personal Communication; Nyaundi, 2004, Personal communication). In traditional Kenyan societies, cohabitation was rare and cohabiters were regarded with scorn until the couple formalized their marriage. In modern sectors of Kenya, an increasing number of young people are postponing marriage and opting to live together without formalizing their marriage (Frederick, 2000). Cohabitation is also widely practiced among adults working in urban centers who are not living with their spouses (Kenya, 1999).

Some other emerging family patterns include complex blended families in various forms. For instance the multiparent, multigenerational blended families composed of the remarriage of older widows and widowers to younger spouses and the recombinant complex stepfamily involving children of both the first marriage and of the remarried couple. Emergent patterns are unconventional multigenerational mixed-age marriages of couples with a large age range (i.e., forty years or more) between the spouses who would otherwise be closer to a grandparent-grandchild relationship than a married couple relationship. In traditional communities, grandfathers married women as young as their granddaughters and it was culturally sanctioned. Nowadays, even some grandmothers marry much younger men who are the age of their grandsons. This is considered unconventional in the sense that childbearing, which is so highly emphasized in the institution of marriage, is precluded in this type of marriage due to the advanced age of the bride.

The HIV/AIDS pandemic has produced an emergent recycled parent-grandparent pattern. In such families, the grandparent(s) can be provider and nurturer to his or her sickly and dying HIV/AIDS infected adult children as well as parent to their orphaned grandchildren upon the death of their parents.

CONCLUDING COMMENTS

Contemporary Kenyan families are undergoing a sociocultural transformation from a relatively rigid and basically collectivistic family system to a more flexible and more individualistic family system. This has resulted in divergent family patterns in search of the best fit between the older and the younger generations and taking into consideration myriad factors influencing families. This chapter examines diversity in family patterns by such factors as ethnicity, rural-urban residence, religious affiliation, age and generation, education and socioeconomic status, and legislation or formal systems ranging from traditional customary law to secular codified law. Multiple factors have transformed the traditional patriarchal extended family system into divergent patterns that include the classical nuclear family pattern, the classical extended family system, and modifications of each type leading to a modified nuclear-extended family pattern and a modified extended-nuclear family, and complex blended stepfamily households.

The influence of Western culture, modern religions, formal education, industrialization, and urbanization has given rise to diversity in couple formation from the typical collectivistic, parent-arranged mate-choice as evidenced by child betrothal, child marriage, and bridewealth exchange for marriage, to a more individualistic mate selection associated with love marriage, elopement, and cohabitation. There are also a variety of marriage forms ranging from monogamy to polygamy and its variants such as sororal polygyny, nonsororal polygyny, fraternal polyandry, levirate, and widow inheritance, bigamy, and gynaegamy.

Marriage and family transformations have given rise to emergent family shifts and trends from large to small family size, a decline in total fertility rate, an increase in abortions, postponement of marriage to a later age, an increase in cohabitation and nonmarital families, emergence of one-person households, recycled parent-grandparent and elderly caregivers, mixed-age couples, and multigenerational complex blended stepfamilies. Contemporary Kenyan families are faced with new challenges alongside rapid global changes that include poverty, HIV/AIDS, and an increase in the aging population. The gaps in knowledge for further study include understanding the impact of the new challenges on the quality of life of contemporary families in the face of rapid social transformations.

MIDDLE EAST:
FAMILY LIFE IN TURKEY AND IRAN

Chapter 10

The Family in Turkey:
The Battleground of the Modern
and the Traditional

Dilek Cindoglu
Murat Çemrek
Sule Toktas
Gizem Zencirci

INTRODUCTION

Turkey is a secular, Muslim society with rapid social change (Aytaç, 1998; World Factbook, 2006) and the uncommon combination of a European modernism and traditional agrarian patterns like those found in developing nations (Aykan & Wolf, 2000). Urbanization, industrialization, employment in the service sector, and the demographic shifts leading to a larger number of children and young people (even as the population ages) all have brought about changes in family structure and life in the last decades (Aytaç, 1998; Vergin, 1985). Rural-to-urban migration has produced the mixture of Islamic traditionalism with urban-based Western values and lifestyles (Erman, 1997). Governmental reforms, resistance by some groups, and the process of social change results in a society characterized by both modernism and traditionalism (Aykan & Wolf, 2000; Aytaç, 1998) with Islamic traditions evident in some regions (e.g., eastern and southeastern areas, in smaller communities, and among the less educated). Indicators of traditionalism are seen in arranged marriages, paying of bride price, religious weddings, attendance at religious schools, and women's head coverings (Aytaç, 1998).

Turkey has approximately seventy million people located between Asia and Europe. The population is 80 percent Turkish and 20 percent Kurdish speaking; most people are Muslim (99.8 percent, mostly Sunni) (World Factbook, 2006). Kurdish-speaking people lived originally in the eastern part of Turkey but now live throughout. Slightly larger than the U.S. state of Texas, its territory borders the Black, Aegean, and Mediterranean Seas. Most industry is located in the western part where the major city is Istanbul. About 30 percent of the land is arable and Turkey has been a land of small and medium-sized agricultural enterprises, an economy with modern industry and commerce along with traditional crafts (World Factbook, 2006). The country has been predominantly a peasant society, and in many areas, still is.

Due to a rural exodus, from the 1960s through the 1980s, Turkey was characterized by a vast population movement that continues to some extent today. There is rapid urbanization. Over two-thirds of Turks today live in urban areas, compared with one-quarter in the 1960s. Approximately 75 percent of the population in the western part of Turkey lives in urban areas, compared with 36 percent in the eastern portion (State Institute of Statistics [State], 1995; United Nations Development Programme [UNDP], 2006; Vergin, 1985). Poverty and tradition increase from western to eastern Turkey (Erman, 1997; Ilkkaracan and Women for Women's Human Rights [Ilkkaracan], 1998; State, 2001; Vergin, 1985). The State Planning Organization estimates that a per capita income equivalent to US$60 per month is necessary to escape poverty. This represents the cost of purchasing 75 percent of 3,500 calories of food per day. In 1997, 24 percent of the population was classified as poor and this increased to 27 percent in 2003. The poverty rate is two times higher in rural than urban households. The highest rates of poverty are found in the east and southeast Anatolia, followed by the Mediterranean region. There are indications that more recently the poverty rate may be falling (State, 2001; UNDP, 2006). Turkey is considered to have a medium level of human development, and ranks ninety-second of 177 nations.

Primary school education has been mandatory since 1927, but still the literacy rates are not advanced. Overall, the literacy rate is 87 percent (male, 94 percent; female, 79 percent) (Turkish Demographic and

Health Survey [DHS], 1999; World Factbook, 2006). In 1970, 6 percent of women had graduated from at least high school. By 2000 this had risen to 18 percent. For men, the increase was from 13 to 27 percent (State, 2001). A revision to the civil code makes it mandatory for children to attend school through grade eight. Most villages have primary schools but lack middle and high schools. Mostly only males go to urban areas for schooling after the primary level. There is a tradition of keeping girls home and thus lagging in education (Aytaç, 1998).

In western Turkey, nearly 40 percent of women work for pay while in the east approximately 90 percent of women perform unpaid family labor (Ilkkaracan, 1998). Turkey has a strong and rapidly growing private sector. The most important industry and the largest source of exports are textiles and clothing (Berik, 1995; Eraydin, 1999). The unemployment rate in 1997 was 7 percent. In 2005, it was 10 percent with an additional 4 percent under employed (World Factbook, 1997, 2006). In 2001, Turkey faced an economic crisis, inflation soared, and the economy contracted. The country has since adhered to a strict monetary program. GDP grew by close to 8 percent in 2002 and 6 percent in 2003, and was projected to grow by at least 5 percent in 2004. Inflation has fallen to its lowest levels in decades (International Monetary Fund, 2004).

Turkey is a candidate for membership to the European Union; 70 percent of Turks support this decision. To this end, new reforms and laws have been passed. For example, the Turkish parliament approved revisions to 116 articles of the 1,030 article Turkish Civil Code that has been in force for seventy-five years. These changes radically alter the status of women and change the balance of legal and traditional relations between wives and husbands and influence family life. The economic situation, urbanization and Westernization, and the development of employment in the service sector, as well as related development policies, influence family functioning and organization, including possibilities for a better quality of life as well as standard of living.

Husbands are no longer heads of families. Men and women have equal status and both can represent the family in legal matters. There have been increases in the legal age of marriage, women are permitted to use their maiden names in addition to their husbands' family names, and women do not have to ask their husbands for permission to be employed. Women are now entitled to an equal say about where the family will live. Shared financial responsibility for the family will ensue, replacing the concept of the husband's responsibility to provide for his wife and children. The mentally retarded can wed, as long as medical reports show that there are no impediments for the person. Other changes include children born outside wedlock having equal inheritance rights, single persons being allowed to adopt, the age for being able to adopt dropping from thirty-five to thirty years, and changes to the divorce process giving women more protection ("Parliament Approves," 2001). The revision does not mention issues such as surrogate motherhood, marriage between same sex couples, or legal provisions for couples cohabiting.

Family in Turkish Context

Family and kinship are important aspects of Turkish society and social functioning (Aytaç, 1998; Erman, 1997; Ilkkaracan, 1998; Vergin, 1985). In the past (e.g., seventeenth century), some wealthy families established multigenerational families in their *konaks* (large two or three story homes). At the same time, conjugal families predominated. The extended family symbolizes material comfort, prestige, solidarity, and family support, and a nostalgic ideal.

> The new bourgeois society prevents the extended family from spreading its wings except in nostalgia and imagination. Because of the commitments created by the modern society, the communal life and solidarity as a basis for the 'real family,' the repository of Islamic values . . . , is at present for most city dwellers but a remote idea and frame of reference. (Vergin, 1985, p. 572)

However, little is known about intergenerational relations in Turkey (Aytaç, 1998).

While the extended family might be an exemplar for working-class families, most households (perhaps 60 percent or more) are nuclear (Aytaç, 1998). Nuclear family households are most common among the landless, those with more education, and migrants (Aytaç, 1998). In cities, the extended family as a housing unit has in many ways disappeared among the middle and upper classes, but it is common for members of a family—siblings, parents, cousins—to occupy separate flats in the same building. Nuclear households form "functional extended families" (Aytaç, 1998, p. 242). Emotional bonding and contact among family members are strong. For example, people migrating to urban areas typically receive material and emotional support from rural and other kin, as well as having frequent social contact with their family members.

Family type is related to property ownership. In the villages, extended households are less than 50 percent of all households. Extended family households are the "prerogative of large landowners" (Vergin, 1985, p. 571). At the same time, in some areas such as near the Mediterranean, many peasant families are organized into extended households as they either own land or work on large estates. Living close to relatives, especially parents, is common (perhaps half of households). This suggests that families prefer to maintain some privacy while maintaining close family ties (Aykan & Wolf, 2000; Aytaç, 1998; Vergin, 1985).

Family ties are strong (e.g., about 70 percent of adult children either coreside with parents or live nearby) (Aytaç, 1998). Several factors link coresidence of adult children and their parents, that is, living in extended family households. These are indicators of a more traditional set of values and include arrangement of marriage by family rather than the couple, payment of bride price, and the wife having rather traditional views of husband-wife relationships. Couples living in Turkey's least developed regions are the most likely to coreside with parents while those living in the most developed regions are least likely to. Rural people are more likely to live in an extended household than are city dwellers. The likelihood of coresidence increases if the husband's father has died. The married couples in such cases are presumably providing assistance or companionship to the husband's widowed mother. Due to the changing nature of Turkish society, the prevalence of parent-child coresidence might decline in the future. As urbanization spreads, education attainment increases, modern practices regarding marriage become widespread, and perceptions of family roles turn less traditional, then coresidence can be expected to become even less common in Turkey (Aykan & Wolf, 2000; Aytaç, 1998).

The adoption of surnames became obligatory as part of the modernization process. The Family Names Act of 1935 upset, in many ways, the traditional concept of family and pushed Turkey in the direction of a Western model with increased emphasis upon individuals. Until this time, the person's first name preceded his or her father's first name. For sons, this was often followed by the patronymic suffix *oglu,* meaning "son of." With this law, old surnames (*lakab*) used in rural areas showing that one belonged to a *sülale* (or lineage) were outlawed. People were required to take a family name. An entire nation of people had to change their names or find new ones. Some suggest that this was the beginning of a search for a new identity—for the "new" individual within the new, secular Turkish society (Vergin, 1985). Another change is taking place. Women now have the right to keep their maiden names after marriage.

COUPLE FORMATION AND MARITAL DYNAMICS

The majority of women (63 percent) in Ilkkaracan's study of eastern Turkey (1998) were married with 0.6 percent divorced, demonstrating the infrequency of marital dissolution in this region. Seven percent were widowed, somewhat higher than the average in Turkey (4 percent), perhaps because of the armed conflict in the region. Almost 4 percent were separated and 26 percent were unmarried. In Ilkkaracan's sample, 97 percent of the women over twenty-four years of age, and all women over thirty-four years of age, were or had been married. This suggests that marriage is virtually compulsory for women in this region. In western Turkey, 27 percent of women are unmarried and 64 percent are married. Nationwide, 69 percent of women are married (HS, 1999).

Marriage Age and Type of Ceremony

Up to the mid-1980s, marriage took place at a relatively young age; fourteen to eighteen for girls and twenty to twenty-two for boys (Vergin, 1985). According to the Turkish Civil Code, the minimum age for a civil marriage, the only legally valid marriage ceremony, had been seventeen for men and fifteen for women. The age of majority for all other legal procedures is eighteen. Despite this, 16 percent of women living in the eastern region are married before the age of fifteen in a religious ceremony—even while it is against the law to hold a religious ceremony of marriage before a civil ceremony has taken place. A revision to the code (2002) raised the age of marriage to eighteen for both males and females.

Early marriage and polygyny are still prevalent in eastern Turkey (Ilkkaracan, 1998). Religious marriage, which is not legally binding, still takes place frequently, occurring sometimes in addition to civil marriages. Forced marriages still occur and arranged marriages are still in the majority, though younger women today increasingly expect to be able to choose their partner. Nevertheless, arranged marriages are still common as "they foster family unity and protect property, political linkages and patriarchal authority within extended families" (Aytaç, 1998, p. 245).

Conducting a religious ceremony before the girl reaches the age of fifteen has been a strategy used by families to evade the civil law (Ilkkaracan, 1998). The tradition of betrothing girls while infants appears to be disappearing, although continues to be practiced. Approximately 20 percent of Ilkkaracan's respondents had only a religious marriage and no civil marriage. This percentage is higher than average in Turkey (8 percent). Approximately 74 percent had a civil and religious marriage, and 1 percent had neither.

Mate Selection

Traditionally, endogamy and marriage with the paternal uncle's daughter were practiced, but less so than in Arab Muslim societies (Vergin, 1985). The 1993 Turkish Demographic and Health Survey indicated that being married to a first-degree relative was most common in the east (about 25 percent) and least common in the west (about 15 percent) of the country (Aykan & Wolf, 2000). The tradition of bride price or "bridesmoney" (i.e., sum of money or goods and services given by the man to the wife's family prior to marriage) is still widespread, more so in Turkey's eastern region (Aykan & Wolf, 2000). The money paid affects the grooms' attitudes. Men assume that through this payment they have rights to their wives' sexuality and fertility. This tradition of bride price can be considered as women being sold into marriages by their families.

Although 79 percent of married women indicated they were against the bride price tradition, 61 percent reported that their husbands paid bride price for them (Ilkkaracan, 1998). Paying bride price varies by region: about 55 percent of current marriages for women between the ages of fifteen and forty-nine in the east; 25 to 30 percent in the south, center, and north; and 15 percent in the west. The payment is more common in rural (37 percent) than urban (21 percent) areas (Aykan & Wolf, 2000). Families who cannot afford to pay sometimes use the *berdel* (i.e., the families exchange daughters as brides for the sons or fathers of the families). In effect, a woman is offered as compensation to the family of her father or brother's wife (Ilkkaracan, 1998).

In societies like Turkey, the extended family dominates the individual member's choices and actions (Cindoglu, 1997). Men relate a woman's "value" to her noncontamination. Virginity is an asset for the woman and her family. Consequently, the whole family is involved. Likewise, Muslim women are expected to only marry Muslim men. Men, however, can marry non-Muslims (Bodley, 1997). There are few mixed-ethnicity marriages in Turkey. Among married women aged fifteen to forty-nine, 97 percent of Turkish, 92 percent of Kurdish, and 80 percent of women of other ethnic origins (e.g., Arab) are married to men of their own ethnic background (Aykan & Wolf, 2000).

The Turkish Civil Code states that the consent of both the woman and the man is a precondition for marriage. Regardless, women often have no influence over the choice of their spouses and often marry against their wills. Even when consulted about the choice of husband, social control over women's sexuality is maintained through a taboo on premarital sex. Religious and cultural values and norms, as well as violence, also control women (Acar, 1995; Ilkkaracan, 1998). The result is that while women have a right to consent, the ability to exercise this right is often limited. Even when the couple arranges the marriage, the agreement of their families is often a precondition for the marriage (Ilkkaracan, 1998).

In Ilkkaracan's study (1998), the families arranged most marriages (61 percent); the couple themselves arranged only 25 percent. Half the women were married without their consent, and 46 percent were not consulted about their partner and the marriage. Fifty-one percent had not met their husbands before the marriage. In 5 percent of the marriages, it was a *berdel* exchange.

Five percent of women had asked their husbands to kidnap them or had eloped of their own free will (Ilkkaracan, 1998). This is a strategy used by women when their families do not allow them to marry the person of their choice, or when the men are unable to pay the bride price requested. Although this would seem to be effective, allowing women to select their own partners, there can be high costs for the women as their families can reject them. In tribal cultures of eastern Turkey, women who have been "kidnapped" or "abducted" by their husbands are usually considered to have eloped by the families of their husbands. This leads to loss of prestige and status and even to violence against these women (Yalçin-Heckman, 1993, 1995). In the western part of Turkey mate selection is relatively more liberal, yet examples similar to eastern Turkey are also present. The *berdel* practice, however, is a unique characteristic of the east.

While many mothers indicate that they expect their daughters to have a say in their marriages (Ilkkaracan, 1998), another study found that the majority of current marriages of women aged fifteen to forty-nine were arranged (Aykan & Wolf, 2000). The highest proportion (70-80 percent) is in the east, south, and center regions, followed by the north and west (60 percent). Rural-to-urban migration possibly inflates the proportion for areas such as the west. Love marriages are a recent phenomenon in Turkey. Characteristics of love marriages include exposure to urban life during adolescence, education beyond primary school, and later age at marriage for women (i.e., twenty or higher). Love marriages, compared to arranged marriages, are also related to more egalitarian relationships between spouses (Aytaç, 1998; Hortaçsu, 1997).

Monogamy—Polygyny

In the eastern region of Turkey, 11 percent of marriages are po-lygynous, although polygamy was banned in 1926 (Ilkkaracan, 1998). Even in the eighteenth century, polygamous families were rare (more common among the urban rich) and disrespected. The monogamous family was the ideal. Given the law today, only one wife in a poly-gynous arrangement can have a civil marriage whereas the others can only have religious marriages. The second wife (known as the *kuma*) is married only in a religious sense. A religious marriage ceremony confers no legally binding rights under the Civil Code, such as related to divorce, maintenance, or inheritance from the husband. Religious marriages must have the obligatory civil marriage before the religious ceremony. Without the civil ceremony, these are not regarded by the state as legally binding. Many of the religious only marriages involved a *kuma* who thus became a wife legitimate in the eyes of religion while being illegitimate by the norms of law (Vergin, 1985).

In one study of the women in polygynous marriages, 58 percent lived in the same house as their husband's other wives, and 65 percent of these women said they had serious problems with the other wives. Despite all the issues involved in polygynous marriage, half of the women in such a marriage were involved in creating the arrangement or entered it willingly. This indicates the acceptance of polygyny by women. The Islamic injunction that a man may marry up to four wives, and the cultural atmosphere that polygyny is a man's natural right, support the acceptance of polygyny by women (Abd Al-ati, 1995; Ilkkaracan, 1998).

Economic factors help sustain the persistence of polygyny. In rural homes, the wife is an economic asset, essential for the success of agricultural work. A man might seek a second (or subsequent) wife as a means of securing a larger workforce. Vergin (1985, p. 573) explained: "The *kuma,* always younger and more robust than the first wife, comes, then, to help with the domestic work. Sometimes the first wife herself asks her husband to provide her with a helper, but we must not therefore conclude that the arrival of the *kuma* is a godsend to her."

Living Arrangements

Patrilocal residence (i.e., living with the groom's parents) and agnatic relationships (i.e., relatives on the father's side) are favored (Aykan & Wolf, 2000; Vergin, 1985). In the mid-1980s, the average household was 6.5 people, slightly higher than in industrialized Western societies during the same period. Three generations of families living under the same roof and "sharing the same dish" were rare (Vergin, 1985, p. 571). The prevalence of extended household is dependent upon conditions (e.g., number of children surviving to marital age, age of parents and their longevity, and rules about inheritance and the division of family land). Especially important is the age at which parents die, as it is not so much marriage of children that leads to large extended households, but the life and death of the head of the family (Vergin, 1985).

The 1993 Turkish Demographic and Health Survey showed that one-fourth of married couples (wives aged fifteen to forty-nine) lived with at least one parent or parent-in-law. The most common (54 percent) residence pattern was coresidence with both the husband's parents followed with coresidence with the husband's mother only (34 percent). Only 7 percent of couples lived with the husband's father only. Therefore, while most couples live independently, the vast majority (95 percent) of coresiding couples live with the husband's parent(s). As the likelihood of having both his parents alive is highest early in the couple's marriage, this is when coresidence is most likely to occur. Later, they are more likely to live with one parent (Aykan & Wolf, 2000).

Extramarital Relationships

There are no laws in Turkey restricting a woman from engaging in a relationship with a man or woman of her choice before, during, or after marriage. Regardless, extramarital relationships are a definite taboo for women in the eastern region. At the same time, men's extramarital affairs are widely accepted. The customary penalty in the eastern region for women suspected of pre- or extramarital sex is death (i.e., so-called honor-killings). In Turkey's eastern region, the majority (67 percent) of women believed that, even with today's law, they could not divorce their husbands if they committed adultery; 67 percent of women thought that their husbands and/or families would kill them if they committed adultery. This perception was found more often among those with only religious marriages, little or no education, and in rural areas. Most women who believed that their husbands would do something other than divorcing or killing them expected to be badly beaten if they were suspected of an extramarital affair (Ilkkaracan, 1998).

Divorce

Divorce is rare in Turkey (2 percent of women; DHS, 1999). Consequently, there are few single female-headed households (Erman,

1997). Divorces represent about 6 percent of all marriages in a year (UNDP, 1999). Divorce at the request of the wife has a long tradition in Turkey, at least since 1917. Traditionally among Muslims, a wife cannot divorce her husband. He can, however, divorce her by repeating the formula "I divorce you" three times (called *talaq*). According to Shiite law this must be pronounced in the presence of two witnesses. In Sunni law the pronouncement can be either oral or in writing. No reason need be given. The wife does not have to be notified (Divorce, 2001). Divorce by repudiation is uncommon (Vergin, 1985).

As noted, religious marriages are legally invalid. Consequently, people in such marriages (e.g., polygyny, women married before the minimal legal age) have no rights to legal divorce. Thus women with only a religious marriage believe that they are less able to divorce than those in civil (and legal) marriages, but the difference is not great (Ilkkaracan, 1998). Women with secondary or higher education are more likely to believe that they could obtain a divorce because of the adultery of their husband, but still about one-third believe this would be impossible.

When a wife obtains divorce, the husband is obliged to pay the *mehr-I müeccel* to provide for her needs. In many Muslim societies the custom of *mehr* is observed; in Turkey, it has rarely been used in divorce litigation. In rural areas there has been a counterpart, known as the *baslik,* derived from Turkish customary law. The *baslik* is a sum paid to the father of the bride by the father of the groom. It can be seen as compensation for their loss of the daughter's labor. As an aspect of bride price, it belongs to the family and not personally to the bride as in the case of the *mehr.* The amount varies according to the prestige of the bride's family as well as her characteristics (e.g., health, age, and beauty). The amount and presence of the *baslik* are often the reason for kidnappings and abductions sometimes with the girl's consent. When this happens, the father is obliged to give his daughter in marriage without any compensation. The State has deemed *baslik* illegal and has tried to convince peasants to abandon the practice. It remains, however, a powerful tradition that helps to maintain village economic life, a visage of family honor, and helps to maintain couple and family solidarity (Vergin, 1985). Upon divorce, the amount stays with the bride's family if the husband is at fault, but paid back if the wife is at fault.

There must be a legal separation for six months before the couple can file for divorce. Assets accumulated during the marriage are to be equally divided unless the couple decides otherwise ("Parliament Approves," 2001). The divorce proceedings can be held in a closed court session at either spouse's request. Due to social values, despite various negative conditions within the marriage, many people still choose to remain married. However, while people do not get divorced easily or frequently, people also do not get married easily. According to the statistics of 1960, 12 percent of women were unmarried and in 1998 this percentage increased to 29 percent (DHS, 1999; *Türkiye'de Nufus ve Saglik Arastirmasi, 2003, on rapor* [Türkiye], 2004).

FAMILIES AND CHILDREN

The highest fertility rate is in the eastern region (3.65 versus 1.88 in the western region and 2.23 in the country as a whole) (Türkiye, 2004). Approximately 11 percent of women living in the east begin their childbearing between fifteen and nineteen years of age. In the western part of Turkey the figure is 8 percent (Ilkkaracan, 1998). In 1992-1993, Turkish women forty to forty-nine years old had an average of 4.6 children and the fertility rate for the age group fifteen to forty-nine ranged from 3.65 children per woman in the east to 1.88 in the west (Ergöçman, Hancioglu, & Ünalan, 1995). Several reasons account for the elevated desire for children in the East—wanting a powerful tribe, expectations of family elders for having additional male children in the family, and a belief that Allah will provide enough food for each person. Boy children are especially valued (Ilkkaracan, 1998). Fertility rates also differ by rural-urban residence and educational level. Women living in rural areas will have, on average, one more child than women living in urban areas. Women without education have approximately one child more (4.2) than women with primary-level education and almost two more children than women with secondary-level education (2.4) (Aytaç, 1998; Türkiye, 2004). The total fertility rate declined from five children per woman in the 1970s to 2.7 in 1993, and to 1.9 in 2006. Women with secondary or more education have an average of 1.7 children. The birthrate is 16.62 (Aytaç, 1998; World Factbook, 2006).

Knowledge of modern family planning methods is almost universal among Turkish women. In this context, regional differences are substantial. The levels of current birth control usage are 57 percent in the east and 74 percent in the west, with over 70 percent usage in most other regions (Türkiye, 2004). Of currently married women, 90 percent have used a method sometime during their life. Overall, 71 percent of currently married women are using birth control and among them, 42 percent use modern methods. Most people using contraceptives obtain them from a state hospital (57 percent) or clinic (39 percent). The rest use pharmacies. The IUD and condom are the most widely used methods among married couples, followed by the pills and female sterilization (Türkiye, 2004).

Abortion

In the five year period preceding the 1998 Turkish Demographic and Health Survey, almost 25 percent of pregnancies resulted in other than a live birth with 15 percent being induced abortions. More than 25 percent of ever-married women report having had an induced abortion with women in the east and in rural settlements being the least likely. The law (1983) legalizing abortion guarantees safe conditions for terminations of pregnancies during the first ten weeks of gestation, for a woman who wants the service, at government hospitals for a nominal fee, and from the private sector for a fee. Around 75 percent of abortions are in private clinics (DHS, 1999).

Infant Mortality

Infant mortality varies by region (i.e., east 60.0 and west 42.7) (Aytaç, 1998). The infant mortality rate was estimated at thirty-eight per 1,000 live births, and the under-five mortality rate at forty-four during 1998-2003, and forty for 2006 (Türkiye, 2004; World Factbook, 2006). Infant and child mortality have declined rapidly in recent years; while encouraging, the rate is considered still unacceptably high because countries with a GNP equivalent to Turkey typically have much lower rates (UNDP, 2006).

There are significant differences in infant and child mortality between regions and urban and rural areas. Medical maternity care and educational level of mothers are important correlates of mortality (Türkiye, 2004). The health care system is modern and Western.

Therefore, the access to and use of appropriate techniques and methods decrease the mortality rates. As mothers' education level increases, the infant mortality rate decreases (Cindoglu & Sirkeci, 2001).

Parenting Practices and Outcomes

Couples tend to become parents more quickly in family arranged marriages than in couple arranged marriages. After becoming parents, couples are often less involved with their families-of-origin and have more conflict with them. Wives also gain more dominance, especially in the domestic sphere and relative to children (Hortaçsu, 1999). Breastfeeding is widespread (95 percent of children) but this falls to 66 percent at the end of the child's first year of age. The median duration of breastfeeding is fourteen months while supplementary foods and liquids are introduced at an early age. Almost all children receive supplementary food after six months of age (Türkiye, 2004).

Lower SES families often display more conservative child-rearing practices (Hortaçsu, Ertem, Kurtoglu, & Uzer, 1990). Parenting practices in lower and middle SES families have different effects on children compared with higher SES families. More educated parents are more individualistic, more internally oriented, and have fewer traditional values and expectations concerning children (Hortaçsu et al., 1990). Values and expectations held for girls are more family oriented and less individualistic than those held for boys. Girls' self-concepts appear to be more affected by parents' behavior (Hortaçsu, 1989b).

Mother's education level is one of the best predictors of primary school academic performance. Individual characteristics of children also relate to school performance. For example, the extent to which girls feel lonely has a bigger impact on their school grades than for boys. In higher SES families (fathers having university degrees), these individualistic characteristics become more important. For lower SES families, family factors are more important. These observations support the notion that in Turkey, different SES families adhere to different child-related values and practices. Families with more education seem to encourage more progressive and individualistic tendencies in their children (Hortaçsu, 1995).

The amount of positive praise by parents influences child loneliness, self-concept, and academic performance especially for girls.

Father's education shapes the amount of praise and extent of loneliness. Turkish families are patriarchal, but educated fathers interact more warmly with daughters; uneducated fathers ignore daughters to a greater extent. Some fathers, when answering the question, "How many children do you have?" count only sons. For example, "I have two children and two daughters" (Hortaçsu et al., 1990, p. 542).

Adolescents are expected to demonstrate familial allegiance while being modest about personal qualities. In-depth interviews with adolescent girls and boys attending high school in Ankara, representative of lower SES families that were more traditional in orientation, showed group membership (e.g., sports teams, friendships) and role fulfillment were two major elements of social identity (Güneri, Sümer, & Yildirim, 1999). Students indicated that they felt secure and close to their friends, some more so than with parents. Peer acceptance was important for self-definition, and friendships allowed for developing social competence. While having a girlfriend or boyfriend can be an important source of positive validation, among those interviewed (ages fifteen and sixteen), some said it was too early for such relationships. Some commented that love can bring happiness, but can also lead to disappointments. While girls and boys believed they may have opposite sex friends, they are more secure with same sex friends. These students were proud of being Turkish and tried to be good citizens. Being a Turk also means being Muslim and religious values were apparent among these youth. Some used religious values to guide everyday life; not smoking, for example, because it is sinful. Self-identity among Turkish adolescents incorporates well-defined values derived from political and religious orientations.

Family has an important influence on Turkish youth self-identities. The interviewed students valued their parents. As one said, "Although I don't agree with what they think and do most of the time, I believe in their good intentions" (Güneri et al., 1999, p. 543). Lack of family relationships is problematic. For those without a father, loving and supportive relationships with their mothers were related to strong family identity. Parents especially guide females in such areas as opinions about what is right or wrong. Girls perceived that their parents control their social life, including strict limits on relationships with boys. Overall, strict conservative principles of their parents restrict the activities of teens in many ways, especially relations with friends. Nevertheless, parents were perceived as warm, caring, and loving. "Although students sometimes were in conflict with parental authority, they felt that their parents were doing what parents are supposed to do. Thus, beyond any particular disagreement with parents, there was a certain level of understanding of good intention" (Güneri et al., 1999, p. 544).

Older adolescents (aged sixteen to twenty) have their closest relationships with same sex friends followed by parents (Hortaçsu, Oral, & Yasak-Gültekin, 1991). Boys are closer to their fathers than are girls. Some studies indicate that male and female adolescents are about equal in the degree of closeness to mothers and same sex friends. Other studies, however, indicate a gender difference, with girls having closer relationships with mothers and friends (Hortaçsu, 1989a). For older adolescents, the relationship with the mother is a good predictor of the quality of the relationship with the father. This is possibly a reflection of the focal role played by mothers in Turkish families. If the relationship with the mother is good, the relationship with the father is good. However, a bad relationship with mother does not seem to be compensated for by a good relationship with father; both relationships tend to be of poorer quality (Hortaçsu et al., 1991).

Social and familial dimensions are influential in contributing to adolescents' definition of self. Physical and personal dimensions were less influential; family and social aspects of self-identity circumscribed these to some extent. Researchers argue that in line with parental expectations, teens had close friends of the same sex and believed they were too young for romantic relationships. This conformity can be problematic as difficulties in the social and familiar realms can lead to distress and emotional disturbances. At the same time, shortcomings in other areas, such as in social identity, can be accommodated to an extent by an emphasis on familial identity, and vice versa. When problems are faced in both areas, more serious identity crises can result. Overall, it can be said that Turkish adolescents have friendships similar to their Western counterparts. Over time, the relationship with parents decreases in intimacy paralleling that found in European societies. Some differences do stand out, especially the important role of the mother, greater control over the adolescent's social life, and a lower level of communication between children and their fathers than reported in studies done with Western families.

Value of Interdependency

Turks place positive value on family interdependency (Vergin, 1985). Close relationships are especially esteemed in lower SES families because of the economic dependency of the individual on the group. Mutual aid and family solidarity are more important than the success of a person independent of his or her family (i.e., familism). Social mobility of a person is a way of enhancing the status of all family members, as the upwardly mobile relative has the duty to come to the aid of the family. Interdependency, implying sharing material and social success, is essential to a family's honor as well as survival in precarious economic times.

In middle and upper SES families, there appears to be no reduction in the quality of interpersonal relations among parents, children, and other relatives. This is true even as it is clear that in these families there is less economic dependency. Contrary to what might be expected with modernization and Westernization, in Turkey, intergenerational relationships have become more interdependent on an emotional level (Aytaç, 1998). There appears to be no loosening of family ties, but perhaps even more withdrawing into the family circle as a means of coping with any difficulties associated with social change. Kinship and neighborhood relations are powerful forces in the lives of urban families—both those newly arrived as well as upper SES families.

FAMILIES AND GENDER

Turkey is in the "belt of classic patriarchy" (Erman, 1997; Kandiyoti, 1995) and is also a Muslim society. In fundamentalist Islamic views, women are considered as legally and morally inferior to men. Husbands and close male relatives must protect women. Staying out of public life and focusing upon domestic roles is prescribed. Legally, in many Muslim societies, women are at a disadvantage. For example, daughters inherit less than sons. Women can have only one spouse at a time whereas men can have up to four as long as they can be provided for and treated fairly. In some societies, female seclusion is required. In some cases, males and females are segregated in employment and education (Abd Al-ati, 1995; Bodley, 1997).

Men, Women, and Social Status

Since the founding of the modern Turkish republic (1923) by Mustafa Kemal Atatürk, Kemalist Reforms have directed Turkey to western Europe (Aytaç, 1998; Vergin 1985). These reforms were the tenets of a cultural revolution of a traditional society turning into a modern one. With this aim, the State: abolished the *Sharia,* replaced the Arabic alphabet with the Latin; closed the free schools of religion and installed secular, scientific, and coeducational schools under the Ministry of Education; banned religious brotherhood activities; restricted the wearing of traditional attire and supported Western modes of dressing for both women and men; and imported the Swiss Civil Code (in place of the Ottoman one) that established Western modes of living. Minimum ages for marriages (fifteen for girls and seventeen for boys) were established and suffrage for women occurred in 1934. The restriction of polygamy and enabling property rights for women were brought by the new Code.

Secularization measures have influenced family relationships. Many perceptions have changed and the status of the head of the family, seen at one time as unshakeable, has been challenged. While judicial changes have reshaped family, research through the 1980s showed that in daily family life, perhaps less had changed. Husbands tended to maintain their authority as Turkish families maintained their hierarchal, patriarchal nature. There are some changes evident in the family relationships among the upper, and more liberal, classes. A spirit of camaraderie is developing in the relationship between spouses and between father and child. This has been influenced by Western values in the media (Vergin, 1985).

Peasant women have had less advantage from these reforms. Changes such as emergence of consumption patterns (e.g., availability of washing machines, speedy transportation to the markets), increase in access to communications technologies (e.g., TV, radio, telephone), and utilization of modern energy sources (e.g., electricity and petroleum), are due to Turkey's incorporation into the world market and the resulting penetration of capitalism into rural areas (Weiner, 1995).

There is rigid gender segregation and an ideology linking the virtue of women with family honor (Moghadm, 1993). Women are "status demonstrators" for their husbands and families. The Muslim concept of *izzat* (i.e., family honor) encompasses the modesty and virtue of the wife, daughters, and sisters of a man (Bodley, 1997). Under the classical system, a young bride will live with her husband's family and work under the control of her mother-in-law as well as the more senior female members of the household. She will also labor in the fields and tend to farm animals (Erman, 1997). In rural areas the family home (*hane*) is the economic unit for production and consumption. Activities are organized by the age and sex of members (Vergin, 1985).

In eastern Turkey, property and power are exclusively in the control of men and women are traditionally oppressed and controlled by the preeminent extended family structure. As men are responsible for women's honor in Islamic societies, this legitimizes their control and power. Husbands and other men in a family thus exercise control over women, especially in rural Turkey where religion is an important force around which society is organized (Erman, 1997).

Gender in Rural-to-Urban Migrant's Households

Modernization has mostly addressed women's public roles, while gender roles, especially those within families, have been questioned less. Primary roles attributed to women are those of being a good wife and a mother to the family. The private realm is the province of women, and the public realm is the province of men. While women have their own hierarchy based on kinship, fertility, and age, within traditional Islamic discourse women live in a "limited space" (Cindoglu, 1997). However, when opportunities are available, women seek to improve their situations. Risks are taken. Women might not openly challenge the patriarchal ideology, yet still go against their husbands as they perceive that such action would provide better life chances for their families (Erman, 1997). One arena for challenging the patriarchal authority and for improving the material condition in which families live, is rural-to-urban migration. Turkish migrant women have a strong preference for city life (Erman, 1997). Women regard the city as a better place partially because they enjoy some comfort there (e.g., educational opportunities, better transportation, less work, and greater availability of consumer products). To many, village life means a lot of hard, filthy work. Village life also means oppression.

When people migrate to urban areas, they often live in one-story dwellings in areas know as a *gecekondu* (i.e., shantytowns or "shabby suburbs"). This is the term used for squatter houses and translates in English as "landed overnight" (Erman, 1997, p. 272). Such housing is incorporated into the housing options sanctioned by the government because of its inability to provide legal housing. Some *gecekondu* owners have been able to obtain title to their lots. These conditions are in sharp contrast to the modern high-rise apartments of the upper-class districts. The household type common among migrants is the nuclear family (Briar-Lawson, Lawson, Hennon, & Jones, 2001; Erman, 1997).

The participation of women in the labor force has declined. In the 1950s around 70 percent of women were in the labor force, but by mid-1990 the rate had dropped to around 30 percent. Much of this decline relates to the high rate of rural-to-urban migration. In rural areas women work in agriculture. After migration to urban areas, women with less education find it hard to obtain employment in the formal labor force (Ilkkaracan, 1998).

Turkish women generally approve of female employment but men hold more restrictive attitudes, views reflecting the ideology that men are to be the sole breadwinners (Erman, 1997). Economic opportunities are restricted for women, especially those with limited education and job skills. While paid work is thus unattractive for migrant women, they do work when family economic conditions warrant it. They will often take on cleaning jobs within the homes of the better off urbanites, or perhaps cleaning offices. Some will also work in the grocery stores that are part of or close to their homes (often run by their male family members). Some women have employment as home-workers producing machine-knitted garments or sewing. Some women also start their own businesses, such as small stores or day-care centers (Erman, 1997; Esim, 2000). Second generation migrant women might have jobs as civil servants. However, as their family financial situation improves, women often cease their employment (Erman, 1997).

Many women seem to have more power relative to men than might be expected; religion and residence appears to be important in this regard (Erman, 1997; Tekeli, 1995). Among the Alevis, the religious group of the heterodox Islamic interpretation, women are often influential in the decision to move their families to urban areas. In some cases women are also enterprising and entrepreneurial in establishing homes, finding jobs, and starting businesses. Urban living also appears to shape household division of labor and decision making.

In urban areas, as men see other men helping their wives, there is less reliance on conventional ideologies to support gendered and age graded divisions of labor. In addition, the wife having a paid job brings some sense of equality to the marriage. Even those without paid work handle money in order to run the household. Likewise, urban households tend to be nuclear in form, and thus lack the extended family matrix for reinforcing gender roles. Even in those cases where parents live with, usually, a son, or visit for part of the year, the relationships tend to be of a different nature than found in village households. Yet, some women seem surprised by another woman mentioning that her husband contributes to housework (Erman, 1997).

Traditional gender roles of migrant families might still remain intact ideologically, but urban living produces changes in family organization and functioning that can be beneficial to women (Tekeli, 1995). Wives become companions and husbands become more dependent upon their wives in the more competitive urban environment. Both spouses need each other's cooperation and support, more so than when living in a village. They also spend more time together, and men are more inclined to ask for their wives' opinions on a variety of matters (Erman, 1997).

In conclusion, while there is some change in gender relations among those who migrate from rural-to-urban areas, it can be argued that radical changes in gender roles on an ideological basis are not taking place. Rather, husbands help their wives when conditions require it. They do not want to publicize their help in order to protect their male image ("invisible helping men"). While the changes might seem trivial or not positive, placing a "double burden" on women, the women themselves perceive the changes as significant improvements (Erman, 1997).

FAMILIES AND STRESS

Violence is used to socially and sexually oppress women. Many husbands subject wives to domestic violence (Yuksel, 1995). In many regions there are no shelters or institutions offering help to victims.

Almost none of the women in one study had sought legal recourse against domestic violence or marital rape, though these were commonly experienced (Ilkkaracan, 1998). Customary and religious laws and practices, such as religious marriages, are often contrivances for controlling women's sexuality and maintaining the imbalance of power. Turkish is the official language. That 19 percent of the women in the study could speak little or no Turkish, but rather an ethnic language such as Kurdish or Arabic, meant they had little possibility of applying independently to legal institutions in case of violations of their rights within the family.

In Turkey, women and their bodies are controlled. The control sometimes takes a more violent course. "The crime of honor is the killing of a woman by her father or brother for engaging in, or being suspected of engaging in, sexual practices before, or outside marriage" (Abu-Odeh, 1996, p. 141). These kinds of events occur in families with low-income levels. Social pressure frames the violence in the light of honor. This kind of savage crime can occur because of thoughts of being honorable or to walk with one's head held high. One of most insidious aspects is that those who are not yet of major age are used as executioners in these murders. By this method, the imprisonment process decreases to two to three years with extenuating reasons like good conduct at the court and maximum provocation. It is argued that honor crimes and the way that they are dealt with are new ways of reproducing an old ideology (Abu-Odeh, 1996). In other words, although the legal systems and jurisdictions are different in the Arab and Turkish societies, dealing with honor crimes end in the same results. The Arab and the Turkish jurisdictions do not provide full punishment in the cases of murders; instead, they provide an excuse, exception, or reduction for the punishment on the grounds of honor and tradition.

Provocation is a concept in every country's legal system, but in the Western countries there is nothing like honor as a reason for provocation. In the Universal Law, every human being can use his or her body however they want. This is a basic human right. If this use is against marriage rules, then it is possible to be divorced. However, with this reasoning, if someone commits a crime, his or her imprisonment is not reduced. As long as Turkey's perspective of killing women for honor is not changed, this society will have many victims.

Akman and Yirmibesoglu (1999) concluded that: (1) Judges under the coercion of traditions and aspects in the criminal law and unapplied laws even promote honor crimes; (2) women (typically those with inadequate education) can kill their own daughters with the decision of the family assembly; (3) doctors cooperate with criminals when giving medical reports for women who are badly beaten, and then their husbands are released; and (4) when women go to a police department to complain, they are faced with comments from police officers like, "he is your husband, he can both beat you and love you."

FAMILIES AND AGING

In Turkey, life expectancy at birth is 72.6; for males 70.2 and for females 75.1 (2006 estimate). The age structure of the population is 26 percent between birth and age fifteen and about 7 percent above the age of sixty-five years (UNDP, 2006; World Factbook, 2006). A number of factors influence life expectancy, such as health care and morbidity. High infant mortality contributes to a lower average life expectancy.

The retirement and pension system is state administered and financed. Private pensions began in the 1980s but could not replace the state. The law restricts working after retirement in order to provide job opportunities for younger generations, but the pensions are low and retired people seek jobs to support themselves. The law on retirement and pension changes frequently. After nearly every election, the government tries to install a different program for social security. The retirement age for women is fifty-five and for men sixty. These previously were forty-five and fifty, but the law was changed due to high unemployment and scarce national budget for pensions.

Caregiving

There is limited research on aging and family life, especially in regard to caregiving (Aytaç, 1998). The treatment of the elderly varies by family SES. As Turkey is not a welfare state, the number of public retirement homes is insufficient and private homes generally target higher SES groups as clients; less than 1 percent of elderly Turks live in nursing homes (Aytaç, 1998; Toktas, 1997). The support provided within the family and kinship group remains the only choice for many people. Generally, daughters and daughters-in-law look after the elderly. This traditional expectation will likely decrease as the modernization and institutionalization of the models of caring develop (e.g., establishment of more retirement homes and the use of paid women labor for domestic care) (Aykan & Wolf, 2000; Toktas, 1997).

Historically, based on Islamic precepts and cultural values, older family members were provided and cared for regardless of whether they were living in an extended or nuclear family household. While women often provided the daily care, sons especially were seen as security in old age. Increases in the aging population are challenging these traditional values (Aytaç, 1998). However, data suggest that due to the prevailing gender roles, men continue to work as the household breadwinner and are unlikely to give physical care to their elderly parents. Their wives or other female relatives do the caregiving for the elderly (Aytaç, 1998).

Consideration of the family life cycle can help explain traditional coresidence patterns. A newlywed couple will first live with the husband's parents (patriarchal extended). At some point, perhaps with the birth of the first child, the couple forms their own household (nuclear). Later, as parents become old and need care, they might live with the man's parents again, perhaps this time in the couple's household. Over time, this pattern repeats as the couple ages and their children grow, marry, and have children of their own (Aykan & Wolf, 2000). This coresidence with children is a manifestation of the "old-age security" motive for having children.

OTHER FAMILY SITUATIONS

Women are the carriers of tradition in Turkey, but there is rapid social change through exposure to Western lifestyles through media, tourism, and migration. One way Islamic patriarchal societies cope with this change is by keeping a close watch on the lives, bodies, and sexuality of women. Women's bodies are sites where gender identities are constructed and reproduced. With social change, a woman's sexual purity and family's control over her sexuality produce more anxiety than before. In addition, with social change, these personal and family acts are no longer local events. Local media attention and that of various organizations focuses on issues of importance to women.

Sexuality—Women's Bodies and Control

Virginity is a crucial arena that provides useful information in understanding the family institution in Turkey. Despite the State directed modernization project, the material conditions in which people live change more easily and speedily than the values that people have. Traditional values continue to persist though the forms as well as their adaptations differ. The virginity issue is significant in that although families modernized, traditional values including those that require women should be virgins at the time of marriage, still prevail.

Research in other countries suggests that it perhaps is a mistake to perceive young women as helpless victims under male control of sexuality (Holland, Ramazanoglu, Sharpe, & Thomson, 1998). Similarly, it is argued that Turkish women are not in so vulnerable a situation as perhaps anticipated. At least for higher SES women, sexuality can be not only the means of subordination and exploitation, but also an arena of power. Women are not passive victims of their destiny.

There is control by kin members over women's heterosexual desire. In Middle Eastern societies, women's heterosexual desire poses a threat to patriarchal, penetration-oriented, sexuality. It is dishonorable for women to become sexually active before or outside marriage. Conversely, such activities are a cause for celebration among men. The control over women's bodies is reproduced through shame and honor codes. Honor is primarily concerned with the legitimacy of paternity (his "seed" in her "soil"). A man's honor is related to his power to protect what is his (Cindoglu, 1997). Social recognition of a woman's purity depends upon the men under whose protection she falls. Significant means to create and reproduce this control are religion and modernization which interact in interestingly, collaborative ways. Modern institutions such as law—jurisprudence and medicine cooperate with tradition and religion to reproduce the patriarchal control over women's bodies. This concern and patriarchal control has led to two interesting medical procedures—virginity tests and virginity surgery.

Modernity and Virginity

Women's relationship to their bodies in Islamic countries is multi-layered and highly complex (Abu-Odeh, 1996). Women's bodies seem to be a battlefield. The Western attire, which covers their bodies, carries with it the "capitalist" construction of the female body—sexualized, objectified, and commodified. However, these bodies are simultaneously constructed as trustees of family (sexual) honor—conservative and asexual. As one of the first modernizing nations in the Middle East, Turkey carries traditional Islamic, nationalist, and liberal discourses simultaneously. This cohabitation of traditional and Islamic gender ideology, along with a liberal gender ideology, is crystallized in virginity tests and virginity surgery (Cindoglu, 1997).

In contrast to traditional expectations, some women do not wait until their wedding nights for their first sexual intercourse. The wedding night often turns into a nightmare for a woman, as the husband and families discover (or perceive) that she is not a virgin and virginity is still an asset in contemporary Turkey and the rest of the Middle East. Suspicion over a woman's purity can lead to the bride being required to provide proof of virginity (i.e., through a medical report) even after the wedding night. "Women's purity before marriage is not only an individual choice but a family matter. Therefore, the family controls women's bodies. The virginity of the women is not a personal matter, but rather a social phenomenon" (Cindoglu, 1997, p. 254).

Virginity tests have a legal status in Turkey. When there is a legal dispute, such as in the cases of attempted rape or the absence of bleeding on the first intercourse with one's spouse, the Forensic Medicine Department of the Ministry of Health can take up the issue (Frank, Bauer, Arican, Fincanci, & Iacopino, 1999). While this Department has the only authority to furnish a report, virginity tests are widely conducted in hospitals and in private practices. Examples of how virginity tests have been used indicate that women are considered the responsible party in heterosexuality (Cindoglu, 1997). Even in order to protect women from male abuse, women's bodies need to be controlled, rather than those of men.

However, in some ways, women now have some control over their bodies and destinies. Due to the social anxiety and the structural transformations that women are experiencing, women have come to use medicine to "repair" their virginity. For a woman with premarital sexual experience, repair by a physician through reconstructive virginity surgery becomes necessary if she is to exist "properly" in a patriarchal society. She becomes "pure" again, and the honor of her family, as well as her hymen, is repaired (Cindoglu, 1997).[1]

There are different ways to conceptualize her choice. One is that it is empowering, allowing her to have some control over her life, sexuality, and marriage chances. Another is that her choice is made within and as a reflection of a patriarchal society. She can have sex before marriage, but she must be a virgin at marriage. Thus the choice of having the surgery is made under duress and due to perceived negative consequences if not a virgin.

CONCLUDING COMMENTS

In Turkey, the local values about sexuality and honor clash with the now commonly known Western code of ethics. Traditional closed communities are no longer closed. In the last decades, massive migration to the urban centers and internationally have exaggerated anxiety over women's purity. When the community borders blur due to physical mobility of people through migration and exposure to Western media and Western people through tourism, women's bodies become the arenas to reproduce the cultural boundaries. Women's possible promiscuity becomes the most threatening aspect for the social and biological reproduction of the community and becomes a contested arena.

This anxiety produced through modernization and globalization results in brutal local responses to women's bodies, as in the case of honor crimes. Usually, it is a family decision to clean their honor by her blood and usually a young male in the family is appointed for the task to avoid long-term jail imprisonment. Paradoxically, globalization on the one hand brings the formation of a single universal identity, while on the other hand, ethnic, religious, and national identities gain dominance in local politics.

The relations within families and the relationship of families with society compose a matrix where practices and worldviews are at stake in different regions and socioeconomic classes. The tension between modern practices and traditional worldviews certainly affects family life and family structure. However, the path that families will take in their attempt to harmonize traditional values with the threat perceived by modernity will probably lead the family structures in Turkey to develop a hybrid-like structure. That is, new meanings, resistances, and practices will continue to develop through the tension between tradition and modernity.

NOTE

1. Virginity surgery (hymenoplasty) consists of stitching together what remains of the hymen. After being sutured, the hymen heals, will often then bleed after the next intercourse, and thus the woman becomes virgin-like once again.

Chapter 11

Family and Family Change in Iran

Akbar Aghajanian

INTRODUCTION

The Islamic Republic of Iran is 89 percent Shiite Muslims, which differs from the Sunnite of most Arab countries. Iran is slightly larger than the U.S. state of Alaska with a population of sixty-eight million. About 67 percent of the population is urban. Languages include Farsi and its dialects (58 percent), Turkic (26 percent), Kurdish (9 percent), and several others spoken by small groups. According to the Human Development Index, Iran has a medium level of human development, ranked at ninety-sixth of 177 countries, an improvement over the 101 rank in 2004 (United Nations Development Programme [UNDP], 2004, 2006; World Factbook, 2006).

Iran inherited the Persian culture and language from the pre-Islamic era. Formerly known as Perse, Iran emerged as a strong and rich civilization. The Iranian sociocultural system evolved through interaction of the Islam and the pre-Islamic Iranian civilization. During the spread of the Islamic Empire, Iranian society made great contributions to Eastern culture, literature, philosophy, and science. However, devastations, such as Mongol and Timurid invasions and destruction, moved Iran into the twentieth century with an underdeveloped economy, weak central government, and strong interference from European colonial powers (World Factbook, 2005).

Outside impacts started in Iran early in the nineteenth century and led to Westernization by the 1970s (Banani, 1961; Menashri, 1992). Fueled by oil exports and public spending, Iran was characterized by rapid economic growth and modernization during 1955-1979 (Bill, 1988). Industrial development and modernization of the infrastructure occurred along with the growth of a strong modern army, secular educational system, and strong nationalistic ideology (Abrahamian, 1982; Lapidus, 1988). Structural changes in the economy accompanied social reforms (e.g., redistribution of land) to provide favorable conditions for economic development. Legal and symbolic changes enhanced the status of women and increased their participation in domains outside the home. These changes included the rights of voting and political participation, and placed women in high positions within government. A new set of laws improved the legal status of women within marriages and families (Bill, 1988; Pakzad, 1994). These changes were aimed toward promoting the status of women and toward affecting family formation and levels of fertility and family growth.

Despite relative improvement in the well-being of the urban population, modernization by the monarchy generated widening regional and ethnic polarization (Aghajanian, 1983). While there was remarkable improvement in economic growth, the society faced a growing ethnic, regional, and class inequality in the 1970s. Other divisions were created by the infiltration of Western culture, especially components that were at odds with the Iranian Islamic traditions. Cultural, religious, economic, and social discontent accumulated over the years culminating in the Islamic Revolution and proclamation of the Islamic Republic of Iran on April 1, 1979.

The Revolution was a turning point that changed the society and economy of Iran through policies for renewal of Islamic values. Mass media, especially television, and formal and informal educational programs reinforced the legal changes. Eight years (1981-1988) of war with Iraq (Chubin, 1988) drained social and economic resources that could have been available for development of infrastructure and social programs. Since the war there have been economic development and reconstruction efforts. The government has improved the standard of living and provided basic amenities to rural areas. A new economic development plan has been implemented and a strong program of basic health care and family planning has been established (Abbasi-Shavazi, McDonald, & Hosseini-Chavoshi, 2003; Aghajanian, 1994, 1995).

Family in Iranian Context

Families today are influenced by pre-Islamic civilization, Islamic values and prescriptions, the 1960s and 1970s modernization efforts, the Islamic Revolution, the eight years of war, and recent efforts toward economic development. In addition to historic influences, the physical and ethnic diversity of Iran have influenced aspects of marriage ceremonies and family relations. The inhabitants of Iran have neither ethnic nor linguistic unity, but over 99 percent are Muslims. The largest ethnic groups are the Persians, Azeri, Turkish, Baluchi, Arabs, and Kurds. Except for Tehran, the capital, and some other industrial centers that have drawn migrants from various ethnic groups, the regions of the country are homogenous in ethnicity and language. Three provinces in the northwest contain Turkish communities, two in the west contain Kurdish communities, and a mixture of Arabs and Persians live in three provinces on the Persian Gulf. In the east, Baluchis live in the province of Baluchistan. Persians populate the central plateau.

While there is some regional and ethnic variation most of the structural and functional aspects of families presented here are common across groups (Azadarmaki & Bahar, 2006). The Iran Statistical Center (2002, 2003) reported 83 percent of households to be nuclear families. In urban areas, 83 percent of households are made up of nuclear families while in rural areas this figure is 80 percent. About 5 percent of households nationwide include the head of household and children but cross-tabulation by sex of the head of household and the type of household are not available. The contributor's observation suggests that most of such households are female-headed and are increasing. Other household types include those containing members other than children of the head and the spouse of the head. Some of these members might be nonblood related. These are considered extended households. About 18 percent of all households are extended; in rural areas, about 20 percent are extended (Iran Statistical Center, 2003).

In Iran, it is difficult to classify households by standard family types (nuclear, extended, and joint). Separation by residential dwelling does not prevent a large network of extended family members of various generations sharing social and economic resources and responsibilities, and considering the affairs of a nuclear family as their concern (e.g., a business can be shared by a man and his married sons who have their own households; land can be cultivated by several nuclear families that economically make up a large family). Divorced women result in shame and stigma to their fathers, brothers, and other family members living in other households. The kinship network, especially from the father's side, is important in the life of the individual although the typical individual lives in a nuclear family.

Patrilocal residence has been historically common among various communities and ethnic groups in Iran (Aghajanian, 1999). Postmarital residence may be in one or more rooms of the husband's father's compound. Several sons could live in the compound with the parents, with a few rooms allocated to each son's family. Usually, meals are prepared and eaten together during the first months of marriage. There will be a time when the new couple will be independent in this regard, yet the complex of economic and social interactions continues. If the new couple does not reside in the same compound with the husband's parents, they typically will be in a dwelling unit in close proximity. There are some variations in the distance to the husband's residence in urban centers where housing has become a serious problem for the younger generation (Aghajanian, 1999). Nevertheless, patrilocal residence is the common pattern.

The common pattern of descent and authority among all ethnic groups is patrilineal and is reinforced by civil law and tradition (Azadarmaki & Bahar, 2006). Primacy is given from fathers to sons and to male relatives. By law, the family name of the child shall be that of the father (Pakzad, 1994). The Iranian legal and sociocultural system is developed within an ancient patriarchal social organization.

COUPLE FORMATION AND MARITAL DYNAMICS

In Iranian society, sexuality is controlled by strong sociocultural and religious beliefs that treat sex outside of marriage as taboo. Adultery is considered a great sin and is harshly penalized (Afkhami & Friedl, 1994). Cases of adultery are punishable with death by stoning. While punishment for adultery is harsh, the rules and regulations for proving it are very tight and require trusted witnesses. At the same time, the sociocultural system and Islamic penal codes support and encourage marriage and family formation. Traditionally, marriage occurs relatively early and is a near universal phenomenon for women. Women must keep and prove virginity until marriage. Women's dignity and status, and their families' are at risk if they are sexually active and lose virginity before marriage (Afkhami & Friedl, 1994; Mohammadi et al., 2006).

The Timing of Marriage

Early marriage for men and women was common in Iran (Moezi, 1967; Shaditalab, 2005). According to nineteenth century travelers, children were often betrothed when they were young, although the wedding did not take place for some years (Rice, 1923). Children were occasionally betrothed in infancy and would become couples when the girl was fourteen and the boy sixteen (Piggot, 1874). Although such young marriages have not totally disappeared, the legal and actual age of marriage have increased significantly compared with the historical description of child marriages. Increase in age at marriage has been influenced by legal and social changes. Secularization of the marital ceremony and civil registration of vital events are major developments in the timing of marriage. For many centuries marriage was a religious act recorded by local religious trustees. In 1930, along with other changes introduced by the government of Reza Shah, recording of vital events (birth, marriage, divorce, and death) became secular. The age of marriage also became part of civil law (Momeni, 1972); marriage of females before age fifteen and males before eighteen is forbidden. In cases where reasons justify it, exemption from the age restriction can be accorded.

Even with the legal changes, the age of marriage was still low in the middle of the twentieth century. A national sample of women showed that more than 50 percent were married by age sixteen (Aghajanian, Gross, & Lewis, 1993). Some changes in the actual age of marriage occurred in the 1970s and 1980s (Shaditalab, 2005). The percentage of ever-married among women fifteen to nineteen years of age declined 34 percent in 1976 (Higgins, 1985). However, in the 1990s, the increase in the age of marriage was remarkable. The data from the 1966 census to the present show the age of marriage for females has been sharply increasing (Iran Statistical Center, 2002). Between 1986 and 1996, mean age at first marriage increased from 19.8 to 22.4 for females, and from 23.6 to 25.6 for males. The percentage of females aged fifteen to nineteen who had ever been married fell to 19 percent (Mohammadi et al., 2006). The norm for the timing of marriage is becoming the time after women finish their high school education.

While there have never been any legal barriers for men to marry before age twenty, the rate of such early marriages is small (Azadarmaki & Bahar, 2006). In 1996, 2 percent of the male population in the age group fifteen to nineteen was ever-married (Iran Statistical Center, 1997). Even in the years before the Revolution of the 1970s, only about 6 percent of men were married before age twenty (Abbasi-Shavazi, 2002; Iran Statistical Center, 2002). It appears that men have been marrying in their twenties and the proportion of those marrying below age twenty has been decreasing.

Mate Selection—Marrying a Relative

Mate selection has been a familial and tribal action rather than an individual decision. Marriage by arrangement has been the norm and continues today with some variation from the past. Free-choice in mate selection has been rare but is emerging. In the end, it is family elders who decide whom adult children should marry. In Iran, endogamy has insured accumulation of power and wealth. It was common for a newborn to be betrothed to his or her first or second cousin (Tapper, 1979). Islamic tradition encourages marriage of parallel or cross cousins. Several ethnographic studies, sample surveys, and censuses report kin marriage as common (Bradburd, 1984; Tapper, 1979). For example, based on the 1966 census, the incidence of kin marriage ranged from 25 percent in Tehran to 33 percent in rural areas (Behnam & Amani, 1974). Iran's fertility survey data from 1977 showed that 40 percent of women were married to relatives (Given & Hirschman, 1994). Rural women were more commonly married to relatives than urban women. Young age at marriage and marriage to a relative are highly correlated. The 1977 survey also revealed that the rate of kin marriage among recent marriage cohorts is higher than the rate among old cohorts of women. However, higher education for women and white-collar jobs for men were related to being married to nonrelatives (Given & Hirschman, 1994). The educational attainment of women and age of marriage has been increasing markedly in recent years

(Abbasi-Shavazi, 2002; Aghajanian, 1985). As previous studies show older age at marriage and higher education for women are negatively related to marrying a relative, it can be expected that mate selection has become more exogamous in Iran. This was supported by data collected in 1995 and 2003 which indicated that compared with their parents, young men and women are less likely to marry a relative (Aghajanian, Tashakkori, & Mehryar, 1996; Ahmadnia & Mehryar, 2004).

Mate Selection—Matchmaking

Iranian marriage often involves a matchmaking process (Price, 2001). Often the initial "go-between" is the mother and sisters of the prospective groom, who search for a potential bride at public, religious, or traditional gatherings. In villages and small urban areas, there is a good chance that the potential bride can be found among first and second cousins or other relatives and neighbors. In urban areas, families first target extended family and members of their trade and business, and make inquiries from neighbors, friends, business partners, and acquaintances for the "right bride" for their son. There are also hired go-betweens, or matchmakers, usually middle-age women who provide assistance in making the arrangement. The matchmaker provides initial information to both families (e.g., reputation, occupation, and wealth). Next the groom's family and the groom visit the family of the prospective bride. Traditionally, this would be the first time the bride and groom see each other. The acceptability of physical appearance not only to the prospective bride and groom, but also to their families, is the main issue in this first meeting. The contributor's recent observations suggest significant changes to this traditional pattern. In the cities, young men have started to look for their own bride before they ask their family to step in for familial negotiations. Having several supervised visitations in the bride's house and permission for private exchange of views are becoming popular, at least in large cities.

Despite changes in the pattern of finding the right mate, marriage is still a familial contract and members of the extended family negotiate on behalf of the young couple (Abbasi-Shavazi et al., 2003). If both families are ready to negotiate the terms of marriage after the initial stages of exchange of information and acceptance of physical appearance, there is a meeting of elders (usually grandfathers and grandmothers, granduncles, fathers, and mothers) from both sides in the house of the prospective bride. The groom accompanies his elders to this meeting. Each side tries to get more information, directly or indirectly, about the social and economic status of the other family and evaluates the extent to which the marriage will improve the social and economic standing and reputation of their family (Drew, 2006). Sometimes during this visit, the prospective groom and bride have a short conversation and thus a chance to evaluate each other's physical appearance. If the prospective bride and grooms are relatives, they have already had opportunities for evaluating each other's physical appearance. In the majority of situations, the prospective bride covers herself with a veil over her full clothing. Modern middle-class families feel less restricted by social and religious norms. Typically among these families, the future bride is not covered with a veil and she wears clothing that reveals her figure.

After the first visit, the families continue to gather information about each other's social and economic situations and the reputations of the prospective marriage partners and their families (Afkhami & Friedl, 1994). If both families are satisfied, the groom's father talks to him to see if he wants to continue with the process. The family makes the case that this girl is appropriate based on the information gathered. In the end, what they really want is his approval of the physical appearance of the girl. If he finds her attractive and the family is satisfied, they request a second visit for formal marriage negotiations. In response, if the girl's family, based on the information gathered, is happy about the standing of his family, they ask their daughter's opinion about the young man as her future husband. The more the girl's family is convinced about the economic situation and reputation of the groom's family, the more they try to sway their daughter for her approval. In the end, socioeconomic status and the reputations of the families of the prospective bride and groom play important roles in the process of mate selection.

During the second visit with the bride's family there is a request made by the groom's elders for the marriage to the young woman. A male elder representative puts the proposal to the girl's family that "it is his family's honor to request that the two families join by marriage."

The male elder of the girl's family, in response, would express that "it is an honor to have a son of your family as our son-in-law and he will be treated like our own son" (Afkhami & Friedl, 1994). After this ceremonial conversation, the negotiation starts on the important issue of *mahr.* This is the sum value of cash and jewelry which is payable at any time requested by the wife, to the bride (Moghadam, 1994). Note that this amount is not paid, but can be legally requested at any time by women. This traditionally protected women against unilateral divorce. It still continues to be a major tradition and is in fact becoming a symbol of value and prestige for women.

Mahr and Jahaz

The tradition of *mahr* comes from the original Islamic custom of *Mahr-a-Sonah* that prescribes the groom to provide the bride with an agreed amount of valued items, which can be in the form of currency or gold (Moghadam, 1994). The original custom emphasized a small amount (Maqsood, 2005). However, in Iran, *mahr* has been used as a safeguard against the unilateral divorce right of men, especially for capricious reasons. With divorce, the husband is required to pay the *mahr* in full. It can be assumed that the larger the amount of *mahr,* the more reluctant a man would be to initiate a unilateral divorce. Likewise, if divorce occurs, the higher the amount of *mahr,* the more economically protected the woman will be. Divorced women who have small amounts of *mahr* will be economically dependent on their parents and brothers.

In the process of negotiation, the bride's family knows that the higher the amount of *mahr,* the more the *jahaziyeh* they should send with their daughter to the groom's house (Maqsood, 2005; Price, 2001). *Jahaziyeh* is the household items including furniture, appliances, kitchen items, carpet, and curtains delivered to the groom's house a few days before the wedding. The original tradition was based on familial support for the new couple to establish their new home. Through time this has become a serious way to show class and wealth distinction for the bride's family. The bride's family gains prestige by the size and variety of items they send with their daughter at the beginning of the marriage. The more items and the more expensive the brand names, the higher the pride of the new bride and the more the groom's family can "show off." In the past, *jahaz* was a practical boost to the young couple starting their married life and needing economic support. In contemporary Iranian society, this has become an important sign of prestige and pride. Owing to this tradition and its significance in individual and family recognition, the bride's family takes much time and planning in the preparation of *jahaz*. This tradition is so important that families start to prepare for the items that will go with their daughter long before she gets to the marrying age (Price, 2001). However, given the high cost of modern appliances, families are having a hard time providing such items. In turn, this has become a source of stress for families and frustration for girls from families who cannot compete with emerging standards. With the expansion of market economy and increase in the number of modern household appliances and items, the tradition that was originally established for the purpose of helping the new couple start married life, has become a serious burden for families.

Weddings

Once the negotiations for *mahr* are finalized and the families agree on the contract and any prenuptial conditions, the religious ceremony will be performed and the representative from the Civil Registration Organization will record the marriage contract. The wedding, which is a big dinner party and marks the time the new couple starts their married life, is usually from six to twelve months after the religious ceremony and the recording of the marriage. A large number of family members and friends are invited to this party and they bring gifts, usually household items.

As the families prepare for the party, they agree on a date and day for the wedding (Price, 2001). On the night of the wedding, the groom's family goes to the bride's family to bring her to her new home. However, today there is some variation. The young couple might live on a separate level and have their own household in the same house where the groom's parents live. They might live on one side of the house separated by a courtyard. They might even live in an apartment in the same neighborhood. It is a stigma for a groom to move to his in-law's household or depend on them in any way.

Personal Mate Selection

In the past the opportunities for personal mate selection were limited. Observations by social scientists in Iran suggest that the number of marriages based on personal mate selection has been increasing (cf. Drew, 2006; Price, 2001). With the growth of women in higher education and the labor force, opportunities for personal mate selection have increased. However, the prospective mates ask their families about the appropriateness of the person as a marriage partner. Parental primacy in mate selection is strong (Aghajanian et al., 1996; Ahmadnia & Mehryar, 2004). Few adolescents want to leave parental influence out of their mate selection. This is not surprising as the social contract of marriage is still among the families of the bride and groom (Azadarmaki & Bahar, 2006). It is the larger network of family that is responsible for the outcome of marriage.

Divorce

In Iran, divorce is a stigma for a woman and her extended family, especially the male members (Aghajanian & Moghadas, 1998). As if divorce is always her fault, she is blamed for being insalubrious and intolerant. The taboo of divorce is reinforced in a newlywed woman by the saying, "that once married, a good woman stays with her husband until her death and it is only death that separates them." Islamic principles advise against divorce and support it only as the last alternative. The Islamic judge acts upon divorce only when confident there is no room for reconciliation. Family elders will always interfere to try to prevent a divorce in their family.

Divorce has always existed in Iran despite familial, social, religious, and economic safeguards for prevention. Divorces are not as widespread as in Western countries. However, the rate is gradually increasing; 60,559 divorces were registered in 2001 (Iran Statistical Center, 2002). The estimated crude divorce rate is less than one divorce per 1,000 population. The crude divorce rate in most Western countries is four to eight times this rate (McKenry & Price, 1995).

Divorce is more common in urban areas. Some differentials in divorce are observable from the few studies available (Aghajanian, 1986b; Aghajanian & Moghadas, 1998). Divorce is more frequent among women with no education and women with college educations.

Employed women are more prone to divorce as are couples without children. Infertility is an adequate cause for a woman to be divorced, but few childless divorce cases are due to infertility (Aghajanian, 1986b).

In the pre-Islamic era, divorce was accepted. It could be affected by mutual consent or if the wife was barren or guilty of a deadly sin/ offence (e.g., sex with another man) (Encyclopaedia Iranica, 1995). In the Islamic era, divorce has been the unilateral right of men but they are strongly advised against it. In the twentieth century, there were some modifications in the laws to improve the situation of women with respect to divorce. While a 1930s divorce law required the registration of divorces in the state registries, it continued to give absolute divorce power to men. In 1967, a legal act designed for family protection was introduced which prohibited men from exercising their former absolute right of divorcing a wife (cf. Family Law Provisions, nd). The law sought to restrict divorces to cases of proven irreconcilability by the secular court.

The law allows couples agreeing to divorce (*Mubarat*) to register their divorce before two witnesses in an office of a notary public (*Mahzar*). To protect women against coercive consent, the law was recently amended to give women the chance to bring their cases to court if they disagreed with divorce. The Special Civil Court (*Dadgahe Madanie Khas*) handles such divorces. Islamic judges in Special Civil Court are to do their best to convince the husband and wife to reconcile (Encyclopaedia Iranica, 1995). Only after a judge has been unsuccessful in bringing about reconciliation will the court investigate the case and make a decision concerning the divorce. The court will also consider cases where the woman has initiated a divorce request (such as a *Khul'a* divorce) for reasons such as being in a physically abusive relationship with the husband (Family Law Provisions, nd). The husband often does not want to divorce his wife in such cases, but the court can order him to act on the divorce. In many such instances, the abused wife will forfeit her *mahr* as an incentive for the abusive husband to divorce her (Aghajanian & Moghadas, 1998). There is not much systematic research, however, about the extent and level of domestic violence and wife abuse and their relation to divorce in the Iranian society.

The economic resource a woman has after divorce is what she receives as part of her *mahr.* She might not be able to get all of her *mahr* if her husband brings evidence of his inability to pay. He might agree to pay in installments or skip installments. After divorce the woman is entitled to receive alimony for three months and ten days. She is expected to remain unmarried during this period so if she is pregnant, the paternity of the child can be established. In general, the situation of a divorced woman deteriorates and she will be economically dependent on her parents and relatives (Aghajanian & Moghadas, 1998; Nassehy, 1991).

After divorce fathers are responsible for their children and have the choice of custody. Boys from age two and girls from age seven can be legally removed from their mother (Pakzad, 1994). It is most often the mother who takes care of the children (Aghajanian & Moghadas, 1998). Mothers often pursue this because they cannot tolerate the authority of stepmothers over their children. This arrangement can help mothers' economic situation, as fathers are responsible for the living expenses of their children. The children living with their mother could be practical for the father's new marriage; it is easier to get along with a new wife if the children are not around.

FAMILIES AND CHILDREN

In Iranian society, children are God's blessing and they are inevitable. Their presence is expected and normal; their absence has to be explained (Friedl, 1985). Historically and religiously, more children meant more followers of Islam who can stand against the nonbelievers and conquer new territories for Islam. This ideology was advocated by the Arab Muslims who conquered many pre-Islamic civilizations and spread Islam across the Persian Empire in 637 (Lapidus, 1988). The spread of Islam needed military personnel and that was only possible through increasing population through early marriage and procreation.

Proverbs (e.g., "Couples without children are like trees without fruit—The only benefits of such trees are for use as firewood," or "It has to have branches to be a tree" (Friedl, 1985)), are a reflection of pronatalism in Iranian culture. Children have been the center of family organization and cohesion within the extended family structure.

It is a cultural norm that at the proper time people will be married and have their first child within a year, preferably a son. Ability to have children must be established soon after marriage, especially for women. Traditionally, son preference has dictated the pattern of individual fertility. Women continue to have children as long as they do not have sons. A preference for sons has contributed to the high level of fertility.

Value of Children

In Iran, children have been perceived as valuable economic assets in addition to their social and psychological significance. Children have been the main source of old age security across all classes and groups, and have been a significant source of family labor and income from wage-earning jobs (Aghajanian, 1986a). In rural areas, children did productive household activities (e.g., bringing water and fuel wood, taking care of livestock, and carpet weaving). As they grew older, children continued to contribute through unpaid labor or through wage-earning jobs. Importantly, children took care of their elderly parents. Male children have traditionally been considered more economically beneficial than female children, as there were fewer restrictions on their economic activities as young adults. The activities of female children became mostly limited to those within the household as they became teenagers, and were expected by religious norms to be segregated from male strangers. In addition, female children will leave the parental house after marriage and thus have limited opportunity to provide economic help to their parents.

In urban areas, children have less value in terms of labor contribution at a younger age, but have been considered valuable as they get older and participate in wage-earning activities. Children contribute to their family through the wages they earn and support their parents during old age. Until about two decades ago, urban parents reported strong economic and old age security values in children (Aghajanian, 1988b). Recently, parents are more concerned about the cost of raising children and financial pressure on the family (Abbasi-Shavazi et al., 2003).

Fertility Issues

In the past low child survival and the high social and economic value of children led to larger families. As late as 1976, 10 to 20 percent of children died before their first birthday (Aghajanian, 1993). Child mortality (i.e., mortality rate before age five) was also high. This meant to have more children might result in the number of surviving children desired.

High expectations for social and economic values of children (especially sons) combined with high rates of infant/child mortality supported high levels of fertility for a long time. Women started childbearing early and continued to the end of their reproductive period. As late as 1966, the average woman would have seven children (Aghajanian, 1991). During the 1970s, urban women reduced their desire for a larger family size as child mortality declined and the social norms supported lower family size especially among educated women (Raftery, Lewis, & Aghajanian, 1995). The availability of contraceptives allowed women to regulate their own fertility. During the 1970s, the monarchy-subsidized contraceptives and information about them spread to cities and villages (Aghajanian, Agha, & Gross, 1996). This however, was limited to about 35 percent of eligible women by 1977 (Aghajanian, 1995). In the first part of the 1980s, revolutionary changes toward the policies of the monarchy affected the supply of subsidized contraceptives. Furthermore, social and political issues related to the participation in the war with Iraq and large number of causalities to young men and rationing based on household size, stalled the decline of family size that had started in the 1970s (Aghajanian, 1991, 1999).

Since the war ended in 1988, the Islamic Republic entered an era of postwar reconstruction and development; families are encouraged to have two to three children. Starting in 1989 the government has encouraged lower family sizes. The family planning program sponsored by the government supports education about, and easy access to, a variety of contraceptives for married women. Official policy is clear and strong in support of small family size for improving the quality of life for parents and children. The contraceptive prevalence rate (for married women aged fifteen to forty-nine) is above 70 percent (UNDP, 2006).

The government has also expanded a network of primary health care units. One result has been a significant decline in child and infant mortality. This is especially so in rural areas where the government has expanded basic health services and provided better water facilities as well as other amenities. The rate of infant mortality has declined to a level around twenty-nine per 1,000 live births (Ministry of Health and Medical Education, 2003). The observed rate in 2000 is almost three times less than the prevailing rate of 112 per 1,000 births in 1977 (Aghajanian, 1993).

As child survival has improved and the size of the families has unexpectedly increased during the last decade, the cost of raising a family has drastically increased. Children's education has become an important need for people of all social classes. Parents aspire to education for their children regardless of gender. The changing agricultural society and fast rate of urbanization have decreased the economic and labor values of children. In addition, a formal social security system is spreading across various classes, reducing the need for children as old age security. There are clear indications that the focus of most families is more on the quality of children rather than on the quantity. The emphasis on education, desire for high educational attainment for females, and the high cost of raising children have convinced parents to have fewer children. Iranian women are not only marrying later but they are having fewer children once married. The new cohorts who marry have a longer interval between marriage and the birth of the first child. It is estimated that total fertility has declined from a high of 6.2 children per woman in 1986, to 3.5 by 1993, and to between 2.1 and 1.8 in 2006 (Fouladi, 1996; UNDP, 2006; World Factbook, 2006). The future trend is toward a fewer number of children in a family.

FAMILIES AND GENDER

Property Rights

Property rights are not legally limited for Iranian women. Islamic norms sanction ownership of private property or business by women and men. In fact, the groom's family transfers part of the ownership of the house to the bride as a precondition to marriage in some areas (e.g., Isfahan Province). Civil law has reinforced the equality of property rights of men and women, however, men and women do not own property equally. As in many other societies, men own more property than do women because opportunities to acquire property for women are limited. Women inherit less property from their parents. Once in their husbands' homes, women only own what was agreed to in the marriage contract. A widow receives a trivial share from her husband's property unless he transferred property to her name before dying (Pakzad, 1994).

Earning income is an important channel for acquiring property. Until recently, a small percentage of women were involved in wage and salary earning activities and had less access to economic resources for acquiring property. In recent years more Iranian women have entered the formal labor force and have attained postgraduate education; it is expected they have also increased their share of ownership of property and businesses. Women are increasingly demanding legal and other rights (Azadarmaki & Bahar, 2006; Osanloo, 2006; Shaditalab, 2005).

Polygyny

Islamic tradition and law (Islamic code) allow polygyny. At the same time, there have been strong Islamic restrictions on the practice of polygyny. Given the religious conditions to be satisfied and the economic requirements, the best estimate is that polygyny was limited in traditional Iranian society. In 1956 at the time of the first census of Iran, a low rate (about ten out of 1,000) of married men were married to two women (Momeni, 1975).

Although the practice of polygyny was limited, the 1967 Family Protection Law sought to prevent polygyny by requiring the consent of the first wife (Bagley, 1971). This law was appealed in 1980 and allowed men to be married to more than one woman simultaneously. Yet, even with the religious support and with no legal restriction, there is no sign of a significant increase in polygyny, based on the Iranian censuses since 1956. In 1994, there were 8.5 men married to more than one woman for each 1,000 married men in Iran (Iran Statistical Center, 1996). It appears that the economic realities strongly limit having a second wife, and many women are opposed to polygyny (Shaditalab, 2005).

Dress Codes

A variety of dress codes exist for women in most Islamic societies, including Iran. There is no one pattern to these; they vary according to rural-urban, social class, policies, attitudes, and interpretations of the ruling governments in these countries at various times. Throughout Iran's history, the ruling dynasties with various levels of dedication to the fundamentals of Islam, have behaved differently in implementing the Islamic codes of dress. Rural Iranian women have never been able to follow the restrictive dress code and gender segregation as the nature of rural life and work is not compatible with such limitations. Urban women have been segregated and restricted with respect to the dress codes in public places (Higgins, 1985).

Education

Iranian families traditionally allocated more of their resources to educate sons (Aghajanian, 1994) because sons are required to care for parents in their old age and stay with the family. Daughters marry and move to another family. Whatever material and human capital daughters have by the time of marriage will benefit their husband's family. In addition, daughters usually have to take household items (*Jahaz*) with them to their new household.

Education of girls is catching up with that of boys. Parents increasingly support the education of their daughters as well as their sons (Shavarini, 2005, 2006). In 1994, the estimated literacy rate among the female population fifteen to twenty-four years of age was 90 percent. The rate for male literacy in the same age category was 96 percent (Iran Statistical Center, 1996). Another estimate for 2003 gave the estimated literacy rates (age fifteen and over) of 86 percent for males and 73 percent for females (World Factbook, 2006). The enrollment rate of female children has increased at all levels especially those in the age group of fifteen to nineteen. The school enrollment of females in this age group increased from 26 percent in 1976 to 48 percent in 1996 (Iran Statistical Center, 1997). The combined primary, secondary, and tertiary school enrollment rate for females in 2002 was 65 percent (compared with 72 percent for males) (UNDP, 2004). About 90 percent of all children reach grade 5 (UNDP, 2006). Families are sending their daughters to high schools and universities at such a rate now that more than half of the university system enrollment is female and more female students pass the entrance test for medical school than males.

Domestic and Economic Roles

The primary domestic roles of women in Iran have been mother and wife. In general, this is consistent with the teachings of Islam that encourage women to be good wives and nurture generations of good Muslims (Shavarini, 2006). Yet, Islam does not prohibit nonhousehold roles for women. A married woman can be gainfully employed. However, if the nature of her occupation is not compatible with her family's interest or dignity, the husband can prevent his wife from engaging in such an occupation, provided he can prove such incompatibility in the Special Civil Tribunal (Pakzad, 1994; Shavarini, 2006).

Women have also always contributed to the economic activity of the household. In rural areas, a number of family chores are essential economic activities. In addition, women contribute their labor to agricultural production, mostly in terms of being unpaid family workers. Urban women might bring extra income to their families by weaving carpets or participation in home industries and trade (Moghadam, 1988). In most cases, the income generated by these activities is spent for the family and is invested in various needs of the family, including preparations for the wedding of a daughter or son. Women with domestically generated income might have slightly more access to economic resources than do women without their own incomes. This does not necessarily mean they have more authority and power in family decision making. They are, however, more prepared financially for old age.

Saving for old age has been important for women. Due to husband-wife age differentials, women spend a large proportion of their adult lives in widowhood. As inheritance from their husbands is limited, women should prepare for widowhood, especially if they do not have sons to take care of them. There is a dearth of knowledge about the economic situation of the elderly in general and female elderly in particular in the current Iranian society.

The opportunities for women's participation in the formal economic sector have only emerged in the second half of the twentieth century (Aghajanian, Agha, & Gross, 1996). It seems that slowly but consistently, changes in roles of women are emerging and women are combining familial with economic roles (Zahedi, 2006). Among adolescents, 95 percent of girls and 65 percent of boys consider working outside of the household for married women as desirable and acceptable (Aghajanian et al., 1996). According to the labor force survey in October 2003, approximately 12 percent of women were economically active (Iran Statistical Center, 2004). This rate must be viewed in the context of the existing large underemployment rate for both men and women in the current decade when the boom cohort of the early 1980s is getting ready to enter the labor force.

FAMILIES AND STRESS

Throughout history, social crises and changes (e.g., invasions, wars, revolutions, Westernization, and modernization) have put an extra burden on families. Some aspects of Iranian families have changed in response to these societal pressures. Nevertheless, the family has remained and continues to play a major role in society and the lives of individuals (Shavarini, 2006). Despite the strong endurance as an institution, families have been under some stress during recent decades. Among these stressors are an increase in the number of dual-earner families, ideological differences among family members based on generation and gender, eight years of war with Iraq, and most recently a harsh economy with high inflation.

Dual-Earner Families

Traditionally, women's roles in the Iranian society have been limited to wife and mother. A shift from this division of labor emerged from the 1970s. Married women have been joining the labor force. About half a million families have been affected by this new pattern, and currently about 15 percent of women are in the labor force (Weiskopf-Bock, 1985; Shavarini, 2006).

Traditional society, especially in relation to men and women's roles inside the household, is changing and increasing stress on families (Shavarini, 2006). Employed married women expect a different division of labor requiring men's involvement in housework and child care. Yet, it is totally unacceptable within the family network and society for a man to do housework such as cleaning, washing, or changing diapers. Hence husbands and wives in dual-worker families are much more in conflict and can have more strain in their relationships. From the limited available data, it is apparent that married women with professional jobs report more conflict and quarrels with their husbands than other groups of women (Aghajanian, 1988a). Married women employed part time and those who do not have preschool children report less conflict.

The best predictor of stress among these families is the amount of housework done by the husband. The reported conflict is 50 percent less for employed women who report that their husbands help with the housework (Aghajanian, 1988a). The speculation is that most quarrels and fights relate to the division of labor within the household. In many cases, although the husband is not against his wife working in the formal sector, he does not want to contribute labor to household chores. There is a need for serious studies of this issue in a society that is swiftly changing in some ways while some traditions such as gender-based household roles strongly persist. Undeniably with increasing education and improvement of opportunities for women in paid work outside the house, the stress on the family will continue, as the societal norms toward men's involvement in domestic chores remain unchanged.

Ideational Differences

Probably the least documented stress on Iranian families is ideational differences based on generation and gender. Differences have emerged from the conflict between what older generations (parents and grandparents) consider Western cultural invasion and younger generations (adolescents and young adults) consider modernization and adoption of new values (Mohammadi et al., 2006; Shaditalab, 2005). These controversial cultural elements include such things as clothing fashion and style of music, films, television shows, and perhaps dating and sexual activity. The availability of modern technology and expansion of mass media, especially television programs through satellite technology, have accelerated the diffusion of non-Iranian culture among younger generations. The adoption of new ways of behaving based on this non-Iranian cultural influence has been a great source of generational conflict within Iranian families. The Islamic revitalization since 1979 has been more demanding for women than men to return to traditional ways (Shaditalab, 2005). This revitalization of Islamic values began with circumscription of roles of women and their societal participation. Religious and political leaders emphasized that domestic roles and raising generations of good Muslims best suited the dignity of women. Regulations were introduced governing the public appearance of women and their clothing. The segregation of women was enforced in public places, universities, and offices. Women were praised above all for being good mothers and wives. This has been the source of stress for middle-class, educated, urban families. It has been argued, convincingly, that urban, well-educated families were not the norm at the time of the Islamic Revolution (Hegland, 1990; Higgins, 1985). Hence, the revolutionary changes were not new to the majority of women who were already following the traditional religious values. However, there were, even then, middle-class, urban, educated families and their number has been growing since with the increasing level of education of women (Azadarmaki & Bahar, 2006; Moghadam, 1988).

War

Families in Iran were forced to deal with the eight years war with Iraq (Zahedi, 2006). More than fifty cities and 4,000 villages were damaged and over 2.5 million people were forced to migrate to war-free zones and live in refugee camps. The war uprooted families from their communities where they had a long history of respect and recognition. In the process of moving and being forced to live under a new situation with many strangers, men and women lost their networks of relatives and the social and economic exchange with the extended family. Refugees were housed in camps and dorms where each family lived in one room or part of a large room shared with other families. The shelters were limited in such facilities as kitchens, baths, and toilets. There was high physical and psychological density in these shelters. Privacy and personal space were practically nonexistent (cf. Iran-Iraq War, nd).

The process of uprooting from villages and communities and refuging to large cities put a large number of war-migrant families in a state of social disorganization and status inconsistency. This was an important source of stress for these families. Some of the effect of stress is reflected in the increase in family break-ups and divorce. During the war, the divorce rate increased (Aghajanian, 1986b) and for war-refugee families, the divorce rate was about 40 percent higher than the national rate (Aghajanian, 1990).

War deaths have also stressed families. Estimates of the number killed in the Iran-Iraq war range from 217,000 to over 1 million (Zahedi, 2006). These estimates indicate a large number of parents lost their sons, many of them below age twenty. Many women became widows. For parents, the adjustment to the death of a young son(s) was difficult and many young widows might want to remarry. However, remarriage by women in Iran is difficult, as virginity is an important factor in marriage and mate selection (see previous text). It is not dignified for a man to marry a woman who is not a virgin although some men married war widows as second wives. Many of these women preferred to stay unmarried rather than become a second wife. In addition, many of these widows have children. The Foundation for Martyrs partly supports the women and their children (including establishing a marriage matching service), and many have achieved a degree of economic independence. While there is economic support, single parenthood in Iran is odd and difficult to adjust to even with the organized social and economic support for widows of war martyrs. Given that there is little study on the consequences of war widowhood and the situation of children of war widows, the extent of continuing stress among these families is not known. There are indications of ongoing divorce among war widows (Zahedi, 2006).

Economic Pressure

The foremost stressor for Iranian families today is economic due to high inflation. Further, about 40 percent of people live in poverty and unemployment is 11 percent (World Factbook, 2006). The war and political division during the 1980s hurt the Iranian economy. The economy experienced a significant decline during the 1980s (Amirahmadi, 1990). During the same period, average family size increased, as the social surrounding of the Islamic revolutionary society was pronatalist. Many high parity women (i.e., those with four or more children), gave birth to another child for the revolutionary society (Aghajanian, 1991). The decline in family income in the face of a growing family size led to a drastic reduction in living standards. With the cease-fire, economic restructuring, and devaluation of Iranian money, inflation was over 30 percent, although the current estimated inflation rate had dropped to 14 percent (Hoogland, 1995; World Factbook, 2000, 2006).

The value of Iranian money drastically declined during the 1980s (Amirahamadi, 1990). Iranian families depend on foreign exchange from the sale of oil for almost anything from basic staple food to clothing and medical and health products. Despite earnings from oil revenue increasing, the increase in the size of the population and higher cost of imported products means retail prices continue to rise and increase economic stress for the majority of families.

FAMILIES AND AGING

While aging is biological, the concept of elderly is social and varies by society. The Iranian census defines "elderly" as the population sixty-five years and older. Like many other developing countries, only a small portion of the population is old by this definition. In 1996, 4 percent of the population was classified as elderly and also in 2003. At birth, male life expectancy is 69.2 while females can be expected to live to 72.3 years (Iran Statistical Center, 1997; UNDP, 2006).

The elderly have held special respect and authority within families (Abd Al-ati, 1995; Aghajanian, 1988b). However, authority can vary depending on the prestige and power that an older man has through access to wealth and political power. Female elders have the respect of younger generations but limited access to material and community resources limits their power and authority. Members of the immediate family, grandchildren, and younger members of the family at large, are to respect the point of view of the elderly and be guided by their wisdom and experience. In reality, affairs within the economic domain and related to decisions for activities out of the household, are guided by the male elderly. An example of this is considerations of opening a new business by younger household members. Older women and men share affairs centered within the household (e.g., selection of a mate for a younger member). Respect for older generations is not limited to members of one's own nuclear family—young people should respect all elderly people in the extended family and the community at large (Abd Al-ati, 1995).

Family Caregiving

The elderly are supported and cared for within their families (Sheykhi, 2006). In many situations, they control the economic resources until their death to protect their status in the family (Aghajanian, 1988b). Islamic principles reinforce cultural expectations for taking care of elderly family members and remind people that good Muslims ensure that elders are able to lead decent lives. While norms and sanctions have been strong, it is plausible that the practice of caregiving within the family has been declining given the social and economic changes in the last decade, especially stressful economic situations and high unemployment rates among younger family members.

The sex ratio of the elderly is 114 men for every 100 women (Iran Statistical Center, 2003). The high male to female sex ratio among the elderly is consistently observed across the censuses in Iran. The implication is that females at one stage of life have a higher mortality. This might be due to early childhood mortality and mortality during the reproductive period (maternal mortality rate of thirty-seven (reported) to seventy-six (adjusted for underreporting) per 100,000 live births; UNDP, 2006).

Living Arrangements

Another way to look at aging is to examine living arrangements (Weeks, 1996). About 92 percent of the male elderly are heads of households and most live with their wives (Iran Statistical Center, 1998). Despite the high sex ratio previously noted, two factors allow this situation for older men. First, the husband-wife age differential favors men. Second, it is easy and common for widowed men to marry for a second time, and to marry a younger woman.

Among elderly women, only 33 percent live with their spouses. Once widowed, remarriage is rare; women either head their own households or join the household of a son. About 30 percent of elderly women live with their children who are heads of households (Iran Statistical Center, 1998). It is clear, then, that differences exist between male and female elderly in relation to dependency during old age and for living arrangements. Men are mostly married and are living with their wives. Women are mostly widows and are living with their children, usually a son. The pattern of living arrangements indicates that elderly women are more economically dependent than are elderly men. Another indication of this differential dependency is that many elderly men report employment while few older women work. Except for the men working in the formal sector of the economy where the law requires retirement at age sixty-five, most men continue to be employed during their old age, working until they die (Iran Statistical Center, 2003). Employed elderly women probably work because of economic need, whereas many men might work because they do not want to lose their hold on economic power (Aghajanian, 1988b).

As fertility and mortality decline, there will be an increase in the number of elderly people in the Iranian population. Around 80 percent of women and 72 percent of men born during 2000-2005 are expected to survive to age sixty-five and the proportion of the population aged sixty-five and over is expected to increase to 5 percent by 2015 (UNDP, 2006). There is, however, limited data for examining the situation of the elderly in this transitional society (Sheykhi, 2006).

OTHER FAMILY SITUATIONS

Temporary marriage, *mut'a,* was a matrilineal form of marriage, and one among several marital forms practiced in pre-Islamic Arabia (Haeri, 1994). *Mut'a* has been legally permitted and religiously sanctioned among the Twelver Shiite (*Ithna Ashariyya*), most of whom live in Iran (Haeri, 1994).[1] In its present form, *mut'a* or *sigheh* is a form of contract in which a man (married or unmarried) and an unmarried woman (virgin, divorced, or widowed) agree, often privately and verbally, to marry for a specified period (one hour to ninety-nine years) (Family Values, 2003). The couple agrees on a brideprice and at the end of the agreed period, the couple parts without a divorce.

After the dissolution the temporary wife must observe a period of sexual abstinence in order to prevent problems in identifying a potential child's legitimate father. This makes the practice different from prostitution, as the child is both legitimate and can inherit (Bowman, 1998). However, attitudes toward the practice are ambivalent.

Temporary, in contrast to permanent, marriage, is invisible. For some, this raises questions of whether women are exploited and without legal recourse (Bowman, 1998; Family Values, 2003). The temporary marriage contract is not recorded and it does not require any witnesses. Surveys and censuses in Iran do not ask questions regarding temporary marriages. Hence, how extensively temporary marriage has been and is currently practiced is not clear and any speculation would be misleading. Ethnographic research indicates that "the institution is alive and well among lower socioeconomic strata in the society. Women who contract temporary marriages tend to be primarily young divorced women from lower-class backgrounds, but middle-class women occasionally do so as well" (Haeri, 1994, p. 107).

CONCLUDING COMMENTS

Family is the most influential institution in Iran. There is rarely a major decision or action throughout the life course that is not discussed and evaluated within the network of the extended family. Despite the huge amount of urbanization that has influenced the residence of the extended family, the social and economic interaction among extended family members have remained and will continue to remain (Iran Statistical Center, 1997). The patriarchal line of authority will continue to protect the status of family through guidance and decision-making control of the younger generations.

Islamic values that have shaped life in Iran for many centuries will continue to support the patriarchal family framework for family decision making and individual behavior. Sexual behavior will continue to be controlled within this framework and sexual intercourse out of marriage will be discouraged through strong punishments by family and State. Hence, marriage will continue to be a marked transitional stage in the life of the individual and the family will have primacy in mate selection. Yet, age at marriage and, therefore, age at the time of first sexual intercourse, is increasing for females. Women are marrying later and as the opportunity for education and paid work continues to expand, there will be an increase in their average age at marriage. Later age at marriage and the opportunity to control pregnancy are leading to a lower number of children in the nuclear family (Abbassi-Shavazi, 2002; Fouladi, 1996). At the same time, postponement of marriage and continuation of education for both men and women will prolong residence with the family of socialization.

With the increase in the age at marriage for women, husband-wife age differentials will decrease and this will reduce the period of time women live in widowhood. A shorter period of time in widowhood means better social and economic status for women in old age.

Islamic tradition and civil law allow women to have prenuptial agreements about divorce in their marriage contract. Legally, women can set conditions in marriage contracts under which they can initiate divorce. As women become more aware of and use this opportunity, there may be more divorces for women in abusive relationships. Higher education and formal employment of women are both correlated with divorce. Societal forces such as economic circumstance and the expansion of urban life patterns will contribute to the favorable conditions for divorce.

The accelerated adoption of communication and mass media technology contributes to the acceptance of Western ideals among the younger generations. There is no doubt that this movement of ideas and values will continue to increase in the future, as it is practically impossible to prevent the penetration of information through modern and expanding technology. Adoption by younger generations of Western ideas in all aspects of life will be a continued source of stress for families. This will also reinforce the existing gender-based conflict, as young generations of women will be exposed to the gender egalitarian values from the Western culture.

NOTE

1. Shiites constitute one of the two major branches of Islam. Sunnites are the other and larger branch. Shiism has three main subdivisions. The majority are called Twelvers (*Ithna Ashariyya*) due to recognizing twelve imams, or the Prophet's successors. Other subdivisions are Severers (*Ishmailis*) and Fivers (*Zaydites*). Twelver Shiism became the state religion of Persia in the sixteenth century and today remains the state religion of the Islamic Republic of Iran (Shiites, 2001).

ASIA AND OCEANIA:
FAMILY LIFE IN INDIA, CHINA,
THE PHILIPPINES, AND AUSTRALIA

Chapter 12

Family and Tradition in Modern India

Duleep C. Deosthale
Charles B. Hennon

INTRODUCTION

A land of 1.27 million square miles (24 percent of the world's inhabited land), India has been aptly termed a subcontinent. India shares borders with China, Bangladesh, and Pakistan, some of the world's most populated nations. Demographic growth contributes to poverty and divergence in conditions among India's states. Southern states have lower levels of infant, child, and maternal mortality rates; lower fertility rates; higher literacy; and better health facilities. Northern states have more agricultural development; lower levels of literacy; higher rates of infant, child, and maternal mortality; and higher fertility rates (Hatti, Sekher, & Larsen, 2004; Ravindran, 1999).

There has been a rapid increase in India's population due to swift industrialization and rapidly declining death rates (Mullatti, 1995). India has high fertility and moderate mortality, adding eighteen million people annually (a 2.1 percent annual growth rate) (Basu, Kapoor, & Basu, 2004). Over 1.1 billion inhabitants live in India (about 17 percent of the world's population, next only to China in size), in sharp contrast to the about 340 million of fifty years ago and 846 million recorded in the 1991 census (Office of the Registrar General [Office], 2002). The population growth rate has slowed but could increase to 1.2 billion by 2015 and 1.6 billion by 2050, resulting in India becoming the world's most populated country (Geohive, 2005; United Nations, 2005e). Many of India's thirty-five states and territories

295

rival medium-size nations in population, size, and diversity. India is a plural society of multireligious, multiracial, and multilinguistic groups. There are about 4,735 people/communities making up the population (Raman, 2003).

India became independent of Great Britain on August 15, 1947, after the division of India, Pakistan, and Bangladesh. India has a rich history that stretches back thousands of years. Over the centuries, India has been invaded by Aryans, Greeks, Persians, and Mongols as well as Portuguese, Dutch, French, and English who have all left their imprint (Mullatti, 1995). Thus, understanding India is no small task given its complexities, and its present day social fabric needs to be understood in the context of its history and how it has unfolded into the present. Modern Indian families have undergone many external changes over time, although internally they still adhere to many of the early traditions.

Independence and Unity Through Diversity

During the early period of independence and in the years following, India developed the foundations of a new democracy on the remnants of past empires. State boundaries were drawn and redrawn to reflect linguistic and historical influences, with the exception of Bengal and Punjab where religion played a major role. An attempt to calm fears of regional or religious domination by any one group led India to forsake any national elements. In its stead was born a secular nation that gave equal and official status to all religions. More than 80 percent of the population is Hindu, with about 2 percent Christian, 13 percent Islam (India has the world's third largest Muslim population), 2 percent Sikh, and 2 percent other groups including Buddhist, Parsi, Jainism, and Zoroastrianism (Largest Muslim, nd; World Factbook, 2006). Different marriage and family laws apply for people of different religions. For example, a Muslim man can legally have more than one wife, while for a Christian or Hindu this would be illegal. To appease fears of linguistic domination, India adopted fifteen official languages, including English, which functioned as a compromise language. However, Hindi remains the dominant language spoken by 30 percent of the population (World Factbook, 2006).

Although India is predominantly rural with over 70 percent of the population residing in the over 650,000 villages, more than fifty million people live in the cities of Mumbai (formerly called Bombay), Kolkata (formerly called Calcutta), New Delhi, Chennai (formerly called Madras), and Bangalore. India is seen by many as a land of contradictions—a low per capita income yet one of the ten most industrialized nations and a nuclear power (Mullatti, 1995; Wolpert, 1989). The United Nations considers India as having a medium level of human development (rank of 126 of 177) (United Nations Development Programme [UNDP], 2006).

Families in Hindu Context

In order to understand some of the existing norms and traditions related to family life, it is important to explore the Hindu caste system, a vestige of the Aryans (Mullatti, 1995), as well as the joint family. The *Vedas* [Books of Knowledge] were the religious books of the invading Aryans about 4,000 years ago. Caste, or *jati,* refers to an endogamous, ranked, occupationally defined group (Bodley, 1997), based on the division of labor and the banding together of groups in four similar broad occupational categories plus the "untouchables." One reason castes and subcastes continue to exist so strongly is that every Hindu family last name reflects the caste and subcaste to which a person belongs. Any attempt to abolish the system would necessitate a restructuring of society and obliterate India's heritage of thousands of years.

Caste organization and related concepts of ritual purity shape Hindu marriage and family life. Intercaste marriages have been legal since 1956, but in practice caste endogamy requires marrying within one's caste. It is somewhat more acceptable for lower-ranking women to marry higher-ranking men (called *anuloma,* or hypergamy), than for women to marry lower-ranking men, *pratiloma,* which is a taboo (Bodley, 1997; Mullatti, 1995). This can be problematic for higher-ranking women and in rural areas where a family faces ostracism if a member selects a partner outside his or her caste and religion. Resisting endogamy has been linked to suicide or other tragic consequences (Verma & Saraswathi, 2002).

The traditional Indian family is a joint family containing two or more married sons, their wives, and their children (Bodley, 1997; Niranjan, Nair, & Roy, 2005). Besides sharing one roof and hearth, they share production and consumption through business, crafts, or agriculture. There is strong interdependency with more emphasis on the family than the individual, with the family seen as fulfilling many needs of the individual. This view emphasizes the importance of patrilineality and of the familial and fraternal relationships while de-emphasizing the spousal and parent-child relationships. In collectivist-oriented societies such as India, there is an orientation toward roles (especially kinship) rather than the pursuit of personal goals. Typically the eldest male is the most powerful. As the senior male's eldest son matures, some authority is delegated that helps him prepare for his future role as head of the household. The eldest male can also share some authority with the eldest female, allowing for effective household management. Women often exert authority covertly through their husbands (D'Cruz & Bharat, 2001).

The Vedic scriptures define the joint family as the house in which a family lives, the land on which the house is built, any crops grown, and the social rights and moral obligations of each member of the family in the larger context of the household (Ahuja, 1999). People can be within a joint family but not a joint household (Ahmad, 2003; Dasgupta, Hennessey, & Mukhopadhyay, 1999; Niranjan et al., 2005). With industrialization, urbanization, migration, and widespread education and employment of women, "structural change has occurred but functional jointness continues" (D'Cruz & Bharat, 2001, p. 172). Rather than moving to a conjugal nuclear family system, there has been movement toward an adaptive extended family system. As family/household composition and living arrangements are changing, the jointness, notably in terms of major decisions, remains for the majority of families (Verma & Saraswathi, 2002).

Nevertheless, some factors have helped the break-up of the traditional notion of the joint family. Foremost is education, a sense of self-realization, and a desire for a son to move with his wife to a more lucrative job to another city. Another factor is that the joint family pools the resources from all working members and distributes the resources among those who live at home. A son with less earning power could receive more from the pool because he has a larger family, resulting in a questioning of the fairness of the system and the "I" form of thinking that quickly replaces the "we" of the joint family (Ahuja, 1999). As the incentive to achieve something based on personal merit receives scant attention, family conflict can result. This largely materialistic motivation allows many younger couples to exercise independence and become masters of their own destiny. The cost of maintaining a large household and the desire for fewer children have also made joint households less desirable (Banerjee, 2003).

COUPLE FORMATION AND MARITAL DYNAMICS

Several aspects characterize the uniqueness of marrying and married life among the Hindus of India. While dating is becoming acceptable, it is not common nor is it love-based, free choice marriage. The caste system structures mate selection and this is reflected in the marriage arrangements, the dowry system, and in the patriarchal nature of marital dynamics. Divorce is uncommon and the associated shame for women makes living in an unhappy marriage better than a divorce.

Dating

The concept of dating is almost nonexistent (Derné, 1994; Sastry, 1999). From an early age, boys and girls are segregated in play and early school years. Although there has been a change with boys and girls in the same school classes, especially in higher education, an unspoken code separates the two. A nonmarriage relationship with any display of affection is indecent, and can result in gossip, or even ruin the status of a family and careers and jeopardize marriage prospects, especially for girls. Families still take pride in their children, especially girls, not having been in contact with the opposite sex. One reason to explain this behavior of being distant is the absence of public displays of emotion between two people who are married (Derné, 1994). This does not mean that Indian culture lacks affection and emotion in regard to love, but display of such an emotion in public is suppressed. Religious ideology influences interpersonal relationships with the purpose of marriage being for procreation (Dhruvarajan, 1988). In urban centers, heterosexual interaction, dating, and romantic involvement, especially in the upper social classes, are more likely (Abraham, 2002; Verma & Saraswathi, 2002).

Love, in an orthodox Indian system, is born after the union of two individuals. Marriage is the most important Hindu ritual, involving great expenditures on the part of the bride's family. However, the first pregnancy, naming of the child, and death are also important life cycle rituals (Mullatti, 1995). Marriage is concerned with ritual purity and status, with chastity a ritual requirement; however, some youth do have sexual relations outside of marriage (Jamshedji-Neogi & Sharma, 2003; Tiwari & Kumar, 2004). The establishment of a family is believed to be primarily for fulfilling religious obligations, including ancestor worship, begetting a male child, and passing traditions to the next generation (Mullatti, 1995). For women, interaction with men, including their husbands, is usually minimal because of gender segregation and male superiority, resulting in inequality between the spouses and low companionship (Ahmad, 2003; Derné, 1994).

The Arranged Marriage

Traditions continue to be the foundation of Indian society and one of the most time-honored is the institution of marriage. Perhaps 90-95 percent of marriages are arranged by the family (Flanigan, 2000; Sastry, 1999), considering it "cannot be left to the caprice and immature judgment of the young" (Tyler, 1986, p. 131).

Although the 1956 India Marriage Act allowed for intercaste and interreligious marriages, "parents look for religious and caste endogamy and consider exogamous rules . . . occupational and cultural compatibility, class compatibility and moral history of the family are well studied by parents" (Mullatti, 1995, p. 190). Arranged marriages give parents control over family members, offers an opportunity to strengthen the kinship group, enhances preserving and continuing the ancestral lineage, allows consolidation and extension of family property, and enables the elders to preserve the principle of endogamy (Flanigan, 2000).

When a son reaches marriageable age, his family begins the search for a bride, using relatives, friends, acquaintances, and others who provide information to the parents about who would make an ideal bride. *Murai payyan* (marriageable kin) such as cross cousins and even uncle-niece marriages are acceptable and sometimes encouraged (Ravindran, 1999). Matchmakers (*nayan*) serve two purposes: scouts who attempt to find possible matches, and negotiators who negotiate between families. Matchmakers consider family background and reputation, economic position, the value of the dowry, possible effect of alliance on property, and other matters (Flanigan, 2000). Caste, and sometimes subcaste, continues to be one of the first issues addressed. Horoscopes are consulted before any decisions are made. Once a match is found, the family is notified and communication is arranged through the *nayan* until an agreement is reached. In urban areas, the mass media also serves as the go-between. The matrimonial sections of the classifieds in newspapers, as well as magazines devoted to matchmaking, the Internet, and television ads, serve as the "modern *nayan*." In some areas, marriage fairs are held (Pache, 1998).

Once a tentative match is found, the parents of the boy will entertain requests and communications from the parents of prospective brides. The parents of the girl determine her future spouse and they become mediators on her behalf. In essence, the matrimonial search is the prerogative of the parents, with little or no input from the prospective bride and groom. However, more recently both women and men have had some influence on spouse selection.

The first meeting between the parents is to determine the compatibility of the prospective mates. Factors include horoscopes and the alignment of the stars at the time of birth, usually drawn up by an astrologer or a temple priest familiar with the system. If this stage is promising, each family gives serious thought to continuing discussions on the possibility of marriage. At this point the process moves to a more formal level. The prospective bride is introduced to family members of the groom. This is a critical moment, because the girl's capabilities and talents are showcased and factors such as physical attributes of height, weight, and skin color, as well as her ability in cooking, housework, and caregiving, are considered.

If there are no complications or objections, the marriage union is discussed. Sometimes the groom accompanies his parents to see the prospective bride, and the prospective mates are left to themselves for a few hours so they can get to know each other. However, there are couples who do not meet until the day of their marriage or even until the marriage ceremony. Tradition generally dictates that the parents' decision is final.

Should the girl be less attractive or have a disability, older than usual (over twenty-five), or highly educated, finding her a suitable mate is more difficult and requires a higher dowry to compensate (Ahmad, 2003; Naik, 1996). Likewise, if the girl has positive attributes such as being physically attractive, the parents may be able to arrange her wedding to someone financially secure or of a higher subcaste. The parents of a family with many daughters can find it difficult to arrange for suitable mates, especially if dowry is an issue.

Women are having more influence on marriage. They are at least asked for their consent and sometimes have the ability to veto the arrangement (Ahmad, 2003; Ravindran, 1999). Consent is sometimes given because they believe that parents know what is best. Romantic love recedes as the majority of young men and women consider their parents' choice appropriate and preferred. Even within the Westernized, upper-middle class there is still considerable support for arranged marriages. One study showed over 70 percent of teenage girls and 60 percent of teenage boys preferred arranged marriages (Verma & Saraswathi, 2002).

Regardless of which side initiated the search, the bride's parents are to assume most, if not all, of the financial expenses associated with the wedding. The costs include housing the family members of the groom's side of the family, meals for all guests, the marriage ceremony, trousseau, and other expenses (Ahuja, 1999). Ritual importance is linked to matrimony.

Age at Marriage

The Child Marriage Restraint Act of 1929-1978 sets the legal age for marriage at eighteen for females and twenty-one for males. Even with this law many children aged fifteen and sixteen are married in a "cultural" sense. These marriages are not void under Hindu religious law as long as they are not consummated until the legal ages (Flanigan, 2000). Hindu religion prescribes the marriage of a girl before puberty, a norm related to the valuing of virginity. At one time child marriages were common but now occur at a considerably lower rate (Center for Reproductive Rights, 2004).

Between 1951 and 1991, the mean age of marriage increased by about four years for men and six years for women, and the average age difference between males and females decreased from seven to five years. In the 1990s, the average marriage age was nineteen for women and twenty-four for men with the average age difference between brides and grooms being almost five years (Medindia, 2005; United Nations, 2000). The 1998-1999 National Family Health Survey revealed that 30 percent of women between the ages of fifteen and nineteen were married. Half of India's married women have their first child before the age of twenty and one out of eight births takes place within eighteen months of the previous birth (Mehta, 2001).

In 2001, the number of married women aged fourteen or younger was 1,511,937, and about 25 percent of all females aged fifteen to nineteen were married. This proportion was slightly higher for Hindus and slightly lower for Muslims, with other religious groups having lower percentages of girls this age married. In general, age at marriage is lower for both men and women in nuclear households (Reddy, 1991). In urban areas, boys marry after completing college and the ability for economically supporting a family is established. Men and women with graduate or postgraduate degrees marry at a later age, perhaps twenty-five to thirty-five for men and twenty to thirty for women (Mullatti, 1995).

Patriarchal Influences on Roles and Power

A daughter is always considered to be *paraya* (someone else's), the Hindi word to describe it rather melodramatically. She is brought up to be given away in marriage. Once the marriage is complete, there is a symbolic breaking of the ties between the daughter and her parents with an emotional good-bye, or the Hindi word *bidaii*. This situation appears in countless Indian movies that revolve around the theme of relationships. Upon marriage, she becomes the responsibility of her husband and his family and often must seek her husband's permission to visit her own family, which her husband could deny. If she goes against his will, he can order her to never return to his house, the worst insult she can suffer. This is also true if he orders her to return to her parents, in essence ending their relationship. Her own parents can deny her entry or help because she is no longer their responsibility.

To avoid such situations, brides in the initial years of their marriage tend to be passive and subservient to the needs of their spouses and in-laws.

These extremes in an otherwise forgiving philosophy can be explained through the religious ideology of role relationships. *Pativratya* (serving the husband) is the complete submission of the wife to the needs and desires of her husband and that her true happiness lies in his happiness, "that her salvation lies in the devotion to her husband and to him only" (Dhruvarajan, 1988, p. 274). The relationship in this ideology is the acceptance on the part of women that "men are ritually pure, physically strong, and emotionally mature; women on the other hand are ritually pollutable, physically weak, and lack strong will power" (Dhruvarajan, 1988, p. 274).

Male authority is maintained in all castes. For example, when an upper caste man marries a lower caste woman, sons will continue to bear his lineage rather than her lineage. Property, too, is inherited through male heirs and "husband-wife relationships are not based on the development of a companion relationship but one of authority relationship" (Dhruvarajan, 1988, p. 280).

Much has changed and there is a balancing of power in gender relationships especially with the development of a nuclear family. There has especially been a shift from traditional roles toward more conjugal relations and quasi-egalitarian roles among urban, educated, higher income, dual-earner families (especially in southern India) and women have been experiencing more autonomy (Raman, 2003; Ravindran, 1999; Suppal & Roopnarine, 1999). Opportunities for employment and education, challenges to patriarchy, and changes in technology have contributed to improving the status of women and to greater involvement of men in child rearing (Ahmad, 2003; Ravindran, 1999).

The increase in literacy, 52 percent in 1991 (men 63 percent; women 39 percent), to 61 percent in 2004 (men 73 percent; women 49 percent), is a factor influencing gender relations (Ahmad, 2003; Office, 2001; UNDP, 2005, 2006). The current literacy rate of those between fifteen and twenty-four years is now over 75 percent (UNDP, 2006). Women working outside their homes are no longer a novelty and over 30 percent are active in the labor force (Mullatti, 1995; UNDP, 2006). Education has become a significant tool of independence, perhaps even of resistance, for Indian women and helps in challenging some of the traditional ideas regarding women's autonomy and self-determination (Center for Reproductive Rights, 2004; Mukhopadhyay & Seymour, 1994).[1]

The Dowry System

Efforts to dismantle the dowry system in modern India have met with little success (Center for Reproductive Rights, 2004; Flanigan, 2000; Indian Child, 2004). While many modern couples and liberal families do not ask nor accept it, the tradition of the dowry is far from eliminated and is often an integral part of marriage negotiations. Some believe that a key reason why dowry has taken on increased importance is that families think it is a guarantee that the bride will be treated well in the house of her husband and in-laws. "If we don't give dowry our daughters would suffer, if we give they will live well. Don't we hear stories about stoves bursting and girls burning?" (Ahuja, 1999; Ravindran, 1999, p. WS 39).

In middle and lower castes, expensive dowries have helped raise the marriage age because families are unable to meet dowry demands, and has also forced some families to transcend their caste groups, finding bridegrooms from other castes or subcastes (Flanigan, 2000). The dowry system inflicts significant pain and anguish on the bride's family and causes monetary harm that can be at times insurmountable. It has been argued that the cost has led some girls to commit suicide to rid their fathers of the financial burden (Flanigan, 2000). The number of "bride burnings" or "dowry deaths" also demonstrates the gravity of the issue of dowry (Center for Reproductive Rights, 2004; Stone & James, 1995; Vindhya, 2003). UNICEF (2000b) estimates 5,000 such deaths each year. This generally happens when promises made by the bride's family are not honored, and either the husband, his parents, or both "torch" the bride. While aware that such a crime carries a legal punishment of up to a life sentence, this has not deterred people from inflicting such harm.

Unlike most dowry-oriented societies where payments have declined with modernization, India has seen a significant increase in the cost of dowry payments over the last five decades (Anderson, 2003). The problems associated with dowry contribute to the lack of a family's celebration for the birth of a girl (especially beyond the first) and can lead to female infanticide, neglect, suicide, and a high female mortality rate (Simon & Altstein, 2003).

Intercaste Marriages

Although intercaste marriage has been granted legal sanctions, it is still not common (Ahuja, 1999; Mullatti, 1995) because the parents still control the decision regarding their sons' and daughters' life partner. What are at stake are not just the marriage, but family status and standing. Society believes that those from similar backgrounds adjust to each other with greater ease and bond better, including the extended families. While there is limited intercaste marriages between the three upper classes, marriage between the upper three and the lowest caste is extremely rare as there are few opportunities for these two groups to interact.

Divorce

Empirical work on divorce in India is scant. Each religious group has different laws for marriage and divorce (Garg, 1998; Kusum, 2001; Simon & Altstein, 2003). In traditional Hindu society, marriage is a religious sacrament and divorce is not accepted. However, the Hindu Marriage Act of 1955 made divorce easier to obtain for women and in 1976 it was further revised to a no-fault divorce (Amato, 1994). Civil and interfaith marriages are covered by the Special Marriage Act of 1956. Recently, the law was changed allowing Christian women to obtain divorce on the grounds of cruelty and desertion without the need to also prove adultery. Hindu, Parsi, and Muslim marriage laws have previously undergone several changes including the recognition of divorce by mutual consent (Legal Service India, 2005; Raikar-Mhatre, 1997; Simon & Altstein, 2003). Given the prevalent "son preference," it is no surprise that having at least one son is associated with a lower risk of divorce (Bose & South, 2003; Hollander, 2004).

Factors associated with divorce include having been married for only a short time, sexual incompatibility related to early age at marriage for females, and large differences in the ages of the spouses. Lower castes are more tolerant of divorce (Rao & Sekhar, 2002; Singh, 1996). While much has legally changed in the last five decades, the negative social consequences for males and females far outnumber the benefits of divorce. The 1981 census showed that only 0.74 percent of men and women between the ages of fifteen and forty-four were divorced (Amato, 1994). Other estimates place the rate between 2 and 8 percent (*Arranged Marriages,* 2004; Ravindran, 2001). Research in the rural north of India indicated that the incidence of divorce was similar to Western societies (Singh, 1996). However, the official divorce rate might mask informal terminations. Some wives are simply sent back to their parents' home without a legal divorce, some couples in unhappy arrangements might continue to live in the same home but not as wife and husband, and in small towns and villages (where most people live), some marriages are unofficially dissolved (Ravindran, 2001). In rural areas efforts are made by caste *panchayat,* or councils, to reunite estranged couples (Tyler, 1986). Less than 10 percent of households are headed by women (Center for Reproductive Rights, 2004).

Quite simply put, for a Hindu family when two people marry, they make a life commitment and nothing is supposed to come between them. If anything does, it must be accepted as part of their married life. There is a belief based on *karma,* that when a marriage does break up it is considered to be the fault of the wife regardless of the husband's behavior. Deserted or divorced women are the subject of contempt and perhaps a little pity (Banerjee, 2003). Upper-middle class divorced women experience more disapproval than lower-middle class women. Some lower castes have been more tolerant of divorce, thus these individuals experience relatively little rejection from others following their divorce (Amato, 1994).

Divorced men seem to get the benefit of the doubt and society condemns the divorced woman to greater economic, social, and psychological hardships. Divorced men experience few economic problems while economic hardship has an impact on women who have custody of children (Amato, 1994). Given the close relationship among family members, one might assume that divorced women could turn to their parents and siblings for help and support. However, parents might believe that they have completed their obligations by getting their daughter married and providing her dowry, and may be unwilling or unable to provide support. Owing to "negative community attitudes toward the remarriages of women" in India, many resign "themselves to remaining single for the rest of their lives, especially if they have children" (Amato, 1994, p. 211).

FAMILIES AND CHILDREN

One way to consider family structure in India and the importance of children is to contemplate the following (Krishna Mohan, Khan, & Sureender, 2003, p. 21).

> The status of the family usually depends on the number of children it has in India because of the strong belief in religion and in concepts like salvation after death and rebirth. According to Indian social customs, every man has to go through the *Grushasthashrama* or "householder" stage and significance is attached to bearing offspring in order to fulfill one's religious duties.

Fertility, Contraception, and Abortion

Currently (2000-2005), the total fertility rate per woman stands at 3.1. In the early 1970s, the rate was 5.4. Limiting the number of children allows for focusing on the quality of life in an urban environment, the choice destination for those leaving traditional families (Krishna Mohan et al., 2003; Ramu, 1991; UNDP, 2005). Most married women, regardless of educational level or living in urban or rural areas, want only two children (Mehta, 2001). Furthermore, the 1998-1999 National Family Health Survey indicated that 28 percent of married women did not want more children and 20 percent wanted to delay the next birth by two years or more (Joseph, 1998).

The current contraceptive prevalence rate is 48 percent (UNDP, 2005). The use of contraceptives increased between 1991 and 1999 with one-half of those in the fifteen to forty-nine age group using contraception. The National Family Health Survey showed that about 2 percent of married couples used the pill or IUD, 3 percent used condoms, and sterilization is the preferred method (34 percent), which accounts for over 70 percent of total contraceptive prevalence (Banerjee, 2003; Mehta, 2001). Over 80 percent of women have used no other method of birth control before being sterilized (Mehta, 2001). Counseling in family planning is important (Baiju, 2003). Barriers to contraception use include poor accessibility, lack of autonomy of women, and preference for sons (Health Watch UP, 2004; Lane, 2004). It appears that economic circumstance explains fertility differences, rather than religion, even among the "scheduled tribes" (sometimes called "scheduled castes") (Basu et al., 2004; Iyer, 2003).

An estimated 6.7 to 11 million abortions occur annually in India, with about 80 percent being unsafe. The number of abortions appears to be increasing. While abortions have been legal for about thirty years, the number of providers is relatively small and scattered. Consequently, many women use illegal sources (e.g., herbs or *safai ki batti,* a type of stick introduced through the cervix into the uterus) and these are not reported in official statistics (Health Watch UP, 2004).

One-fifth of the global maternal deaths because of unsafe abortions occur in India ("India," 2001). Unsafe abortions are one of the greatest health risks confronted by Indian women and are responsible for 10-20 percent of all maternal deaths, and one-half of maternal deaths in the fifteen to nineteen age group. There are about forty-six abortions (induced and 4.5 spontaneous) per 100 live births ("India," 2001; Joseph, 1998; Mehta, 2001). The Population Council has promoted safer medical, rather than surgical, abortions as well as family planning initiatives, some involving men as joint birth control decision makers (Population Council—Asia, 2006; Sharma, 2003).

Abortion rates are higher in urban areas and more common among wealthier women who desire smaller families (Babu, Nidhi, & Verma, 1998). Higher abortion rates in some states (e.g., Delhi and Tamil Nadu) could reflect the higher usage of modern sex-selection tests (Babu et al., 1998). Sex-selection abortion is more common among women who already have daughters, urban women, women with middle school or higher education, and women living in households with a high standard of living, and is often condoned by the community (Arnold, Kishor, & Roy, 2002; Hatti et al., 2004; Health Watch UP, 2004; Visaria, 2005).

Child Rearing

The study of childhood is relatively new in India and tends to be limited to studies of tribal communities. Some recent interest focuses on girls, especially intrafamily discrimination with regard to violence, child labor, child marriages, and access to education and nourishment (Raman, 2003). Suppal and Roopnarine (1999) pointed out that:

> Within the context of traditional role expectations, the socialization of daughters hinges on being a successful wife and mother

with characteristics of docility, fidelity, thrift, nurturance, and skill in domestic tasks. By contrast, boys are socialized to be economically responsible for immediate and extended family members, maintain filial and fraternal solidarity, and uphold the family name and honor (*izzat*). (p. 732)

Each aspect of a child's life, from the right to be born, socialization, and transition to adulthood, is context-determined. Each group has ideas about childhood and the place and roles of children, and the relationship between the divine and the human. While there is an emphasis on the collective versus the individual, the nature of the relationship varies and people incorporate aspects of both collectivist and individualist elements in their psyche (Raman, 2003; Sinha & Tripathi, 2003). Hindu children's early years include security provided by the extended family and kinship systems, close contact and a special relationship with the mother (especially for boys), other adults who perform as mother surrogates, and infant indulgence. These aspects help to form a personality different from one which youth develop in a nuclear family (Raman, 2003).

Recent research shows that at least in urban areas, cultural-historical prescriptions for family roles continue (cf., Raman, 2003; Ravindran, 1999; Sharma, 2003). These prescriptions influence family functioning, including hierarchical organization, traditional customs, traditional religious beliefs, and cultural props for maintaining prescribed roles. These forces work to resist any changes in men's involvement in child care regardless of the employment status of the mother and household type (joint or nuclear). On the other hand, Indian men are more involved with young children than has often been asserted (Suppal & Roopnarine, 1999). For example, fathers in middle and upper-class, urban, nuclear households are more active in caregiving than fathers in joint households (Seymour, 2001). One study found in a sample of middle-class urban families that fathers spent 22 percent of their time with children, 7 percent of this was alone with children, and there was no difference in the amount of time spent with girls or boys (Larson, Verma, & Dworkin, 2001). Middle-class urban parents are becoming more child-centered and responsive to children, and less authoritarian. These parents value their children as a source of love and through them find personal fulfillment. They give more emphasis to the psychological value of children, rather than their economic value as found more often in rural areas (Larson, Verma, & Dworkin, 2003).

Research indicates that even in urban areas, social class is not a significant factor influencing the status of girls (Raman, 2003; Verma & Saraswathi, 2002). Her early childhood is sheltered, peopled by siblings, cousins, and adults in addition to her parents. The young girl is socialized for her future role as wife and mother in another household. Socialization includes doing household chores, caring for younger siblings, and participating in a supportive way in the principle occupation of the family. Schooling is often a luxury depending upon the socioeconomic status of the family. A principal component of the socialization of a girl is an emphasis on her temporary membership in her natal home. She is seen as irrelevant in terms of the perpetuation of her natal group. However, this socialization varies by kinship systems. In the south of India there is more awareness of a woman's rights in her natal home (Raman, 2003).

It is hierarchy that dominates all aspects of family life and influences socialization in joint families (Ahmad, 2003). The authoritarian family structure and the emphasis on conformity means severe child training methods for older children (D'Cruz & Bharat, 2001). A child is exposed to a variety of adult role models and as an infant is somewhat indulged (e.g., many physical, emotional, and/or supportive caretaking acts directed toward the child; responding immediately and positively to a child's crying or request for attention) (Seymour, 2001). This parenting style follows a pediatric model in its directed focus on a child's health and survival.

As noted in previous text, the role of the father is limited while the role of the mother is dominant. However, in joint households many women share the caretaking, such as the grandmother, older siblings, and other wives living in the household. There is a gentle "pushing away" from the mother, as close, intimate mother-child bonds are viewed as potentially disruptive to the collective well-being of the extended family. Exposure to multiple caretakers and an indulgent but somewhat laissez-faire atmosphere of caregiving exposes infants to important principles of joint family living and self-identity, and reinforces interdependence. Children learn they are only one of many household members, not unique individuals who should expect special attention (Seymour, 2001). There is no sharp distinction between spaces for children and adults, as they intermingle throughout the house and other areas. Children receive a sense of being able to count on others. Earlier studies indicated children were breast fed for long periods and toilet training was not systematic, children were seldom left alone, and children experienced a consistency of being with family and a de-emphasis of peer group and peer activities (Raman, 2003).

In nuclear families more emphasis is placed on autonomy and separation. Especially in higher social status families, there is less concern with ritual bathing and holding of infants, more concern with talking to and playing with children, and teaching them to care for themselves. There is also active teaching through verbal instructions. This pedagogical style of parenting includes intentional cognitive stimulation and learning self-reliance (Seymour, 2001). Children experience more psychological differentiation than their counterparts in joint families (D'Cruz & Bharat, 2001). Children are also prepared for competitive schooling and occupational achievement in new types of jobs (Raman, 2003; Seymour, 2001). In middle-class educated families in urban areas, there is more distinction between child and adult spaces.

Joint families stress cooperation for family survival through more authoritarian parenting styles. Nuclear families accord emphasis to individualism and achievement through democratic parenting styles. Socialization in joint families functions to match a cultural model of an ideal family. Seymour (2001, p. 13) noted that this family is

> characterized by principles of patrilineal descent and patrilocal residence; male authority; sexual segregation of many household activities; female purity and seclusion, which represent family honor; early arranged marriage, especially for daughters; and an emphasis on the welfare of the collective family unit over that of the individual.

Middle and upper-status nuclear-family households, which represent in various degrees India's transition from an agrarian to an increasingly urban and industrialized state, often have a parenting style associated with technological modernity. While the value placed on patrilineal decent and patrilocal residence continues, it is sometimes hard to achieve in urban settings.

Even with the changes in family types and across classes and castes, it can be said that Indian parental beliefs concerning child rearing reflect traditional values of familialism, interdependency, collectivistic orientations, gender differences, and respect for elders.

Impact of Marital Conflict and Divorce on Children

Marital conflict can have negative consequences for both the married partners and their children (Bradford et al., 2004; Gill, Sharma, & Verma, 2003). Both covert and overt interparental conflict is associated with antisocial behavior and depression in adolescents, while overt conflict is negatively associated with social initiative. The effects on children is partially due to the impact conflict has on parenting behaviors (e.g., as psychological and behavioral controls and supportiveness) (Bradford et al., 2004).

Adolescents in middle-class single-parent families (including both those resulting from death and divorce) appear to suffer feelings of loneliness, fear, and anger as well as changes in the relationship with their parents. Girls, compared with boys, report that they feel closer to their mothers due to the lack of enforcement of discipline and a higher degree of family cohesion. Boys and girls living in nuclear, single-parent households perceive their mothers as having less control, being less possessive, and being less anxious, while experiencing greater family cohesion, expressiveness, and independence compared with those living in joint family households with their single parents (Gill et al., 2003). Today there are marriage and family therapy programs available, and people are aware of the need for such services (Natrajan & Thomas, 2002; Singh, Nath, & Nichols, 2005).

Child Labor

Globally, India has the largest number of child laborers. While likely to be an underestimate, in 2000 there were ten million children less than fourteen years of age who were working in the home or elsewhere and not attending school (Institute of Applied Manpower Research, 2000). The 2001 census reported that among those aged ten to fourteen years, 5 percent were in the labor force and for those aged fifteen to nineteen the rate was 36 percent (44 percent of males and

26 percent of females) (Verma & Saraswathi, 2002). Those in the informal economy or working without pay in family enterprises are underreported.

Among the poor, especially those below the poverty level, child labor starts early as a way to supplement family income. In the middle-class, it is typically delayed until adolescence because the family can afford to support their children. Some policy makers and others see child labor as a necessary evil which enables these families to raise their standard of living. However, the lack of education will severely limit their occupational opportunities in the future. In this light, the government seeks not to ban child labor but to protect the child, for example, by offering informal educational opportunities. Other groups favor a ban on child labor.

Most youth workers are in agriculture, mining, glass factories, match and fireworks industries, cigarette manufacturing, making locks, handicrafts, carpet weaving, and brass working. Older children labor in restaurants and gas stations, or as car park attendants, porters, and vendors. Some are indentured by their families to pay off debts. Health is a concern as children work in dangerous conditions, for long hours, doing adult level tasks.

Around eleven million children are involved in the street economy, where they also often live and fend for themselves as beggars, rag pickers, shoe shiners, or by selling vegetables and fruits or other items. Others engage in pimping and prostitution, thievery, or selling drugs. These children often come from families with alcoholism, criminality, health problems, unemployment, and strained family relationships (Verma & Saraswathi, 2002).

Adolescents

Adolescence is a relatively new concept and is primarily limited to urban middle and upper-class families in India. The experience of the approximately 200 million adolescents (or 300 million if the age group considered is ages ten to twenty-four) varies widely. For example, more that 40 percent of girls are married by age seventeen and of this group almost 60 percent are mothers or are pregnant (Verma & Saraswathi, 2002). It has been argued that adolescence is a cultural construct, gendered, and class biased. Except for the upper classes, the transition from childhood to adulthood has greater continuity than discontinuity with little opportunity for the emergence of an adolescent culture in India (Verma & Saraswathi, 2002). This is especially the reality for girls, except in the upper classes. Saraswati (1999, p. 230) argued that in India there is a range from

> [c]omplete absence of adolescence in girls who are betrothed in childhood and married before puberty, to a prolonged adolescence that extends beyond the teens; no schooling and direct integration into the workforce to extended and highly specialized expensive education with parental support; sexual restraint as a rule to sexual permissiveness as an exception. Woven into these variations are the dynamics of a society in transition, with a trend indicating that in the decades to come, with greater access to schooling and economic prosperity, adolescence may emerge as a distinct phase cutting across class and gender. For the present, wide disparities prevail.

Or in the words of Verma and Saraswathi (2002, p. 105), adolescents in India evoke "kaleidoscopic images—images of dreams for a rosy future, of dreams that died before they took shape, of privileges and deprivation, of leisure and toil, of hope and despair." The experiences of adolescents are diverse due to religious, social, and economic disparities so attempts to generalize must be tempered.

Even among the urban middle and upper classes, there is continued emotional dependence on the family, especially on mothers, into adulthood. Youth hold to an idea that "parents know best." Occupational success is related to academic success and middle-class boys especially receive firm parental control in this regard. Families set high career aspirations and parents are involved in their teens' academic lives and career choices (Larson et al., 2003; Verma & Saraswathi, 2002). For some adolescents, the educational process is divorced from direct careers and practice and is related to an extended (until the mid-twenties or young adulthood) financial dependence on parents. It also has lead to a longer period of peer-group involvement and identification, and an emphasis on individual development in contrast to collectivistic orientations.

In middle and upper social classes, families see education as a method for upward social mobility and therefore sacrifice to see their sons (and sometime daughters) through school, including the university.

With globalization and changing values, choices and opportunities for the middle-class child have expanded while for the majority they have narrowed (Raman, 2003).

Peer Groups and Peer Culture

Within joint families youth have a large group of kin-related peers, consisting of siblings, cousins, and aunts and uncles of relatively the same age. In upper-social classes, non-kin peer groups are more prominent. However, with the exceptions of the wealthy who have more leisure time, in India in contrast to many regions of the world, non-kin peer groups play a less important role for youth including adolescents. One reason is the cultural restrictions on limiting heterosexual interaction, applying most importantly to girls after puberty, and the emphasis on and availability of family/kin relations. Research confirms the large amount of time youth spend with their families in contrast to the time spent with peers, and that family comes first except for school-based activities. Peers can become part of family gatherings and activities, and even address non-kin by kinship terms (Larson et al., 2003; Verma & Saraswathi, 2002).

At the same time, social class, gender, and geographic location influence the involvement with peer groups, especially in the upper-middle and upper social classes. In such cases, the peer culture includes styles of dress and hair, music, having places to gather or "hang-out," and the use of slang. Two studies showed that among upper-middle class university students, spending time with peers was emotionally satisfying and males and females spent about the same amount of time with peers. However, another study found that adolescent girls in urban slums spent less than thirty minutes a day with peers. The mothers expressed concern about the negative influence that peers could have and restricted the time daughters could spend with them. In rural areas, teen girls might spend up to three hours a day with peers as they do agricultural work in fields or domestic tasks in a courtyard. These young women are accompanied by kin of a similar age (Verma & Saraswathi, 2002). Adolescent girls are less happy than boys and experience a less positive social climate when with extended kin. In nuclear households, girls experience a more favorable family life when mothers are better educated (Larson et al., 2003). Concern has been raised that movement toward a Western style nuclear family means that adolescents spend less time with their families, receive less supervision and control, and display more problematic behavior. The employment of mothers is another concern, seen as further diminishing the cohesiveness and support of families. However, in both joint and nuclear families, where mothers are and are not employed, and across education levels, there does not appear to be a weakening of family ties (D'Cruz & Bharat, 2001; Larson et al., 2003).

FAMILIES AND GENDER

India has had elaborately designed and concrete gender roles that have changed over the last few decades. Education is important in this regard (Sastry, 1999; Suppal & Roopnarine, 1999). The status of women is the focus of a large body of research. The issue of gender in families is discussed in many places in this chapter as gender norms and concerns permeate the culture.

As much of the population lives in rural areas, the husband continues to be the principal provider and the wife keeps house (Sastry, 1999). His responsibility is to bring home a decent paycheck and look after the general welfare of the family. Her job is to see how the paycheck will be used based on the needs of the family. It is well known that while the man is the decision maker outside the house, inside the house the woman rules. Gratification for women is ideally to come through motherhood, especially so with the birth of males (D'Cruz & Bharat, 2001).

About 44 percent of women are in the labor force primarily as schoolteachers, nurses, and politics (women hold 9 percent of seats in parliament), and their earned income ratio (to men) is 0.31 (Center for Reproductive Rights 2004; UNDP, 2006). However, only lately has a father's role in child care increased and help with cooking and chores is rare. Thus, the wife is still responsible for household duties and even career women place family over their jobs (Verma & Saraswathi, 2002).

FAMILIES AND STRESS

Probably an aspect of Indian families least exhibited or discussed, is stress (Sastry, 1999). City life and its quick pace and the changing economic climate have added to existing and underlying stress.

However, in the Indian way of thinking, there is a denial of the existence of stress and the idea of seeking a therapist conjures up images of mental instability, a fact that an average Indian would refuse to accept, leading to difficulty in attempting to resolve stress silently, individually, and internally.

Stress is caused by three probable situations. First, stress is felt by women who have to do the balancing act of being in the labor force and also discharging the functions of homemaker (Kapadia, 1999; Ravindran, 1999; Sastry, 1999; Suppal & Roopnarine, 1999). The dual role that a woman is expected to play has to be kept in low profile, especially if the woman wants to assert some degree of independence. In deference to her husband, she must suffer this alone, as is expected of her (*pativratya*). The fact that she brings in additional income cannot be leveraged as a means of determining any sense of equality in chores done at home.

A second source of stress results from incompatibility between a husband and wife resulting from arranged marriages in which the couple has little input and age differences are large (Bhatti, 2003; Bradford et al., 2004; Isaac & Shah, 2004). However, as noted elsewhere in this chapter, women tend to avoid conflict due to their awareness that long-term security lies in subordinating their own well-being relative to the wishes of male authority figures and, there is considerable social stigmatization of divorce (Kapadia, 1999).

It is in the third case that one sees perhaps the harshest impact of stress: the tense relationship between the wife and her in-laws, specifically the mother-in-law (Ahmad, 2003; Mukhopadhyay & Seymour, 1994; Ruback & Pandey, 1991). An immediate tension develops between the mother-in-law who has the support of her son and the family, and the daughter-in-law who is the outsider who has intruded into their lives. Giving birth to a son, who will carry on the family name, raises the young woman's status. She will give considerable emotional investment to the son, who she might consider her savior in this family situation (Verma & Saraswathi, 2002).

FAMILIES AND AGING

Any casual observer of Indian tradition will note that outside of the marriage rituals, nowhere is the sense of tradition stronger than in the treatment of the elderly who are respected and revered. The elderly in India are to a great extent associated with life experience, which in turn is associated with knowledge. Children are taught to respect their elders, not just their parents and grandparents, but also their elder brothers and sisters (D'Cruz & Bharat, 2001). In nearly all regions of India, respect is demonstrated through the act of bending down and touching the feet of elders, both as a mark of respect and to seek their blessings.

The elderly population and the aging process are usually dealt with internally by families, but this is changing and state-based social security systems have come into existence (Jamuna, 2003). Only 1 percent lives in "old-age" homes but the numbers of these homes (free for those who cannot pay and do not have family to care for them, as well as fee-based homes) are growing (Liebig, 2003).

Given these changes, it is still the convention that as parents become old it is sons, or in many cases the eldest son, who has the moral obligation and social responsibility to provide for the well-being of parents. The daughter is generally not responsible for her parent's welfare—her obligation is associated with attending to her in-laws. However, this is also changing. Gender, degree of adherence to cultural norms, and especially role overload are factors influencing caregiver burden (Jamuna, 2003; Rowe, 2002). Elder care is becoming difficult as a result of the increase in dual-career/earner families, the dwindling of the joint family, a possible alteration in filial piety values, and the increasing life expectancy. This results in a greater chance of a prolonged old age characterized by dependency, degeneration, and poverty. These factors have made the elderly more susceptible to abuse (Jamuna, 2003).

Life Expectancy

Due to advances in medicine, life expectancy of the average Indian has increased. In 2004 it was 63.1 years (65.3 for women and 62.1 for men), an increase of over twelve years since 1970. The probability of surviving to age sixty-five for those born between 2000 and 2005 is 67 percent for females and 59 percent for males (UNDP, 2005, 2006). With mandatory retirement set somewhere between the ages of fifty-five and sixty-two years, the elderly are living beyond their ability to earn. Presently, their children care for most elderly individuals, but as families begin to have fewer children the pressure of taking care of more people is being felt. In the future, it is quite likely that the elderly will have fewer resources on which to depend to ensure their care. With the increase in the elderly population, India, as a developing country, has been unable to manage the needs of the aged. The government continues to introduce programs and nongovernmental organizations are playing a role in highlighting the socioeconomic and health problems of the elderly (Sawhney, 2003).

OTHER FAMILY SITUATIONS

Two types of adoptive families are found in India. The larger group is those adopting due to childlessness. A smaller group adopts for humanitarian reasons. The adoption process confers on the adoptive parents and child basically the same rights and responsibilities existing in biological parent-child families and severs the ties between a child and his or her biological parents (D'Cruz & Bharat, 2001; Groza & Kalyanvala, 2004).

The situation today can be better understood by reference to history and tradition. India has a long tradition of adoption based on Hindu law. Adoption of a male child was practiced because "sons have a special spiritual and secular significance in Hinduism, for repaying the debts to one's ancestors, for conducting the last rites, for continuing the family line and to inherit and manage family property" (D'Cruz & Bharat, 2001, p. 183). His biological father or his mother, if the father had died, could give the child in adoption. The child had to be Hindu and of the same caste as the adopting father. He could not be an orphan or mute. The adoption proceeded through a series of ceremonies and was irrevocable. Adoption was thus not on humanitarian grounds, but rather a pragmatic decision to ensure a male heir and provider.

Since independence there has been a change in the philosophy and practice of adoption, including allowing for adoption of girls. Efforts to legalize adoption have resulted in laws allowing adoption only by mentally sound Hindu males or females with no natural born or adopted children or grandchildren of the same sex as the child being adopted.[2] If the man is married, the consent of the wife is necessary before the adoption takes place. If the woman is married, she can adopt while her husband is alive providing he is unsound and not capable of deciding. Single, divorced, or widowed women can also adopt. Either a male or female child can be adopted if he or she is a Hindu, less than fifteen years of age, unmarried, and not already adopted. An orphan can be adopted if there is a guardian to give the child in adoption and court permission has been obtained. There must be at least a twenty-one years age difference between the child and the adopting parent if the child to be adopted is of a different sex than the parent (Adoption among Hindus, 2003; Bharat, 1997; D'Cruz & Bharat, 2001).

The available research on family dynamics in adoptive families suggests that adoptive parents, by and large, find satisfaction in their parental roles and that the development of the child is normal and satisfactory (Billimoria, 1984). While parents expect the child to care for them in old age, many are uncertain that this will happen. Many parents believe that the child should know about being adopted, but some do not tell the child of his or her adoption due to insecurity. Cultural issues underscore the reluctance toward adoption—the stigma associated with infertility treatment and adoption as the inclusion of a "third party" ruptures the cultural boundaries of family being tied to the conjugal bond (Bharadwaj, 2003).

CONCLUDING COMMENTS

Where does the family unit stand today? Does modernization mean forsaking traditional values? Have the foundations of the family unit been shaken to an extent that a new way is the only way out? Will Western thought and globalization take a toll on India and her people and way of life and provide them with an escape clause from their obligations? Will the status of women, especially that of the wife, change for the better?

Many of the answers to these questions lie in contemporary issues. The lack of education has limited the development and growth of the average individual. In some cases, the inability to access education leads to frustration and a life gone astray. In 1971, with less than 30 percent of its population being able to read and write, India had one of the highest illiteracy rates in the world (Noble & Dutt, 1982). Today, significant efforts are being made to overcome this hurdle.

However, an impediment to change is India's inability to check its population explosion. With one of the highest growth rates in the world, India will overtake China in a few decades as the world's most populated nation, with a landmass that is less than one-half that of China. India's problems consequently become more severe. High population, illiteracy, and a high percentage of individuals living in poverty combine to make India a potential disaster of gigantic proportions. Proactive attempts at curbing population growth have been stalled for a number of reasons. It is often viewed that for every step that India takes toward being an industrial powerhouse, population growth nullifies her advancement.

In spite of these situations, India has been able to develop an aggressive campaign toward success. The closed economy of the past is now significantly open to a competitive market. Joint ventures between Indian and foreign companies have recognized the tremendous potential that lies within India. For example, while Internet connectivity in villages allows accessing and sharing of health, meteorological, agricultural, and other information, technology also means employment and economic growth. With a critical mass of entrepreneurial activities in an area, sustainable momentum for socioeconomic development is generated. India is experiencing a growth in information technology-based economic aggregates. The skills needed for high-tech startups as well as supplying the skilled workers for established businesses has been driving the opening of new universities and the expansion of related services (UNDP, 2001).

Foreign investments have risen and the quality of life of the average individual and family has improved. The brain drain of a few decades ago has been replaced by the sharp minds of young entrepreneurs. What were once considered luxury items—a car, a color television, ownership of an independent company—are today a way of life for many. Ignorance about things foreign has been replaced with an awareness of what is happening in the world. The desire for change is strong and old institutions and traditions have adapted themselves to this change. However, the deep sense of tradition that guides every Indian will not be easy to disturb. India will absorb, adopt the new, and adapt to the changing currents, but the core of India, built on centuries of tradition, will continue to provide the foundation on which thousands of years of civilization have existed.

NOTES

1. Contemporary roles of women and men are based in the *Shastras* (Laws of Manu) and other ancient texts. Suppal and Roopnarine (1999, p. 732) indicated "legends, myths, and moral fables emphasize a strictly traditional dichotomy of male and female responsibilities: women as nurturers and caregivers in the subservient role of wife and mother and men as providers and protector of family honor and prestige."

2. The Hindu Adoption and Maintenance Act (1956) cover Hindus, Buddhists, Sikhs, and Jains as well as those who are not Muslims, Christians, Jews, or Parsis. Muslims, Christians, Jews, and Parsis can take a child as a ward, but not legally adopt except in certain circumstances from an orphanage (Adoption among Hindus, 2003). This is under the Guardianship and Wards Act of 1890. The "adopter" in such cases is only a guardian and upon the child's maturity, the legal relationship ceases to exist. The child does not receive the same status as a biological child. Likewise, the child is not automatically entitled to take the family name or to inherit property (D'Cruz & Bharat, 2001). Attempts have been made since 1955 to establish a uniform adoption code to uniformly apply to all Indians irrespective of religion or caste. Although bills have been introduced in parliament, they have been unsuccessful for a variety of reasons.

Chapter 13

Chinese Family—Developments and Changes

Aimin Wang

The People's Republic of China is the world's most populous country with 1.3 billion people, and comprises more than one-fifth of the world's population. About 40 percent of these people live in urban areas (United Nations Development Programme [UNDP], 2006). There are fifty-six different officially identified ethnic groups. While officially atheist, Daoist (Taoist), and Buddhist are the most common religions; Han nation, the largest ethnic group, accounts for about 92 percent of the population. Not only is China a large and diverse country, it is also an old country. The written history dates back over 4,000 years. During the last century, especially the last several decades, China has undergone tremendous changes. The Communists, under Mao Zedong, established a socialist system after World War II that imposed strict controls over everyday life. Since 1978, Deng Xiaoping and other leaders have focused on market-oriented economic development. Living standards have improved and personal choice has expanded while political controls remain tight (World Factbook, 2006). China has a medium level of human development, ranking eighty-one on the Human Development Index (UNDP, 2006).

It is difficult to provide a comprehensive or typical description of family life in a country with thousands of years of history, many different subcultural groups, and undergoing considerable rapid changes. Until the last century, the Chinese family system developed under the feudal patriarchal system, a system running consistently for thousands of years. The feudal tradition still plays an important role especially in rural areas where change typically lags. Without a minimum understanding of this tradition, it is difficult to understand the real meanings of Chinese families. The emphasis of this chapter, in addition to briefly introducing the traditions, will be devoted to the contemporary families of the major ethnic group.

Family in Chinese Context

The concept of family in China is similar yet different from Western countries (Fei, 1933). Instead of the Western idea that a family is a couple and their unmarried children (i.e., nuclear family), Chinese people consider married children, children's children, brothers, sisters, and many other relatives as members of their families. To distinguish between these understandings, the concept of extended family is commonly used to describe the pattern in China.

The Chinese value loyalty to family. Elders are highly respected. A crucial dimension for evaluating a family or family members is how well they take care of their elderly parents or parents-in-law. Typically, parents should live a better life than their children. Children should provide for their parents, even if parents can provide for themselves. If parents need anything, it should be provided. Children are expected to listen to their parents and respect their opinions, even though the "children" might have children or even grandchildren (D. Zhang, 1993).

Until recently, the traditional extended family pattern had been dominant for thousands of years, and it is still common in rural areas and many cities. The Chinese family has undergone significant changes due to rapid cultural and economic developments. Based on a survey in 1982 in five cities (Beijing, Tianjing, Shanghai, Nanjing, and Chengdu), families can be classified into single person families, nuclear families (a couple and their unmarried children), stem families (two generations with one couple in each generation), joint families (at least two generations with two or more couples in a generation), and other (Li & Shen, 1991; Liu, 1987; Wuchengshi Hunyin yu Jiating Yanjiu Ketizu [Five City Marriage and Family Research Project Group—FCMFRPG], 1985). The stem and joint families belong to the extended family category. Although all of these patterns are not clearly seen as being extended households, Chinese people typically consider separated family units as components of their extended family. These separate units might be independent economically and physically, but they all share many responsibilities with the extended family members. Taking care of their aged parents, for example, is one of these responsibilities regardless of whether or not they live in the same household with their parents.

History, Values, and Customs

In the traditional family, people belonged to individual nuclear families having properties, such as room and land, and cooked their meals separately from other nuclear families. At the same time, they considered themselves members of a larger family and assumed many responsibilities within this extended family. A typical family unit consisted of grandparents, parents, married sons and their wives, unmarried sons and daughters, and unmarried grandchildren (and perhaps great-grandparents). Members in a family were also ranked in a specific hierarchical order. The oldest man in the oldest generation was usually the head of the family. Generation, age, and gender were used to rank people. With few exceptions, the younger generation respected the older; people respected older people within their generation; and males had more privileges than females (Fei, 1933). The first son in each generation had privileges over his siblings and received privileges from the older generations. If his father was the oldest in his generation, the first son's position was usually higher than his father's brothers. Family descent was patrilineal. Each child inherited her or his family name from the father.

Children were expected to show filial obedience to the father and he had the right to do almost anything to his children. To not show filial obedience to one's parents or grandparents was specified as one of the Ten Abominable Offenses that could not be forgiven by the laws in most of the dynasties during the last 1,400 years (Du, 801, republished in 1987). The traditional Chinese family was patriarchal; the father was head and owned and controlled all the people, properties, and income (Fei, 1933). The father made decisions about important family matters such as land, housing, and field products. When he died, his oldest son, instead of his brothers, usually took his position. When the oldest generation died, the brothers in the next generation shared the properties owned by their parents to create individual nuclear families or stem families. The separated families did their own cooking even though they may have lived in their own rooms in the same house or on the same property (D. Zhang, 1993).

Husbands represented the family in interaction with others and provided for their family. Wives cared for and were responsible for the children, cooked, and were responsible for aspects within the family. Though a wife could be influential, the husband usually made the major decisions (B. Wu, 1987). For thousands of years husbands took no direct responsibility for internal family matters. When her son married, the mother became the boss of her daughter-in-law whose life could be miserable if she did not have a good relationship with her mother-in-law (Fei, 1933). Her hope was to hold out until she became a mother-in-law to her son's wife. The relationship with the old mother-in-law would usually not change, but her new role as mother-in-law meant also being dominant to her new daughter-in-law.

Traditional family patterns started to change when the Republic of China, about a century ago, replaced feudal society, but the preponderance of changes occurred during recent decades. Broader and more rapid changes have occurred in large cities and more limited changes in remote areas (FCMFRPG, 1985). It is the contributor's opinion that four main events lead to these changes: the Cultural Revolution from 1966 to 1976; the taking of lands and properties from the rich by force and sharing these with the poor; the adoption of new marriage laws resulting in more equal rights between women and men, changes in the age at marriage, and the emphases on having one child per couple; and the nationwide increase in women's employment.

The ten-year Cultural Revolution changed people's perceptions about hierarchy. It is widely known that people were encouraged, sometimes forced, to challenge authorities at all levels of society, including within families. Many short-lived groups within all levels of society (except the military) claimed power and replaced one another rapidly, either by announcing their existence or by force. People from the working class (e.g., factory workers and peasants) and officers and soldiers within the military became the decision makers at factories, businesses, schools, universities, and so on. No longer observed were values and traditions, such as respecting elders. Family members were not caring for and helping each other, but instead fighting each other over political beliefs. The hierarchy of the family was destroyed in most of China. The generation growing up during the Cultural Revolution learned disrespect, rather than respect, for others, and showing filial obedience was considered as one of the worst aspects in the old values system. Overall, the Cultural Revolution destroyed many long-standing traditions.

Forcefully taking lands and properties from the rich and sharing them with the poor also weakened the hierarchical structure of the family. This happened many times in different regions throughout China's history. The Communist party led the most recent redistribution. It affected almost all of China and has had the greatest influence on people. When everybody in a family had a share of land and property, their status changed to become equal in the family. In conjunction with the perceptual changes during the Cultural Revolution, relationships among family members became less restricted by the hierarchical structure (D. Zhang, 1993).

During the many years of feudal society, the Confucian or feudal ethical code, the emperor's words, and historical precedence played major roles in deciding and judging family matters. The country was perceived as belonging to the emperor. Although there were written laws, the emperor's words were considered as important as the law. People were more likely to expect a person such as a hero, an open-minded emperor, or a higher-ranking government official, instead of the laws, to speak for them when they had a problem or conflicts with others. This tendency lasted after the end of the feudal society. For example, the words of Man Zedong (the former Chairman of the Communist Party and the country) were treated as salient as any of the emperors' in China's history. This tradition was a reason for the instability of the political settings and played a role having tremendous impacts on Chinese families and people's daily lives (Yue, 1994; C. Zhang, 1997; D. Zhang, 1995). Many changes started with the implementation of a policy or a direction by a high-ranking official, instead of an official law.

New marriage laws, published in 1950 and revised in 1980 and 2001, and the Women's Law adopted in 1992, have provided women with the same status and rights as men (B. Wu, 1987). Traditionally, men could have several wives, and women could have one husband. When married, a woman belonged to the man and his family. A man could divorce his wife, but the wife could never divorce her husband.

It was considered a deep shame if a woman was divorced. If a woman was divorced or widowed, it was expected that she would not remarry.

The one child per couple policy, of the early 1970s, restricted each married couple to give birth to no more than one child. This policy plays an important role in the composition of contemporary families and their ideas about family. Being unable to give birth to a son had been one of the "seven reasons" to legally divorce a wife until the early 1900s. Having a son had been a must for the majority of Chinese families. Owing to this policy, the expectation that a family had to have sons to carry on the line or care for the elders could not be met for families that had girls. If there was no son, then the next generation will not continue the name. For older generations, this has been a concern as the function of the family has been to carry on the name. This is especially true for urban families where this policy has been more strictly observed.

Today, women have reached equal status with men in society and family because of the laws that favor women and their employment. The society is no longer strictly patriarchal, especially in the cities. Some children now take their mother's family name. Some women have higher status, more education, or a higher income than their husbands. All of this has greatly improved women's social and economic status as well as their position in their families. With independent incomes, wives are no longer economically dependent on their husbands (B. Wu, 1987). Decades ago, a man would be ashamed if his wife had to find a job outside the home. This indicated that he could not support his family. This changed over the past decades when the government called on all people, except children and aging individuals, to contribute to society by working outside the home. Today, both the husband and wife having paying jobs are viewed as a normal occurrence. This equal status is more likely found in major cities. In most of the rural areas, due to the need for manual labor, men still are considered more important than women and have more privileges. This is a factor in the preference among rural families for having boys.

COUPLE FORMATION AND MARITAL DYNAMICS

Until the past decades, the couple's parents, grandparents, and/or matchmakers arranged marriages. The couple was not involved in the decision. For the proposed bride and groom, especially the bride, to ask questions about the marriage or about the fiancé was considered improper and forbidden. Typically, the couple did not meet until the wedding. The arrangements usually were conducted through a match-maker, who could be a member of one of the families involved. If the marriage agreement was broken, the family who refused to allow the marriage would lose their good reputation. Typically decided by the oldest male in the family, the marriage arrangement could be made years before the actual marriage. It was common that the couple would have been children when the arrangement was made, or even before they were born. A man might talk to another man to arrange their future children's marriage by saying: "If I have a son and you have a daughter, my son will take your daughter as his wife." This is known as *Zhi Fu Wei Hun* (making a marriage arrangement before the child was born; Zhong, 1974), documented by S. Wei (554, republished 1974). If arranged during adolescence or young adulthood, there were still many customs designed to maintain parental control. In most rural areas, strict rules made it difficult for young people to meet potential partners (Yi, 1995).

Economic statuses were equal, or the boy's family had a higher status. The marriage with well-matched social and economic status was *men dang hu dui,* the ideal or typical marriage (Shen & Ma, 1987). Marriage commonly was used for increasing the relationship between families. A wife was for the benefit of the family, not for an intimate relationship. A wife's two major duties were providing the family with a son, and providing good care of her parents-in-law and husband (Dai, 1992; Fei, 1947).

Several laws since 1950 have changed the status of women and men and have had consequences for couple formation. In addition, changes in the role of the family as an economic production unit could have contributed to modifications in the mate selection process (Thornton & Fricke, 1987). Before these changes, family members contributed to the family business. As financial needs changed, people began to secure their own employment. This allowed meeting prospective spouses, thereby restricting the role of parents in arranging marriages.

Love and the personal relationship of the couple have become important. The criteria for a happy family and marriage reported in a survey of 500 people aged twenty-five and older in Beijing, were: honesty (97 percent considered it important), appreciating and respecting each other (95 percent), understanding and tolerating each other (94 percent), sharing family chores (88 percent), and a satisfying sexual life (84 percent) (S. Lu, 1997). These responses indicate that the criteria of a happy family and marriage are from the perspective of the couple. The traditional idea of bringing honor to the family and having lots of sons is no longer on top of the list in the perspective of contemporary city families; research in rural areas report similar findings (S. B. Wang, 1992).

Age at the First Marriage

For thousands of years the average age when a Chinese couple married had been in the mid-teens. The suggested marriage age about 1,500 years ago was fifteen for men and thirteen for women (Dai, 1992). Between the late 1300s and the early 1900s, the government required men to marry no earlier than the age of sixteen and women fourteen years. These examples give an idea of the age norms of first marriage. Early marriage was consistent with the interests of the family. It was crucial for a family to have sons as early as possible and thought that the earlier a person had a son, the earlier the person would enjoy happiness. A wife with sons held higher status than a wife with no sons.

The 1950 Marriage Law helped change the age at marriage within a short period. In addition to treating the sexes equally and speaking against arranged marriage, the law set the minimum age of marriage as twenty years for men and eighteen years for women. Using women's average age at their first marriage as an example, it was 18.3 years in the 1940s, 18.7 in 1950, and 22.8 in the early 1980s (Coale & Chen, 1987; Dai, 1992). The average age at first marriage has consistently been higher in urban compared with rural areas. In 1980, for example, in cities a woman's average age at marriage was 25.2 years; it was 22.5 in rural areas. It is also consistent with factors such as education and employment differences between areas (State Statistical Bureau, 1980).

The family planning program emphasizing "later, sparser, and fewer" played a role in increasing the age at marriage (Dai, 1992). Under this program, a couple would generally not register to marry at their minimum age. The "later marriage age" was adopted to make sure the age of the marriage was appropriate. During that period, approximately 1970-1980, local governments in many rural areas set the marriage age at twenty-five years for males and twenty-three for females. In cities, the age could be as high as twenty-eight for males and twenty-five years for females. The revised marriage law (1980) specified the legal ages of marriage as twenty-two and twenty for males and females, respectively. Although people are encouraged to get married several years after the legal age, due to the change in the law, the average age at the first marriage has decreased (Dai, 1992).

Cohabitation Before Marriage, Sexual Norms, and Behaviors

There was little or no cohabitation before marriage under traditional arranged marriages. A marriage based on personal choice provides the possibility for intensive interaction before the marriage, but many people consider sexual relationships or living together before marriage wrong. The government, although wanting to foster greater freedom of mate choice, did not want to encourage dating or premarital sex. During the 1950s, many recreational facilities were closed. After the 1950s, romantic themes largely disappeared from the media. These actions were taken in hopes of eliminating or reducing the desire for premarital relationships (Yi, 1995).

When people were asked to give one suggestion to an unmarried couple, in two surveys conducted in 1982 and in 1996 in Beijing, over 76 percent suggested, "do not live together if not married" (S. Lu, 1997). However, a significant decrease and age difference in terms of holding this belief is seen when comparing these two surveys. Responses by age groups show 75 percent of the people in the younger age group (thirty-five years old and younger), 88 percent in the middle age group (thirty-six to fifty-five years old), and 98 percent in the older group (fifty-six and older) held this belief in 1982. In 1996, the people with the same belief dropped to 65, 68, and 75 percent in the younger, middle age, and older groups, respectively (S. Lu, 1997). People in their middle ages or older made the largest change in the years between the surveys. In the 1996 survey, more than 60 percent stated that they would not select someone as their spouse if he or she had sexual activity with others prior to the time they dated or married. About 80 percent of the people responded that it was unacceptable if his/her spouse had a sexual relationship with others after the marriage.

While these questions were not included in the 1982 survey, the comparison based on a general question indicated a significantly higher tolerance in a large portion of the population. About 71 percent of the younger age group in the 1996 survey claimed that it was unacceptable to them if their spouses "dated" others after their marriage (i.e., have nonwork-related dinner or other somewhat intimate/social interactions with those of the opposite sex, as well as affairs). The same responses in the middle and older age groups were 74 and 82 percent. The responses to a similar question in 1982 showed 84 percent of the younger group considered "dating" others as unacceptable. The same responses in the middle and older age groups were 95 percent and 98 percent, respectively. In this fourteen-year period, 10 to 20 percent of the people across all the age groups indicated less rejection of "dating" after marriage. However, while people are more tolerant, to a Chinese family, demonstrating loyalty to the marriage is most important for a happy family. The most damaging factor to the marriage is the breaking of that loyalty (S. Lu, 1997).

Dissolution of Relationships

For centuries, the Chinese have considered divorce the last resort, leading to a low divorce rate. Along with China's new openness and reforms, the divorce rate has increased. For example, from 0.35 per thousand people in 1980, to 0.75 in 1992, and to 2.1 per thousand people in 2003 (L. Wang, 2003), more than a 100 percent increase in the twelve years and sixfold increase in twenty-three years. The divorce rate is still lower than many countries (Xinhuawang, 2004).

During the era of arranged marriages, a wife was the "property" of the husband's family. She was expected to follow the husband from the day of their marriage. Expected not to remarry, women would have no home if they were divorced. Going back to their parents' homes was acceptable when their parents were still alive, but it would create a negative impact on the family reputation and make the parents "lose face." These traditional ethics and practices made it remarkably rare for a woman to initiate divorce. A man usually did not divorce his wife either. Tradition and law restricted a man from divorcing his wife without acceptable reasons (D. Zhang, 1993). All this contributed to the extremely low divorce rate in traditional society.

Acceptable reasons for divorce in the feudal society were unfair to women. The criteria to divorce, consistently adopted by many dynasties in the feudal society, were if the wife: (1) did not obey her parents-in-law; (2) did not bear a son to the family; (3) engaged in improper sexual activities; (4) was jealous of others; (5) talked too much; (6) had an infectious disease; and (7) stole others' properties. Exceptions were also considered. If the wife had no home to go to after being divorced, for example, she usually would not be divorced (D. Zhang, 1993).

Reasons for divorcing a wife aimed to protect the honor of the extended patriarchal family and the norms of the society. The couple's individual needs and relationship were not a consideration. It was not the husband, but the family, who divorced his wife. If the parents of the husband wanted him to divorce his wife, he would have to accept this decision. Obviously, the accusation, "did not obey her parents-in-law," was subjectively determined by the parents-in-law. However, this accusation was considered the number one reason to divorce a wife. If the husband did not support his parents' opinion, he would be accused as not *Xiaoshun* (*Xiaoshun* means showing filial obedience to his parents) (D. Zhang, 1993). He would lose his reputation because filial obedience was one of the most important rules in a family. This was also valued by society and the government when selecting officials. Under such circumstances, divorce was not a choice made by the couple.

While divorce has been uncommon for centuries in China, the divorce rate has increased notably in recent years (Xinhuawang, 2004). Instead of the husband's family divorcing the wife, wives initiated 70 percent of the divorces in recent years (D. Zhang, 1993). The predominant reasons for filing divorces are more directly related to the couples themselves. The reasons considered important for a couple to divorce are: spousal abuse (87 percent), dishonesty in marriage (86 percent), drugs or alcohol abuse (76 percent), long-term separation (62 percent), personality conflict (59 percent), difficulty communicating (56 percent), an unsatisfactory sexual life (55 percent), not taking care of the spouse (55 percent), not taking enough responsibilities for the family (51 percent), not getting along with the spouse's extended family members (33 percent), and unable to have children (24 percent) (S. Lu, 1997). In recent years, abuse or family violence and dishonesty in marriage accounted for a significantly reduced proportion of reasons for divorce, while the quality of the couple's relationship became more important (Y. Wu, 2002). Gender and educational level also relate to divorce propensity. Men tend to get divorced more than females if their educational levels are low, and females tend to get divorced more than males if their education levels are high (Zeng, 1995).

The old (before the twentieth century) reasons for divorcing a wife, such as the factors of the spouses' family and whether a woman was able to have children, were still considered important by some people, but were far from the top reasons. In addition, the 33 percent of the people who considered getting along with their spouses' extended family members as important and the 24 percent who considered not being able to have children as important were not considering these as solely a woman's responsibility. Men were facing the same challenges as well (S. Lu, 1997).

Although the divorce rate has been increasing and perceptions are changing (especially with the younger generation), people still tend to expect happy endings. Considerable efforts are made to save a marriage if there is a divorce attempt from either spouse. Although there are changes, the couple usually will undergo a long process involving many people to try to achieve reconciliation (Zeng, 1995). The court will generally not consider a divorce until all of these attempts have failed, except when immediate attention is needed to avoid possible violence.

Children are an important factor for a couple concerning divorce. Many people acknowledge their marriage crisis but continue their relationship mainly for their children's future. More than 80 percent of the people responding to Lu's survey (1997) considered their children's future advantages as the major reason for a couple with a marriage crisis to keep their marriage together. Other reasons, such as family's reputation, "saving face," and needing help from each other, were considered as important by less than 40 percent of the respondents.

FAMILIES AND CHILDREN

Average Family Size

Family size has been three to seven for the past 2,000 years but the average was between five and six. A family with five people, two parents and three children, was considered the typical family. Some extended families had shared properties for many generations. These families could be as large as hundreds or even thousands of people. However, this was never typical in China (Dai, 1992; Liang, 1990; S. Lu, 1997; Ma, 1984; Ma & Shen, 1987). Family size has decreased in recent years. In 1990 about 50 percent of families had three or four people while in 1980 the most frequent family size was four or five. In addition, the percentage of larger sized families has decreased (State Statistical Bureau, 1982, 1991, 2003). Though many researchers predicted that families would develop toward the nuclear type, others argued there was a large portion of nuclear families that did not necessarily conflict with the concept of the extended family (Ma, 1982, 1984; Pan, 1992). The incidence of the nuclear family is high in middle-aged couples but relatively low among both young and older couples (Liu, 1987). One reason for this is the changes in tradition. Parents traditionally stayed with their oldest son's family. This has changed and the older children usually leave their parents' home when they marry or shortly after. The youngest children now stay with their parents after marriage. Instead of decreasing, the pattern of the stem family is predicted to be stable or even increase (Ma & Shen, 1987).

Birth Interval, Fertility Rate, and Population Control

For centuries, couples began their families early. The most frequently occurring birth interval was between one and two years of marriage. Low survival rates due to insufficient medical care and poor living conditions influenced the population's reproduction pattern (W. Chen, 1996).

The fertility rate has been relatively high throughout the history of China. During the year of 1949 when the People's Republic of China was founded, the fertility rate was above 5.5 per couple. This is a representative figure for the fertility rates prior to that year because there is no evidence that the fertility rates changed before 1949. The available figures on fertility rates between 1945 and 1955 support a similar conclusion (Dai, 1992).

The population has rapidly increased due to improved living conditions and medical care. There were 600 million people in China in 1954. The population increased to 700 million by 1964 and 800 million by 1969. The fertility rate in 1963 reached 7.4. High fertility was a major factor for the shortened time period of each 100 million-population increment (State Statistical Bureau, 1954, 1964, 1969). Increasing population threatened the future of China and put pressure on limited natural resources and economic development. Government documents first mentioned birth control in 1957 in the Second Five-Year Plan. However, there was no specific policy until the early 1970s. The recommendation for the number of children was "one is sufficient, two is just right, and three is acceptable" (J. F. Wang, personal communication, May, 1997).

The government started to vigorously advocate a later marriage and birth control policy in the early 1970s. This reduced fertility rates from 5.75 in 1970 to 2.32 in 1980. Since 1980, the majority of couples have been restricted to having only one child. While there were almost no exceptions made in cities, in rural areas there were still many families that had more than one child. Reasons that contributed to the different birthrates include the strong desire for boys in rural families, and the financial punishment for exceeding the one child limit did not work as well. However, while the policy did not prove as efficient in rural areas, the average number of children per couple declined to no more than two or three in most rural families (L. Wang, 1993).

The impact of this policy was tremendous in terms of population control. Researchers, using different methods, predicted that the population in China would be 200 million more than the actual number reported in the statistics, if this policy was not in place (Liang, 1990; Qiao, 1995; J. Wei, 1989; Z. Zhang, 1994). Based on Wu and Xiao's (1994) calculation, the number of children born between 1971 and 1990 was 221 million less than without a birth control policy, a one-third reduction. The slower speed of population increase has allowed time to cope with the difficulties of economic development and has improved living standards (Qiao, 1994).

This policy has influenced the structure of the Chinese family and people's expectations and perceptions of the family—the traditional ideal family with many sons has been impossible for most families since. The continuity of the family name, valued by Chinese society for thousands of years, is being jeopardized. Since the early 1990s, the policy has been relaxed somewhat and allows couples in rural areas to have a second child, especially if the first child is a girl. This is not officially encouraged, but practically accepted.

Sex Preferences

The gender preference has been clear and strong throughout Chinese history. Sons were permanent members of the family; daughters were considered temporary members. Rearing girls was considered a liability and a cost that benefited the families of girls' future husbands. Having at least one son to keep the family line has been considered extremely important. The policy of one child per couple conflicts with this preference and has been one of the major stresses in many Chinese families. It has also led to an unbalanced birthrate ratio between the two sexes.

In the 1960s and 1970s, the sex ratio of newborn boys to girls was 106/100, within the normal range of 103/100 to 107/100 (Gu & Li, 1996; Zeng, Gu, Tu, Li, & Li, 1993). The sex ratio started to increase in the 1980s to 108/100 in 1984 and greater than 112/100 in 1986. The sex ratio reached its highest value of 116/100 in 1991 and dropped to 114/100 in 1993. The sex ratio was higher in rural areas (112/100) than in cities (109/100). As the birth control policy was applied most thoroughly in cities, birth control was not the major reason for this unbalanced sex ratio (Gu & Roy, 1996). The sex ratio was normal among firstborn children. The ratio significantly increased among second and thirdborn children and children thereafter. This pattern was especially true for couples whose firstborn was a girl. The sex ratio was about 150/100 for secondborns for families that had one girl, and was over 200/100 for the thirdborn for couples with two girls (Y. Li, 1993). The major reasons for this unbalanced sex ratio are not reporting the birth of girls (so that the couple might have a chance to have another child), abandoning and neglecting baby girls, and selectively aborting female fetuses after identifying their sex. Abortion was rare in China one hundred years ago, only used in extreme situations. After the birth control policy was vigorously promoted in the early 1970s, abortion has been more frequently used as a method to control the birthrate when birth control practices fail.

The government strongly encouraged couples to use birth control and different levels of government provide free contraceptives to married couples. They can also be purchased from drug stores. There are more women in China using the contraceptive pill than in any other nation (Mehta, 2001). The contraceptive prevalence rate is 84 percent (UNDP, 2006).

Parenting Styles and Practices

In cities, if a mother is employed and the one child per couple rule is observed, she will be allowed to stay home for six months after the birth with full salary and benefits. Her employer will maintain her position. When returning to work, her parents or parents-in-law will usually help care for the infant if they are available. Otherwise, she can hire a babysitter or send her infant to a child-care center. A child usually is in a center from age three to five or six and then goes to an elementary school at age six or seven years. Children in rural areas start school at about the same age, but they typically will stay at home before school age (B. Wu, 1987).

Nationwide research with over 2,000 families found that effective parenting includes having authority as well as respect for children's opinions. Parents emphasize children's development in intelligence, independence, self-control, respecting others, and willingness to participate in labor (Xu et al., 1991; Xu, Wang, Wu, & Min, 1990). Chinese families emphasize discipline and learning. To emphasize discipline means that children are required to be good and to display good manners. This includes displaying respectful behavior to elders, following parents' instructions, being ready to help others, and being able to get along with siblings, cousins, friends, and others. To emphasize learning means that parents want their child to learn and learn well. They want to help their children to have the best possible future, and be proud of their children and themselves as parents (Jiang, Teng, Wang, & Qian, 1991).

Scholastic Achievement

Chinese children have the highest scholastic achievement in comparison with Japanese and American children, while their parents' satisfaction level about their children's scholastic achievement is the lowest (Stevenson, Lee, & Stigler, 1986). Tradition is a reason for this high expectation. China has been a society emphasizing cooperative behavior and placing a high value on getting along with others. Meanwhile, there is a consistent and often silent competition between people in most areas of life. Satisfaction comes only from being the best at something.

Since the Tang Dynasty 1,400 years ago, passing a series of entrance exams at different levels in order to qualify for a government office became almost the only way to start a career (Du, 801/1987). This system was used until the Qing Dynasty, which ended about one century ago. As few exams were given (e.g., once in three years for the highest level) and only a few would be selected from each exam, performing at a high level was crucial. People had to study well to be selected. Even today this system makes many families consider education to be the most important activity for their children. People will work harder or skimp on their food, clothing, and even health care to help their children go to school. They expect their children to have success and bring honors to the family. Parents' high expectations are partially due to competition for limited opportunities of high school, college, and university, coupled with limited opportunities for the most desirable jobs.

In the past decades, financial considerations have not been a major factor for Chinese families. The government provides all children with a free education for nine years, until the end of middle school. Further education is free, but it is not available to all because resources are limited. Only some children who succeed in a competitive exam are admitted in high school. An even smaller proportion will be accepted for college and university (Jiang, 1977). Until recently, state supported universities provided free room and tuition. Though there have been small "tuition" charges in recent years, a large portion of this money is used for scholarships to the highest achieving students and those needing financial support. If a student does not score high enough to be accepted by a state school, he or she can pay a much greater amount to go to "self-supported" schools. Typically students are "full-time" and do not work, putting a financial burden on families (Y. J. Su, personal communication, January 14, 1998). This burden increased significantly in low-income families due to the rapid increase for receiving college education.

Parents, especially in cities, start to prepare their children for this competition at an early age. They typically compete for enrollment in the best child-care centers. The best centers will prepare them to compete for the best elementary schools that will prepare them to compete for the best middle schools and so on through to the best high schools whose job is to send as many students to university, especially the well-recognized universities. It is believed a child will have a small chance to be prepared for the future competition if he or she was not able to start with a good child-care center because of this continuous competition and selection process.

Parents usually do whatever they can to help their children; many give all the time and money they can afford to provide their children with opportunities to learn better. Meanwhile, parents need to convince their children that all of the learning activities are important. To motivate children, parents have to do more than just provide the opportunities. Parents use modeling, reinforcing, restricting, and internalization techniques to varying degrees to help children keep up with schoolwork. Among them, parents' modeling is the most emphasized (Jiang et al., 1991).

FAMILIES AND GENDER

As noted throughout this chapter, the status of girls in families has traditionally been much lower than boys. Women's roles in families were typically concentrated on the household chores and taking care of elders and children. A family or several families together, would hire a mentor to teach sons but would not do so for daughters. If a girl could receive any education, she would usually benefit from her brothers' learning and be taught by her brothers' mentor.

This situation started to change in the early 1900s as public schools emerged. Women started to seek the right to education and schools began to accept female students. Today women and men have similar opportunities to receive education and employment. According to a

1987 survey, about 50 percent of wives and 43 percent of husbands had at least a junior high school education. About 40 percent of wives and 34 percent of husbands had a high school or equivalent education, and about 10 percent of wives and 20 percent of husbands went to college or graduate schools. Among them, 62 percent of the wives and 61 percent of the husbands worked in jobs that were labor intensive. Others were doing white-collar jobs (Ma, Liu, Sheng, & Meng, 1992).

The increase in education and employment has greatly increased women's independence and status in the family. Women typically participate in most of the decision making regarding their families. The pattern of making decisions on family matters has changed from husbands making decisions to joint decision making. In cities, more men share or take major responsibility in caring for children, cooking meals, cleaning, and doing other household chores, even though these responsibilities are still predominantly taken on by women. In rural areas, most of the employed women still do most of the housework (Z. Lu, 2000; Xu, 1992; Xue, 1992).

Marriage and family oppressed women; this has diminished greatly in the past decades. The marriage law (1950 and revised 1980), indicated that men and women have equal rights in the family and should be treated equally, and that daughters have an equal right to inherit family properties. Included in the marriage law (Renda Changweihui, 1994a) are

- The wife can be a member of the husband's family after the registration of marriage according to mutual agreements; the husband can also be a member of the wife's family
- Children can be named after either the husband's or the wife's family name
- The husband is not allowed to propose a divorce during the wife's pregnancy and within one year after childbirth. However, the wife can divorce her husband during this time
- After divorce, each party gives economic support to the other if there are difficulties.

The Women's Law (1992) specified protection of women's rights in the following six ways (Renda Changweihui, 1994b):

- Political rights, which guarantee a woman's right to participate in politics;

- Cultural and educational rights, which guarantee a girl's right to receive an education;
- Labor rights and interests, which guarantee a woman's right of employment;
- Property rights and interests, which guarantees a rural woman's rights and interests to the field and courtyard in which the family grew crops;
- Personal rights, which guarantee the rights and interests of abducted women, those forced into prostitution, and infant girls; and
- Marital and family rights and interests, which guarantee a woman a residential house after divorce and her rights and interests to reject a second pregnancy, and so on.

These laws played important roles in increasing women's status, in both family and society. In the early 1950s, for example, few women worked in natural sciences and technology. In 1984, more than 30 percent of the people in these areas were women. Women also held 40 percent of the positions in education, music and art, medical and health care, and social welfare (Dai, 1992). Marriage based on personal choice has also significantly increased. A study of couples from five major cities reported that parents arranged the marriages of most women who married before 1937. However, there were few arranged marriages after 1965 (FCMFRPG, 1985).

The Marriage Law was further revised in 2001 and explained by the Supreme Court in 2002/2003 creating changes in marriage, separation, and divorce procedures in China. Among these, the law required mutual loyalty between spouses. It also prohibited a married person from living with a "non-spouse," and prohibited family violence. It also stipulated that individual property is property that belongs to someone before marriage, and the law specified that individual property be protected if a divorce were to occur. The law also decreased the separation period before filing for a divorce from three years to two years (Standing Committee of the National People's Congress, 2004).

Fault compensation was also allowed so that during a divorce, one party may be found to be at fault, and the other party may be entitled to compensation. Fault compensation is typically due to double marriage, a married person living with a "non-spouse," family violence, and abuse or discarding of family members. Except for living with a non-spouse, all of the faults mentioned previously can be subjected to criminal charges. Both spouses are required to assume responsibility for the support and welfare of their children after a divorce. They must both foster and support a child's education. Parents both have the right and the responsibility to visit children, regardless of which spouse has custody of the children. If a parent does not meet the requirements of support, they can be subjected to civil and/or criminal charges. However, the forced visitation that applies to parents does not apply to children. If a child does not want to see a parent after a divorce, the child has that particular right (Standing Committee of the National People's Congress, 2004).

Overall, the revised laws protected the weaker sides of the marriage, usually women and children. It also helped reduce the difficulty of finding spouses who are military personnel, as it was difficult to divorce a person serving in the military and therefore discouraged individuals to consider marrying military personnel. The spouse of an in-service military personnel is still required by the Marriage Law of 2001 to obtain a spouse's agreement before proceeding with the divorce procedure. However, the law also defined the situations in which this requirement will not be observed, such as when in-service military personnel has made serious mistakes, such as double marriage, family violence, abuse, or discarding of family members.

FAMILIES AND STRESS

Several factors lead to family stress, including aging of the population, difficulty of mate selection due to a highly unbalanced sex ratio— tens of million of males will not find wives because there will be many more males compared with females (Gu & Roy, 1996; P. Zhang, 1992), competition for employment and education opportunities; conflict between traditional and present practices of raising the only child; and rapidly increased unemployed population along with the economic reform in recent years. Two of these are discussed here.

Supporting an Aging Population

There were about 100 million people over age sixty in 1991 (about 10 percent of the population). It is predicted that the aging population will increase at a rate of 3 percent per year. By the year 2025, there will be 280 million people over age sixty (19 percent of the population) and by 2050, the aging population will be over 27 percent. The average age will also become older. The proportion of elderly people aged sixty to sixty-nine will drop from 62 to 47 percent from 1990 to 2050, while the proportion above seventy years of age will increase from 38 to 53 percent (Ma, 1988; Tang, 1995; Tang & Yie 1994; S. Wang, 1996; C. Zhang, 1997).

Throughout history, families have played a major role in supporting their aging members. Families will continue to play a major role for a long time as the extraordinary speed of the population aging increases and because of the social and economic development level in China (Liang & Zhai, 1996; Ma, 1988; Tang, 1995; Tang & Yie, 1994; Z. Yang, 1997; Yie, 1993; C. Zhang, 1997). However, supporting an aging population this large is a challenge for families and will increase in the future. In Chinese tradition, parents are always considered members of their children's families. Adult children are responsible for taking good care of their parents, and they will be disrespected if they do not provide adequate care (Chou & Zheng, 1987). The Marriage Law (2001) requires that in situations where their parents either died or were not capable of supporting grandparents, the grandchildren should support their grandparents (L. Wang, 2003).

Several factors contribute to the increase in the aging population. Two major factors are improved living standards and medical care that have significantly extended lives, and enforced national population control that has reduced the proportion of the younger population. Looking at a three generation family and assuming that the one child per couple policy was strictly observed, there would be four people in the generation of the grandparents (two on the father's side and two on the mother's), two people in the generation of the parents (father and mother), and one person in the child's generation. This pattern is described as 4:2:1. When a child marries a child from a similar family, this couple would have four parents on both sides and eight grandparents (Jiang et al., 1991; Sheng, 1992; A. Wang, 1989). This 4:2:1 pattern will transform into a four-generation family pattern of 2:4:2:2. This is because a couple is allowed to have two children if they both are the only child of their parents and because of the increased longevity of the aging generation. It is predicted that this problem cannot be completely solved until after the parents of the single-child generation pass away in about 2020 to 2030 (Yie, 1993).

The financial support for aging people in rural areas is predominantly from their families, including spouse and children (Tan & Li, 1997). In cities, family support accounts for more than 50 percent of older people's three basic sources of income (i.e., a retirement stipend, support from children, and support from spouse). Many aging individuals in cities find other jobs after retirement in order to contribute to society and earn more money.

Many aging individuals in cities enjoy complete or partially free medical care supported by the units (e.g., companies, factories, schools) for whom they have worked. The individuals who have never been formally employed (e.g., small portion of women in urban areas and most of the aging people in rural areas) are predominantly supported by their spouses and their children (Chou & Zheng, 1987; Huang & Tao, 1987). Socialized resources for supporting senior citizens is highly recommended, which includes resources from family units, social security funding, and personal savings. Senior housing and nursing homes have been developing rapidly. Senior citizens in rural areas may also opt to exchange social security for land, a transactional process in which rural workers who are too elderly to work the land can trade the land for a certain amount of compensation that could be used to cover social security.

The government provides minimum support when individuals have neither retirement income nor children. Depending on the level of economic development in the region, the support varies from minimum to sufficient (Huang & Tao, 1987). Families, whose income is below the minimum average income as determined by the government, also receive this minimum support. Financial supports will make these families' incomes match the minimum average.

Increase in Unemployment

Owing to economic reforms, government owned businesses have significantly changed. Transitioning from a government controlled to a market controlled economic system means businesses have to rely on their resources to compete in the market place (Q. Li, 1997). Economic reform has led to many factories and businesses closing resulting in many people being laid off or losing their jobs (F. Yang, 1997). Over ten million people have received lower wages or lost their jobs since the beginning of reforms (Theory Department of Chinese Employment Committee [TDOCEC], 1998). The rapid increase of the unemployed has put more families in stressful situations due to significantly decreased family incomes. It is expected that one-third of the employed population would face potential unemployment (F. Yang, 1997).

In cities, the unemployment rate in 2001, according to the registry, was 3.6 percent (Laodong He Shehui Baozhang Bu & Guojia Tongji Ju, 2003) though a significant proportion of the unemployed did not register so the actual unemployment rate is much higher. The Labor and Career Development Report in June 2002 reported a 7 percent unemployment rate. The latest report, published in May 2004, indicated that there was a total of 8.1 million registered unemployed. In addition, 250 million people in rural areas were reported to not have full employment. About 100 million of them found jobs in cities, the rest are technically unemployed. The unemployed rural population is not included in the statistics of unemployment. If this number is included, the unemployed population in China could be over 10 percent (Zheng & Wang, 2003).

When this large population "retires" or is laid off, youth are forced to compete with experienced, newly laid off workers. Finding a job becomes ever more difficult for young people who are entering the job market. Unemployed youth are more likely to create problems for the society and for their families. In order to provide jobs for these young people, parents retire in their early fifties or at younger ages to let their children take their jobs if such exchanges are permitted (TDOCEC, 1998). It will be a substantial relief to these families if unemployment can be solved in the near future. Until then, unemployment, in conjunction with the responsibilities of supporting their children, their parents-in-law, and maybe even their grandparents and grandparents-in-law, will continuously create stress for many families in China.

FAMILIES AND AGING

Until several decades ago, aging people owned family property, ruled the family, and were considered as the most valuable resource to the family because of their experience and wisdom. This situation has changed because of changes in society and the development of technology.

Retirement

Employed people in cities usually retire at the ages of fifty, fifty-five, sixty, or sixty-five depending on their job. Women usually retire five to ten years earlier than do men (Y. Wang, 1996). Many find another job after retirement to improve their living standards or to support their adult children's families, or to contribute more to the society (e.g., financial support and help taking care of their grandchildren). Aging people in rural areas are more likely to be involved in family production activities throughout their lives because most of these activities are conducted at home. To most of these people, there is no retirement. On the other hand, when they are unable to be fully involved, older people will take some lighter duties or do something they wanted to do.

Aged women have lower socioeconomic status compared with aged men. Based on research in urban areas, 64 percent of over 7,700 men surveyed received retirement incomes compared with 36 percent of women. In rural areas, 6 percent of females received retirement income among the 600 people who reported receiving retirement income. Women's average retirement income was about two-thirds of that of men. A similar situation is seen regarding free medical care. Over 80 percent of aged males in cities received free medical care while the percentage for females was fewer than 50. In rural areas, families provided the funds for medical care for about 84 percent of the aged males and 92 percent of the aged females (S. Wang, 1996).

Laws and Other Supportive Interventions

China has recently adopted the Aging Rights and Benefits Protection Law. It provides constitutional supports to older adults in addition to the supports specified in the National Law and policies specified in Retirement Regulations, and *WuBao* Regulations (Z. Yang, 1997). However, supports to the aging population are not adequate, overall (Family Aging Supports [FASSS], 1996a; Liang & Zhai, 1996; Tang, 1995; Tang & Yie, 1994; Y. Wang, 1996). A survey (with a sample of 606 people aged from sixty to eighty-five conducted by FASSS

(1996a, 1996b)) reported that beyond financial and medical inade-
quacies, many other needs are not met (e.g., 4 percent received on-
call services, while 45 percent indicated need for this service; Nursing
homes were available for less than 1 percent of the sample while the
need was close to 20 percent).

Researchers have been calling attention to the comparative poverty
of the aging population (Z. Wei, 1992). A national law on aging individuals is considered necessary to protect their rights and interests. A
security system in conjunction with family supports and neighborhood
service networks to provide better supports for the rapidly increased
aging population in China has also been suggested. Numerous recent
studies suggested or explored a variety of possible solutions to support
this aging population (Q. Chen, 1994; FASSS, 1996a, 1996b; Gao,
1995; Z. Lin, 1995; Ma, 1988; Xiong & Dong, 1996; Z. Yang, 1997;
Yie, 1993; M. Zhang, 1995). These research studies agreed that supporting the aging population was a great challenge to the families, to the
aging people's previous working units, to the society, and to the governments. A combined effort from all these sources is required because
none of these sources alone is able to support this huge and rapidly
growing aging population. Examples of detailed suggestions include:
(1) mandatory aging insurance paid by both the individual and their
work unit; (2) neighborhood supports (e.g., aging service centers, nursing homes, senior citizen centers, etc.); (3) family supports (i.e., the
law indicates that supporting aging parents is the duty of their children
and/or, children-in-law, and sometimes grandchildren); and (4) young
aging individuals helping older aging individuals in order to save cred-
its for future free services from aging individuals who are younger
when these "young old" are in need of these services in the future.

OTHER FAMILY SITUATIONS

There is a matriarchal family system observed among the Naxi ethnic group (also known as Nari or the Mosuo), approximately 178,000
people living in northwestern Yunnan Province (Yuan & Mitchell,
2000; Zhao, 1995). These people call their living unit *Yidu,* meaning
a house and its occupants. The head is usually the eldest or the most
capable woman. The household contains several matrilineal descent
generations. Naxi people desire daughters more than they desire sons.

Children live with their mothers and all household members take care of them.

Naxi men and women do not marry; each mating partner always remains at his or her mother's house. Around the age of twelve years, a girl has a coming-of-age ceremony. After puberty, she can receive male visitors. The boy comes to the girl's house in the evening, stays the night, and returns to his home early the following morning. People called this relationship "walking back and forth" or *sisi* (Yuan & Mitchell, 2000; Zhao, 1995), or in Chinese the arrangement is called *zou hun* (walking marriage) or *azhu hunyin* (friend marriage). These informal unions can end at any time. A man might have several relationships at one time. Women might have children from more than one walking marriage.

The Naxi did not have a word for father until the early twentieth century when the term *ada* for father was created, but people seldom use it. Children generally do not know their father's identity. In longer lasting mating relationships or from villager stories (seldom from their mothers), children may come to know their father, but seldom establish close relations with him. If the relationship between father and child is close, it involves no economic or social responsibilities. The males that look after a female are her brothers (uncles) (X. Yang, 1993). The man's sister's children will care for an older man (Yuan & Mitchell, 2000).

Naxi note several advantages of this system including all children helping the mother's household, larger extended families that can produce more than can a nuclear family, less conflict between children, and relationships based on love rather than money or dowry. During the Cultural Revolution, Naxi were forced to marry and practice monogamy. During this time, the couples held marriage certificates and lived with the wife's mother. The man, however, returned each morning to his mother's household to work. When the period of the Cultural Revolution was over, the people soon returned to their former system (Yuan & Mitchell, 2000).

CONCLUDING COMMENTS

China, with thousands of years of history and more than one-fifth of the world's population, has been closed to the rest of the world for a long time. Chinese people value loyalty to the family and its members. Family systems are dominantly patriarchal. However, there are many variations. Matriarchal families can be found as well, though restricted to a small region. Modern Chinese families follow the stem and the nuclear family patterns. For centuries, women had the lowest status in a family. Recent laws entitle women to equal status and rights.

Chinese couples tended to get married early and to have many children. Providing sons for the extended family had been one of the major traditional duties of a married couple. The restriction of one child per couple has changed this tendency and tradition. Chinese parents emphasize learning and discipline in raising children. As there is only one child in many cases, parents' hopes and aspirations cannot be shared by siblings; parents' expectations for their one child's achievements become higher. These high expectations put pressure on children.

The Chinese family has undergone tremendous changes in the past decades. These changes include family formation, the concept of family, relationships within a family, and the expectations of family members to each other. Among these changes, the improvement of women's status in a family, women's employment, and the 4:2:1 generational pattern influenced by the one child per couple policy are the most significant aspects. Developing from a system that has thousands of years of history toward the family patterns found in a modern society bring both positive and negative impacts to the family. While families and their members tend to live more independent lives, enjoy equal status and more freedom, there are also challenges.

Population control helps in reducing the pressures of a huge population. It has also provided China valuable time to produce a rapid economic development. This significantly increased the living standards of Chinese families. Along with these positive changes, population control has also led to a largely unbalanced sex ratio, which is changing many aspects of marriage, and has disproportionately increased the aging population. Although population control has been considered a move in a positive direction for the long run, it is also predicted that this factor will have its greatest impact on Chinese families in the following decades.

Chapter 14

The Family in the Philippines

Belen T. G. Medina

The Philippines is an archipelago of over 7,000 islands in the Southeast Asia region. The terrain is mountainous with narrow to extensive coastal lowlands. The climate is tropical marine with monsoon seasons and typhoons. About 19 percent of the land is arable while forest covers about 46 percent. Of the population of 81.6 million, many (40 percent) live in rural areas and engage in agricultural production (about 45 percent of the labor force). Population growth is around 2.3 percent but is expected to be 1.6. By the year 2015, the population is estimated to be 96.8 million (United Nations Development Programme [UNDP], 2006; World Factbook, 2006).

The inhabitants are largely of Malay stock but include hundreds of ethnolinguistic groups. Christians (mainly Roman Catholic) who occupy the lowlands of the major islands (often referred to as lowland Christians) are the majority (90 percent). Minority communities consist of Muslims in the south, the indigenous pagan tribes in the Cordillera Mountains in the north, and some other tribes scattered in the more isolated sections of the islands (World Factbook, 2006).

In 1998, the Philippine economy was a mixture of agriculture (14 percent of GDP), industry (33 percent), and services (53 percent) but has since deteriorated due to spillover from the Asian financial crisis and poor weather conditions. There was a recovery between 2002 and 2005. Unemployment was 8.7 percent in 2005 (World Factbook, 2006).

The National Capital Region of Metropolitan Manila contains more than ten million people. Quezon City has the largest population (2.17 million), followed by Manila (1.58 million), and Caloocan City (1.18 million) (36 percent of the population was urban in 1975, increased to 60 percent in 2002, and by 2015 is expected to be 69 percent; National Statistics Office, 2002; UNDP, 2006). As the center of trade, transportation, education, and culture, Metropolitan Manila attracts migrants from the provinces. It is here where people from all walks of life and various backgrounds are found. It is also here where the great inequalities in social class are highly visible, with squatter shanties standing along side mansions. In 2000, 34 percent of the country's families lived below the official poverty line with 38 percent estimated for 2004 (Philippine Statistical Yearbook, 2002). About 16 percent of the population lives on the equivalent of US$1 per day, and 48 percent on US$2 per day. The United Nations places the Philippines in the medium human development category, ranked eighty-fourth of 177 nations. The Human Development Index scores have been increasing steadily since 1975 (UNDP, 2006).

The country has a long history with Indian and Chinese traders, as well as with neighboring peoples from Indonesia and Malaysia. Spain, the United States, and Japan successively colonized the Philippines. Spain ceded the Philippines to the United States in 1898 following the Spanish-American War. After occupation by the Japanese in World War II, independence was obtained in 1946. A quarter-century-old guerrilla war with Muslim separatists on the island of Mindanao ended with a treaty in 1996, but the government continues to struggle with insurgencies in the south (World Factbook, 2006). Communist rebels in isolated regions of the country also stage sporadic attacks.

The most important Spanish legacy of 300 years is Catholicism (81 percent of the population is Roman Catholic, 12 percent Protestant, 5 percent Muslim, and 2 percent other) with its religious festivals, pageants, and rituals surrounding birth, death, and marriage (World Factbook, 2006). The United States left its mark on the government and education systems and brought about the widespread use of the English language, a taste for American consumer goods and pop music, and the Western concept of dating and romantic love. Today, the Philippines is a busy Pacific international hub of trade, transportation, and communication, as well as a tourist attraction.

Families in Filipino Context

Owing to contacts with the outside world from precolonial times, the Filipino culture is a mixture of East and West, of traditional and modern. There are diversities among Filipinos with respect to ethno-linguistic origin, socioeconomic background, religion, rural-urban residence, and degree of modernity. Thus there is no typical Filipino family. However, because lowland Christian families constitute the majority, and their modal patterns and traits are commonly perceived and accepted as typical, they are referred to as "the" Filipino family in this chapter. Moreover, because of similarities with Muslims and the indigenous pagan families, the patterns describing the Christians can apply to non-Christian families. When the basic characteristics of Filipino families are examined, "far greater similarities than differences stand out" (Jocano, 1972, p. 25).

One characteristic common to Filipino families and most families in Southeast Asia is bilateral extension. Close bonds extend beyond the nuclear family to include the relatives of both husband and wife with equal recognition and closeness to both paternal and maternal kin. The nuclear family is oriented toward the wider extended family of grandparents, aunts, uncles, and cousins. Frequent reciprocal visits and close interaction keep the bonds strong (Medina, 2001).

Another Filipino family characteristic is egalitarianism promoted by the bilateral structure (Medina, 2001). Both spouses, after marriage, are integral parts of their families of orientation. Although residing independently, they continue to interact with their kin and receive support and protection. The families of orientation maintain their interest in the affairs of the couple. They intervene when there is a quarrel or spouse abuse. Equality is preserved by virtue of the two kin groups who are to be on an equal relation to the couple, serving as watchdogs for maintaining the balance of power between the spouses and between the kin groups. There is no favoring of husband's or wife's kin or gender discrimination in property ownership and inheritance. All children inherit equally from their parents (Family Code of the Philippines, 1987).

COUPLE FORMATION AND MARITAL DYNAMICS

Mate Selection

In traditional Philippine society, kin involvement and control characterize courtship. Marriage is viewed as an alliance of two families, not merely two individuals. Parents try to control the choice of mate due to concerns about the family into which their children are marrying. Furthermore, young people cannot interact among themselves without a chaperone, partly to keep girls chaste because of concerns about family honor, for premarital pregnancy brings shame to the family (Hunt, Quisumbing, Espiritu, Costello, & Lacar, 1987; Medina, 2001).

The extended family has slowly relaxed its hold on individuals. Today some traditional courtship patterns remain among rural residents, while emerging patterns in urban areas differ in that young Filipinos exercise freedom of mate choice although they still regard parental approval as important and necessary. Romantic love has replaced the chaperone system (Medina, 2001).

Choice of a marriage partner is primarily a prerogative of individuals, but laws and preferential mating rules place restrictions on the group from which a mate is selected. The New Family Code fixes the minimum age for marriage at eighteen for both men and women but requires written parental consent for those ages twenty-one and below (Family Code, 1987; Feliciano, 1994). The law also provides for monogamy except for non-Christians who may follow their own customs and traditions (Mastura, 1994). The law further prohibits marriages between ascendants and descendants of any degree, between brothers and sisters whether of full or half blood, between first cousins, and between a person and his or her aunt/uncle.

There are no legal restrictions to racial, national, or ethnolinguistic intermarriage, but Filipinos generally prefer endogamy (Medina, 2001). Parents often advise their children to marry those from the same town, religion, nationality, and race to make marital adjustment easier. Even among young people, there is a preference to marry within the same religious, racial, socioeconomic, and linguistic group. There are indications that endogamy is breaking down. A considerable trend toward crossing of regional lines, as well as a tendency to ignore ethnicity as a basis for mate selection, has been noted (Feldman, 1994; Medina, 2001).

In the Philippine traditional courtship style, the man is the pursuer. However, patterns of initiative in courtship are no longer clear-cut. Although the man generally does the wooing, it is not uncommon for the woman to encourage the man by making phone calls, text messaging, or by invitations to a party or ball game. Pairing off is not the style unless the couple is going steady. Rather, there is increased emphasis on group activities (e.g., informal get-togethers, conversational gatherings, video viewing, and singing). The Western pattern of "hanging out" where young people meet without the need for formal introduction or invitation is the trend.

Young people have many opportunities to interact. Coeducation has given young men and women the chance to meet and participate in classroom and school activities (e.g., programs, sports fests, and other celebrations). In urban areas, young people go to parties, picnics, and other social gatherings, or meet in the malls, restaurants, movie houses, or at work. In rural areas, planting and harvesting seasons offer opportunities for young men and women to be together. They also interact during town fiestas, wakes for the dead, or baptismal and wedding parties.

While adolescents accept single dating as a practice, some parents are still strict and allow their daughters to go out only with a group or at least in a foursome. This is especially true in the rural areas where pairing off is still frowned upon. Urbanites have a more liberal attitude and allow paired-off dating. The most favored dating places are movie houses, shopping malls, parks, discos, and restaurants (Medina, 2001).

Sexuality

Like in any other society, there are certain restrictions on sexual behavior. Ideally for Christian Filipinos, one may have sex only with one's spouse. Consequently, premarital and extramarital sex is not approved. For some non-Christian tribes, a wide range of sexual activities, both premarital and postmarital, is approved (Hunt et al., 1963). Among some cultural communities like the Muslim Filipinos, a man may have as many as four wives.

A double standard of morality characterizes Filipino sex life (Medina, 2001). Men have greater freedom than women while women have to live up to a stricter sexual code, one of being modest and chaste. Thus, virginity is ideally required of women before marriage, but not of men. In urban areas young people have more opportunities to interact outside the home and enjoy more freedom in sexual expression, as well as independence from strict parental control. Furthermore, mass media—movies, television, and so on—provide sexual stimulation (Medina, 2001). Young people are no longer as prudish. Holding hands and "necking" are now a common sight in Metropolitan Manila, especially in university campuses. Young people engage in intimate behaviors such as passionate kissing, petting, or sexual intercourse, although these are done clandestinely and are frowned upon by adult society. The prevailing sexual ethic among youth relates to the amount of affection within couples. Permissiveness with affection is not promiscuity or acceptance of sex per se. These conditions include maturity, strong love, security of the relationship, and intention to marry (de Guzman & Diaz, 1995; Raymundo, 1984).

In a 2002 study with a nationwide representative sample of young people fifteen to twenty-four years old, it was found that 23 percent had premarital sex experience. The overall percentage increased with age, from 12 percent among fifteen to nineteen-year-olds to 40 percent among the twenty to twenty-four-year-olds. Premarital activity consistently increased with age for both males and females, although females reported lower prevalence than males at all ages. Nearly 35 percent of all respondents who had premarital sex reported relations with at least one person aside from the first partner. However, almost one-half of the males but only 11 percent of the females had more than one sex partner. The percentage with more than one sexual partner increased markedly with age among males but remained at the same low level across age for females (Natividad & Marquez, 2004). This sex differential in premarital experience is in line with the double standard of morality.

Rates of premarital sex activity are increasing. A nationwide study in 1994 showed 18 percent of the youth ever having premarital sex experience compared with the 23 percent in the 2002 study. The increase is manifest among males and females alike but the magnitude of change is higher for females than for males. In terms of levels, however, prevalence among males remained higher than for females (Natividad & Marquez, 2004).

Increasing liberalization of attitudes toward premarital sex activity was found (1994 to 2002) for males' approval of males engaging in premarital sex (increase from 41 to 46 percent), and their approval of females engaging in premarital sex (from 19 to 31 percent). This shows a double standard of morality, as does the 34 percent overall approval for males engaging in premarital sex compared with 22 percent for females (Ventura & Cabigon, 2004). Despite these findings, Filipino society is largely conservative and virginity still valued, especially in the rural areas. Informal social pressure such as gossip exerts a strong coercive force to conform to the ideal of sexual morality in rural areas (Medina, 2001). Thus, the highest percentage of youth who engaged in premarital sex (30 percent) was found in the National Capital Region while the lowest (14 percent) was in the rural Cagayan Valley (Natividad & Marquez, 2004).

Cohabitation

Cohabitation arrangements are generally frowned upon and are not considered acceptable as an alternative to marriage. Cohabitation also goes against the dictates of the Catholic Church and puts a social stigma on cohabiting couples (Berja & Ogena, 2004). However, there are indications that cohabitation is increasing and gaining acceptability because the 1995 census formally recognized this as one of the categories of marital status. The 2000 census, however, dropped this category and put in its place Others and Unknown, presumably to soften the stigma attached to cohabitation. Nevertheless, a comparison of the 1995 and 2000 census data shows an increase in cohabitation and a decrease in the number of single and married people.

Young people (fifteen to twenty-four years old) are increasingly involved with live-in arrangements, from 28 percent in 1994 to almost 40 percent in 2002. Moreover, 18 percent of adolescents (11 percent of the females and 26 percent of the males) in the latest survey think it is all right to live together even if there are no plans to marry. Focus group discussions revealed the advantages of cohabitation as allowing couples time to get to know one another and "getting out of cohabitation is easier compared to marriage" (No More Weddings, 2002).

Other reasons why couples resort to cohabitation are the expense and inconvenience of a marriage ceremony, parental objection to the match, or because one or both of the partners are already married. Divorce is not provided for by law, so a married person may not contract another marriage lest he or she be charged with bigamy. However, unless there is a legal impediment, most young people who are living together plan to marry eventually when they have saved enough money or when they are of age. Furthermore, friends and relatives encourage the couple to marry in order to give legal status to the children and to safeguard and protect the rights of all concerned (Medina, 2001).

Marriage

When a couple decides to marry, the parents are informed and preparations are made for the *pamanhikan*. This is the formal visit of the groom's parents to the bride's parents to ask officially for her hand in marriage. At this time the wedding date, place, and details are decided. This is a joint decision of the couple and their families (Hunt et al., 1987). Filipino weddings are ideally solemnized in church. Even when a couple elopes or has a secret civil marriage, a church wedding usually follows later when the parents have been pacified. The groom's parents generally shoulder the wedding expenses, but if the bride is rich and wants a big wedding, her parents usually offer to split the cost. If the couple is older and each has a steady job, they might shoulder all expenses and free their parents of any obligation.

The trend is to postpone marriage until the couple have saved enough and are ready to stand on their own. Hence, there is an upward trend in age at marriage for both sexes with men marrying at an age that is almost three years older than women. By 2000, the mean age at first marriage was 23.9 years for females and 26.5 years for males (Cabigon, 2001).

The residence pattern in Filipino culture is bilocal, meaning that the newlyweds may live with or close to either the groom's or the bride's family. The ideal is to live independently as soon as they can afford to do so. The Filipino family is characterized as "residentially nuclear but functionally extended" (Castillo, 1979, p. 116). This means that each nuclear family lives in a separate dwelling from other kin, but the bonds remain strong. Relatives pool resources, participate in joint activities, share responsibilities, and assist each other financially and emotionally even while not sharing a common residence.

FAMILIES AND CHILDREN

Filipinos see children as a natural feature of marriage. Children are highly valued for many reasons including their economic contribution to housework and child care, financial additions to the family and support during the parent's old age. As early as the age of five, especially in the rural areas, children take active roles in the families' production and maintenance activities. Most are unpaid family workers, performing domestic tasks (e.g., babysitting, cooking, running errands, or working as farmhands during planting and harvesting seasons) (Medina, 2001).

Children provide socioemotional benefits to parents (e.g., companionship, love and happiness, play and fun). Their psychological value includes furnishing incentives for success, satisfying the drive for achievement or power, and providing a sense of fulfillment or meaning in life. For men, the number of children measures masculinity, which is highly valued in Filipino culture. For women, to bear a child is the fulfillment of womanhood. Some wives also believe that one way to hold a man is to have his children. Many wives also try hard to keep the marriage intact "for the sake of the children." When there is a serious quarrel between husband and wife, children often help bring about reconciliation. Children, therefore, indirectly cement the union of their parents by helping strengthen the marital bond (Medina, 2001).

Children are believed to bring good luck. The more children, the more blessed is the union. A child is seen as a gift of God and a sign of grace. Accordingly, contraception is considered sinful and often not used; the contraceptive prevalence rate among married women is 19 percent (Lee, Lush, Walt, & Cleland, 1998; Mason & Smith, 2000; UNDP, 2006). One study discovered that in about one-half of the couples surveyed, both husbands and wives together were the birth-control decision makers. In 15 percent of the couples the husband made the decision and in 18 percent the wife (Sanchez, 1994).

Children also perpetuate the family name. For this reason, there is some preference on the part of the father for the firstborn to be a boy (Dalisay, 1983; Davies & Zhang, 1995). However, mothers might prefer a girl for the firstborn for the help she can give with household tasks. Overall, the ideal is to have an equal number of sons and daughters.

Fertility

The estimated birthrate for 2006 was 24.9 births per 1,000 population while the infant mortality rate for the poorest quintile of the population was 49 and 21 for the richest quintile. In 2003, the infant mortality rate was estimated at twenty-seven deaths for each 1,000 live births, a big reduction from the infant mortality rate of sixty in 1970 (UNDP, 2005, 2006; World Factbook, 2006). The under age five mortality rate is also improving, being ninety in 1970, but forty-two in 1999 and thirty-six in 2003. In 2004, the rate was eighty for the poorest quintile of the population and twenty-nine for the richest quintile. Maternal mortality remains relatively high at 170 per 100,000 live births (adjusted to 200 for underreporting in 2000) for the 1990-2004 period (UNDP, 2004, 2006).

The Philippine population is young (median age of twenty-one) because children are valued and there is a relatively high birthrate. According to the 2000 census, 37 percent of the population were fourteen years old or younger (National Statistics Office, 2002). There is, however, a declining birthrate partly attributed to an increased age at marriage and the increasing acceptance of family planning, especially among the more educated and those of higher occupational status. Consequently, the fertility rate estimates declined from 6.0 for the 1970-1975 period, to 3.6 for 1995-2000, and 3.2 for 2000-2005 (UNDP, 2004, 2006). The average number of children to ever-married women declined from 3.27 in 1990 to 2.82 in 2000 (National Statistics Office, 2003).

Child Rearing

Responsibility for the care and discipline of children rests mainly with the mother. The father assumes more responsibility in socialization as the children grow older, especially with respect to sons. Farmers train their sons to cultivate the fields and care for the carabao (water buffalo or work animal); in urban areas, fathers teach sons the skills needed in business.

Parents invest in child rearing not only because of love and concern for children's welfare, but also because of community expectations. Children's behavior is regarded as reflective of upbringing. When children go wayward, it is said that the parents did not guide and discipline them well. Conversely, when children do well, family honor is enhanced (Medina, 2001).

In general, child rearing among Filipinos is nurturant and indulgent. There is a tendency to be overprotective because of great love and concern for the health and safety of children. As the children grow older, however, discipline becomes stricter. Children are raised to honor and respect their elders (Ingersoll-Dayton & Saengtienchai, 1999). They are taught to be humble and submissive, to be self-reliant and industrious, and to help in family activities when not in school. They are not supposed to do their work grudgingly and are prohibited from talking back to their parents. A good child is an obedient child.

Corporal punishment is traditionally common and considered the most effective method of discipline (Medina, 2001). Parents consider the best time to start corporal punishment is when the child is still young. Values inculcated early in life are thought to be more lasting. Moreover, bad behavior and habits, if allowed in childhood, are difficult to change later.

Parental strictness depends on the site, the occasion, and birth order. Parents are strict if the behavior or place is hazardous to health and safety, permissive if the child plays within sight, but apprehensive if he or she goes further away. The youngest child is pampered for a longer time not only because nobody else comes after him or her, but also because parents have become more liberal by this time. The eldest bears the greatest demands and expectations from everyone. However, the eldest receives special attention and privileges; as parental surrogate, the eldest has authority over the younger ones (Mendez, Jocano, Rolda, & Matela, 1984).

There is little gender differentiation in activities and behavior before puberty; boys and girls mix freely and have similar tasks. Both boys and girls wash dishes, feed the chickens and pigs, and go to the store on errands. Older siblings are quite adept at rocking or lulling the baby to sleep, or playing in the neighborhood with the younger sibling carried on the hip. Among the urban middle class, children have more time to play because the family can afford house help to do the chores and a nanny to care for the baby (Medina, 2001).

Gender differentiation in behavior and activities becomes more marked by puberty. A son is told not to play with dolls because he will look like a sissy. A daughter is told not to play rough games because it is unbecoming in a girl. Boys can spend more time with other boys and come home late, while girls are more restricted. This differential treatment in puberty orients boys and girls gradually to their adult masculine and feminine roles as prescribed by Filipino culture.

Stereotyped gender traits are inculcated so that girls are developed to be modest and refined, and boys to be strong and healthy (Liwag, dela Cruz, & Macapagal, 1999).

Parental authority over their children seems to be declining. Complaints that children are less submissive and obedient are now heard. On the other hand, children today complain that their parents are unreasonable and strict and not adaptive to change. They are extra-sensitive to the slightest scolding, sometimes answering back with disrespect. In response to modernization, parents are becoming increasingly permissive and liberal with their children. They allow their children to reason out and express themselves, to raise questions, to think for themselves, and to plan their own future. The observed trend in child-rearing behavior today is a shift toward a more liberal, less authoritarian, less restrictive, and a less controlling orientation (Medina, 2001).

FAMILIES AND GENDER

Filipino couples traditionally follow a division of labor or task allocation where the husband is the breadwinner and the wife is the domestic. The ideal husband is faithful to his wife and works diligently to support his family. In return, he enjoys a position of authority, respect, and headship of the household. The Filipino wife has the important responsibility of being the treasurer of the household and is expected to be efficient at budgeting for the family needs. She is also to love her husband and children and be concerned about their needs (Medina, 2001).

Socialization practices promote continuities in gender role differentiation. A review of 131 studies on child-rearing practices and gender socialization confirmed that women are essentially perceived as wives, mothers, and homemakers while men are expected to be the family's primary source of financial support (Liwag et al., 1999). Socialization differs upon reaching adolescence. Boys participate in many affairs with more freedom, tolerance, and understanding. Girls generally stay home taking care of their siblings and doing other "womanly" chores (e.g., laundry, cooking, and other chores related to upkeep of the house).

Contemporary Adult Role

The role of the contemporary Filipina is changing. She not only plays the traditional wife/mother role, but she is a companion to her husband and children in recreational activities. She participates in religious, civic, political, and other community affairs. She is an equal partner to her husband in providing economically for her family. In a study of low-income families in Metropolitan Manila, the wife's income was a source for 95 percent of the households, of which 33 percent depended solely on her earnings (Castillo, 1993). In rural areas, wives engage in farming and selling produce, and raising livestock. They often engage in cottage industries and other small-scale businesses aside from the usual farm work.

Known for creativeness, business acumen, and competence as entrepreneurs, Filipinas' contribution to the family often exceeds that of husbands. Statistics of the Department of Trade and Industry show 80 percent of registered enterprises were owned, run, or operated by women (Japa, 1999). Likewise, many overseas migrant workers commend their wives for singularly assuming the responsibility of household management and at the same time running the enterprise established by their overseas earnings. Wives keep the family intact while successfully maintaining and expanding household entrepreneurial activities (Medina, 2001).

Many wives are in the labor force for economic reasons (Tiefenthaler, 1994). Lower-class women, in particular, work to help sustain basic subsistence requirements The wife's outside work is now considered an extension of her traditional role that demands contributing her share for the economic survival of the family (Medina, 2001).

Women are employed mainly in export-oriented manufacturing, in contractual, part time, and casual work, and in overseas jobs. Many are in the informal sector engaged in micro enterprises (e.g., operators or workers in sidewalk eateries, small retail stores, stalls in public markets, and services like laundry, sewing, and cleaning) (Ofreneo, 1999). More educated wives are employed in various government and private agencies as clerks, typists, supervisors, managers, and the like. College-educated wives are often self-employed as professionals. Hence, whether on the farm or in the city, wives share in their husband's economic responsibilities.

Household Division of Labor

Employment of the wife, however, does not change the pattern of task allocation in the household. Families follow the traditional division of labor including the dominant role of the male "head-of-household." Therefore, the wife has the dual burden of employment and home management. The social structure of the Filipino family, however, lightens the burden of the employed wife somewhat in allowing for mother substitutes such as grandmothers, aunts, cousins, and older siblings. Even neighbors, who, in the rural areas are usually also relatives, are sometimes asked to look after the young children when parents are away. Furthermore, older siblings often act as mother surrogates to the young. While the presence of young children is a constraint to a married woman's working outside the home, the presence of older children is a positive factor for her employment (Medina, 2001).

For those who can afford domestic help, house help and nursemaids clean the house, wash the clothes, do the cooking, and other household chores including child care. However, there is a growing scarcity of good help because of the attraction of factory employment as well as overseas opportunities as domestics (Bagley, Madrid, & Bolitho, 1997).

One indication of the growing concern for employed wives and mothers is the enactment of Republic Act No. 6972 establishing a day-care center in every village (Tapales, 1997). This should help ease the problem of child care while the mother is at work. However, full implementation of this law is not yet realized. A law which is being implemented is the Republic Act No. 8187 that entitles a married male employee to a paternity leave of seven days with full pay for the first four deliveries (childbirth or miscarriage) of the legitimate spouse, in order to enable him to share child care and household chores with his wife.

Surveys indicate a prevailing view and gradual acceptance of the idea that modern husbands should lend a hand in house chores when their wives are employed. One study showed that the more educated the husband, the more time he gave to housework and child care. Moreover, professionals spend the longest time at home compared with production and agricultural workers. Husbands, however, were quite selective in what chores to do like babysitting, repairs, and fetching water; they were less likely to wash dishes or scrub floors (Tan, 1997). One comparative study showed that 43 percent of wives in the Philippine sample had husbands regularly helping with housework. This was higher than reported in the Javanese, Sundanese, Taiwanese, and the United States samples, and lower than the proportion reported in South Korea (Sanchez, 1994).

Nevertheless, husbands do not agree to a reversal of roles to become househusbands that would run counter to the traditional masculine image they want to maintain (Medina, 2001). Thus, the major responsibility for homemaking still falls in the hands of the wife. In order to eradicate this traditional gender typing and gender role inequality, an innovative curriculum has been implemented in both public and private schools. A practical arts subject teaches skills like homemaking and carpentry to both girls and boys (Ordonez, 1988). Boys learn how to cook, sew, and take care of babies, while girls learn furniture repair and electronics. This curriculum is to help promote equality and sharing between the sexes.

Egalitarianism

Filipino families are egalitarian in relation to decision making. The most common pattern among both rural and urban couples is the joint-mode, where the husband and wife share in the process. This joint decision making has been found in the areas of child rearing and discipline, choice of child's school, business and investments, house improvement, purchase of appliances, birth control, and choice of recreation and vacation place (Alcantara, 1994; David, 1994; Illo, 1989; Mendez et al., 1984; Sanchez, 1994).

Filipino husbands are acknowledged as heads of households. Wives assume headship when widowed, separated, or divorced. However, women not only have power derived from their authority as treasurer of households, but also as silent but influential partners to their husbands; thus, the reality is shared headship. Regardless of the monetary contribution of wives to household income, and no matter who brings in the larger income, wives predominate in household allocation as well as fertility decisions (Alcantara, 1994).

Equalitarianism of Filipino couples dates back to the pre-Spanish colonial era. At that time the laws gave women equal rights to men for ownership, inheritance, trade and industry, and to serve as village chief when there was no male heir (Agoncillo & Guerrero, 1977). Men showed respect for their women by walking behind them. Furthermore, pre-Spanish Filipinas retained their maiden names after marriage and were consulted by husbands in many matters, including state affairs (Romero, 1978). Women also had the exclusive right to give names to their children.

It was under the cultural influence of the Spanish that some patriarchal aspects of the family developed (Feliciano, 1994; Hunt et al., 1963). Only the male members of the family, then, were allowed to pursue higher education because "girls would marry eventually and their activities would be limited to home and childcare" (Mendez et al., 1984, p. 114). American libertarian policies later boosted women's social position somewhat but these influences were not sufficient to erase the deeply ingrained image of women as inferior (Miralao & Dongail, 1984).

More recently, views have changed. Parents seem to rely on their daughters more than their sons to study conscientiously, keep stable jobs, and provide support in their old age (King & Domingo, 1986). Nationally, in both rural and urban areas, literacy rates in the last two decades have been on an upward trend for both sexes, but more so for women. Estimates for 2002 showed a gain for both sexes, to 93 percent overall (World Factbook, 2006). In fact, more women than men reach and complete high school and college education. Consequently, women have entered occupations and activities traditionally reserved for men.

FAMILIES AND STRESS

Modernization and its related processes of urbanization and industrialization have brought about changes in Filipino society that affect families. Among these changes is the increased participation of women entering the labor force, and continuing employment after marriage and through the childbearing years (Filipino Women, Issues and Trends, 1995). Many wives face the double burden of domestic responsibilities and employment. Other sources of stress for Filipino families include changing sexual values and relationships with in-laws.

Double Burden of Wives

Whether the wife is employed, self-employed, or engaged in entrepreneurial or farm activities, the responsibility for household management is still mainly hers. She carries the primary responsibility of child rearing and housework. In the formal sector, this double burden necessitates waking at dawn to do chores before rushing to her work place and continuing with housework till late at night (Medina, 2001). For the informal sector, the double burden is even heavier. Wives extend their domestic chores to include farm activities from planting, transplanting, and harvesting to hiring of farm laborers, selling of produce, and raising livestock to augment the household budget. Being a co-breadwinner and household manager can cause strain on the wife, thereby affecting her relations with the rest of the family.

Evidence that many wives are strained and how this relates to family life comes from a stress management seminar for women managers, sponsored by the Department of Labor and Education. Women shared that their significant stressors were mostly family related (e.g., long commuting hours, domestic chores before and after work, the children's illnesses requiring being absent from work, and the caring for aging parents expected of daughters) (Peñano-Ho, 1999).

The stress arising from wives' double burden compounds if husbands are unemployed, underemployed, or incapacitated. Male inadequacy as a breadwinner is counter to the traditional machismo role expected of a husband and can hurt his ego. Premature deaths from heart diseases are eleven times more frequent among under-achieving husbands whose wives are over-achievers, than otherwise (Cabatit, 1998). This shows the great psychological hurt to the husband's ego when his inadequacy undermines his masculinity. Role reversal is something that husbands find hard to accept and is often a source of conflict and stress in the family.

Changing Sexual Values

A consequence of modernization and the shift from agricultural to industrial production is the influx of migrants from rural to urban areas, particularly Metropolitan Manila. Migrants come in search of employment, or for young people to go to college, and are exposed to mass media that glamorize sex and Western values. There is a lack of ideal role models in media; many matinee idols have children out of wedlock and move from one partner to another (Mercado, 1990). Furthermore, the 2002 Young Adult Fertility and Sexuality Study (YAFS III) revealed that one of three of the adolescent population has been exposed to pornographic media materials, either through film, video, or literature. Two-thirds of the young people from the National Capital Region, particularly, have watched X-rated movies or videos while one-half have read pornographic materials. In addition, the Internet (fast becoming a major part of young people's everyday life for on-line dating and love affairs) is used for sexual exploitation and harassment, as well as a source of pornographic materials and information (Raymundo, Kabamalan, Berja, & Laguna, 2004). Consequently, more and more young people engage in premarital sex despite moral questions and stigma that go with this behavior. The result is unwanted pregnancy and early marriage even if they are not ready. Family life is thus adversely affected.

The change in sexual values is also evident in the increasing number of consensual unions and extramarital affairs. Marital infidelity seems to have become pronounced in the city. This is due to increasing permissiveness as well as the availability of contraceptive devices and the presence of hotels and motels where illicit relations can conveniently take place (Medina, 2001).

Most studies of marital conflict mention infidelity as a common cause (Bautista & Roldan, 1995; Dayan, 1994; Mendez et al., 1984; Vancio, 1980). This is also the ground cited in the majority of suits for marriage annulment filed in two Metropolitan Manila Family courts in 1986-1990 (Bernardo, 1990). The fact that mostly wives filed the cases indicates that husband marital infidelity is more common. However, in a study of court applications for annulment filed by husbands, the most common ground was adultery on the part of the wife (Tinio, 1994).

A more recent study of 148 resolved cases of annulment in two Quezon City Family Courts from 2001 to 2003, showed that the majority of the causes of action fell under psychological incapacity and bigamous marriage (Africa & Disangcopan, 2004). Psychological incapacity covers just about every ground and is left to the courts to interpret based on psychiatric tests. Bigamous marriage includes cases where an overseas worker finds another partner abroad or cases where an overseas worker's spouse left in the country squanders financial support over another partner. Another ground cited by annulment petitioners is sexual infidelity or perversion.

In-Laws

Another family stressor is the problem of in-laws. Owing to the strong and close-knit extended family system in the Philippines, conflict with and over in-laws is often unavoidable. Very close ties with parents threaten security feelings and hurt the ego of the spouse. Some spouses feel that their in-laws receive more attention and support than what they get, and that they are left out. The problem is compounded when parents-in-law continue to advise, control, and monitor their children and grandchildren as traditionally expected. Even if done in good faith, many couples consider this as interference in their private affairs (Medina, 2001).

Coping with Stress

How do Filipino couples cope with stress? Employed wives usually set aside time during weekends and free time during weekdays for their families. Wives personally attend to the children whenever possible, even to the point of being absent from or stopping work temporarily when the children are ill. As noted earlier, husbands are now more willing and able to share household work, especially if the wives are employed.

To prevent young hasty marriages, the New Family Code has raised the age at marriage to eighteen; further it requires parental consent of those who are eighteen to twenty-one years of age, and parental advisement for those who are twenty-one to twenty-five years old. Another requirement is attendance at a marriage-counseling seminar for those below twenty-five years of age before a marriage license is issued (Family Code, 1987).

Wives are the stabilizing element in marriage. They invest more of themselves emotionally and completely in the marital partnership, and are more tolerant of husbands' lapses. When parents, relatives, and friends try to reconcile the couple for the sake of the children, wives are often willing to give in (Medina, 2001).

Some options are open to Filipino couples when conflict continues unresolved. One is legal separation that permits spouses to live separately. Neither spouse can remarry, as the marital bonds are not severed. Couples divide their conjugal property and the children are placed under custody of one of the parents. Another option is annulment, which voids the marriage and therefore allows the spouses to marry new partners (some Catholics also receive church annulments). The bulk of troubled couples, especially the poor, merely separate informally by mutual consent (Medina, 2001). There is no law permitting divorce nor is divorce recognized, except among non-Christians who are allowed to follow their own customs.

FAMILIES AND AGING

Four percent of the Philippine population is sixty years old and over (National Statistics Office, 2002). This number is expected to grow because of the increase in life expectancy. By the year 2015, 5 percent of the population will be aged sixty-five or older. Life expectancy has improved from 58.1 years in 1970-1975 to 70.2 years in 2000-2005. The excess of females over males among the elderly population reflects the higher life expectancy for females (estimated to be 72.8 for females and 68.6 for males). Of those born during 2000-2005, 79 percent of females and 70 percent of males are expected to survive to age sixty-five (UNDP, 2006). Most older men are married while older women have almost the same proportion of married and widowed. The large proportion of widows compared with widowers is due to the longer life expectancy of women and to the greater propensity of widowed men to remarry. There are generally more unmarried women than there are bachelors among the elderly, probably because men prefer to be married (Cruz, 1999). Approximately two of three Filipino elders live in a rural community. This pattern is stronger for men than women and for the "young-old" rather than the "old-old." This concentration of the aged is due to out migration of young adults (Costello, 1994).

The notion that the elderly are helpless and dependent is refuted by the reality that more than two-thirds are still earning some or all of their household's income. Men dominate farming as an occupation in the rural areas while women dominate sales or commerce in the metropolitan areas. The most active on the job are those who have excellent or very good health. In addition, the elderly are active in household tasks such as cooking, light housework, managing family funds, and taking care of children (Cabigon, 1999).

Respect for the Elderly

In the Philippines, as in most developing countries, the family is the traditional institution for care and support of elderly. The rapid rise in the elderly population is not seen as a crisis. From the Filipino cultural viewpoint, aged family members are not a burden. Rather, they are assets to the family and community for their wisdom, skills, and experience in social, economic, and political affairs. The elderly are highly respected and consulted on important matters (Ingersoll-Dayton & Saengtienchai, 1999; Lindy & Domingo, 1993; Medina, 2001).

One of the most important values imparted to children early in life is filial respect and *utang na loob* (debt of gratitude) to parents (Medina, 2001). Children not only feel that they owe their parents respect, obedience, and love, they also feel eternally grateful for having been brought up and supported by them. It is the filial obligation of children to provide their parents protection, love and care, and give them the same kind of attention they themselves received as children. The community condemns a socioeconomically well-placed person who does not share resources with parents. It is a disgrace to neglect or leave aged parents in the care of strangers.

Grandparents play an important role. The grandmother, in particular, is a familiar figure in the household as domestic consultant to her daughter or daughter-in-law, as supervisor of the house help, as babysitter, or more often as the housekeeper if both the husband and wife are employed. Consequently, the relationship between the grandparents and the grandchildren is close. Many grandchildren feel that their grandparents are more loving, caring, and understanding than are their parents. Grandparents act as intermediaries and side with or intervene for their grandchildren when the latter are scolded or confronted by their parents. There is a tendency for grandparents to spoil or pamper their grandchildren (Medina, 2001).

Living Arrangements and Caregiving

Living arrangements of elders mirror the import of family care giving. Only about 6 percent of the elderly live alone and most have children living nearby and/or are in frequent contact with them (Cruz, 1999; de Guzman, 1999). Children typically live with their elderly parents rather than the reverse because the majority of the elderly, especially in rural areas, own their house. Coresidence is not necessarily beneficial only to the elderly. There is much evidence suggesting a reciprocal flow of support. The elderly have younger family members available to look after them, to run errands, and so on. The younger members live in the older person's home and receive guidance and financial as well as moral support (Perez, 1999). While some say it is the obligation of children to care for them, other parents say that adult children need to be cared for and to receive their guidance (Medina, de Guzman, Roldan, & Bautista, 1996).

Less affluent elderly and those no longer employed are dependent on their children and other relatives for financial support. Children who have left home, especially those who have migrated within or to another county, are the main sources of financial support. Children also supply nonmonetary support, such as food, clothes, and other basic needs. The coresident children, particularly the unmarried daughters, provide material support and physical care. Overall, the Filipino elderly prefer to coreside with an unmarried child, particularly an unmarried daughter, with a married daughter as the second choice (Medina et al., 1996). The prevailing belief is that daughters are capable of providing more care, attention, and love. Some elderly, especially the more affluent, prefer to be with a married son because there is no foreseen problem with him as head of the family. Living with a married daughter places them in an awkward position of relating to the son-in-law head of household.

While coresidence is the most acceptable and beneficial arrangement for both the elderly and their children, it can also generate conflict and problems (Domingo & Asis, 1995). An aged parent might have to give up some peace and quiet, and can either feel the financial cost of supporting dependent children or feel uncomfortable being a burden to the children. Conversely, the children might have difficulties in meeting the needs of the elderly, both materially and physically.

The unmarried daughter is torn between domestic work and filial obligation on the one hand and economic activity on the other. The married daughter is caught between conflicting responsibilities of child rearing and elder care. She could have conflict with her spouse and in-laws regarding time, energy, and resources spent in elder care. The married female elder, on the other hand, who is often a caretaker to her aging husband, is in need of care and support herself. Owing to increased life expectancy, another problem is that younger relatives, mainly daughters, are expected to take care of their older kin, but are more likely to be already within the sixty years age group themselves and might need care and attention (Troisi, 2003). In spite of all these problems, the family's obligation to care for the elderly is still well established in the mores of the culture. To confine the old in homes for the aged is considered "unFilipino" and unnatural (Domingo & Asis, 1995). Thus there are only twenty-one such homes in the country with only a few residents who are poor and without family, or abandoned by relatives (Medina, 2001).

A growing concern is that, with the increased rate of female migration to the urban areas and overseas and with the higher levels of participation of women in work outside the home, there might not be caretakers left at home for the elderly.

OTHER FAMILY SITUATIONS

The nuclear household is prevalent in the Philippines. The mean size of households declined from 5.9 in 1970 to 4.9 in 2000. The percentage of households with five or more members has also declined. This reflects partly a declining fertility but more importantly a growing detachment of individuals from their family of orientation and a breaking up of extended households. In the Philippines the trend is toward nuclearization and smaller-sized households at the same time that extended family households still thrive in urban areas (Medina, 2001).

Solo-Parent Families

Emerging variations to the usual Filipino family structure and composition include several new forms including the solo-parent family.

There are several types (Medina, 2001): (1) widow or widower and his or her child/children; (2) single man or woman and his or her adopted child/children; (3) unwed woman and her child/children; (4) mistress and her child/children by a married man; and (5) separated parent and his or her child/children.

Female-headed households increased from 11 percent in 1990 to about 14 percent in 2000 (Raymundo et al., 2004). By cultural definition, the oldest male member of the family is automatically acknowledged as head. It is only when the man of the house is gone that the woman assumes headship; thus most of these female heads of household could be widows or separated. Overseas employment of husbands could also contribute to the increase in female-headed households, resulting in the wives being solo-parents, at least temporarily.

Much of the temporary separation of couples results from migration of one spouse, usually for economic reasons. In the Philippines, modernization and the shift from agricultural to industrial production has resulted in rural to urban migration, the principal destination of which is Metropolitan Manila. In addition, overseas employment is an alternative option chosen by millions of Filipinos. The Philippines is one of the world's major exporters of labor. Mothers and fathers are compelled to work in international labor markets due to the twin problems of unemployment and low wages, as well as noneconomic motivations of adventurism or to escape from marital problems (Aganon, 1995; Bagley et al., 1997).

Overseas work brings many advantages to the migrant's family. In communities of migrant workers there are visible signs of progress: houses newly built or refurbished, purchase of durable consumption goods, children getting quality education, and evidence of thriving family business. However, there are also many problems: the psychosocial costs of surrogate parenthood including faulty development of self-concept among children, the likelihood of juvenile delinquency, marital breakups, role alteration of the parent left behind, changing lifestyle and values such as the desire for conspicuous consumption, the loneliness and trauma of separation, and other psychosocial and emotional consequences (Aganon, 1995).

Despite all the difficulties, the Filipino solo parent seems to be coping. In a survey in selected rural, urban, and Metropolitan Manila communities, the majority of widows and separated women claimed that they had no problems except a few who mentioned financial problems, children's educational needs, children missing their father, children's emotional problems, and need for romance (Medina et al., 1996). The majority did not plan to remarry because of reasons such as already old, need to take care of the children, no appropriate mate, happy with the present situation, promised deceased spouse not to re-marry, children need parent, and it is another headache to remarry. Remarriage is unpopular. In the last census nearly all marriages (99 percent of brides and 98 percent of grooms) were first marriages (World Bank, 2004).

Other Household Types

There are also other types of households (Medina, 2001). The first three of these are small in number. They include: (1) step or blended-family households; (2) siblings without parents households where the siblings are orphaned or their parents are overseas workers; (3) one-person households; and (4) extended family households. There are many urban extended family households, especially those of Metro-politan Manila, which include such kin as parents, grandparents, sons/daughters, grandchildren, nieces, and nephews. One explana-tion is the tendency for rural relatives to join the urban household because they want to study or work in the city. It is difficult and costly to construct a separate house in the city where land values are high (Medina, 2001).

According to the respondents of a study on living arrangements in Metropolitan Manila, relatives stay with them because there is no one else to stay with, they grew up in that family, it is more economical to stay together, they are underage and financially unstable, or they are newly married (Medina et al., 1996). The benefits of having kin in the household include help in the house/business chores, help in earning a living, provision of parental guidance, and help to take care of the aged. The extended family household in the city is reflective not only of the capacity and willingness of the family to provide support to relatives but also of the solidarity and strength of kin ties for which Filipinos have been traditionally known.

CONCLUDING COMMENTS

Philippine society is in a period of transition from traditional peasant to a modern industrial society. This modernization process has repercussions on families. Industrialization has made possible the employment of young people away from the watchful eyes of parents while improvement of transportation has increased their mobility and participation in recreation activities far from home. Coeducation has drawn boys and girls together over long periods. Urbanization brings together people of different religions, regional and ethnolinguistic backgrounds, nationalities, and racial origins. The mass media has introduced the Western concept of romantic love; the choice of marriage partner now is the prerogative of the individual. A trend toward intermarriage across regional, ethnolinguistic, nationality, and racial lines is observed. These are just some of the recent trends that are influencing family life.

Family tension is a problem of a rapidly changing society like the Philippines. The modern-day strains are but part of the adjustment to new conditions. Despite its problems, the Filipino family as an institution has proven to be resilient and adaptable in coping with these stresses. People have not lost faith in the family as an institution. The majority marry and have children. Indications point to a generally cohesive and stable family and a mutually supportive and close-knit kin group. Families might change in size, form, and lifestyles, but ties of obligation and affection within and among generations of families will remain strong and important.

Chapter 15

Australian Families:
Social and Demographic Patterns

David de Vaus

INTRODUCTION

The Commonwealth of Australia, geographically the world's sixth largest nation, is in Oceania between the Indian and the South Pacific Oceans. With the establishment of a penal colony by Britain in 1788, the white settlement rapidly destroyed Australia's indigenous population and replaced aboriginal culture with a British legal system and popularly elected governments. Since 1901, Australia has been a federal system of states, territories, and a central government. Federal and state governments share service delivery to families, but because family law and taxation powers reside with the federal government, family policy is relatively uniform. The population is about 20.5 million (about fiftieth worldwide), 90 percent urban, and situated mostly along the southeastern and eastern coasts (United Nations Development Programme [UNDP], 2006).

Although having a mixed economy with government owning some large businesses in the finance, transport, and communications sectors, the private sector is easily dominant. Recently governments have been divesting themselves of businesses, a trend that reflects a move to smaller government. This trend has also seen a reduction in government family support, an expectation that families will provide for their own members, increased financial pressures due to a new "user pays" philosophy, and much greater targeting of family support to needy families based on stringent rules concerning family income and assets.

Unemployment remained high for much of the time since the late 1970s at between 8 and 11 percent, but in recent years fell to 5.8 percent. The 2006 estimate is 4.9 percent (Australian Bureau of Statistics [ABS], 2000b, 2004; World Factbook, 2007). Many women have joined the workforce, but high rates of youth unemployment have persisted and unemployment and early retirement among older people are common. Those employed are increasingly working in part-time, temporary, and casual jobs. Economic restructuring, globalization, and tariff reduction have led to a decline in manufacturing and rural industries, loss of jobs, and increased pressure to reduce wages and remove many benefits (e.g., leave, overtime, job security, injury insurance). Australia ranks third on the United Nations Human Development Index (UNDP, 2006).

With a tradition of individualism, free enterprise, and a suspicion of government, Australians resist the intrusion of government into the private sphere and stress individual rights. However, there is a parallel tradition of state paternalism involving a centralized wage fixing system, compulsory voting, subsidized university education, and a universal health scheme. There is no established church and there is a separation of church and State with religion playing little role in the public and political discourse. Although protestant Christianity is the dominant religion and two-thirds identify as Christian, Australia is relatively secular with one-quarter not claiming any religious affiliation (2001 census) and only 19 percent regularly attending religious services more than monthly (Gibson, Wilson, Denemark, Meagher, & Western, 2004).

Indigenous Australians (i.e., aboriginals and Torres Strait Islanders), representing just over 2 percent of the population, are disadvantaged in terms of health, income, employment, and housing with many being dependent on government welfare support. Since 1945, mass immigration has increased the urban ethnic diversity, but until the early 1970s the "White Australia Policy" meant that most migrants came from Europe—still mainly Britain but with substantial numbers coming from non-English speaking southern European countries. Recently, Asian migration has increased sharply but the largest overseas born group of Australians comes from Britain and Ireland (Bureau of

Immigration and Population Research [BIPR], 1994). Over 90 percent of the population is Caucasian and English is spoken by 80 percent of people. The population growth rate is low (0.85 percent) as are standard indicators of well-being such as low infant (5) and maternal mortality (8) rates (UNDP, 2006; World Factbook, 2007).

Family in Australian Context

The nuclear family—"mum, dad, and their kids"—is the dominant cultural image of the Australian family: most people aspire to a permanent, monogamous, heterosexual couple relationship with children. Determining how typical this family form is, however, not straightforward. While most people spend significant parts of their life in such families, they also spend parts in different family forms. There is considerable diversity in types of household-based families (many families extend across households because of divorce and grown children leaving home). In 2001, the largest proportion (83 percent) of households containing a family was couple families, 15 percent were one-parent families, and the rest were "other." Couple families come in diverse forms. Many (just over half) have no dependent children present, some are step- or blended-families, and around 12 percent are cohabiting de facto couples (i.e., a couple living together without being formally married). Of all households, only about one-third consists of a couple and at least one dependent child. Furthermore, one-quarter of all households consist of one person living on his or her own (ABS, 2003d).

Although the mum, dad, and the kids family is not the main household form (as seen in the figures mentioned previously), it is the most common and the most frequent from the perspective of children. Couples with dependent children account for over 60 percent of all family households in which there are any children. While over 30 percent of children spend part of their childhood up to the age of eighteen years in a one-parent family, most spend the greater part of their childhood living with both their natural parents and a sibling. Nearly all of the other households types were at some point a mum, dad, and the kids family or will be at some future point (de Vaus & Gray, 2003).

Identifying the typical family depends on definitions. Focusing on household families ignores the fact that people typically have a family that extends "beyond the front door." Although only 3 percent of Australian households consist of more than one related family, contact with wider family members—especially parents, adult children, and siblings—remains an important source of identity, interaction, and support (de Vaus, 2004). For some people their families are entirely outside of their household. Almost 15 percent of Australians do not live in household families; some live in institutions (3 percent), alone (9 percent), or in group households (3 percent) (ABS, 2003d).

COUPLE FORMATION AND MARITAL DYNAMICS

In this section several aspects of how couples form and the dynamics present in typical Australian families are explored. Free choice of marriage partners is the norm. Some couples live together without legally marrying. The majority of young people are sexually experienced by age seventeen. The marriage rate is low, yet love remains the firm basis for marrying. Divorce has become more common at the same time that the majority believes that marriages should last a lifetime.

Mate Selection

Choosing a partner is a matter of the individuals concerned and arranged marriages are rare. Less than 5 percent of Australians believe that a person should not marry if their parents disapprove of the marriage (de Vaus, 1995). The law requires parental consent for marriage only for those under eighteen years of age, but older individuals will normally seek and value parental support for a marriage. The majority of people (83 percent) say that love is the most important factor in choosing a partner (de Vaus, 1995) although young people also stress similar goals, good personality, and physical attractiveness (Glezer, 1991).

De facto marriages, that is, a couple living together as a married couple without being formally married (i.e., cohabiting), are not always treated the same in law as are formal marriages. This situation is due to the federal government having legislative authority over marriages and children of relationships, while individual states have legislative authority over de facto relationships. Social security entitlements (which are paid by the federal government) regard established de facto partners much the same as legally married partners. The parental rights and responsibilities of de factos are the same as for legally married parents but, because property and maintenance of de factos is a state responsibility, there are differences between married and de factos in some states. In general however, laws and entitlements are moving to minimize any distinction between de facto and formal marriages.

The average age of first sexual intercourse is sixteen and young people become sexually active at about seventeen or eighteen (Rissel, Richters, Grulich, de Visser, & Smith, 2003). Most adolescents approve of premarital sex within a committed and monogamous relationship; those in their twenties see monogamy as essential to commitment (Moore & Rosenthal, 1993).

Australians are less likely to marry now than at any time since the 1930s. There has been a steady decline in the crude marriage rate (number of marriages per 1,000 population in a year) from 9.2 in 1971 to 5.4 in 2002. On current patterns, it is estimated that only 72 percent of today's young men and 77 percent of the young women will ever marry (ABS, 2003f).

Marriage is no longer a prerequisite for living together or having children. In 2002, 73 percent of couples that eventually married lived together first and many had children before they married (ABS, 2003f). Less than 30 percent of people disapprove of living together even if the couple does not plan to marry (de Vaus, 2004). Almost one in three children are born to parents who are not formally married (ABS, 2003b). The majority of these parents are living together in de facto relationships, but some (11 percent) are single mothers (de Vaus, 2002).

Few teenagers marry and adults are delaying marriage. Between 1974 and 2002 the median age at which men first marry increased from 23.3 to 29 years and increased from 20.9 to 27 years for women (ABS, 2003f). Delaying marriage, however, does not mean that people delay forming marriage-like relationships. Much of the increase in the age of marriage is because couples live together for a time before they formally marry. When people do marry, many do not have a religious marriage. While almost all (90 percent) marriages in 1966 were religious, less than one-half (45 percent) were performed by a religious celebrant in 2002 (ABS, 2003f). This change reflects the growing secularization of Australia where fewer and fewer people are involved in churches or acknowledge the church's right to regulate their lives. It also reflects the increased number of marriages in which one partner has been previously married. In such cases, some of the major Australian churches continue to be reluctant to marry previously divorced people.

Cohabitation is becoming increasingly common but living together is usually part of a relatively short-term relationship or is a precursor of marriage. Between 1976 and 2002, the rate of couples who lived together before they married rose from 16 to 73 percent. Cohabitation is more common among younger couples. Eighty-two percent of couples in which one partner is a teenager are cohabiting compared with 34 percent of those in their late twenties and around 10 percent in their early forties (Dempsey & de Vaus, 2004). Cohabitation depends partly on cultural background. While 12 percent of all couples in Australia are de facto relationships among indigenous couples 36 percent are de facto relationships, while less than 4 percent of couples from non-English speaking countries are in a de facto relationships (ABS, 2003d; Dempsey & de Vaus, 2004).

Marriage Values

Love is regarded as the prerequisite for marriage and almost all Australians (98 percent) rate faithfulness as extremely important for a successful marriage (de Vaus, 1997c). Most people (85 percent) condemn extramarital sex but are more accepting of premarital sex. Only about 20 percent condemn premarital sex if the couple is in love, but 60 percent condemn casual premarital sex (Kelley, Bean, & Evans, 1993).

There is a growing tolerance of homosexuality. One-third of adult Australians believe that the law should recognize same sex-relationships, 42 percent regard a same-sex couple with children as a family, and 20 percent regard a same-sex couple without children as a family (Gibson et al., 2004). Furthermore, 20 percent believe that homosexual couples should be allowed to adopt children. Fifty-seven percent of adults regard homosexuality as being always, or nearly always, wrong, (Kelley, 2001). Younger people hold more liberal views on these issues and women are a little more tolerant of homosexuality than men, but women are less accepting of premarital or extramarital sex.

Dissolution of Relationships

Divorce has become more common since the 1970s. With the 1976 Family Law Act, which enabled no fault divorce, there was a jump in the rate of divorce from 4.2 divorces per 1,000 marriages in 1971 to 18.9 divorces per 1,000 marriages in 1976. This jump partly represented the formalization of long-standing marriage breakdowns and, after the initial rise, the divorce rate stabilized at between 10.9 and 12.7 per 1,000 marriages (ABS, 2002b; Carmichael, Webster, & McDonald, 1997).

Divorce is more likely in the early years of marriage. Currently, about 9 percent of marriages end within five years of marriage, 20 percent within ten years, 25 percent within fifteen years and 32 percent within twenty-five years (ABS, 2000c). Men are most prone to divorce in their thirties and early forties while women are most prone to divorce in their late twenties and thirties. Living together before marriage has done nothing to stem the divorce rate. Those who marry without first living together and those who live together before marrying have a very similar probability of subsequently divorcing (de Vaus, Qu, & Weston, 2003).

Many people who marry have been married previously with about one-third of marriages involving a previously divorced person (de Vaus, 2004). These marriages are a little more likely than first marriages to end in divorce. When couples divorce, a central concern is the financial, emotional, and psychological impact on children. Over the last thirty years the proportion of divorces involving dependent children has declined from 64 percent in 1966 to 51 percent in 2001. This is a change that reflects an increase in divorce among older people whose children have left home, delays in childbearing, and increasing levels of childlessness (ABS, 2002b).

Despite many children being affected by parental divorce or separation, most children (72 percent) spend most of their dependent years (up to age fifteen) with both of their natural parents. Overall, children spend 82 percent of their first fifteen years of life living with both biological parents. Of course some spend all their time with both parents and some spend very little time, but the bulk of childhood is still spent living with both biological parents (de Vaus & Gray, 2003). Remarriage involving children produces blended and stepfamilies. About 40 percent of remarriages include a partner who has a dependent child from a previous marriage (ABS, 1999c). This results in at least 8 percent of couple families with dependent children being either blended or stepfamilies (ABS, 1998a).

The reasons for which Australians divorce are many and varied. A recent study using a representative sample of people between 1988 and 1997 revealed the most common reasons for divorce are affective issues such as communication problems, incompatibly or drifting apart, and an affair. Less noted reasons were abusive behaviors and external pressures such as financial problems or employment issues (Wolcott & Hughes, 1999).

Divorce is more common among some cultural groups than others. Among immigrants from southern Europe and the Middle East, the divorce rate is between four and five per 1,000 married people (compared with around twelve per 1,000 married people for the population as a whole). However, among immigrants from China, Philippines, North America, and New Zealand, the divorce rate is higher. In international terms, Australia has a high divorce rate. It is higher than in most European countries, Latin America, and the developed Asian countries. However, the Australian rate is much lower than the United States and is similar to that of Canada and Britain, both cultures with which Australia shares considerable similarities (ABS, 1999c).

Although a great many Australian families are directly or indirectly affected by divorce, the majority of people (80 percent) believe that marriage should be for life and almost everyone agrees that it is wrong to enter marriage thinking that if it does not work out they can divorce. Most Australians believe that divorce is easy to obtain and one-third say that it is too easy, especially where children are involved (de Vaus, 1997b). However, while adult Australians say that marriage is for life and should be approached seriously as a lifelong commitment, there is a recognition that things can and do go wrong. Almost 80 percent agree that couples should be able to get a divorce if they wish. Essentially the commitment to marriage is contingent on personal happiness, growth, and fulfillment; people regard these of higher value than a lifelong marriage.

FAMILIES AND CHILDREN

Like many countries, Australia's fertility rate has declined since the postwar peak in the early 1960s, to a current record low level. Since the early 1960s when the average number of children women had was 3.6, it declined to 1.9 in the mid-1980s, and 1.7 by 2005 (ABS, 2003b; UNDP, 2006). This average suggests the two-child family as the norm. However, the reality is more varied. In 1998, 11 percent of women who had completed their childbearing (those aged forty-five to fifty-nine years) were childless, 10 percent had an only child, 37 percent had two children, and 40 percent had three or more children (ABS, 1999b). The overall birthrate is 12.1 (World Factbook, 2007).

The decline in fertility is due to factors including more women remaining childless, later marriage, and workforce participation influencing decisions to delay or have fewer children. Effective means of controlling fertility makes this possible. Legal, publicly funded abortion is widely available throughout Australia. Although only limited abortion statistics are available, it appears that for every 1,000 women aged fourteen to forty-four years, about 17.8 have an abortion in any one year. The rate is double for women aged twenty to twenty-four years (Chan, Scott, Nguyen, & Keane, 1999) while about one-half of all teenage pregnancies end in abortion (Adelson, Frommer, & Weisberg, 1995). The pill is the most common form of contraception for those under age thirty-five, after which sterilization is the favored form of contraception (de Vaus, 2004). While women were once far more likely than men to be sterilized, recent years have seen a decline in female sterilization and a rise in male sterilization so that among those younger than forty-five, males and females now have similar levels of sterilization (de Vaus, 2004; de Vaus, Wise, & Soriano, 1997).

Despite the decline, Australia's fertility rate remains substantially higher than many European countries (e.g., Italy, Spain, Greece, Austria, and Germany) and the developed Asian countries (e.g., Japan and Hong Kong). Australia's rate is comparable to that of Canada, Britain, South Korea, and some Scandinavian countries, but lower than that of the United States (ABS, 1999b).

Fertility varies between ethnic groups in Australia. Among indigenous (aboriginal) Australians, the fertility rate in 2002 was 2.2 births per 1,000 females compared with 1.75 overall. Women born in the

Middle East and North Africa (e.g., Lebanon, Egypt, Turkey) have the highest fertility rates (3.0) while those from the developed countries in southeast and northeast Asia, many of whom are students in Australia, have low fertility rates at around 1.3 births per 1,000 females. Similarly, women who migrated from Europe have the lowest fertility rates (e.g., Yugoslavia, 1.2; Ireland 1.3; Italy and Greece, 1.4) (ABS, 2003b).

Not only are women having fewer children, but their childbearing is within a narrower band of years. They are older when they have their first child and younger when they have their last child. Over the last quarter century, births to women from teen years to early twenties, and to those in their forties, have declined sharply. The main childbearing years for women are now between the ages of twenty-five and thirty-four years. The average age for their first birth within marriage (first nuptial birth) increased from twenty-three years of age in 1966 to 30.1 years in 2002 (ABS, 2003b).

With contraception and the demands of work, childlessness is an option for Australian women. In 2001, 13 percent of women aged forty-five to fifty-nine, were childless (de Vaus, 2004). It is unclear how many of them were voluntarily childless, but childlessness is higher among women with higher education and higher status occupations. Among women aged forty-five to fifty-nine, around 20 percent of those with professional jobs and with university level qualifications are childless. This is about double the Australian average (ABS, 1994b, 1999b). Today 28 percent of young women remain childless—the highest rate since the early 1900s when about 25 percent of women remained unmarried and childless (ABS, 1999b; Rowland, 1998). Childlessness is more common among Australians born of an Anglo-Saxon background than among indigenous Australians (8 percent) and those from Eastern and southern Europe and the Middle East (around 4 percent) (ABS, 1999a).

Attitudes do not demand that women have children. Only 15 percent of Australians believe that a woman must have children to be fulfilled and only 10 percent say that a couple need children to be happy (de Vaus, 1997b). However, virtually no Australians (0.3 percent) say that childlessness is the ideal family size and less than 1 percent (0.8 percent) say that one child is ideal. Almost half (49 percent) say that two children are ideal and 45 percent prefer three or four children

(Inglehart, 2000). Men and women have much the same views about desirable family sizes.

Teen Births

Delays in childbearing are reflected in a marked decline in teenage parenting. Since 1971, the teen birthrate has dropped by two-thirds and the number of births to teenage women has halved from over 30,000 to just 11,423 in 2002. In 1978, 10 percent of first-time married mothers were teenagers. By 1998, this had dropped to 1 percent (ABS, 1999b). Although there has been a sizable decrease in births to teenagers, it is now more accepted for an unmarried teenage girl to have a baby and the majority of births to teenagers are to unmarried teenagers (92 percent in 2002 compared with 33 percent in 1971). The teenage "shotgun wedding" (i.e., those who have a child within seven months of marrying) has almost disappeared, declining from 40 percent of teenage marriages in 1971 to just 4 percent (ABS, 1994a). Most unmarried teenagers now keep their babies rather than making them available for adoption.

Births to teens are more common among some groups than others. While half of 1 percent of all births in Australia are to teenage women, about 20 percent of births to indigenous women are to teenagers (ABS, 1999b). Among teenagers from non-English speaking backgrounds such as southern Europe and Asia, births are less common than the Australian norm (BIPR, 1994).

Parenting Styles and Practices

Australians say that socializing children for specific gender roles is not important and indicate acting like a boy should/acting like a girl should is the least important of a set of thirteen qualities (de Vaus, 1995). Both girls and boys are encouraged to obtain a good education. Most girls grow up expecting to have paid jobs, but if current practice is any guide, jobs will rank behind home and child-rearing responsibilities.

The majority (two-thirds) of Australian parents consider parenting to be their own business and reject the right of governments or anyone else to tell them how to rear their children. The majority (70 percent) opposes governments making it illegal for parents to hit their children and only 12 percent totally reject the use of smacking by parents. However, most parents (80 percent) believe that children should be taken from their parents if they are seriously neglected (de Vaus, 1995).

Independence for both boys and girls is highly valued. Virtually everyone agrees that children should be encouraged to express their opinions, question things, and be curious, and two-thirds agree that a thirteen-year-old should be learning to be independent of his or her parents. There is general support for a child's right to privacy with the great majority of adults (90 percent) saying children should have their own room. At the same time, people feel that it is the parent's responsibility always to know the whereabouts of a thirteen-year-old and the majority (86 percent) believe that children of this age need strict, well-established rules. The characteristics adults see as most desirable in children are those associated with being a "good person": being honest, having good manners, having good sense and sound judgment, being considerate, and trying hard (de Vaus, 1995).

Although adults play down the importance of gender specific behavior for children, there is in practice a traditional gendered division of domestic labor. Boys do less around the home and their main activities are restricted to "male" tasks such as mowing lawns. Girls assume the routine tasks (e.g., bed making, dishes, cooking, vacuuming, laundry). Both boys and girls resent being asked to do a household chore that "belongs" to the opposite sex (Dempsey, 1992).

Child Care

Australia's extensive system of child care gives special emphasis to enabling women's labor force participation. In 2002, almost half of all mothers with children four years and under were employed, mainly in part-time positions (ABS, 2002a), and this creates considerable demand for child care. There is a variety of types of child care, but they fall into two broad categories: formal and informal care. Governments provide substantial child-care subsidies for employment related formal care in government accredited child-care centers. Despite a well-developed and supported formal care system, informal care, which is mainly provided by grandparents, friends, and neighbors, remains the backbone of the child-care system (Millward & Matches, 1995).

Nearly one-half of children aged birth to twelve years receive regular formal or informal child care. Of these, 60 percent are exclusively in informal care and one-quarter exclusively in formal care, with the balance receiving a combination of formal and informal care (Wangmann, 1995).

In 2002, nonparental child care of children under one was relatively uncommon. Just 7 percent received any formal child care and another 30 percent received some informal child care, but two-thirds of children under one were cared for by their parents. However, a quarter of one-year-olds received formal child care and 40 percent received informal care. By age three, 75 percent of children received some formal or informal child care and among four-year-olds, 88 percent received some child care (ABS, 2003c).

Preschoolers take up most of the formal child-care places (Wangmann, 1995). For primary school-aged children, formal before and after school programs are available, but informal care is more heavily used. Nevertheless, 17 percent of primary school-aged children whose parents are working are regularly left on their own without adult supervision. This is mainly because the parents do not have relatives nearby or they do not know people in the local community well enough (de Vaus & Millward, 1997).

Other Government Family Support Programs

In addition to child-care subsidies, the federal government provides income support through the welfare and taxation systems. The majority of families with children receive a means tested Family Payment for each child. Parents not in the workforce who care for children receive a means tested Parenting Allowance. Australia does not have a system of compulsory paid maternity leave to help mothers remain out of the workforce to care for a baby, but mothers receive a one-time lump sum of less than US$600 on the birth of a child. Sole parents are eligible for the sole-parent pension and governments support training schemes and provide child care to assist lone parents to obtain paid work. To assist dependent children affected by divorce, the government administers a Child Support Scheme whereby it collects money from nonresident parents to financially support their dependent children. Finally, families with children receive taxation concessions to help support parents in their child rearing.

FAMILIES AND GENDER

Gender Differences in Education, Employment, and Leisure

Despite some recent changes, large gender differences remain in the areas of education, employment, and leisure. While overall Australian women (aged fifteen to sixty-four) have lower educational qualifications than do men and more men have trade qualifications, women are slightly more likely than are men to hold a university degree (22 percent compared with 20 percent). An earlier pattern of male educational advantage is reversing. More girls than boys now complete secondary schooling. In 2000, the school retention rate to the end of secondary schooling was 79 percent for women but 66 percent for men (ABS, 2001a); more women than men go on to higher education (ABS, 2003d). Among young adults age twenty to twenty-nine, more females have university degrees (29 percent compared with 19 percent) (ABS, 2003d). However, men and women continue to obtain postschool qualifications in very different fields, which in turn affect career opportunities and income. Women are concentrated in the arts and humanities (59 percent female), education (73 percent female), and health (78 percent female), while men study in business (64 percent male), engineering (93 percent male), and science (63 percent male) (ABS, 1999a).

Australia has a long history of pay discrimination institutionalized through a centralized wage fixing system. In 1919, the female basic wage was set at 54 percent of the male equivalent. This was based on a male breadwinner model setting the male wage to support a family while the female wage was set to support a single person. In the 1960s, a policy of equal pay for equal work was phased in as formal barriers to workforce participation of married women were phased out. From 1972 to 1975, the introduction of equal pay for equal work value narrowed the male/female wage gap, but partly because of job segregation, a significant gender-based pay differential persists. For full-time employees the average wage of women is about 80 percent that of the average wage of men.

The workforce participation rate of women is lower than that of men, but the gap is narrowing. In 2002, the gap was 16 percent compared with a gap of 48 percent in 1966 (ABS, 2003e; Wolcott, 1997). Increasingly, women with young children are employed frequently on a part-time basis. Among older men and women, gender differences in employment are also narrowing as more women in their fifties and fewer men have paid work (de Vaus, 2004).

The Australian workforce has high levels of gender segregation that show little sign of diminishing. Women work mostly as clerks and in sales and personal service areas where wages, conditions, promotion ladders, and access to training and education are fairly poor (Lambert, Petridis, & Galea, 1995). Men are more likely than are women to be employed in managerial and administrative positions (12 percent of employed males compared with 6 percent of employed females), as tradespersons (20 percent compared with 3 percent), and as production and transport workers (13 percent compared with 3 percent). On the other hand, women are far more likely than are men to be employed as middle and lower level clerks, in sales, or as personal service workers (41 percent compared with 13 percent) (ABS, 2003d). More recently, this gender segregation is affecting the opportunities for men in unskilled and semiskilled jobs. Economic restructuring and the decline in manufacturing have undermined opportunities for these men.

The shape of men and women's leisure also differs. Women in paid work who have children spend about five hours a week less in leisure activities than comparable men and women not in paid work (Ironmonger & Richardson, 1991). Men spend more time in active leisure activities such as sport, while women engage more in passive leisure such as reading and talking (ABS, 1998b). Among children and teenagers, boys spend more time watching TV, playing sport, and playing video games while girls spend more time reading, listening to music, drawing, and writing (Cupitt & Stockbridge, 1996).

Distribution of Power

Most adults say that husbands and wives should jointly make decisions (de Vaus, 1997b), a considerable change from the 1950s when there was widespread acceptance of the legitimacy of men's traditional authority in the home (Dempsey, 1997). However, the belief in equal decision making does not always translate into practice.

Research on inequality in Australian marriages demonstrates that for husbands and wives, joint decision making does not mean equal power (Dempsey, 1997). For many couples, joint decision making means being consulted, or each partner making decisions in a particular sphere of competence, or in implementing decisions that the main power holder has delegated. Despite attitudes to the contrary, husbands more often have the final say in important decisions, especially those involving large expenditure. The majority of wives only take decisions on their own when it involves little or no expenditure and normally they are simply implementing rather than making the decision. Commonly, the decisions made by women relate to areas associated with their traditional areas of responsibility such as shopping, arranging social activities, and minor decisions regarding children. Research confirms continuing inequality in decision making within Australian marriages but does observe that the inequality appears to be less today than in the 1950s (Dempsey, 1997).

Division of Labor in Households

Australian men and women are increasingly likely to agree that men ought to take a fair share of responsibility for tasks around the home. Especially where women are in the paid workforce, most (93 percent) men and women agree that there should be an equal, or at least fair division of domestic tasks (de Vaus, 1997b). However, Australian wives are spending about double the time in unpaid work as their husbands (Dempsey, 1997). Over the last quarter century, the gap between the time men and women spend in domestic work has narrowed but this is due more to women spending less time on domestic work than men spending more. Women still contribute about 70 percent of the unpaid domestic labor (Bittman & Lovejoy, 1993; Dempsey, 1997).

Even employed women do far more than their share of the domestic tasks and undertake what Hochschild (1989) called the "second shift." When wives are in the paid workforce, Australian husbands do not take over much of the domestic load. When they do help, the nature of the domestic tasks they undertake differs from that undertaken by women. The differences between the nature of men's and women's domestic tasks in Australia can be summarized in the following ways: men's domestic tasks occur less frequently and less regularly; men have more discretion over the time and frequency of performing their tasks; men's tasks have a more defined beginning and end (mowing the lawn versus child care); men's domestic tasks are generally less boring, are given greater status, and give greater opportunity to achieve affirmation; and men help with "feminine" tasks rather than taking responsibility for them (Dempsey, 1997).

Men spend more time caring for children today (Wolcott, 1997), but so do women; children now take more of both parent's time. Furthermore, men have mainly increased the time they spend playing with and minding their children rather than in routine caring. Mothers continue to spend far more time than fathers feeding, clothing, teaching, assisting with homework, looking after sick children, and providing emotional support. Australian women, including those in the paid workforce, continue to take the major responsibility for child rearing. Taken overall, the Australian situation in the 1990s concerning child care remained similar to that in the 1940s—while fathers come and go, mothers remain the abiding presence for their children (Dempsey, 1997).

Work and Family Patterns

Australia has experienced a steady increase in the proportion of women in the paid labor force. Between 1966 and 2002, female participation increased from 36 to 57 percent (down from 84 to 73 percent for males) (ABS, 2003e). In 2002, 63 percent of married women with dependent children, were employed and 48 percent of lone mothers with dependents were in the workforce (Gray, Qu, Renda, & de Vaus, 2003). Women with family responsibilities have to juggle the competing demands of employment and family with little reduction in their domestic load (Dempsey, 1997).

In Australia, the organization of employment—the hours, the scheduling of jobs, and what it means to be committed to work—are based on assumptions that most full-time workers are men whose partners take responsibility for day-to-day family matters, or that they have no family responsibilities (Wolcott, 1997). It is difficult for families with children to manage their family responsibilities when both parents are employed full time. It also means that lone parents find it extremely difficult to maintain a full-time job, a fact that contributes to the poverty in which many lone parents find themselves.

The main way that families manage the competing demands of work and family is for women to reduce their hours of employment (Wolcott & Glezer, 1995). In 2002, only 37 percent of mothers in couple families with dependent children and 21 percent of comparable lone mothers were employed full time (Gray et al., 2003). Many mothers prefer to be employed part time as the way of dealing with the demands of both work and family. The 1991 Family Formation Survey found that of mothers who were employed full time, the majority (60 percent) wanted to work part time and 14 percent preferred not to work at all. Of those working part time, the majority (71 percent) were happy with this level of employment, while 10 percent wanted full-time employment and 19 percent preferred not to be employed. Of those not employed, one-half wanted part-time work and 8 percent full-time employment (Wolcott & Glezer, 1995).

A number of industrial award conditions (i.e., conditions employers are required to provide to employees) and workplace arrangements assist parents with family responsibilities. For example, most workers are entitled to fifty-two weeks-unpaid parental leave after the birth of a child. This total of fifty-two weeks can be shared between mothers and fathers (i.e., some of the weeks can be taken by the mother and the balance by the father). Anecdotal evidence suggests that relatively few fathers avail themselves of this opportunity. Most workers are also entitled to several days of paid leave a year for family care purposes. Many workplaces have introduced paid maternity leave (especially in the public sector), additional sick days for family care purposes, and flexible work hours (e.g., flextime, job sharing, part-time employment). Over 60 percent of workers can get flexible working hours if necessary and three-quarters can leave work for short periods for personal and family reasons. Some parents, especially women, combine employment and family responsibilities by working from home, a pattern that is becoming increasingly popular and viable (ABS, 1996).

FAMILIES AND STRESS

Australians place great weight on the importance of family life and express general satisfaction with it. In the Australian Living Standards

Study, adults rated their family life (relationship with partner, children, and children's relationships with one another) as the most satisfying aspects of their lives (Weston, 1997). For many Australians, their family is a "haven in a heartless world" (Lasch, 1977).

However, family life is not insulated from the wider society and is therefore subject to many stresses and strains. This is especially so when economic change is both substantial and rapid and the postmodern culture creates uncertainty about values and a strong strand of individualism challenges the notion of commitment and responsibility to others. In an era where the role of government is being redefined and the store of social capital is being eroded, where families are expected to take more responsibility for their members, it is hardly surprising that many families are stressed. The challenge for families, the community, and governments is to provide sufficient and appropriate support as families confront these strains.

A national survey asked adults what the greatest pressures were that they faced (Australian Institute of Family Studies, 1997). Although people identified several kinds of pressures, an underlying theme was uncertainty about the future. In an era of rapid change, Australian families are experiencing the uncertainty and the end of tradition firsthand (Beck, Giddens, & Lash, 1994). Other common areas of stress include lack of time, young adults living with their parents, caring for the elderly, marriage breakdown and stepfamily life, negotiating an appropriate division of labor, and balancing employment and family.

Uncertainty

The deregulation of the labor market has made jobs less secure. Sharp reductions in public sector employment, the decline of manufacturing and manual work, the contraction of middle management, and reduced government funding for education and welfare means that few people feel safe in their jobs. Although families might be managing on their current incomes, they have little confidence about future income. Concerns about job insecurity make families feel financially vulnerable. Frequent changes to government income support, tightening of entitlements to the old age pension, and changes to superannuation tax concessions make planning for old age difficult. In sum, the climate of change makes the future unpredictable and planning difficult. These conditions inject in families a sense of lack of control. This lack of control in turn places great stresses on families.

Employment and Unemployment

The polarization of employment creates further family stress. There has been an increase in families where both partners are employed and in families where neither is employed. In 2002, in 57 percent of couple families with dependents, both parents were employed (Renda, 2003). Among those employed, the increasingly competitive work culture means that although fewer people are working, those that are employed full time are working longer hours. This, in turn, stresses families as they cope with their responsibilities. In other families no adult is employed. In 2002, of two-parent families with dependent children, 7 percent had neither parent employed (Renda, 2003). Among lone-parent families with dependent children, 50 percent of the parents were not employed and a further 25 percent had part-time work only (Renda, 2003).

Lack of Time

For many families, especially those where both parents are employed (or in sole-parent families where the parent is in the workforce), lack of time is a significant problem. Parents in the Australian Living Standards Study identified the lack of time to do what they want as well as the pressure they feel, as among the greatest sources of dissatisfaction (Weston, 1997). Of couples with dependent children, 53 percent felt that they were always pressed for time. This contrasts with only 25 percent of couples without children who regularly felt pressed for time (ABS, 1998b). Pressure of time was especially a problem in families where both partners were employed full time and for long hours. Recent years have seen an increase in the hours that some families, especially those with managerial or professional occupations, are working. In addition, as the State provides fewer family support services, families must find time to care for elderly members and those with a disability. This places special time pressures on middle-aged women who are caught between the multiple pressures of paid work, unpaid caring, children living at home for longer periods, and the responsibility for a major portion of the domestic work (Brody, 1990; Schlesinger & Raphael, 1993).

Young Adults Living with Their Parents

Having adult children living in the parents' home is another source of stress for some families. As participation in higher education increases and entry into the labor force becomes more difficult, the period of economic dependence of young people on their parents is extending. This results in young adults delaying family formation while continuing to live with their parents. Interim cohabiting relationships and the casual, insecure, and lowly paid work that many young people initially obtain, mean that when young people do leave home, it is often temporary. Insecure employment also makes it difficult for young adults to enter the housing market.

For young adults, an extended period of living with their parents can require what can be a complex renegotiation of roles, rights, and responsibilities both for the young people and their parents (Hartley, 1993). Privacy and lifestyle issues such as sexual behavior and use of alcohol and drugs within the parent's home can lead to additional family strains.

Caring for Elderly Family Members

In other families, the financial and emotional strains of caring for elderly family members (or being cared for) produce additional pressures, especially on top of the many other demands that these carers must face. Almost one-third (31 percent) of primary carers of elderly or disabled parents or partners report feeling depressed, and often worried, and one in six (17 percent) say they often feel angry and resentful because of their caring responsibilities. About one-quarter of carers report that their financial situation has suffered because of caring (ABS, 2000a).

Marriage Breakdown

Marriage breakdown is, of course, a severe stress for family members and those around them. The stress is emotional, psychological, and financial (Weston & Funder, 1993). Over time, however, individuals who experience marriage breakdown adapt to their new situation and construct new families (Funder, 1996). Although the financial situation of sole parents with dependent children often remains precarious, this improves over time as children grow older or parents repartner. Living in a reconstituted family produces stresses on many children, parents, and stepparents, and parents rate relationships with stepchildren as the least satisfactory relationship in their family life (Weston, 1997).

Negotiating the Division of Labor

Negotiating an appropriate division of labor can be an important source of stress and conflict within marriages. Despite widespread agreement with the theory of gender equality, there seem to be some difficulties implementing this in the domestic sphere. However, the major stressor here is often not the unequal division of labor or even the gendered nature of the division of labor. Rather, it is whether it is perceived to be fair and whether the person doing more feels appreciated. The male partner's willingness to help and his recognition and appreciation of the contribution of his wife is critical to whether the uneven division of domestic work creates relationship difficulties (Baxter & Western, 1996; Dempsey, 1997).

Balancing Employment and Family

A major stressor for many families is balancing the demands of family life and dual careers or jobs. Men and women, particularly women employed full time, report the negative effects that paid work has on their relationships with their partners and children, and on household management. Close to one-half of mothers employed full time report how exhaustion affects their capacity to do things with their partner, to parent, or get much done around the house (Wolcott & Glezer, 1995). Working part time alleviates these problems for many women to the extent that only 20 percent of women employed part time reported these sorts of work-related family difficulties.

FAMILIES AND AGING

The postwar baby boom and declining fertility mean that Australia's population will age significantly over the next forty years, with the population aged sixty-five or over doubling from 12 percent in 1995 to 22 percent in 2041. As the population ages, the pool of caregivers will decline; there will be fewer carers for a larger number of older people. In Australia, women in their fifties are an important source of elder care, but over the next twenty years the ratio of women in this age group to those aged over eighty will halve (Rowland, 1998). The proportion of working women will increase as will the "women in the middle" phenomenon. This situation reflects middle-aged women caught between the demands of elder care, workforce participation, domestic responsibilities, and extended dependence of their adult children, and grandchild care.

Population aging will significantly increase the costs of elder care, income support for the elderly, and health costs to the government. Accordingly, governments have moved to minimize these costs. A savings system has been introduced whereby most workers are required to contribute to superannuation schemes to make them more self sufficient in old age. Means and assets testing have substantially curtailed access to the once universal aged pension system. Compulsory retirement has been largely abolished and incentives to continue working have been introduced to encourage older people to continue earning their own income.

Access to subsidized institutional care has been made more difficult and is targeted at those in most need. The user pays philosophy for elder care and the introduction of substantial entry fees for nursing homes are designed to limit the call on expensive forms of elder care. Increasingly, elder care is being deinstitutionalized and replaced by the much less expensive Home and Community Care (HACC) program whereby care for those in need is provided in the community. This involves governments providing limited funds to purchase services such as meals, transport, personal care, and home maintenance to enable the needy elderly to stay in their own homes.

Caregiving Arrangements

Apart from the fact that it is cheaper, people typically prefer community care. It also reflects the general trend in government policy to minimize expenditure, to withdraw from the direct provision of services, and to foster self-reliance. With elder care, this translates into family self-reliance whereby elder care is to be the responsibility of families, not governments. In reality, families have always been the main providers of elder care. Elder care consists of a wide variety of tasks including personal care, health, verbal communication, home help, home maintenance, meal preparation, transportation, and the like. In Australia, family members provide 80 percent of the assistance to people aged over sixty. A family member in the same household provides almost 60 percent of all assistance, frequently to a partner (Millward, Wolcott, de Vaus, & Soriano, 1997).

Family care of the elderly falls more heavily on women and mirrors the typical household division of domestic labor. Daughters are generally regarded as the appropriate caregivers (Evans, 1996) and provide personal care, meals, health care, transport, and the like while sons assist with less routine tasks such as home maintenance and financial assistance. Sons help parents financially while daughters provide domestic labor.

Policies that rely on families caring for their own assume that families are available and willing to do so. Divorce can disrupt kinship ties and produce ambiguity about kinship obligations. Divorced men, in particular, lose contact with their families and have few family members either available or willing to provide support in their old age (Furstenberg & Cherlin, 1991; Millward, 1997; Rezac, 1994, 1998).

Australian culture promotes individualism and places less emphasis than some cultures (e.g., Asian, southern European, and Middle Eastern) on the mutual obligations of family members. While Australians agree that children should assist needy elderly parents, their support is both conditional and equivocal. They agree that adult children should care, contact, and help their elderly parents, but when this interferes with their own life and other responsibilities, far fewer accept that parental needs should take priority. There is little support for accepting major obligations such as sharing a home (less than one-third), living nearby (18 percent), or a daughter giving up employment to care (10 percent). Young and old alike accept that adult children should keep in touch with their parents but not that they should live nearby. They accept that adult children should help their parents, but not if it causes hardship. They accept that children should provide care, but not if it affects the rest of the family (de Vaus, 1996). Elderly

Australians, overall, want to remain independent and do not want to be a burden to their grown children (Day, 1989).

Of course, not all Australians share the same views on these matters. Although men and women and the young and old share similar views, migrants from Asia, the Middle East, and southern Europe place more importance than those from Anglo-Saxon backgrounds on the responsibility of families for elder care (de Vaus, 1996).

Institutional care of the elderly remains the exception rather than the rule. Almost 94 percent of those sixty-five or over live in private houses and most live in a family. Even among those aged eighty-five or older, more than 80 percent live in a private dwelling. Of those in their late eighties, more than 40 percent live alone and another one-third live with other family members (ABS, 2003a). It is only among those aged ninety-five or over where more than one-half are in institutional care. As the ninety-five plus age group is a tiny proportion (7 percent) of all older people, few older people are in institutional care.

It is relatively unusual, however, for older Australians to live with their grown children. They are far more likely to live with their partner or alone. Just over 3 percent of Australian households include an elderly parent living in the home of their adult child. These arrangements are more common among indigenous aboriginal families (where about 10 percent of households are multifamily households containing an elderly parent) and among families from southern Europe, the Middle East, and Southeast Asia (Millward & de Vaus, 1997).

Frequently the aging of the population is portrayed as a problem, no doubt because of concerns about the cost of elder care. However, concern reflects an unbalanced picture of the elderly. The bulk of elder care is provided by other older people (partners, friends, and other older relatives) and the period when older people require relatively intensive and more costly care is typically limited to the last two years of life. For the small numbers who enter nursing home care, the average duration of care is just six months. In the main, elderly people remain independent and contribute significantly to the community. In addition to being the core caregivers for the elderly, older people also contribute to child care with grandparents being the single most important providers of informal child care (ABS, 1993; Millward & Matches, 1995). Taken overall, older people are net providers rather than consumers of care. Furthermore, older family members also provide a range of economic and in-kind transfers to younger family members (de Vaus & Qu, 1998). The value of the unpaid work of older people in 1997 was estimated at $A39 billion. In an economy with a GDP of $A550 (in 1997) this represents a major, but often unrecognized, contribution (de Vaus, Gray, & Stanton, 2003).

The aging experience is quite different for men and women in Australia. Owing to the greater longevity of Australian women (average of eighty-three years for women and seventy-eight for men in 2004), women are more likely than men to spend some of their old age as widows living alone (UNDP, 2006). Nearly 60 percent of women (20 percent of men) seventy-five to eighty-four years of age and 80 percent of women (40 percent of men) aged eighty-five and over are widowed (ABS, 2001b). Not only does this mean that many older women will spend some time living alone, it also means than many older women will spend time caring for their ailing husbands. Older men are likely to be cared for by their partner while older women are more likely to be cared for by daughters or have to manage on their own.

OTHER FAMILY SITUATIONS

Earlier in this chapter, it was noted that there recently has been an increase in the average age when a mother has her first child within a marriage. This is partly due to more unmarried women having children (ex-nuptial births). In 2002, 31 percent of births were to unmarried women, a sharp increase from 5 percent in the early 1960s (ABS, 2003b). Many of these ex-nuptial births, however, are to couples who are living together in de facto relationships and only about 11 percent of children are born to lone mothers (Australian Institute of Health and Welfare, 2003; de Vaus, 2002). How many of these parents eventually marry or the extent that the rise in ex-nuptial births represents a reordering of the life stages of family formation is not known.

As ex-nuptial births have become more common, the stigma once attached to the unmarried mother and child has declined. However, one-half of the population (more among those over age forty) do not approve of having children without being married (de Vaus et al., 1997).

Ex-nuptial births are more common in some ethnic groups than others (ABS, 2003b). In 2002, while 34 percent of births to Australian born mothers were ex-nuptial, about 6 percent of births to Australian mothers who were born in the Middle East, North Africa, south Asia, northeast Asia, and parts of Southeast Asia were ex-nuptial. Around 15 percent of births to women born in southern, central, and Eastern Europe were ex-nuptial. Overall, the higher rates of ex-nuptial births are among mothers who migrated from English speaking countries and from western Europe. However, the highest rate of ex-nuptial births occur among indigenous Australian women than among Australian women overall. Of registered births to indigenous mothers in 2002, 82 percent were ex-nuptial (ABS, 2003b).

CONCLUDING COMMENTS

In recent decades, the general social and economic context in which Australian families go about their business has changed radically. Families themselves also have been changing significantly. Some of these changes have centered on the personal dynamics of family life; the way people form families and organize their tasks and responsibilities. Other changes have taken place as families have responded to external economic and social changes. It appears that both sets of changes will continue in this new millennium.

Rather than talking of "the family," it is more helpful to talk about families and to be alert to the wide diversity of family forms. Family structures and dynamics change over the life course of individuals as they respond to economic and social change in the societies in which they are embedded. Patterns of family formation, in particular, are changing. Men and women are marrying later, having fewer children, divorcing more often, and living in de facto marriages. Expectations of gender equity between partners have increased and more children are being born to unmarried parents or are being raised in sole-parent or blended families. Understanding of families must be informed by an awareness of the diversity of family forms and the recognition of different responses of family members to challenges along their life course.

As Australia continues to engage with the effects of economic restructuring, globalization, economic rationalism, smaller government, and cutbacks in social and community programs, there is increasing reliance on the private, community, and voluntary sectors as well as on families themselves to fulfill care and support functions previously undertaken by the State. This, and a user pays philosophy, will place increasing pressure on low-income families, women, and others reliant on government benefits. Persistent high unemployment and underemployment, the casualization (i.e., the move toward work that is temporary, paid by the hour, and that attracts minimal nonsalary benefits) and insecurity of work, and the difficulty for young people as they try to enter the labor force and establish families of their own, pose particular challenges for contemporary families. These families face a very different world to that with which their parents had to cope.

Changing patterns of family structure and formation—the formation of marriage-like relationships, changes in childbearing and fertility patterns, attempts to change gender roles, single parenting, the intrusion of paid work into family life, and family breakdown—are bemoaned by some as constituting the decline of the family as we know it (Blankenhorn, 1995; Popenoe, 1988, 1993; Sullivan, Maley, & Warby, 1997). Others regard these changes as positive indications that an oppressive and patriarchal institution is disappearing (Cooper, 1972; Eisenstein, 1984; Laing & Esterson, 1970; Leach, 1968). Yet, others argue that past evidence shows families to be resilient, with the capacity to respond adaptively in the face of demands for change. Such commentators argue that the changes seen are constructive, reflecting the strength, durability, and adaptability of the family and will ensure that families remain the basic social units of society (Fletcher, 1993; Parsons, 1943; Shorter, 1971). It remains uncertain how Australian families will address the pressures they face. Perhaps there will be additional "breakdown," but at the same time, it is possible for families to pull together and be strengthened. Time will tell.

LATIN AMERICA:
FAMILY LIFE IN BRAZIL,
MEXICO, AND CUBA

Chapter 16

Brazilian Families in the Confrontation Between Hierarchy and Equality

Maria Lúcia M. Afonso

INTRODUCTION

The Federative Republic of Brazil is the largest South American country with a population of 183.9 million (84 percent urban). The political system has been a democracy since 1985. However, Brazil suffers from an unequal society, with social disparities deepened by four centuries of colonialism (1500-1889) and another of many authoritarian regimes. Since 1998, the law guarantees free access to education through high school. The enrollment rate for adolescents fifteen to seventeen increased from 60 percent in 1992 to 81 percent in 2001. Even so, 71 percent of youth from poor families compared with 95 percent from the more wealthy families were in high school in 2001.

This chapter is dedicated to the memory of Mateus Afonso Medeiros, my son. Since Law School, Mateus was a dedicated worker for human rights in Brazil. In 2000-2001 he was the Coordinator of the Human Rights Public Office, in Belo Horizonte. He received a Fulbright Commission scholarship to spend the 2001-2002 academic year as a visiting scholar in the Human Rights Institute of Columbia Law School, New York. In 2002, Mateus became a lawyer of the National Committee on Minorities and Human Rights in the Brazilian House of Representatives, Brasilia. In that position he contributed to the *Brazil 2003 Global Justice Annual Report* as well as contributing to the *Report on Conflicts About the Land of Native Brazilians,* sent to International Amnesty in 2004. In January 2005 Mateus was hit by a car while riding his bike on a Sunday afternoon in Brasilia. He was twenty-nine years old and about to finish his masters degree in political sciences at the University of Brasília.

In 1999, 12 percent of the population was illiterate and 29 percent had less than four years of education. More recently, the illiteracy rate (age fifteen and older) was 11.4. These are examples of contradictions in Brazilian society. The United Nations reports that Brazil has a medium level of human development, ranking sixty-nine by use of the Human Development Index (Instituto Brasileiro de Geografia e Estatística [IBGE], 2002; United Nations Development Programme [UNDP], 2006).

From its Portuguese colonial rule, the country inherited Roman Catholic Christianity and the Portuguese language. Slavery of Africans ended in 1888. Native Brazilians had been almost exterminated until policies were created in the second half of the twentieth century to protect their land. Afro-Brazilians and immigrants in the twentieth century from European, Eastern, and Oriental countries have contributed to the Brazilian cultural identity. The population is 54 percent whites, 6 percent blacks, 40 percent *pardos* (a wide designation, adopted for use mainly in statistical analysis, for people with mixed racial characteristics), and less than 1 percent Orientals and native Brazilians (IBGE, 2001; World Factbook, 2007). Cultural differences are expressed by a richness of rituals, culinary tastes, dance, music, and so on. As it has been scarcely studied, it is hard to say whether cultural diversity affects everyday family life, except for native Brazilian groups. Descendents from immigrants speak their languages within small cultural communities: Banto (spoken by descendents of slaves from the African Banto tribe), German, Japanese, and others. The main language is Portuguese. Catholicism is the declared religion for 74 percent of Brazilians (Folha de São Paulo/Datafolha, 1998). Other Christian sects include forms of Protestantism (15 percent), Kardecism (spiritualism based on the teachings of Alan Kardec), Afro-religions, and belief systems with the common basis of Christianity (World Factbook, 2007).

Brazil presents a high degree of racial miscegenation side by side with an ideology that has been named "cordial racism." That is, discrimination is denied and disguised under soft manners in personal relations at the same time that blacks suffer from discrimination and exclusion (Folha de São Paulo/Datafolha, 1998). For instance, the infant mortality rate is thirty-five per 1,000 live births, but reaches sixty-two among black and *"pardos"* and is eighty-three for the poorest

20 percent of the population, and twenty-nine for the richest 20 percent (IBGE, 2001; UNDP, 2006). The majority of blacks are poor. Racial discrimination and social inequality are intertwined and it is easier to identify racism when blacks and whites compete within the same levels of education and employment.

Families in Brazilian Context

While considering the colonial past in order to understand the Brazilian family today is important, it is even more important to describe the twentieth century processes that influenced families and shaped contemporary characteristics. During 1960-1980, Brazilian families went through a "modernization" process, as did the country. There was an expansion of mass communication, of the public school system, and of women's participation in the labor market and in politics. Initiated by a military right-wing dictatorship (1964-1985), the Brazilian modernization process was marked by social inequality and thus by an increasing differentiation in lifestyles and in access to information by different social classes.

While modernization varied among classes, ethnic groups, and geographic regions, some changes reached all social groups. The main changes in families in the 1980s were a decrease in average family size, growth in percentage of couples without children, and an increase in the percentage of single-parent and female-headed families (Berquó, 1989; Goldani, 1993; Oliveira, 1996). The fertility rate dropped from 6.2 in 1960, 4.7 in 1975, 3.3 in 1990, to 2.3 in 2005. The differences between social classes are gradually diminishing. In 1999, the fertility rate was 3.2 among women of low educational level and 1.6 among women of middle and higher education levels. The birthrate is 16.6 and the population growth rate is 1.04. Life expectancy grew from 53.5 in 1970 to 70.3 in 2005. With the drop in fertility rate and increase in life expectation, projections are that the proportion of children will diminish and the percentage of elders will grow in the following decades (Goldani, 1994; IBGE, 2002; UNDP, 2003, 2004, 2006).

The majority of the Brazilian families are "nuclear," organized around the couple and their children. However, other arrangements are common, especially among the poor. In 1992, approximately 72 percent of all families consisted of couples with or without children.

Fifteen percent were single-parent families. In 2001, the nuclear family was still predominant (67 percent), single-parent families (women and their children) increased (18 percent), and 9 percent of households were of individuals living alone (42 percent of which were elderly) (IBGE, 2002).

Economic development that enhanced inequality and social exclusion had an impact. Most female-headed families are of black or dark-skinned women and belong to the poorest sectors of society, with 29 percent below the poverty line (IBGE, 2002). Social inequality is also shown in the monthly income among families. In 1999, 28 percent of Brazilian families lived with less than US$272 monthly income (below poverty line); 32 percent had a monthly income between US$272 and US$680; 19 percent were between $680 and US$1,360; 10 percent between US$1,360 and US$2,720; and 6 percent more than US$2,720 per month (IBGE, 2001). Between 1990 and 2003, 21 percent of the population lived on less than US$2 per day and 22 percent were below the poverty line (UNDP, 2006).

Changes in families influenced values and practices. There was: (1) a weakening of the association between marriage and family, and between marriage and reproduction, with the legal acceptance of other family and union arrangements; (2) more flexibility in gender roles, including women in the labor market as long as motherhood remained a priority (but the authority of the father remained an ideal in the nuclear family, and outside work and household chores overburden women); and (3) with the spread of psychology and pedagogy, new values related to child rearing emerged (Ribeiro & Ribeiro, 1994).

Transformations in families happened in a context of social conflict between authoritarianism and democracy, between traditionalism and modernity, reaching all spheres of social life. Families are in the forefront of a confrontation between hierarchy and equality. The struggle for political democracy encompassed the claims for women and children's citizenship at the same time that socioeconomic changes provoked changes in family structure. Claims for equality and citizenship (recognition and full participation, with associated rights and responsibilities, as citizens in society) have entered private life. Gender roles and child-rearing practices have changed. At the same time, poor women and children face violence, poverty, and exploitation. In such a context, new social policies, focused on families, have emerged.

After the United Nations declared 1994 the International Year of the Family, Brazil created an interministerial National Committee on the Family made up of government and nongovernment organizations, to propose a national social policy. The Committee agreed that the traditional organization of families had been dismantled and that many were exposed to poverty and exclusion. It defined family as, "the couple, the couple and their children and/or other relatives, each parent and his or her children, grandparents with their grandchildren, and other relations that are characterized by consanguinity and/or affection, whether or not they are formalized through legal actions" (Comissão Interministerial para a Formulação da Política Nacional da Família [Comissão], 1994, p. 6).

According to the National Committee on Family, the State assures families: the rights of citizenship, respect for pluralism of family structures and family ties, equality of rights between men and women, and the right to family planning and to responsible parenthood. The Committee also reaffirmed the importance of families for the support and protection of children, adolescents, and the elderly. Ideally, a social policy should provide an effective social intervention in the defense of such rights, at the levels of cities, states, and the federation. The defined strategies were support for Family Councils—created in the states and counties in order to promote social programs directed to families—and the allocation of resources (e.g., support of family social programs, especially those focused on income generation and the defense of basic rights). There is a special concern for citizenship rights of women, children, adolescents, and the elderly. In this sense, two points are highlighted. First, a change in the official discourse about families that has become open to acceptance of cultural plurality and claims to citizenship. Second, is the distance between official discourse and effective action. For example, there are no consistent and effective social policies to fight poverty. To illustrate, in the north of Brazil, only twenty-six pregnant women had access to seven sessions of prenatal care while the national mean is 46 percent (IBGE, 2002).

The weakness of the policies questions whether there will be a welfare state policy in Brazil. The "family" policies still focus on individual needs more than the family group, even though the family network is essential among the poor (Carvalho, 1994).

Purposes of This Chapter

Three main points are argued in this chapter. First, recent changes can be understood by analyzing the polemic between hierarchical and egalitarian points of view about the organization of private life.[1] Second, the family can be revalued as an important institution for a democratic society as far as citizenship of women and children is protected, family diversity is no longer discriminated against, and policies offer support to family ties and enhancing the quality of life. Third, the promotion of democratic values and relations within the family will be only possible with the surpassing, or lessening, of social inequality and exclusion. It is argued that egalitarianism and democracy in family life has to be supported by social democracy and so cannot depend on a single model of family. Furthermore, at each shift in family relations, new contradictions arise, in a lively movement toward new arrangements in family and society that presupposes communicative action and negotiation, in public as much as in the private spheres of life (see Habermas, 1984). In this sense, no one model could be, in itself, the "ending point" of a democratic family life. Furthermore, social exclusion and poverty are to be surpassed in order to prevent violence as well as to reveal the potentialities of family life.

COUPLE FORMATION AND MARITAL DYNAMICS

Three types of conjugal arrangement could be identified in the colonial period in Brazil. In the "patriarchal family" of powerful landowners, there were strictly defined gender roles and hierarchical patterns of authority between husband and wife and parents and children. Marriage was for a lifetime. On the other side of the social structure, slaves needed permission to marry and ran the risk of separation from their families. Free unions were more frequent among slaves. It was difficult to maintain family values far away from their own culture. Among the small nonproprietor free population linked to trade and mines, marriage presented more flexibility regarding conjugal roles, free unions, and marital separation. Women participated in commercial activities and contributed to family income. Legally, marriage was a lifetime commitment. However, since the end of the nineteenth century, legal separation was possible in case of violence or infidelity. At the beginning of the twentieth century, medical doctors began to spread a new worldview among the upper-class families. This view included conjugal fidelity to prevent syphilis as well as a good understanding within the couple for the sake of their children's health and moral education (Figueira, 1987; Foucault, 1980; Genofre, 1995).

Until the first decade of the twentieth century, and later for some rural areas, marriage was a matter of family interest rather than individual choice. Marriage was monogamous. There was a double standard and a tolerance of male extramarital sexual life. The ideal of romantic love grew among educated groups, combining with moral commitment within marriage. The double pattern of sexual morality remained among the population (Ribeiro & Ribeiro, 1994; Trigo, 1989).

More radical changes came in the second half of the twentieth century. After industrialization in the 1950s and authoritarian modernization in the 1960s, women enlarged their participation in labor markets and new patterns of consumerism arose. Husbands were no longer the only providers, nor always the head of the couple. The expansion of health services and birth control created a choice for having fewer offspring, and of shortening the period dedicated to raising children. The struggle for citizenship in the 1980s encompassed women's rights inside and outside the family, including egalitarianism in marriage.

Divorce was legalized in 1977, but with conditions such as having to get a legal separation and waiting at least two years to divorce. The new Civil Code (2001) reduced this to one year. In the 1988 Constitution, husbands and wives reached equal rights in marriage and divorce. Cohabitation acquired legal status. In 1996, Congress regulated informal marriages, granting to the partners some conjugal rights (such as legacy) to those together for at least five years (Genofre, 1995).

Since the 1970s, there has been a continuous decrease in wedlock and an increase in divorces and separations, suggesting that the traditional marital contract has undergone change. From 1980 to 1988, the rate of wedlock dropped from 7.8 to 6.7 per 1,000 inhabitants (Facultad Latino Americana de Ciencias Sociales [FLACSO], 1993). Considering only legal conjugal arrangements, in 1991, 21 percent of marriages ended in separation or divorce. This has been more pronounced in large urban centers (Oliveira, 1996). In 2001, the wedlock rate dropped to 4.1 while divorce and consensual separation reached 1.3 per 1,000 inhabitants (IBGE, 2002). In the 1990s, the average age at first marriage was 22.7 for women and 25.8 for men. While only 3 percent of men aged fifteen to nineteen years were married, 23 percent of women of this age group were married.

There was an increase across the 1980s in nonlegalized marriages even after the legalization of divorce (Oliveira, 1996). The choice of informal marriages can no longer be attributed to the difficult access to legal procedures. The Civil Code (2001) guarantees free access to legal marriage if the couple cannot afford to pay. Although informal marriages had always been common among the poor, their percentage rose among the middle and upper classes. As they tend to be unstable, informal marriages might express a new way of changing partners in a society where men traditionally have had lovers. Statistics show that compared with women, men have a greater chance of remarrying, whatever their age (Oliveira, 1996).

The choice of informal marriage could also be based on the changes in gender relations—which became more egalitarian and demanding—and in marriage bonds that carry new demands such as greater communication and identity between the partners. The tolerance toward informal marriages can be related to the increasing importance given to individual choice in couple formation and relationships (Figueira, 1987). Furthermore, the importance of individual choice to contract and maintain marriage has grown along with a new idealization of the conjugal relation. Married partners are expected to love each other and continue to feel sexual attraction to maintain the marriage. These reasons have become more important than raising children or defending family interests. Individual's feelings and choices introduce demands in the marital bond. If these create the possibility of fulfilling relationships, on the one hand, they can also create tension that can lead to the breakdown of the bond on the other (Heilborn, 1992).

Changes in conjugal roles and ideals affected Brazilian society. However, these changes and resulting patterns vary by gender, class, race, ethnicity, and religion. In general, the changes have not resulted in men and women fulfilling the same gender roles.

Social and Cultural Differences About Marriage

One can see in statistical data that women can expect to spend a larger period of their lives out of conjugal arrangements, and that this period tends to be even broader for poor and black women (Goldani, 1994). In 1988, 56 percent of women over fifteen years of age had a marital or other partner, while 31 percent were single, 3 percent divorced, and 8 percent were widows. For people aged sixty to sixty-nine years, 17 percent of men and 45 percent of women lived alone. Today, life expectancy is higher for women (74.8) and men are older (three years on average) in most couples. Life expectancy for men is 67.0 (FLACSO, 1993; UNDP, 2006; United Nations, 2000).

Social differences can also be identified in the value of marriage. Among the poor, legal and religious marriage is considered morally superior, conferring respectability and legitimacy (Sarti, 1996). Nevertheless, due to its financial costs, legal marriage was never a common practice among the poor, until now. Although there is a low percentage of legal divorce, there is a high percentage of separation and remarriage—both from legal and informal marriages—including when men or women have children of their own. Single mothers, even those never married, might live with different partners during their lifetimes without exposure to social shame (Sarti, 1996).

In a country with many regional differences, it is not possible to analyze "the poor" or the "working class" as a homogenous group. Even so, research has pointed out two contradictory characteristics: marriage and family are highly valued among the poor at the same time that poverty has a destructive impact on the marital bond. In working-class families, authority is defined by men (husbands or another male relative) and is adult-centered (Sarti, 1996). Family can be understood as a "moral universe," wherein the identity of men is linked to the public sphere while the identity of women is related to the home. Familism rather than individualism is the main value for family life. The family defines a network of moral obligations whose ties are stronger than the marital bond. The breakage of the marital bond means a rupture with the family network. Others, such as Woortmann (1984), described the instability of the marital bond in the slums, but affirmed that in the so-called female-headed families, if a man joins in the role of "husband" he will become the "head" even if he is not the main provider. Nevertheless, if he does not manage to provide for the group, he will be excluded from it, sooner or later.

This contradiction suggests that poverty erodes the strength and quality of the marriage relationship by preventing men and women from fulfilling the most basic mutual expectations. In addition, it is hard to know if peoples' actions are based on values and beliefs, or on immediate survival. Considering that between one-quarter to one-third of Brazilian families live in poverty, one can imagine the impact of such a situation on the stability of conjugal bonds. Nevertheless, poverty is not the single reason for the changes in the strength or fragility of marital bonds. After the 1960s, individualism as a worldview expanded in Brazilian society, especially for the intellectual, urban, upper and middle classes (Figueira, 1987). The emphasis on individual freedom and rights strengthened the ideal of romantic love and individual choice in relationships. The traditional influence of religion upon sexual and affective life decreased and a greater flexibility in gender roles became accepted (Figueira, 1987; Nicolaci-da-Costa, 1985).

Different social agents began to question traditional marital dynamics. The feminist critique denounced marital hierarchy, domestic violence, and women's social and economic subordination. Feminist groups were an important influence on the legal reform of marriage that occurred with the new Constitution of 1988 (FLACSO, 1993). It is very possible that large sectors of the urban working class are incorporating these new values through schooling and with the presence of women in the labor market.

Since the 1980s, the Catholic Church has reviewed its interpretation of the marital bond. Maintaining the ideals of monogamy and indissolubility of marriage, the Church recognized sexual life as essential not only for procreation but also for the stability of the couple and the family. It forbade the use of contraceptives except for "natural" methods. It stressed the importance of responsible parenthood, refused the moral reference of individualism, and insisted on the importance of "the bond" in family/marital life (Nunes, 1994; Ribeiro & Ribeiro, 1994).

Nowadays, the marriage bond can be said to be surrounded by differences of gender, race, class, and the individualist perspective, as much as by ideals of equality and reciprocity. Data suggest that, as an institution, conjugality is now weaker and more precarious. As citizens, individuals can improve their autonomy and freedom. However, the expansion of rights and autonomy begs for new social and moral references to fulfill the functions of marriage and its importance for other family functions.

FAMILIES AND CHILDREN

Children under age fifteen compose 29 percent of the population; those who are fifteen to seventeen years of age comprise 6 percent (IBGE, 2002; UNDP, 2006). Projections indicate a decrease in the population aged birth to fourteen to where they will represent 26 percent of the population in 2010 and 23 percent in 2020 (IBGE, 2002). Two issues reflective of these data should be highlighted. First, the drop in the fertility rate since the 1960s indicates a shift in parenthood, and second, there was a shift in the children's place within families and society. In 1991, 68 percent of the female population believed that the ideal number of children was two or three (Goldani, 1994). This belief was associated with other ideals offering more possibilities to their children in terms of health, education, and consumer patterns.

There was also a widening in birth intervals, suggesting an increase in time dedicated to each child in its infancy and that women plan their offspring. At the same time there was an increase in pregnancies outside of marriage and a decrease in the average age of the mother at the birth of the first child. This suggests that changes in the timing and other aspects of motherhood were related to the changing status of women in family and society (Goldani, 1994). Both parenthood and childhood were experiencing change.

Family planning was declared a right in the 1988 Constitution, but the public health system is not organized to provide for the majority of people. There is no legal restriction on the production and sale of contraceptive devices and no medical control over their sale, and no laws about reproductive technology, such as artificial insemination. Currently, the contraceptive prevalence rate is 77 percent (UNDP, 2006). In the early 1990s, 34 percent of married women fifteen to forty-four years of age did not practice contraception, 27 percent were sterilized, 25 percent used contraceptive pills, and 14 percent used other methods. Among married women using contraception, 44 percent chose sterilization (4 percent of men) (Scavone, Brétin, & Thébaud-Mony, 1994).

Although defined as a crime, since 1942 abortion has been allowed in the cases of rape or if the mother's life is at risk (Genofre, 1995).

Around 15 percent of women between thirty and thirty-nine years of age who had been pregnant report having had an interruption of pregnancy; this does not differ by socioeconomic level. However, as abortion is forbidden, this number is likely even higher (Monteiro, 1994).

Value of Children

Children and youth are important to Brazilian families, which is organized around "raising the kids." Adult-centered authority was the prevalent model, inherited from the colonial past. However, new conceptions of social rights and psychological needs influence child rearing, with some differences among classes. The 1988 Constitution gave all children the rights to parental recognition, whether conceived or born outside or within their parent's marriage. Moreover, the concept of family widened to include "any of the parents and his or her descendants."

Health indicators include 6 percent of children being underweight and 10 percent of infants with low birth weight. The under-five mortality rate was thirty-six per 1,000 live births in 2001, compared with 135 in 1970. For the lowest 20 percent of the population the under-five mortality rate is ninety-nine, and thirty-three for the richest 20 percent. The infant mortality rate has improved, from ninety-five per 1,000 live births in 1970 to thirty-five in 2004. The maternal mortality ratio (per 100,000 live births during 1990-2004) remains high at 64 (reported; adjusted rate is 260) but has likely dropped over the past years (UNDP, 2001, 2003, 2006).

Child-Rearing Practices

Children are valued in working classes and parents invest their hopes and have expectations about their children's' gratitude. The adult-child relationship is within the family web of duties and obligations. It is supposed that when efficiently providing for their children, parents can choose the methods of raising them, including forms of punishment. Love is expressed by the fulfillment of basic needs and is not considered contradictory to physical punishment (Fonseca, 1995). In working-class black families, children are cared for and loved, but adults are not expected to play with them or to share in their activities. Parents think they must give to their children all they can. The mother-child bond is understood as stronger than that of the father-child bond (Pacheco, 1986).

The central role of mothers derives from a social bond according to which they provide the link to the internal relations of a family. In case of the absence of the mother, another woman, likely to be a relative, is in charge of the children and the home. There are few cases of single-father families in the working class, unless there is a child who can act as a substitute mother (Afonso & Filgueiras, 1996). Ethnographic work with lower classes shows that when the father keeps the children (i.e., divorce or separation), a female relative (such as the grandmother or an aunt) cares for the children's daily arrangements. Children are reabsorbed within their father's kinship organization, eventually at the expense of contact with their mother's. Indeed, the role of the extended family in the care of children is strong. Relatives are expected to help if parents are facing difficulties in performing their duties (Filgueiras, Afonso, Carvalho, & Ladeira, 1995; Fonseca, 1995).

Under the influence of psychology and pedagogy, middle and upper classes have developed a new model of the parent-child relationship. This model includes closer communication, more intimacy, and softer discipline. There is a new consciousness of children's needs and rights since the 1960s; children are now allowed to participate more in the decisions regarding themselves and their families. This consciousness also questions physical and moral punishment, largely used in former generations, and argues for more enlightened, responsible, and nonviolent methods for raising children (Moukachar, 1996).

In the middle and upper classes, the needs of children have been largely associated with patterns of consumerism (toys and clothes) as much as with the expansion of educational opportunities (e.g., preschooling, arts). In the lower classes, there has also been a search for educational opportunities, including preschool and child-care centers. While in the 1970s child care would be considered a "lesser evil," during the 1980s it became a "women's right," and from the 1990s as a right of the child and an option of the family. In 1996, a law established that children from birth to six have the right of free public education, a right that has not been fulfilled for the majority of the population.

For poor families, public day care means that children will be fed, cleaned, and stimulated in their social and cognitive development.

Data from Belo Horizonte (one of the larger cities in Brazil), for instance, show that the number of undernourished children lessened with the development of a network of public-supported child-care centers (Prefeitura, 2000). Malnutrition is an example of how the end of violence against children has to be linked to the lessening of social inequality, as it has many intertwined causes: family income, nutritional information, quality of child rearing in the family, health care access, and so on.

Children's Rights

The concern with the rights of children and adolescents, especially the poor, led to important social movements in the early 1980s, including the *Movimento Nacional de Meninos e Meninas de Rua* (National Movement of Street Boys and Girls) and the *Pastoral do Menor* (Child Ministry of the Catholic Church). In 1990, a new set of rules and principles published in Law 8069/90 (the Statute of Children and Adolescents' Rights) intended to guarantee civil rights and social protection to children and adolescents. Abandonment, exploitation, and violence have existed since colonial times—that they are now being considered a social problem is the novelty. Raising a child has become more than ever a "social issue." The National Movement of Street Boys and Girls and other movements denounced the violation of children's rights, child prostitution, domestic violence, and child labor. The defense of children and adolescents' rights required the redefinition of social policies toward childhood and families (Costa, 1990). During the 1990s, there was the implementation of the Committee on Children and Adolescent Rights in each city, linked to public local administration. The committees advise and orient families and can receive accusations of child abuse.

In spite of the decrease in family size, among the lower classes and black families there was an increase in family members entering the labor market to provide for the family. These workers include not only married women, but also children and teenagers (Goldani, 1994). Such contradiction expresses the ambiguous situation of children and adolescents. The struggle against child labor, for instance, has to include support for poor families as well as changes in cultural patterns. Social policies directed toward families are mostly intended to protect and guarantee child and adolescent rights and quality of life. However, contradictions arise. Contemporary laws established that youth under age sixteen cannot work. For many poor families it is difficult to obey the law either because of their low income or because they hold different beliefs on the issue. So, there is a paradox.

FAMILIES AND GENDER

The changing status of women in the labor market and in education not only has led to changes in the roles of wives and mothers but has also affected the status of daughters, grandmothers, and single-adult females. The control of family relations was part of the Colonial system. White women in rich families would marry during adolescence; if not, they could be considered too old for marriage, becoming a "single old aunt," and expected to help relatives with their children. In the nineteenth century, the permission to install convents in the colony (i.e., Brazil) introduced the choice of religious life. Women from the free-white-not-rich segments of the population would eventually help their families in commercial activities, sometimes heading business (Figueiredo, 1993; Hennon & Medina, 1993). Under the control of masters, slave women had little power. Nevertheless, in the culture of some African-Brazilian groups, women had an important role in family and religion. The nineteenth century saw the first claims in the defense of women's education and autonomy, through feminist newspapers.

During the twentieth century, women acquired a set of civil and social rights having a stamp on their family roles. By the mid-1900s, there was a shift in women's demands which included egalitarianism in the labor market, education, and political participation; access to child care; availability of public services; access to birth control; and the reform of family laws. By 2000, women had almost the same access to higher education as men.

The rate of economic activity (i.e., employed or available to provide economic activity) for women was 47 percent in 1992, 49 percent in 1999, and 56 percent in 2004 (IBGE, 2001; UNDP, 2006). In the formal labor market, pregnant women have the right to job stability and can apply for a maximum of 120 days of leave of absence, receiving full payment. In the case of abortion, the woman can request a fifteen-day leave of absence. Companies that employ more than thirty women over sixteen years old are required to facilitate proper child care until children are six months old. During the nursing period, the mother can demand two one-half hour intervals, during her day's work, to breastfeed her child. However, the gap between law and reality is large, especially among the poor and in rural areas.

Black women have the worst labor market conditions. Women have mostly been active in the informal economy, without legal registration and earning much less than men doing the same job (Abreu, Jorge, & Sorj, 1994; Bruschini, 1994; IBGE, 2002). Although women have increased their participation in the labor market, and the percentage of single-parent families has grown, men are considered the main providers for their families. Employed wives are considered "second providers" and their professional life should be adapted to family needs. Employed wives should be hierarchically submissive to their husbands' careers (Coelho, 1996).

The 1988 Constitution declares equal rights for men and women. Legally, both spouses are "heads" in their family. However, there exists a hierarchical structure in which male roles are related to the public world and rule over female roles that are defined within private life, even when women are employed. Research demonstrates that this is especially so in the lower classes. House chores are largely a female duty. The association of women with the home is a value deeply rooted in Brazilian culture, pointing to the importance of the mother in the organization of the family group and daily life (Sarti, 1996). In spite of the rhetoric about the defense of women's citizenship, policies are still formulated as if women were full-time mothers and housewives. Women are expected to be in charge not only of the children during out of school periods but also of the elderly and of the sick (Afonso & Filgueiras, 1996).

Research on middle-class couples also emphasizes that domestic organization is largely a duty of wives. While women verbalize the value of equality, their practices are linked to a traditional family organization (Coelho, 1996). The increasing equalization in the access to education might lead to the lessening of differences in the socialization of sons and daughters. However, domestic chores and acceptable patterns of sexual behavior remain linked to traditional views (Filgueiras et al., 1995). While there is some degree of flexibility, gender stereotypes in

children's socialization persist. During adolescence, gender stereotypes become stronger, acting upon their sexual and affective life and
influencing their aspirations (Afonso, 1995, 2001; Filgueiras et al.,
1995; Stengel, 2003).

Double Sexual Standard

The double sexual standard is an important reference in large segments of society, giving greater tolerance to male sexuality in and out
of marital arrangements (Coelho, 1996). The "culture of ambivalence"
values and censures female sexuality (Parker, 1991). Feminine sen-
suality is praised in the media, in fashion, and in many celebrations
such as Carnival, but the cultural patterns are restrictive about women's
autonomy over sexuality and reproductive life. It is generally believed
that men have more sexual needs and less control of them, while women
who express a deeper knowledge of, and autonomy over, their own
sexuality and reproductive life can be viewed as dangerous or as
prostitutes.

The double morality is seen in the difficulty of women to negotiate
about the choice of contraceptive methods and the use of the condom
as a protection against sexually transmitted disease. It is no wonder
that Brazil figures among the top three countries in the world in terms
of the number of AIDS cases. The rate of infection was 5.4 for 100,000
inhabitants in 2001. Although the majority of infected are men (66
percent), rates have been growing among married women and those
with low education (Barbosa & Villela, 1996; Campos, 1996; IBGE,
2002; Santos & Munhoz, 1996). Approximately 220,000 women aged
fifteen to forty-nine are living with HIV/AIDS, and 13,000 children
(UNDP, 2003).

Changes in Gender Roles

The new generation expresses some timid changes in views of
gender relations. For example, in Belo Horizonte, 79 percent of high
school students support equal sexual rights for men and women.
However, 63 percent believe that sexual needs are different for males
and females so that the defense of equal rights is modified by the
belief in "different needs." Under the disguise of a liberal discourse, the
double standard is reproduced. All the same, 35 percent of teenagers

believe that men should be the main family providers and 47 percent maintain that women are responsible for household chores. The majority thus believes that men are not necessarily the main providers and women should not necessarily be the housekeepers. Women and individuals from the upper and middle classes hold more egalitarian values. For instance, female premarital virginity is important for 57 percent of women and 63 percent of men in the lower class, and 19 percent of women and 23 percent of men in the upper class (Afonso, 2001).

Male roles in families have also been the subject of discussion by intellectualized upper and middle classes. The media reflects signs of these new concerns, especially when parental roles are affected. Fathers are encouraged to be emotionally and directly involved in their children's daily life.

Since the 1960s, women have enlarged their social and political participation. These changes are more often expressed in more developed regions, large urban centers, and more privileged social groups. Indeed, inequality among women of the various social classes has increased, in spite of similar claims for social and civil rights. One may ask whether inequality would eventually provoke different demands or whether the similarity of demands would challenge inequality. This tension can be better understood as families become the focus of social policies with the basis on equal rights for their members.

FAMILIES AND STRESS

The modernization of the Brazilian family as an institution has had a different impact on various groups, especially because economic development has been deeply based on social inequality. Lower-class families seem to have suffered with the weakening of the traditional family web of obligations that provided support for the individuals in daily life. Three major problems have been identified among the poor: children who live or work on the streets, the institutionalization of children and the elderly, and violence—both the impact of social violence on family life and domestic violence (Vicente, 1994). Violence is also a stressor related to the rapid changes in family values, especially those related to parental authority and gender roles.

Poverty and Social Exclusion

Poverty and social exclusion are major stress factors. Especially in families below the poverty line, the struggle for survival modifies affection and authority. In poor families, to whom birth control is far from being a reality, parents cannot provide basic care for their children. Unemployment also generates an environment of instability. The family has difficulty establishing relations with other social institutions in order to guarantee health care, housing, schooling, and a family routine for their children. The social basis for parents' authority within the family is eroded and adults can find difficulty performing their family roles. Consequently, family relationships can become unstable.

A significant number of children are forced into the labor market even below the age of fourteen years, sometimes leaving their family and sometimes becoming the main family providers. There are children who live in the streets and children who just work in the streets. In São Paulo, 47 percent of the children that are "on the streets" attend school, 62 percent go home at least once a week, and 49 percent sleep at home every night (Lozano, 1997). The majority of the children in the streets are black and *"pardo."* The new policies, initiated after the Statute of Children and Adolescents' Rights, include programs of family support to take children off the street and reinsert them in schooling. Those who do not have a family are to be cared for in social institutions and eventually adopted. Most of these programs are developed by a joint effort of counties, states, and the federal government. In 2003, the government initiated the "Family Income" policy aiming to reach 11.4 million families at the end of 2006. Three premises were embedded in the program: families will receive a minimum income (as a provisory financial help), there should be complementary programs of family development and income generation, and there should be access to universal citizenship rights such as health and education (Cohn & Fonseca, 2004). Nowadays the program is implemented in the majority of the intended areas but presents two main problems: the control of resources and the definition of goals and methods to promote "family development" and orientation in such a large program.

With the growing violence of drug dealers in Brazil, especially in the slums, poor families are at risk because children are easily co-opted by the promises of money and their homes are located in the territory of violent conflicts. Sometimes it is hard for social workers to make contacts with families in the poorest areas due to the risk involved. Public policies have to face the new problem in order to reach and mobilize families.

Domestic Violence

Three factors assist in the analysis of domestic violence in Brazil: (1) if poverty is not sufficient, necessary, or the single cause of violence, it certainly can help the deterioration of family ties; (2) social violence has increased in the last two decades and there is no reason to suppose that it would lessen in the private spheres of life; (3) social movements in defense of women and child rights have been mobilizing public opinion or helping to formulate laws and programs against domestic violence. In Brazil, family violence intertwines with social violence and inequality, and relates to the change between traditionalist and modernizing worldviews that establish the framework for the organization of family life. This is true for the perception and conceptions of violence and for the chosen ways for fighting it—thus the struggle against domestic violence is not limited to legal action but includes educational and cultural action.

The influence of psychology and pedagogy has contributed to a new consciousness in the upper and middle classes on the issue of violence against children at home. In the lower classes, the realization of children's rights is in the struggle for basic rights: food, health, education, and housing, the lack of which is a form of violence in what is a very unequal society. The presence of children in the labor market, in harsh conditions, is a huge problem in Brazil. It is not enough to blame parents, because poverty overburdens the family, especially in periods of high unemployment. In 2001, in 17 percent of the families with children and adolescents there was at least one child or adolescent in the labor market. As the law forbids child labor until the age of sixteen, these individuals are in the informal market. Occupations vary, for example, from helping parents in family businesses to washing cars in the streets, and to digging mines in harsh conditions (IBGE, 2002).

When a denouncement is made, there are legal consequences for employers and the family through a legal system constructed to protect children and adolescents. However, poverty continually generates transgression of the law. The surpassing of exploitation and child labor demands that policies grant a "minimum income" to families, prevent children from quitting school, and offer activities to stimulate their psychosocial development.

Consciousness of physical and sexual abuse of children is just beginning. In the 1990s, the media, educators, and nongovernmental organizations became involved in constructing a deeper social understanding of the problem. Although abuse can provoke indignation, a large number of families believe that spanking and even beating is not child abuse. Research with lower-class teenagers shows that 47 percent consider physical punishment as a normal method for parents and 33 percent accept that adolescents can also be physically punished (Assis, 1994). Methods of child rearing in Brazil thus include corporal punishment as normal. The line between discipline and abuse is never defined due to the cultural belief that parents would not cause real harm to their children. Abuse is usually considered only if the child suffers physical injury (Filgueiras et al., 1995). Sexual abuse and incest are involved in a "culture of silence" that denies their existence (Filgueiras et al., 1995; Grossi, 1994). While rape is considered a revolting crime, other forms of sexual abuse are rarely perceived and identified.

Law 8069/90 (the Statute of Children and Adolescents' Rights) defined and outlawed many types of physical and sexual violence (Costa, 1990). The women's movement tried to propose changes in the Criminal Law aiming, for instance, at creating the legal term of "sexual abuse" and to expand the concept of rape to include oral and anal sex. Sexual and physical violence between partners should not be treated as belonging to the privacy of the couple. As women overcame barriers to social rights, family violence gained visibility and began to be denounced. After 1978, the women's movement started a campaign against domestic violence. Police stations specializing in crimes against women were created in many cities. Among reported acts of aggression against women, husbands, male relatives, or acquaintances commit 65 percent of such acts in the women's homes. In spite of Brazil being a signatory of the UN 1979 Convention on the Elimination of All

Forms of Discrimination Against Women, criminal law still labels rape and sexual abuse as "crimes against social customs." For several years, without a decision, Congress has discussed labeling these crimes as "crimes against persons" (Pimentel & Pierro, 1993).

FAMILIES AND AGING

Elderly people comprise 9 percent of the population; 13 percent of these elderly are living alone, 25 percent as a couple without children, and 62 percent with their families. Sixty-five percent of the elderly are considered to be the heads of their families even when not the main provider. This is consistent with the values of Brazilian society (IBGE, 2002).

The 1988 Constitution establishes the right of elders to be supported by family, society, and State. Adult children can be legally requested to provide food, housing, and health care for their aged or ill parents. Once more, there is a gap between law and reality and the care of the elders becomes an important issue in a country where the population over age sixty grows at twice the rate of the total population (Debert, 1994). In this context, the "aged" have become important political actors, demanding rights and care from the State and society. Such importance is reflected in the promulgation of the "Statute of Elders" (Law 3561) in 1997.

In 2001, 13 percent of elders lived in families with a per capita income lower than US$40 per month. At the age of sixty to sixty-nine, 50 percent were retired but among those, 73 percent remained in the labor market. At the age of seventy to seventy-nine, 36 percent were retired but among those "retired," 31 percent kept working (IBGE, 2002). The majority of the retired receive a pension from the State after having paid a contribution to the social security system for thirty or more years. The Associations of Retired People have gained political visibility since the 1980s. They mobilized and demanded from the State an increase in their pensions to be equivalent to the wages of the workers in the same professional category that they once held (Debert, 1994).

For the following decades, a growing number of Brazilian families will have to face the challenge of taking care of their elders. As the family structures change, caring for the elderly becomes a crucial problem and new demands for more and better public services will probably emerge. The elders of tomorrow will probably exercise different values about individual independence and family ties. Indeed, many newspapers and magazines picture elders as independent, healthy, and active persons. Old age (or the third age) is presented as a privileged period for personal satisfaction and accomplishments. Brazil might be in a process of changing the social representation of the third age (Debert, 1994). Side by side with traditional values, it is possible to find different styles of living in later life. In the urban higher and middle classes, the elderly who had always been economically independent might seek independence in daily life from their families. However, most people reinforce ties with families when old (Barros, 1987).

According to tradition, families would consider it their duty to take care of their aged members. The number of public and private nursing homes has grown, receiving people from all socioeconomic levels. The care of the elderly, especially if they have special needs or a health condition, is difficult due to the financial expense, time, housing conditions, and health assistance required. The growing participation of women in the labor market, without significant changes in their household chores, prevents them from holding more responsibilities such as the care of the elders, as they would do some decades ago. Among the poor, there are more elderly people living in the streets, without public or family protection (Villaméa & Quintanilha, 1997). In 1994, the federal government created the "Continued Benefit Program," a social policy for elderly in households with per capita income under US$20 per month. The benefit (US$90, the same as a minimum wage of 260 reais) is given for lifetime to those older than sixty-five living in poverty. (Minimum wage was 300 reais and should rise to 350 in May 2006).

Grandparents

The relationship of grandparents with their grandchildren is a special one in Brazilian families. The network of grandparents includes the frequent contact not only with their children and grandchildren, but also friends (Barros, 1987).

The grandparents' home is an important space for the family to be together. Grandparents help raise their grandchildren and offer financial support for their children. In this way, they restore a model for family living that has become menaced by the independence of the second generation. The birth of a first grandchild starts a new period in life. In addition, grandparents act as socializing agents for their children's new motherhood/fatherhood. The relationship with sons-in-law and daughters-in-law can be viewed "as they were children," but is usually marked with some distance that reaffirms the difference between the linkages of consanguinity and of affinity (Barros, 1987). Grandparents exercise authority in an indirect way. There is a renewed closeness between grandmothers and their daughters as they become mothers. This closeness renews the female network of family care. However, conflicts can be generated when the daughters have professional projects that grandmothers might not support (Barros, 1987). In the middle and upper classes, recent changes in families have provoked conflicts among generations over values and practices (e.g., child rearing, gender roles, divorce) that can create adjustment problems for the elderly (Barros, 1987; Nicolaci-da-Costa, 1985).

Gender Differences

Some gender differences in the aging experience can be highlighted. In 2004, life expectancy at birth for females was 74.8 and for males was 67. 0 years (UNDP, 2006). Among those who are living alone, 51 percent are women. Among those women, 72 percent are aged fifty or older. Among men living alone, 49 percent are between twenty-five and forty-nine years of age (IBGE, 2002). Having had an important role in sustaining family ties throughout their lives, older women are probably more adjusted in their family network. However, as they get older, they face more difficulties in finding a male partner. Men, having always been more involved in the labor market, might suffer adjustment problems when they retire. Research reveals the loneliness of older men, especially in lower classes, some of whom have a history of family ruptures (Boff, 1995). As the main family bond in the working class is that between mother and child, fathers can become distant from their children if the link between mother and father is broken.

OTHER FAMILY SITUATIONS

This chapter intends to help the reader comprehend the main characteristics and tendencies of change in Brazilian families. Diversity is thus as important as the identified cultural norms and "typical" patterns. To consider situations others than those already presented is to reflect on those singularities that could point to social change in defined terrain, such as those of gender, ethnicity, or social class.

Gender

In the terrain of gender relations, Brazilian families are not only showing more flexibility about gender roles but are also opening to new situations. It is possible to see this in the slow but consistent change in the joint-custody or custody of children by fathers in divorced couples. Despite the legal assertion of egalitarianism, child custody was requested by and given to mothers in 85 percent of the cases after divorce in the 1990s. In addition, joint custody represented only 4 percent of legal custody in the country. In spite of the idea that little children need to stay with their mothers, equality can be the reference in court decisions (Petrucelli, 1994). A small number of single-parent, male-headed families can be seen, especially in the big cities.

It is also worth noting that there is a project to be voted on by Congress, according to which homosexual marital contracts can be legally recognized under the name of "civil partnership." It allows, among others, some rights to the partners as a couple: health insurance, the right to gain the Brazilian citizenship of the partner, social security benefits, and the right to inherit common patrimony in the case of the death of one member. The project does not allow the couple to adopt children, but each partner maintains his or her right to adopting as an individual. It is hard to say how Congress is going to vote.

Ethnicity

In the terrain of ethnicity, the social mobility of blacks and *"pardos"* families to upper and middle classes generates new conflicts and answers. Black families complain about discrimination of their children in school and other social environments (Cavalleiro, 2000). However, it is rare to approach the issue of prejudice—or the resistance against it—during their daily life or in the socialization of their children. Silence is the answer. A changing pattern would be the construction of new values and practices in order to identify racism and demand non-discriminatory treatment of children at school.

Studying black families in a poor community in Niterói (in the State of Rio de Janeiro), Pacheco (1986) emphasized that interracial marriages are frequent. However, there is also an "ideology of whiteness," according to which it is good for a family to become more and more "white" through interracial marriages. A change could be to continue the flexibility toward interracial marriages while a new value of plurality emerges against the ideology of whiteness.

In families with interracial marriages, mothers and fathers have defined roles: fathers are providers and mothers are caretakers, even when employed. However, both have equal authority in the group. The relationship between mothers and children is stronger than that of father-children, and the oldest brother is an authority for his siblings, eventually substituting for the father figure. Among those families studied, Pacheco (1986) did not find grandmothers who were in charge of raising their grandchildren.

Social Class

In the terrain of social class, research on working-class families shows alternative practices for the care of the children (Fonseca, 1995). As lower-class families are subject to many sources of instability, the values and practices of raising children must be adaptable. The practice of "child circulation" in which a child is "given" by his or her mother or father to a relative (for a short or an intermittent period, years, or for good), is one such adaptation. In the majority of these cases, the child stays inside the larger family and maintains a relationship with his or her parents that includes filial love and gratitude. This practice can be qualified as "fosterage" and not as abandoning or adoption. Mostly, fosterage is due to financial or housing difficulties, especially among single mothers. However, fosterage can also occur with separation or remarriage. A child could live with a relative to have better conditions for studying or working (Filgueiras et al., 1995).

There can be three types of relationship to substitute families: (1) the *guarda* (care) that is given to a family while the petitioners are waiting for a court decision about tutelage, adoption, or in cases of suspension of parental rights; (2) the tutelage that implies the duty of caring for the child and administering his or her properties; and (3) adoption that recognizes the status of parents and children, with all its consequences.

Fosterage creates a double link of moral obligations between the biological and the fostering parents, because the child represents not only a duty but also a "gift." This reveals elasticity in the conceptions of mother and father, which are the terms that the child can call both her or his biological and "foster" parents, both of them deserving gratitude. However, the child might also call the foster parents by their first names, or by their relatedness (uncle, grandparent, and so on), and consider them as "second parents." In these situations children perceive the existence of one "blood bond" and one "upbringing bond," each one creating a special type of attachment (Fonseca, 1995). However, there is a lack of quantitative data about fosterage in Brazil.

CONCLUDING COMMENTS

Brazil has undergone a modernization process with an impact on families. There has been the emergence of new social facts, such as the increase in divorce rate. Other phenomena, linked to poverty throughout Brazilian history such as the exploitation of child labor, remain a problem. The big shift is the creation of laws to protect the rights of women, children, and elders. The process of family change can be seen as a crisis involving a clash of hierarchical views and those emerging values based on the ideal of equality and citizenship. It has been questioned whether and how families could maintain, reinforce, or even acquire their protective functions toward their dependent members.

Changes in families have been experienced differently by social groups. Mutual support has been weakened in lower classes. Individualism has been strengthened in the middle class. The association between individuality and citizenship has brought about new tensions. Families are to reshape their patterns and values regarding authority, care, gender relations, and so forth. However, especially among the poor, these changes require public support and the redefinition of responsibilities among families, the State, and society (Acosta & Vitale, 2003; Cohn & Fonseca, 2004; Fonseca, 2002; Sarti, 1995, 1996; Vitale, 1995).

In 2004, the Social Welfare System was reformed to propose a family-centered orientation in the provision of services and in the socio-educative methods to prevent social risk, to promote autonomy, and to reinforce the care and the rights of children, adolescents, elders, and people with disabilities. The new policy supports social participation, through organized councils with citizen's participation to control social policies. However, this has to include advancement in the identification of the vulnerabilities, risks, and strengths of families, and the ways in which they can be effectively helped within a perspective of respect for multicultural values (Ministério Do Desenvolvimento Social E Combate À Fome, 2004). The biggest difference in this new policy is its alignment to the defense of social and human rights. Will it be transformed into consistent practices? Will it contribute to lessen poverty, social exclusion, and violence? Or will it just expand the State's control over society?

Brazilian families have experienced modernization partly as an achievement and partly as a crisis. It is important to develop social policies not only to protect individuals' rights but also to defend their family and social bonds. In this way, families can become strengthened and help to promote a more democratic society.

NOTE

1. The hierarchical view includes traditional ideas such as those present in double sexual standards for males and females, rejection of contraceptive practices, reinforcement of parental authority, and rejection of the existence of varied family arrangements as "families." Egalitarian views are marked by the defense of equality between women and men, of children's rights, of reproductive rights, of the lessening of religious influence over sexual and reproductive life, flexibility in laws about divorce, and so on. Egalitarian views are linked to progressive social movements, but could also be present in progressive, dissenting segments of the Church and of governmental and nongovernmental organizations.

Chapter 17

Mexican Families:
Sociocultural and Demographic Patterns

Rosario Esteinou

The United Mexican States (thirty-one states plus the federal district) is a republic of about 105 million people bordering the Caribbean Sea, the Gulf of Mexico, and Pacific Ocean between Guatemala, Belize, and the United States. The annual population growth rate is 2 percent and 76 percent of the population is urban. Mexico has a free market economy of modern and outmoded industry and agriculture. An economic recovery has been in progress. Since the implementation of NAFTA in 1994, and recent free trade agreements with other nations appear promising, trade with Canada and the United States has tripled. There are concerns including low wages, underemployment, and poverty, and restricted opportunities for the Amerindian population living in the impoverished southern states. About 13 percent is arable land. About 90 percent of the population is Roman Catholic, 6 percent is Protestant, and the rest is "other." Spanish is the main language, with a few people speaking various Mayan, Nahuatl, or other regional indigenous languages (World Factbook, 2006).

To understand the family patterns that have been developing in Mexican society, one must consider the evolution of kinship and family arrangements. For example, Mexican society has always had a sizable indigenous population and kinship has played a central role in social organization. Likewise, the nuclear family in Mexico differs in

---

This chapter is dedicated to the memory of my mother, Sara.

many ways from the Western model (Instituto Nacional de Estadística, Geografía e Informática [INEGI], 2004).

Before the Spaniards conquered Mexico in the sixteenth century, the main pattern was extended and joint families. In the central region, families were larger and composed of the nucleus and relatives, or by more than one nucleus. The kinship network's role was so important that families tended to live in the same *"patio"* (different related domestic groups living next to each other and sharing a common space). The term family did not exist, and instead *cemihualtin,* which means those who live in the same *patio,* was used. The concept of family, as used today, was unknown. Family was defined in terms of coresidence and economic cooperation rather than relationships of love, freedom, and emotions (Carrasco, 1993; McCaa, 1996). Authoritarianism and respect for adults, parent arranged marriages, and patrilocal residence prevailed, as did economic, social, and political functions regarding the *calpulli,* a social, economic, and political unit.

During the Spaniard's rule (sixteenth to eighteenth centuries), family among indigenous people followed a process of nuclearization while among Spaniards the extended family was more frequent. Different ethnic and social groups followed different paths. One effect of the conquest was the disorganization of previous patterns, the resilience of others, the combination of existing norms with those brought by the Spaniards, and the gradual introduction of the later. Diversity was characteristic. The Church molded behavior, playing a crucial role in introducing some new traits, mainly among Spaniards and *Mestizo* (Spanish and indigenous blend), and to a lesser degree among indigenous people. The Church promoted personal freedom in mate selection and established the "promise to marry." Such promising by men was considered to be "engagements" and considered as a binding social contract. When a man gave his word to marry one woman this meant they could then have sexual intercourse without any sanction, since it was assumed he would fulfill his promise. The "promise to marry" was then a way to validate unions. However, this practice encouraged seduction, kidnapping of the bride, eloping, concubinage, and other illegal unions (Lavrín, 1991). Gradually, the Church's ruling over marriage had an impact among the Spaniard and *Mestizo* populations (Carrasco, 1975). Freedom of choice concerning one's partner infringed on how family and community intervened in the process.

A result was a reduction of kinship and community bonds in family formation and the development of more restricted family groups with more autonomy. Consequently, greater individualization (partner freedom of choice) and a family nucleus regarding the kinship network developed.

Catholic marriage did not eradicate native customs. Catholic marriage spread, but only superficially. As monogamist unions were common, the regularization of unions through the Catholic ritual did not mean the abandonment of their practices. Consequently, although married by the Church, indigenous people did not wholly embrace Catholicism. To this day in rural communities, a traditional family behavior prevails in which paternal authority rules, families intervene in partner selection, the mediation of matchmakers is common, and kinship loyalties are respected (Gonzalbo, 1998). Patrilocality also persists.

Couple and parent-child relationships were vertical during the colonial period. Women were subordinated legally and socially to their fathers and partners. By law, male spouses protected their partners but could also discipline and punish. Parent-child relationships were strict, respect for adults was the rule, and children, as such, did not have a central role in the family. The idea of children as people needing care and nurturance was lacking. At twelve years of age females were considered to be adults; males were considered adult at fourteen years of age when they could marry.

During the nineteenth century, secularization developed and influenced family formation and development. A transition from a Christian morale to a more secular one influenced family relations. The "promise to marry" was abolished and marriage was conceived as a civil contract with freedom of choice. Marriage, as the new base of family relationships, was to be ruled over by the State, not the Church (Ramos, in press). Increasingly marriage stressed individualism and the civil nature of marriage. Family relationships followed a Catholic conception of marriage.

These trends encouraged family relationships that matched the depiction of the Western nuclear family. By 1900, one can observe family relations similar to the nuclear family with father, mother, and child. Sexuality and marriage became more central as individuals saw themselves being freed from dependencies on family-of-origin and community due to freedom of partner choice. The couple concentrated on the welfare of the family nucleus. Romance and domesticity emerged as women's roles as the mother-housewife-woman developed. The domestic sphere, free of economic interests and influence of the family-of-origin and the community, also emerged.

Family patterns followed these trends during the twentieth century. Nevertheless, Catholic and communitarian conceptions still strongly influenced this nuclear type of family, so individualism was limited. Communitarism found a way to persist among indigenous people as well as in *Mestizo* and Spanish groups, and Mexicans tended to be strongly oriented toward the family. This prototype of nuclear family spread from 1930 until 1970. The family was the father, mother, and children; the couple tended to marry by both church and State; a strict division of labor prevailed with women generally not working outside the home; and a strong Catholic adherence marked most individual and family behavior.

Family in Mexican Context

Particularly in the past three decades, Mexican society has experienced important changes that have influenced families. These include economic crisis and change in the structure of labor markets, demographic shifts, and an accelerated openness to modernization and globalization. From an economic perspective, abundant literature has documented the strategies developed by households and families for managing their resources in order to maintain their standard of living during difficult socioeconomic conditions, when facing changes in the labor market and deteriorating income (Cortés, 1995; Cortés & Rubalcava, 1995; Molina & Sánchez, 1999).

One strategy has been the maximization of the family labor force as well as additional economic activity or longer working hours for the head of the household. This has resulted in more family members (especially women) entering the labor market. The presence of women in the labor market is significant. In 1940, the figure was 8 percent, in 1993 the figure fluctuated between 24 and 41 percent in different states, and projections for the year 2010 are 28 to 45 percent (Consejo Nacional de Población [CONAPO], 1998).

This pattern is important as it is not only the single, widowed, separated, and divorced women, entering the labor force, but also mothers-housewives. Within this latter group, those with small children, who previously were a very small proportion of the economically active population, have increased considerably in the last decades (García & De Oliveira, 1994). The growth of married women in the workforce has increased so fast that by 1995 it reached almost 30 percent; and of divorced and separated women it was 69 and 74 percent, respectively (López, 1998). A relevant consequence is that family roles are changing and new family forms, such as dual-earner and dual-career, are evident in greater proportions. These new forms, although often having a nuclear structure, imply different forms of organization and values.

Other demographic tendencies have influenced families. There has been a surprising decrease of the Total Fertility Rate (TFR). The TFR, the expected number of children born to women in their lifetime, reduced by more than half between 1974 and 1999 from 6.11 to 2.4 where it remains today, implying women have greater freedom and control over their lives as they spend less time rearing children and more time to developing other activities (CONAPO, 1999; Gómez de León, 1998; United Nations Development Programme [UNDP], 2006). There has also been a decrease in mortality rates due to changes in health policies (despite the remaining maternal mortality due to unsafe abortions; Population Council, 2006). One important result is the rise in life expectancy. While in 1930 this was thirty-five years for men and thirty-seven for women; today it is 72.8 and 77.8 (UNDP, 2006). This increase has had important consequences when combined with sociocultural changes, as it leads to changes in the way that individuals and families live out, share, and understand their lives. A third demographic tendency is changes in marriage and dissolution patterns, discussed below under the section Couple Formation and Marital Dynamics.

A series of changes in the sociocultural area has been having a great influence on the family institution. In the last decades, Mexico has experienced a process of modernization on the economic as well as the sociocultural levels. The country is considered to have a high level of human development, ranking fifty-three of 177 nations (UNDP, 2006). As in other Western countries and in an increasingly globalized world, Mexico has been the object of a greater differentiation and multiplication of coexisting sociocultural subsystems. However, these processes are less widely extended and not as deep as in Western industrialized societies.

A national survey revealed that along with old native cultural codes there is the development of values associated with market economy, formal democracy, and individualism (Beltrán, Castaños, Flores, Meyenberg, & del Pozo, 1996). Nevertheless, the expansion of such diverse values has been somewhat limited for individual options and different lifestyles given communitarian or "collectivistic" value orientation. People hold value orientations such as tolerance, respect for differences, and planning of life. These coexist with deep-rooted conceptions about nepotism as a way of social mobility, sexuality, and gender roles associated with biological nature, and the family as a group that dominates individual life, even at the cost of individuality. The impact is heterogeneous among regions, social classes, and ethnic groups. Mexicans are now more exposed to a plurality of cultural codes and patterns.

These codes and patterns have an impact on identity by differentiating it, and this process can generate tensions (Esteinou, 1999a). For example, an employed housewife can experience tension when she tries to reconcile "home" values (of devotion and sacrifice for the family) with values enhancing individualism and gender equality in the work world. Even so, with resistance, conflicts, and tension, women's work outside the family is beginning to be valued positively rather than negatively as it was in the past (Beltrán et al., 1996; Esteinou, 1996).

Family planning programs implemented by population and health policies have also promoted cultural changes in the family. Specifically, population policies have favored a "demographic culture" about issues such as birth control and family planning, and making the population aware of their advantages. Campaigns such as "the small family lives better" and "fewer children to give them more" have clearly induced rationalization and individualization processes, modifying the weight of meta-individual (i.e., family, community, and social environment) and meta-family (i.e., Catholicism) themes (CONAPO, 1998). Men and women understand that they have more control over their lives. Couples, for example, can plan the number and the spacing of births and women can involve themselves in the labor market or other activities due to having greater individual freedom.

The lengthening of life expectancy has increased the individual's and the family's view of the future and perhaps places new burdens on marriage. The number of years that a couple can live together has risen, and families and individuals are exposed to different patterns and conceptions about what the couple, the family, sexual life, and child rearing should be. Tensions, uncertainty, and anxiety often result. More couple dissolutions will likely occur in the future.

The nuclear family is the dominant family form, but in recent decades this form has diminished because of important changes in economic, demographic, and sociocultural trends. For example, in 1990 around 75 percent of households were nuclear families while in 2000, 69 percent were nuclear families. The decrease of the nuclear family accompanies an increase of the extended and one-person households. In 1990, 24 percent of households were extended families, while in 2000, 31 percent were extended; one-person households registered one percent in 1990 and 1.5 percent in 2000 (INEGI, 2003a). The economic crisis and the deterioration of family income have influenced the increase of extended families because gathering more economically active family members under one roof becomes a strategy to overcome economic difficulties.

COUPLE FORMATION AND MARITAL DYNAMICS

The majority of Mexicans follow a pattern of free choice in choosing their partner and marriage is the main path for forming a family. The way in which marriage is established differs from that in the past. In 1930, the State established that all religious marriages had to be legally established first as a civil contract registered by the State, successfully imposing a secular pattern of marriage along with the religious one. In 1930 only 48 percent of persons validated their marriage by the State, while in 1990 the percentage was 82. Currently, the majority of Mexicans marry under both secular and religious systems. The secularization of marriages contributed to institutionalizing consensual unions (Quilodrán, 1996).

Mexico has not reached the second demographic transition characterized by a decrease in the marriage rate and an increase in divorce rates and consensual unions (cohabitation), but here are changes pointing toward this tendency. Between 1976 and 1995 there was a continuing trend of lower marriage rates, a rise in the numbers of consensual unions and divorce, and an increase in the median age at the first union (from 19.5 to 24 years) (Gómez de León, 2001). In 1995, the mean age for women for the first union (married or cohabitation) was 22.9 years and 25.1 for men. The age differential of the partners at the first union has been reduced, meaning that relationships that are more equal are being established (Quilodrán, 1996, 2001; Samuel, 1996).

Consensual unions have increased. These unions have roots from the precolonial period and have persisted within the socially accepted forms of couple formation. In 1982, consensual unions constituted 17 percent of unions, while in 1996 they reached 27 percent and are more frequent among younger than older people (CONAPO, 1999). There are two patterns. In one, cohabitation is an alternative to legal and religious marriage. This is a more traditional tendency and it is more frequent among those with lower educational attainment. In the second pattern, cohabitation is a modern prelude to marriage (Gómez de León, 2001; Quilodrán, 2001). Various factors influence the marriage rate. Within cohabiting relationships, the woman becoming pregnant favors a rate of marriage four times higher than if a woman is not pregnant. However, in rural areas, there is no greater stigma on having children out of wedlock.

Women with more education have a lower marriage rate and a tendency to marry at a later age, but when they cohabit they tend to eventually marry; women with less education, tend to maintain the consensual union (Gómez de León, 2001).

Historically parents and other family members arranged marriages in most rural families. This behavioral norm implied the transfer of a woman from her home to the bridegroom's home. By 1930, arranged marriages were disappearing and freedom of choice started to dominate, though in a limited way. Women could only approve of the marriage in a "formal" manner and in reality had to accept their parents' decisions. The ritual of "asking for the hand of the bride" emphasized freedom of choice, but the options were limited and parents had influence. The woman could only choose among the candidates who "asked for her hand" and the possibilities of meeting and getting to know each other were limited. Under strict surveillance, fleeting and secret encounters were the main way of meeting before the union. Virginity was so valued that when women reached puberty their movements were controlled in order to avoid contact with men. Daughters left home only through a "good marriage." Religious marriage was important in that it was legitimated before God and the community. Parent's enhanced surveillance after the "asking for the hand of the bride" was settled. The bride was taken to her future in-laws' house to make *tortillas* as a way to prepare her for the marriage. The bridegroom had to spend some time serving his future father-in-law by helping in the fields. The bridegroom's parents gave presents to the bride's parents. This, and the bridegroom's work, was symbolic compensation for the parent's loss of their daughter's help with family matters (González, 1996; Robichaux, 2003).

This pattern has been changing since 1980. Now, girlfriends and boyfriends appear in public, and a period of courtship is accepted, giving more freedom of choice. The expenses of the religious wedding can be high so there is a tendency to omit this and have the union established through "stealing the bride." This is typical in rural areas where cohabitation is common. There are two types of stealing the bride. The boy and his relatives, without the consent of the bride, carry out the first type. This was frequent in the past but now rare. The second type is where the boy and girl elope and she goes to live at her parents-in-law's home. After the relationship has been consummated, the bridegroom's parents tell the bride's parents that she is with them and they can start the ritual of asking for the bride's hand. The ritual is simplified: her hand is only asked for once, instead of many times as in the past, they give fewer or no presents, and the work of the bridegroom and the bride has disappeared (González, 1996; Robichaux, 2003).

The Diminishing Role of the Nuclear Family As a Symbolic Referent

The majority of Mexicans regard love as a prerequisite for marriage and faithfulness is deemed a fundamental ingredient for a successful marriage (Beltrán et al., 1996). However, three elements have influenced the weakening of the conjugal nuclear family as a symbolic reference: the significant presence of women in the labor market, the changes in family role structure, and the fragility and openness regarding the marriage bond. The significant presence of women in the labor market has favored the development of the dual-earner family. More than 30 percent of married women with young children are employed. This family type is growing in proportion and is leading to important changes, for example, in individuals' role structures (Esteinou, 1996;

López, 1998; Tuirán, 1993). Women with paid jobs gain economic independence, but can experience an overload of roles and difficulties in conciliating domestic demands and expectations such as taking care of children. The overload expresses itself in pressure. The overload is less in women with part-time jobs or who have more flexibility in terms of schedules.

Employment and the resulting tensions are creating conflicts among partners, sometimes leading to dissolution of the relationship. Social identity now depends less on marriage and family, and more than before on the job held, partly a consequence of the decreasing economic interdependence among family members. Family relationships are more intense and more fragile (Esteinou, 1999b). Individuals often evaluate their lives as a couple based on affective and emotional satisfaction. Economic interdependence, the significance of the family group, and religion are less compulsory for maintaining their bond.

Dissolution of Marriage

The most frequent cause of dissolution in the past was the death of one of the partners. In Mexico, there is scarce statistical information on divorce that would allow a comprehensive view of this phenomenon and vital statistics do not capture separations that constitute the most frequent form of dissolution (Ojeda & González, 1992). However, available information points toward an increase. Divorce rates once low, have increased since the 1950s when it was 4.4 percent. In the 1990s it was 7.2 percent and in 2001 it had increased to 8.6 percent (INEGI, 1997, 2002a). Other sources estimate the dissolution rate as 14.5 percent in recent years (CONAPO, 1999). If unions that are not legally sanctioned and often not registered are considered, the proportion of dissolutions is presumed greater. The National System for the Integral Development of the Family (Sistema Nacional para el Desarrollo Integral de la Familia [DIF], 1998) estimated that separations or informal dissolutions reached nearly 23 percent in 1996. The data have to be taken cautiously as they include different cultural patterns. Anthropological studies show that marital and dissolution patterns in communities with a strong indigenous tradition follow different rules compared with urban contexts or in certain social strata (Franco, 1995; Robichaux, 1997, 2003).

Despite the deficits in capturing these phenomena, statistics indicate that divorce is mainly an urban phenomenon, suggesting a link to individuation processes as well as to important cultural changes. Divorce occurs more frequently in younger cohorts, pointing to cultural change among generations. The risk of divorce is greatest during the first five years of marriage and, later, after ten years. Divorces after ten years of marriage have recently increased, probably related to cultural changes as well as to the lengthening of life expectancy (INEGI, 1997).

FAMILIES AND CHILDREN

Throughout the twentieth century, Mexico experienced a demographic transition from high levels of mortality and fertility without control toward one of low levels of mortality and fertility with control. Between 1930 and 1970 there was rapid population growth; then a significant deceleration due to an aggressive family planning policy implemented by the State in 1974 (mainly promoting sterilization at the end of the desired reproductive life). Families had about six children at the beginning of the twentieth century and reached a maximum of 7.2 children during the first half of the 1960s. Afterwards, fertility was an average of five children per woman in 1978, four in 1985, three in 1993, and is now estimated at 2.4 children (CONAPO, 2002; Mier y Terán & Partida, 2001; UNDP, 2006). The decrease in fertility ensued sooner in the urban middle and upper classes than it did in lower SES groups and rural areas. The majority of women now report that the ideal number of children is two (INEGI, 2004). Areas with low or very low fertility rates are located in the most highly developed regions in the country. In contrast, regions with high or very high fertility rates are areas with high concentrations of indigenous population and less socioeconomic development (CONAPO, 2002; Mier y Terán & Partida, 2001).

The diffusion of birth limitation and spacing practices and the increase in the use of more effective modern contraceptive methods have led to fertility decline (CONAPO, 2002; Mier y Terán & Partida, 2001; Zavala, 2001). It is estimated that the proportion of married or united (i.e., in consensual unions) women of a fertile age who use contraceptive methods rose from 30 percent in 1976 to 70 percent in

2000. Divorced, separated, and widowed women are less likely to use contraception (less than 45 percent). It is estimated that in 2005, three out of four women would employ some contraceptive method (CONAPO, 2002; INEGI, 2004; UNDP, 2006).

However, not all social groups follow this tendency and there are important differences and high levels of an unsatisfied contraceptive demand. In 1997, 26 percent of the indigenous married or united women of fertile age, 22 percent of women who lived in rural areas, and 22 percent of women without education, used contraception (Population Council, 2006). These social, cultural, and geographical contexts limit the exercise of reproductive rights. Two demographic transition patterns are evident, one related to the more modern social contexts and the other where modernization does not have a massive impact. Rural areas are an example of the latter. Women started to control their fertility after the birth of many children, and they mainly used sterilization provided by the State (Zavala, 2001). The changes in union formation and dissolution patterns have also influenced, though in a limited way, fertility decline. In recent years, the postponement of the age at first union, an increase in the number of consensual unions (with a greater probability of breaking up), and an increase in the separation and divorce rates have had an impact on fertility decline (CONAPO, 2002).

Parenting

Mexican women almost exclusively have had responsibility for children but this has been changing in recent decades. In a survey by Beltrán and colleagues (1996), 56 percent of Mexicans indicated men and women should share care for children. Even though parenting has not been studied widely in Mexico, it appears that the most common pattern in the past was an authoritarian one; parents primarily used orders to elicit the desired behaviors. There was a low incidence of questioning orders and strict rules and measures were imposed to carry out the orders; negotiation was practically nonexistent. Parents used advice to transmit experiences, ways of thinking and of solving problems, and a strong moral orientation. Parents advised children to behave well, to be polite, to obey and respect adults, to study in order to be economically and socially successful, and to value the family (Esteinou, 2005).

This pattern has been changing and authoritative styles are emerging, mainly in urban areas and the middle classes. Communication plays an important role, making parent-child relationships more flexible and less vertical. Orders are used to mark limits rather than as the main technique. While showing themselves as figures of authority, parents are establishing communication, flexibility, and closeness in relationships with their children. Obedience is still an important expectation, but parents make more use of negotiation. Emotional communication represents an important change, particularly among men. In the past men tended to be distant and hesitant to express affection and emotions. Fathers today are much more expressive, not only verbally but also through physical contact (Esteinou, 2005).

There are also shifts in the types of values instilled. One of the most important is the emphasis on the child as an individual with many needs. As a result, individualism is promoted more than in the past and values such as unconditional deference and respect toward adults or older people are loosing ground. There is opportunity for children to express their opinions and emotions regarding their parents, grandparents, kin, and adults in general (Esteinou, 2005).

A national survey in 2000 of youth aged twelve to twenty-nine shows aspects of parent-child relationships from the viewpoint of youth (Secretaría de Educación Pública/Instituto Mexicano de la Juventud [SEP/IMJ], 2000). Nearly two-thirds of the sample lived with both parents and around one-third had left home and was living on their own. In general, youth reported little influence on family decision making. There were some activities where youth had more autonomy to decide and there were others where the parents had control over them. For example, just over 50 percent could decide to have a girl/boy friend and 85 percent could decide about how to dress. However, 65 percent needed permission to go out with friends and 60 percent needed permission to arrive home late. Exercising the greatest level of control, 40 percent reported that they were forbidden to smoke; 41 percent were forbidden to drink alcohol, and 46 percent were forbidden to have tattoos or piercing. The survey showed that boys had greater autonomy and girls had less (Esteinou, 2005; SEP/IMJ, 2000).

These youth reported that parents tend to use more conversation than punishment. The majority talked about their problems with their parents, mainly with the mother. Young people talked little with their fathers. The themes discussed most often with fathers were school or work, while seldom mentioning sex and politics. Young people talked frequently with mothers about school, work, religion, politics, and their feelings. Girls also talked about sex, but boys did not. These young people also gave good evaluations of their families because they found solidarity and support in them, and saw family members as being responsible and good workers. Young people spent most of their free time with their families (Esteinou, 2005; SEP/IMJ, 2000).

Child Care and Other Family Support Programs

In 2000, about 27 percent of boys and girls under age six were taken care of by an institution or a person other than their parents. Of this group, just over 60 percent were cared for by a relative inside or outside of the minor's home. Public child-care institutions provided care for 5 percent and private child-care institutions provided care for about 4 percent of children under six (INEGI, 2004). In Mexico, there is a weak public social service system. Even though many married women are in the labor force, there are few public child-care services. Although the State provides child-care centers for women who work in public institutions, the demand is not satisfied. In 2000, the Mexican Social Security Institute (called the IMSS), which is the largest social security institution, reported that more than 44,000 individuals requested child care services. The second social security institution (called ISSSTE) for state workers reported more than 3,000 unmet requests for child care. Parents have to rely mainly on informal care, provided by grandparents, friends, and neighbors. Children from birth to age three frequently do not attend child-care centers. When used, private child-care centers are the usual choice. It is also common for maids and domestic employees to care for children.

Child care is not always available for families living in poverty. When such parents are working, children are often left without adult supervision. This is due to relatives living far away and parents not having friends nearby or people in the neighborhood they know well enough to ask them to care for the children. Mexico does not have subsidies, such as those found in Europe, to support families rearing children. Mexico has had a pattern of fertility reduction and has financial difficulties in supporting subsidies. Therefore, there are no income incentives through the taxation system, to provide payments for each child who is born, or pensions for single parents. The law guarantees maternity leave, but not for men. There are other kinds of subsidies directed at the consumption of basic products, providing breakfast in schools, scholarships to students, and training. About 20 percent of families receive some support (INEGI, 2000a).

FAMILIES AND GENDER

Opportunities for education, employment, and leisure are related to one's gender. In the past, these gender linked differences were large, but in the last three decades they have diminished substantially. In Mexico, school attendance is concentrated in the group aged six to fourteen years. The percentage of boys and girls who attended school increased between 1970 and 2000, from 66 to 92 percent for boys and from 63 to 91 percent for girls. Beyond age fourteen, school attendance diminishes because individuals drop out, do not attend, or have finished. In 2000, only 25 percent of those aged fifteen to twenty-nine attended school, the proportion of boys (26 percent) and girls (24 percent) was similar. However, between 1990 and 2000 the increase in girls' attendance was larger than that of boys including greater proportions being in high school. Gender differences persist in graduate and undergraduate studies, but they are diminishing (INEGI, 2004; UNDP, 2006).

In 2003, Mexico had almost seventy-seven million people aged twelve and over; 54 percent of whom were in the workforce. Gender differences are evident as 75 out of 100 men and 35 out of 100 women participated in economic activities. Women's participation has increased in recent decades, especially married and united women between twenty and forty-four years of age (32 percent in 2003) (INEGI, 2004). This is an important change; in the past, women usually stopped their employment when they married or otherwise united and had children. Younger women with fewer children participate more in economic activities than do older women with more children. Although the level of education among men is not related to their rate of participation in economic activities, there are differences among women. About

40 percent of women with secondary and 50 percent with higher education are involved in the labor market. In contrast, approximately 25 percent of women without formal instruction, with only elementary school, or with incomplete secondary school education participate in the labor market (INEGI, 2004).

In 2003, 13 percent of men and 19 percent of women received less than the minimum wage. This gap of six points is fairly constant as wages increase up to five or more times the minimum wage (INEGI, 2003b). Large differences in income are observed in ten occupations: women teachers, office workers, service employees, public officers, assistant workers, professionals, domestic workers, merchants, artisans, and industrial supervisors earn between 4 and 36 percent less than men. Only women and men technicians and specialized personnel receive the same income (INEGI, 2001, 2004).

Mexico has an important informal economy, with 25 percent of women and men occupied in this sector. The biggest gap between women and men appears in domestic services (12 percent of women in the workforce versus 1 percent of men) and agriculture and fishing (23 percent of men in the workforce versus 6 percent of women). In the formal economy the gap is smaller, but segregation is present by occupations. Women tend to work in commerce (e.g., clerks, sales) and services (e.g., teachers, secretaries) where wages, conditions, promotion, and access to training and education are relatively poor, as they usually have middle or lower positions. Men are more likely to be in positions having more opportunities in terms of training, education, and income within the fields of business, communications, transportation, agriculture, and fishing (De Oliveira, Ariza, & Eternod, 2001; INEGI, 2004).

In general, the time spent in leisure activities is about the same for men and women. However, men under thirty years of age tend to invest more time in leisure activities than do women, with women aged forty-four and older spending more time than men. There are differences according to the type of family. In traditional families with a strict division of roles (men as breadwinners and women as housewives and mothers), women tend to spend more time in leisure activities than do men. Among families with more flexible or "modern" role structures and where both men and women work outside the home, men spend 20 percent of their time in leisure activities while women spend 15 percent. Among children and teenagers, boys spend more time watching TV, playing video games, and playing sports while girls invest more time in listening to music, watching TV, drawing, and talking and playing with friends (INEGI, 2002b).

Distribution of Power

In the 1950s and 1960s, the distribution of power followed a rigid pattern in which men usually made the majority of decisions and women were subordinate. The increasing participation of women in the labor force and their increasing levels of education have been influencing a change in the distribution of power and authority among couples. However, this distribution depends on the significance women attribute to their labor market work as maternity and the nurturing of children strongly orient their behavior and conceptions about family. More changes in this regard have been observed among middle-class women than lower SES women. Professional employment can represent career or it can be a part of a family project to maintain status. In the first case, working is taken on with dedication and women try to make it compatible with maternity. Women who consider their economic contribution to the family as fundamental, try to incorporate their husbands in domestic tasks, tend to criticize men's authority as the heads of households, change their child care strategies, and to do whatever else is necessary to make the role structure more flexible and to diminish male dominance. In these cases, there is more joint decision making. In the second case, paid work is conceived as complementary, women do not pursue a career nor seek to change the basic role structure, maternity is still the main value that orients their behavior and attitudes, and it is assumed that men are breadwinners and the main figures of authority and power (Esteinou, 1996; García & De Oliveira, 1994).

In lower socioeconomic classes, women see their employment more as a need to overcome economic difficulties than for personal satisfaction or a means to becoming more independent. They do not intend to change family role structures nor the distribution of power. Seeing maternity as structuring life, they work to give their children better conditions, expect men to be the main authority and head of the household, and do not see their employment as an important economic contribution to the family. Inequalities can be strong and women might have to ask permission to get a job, to go out, and in other important situations (García & De Oliveira, 1994).

Division of Labor in Households

The distribution of economic and domestic activities has registered important changes in recent decades. However, many people still endorse the traditional roles of breadwinners and housewives; 30 percent of the male population aged twelve and over develop the role of breadwinner exclusively, and 47 percent of the female population aged twelve or older develop only a domestic role. Participation in domestic activities varies according to age and conjugal state. Between 1998 and 2003, about 95 percent of women participated in domestic activities. However, the gap between men and women declined as men's participation increased from 52 to 62 percent. Participation varied by age, with women aged forty to fifty-nine participating in domestic labor more intensively. Younger and older men were the ones who registered the highest domestic labor participation rates. In 2003, married or united men had the lowest share in domestic labor (56 percent), followed by the single (68 percent), and then by the widowed, separated, or divorced (70 percent). Education does not seem to have an impact on men's domestic labor (INEGI, 2001, 2004). Men have become more involved in child care but do not get involved as much in routine caring and usually play with children and spend time in leisure activities. Women continue to have the major responsibility for child rearing (Esteinou, 1996; INEGI, 2001; López, Salles, & Tuirán, 2001).

Despite the importance of their earnings to family income, women continue to be in charge of domestic responsibilities in an almost exclusive way, including child rearing. In this sense, women have double workloads, inside and outside the home, as men do not share the work at home equally with women. In addition, women's domestic work is continuous while men's work is usually a task with a specific ending. Men choose to participate in activities that are more creative such as cooking but not in those with less status such as cleaning the bathroom. In many activities men "help" women rather than take full charge of the task. This double load is harder for women in lower socioeconomic situations while middle- and upper-class women have an alternative—paying a worker to do domestic labor (Esteinou, 1996; López et al., 2001).

FAMILIES AND STRESS

Family is highly valued among Mexicans and they have a strong sense of commitment to family members. The majority perceive family as something they can rely on and in which they can trust. From family they get economic and emotional support and satisfaction. The word family is associated with positive connotations, such as love, bonds, children, home, welfare, parents, and understanding (Beltrán et al., 1996). For Mexicans, family is not only an institution, but also a value. Most behavior is family oriented.

Families have faced many challenges, especially over the last three decades. Mexican society has experienced rapid changes and it is difficult for families to cope with these changes. In an increasingly modernized society, tradition is loosing ground and certainty in many aspects of life becomes fragile and contingent. At the same time, family matters require more effort and attention and other institutions do not give substantial support. The diminishing role of the State in social life has resulted in families having to face problems on their own. Families, therefore, live with high levels of stress.

Poverty, Unemployment, and Fragility of Jobs

In the past three decades, Mexico has experienced numerous economic crises that have decreased the standard of living and the quality of life. Since 1976 there has been a decrease in real income, unemployment has increased at different times, and there has been rapid development of the informal economy. Increasing informal and flexible processes contribute to labor market instability with very low wages paid to nonqualified workers and proliferation of precarious working conditions (Cortés, 2000; Gordon, 2002). Families have faced income deterioration and have had to increase the number of family members in the labor market or have some family members take additional jobs (Cortés, 2000).

Poverty has been an important problem over recent decades, both in urban and rural areas, though it is greater in the latter. Around 20 percent of the population lives below the official poverty line and about the same percentage lives on less than US$2 per day (UNDP, 2006). Poor households have several characteristics: they tend to have younger members in extended families; household size is greater than the national average with several people who depend economically on one member; and they tend to live in crowded dwellings. Likewise, they are more likely to have children under twelve years old; children attend school less; a greater proportion of adolescents work; and the heads of the households have a low level of formal education (Cortés, Hernández, Hernández, Székely, & Vera, 2002; INEGI, 2000a).

The Diminishing Role of the State in Social Life

Economic policy reflects a diminishing role of the State in social life. Public policies have been directed to certain problems while reducing the investments in other areas such as health and social security. Public health services are relatively inexpensive but insufficient, and private services are expensive. Consequently, health expenses can throw families into a situation of poverty. Although the State has made investments in public education, the quality is low. Poor quality education means lower income during the time one is in the paid labor force so that lack of an adequate education results in inequality from generation to generation (Gordon, 2002). As this places pressure on families to overcome this situation, low SES families often enroll their children in private schools while making sacrifices in order to accomplish this.

Migration

The difficult socioeconomic conditions many Mexicans face have contributed to an increase in migration, mainly to the United States of America, to such a large extent that it has become an important national issue (Hennon, Peterson, Polzin, & Radina, 2006). It is estimated that throughout the 1970s around 30,000 persons migrated annually to the United States while this increased to 360,000 during the last five years of the 1990s. The population of native born Mexicans plus children of Mexican immigrants living in the United States totaled over twenty-three million in 2003, composing the biggest group within the Hispanic population (Tuirán, 2002). Nowadays, one out of ten households in Mexico has at least one member who has migrated to the United States. This is not only typical of rural areas and small cities, but it is also true for some intermediate and large urban areas. One of the most important effects of this migration phenomenon is the economic resources migrants send to their families in Mexico. Estimates indicate that in towns with less than 2,500 people, 10 percent of households received remittances from their relatives in the United States. Remittances constitute the second major source of income in Mexico (Tuirán, 2002).

Migration has a great impact on family life. In small towns, courtships are less restricted and often maintained over long distances. Given the contact young men have with North American culture and greater opportunities women have for meeting men, courtships have become increasingly open in the sense that traditional courtship rules have been eroded and individuals have more freedom to choose their partners. Exogamy is also increasing. Even though the expectation of marrying someone from their own ranch or town is still high, migration has brought more opportunities to meet people from other areas. An increase in the age at first marriage has also occurred. Before they marry, many migrants buy their own house, thus neolocal residence after marriage is becoming more common (Mummert, 1996).

Migration has become an important economic strategy and it has been positive in gathering more resources. However, families have to adjust emotionally to the new and stressful conditions. The risk of family disintegration is increased when family members spend long periods away from home. The pressures to maintain the family usually fall on women, adding additional issues in parenting, care of the elderly, and in managing daily survival.

FAMILIES AND AGING

One of the great challenges Mexican society will face in the twenty-first century is the aging population. At present, Mexico is still a country of young people. The average age of the population for the year 2000 was twenty-seven. However, the demographic transformations experienced over the past sixty years indicate a significant adjustment of the population age structure will be experienced during the following decades with an increase in the number of elderly people among the most important. It is estimated that the numbers of elderly will increase to twenty-two million in 2030 and to thirty-six million in 2050 (Zuñiga & Gomes, 2002). As men tend to die earlier than women due to a set of biological and social factors, there is a "feminization" of the aging process. In 1996, 55 percent of persons older than sixty years and 60 percent of persons older than seventy-five, were women. Today there are about 3.4 million women and 2.8 million men aged sixty-five and over (World Factbook, 2006).

The dependency ratio is also changing. In 1996, there were eleven persons older than sixty years of age for every 100 adults in intermediate ages. This number will increase to 14 for every 100 in 2010, 19 for every 100 in 2020, and 27 for every 100 in 2030 (Aparicio, 2002; Solís, 2001).

Health Problems and Functional Deterioration

The National Survey on Sociodemographic Aging (NSSA) reported that 39 percent of the elderly had some health problems (Solis, 2001). Vulnerability increases rapidly after seventy-five years of age. People who were ill at home increased from 30 percent of those aged sixty-five to seventy-four to 45 percent of those aged seventy-five to eighty-four. Another sign of the deterioration of health conditions is the inability to do certain daily activities. The performance of personal care activities (e.g., bathing, dressing, toileting) is not a problem for the majority of sixty to sixty-five years olds. However, these problems are common for one quarter of persons older than eighty-five years. A similar situation appears regarding the inabilities related to instrumental daily activities, such as shopping, preparing meals, doing housework, or going out.

For many, health problems related to aging start ten or fifteen years after they have entered the so called "third age," so it is important to distinguish between aging without disabilities and the subsequent phase of deterioration and dependency called the "fourth age." Prevalence of health problems and functional deterioration is greater among women and in rural areas. Even though women live longer, their health conditions are less favorable (Solís, 2001; Tuirán, 1999).

Residential Arrangements

The welfare of the elderly is related to the quality of their integration into different groups (e.g., family, neighborhood, and community). The immediate expression of this social network is the people with whom the elderly share their residence. These coresidents are often the main source of affective, material, and economic exchange. The NSSA offered a view about the organization of the households of aging people. The majority (64 percent) were the head of the household and lived in households formed exclusively by the members of their own nuclear family. Among these elderly, 28 percent shared their home with single children; 21 percent lived with their married or united children, and/or grandchildren; and 14 percent lived only with his or her partner. These figures suggest that there are relatively few adults who experience the so called "empty nest" and only 8 percent shared their residence with other people, relatives or non-kin (Solís, 2001).

Those who are not the head of the household do not control the resources of the household. The living conditions of these persons depend largely on the bonds sustained with others. In Mexico in 1994, almost 20 percent of people aged sixty or older were not the head of households and the majority did not have a partner. One-half of these people lived in households where a son, daughter, or a son- or daughter-in-law was the head of the household, while 7 percent lived where their unmarried sons or daughters were the head of the household. The proportion (34 percent) that lived with other relatives heading the household is the second largest group, and 7 percent lived in homes where there was no kinship relationship with the head of the household. For the majority of the elderly who are not the head of the household, the family, and especially their children, represents the main residential option (Solís, 2001).

The census of 2000 reported that 13 percent of men and 22 percent of women aged sixty-five or older formed a one-person household (INEGI, 2003a). The factors related to the risk of persons older than sixty years living alone can be classified into two main groups—those that determine the likelihood of persons living with family (the children, but also close relatives), and those that predict the independence of the elderly. If aged people have children to live with, they would probably not live on their own unless they are physically and economically independent. This probability depends on cultural factors promoting independence and individualism, or family support. In Mexico, the latter is more common and is an important reason why the majority of the elderly live with their family (Solís, 2001).

Caregiving to the Elderly

In Mexico, the family, with the occasional participation of other community support networks, satisfies the needs and demands of the elderly. This includes economic support and medical assistance because the support from the social security institutions is limited. In 1994, 70 percent of persons aged sixty or older received some type of help from a family member, a friend, or neighbor. In-kind help was the most frequent (54 percent); economic support was also frequent (47 percent). A smaller proportion (21 percent) received physical support. In many cases, the elderly simultaneously receive different types of support. Practically all the elderly who received physical support required additional support (Solís, 2001; Wong, 1999). Their children performed most of the caregiving; 52, 54, and 70 percent of the in-kind, physical, and economic support, respectively. The sex of the persons who give support varied according to type. Women were more likely to provide the physical (63 percent) and in-kind support (62 percent), while contributing less (38 percent) of the economic support. This reflects the traditional division of labor with women more often caregivers and men economic providers (Solís, 2001). Often the person who cares for the elderly is the youngest, or one of the youngest, daughters. It is also common among Mesoamerican people that the youngest son stays with his parents even if he is married. He is in charge of the caregiving and in exchange inherits the house and the land (Robles, 2001).

In many cases, caregivers are also aged and in charge of the care of others. Many elderly women care for their partners and sometimes their grandchildren while their daughters work. These women constitute important sources of help, but they can be overloaded with housework and caring for others (Robles, 2001).

Poverty, Work, and Retirement

The aging of the society will impose the need to attend to the increasing demands of social security services, especially for women as they have a longer life expectancy and are socially more vulnerable due to less labor force participation. Women experience aging with fewer probabilities of counting on access to the social security systems (Montes de Oca, 2001). In 2000, 70 percent of the elderly lived in municipalities that had low or very low social development, and of those aged seventy-five or more, none lived in a municipality classified as having a very high level of social development (Aparicio, 2002). Consequently, this age group is the least protected and most vulnerable. The family appears as the only source for survival in many cases.

In Mexico, being old does not mean being retired. Many elderly people (mainly women) never experienced a work life other than one of domestic activities and many are still economically active during old age. The economic participation rates reflect this reality. In the 1990s, 15 percent of women and over 60 percent of men aged sixty or more belonged to the economically active population (Salas, 1999). Another notable fact is that the economic participation rates among the elderly are larger in small sized localities. Forty-three percent of persons aged sixty or older lived in localities under 100,000 and were economically active, while 30 percent of that age group who lived in larger localities were economically active. These differences reflect the structural disparities of the labor markets between metropolitan and rural environments where the coverage of social security systems is more limited. Retirement is more frequent when there are children, basically sons who can provide economic support, and when the elderly live in households where there are more workers (Solís, 2001).

OTHER FAMILY SITUATIONS

One current controversial trend is toward households headed by women. The increase in these families, as well as their experiencing more poverty and vulnerability, has been a subject of introspection by scholars and policy makers. Even though the analysis is still developing, more is known today about the diversity of elements influencing this increase among different social groups and their level of welfare. In 1970, 14 percent of all households were female-headed: a number which increased to 17 percent in 1990 and 21 percent by 2000 (García & Rojas, 2002).

Many households headed by women have emerged due to the increase of life expectancy, as well as to fewer widows establishing new unions. However, there is special interest in analyzing those households in which there are dependent children as a result of separation, divorce, male abandonment, and pregnancy of single women. Many of these are smaller in household size than the average, even though a considerable proportion are extended households. The women who are the head of the family are typically separated, divorced, or widowed, and are older than the average adult woman (García & De Oliveira, 2006).

Until recently, scholars generally thought that this type of household was associated with greater levels of poverty and vulnerability. It was argued that even though the household was smaller, it had fewer members contributing to the family income and had more dependent members to sustain. Also, women who headed the households had lower wages and fewer resources than families headed by men and they were poorer and more disadvantaged because of gender differences. These women had to assume the double load of paid work while also doing housework and caring for the children, and they experienced a lack of time and mobility that affected their opportunities to obtain better jobs (Buvinic & Gupta, 1994; INEGI, 2000b).

The idea that in rural areas female-headed households are poorer and more disadvantaged has come into question as another perspective has developed. This perspective presents a more heterogenous view. In Mexico, female-headed households are not necessarily the poorest, especially in urban areas. When the different sources of income are analyzed, studies show that what makes a positive difference are the sources of income coming not from women's employment but from other members or relatives living either within the household or elsewhere. This suggests that this type of household is formed and maintained because women can, with economic assistance, sustain their households (García & De Oliveira, 2006; Gómez de León & Parker, 2000).

Three elements have been indicated through the analysis of these households in large cities. The first is domestic division of labor and the possible overload women experience. Women assume the responsibility for activities that are fundamental for the organization of family life and combine female activities with other activities typically associated with males. The second is decision making. These women enjoy greater power and do not have to share decision making with other members of the household compared with women who are wives; sharing, if it exists, is limited. The third element relates to the possible presence of domestic violence. The great level of conflict these women experienced in their previous marriage or relationship is relevant and in the majority of the cases this has been a fundamental aspect in dissolving the relationship and forming this type of household. Nevertheless, it is also relevant that in spite of this experience with conflict and violence, the relationship between mothers and children are not marked by violence, at least no more so than households composed of two parents. Therefore, although these women are over burdened, have greater power, and have been exposed to greater violence, these do not seem to affect in a disadvantageous way their children, nor the ways in which women face family conflicts (García & De Oliveira, 2006).

CONCLUDING COMMENTS

Mexico has experienced a set of changes, especially intense during the last three decades, which have affected family patterns. It was not until the beginning of the twentieth century that the development of a nuclear family composed of father, mother, and children was formed. At this time family relations typical of the nuclear family developed and articulated with nuclear family structure. Individualism, freedom of choice in partner selection, and the fusion of sexuality with marriage were institutionalized. Nevertheless, although there were individualism and freedom oriented family behaviors, profound inequalities characterized family relations, particularly between genders and generations. Women had as their main roles mother and housewife and men were breadwinners and had greater decision-making power over all nuclear family members. However, the Mexican nuclear family had other characteristics that establish a specific pattern different from the Western nuclear family model. A strongly communitarian value system puts limits on the development of individualism and freedom. Consequently, for Mexicans the family has been and is a value that rules most of the members' behavior. Roman Catholicism has spread a sense of responsibility regarding family members' cooperation and solidarity.

This pattern dominated family life from 1930 to 1970, then it started to change and another pattern rapidly developed. While also a nuclear family pattern as it maintains a nuclear structure, its relations are different. Owing to female participation in the labor force, the dual-earner family is becoming more prevalent. In this type of family the organization of roles as well as value orientations are changing. Today, negotiated and more equal relations are emerging, individualism tends to be stronger, and there is increased secular behavior involving family matters such as parenting. This family pattern will increase and will probably become the prevailing one if the present socioeconomic tendencies continue.

Along with these patterns, since the 1970s, Mexican society has witnessed the emergence or the increase of other family patterns. These include consensual unions, one-parent nuclear families, extended families, and unipersonal households. These households include modern tendencies as well as traditional ones. Therefore, family formation is in a process of change and, as a result, there is a mixture between modern and traditional aspects. In these processes, individuals and families will face many challenges. Time will tell what the prevailing family pattern will be. Questions that also need to be defined include: "Will Mexico experience a loss of tradition?" "How will families be able to cope with the modernization and globalization processes?" And, "How will tradition and modernity interact with one another?"

Chapter 18

Family, Marriage, and Households in Cuba

Ana Vera Estrada
Teresa Diaz Canals

The Republic of Cuba is a 110,860 sq kilometer archipelago at the entrance of the Gulf of Mexico. Its geographic position provides pleasant weather the year round with an average temperature during winter occasionally falling below 19°C, while on the warmest summer days it barely reaches over 30°C. Cuba has two seasons: rainy (from May to July) and dry (from August to April). The dry season is interrupted by an active hurricane period from August to November that causes frequent disasters. Topography is moderate, with elevations in the western, central, and eastern parts of the main island. The highest mountains, not more than 2,000 meters, are situated on the southeastern coast. Regional geographical differences give rise to microclimates, some that differ significantly from the national averages.

About the size of the U.S. state of Pennsylvania, Cuba has a population of 11.2 million unequally distributed among its fourteen provinces and the special municipality of Isla de la Juventud. Ciudad de La Habana is the country's capital. This province, the smallest, shows the highest population density with approximately one-fifth of the entire population (Oficina Nacional de Estadisticas, 2000; United Nations Development Programme [UNDP], 2006). Measures to regulate domestic migration are in force.

The population is roughly 50 percent *mestizo* (people of mixed European and African heritage), about 40 percent whites, and 10 percent blacks, but skin color is not related to social and economic differences, although it is associated with historical factors determining a cultural component of interest. During the colonial period (i.e., sixteenth to nineteenth centuries), Cuban society was not only organized by classes, but also by racial strata; white, free colored people, and slaves, were not always identified with a given social class (Instituto de Historia, 1993). In spite of the homogenizing effort by the Revolutionary Government since 1959, and equality offered to all Cuban citizens, the reason that the black part of the population lives in worse material conditions can be found in the long period of exclusion and marginalization they suffered (Adams, 2004; Guanche, 1996). Cuba is considered one of the Caribbean's least socially stratified countries (Herrera-Valdés & Almaguer-López, 2005). However, racial differences have no bearing on class differences. The Cuban ethnos is one, regardless of race (Guanche, 1996).

Perhaps 80 percent of white Cubans traced their heritage to the area of the Iberian Peninsula where their ancestors lived before coming to Cuba. Some arrived more recently (i.e., early twentieth century). Settlement of racial groups was influenced by historic forces. In the central provinces and in Pinar del Río, where tobacco plantations thrived, "islets" of white population, mostly from the Canary Islands, can be found. This was also the case in the present provinces of Camaguey and Ciego de Avila where cattle raising demanded the existence of large and medium-sized landowners and free laborers who were mostly whites. The black population was clustered mostly in sugar production to the west and part of the center of the island, where slaves were the main labor force. The greatest number of *mestizos* sought refuge in the easternmost provinces, distant from the central power.

In the past fifty years religions of African origin, especially *santeria,* have widened their influence. The socialist state is secular although all religions are respected. In the past two decades there has been an increase in the number of believers who find relief in religion for their daily anguish. It is said that a high percentage of Cuban society believes in some form of faith, although they do not practice it assiduously (Ramírez Calzadilla, 1995).

Cuba chose the socialist road (since 1961) for development during a period in which international forces were polarized between two powerful blocs, the United States and western Europe on one side, and the Soviet Union and Eastern Europe on the other.[1] This situation left no alternative for an independent path for a small country without significant natural resources. The collapse of the socialist bloc in 1989 forced structural adjustments in the economy to adapt to international markets. This required, among other measures, changes in enterprise autonomy and in agricultural landholding, an opening to self-employed work and foreign investment, a reform in the banking and monetary systems, new forms of incentives for the workforce and, more recently, the reform of the entrepreneurial system in the search for more flexibility (Carranza Valdés, 2002). Sugar, tobacco, and coffee are the main export products. There are reserves of strategic minerals that, together with tourism and family remittances (discussed later in this chapter), are today the main sources of income. Cuba ranks 50 of 177 countries on the Human Development Index, placing it in the high human development category (UNDP, 2006).

Historical Perspective

Blacks and *mestizos,* approximately 40 percent of the population in 1841 (the time of highest concentration of black and mestizo population during the colonial period), suffered the most from the consequences of social exclusion (Instituto de Investigaciones Estadísticas, 1988). The persistence of a racist mentality and racial prejudice, a consequence of colonialism and slavery, pervaded Cuban life throughout the bourgeois Republic. In 1959, President Castro challenged the silence on race and racism, calling for a national debate. The issue resurfaced in the 1990s. In some instances, black persons were not selected for the best-paid jobs. However, when the principal person was black, he or she often preferred to hire black people. Social activism has contributed to exploring the issue. Racial ideologies have remained in the social consciousness of Cubans, but often hidden. There is some concern that racism has reemerged.

The Republic of Cuba was established on May 20, 1902. The Platt Amendment to the Constitution was an agreement imposed between the Cuban president and the U.S. government. This amendment established a national structure subject to the U.S. economic and financial systems and the American imperialist designs in the Caribbean.

The government started improvements to the health care system and the renovation and strengthening of the school system (Instituto de Historia, 1998). The modernization and education work carried out by this government is undeniable as it introduced technologies and opened new labor markets, particularly for women. Owing to the experience gained in fighting colonialism, and perhaps with the influence of U.S. feminism, the end of the war with Spain meant progress for women (Vera, 2004a). This was achieved not without objections from the most conservative sectors of society, which defended the idea that women should be the main caretakers in the family and strive for its preservation under their husbands' authority. According to 1899 census data, not only did women's integration into the workforce increase at the turn of the century but there was also a diversification as to their skin color. Until then most women workers were black and mestizo. That year, 61 percent of the female population was white, but white women formed 3 percent of the workforce, while although their percentage in the population was lower, black and mestizo women were 18 percent of the workforce (Vinat, 2001).

The first aim of the women's movement during the Republican period was the divorce law, representing the desire of higher-class women to liberate themselves from the subordination they had been submitted to. It is also a reflection, contrary to what was the case in other countries in the Americas, of the meager influence of Christian moral principles on the formation of society. The second main aim was women's right to vote obtained in the 1930s, almost twenty years after divorce laws were in force (González Pagés, 2003).

From the 1920s, the women's movement condemned the terrible conditions in which the poorest strata of the population lived. However, their views were dominated by clear prejudices against the lives led by subaltern groups. This underestimation of the culture of the poor did not escape notice by poor women and some intellectuals participating in the women's movement. The 1925 and 1939 Congresses were the scene of debates in which social differences came to the forefront. It was in 1939, however, when several black representatives submitted their demands. Top among them were guaranteeing the right to work, better living conditions, and education for their children (Stonner, 1991).

Another important achievement of the women's struggle during the Republican period was that of illegitimate children whose equalization with legitimate children was formally reflected in the 1940 Constitution, and ratified by an act adopted in 1950. Its final implementation, however, was postponed until the approval of the Family Code by the Revolutionary Government in 1975.

Generalized poverty and its impact on family life were one of the main obstacles that the Revolution Government was forced to face when in 1959 and 1960 it adopted, for example, new social programs such as the literacy campaign in 1961, scholarship programs, job opportunities, and social integration for the poorest women.

Families in Cuban Context

The State guarantees the basic needs of the population. Every household receives a "basket" of rice, beans, meat or fish products, oil, sugar, and coffee at subsidized prices. Children under the age of six and chronically ill people are assigned an additional ration of milk and other products. There used to be a differential quota for the largest cities, Havana and Santiago de Cuba, but this is now being evened out. The composition of the family basket has undergone some modification in price and quantity and is currently limited, although estimated to cover the nutritional needs of children from birth to age six. There are programs for nutritional needs connected to institutions like boarding schools, day-care centers, hospitals, maternity homes, senior citizens' homes, and workers' dining rooms (Ferriol, Quintana, & Pérez Izquierdo, 1999). There is no access to official data that would enable a calculation as to what extent the family basket can compensate for the fluctuations in prices of the products and the marked increase in the cost of living over the past ten years. According to unofficial data, in 2003 a family unit needed to multiply its real income in order to cover all its necessities.

Life expectancy is 76.4 years, although women outlive men (average life expectancy of 78.7 and 74.8, respectively), child malnutrition prevalence (weight for age among children under age five years) is 4 percent, infant mortality rate is 6.2 percent, and maternal mortality ratio (33 in 2,000) is comparable with industrialized nations (Ferriol, 2003; Jones, 2002; Pan American Health Organization, 2002; UNICEF,

2005; World Bank, 2002). The 2005 birthrate was estimated at 12.03 births per 1,000 population, ranking Cuba at 174 worldwide, while the total fertility rate was estimated at 1.66 children born per women ranking 175 worldwide (Index Mundi, 2005; World Bank, 2002).

From 1965 abortion has been available through the national health system, up to the tenth week of gestation (United Nations Population Division [UNPD], 2002). Unlike most of Latin America, abortion is legal in Cuba (Wulf, 2005). Consequently there are fewer complications for women and their reproductive health compared with women having clandestine abortions. Seventy percent or more of women use modern contraception with direct support provided by the government. Approximately 27 percent of women between fifteen and nineteen use no birth control even if they are sexually active (Bardisa Ezcurra, 2003). Even though abortion is a right and it is practiced in hospitals and clinics, efforts have been made to eliminate it as another birth control mechanism, and this appears to be successful as the incidence of abortions has declined. The induced abortion rate was 46.8 per 1,000 women in 1989; in 2001 there were 20.6 abortions per 1,000 women aged twelve to forty-nine, and 49.8 abortions for every 100 births (Acosta, 2002; Pérez Izquierdo, 2000).

More than 75 percent of Cubans live in cities, towns, or semirural communities where they enjoy water, power, and telephone facilities subsidized by the State (Fernández Suárez, 2003; Ferriol, 2003; UNICEF, 2005). The State ensures jobs for most of the active population. National institutions (e.g., Ministry of Public Health, the Ministry of Education, the Ministry of Justice, the Electric Company, the Cuban Telecommunications Company), and organizations like the Federation of Cuban Women, the Committees for the Defense of the Revolution, guarantee a basic living standard for all families. These organizations provide for the home budget in the country's currency, the Cuban peso. The peso buys a limited range of subsidized rationed food items and can be used to purchase fresh produce in the farmers markets.

There is also another official (since November 2004) money system, the convertible peso (CUC or Cuban Unity Currency). It is the only equivalent with international currencies and is equivalent to 24 Cuban pesos. This is used in a wider market where people receiving remittances from abroad or payments in foreign currency buy food, clothing and footwear, personal hygiene products, and household goods in hard currency stores. It is estimated that from 30 to 60 percent of Cubans augment their income with remittances whose total amount reaches a billion U.S. dollars per annum. This shows that although many persons benefit from the socialist system, it does not satisfy the requirements of the population as a whole.

The double currency system, aimed at reviving the economy after the disappearance of the Socialist bloc, involved removing penalties for possession of foreign currency and opening the national market to foreign currency. In 1996, it was estimated that the population's consumption in foreign currency was 300-500 million dollars from overseas remittances. Of this, 100-150 million was through special types of salary stimulus, 50-100 from tourism-related income, and 20-50 million through other means. The current data on overseas remittances are unofficial. According to an AFP story datelined Miami, July 2, 2004, Cuba was receiving one billion dollars a year in remittances. A report by CEPAL estimated that about three billion dollars in family remittances entered the country between 1989 and 1996 (Marquetti Nodarse, 1997).

The Family Code (1975) regulates family life including marriage, divorce, child support, child custody, adoption, and tutelage. Aspects concerning living within the family unit, and with child rearing, motherhood, and other issues are covered in specific legislation. However there are fundamental aspects of family life, such as kin relationship, that follow Spanish codes. Social programs (e.g., family doctors, day care, and welfare workers for families living in poverty) are part of the implementation of the Family Code (Código de la familia, 1979). Cuba enjoys a universal and free health care system emphasizing primary care and prevention. There are about sixty physicians per 10,000 inhabitants and a family physician program covering the population (Herrera-Valdés & Almaguer-López, 2005). Health indicators are comparable with "developed" countries. Youth immunization rates are around 99 percent (Steinmetz, 2004).

COUPLE FORMATION AND MARITAL DYNAMICS

Single mothers were one of the social problems having no effective solution when the Revolution came to power. As Roman Catholicism was the official religion in Cuba, as in other Spanish colonies,

Catholic doctrine was the ideological model that ruled the life of the upper crust of society. Thus, civil marriages—and Catholic religious marriages—were something yearned for, especially by women. However only people with some resources could be married by the Catholic Church as this involved a relatively costly ceremony. Even civil marriages implied an adequate trousseau and lodgings for the new couple. At times, this led to long courting periods where the couple tried to save enough to satisfy these requirements. Many couples opted for common-law marriages and living in tenement houses where a different family lived in each room. The increase in the number of children without a corresponding increase in income created detrimental conditions for their survival as a couple.

Concubinage and female-headed households were distinct traits of family life among the least favored classes in both urban and suburban areas during the entire Republican period (1902-1958) (Vera, 2002, 2004a). The number living together as a couple grew from 31 percent in 1899 to 54 percent in 1953 (Catasús, 1999). For poor women, marriage meant support for their family and a potential rise in their economic and symbolic status. In general, given the moral prejudices of the times, only the poorest women accepted a permanent situation of concubinage; their large number is a reflection of the level of poverty. The average for the period from 1899 to 1953 is one of every two people lived in a consensual union. At the time, consensual unions, which are much more accepted today, were a challenge to public opinion.

Under those circumstances, in the promiscuous conditions of collective housing, instability among couples was widespread. A goal of the Revolution has been to eradicate poverty and marginalization and provide opportunities for marriage. However, social changes do not happen with the same speed that policies are drafted, and the plan to do away with marginal neighborhoods and provide modern housing to the poorest sectors was not achieved in the short term. In spite of the undeniable general social and economic transformations that took place after 1959, individual cultural changes advanced at a slower pace. Today, about 40 percent of the population lives in housing units considered in need of repairs or refurbishing. A study indicated that the deficit and poor housing conditions create a problem impacting families. It is common for three generations to live under the same roof. Lack of privacy and adequate living space, combined with other factors, has lead to a declining birthrate. Difficulty in finding a place to live is one of the factors responsible for, especially young couples', attempts to emigrate (Acosta, 2001).

The topic of legal marriage is not a central concern today. This does not mean that a substantial part of Cubans do not see it as an ideal, above all young women would like to be officially wed. The legal and social support offered by the Family Code and the status women enjoy thanks to their educational level and job opportunities, aided by family networks created by the prevalence of the extended family, reinforce their economic and psychological independence. This contributes to the processes of separation to the point that the term "fatherectomy" has been coined for the relative ease many women do away with the links with their partners when they do not meet their requirements. At times, the forced cohabitation due to shortage of houses for young couples restrains the desire to get rid of inconvenient partners.

The case of couples formalizing their relationship after a period of sexual relations, often when the first pregnancy is underway, is more common in families less interested in ostentatious behavior. It is infrequent that a person marries more than once. After a woman is legally married once, she is considered free to decide her life without having to formalize her relationships. The value formerly attributed to virginity as a guarantee of morality for a marriage contract has lost all value. On the other hand, the absence of common property in the case of younger couples living in the houses of relatives is perhaps one of the factors contributing to the decision to separate when conflicts brought about by living together become more acute.

Cubans tend to marry within their immediate groups. Although data are lacking, some research findings suggest some color endogamy, especially among blacks (Rodríguez, Cañet, & Estévez, 2004). In recent years, some sectors show a trend of looking for partners in a different social stratum, using marriage as a way toward a quick, although not always secure, upward mobility. Generally, the first stable boyfriend-girlfriend relationship results in marriage, precipitated mainly by the girl and her relatives and less by the boy's side. Age at first marriage and the first planned pregnancy have been increasing to around age twenty-five, mainly among couples with higher levels of education and a better planning of their actions and budget. This perhaps, is because they have a more accurate understanding of the advantages and rewards of living as a couple, of the cost of feeding and caring for a child, and knowing that having a child means that they must postpone their professional career at least for a year.

With a higher age at marriage there tends to be a decline in fertility rates, as some of the more fertile years elapse before unions are formalized. Women with low educational levels tend to have children earlier and a large proportion of Cuban children are born to them. Between 1986 and 1996, 83 percent of children were born to mothers between fifteen and twenty-nine years of age (Alfonso, 2003). A substantial difference exists between the age of marriage and the first relationship accepted by the family, although without living together steadily. That is, people often have a relationship (including sexual) before they marry. This is increasingly so even in the case of girls and the person's mother often accepts such relationships while fathers might accept them less so.

Marriage implies the legal formalization of the couple and it takes place when its members are well into their twenties, but sexual relations tend to start much earlier and marriage does not necessarily follow. Sociological research in the English-speaking Caribbean suggests a gradual pattern for couple relations whose validity for Cuba should be explored (Chevannes, 1994).

Couple relations imply an imbalance in functions. Women state that marriage has deteriorated their relationship by making domestic chores their obligation. Daily household chores are still considered women's responsibilities, while the prevailing attitude seems to offer more freedom to men. Also, preparation for life is different for boys and girls. Girls are generally taught to be modest, obedient, diligent, and boys to be courageous, to hide their feelings, and to be independent, all contributing to repeating the traditional pattern in adulthood.

Marriage in general underwent a process of deterioration as the liberation discourse on women's rights became commonplace. Men and women increasingly shared that discourse, although women have continued to be the caretakers of the children and the ill, and are still in charge of most domestic chores. The relation of women with family work is a patriarchal creation with a well-developed and age-old socialization that continues with almost general acceptance, questioned only by certain transgressors.

FAMILIES AND CHILDREN

A key factor for the adequate understanding of Cuban familism is the differentiated weight given to blood and in-law relations.[2] Research on the concept of family with a proportional sample of 2000 adults asked about their most important relatives. Spouses were not often mentioned. This is understood as their nonidentification of this relationship with the notion of family (Vera, 2004b).

The Cuban concept of family is different from North American society. Cubans believe they are linked by family ties to their blood relatives: father, mother, uncles, cousins, sons and daughters, grandfathers, and so on. Partners (such as spouses) are not considered part of their family. A partner is a partner, the father (or mother) of one's child in separated couples, and one's husband (or wife) when the partners are living together and respecting each other. This feeling might change with age. However when people are asked about the concept of family, less than 25 percent include the partner in their answer (Vera, 2004b).

The Cuban concept of family is not based on conjugal unions. Cubans often share housing with others besides a spouse. People live wherever they can in whatever space is available in the home of a relative because few young couples have the means of getting a house of their own. Rather, they resort to dividing the house of the bride or groom's parents. Couples living together offer each other moral and affective support, but they do not always enjoy total economic independence.

Extended family is the typical pattern, although it shows variations in the organization of family life according to place of residence, age of its members, and household composition. Economic differences are fundamental. It is not the same living on a state salary compared with being self-employed; neither is it the same living in an urban or serviced area with running water, electricity, public transportation, and telephone compared with a rural area where daily life mostly depends on manual work and activities take place during the day light hours. Cultural influence is a factor that should also be taken into account. In western Cuba a preference for the nuclear model is often found, although it is not the one prevalent in Cuba today.

The campaign for the legalization of common-law marriages, an initiative to mend injustices, was up taken in the early years of the Revolution. The number of marriages rose between 1953 and 1970 and there was a 142 percent growth between 1957 and 1968 (Hernández, 1973). Speaking of those times, a woman related, "You just had to get married, it was something like a fad." If the effects of the marriage boom are considered vis-à-vis changes in the socialization of the population, the massive number of women entering the workforce, and the political pronouncements on private property as an expression of bourgeois society that should be abolished as an encumbrance, one would be able to appreciate the complex ideological framework that existed when the Family Code was adopted in 1975.

An article, often quoted in the 1980s that analyzed changes undergone by families in the decades after the Revolution, referenced family transitions (Bengelsdorf, 1985). In the 1960s, the family was neglected because of migration, growing collectivization, and the new educational system that trained youngsters away from home thus minimizing the importance of the parents in the socialization of their children. During the 1970s, when the Family Code was drafted, the requirements for a more orthodox social structure imposed a more conservative image on the family that began to be seen as a shelter from the many stresses of social life.

Bengelsdorf (1985) argued that the weaknesses of these studies were their lack of a historical perspective with the capacity to remark and put into a context the various stages transited by the policies of the Revolutionary Government toward the family. Apart from a historical problem, there is a relative lack of correspondence between the legal design of the Code, a policy-making document that set as a model a type of family that was not characteristic of the family organization of most of the population and the real model. The most deeply rooted and extended traditional model is that of a family formed by the parents, the children, and all the relatives, with rare mention of in-laws. This is a cultural problem that has not attracted enough attention from scholars.

The Value of Children

In Cuba, children and youth are considered the most valuable resource and social programs reinforce this value. In rural areas there might not be electricity for cooking, but children will have access to electricity for computers (e.g., solar panels provided by the government). During food or medical shortages, children are the first priority.

Children are recognized as the human capital for the next generation (Steinmetz, 2004). Children play a central role in family dynamics and create close relationships among people whose common bond is having children of a similar age. Thus, maternity and child rearing might become a factor of interesting horizontal and also vertical solidarity, whatever the economic condition of the family.

Child care is relatively inexpensive, but not so in comparison with the lowest salaries, which are about 230 pesos per month. Parents pay 40 pesos per month for each child between one and five years old in *Círculos infantiles* (day-care centers). There, children have daily care from 8 a.m. to 5 p.m., Monday to Friday. These centers are for working mothers and there are not enough places to accommodate all children. Thus some licenses for private child care also exist; and some parents prefer to have their children in private care as they think that children are better cared for.

Parenting

One study of the methods that parents use to control the conduct of their adolescent children indicated that mothers employ better methods and are more persuasive as parents (Suárez, Reyes, Casañ, & Castañeda Marrero, nd). A common pattern is for one parent to threaten the child that he or she will tell the partner about the child's misbehavior. In about one-third of families, being physically and verbally aggressive is characteristic of one parent, while the other parent is persuasive. Boys are punished, particularly with nonpersuasive methods, more than girls. Adolescents report difficulty communicating with parents. A different study indicated that the mothers are more respected by adolescents (Medina, 2001). The largest proportion of adolescents indicated that love was the greatest reason for respecting their parents, with setting an example and reasoning also reported by more that one-half. Punishments, yelling, beating, and obligation were not seen as fostering respect. When parents disciplined adolescents, discussing the problem was the most consistent technique, with silence and yelling the next most frequent techniques. Pushing, pulling hair, and beating were reported by 12 percent or less of the adolescents. In another study, around one-third of youth aged six to twelve reported being beaten with a hand or object (Durán Gondar, Díaz Tenorio, Jiménez, Córdova, & Hernández, 2003).

The efficacy of parenting beliefs can be seen in youth outcomes. Remembering that Cuba is a relatively poor country having comparatively few resources but enjoying what the United Nations defines as a high level of human development, many socioeconomic and health indicators are comparable to those of what might be considered more developed countries. Examples include long life expectancy, low infant mortality, few low birth weight infants, slow rate of population growth, good health status including low prevalence of HIV/AIDS, high rate of literacy, and high educational attainment.

Single-Parent Families

A large number of births are to single mothers and mainly to the less educated. Statistics show a relative increase in the number of teenage pregnancies, mothers insufficiently prepared for maternity, and thus lacking economic independence to face a responsibility of such magnitude. Of the 137,000 births registered in 2003, only 31 percent were from legally married couples. When mothers separate from their partners, and even while living with them, they could still depend on their parents and become, in fact, like sisters to their own children. Additional resources are provided in day care and schools for children from families facing challenges, such as single parenthood. As a result, class or strata differences in childhood indicators are small. Consequently, the relationship between single-parent families, poverty, teen pregnancy, delinquency, school leaving, and substance abuse often prevalent in other countries are not prevalent in Cuba. Divorce or single parenthood is much less of a problem in terms of child outcomes than in some other countries. Having goals of equality, Cuba strives to ensure that children from challenged families do not then reproduce these challenges in a subsequent generation. Attempts are made to avoid a cycle of poverty (Steinmetz, 2004).

Intervention Programs

Studies from many countries point to a lower standard of living and lacking access to resources being risk factors for children and youth (e.g., lowered educational motivation and school leaving) (Briar-Lawson, Lawson, Hennon, & Jones, 2001; Steinmetz, 2004). However in Cuba, class/strata, gender, and race are not related to youth-related problems, school leaving, or illiteracy (Steinmetz, 2004).

The goal of determining the best preventive or intervention for a defined problem (e.g., Attention Deficit Disorder or ADD) is approached as a scientific endeavor. The situations are investigated and preventative and remedial programs are enacted. For example, programs for adolescents and young adults were implemented due to increased rates of STDs (Steinmetz, 2004). Another example is when teenage pregnancy was defined as a growing problem. Programs with early and realistic sex education, combined with contraception availability, were begun. However, a study by González and Miyar stipulated a need for more comprehensive sex education programs and a more effective family planning policy to reduce the prevalence of abortion. They suggested programs that distinguish between birth control for adults in stable relationships to plan families and space births, and for younger people that allows them to optimize the enjoyment of sex while offering protection from pregnancies and STDs (Acosta, 2002). Sexually transmitted diseases were on the rise, especially syphilis and gonorrhea; the rates in 1996 were 143.7 and 368.7, respectively, per 100,000 inhabitants. Work is currently under way to upgrade the prevention and control program (Pan American Health Organization, 2002).

Ritualizing Relationships and Building of the Future

Recently there has been a reemergence of ostentatious behaviors by groups with higher foreign income that influence other social strata. Weddings and birthday parties when girls arrive at their fifteenth year of age have become an occasion to dazzle the community with classic white dresses and a parade of fashionable clothes. Memories are then saved in collections of pictures whose possession and exhibition to acquaintances and relatives constitutes an act of power in which even the poor indulge when having the chance and saving for many years specifically to cover the expenses these rites require. It is common to hear mothers talk about saving for their daughter's fifteenth birthday party from the time the girl turns ten. A larger number of persons would rather pay for the photo album of the teenager or the wedding—something that will inscribe her history in society, that will immortalize her—instead of investing the money in a cultural experience such as a trip that would contribute to her personal development, or in cases of true shortage of resources, buying durable goods such as furniture, the personal items they will require in their new state, or more nutritive food such as meat or milk.

Family rituals with great cohesive value for large families, such as Christmas Eve dinner, have maintained their validity and are still held inside the homes, although resources can be scarce and they do not receive institutional or mass media support. However, the most impressive family gatherings are wakes, where extended families attend in full. It is during these moments of shared sadness that the joy of the unexpected meetings hardly manages to be contained by the moderation imposed by circumstances. Children's birthdays are occasions for relatives and neighbors to spend time together, although they are attended mostly by children of the age group of the child celebrating his or her birthday.

FAMILIES AND GENDER

Two issues are discussed in this section: social programs for women and gender equality and then domestic violence. Some other aspects of gender including the issue of the family division of labor were discussed earlier in this chapter.

Social Programs for Women

Programs are intended to strengthen equality in opportunities for men and women. Today, women constitute 43 percent of scientific workers and researchers, 57 percent of technicians and professionals, 45 percent of university professors, and more than 60 percent of university students. Cuban women have achieved a high level of integration into political and economic life with an increasing level of social and political activity, especially in management positions. At the same time, representation is not adequate in roles in higher-level decision making given their successful performance at various levels of middle management. In 1995, women accounted for 30 percent of people having an administrative position in an enterprise or institution, and in 2000 they reached 32 percent (Informe Central, 2000). Women are not widely present in upper management positions often because they themselves have been unwilling to take them to avoid putting themselves in a work-life situation that does not take into account the demands of family life for women as caregivers (Echevarría, 2003). Their double shift (one at work and the other at home) makes an overly demanding work schedule overwhelming.

From being the Latin American country with the least number of women in the workforce in 1950 (13 percent), in 1990 Cuba was only behind Uruguay and Nicaragua (34 percent). More recently, about 40 percent of the labor force is women (World Bank, 2002). Despite the growth of women's integration into the workforce between the 1960s and the 1980s, the last decade showed a decrease of men and women in state jobs as a consequence of the economic crisis and the rise in the cost of living, with a strong trend toward what Cuban economists call "demonetization" (i.e., sudden and radical decline in purchasing power of currency in the 1990s).

Despite the equality of men and women's rights stated in the Code, the division of labor is unequal. Most Cubans learned in their childhood that child and elder care are the duties of women, and women do most of the household work. The "aid" contributed by men is mostly for shopping and dealing with matters considered to be within the sphere of men's concern. There are men who contribute more, but they are the exceptions. This attitude toward a gendered division of labor is the same across age, race, and social groups.

Family Violence

Daily economic problems are the cause of family conflicts and generate violence, mainly against women. Research into relationship abuse began to gain visibility after the 1990s. Criminal and judicial investigations focus attention on female victimization and have worked on legislation for the protection of women and the identification of risk groups. Findings show a relationship of crimes with gender issues, and place female victimization mainly within couple and domestic environments. Findings also point to the impact of violence learned in childhood homes, reproducing aggressive behavior in adult families (García Méndez, 1998).

In a study carried out in the mid-1990s in Havana, the majority of cases of homicide were females killed by men, while only a few of the dead men were murdered by women. Most of the murdered women were between twenty-one and thirty-five years of age and did not work outside the home. Almost half of the women were murdered by someone who was (or had been) their domestic partners, and most of the murders took place inside the home, whether shared or not with the perpetrator (Pérez González, 2003). One feature to take into account is that there are no great variations as to economic situation, educational level, skin color, or others factors that were expected to create a difference.

One of the causes of conflicts is the unwanted sharing of living space due to the insufficient growth of suitable housing (Garcia & Aquilera, 2004). The Cuban situation includes the growth in the number of families per house. As housing does not grow sufficiently, homes are subdivided to receive new families giving rise to uncomfortable conditions that make life for couples difficult and cause conflict among family members.

FAMILIES AND STRESS

Many issues create stress in Cuban families as in any society. Domestic violence is one issue that is a consequence of traditional role relations and the stressful economic situation. In this section the current economic situation of families and one of its strategies—marrying a foreigner—are reviewed as stressors. Some other factors are discussed in the Concluding Comments section.

The economic crisis in the 1990s resulted in growing difficulties in social and economic life. The collapse of the Socialist bloc brought about changes in the economic policies of the state and for the people of Cuba it meant finding alternatives for survival, mainly mechanisms to obtain CUC (Cuban Unity Currency, valued at about US$0.80) income to face the rising cost of living. Some of these mechanisms include the diversification of family work, self-employment, searching for remittances, searching for support from informal networks (family, neighbors, friends), renting rooms, starting businesses, and marrying foreigners among other alternatives (Arés, 2004). The sale of personal goods, performing work other than that of the professional career, and cooking food to sell directly to consumers or for resale by vendors can be added to this list, as well as the more radical solution, migration. Many informal trades and activities have replaced or complemented salaries from formal work activities in state institutions. In spite of a progressive increase in salaries, now with a much lower purchasing power, these institutions have undergone a decline in staff and clients. It is obvious that self-employment activities generate larger incomes. Under these conditions, most family members work to cover daily needs and still the cost of living exceeds their income.

These strategies to generate income do not exhaust the routes chosen by many who in their search for solutions for an unsatisfactory budget take advantage of opportunities to obtain more by making use of collective resources and goods. This has created a gray area between the legal and the illegal and relaxation of certain values, and explains certain cases of uncritical acceptance of actions like divorcing a spouse to marry a foreigner, hoping to achieve in time the legal migration of the Cuban spouse and children, or at least sending financial help to improve the family's life in Cuba. This pragmatism at times turns people into mere instruments. Love becomes business or a tool to leave the country through marriages of convenience responding to the question, "What do you offer and what do I give in return?" This pragmatism turns the "Other" into an object, and gives rise to relationships where economic and emotional alternatives are at stake that could help foreigners interested in staying in Cuba (Díaz Canals, 2004).

Marriage to a foreigner has become a viable solution to economic problems. The countries with the highest number of persons marrying Cubans are Spain, Italy, Mexico, Germany, Canada, and the United States, in that order. The foreigners are mostly men. Cubans of both sexes marry older foreign partners. A Ministry of Justice survey indicated that most marriages with foreigners in 2003 took place in Ciudad de La Habana province. Second and third were Matanzas and Habana provinces. Most Cuban spouses were twenty-six to thirty years old. Most women were registered as housewives with high school education. Next were professionals and, in fewer numbers, employees, students, technicians, unemployed, and artists. The age of most foreign women and men was thirty-six to forty; they were registered as tourists and had high school educations. Most men were Spanish and most women were Mexican. One should not assume all these marriages have illegitimate causes, but they are sometimes looked upon with certain mistrust and/or complicity.

FAMILIES AND AGING

Cuba's population is rapidly aging (Bertera, 2003; Pan American Health Organization, 2000). People over age sixty comprise 14 percent of Cuba's population. It is estimated that by 2030, 30 percent of the population will be over sixty years old and fewer than 15 percent will be under age fifteen (Alfonso, 2005). According to the 2000 SABE survey, 11 percent of adults in the City of Havana lived alone, 11 percent with a spouse, and a considerable majority (78 percent) lived in the company of other persons (Centro de Estudios en Población, 2003). These elderly have found family reciprocity in giving and receiving help, a method of integrating more dynamically into the complex network of family relations. In 2000, 84 percent of Cuban elders received help from those living with them and 72 per cent of them offered help to their relatives. These percentages are much higher than the help offered to and received from children that do not live with the elderly (Pan American Health Organization/World Health Organization, 2003).

Sixty-nine percent of older people live in Havana. Research in Ciudad de La Habana showed that the educational level of this group was 51 percent elementary school, 39 percent high school, and 6 percent university level. Of these, 76 percent received pensions or social security and 21 percent still worked. Approximately 90 percent had good or not so good houses, but 20 percent lived in overcrowded conditions (more than two persons per room); 73 percent cooked with gas or electricity; more than 90 percent had refrigerators, television sets, and electric fans; and less than 25 percent had a telephone. Over 90 percent received some help in services, food, clothes, or money and 30 percent offered help to their relatives. Women received more money and men more services and objects, and women offered more care and company, while men offered more money. These people had social and health services at their disposal, but these did not cover all their requirements for gerontological medical services, grandparents' day care, social welfare help, food, and housing repairs (Centro de Estudios en Población, 2003).

Cuba is not the country with the largest number of elders in Latin America, but it will be in two decades, approaching the level of developed countries without a development level similar to them. The decrease in the birthrate of the population is linked to a decline in fertility but also to the foreign migratory rate (Alfonso, 2005). The lean years since the collapse of the Soviet Union have hurt the economy and civil society. A lack of resources and infrastructure means Cuba is poorly equipped to cope with a shrinking labor force and an expanding pensioner class. Recent measures to improve pensions and help, and a media campaign highlighting aspects of living with aged people and improving their subjective living conditions contribute to better integration in the home dynamics. These measures favor the positive acknowledgement of the elders' participation in chores and giving not only their time, but their pensions and other help they receive, to activities such as buying and cooking food, sewing, and taking care of children and sick relatives. In this way, they contribute to the solution of specific family problems.

Authorities argue for restructuring of the health system, an expansion of social security, and a review of current policies and legislation related to human resources. For example, the retirement age is fifty-five for women and sixty for men. A decade ago there was consideration that people should retire early to create jobs for young generations; likely Cubans will soon have to continue working until older. Socioeconomic development and using the creative capacities of skilled human resources over the next few decades will allow Cuba to deal with the challenge of an aging population (Acosta, 2003b).

Many Cubans have migrated to the United States. Most of those who did so in the 1960s are now becoming elderly. Approximately 20 percent are over the age of sixty-five (with a median age of 43.6 years). Cubans in the United States are demographically unusual given their average age. Cuban elders in south Florida, contrary to the model of extended multigenerational household arrangement, often prefer to live alone. This could be related to changing family dynamics and household arrangements arising from the processes of migration and acculturation (Martinez, 2002). Some elderly living in the United States have started to visit Cuba.

OTHER FAMILY SITUATIONS

It important to consider exodus from Cuba because of its implications for family life (Acosta, 2004). Family issues and the search for

a better life are present both in legal and illegal departures. State subventions and gratuities for the population in health care and elementary, middle, and high school education do not seem to satisfy equally
the entire population. This explains legal and illegal emigration, mainly
to the United States, by more than a million Cubans during the forty-
five years of the revolutionary process. However, most Cubans still live
in Cuba. According to government data, in 2001 the number of Cubans
living abroad was between 1.4-1.5 million, most of them residing in
the United States. The 1990 U.S. Census recorded 1,043,932 persons
of Cuban origin (Aja Díaz, 2001). The tragic fate of many illegal migrants has made separations from relatives painful. It is estimated
that in the early 1990s, for every Cuban who reached Florida on a raft
or other watercraft another died in the attempt. The paradox is that
family well-being at times depends on a rupture with the family that
brings pain to those that leave and those who stay. This rupture not
only takes place among parents, children, brothers, sisters, grandparents, aunts, uncles, and cousins but also among close friends who are
vulnerable to the feelings of loss, emptiness, loneliness, and nostal-
gia. Some ties are broken while others become tighter with family,
friends, and acquaintances that have migrated before and can become
important sources of support. Many parents do not take their children
when leaving illegally. Instead, family cares for them and parents hope
to claim them later, thus sparing them the risk of the adventure.

This brings about the problem of identity. Parents leaving their children and integrating into a different economic system, perhaps more
prosperous but more restrictive, sacrifice their own values, traditions,
customs, and language without always having fully weighted the emotional consequences for those who undertake the adventure and those
who stay behind. In these cases, family becomes the only effective tie
of emigrants with their own culture, with their country of origin, a
connection that few break completely. The restructuring of widened
and transformed relative networks resulting from changes brought
about by leaving their country is one of the comforts emigrants find
in their new situation (Martinez, 2002). Relations among them is expressed through exchanged values, not only remittances—most of
them to Cuba from abroad—but other types of exchange: letters, gifts,
pictures, visits, phone calls, videos, and other means allowing and
guaranteeing contacts and preserving affection and language. These

contacts are undoubtedly endowed with a strong sentimental component (Martínez, Morejón, & Aja, 1996).

Many consider economic aid through regular remittances a certain kind of obligation of blood relationships (cf. Martín & Guadalupe, 1998). Those living in Cuba with an eye on their emigrant relatives get used to living on remittances and generally think that it is the emigrants' duty to help them financially. Some consider it a duty of their family living in the States to claim them if they also decide to leave Cuba. Although there is undoubtedly a sentimental component on both sides, help can even be demanded and negative judgments made when the desired amount is not received, while ignoring the economic situation of their relatives abroad and their efforts to adjust to their new environment, often not favorable for people just arriving from poor countries.

Family remittances through both formal and informal routes, regulated recently by the U.S. government, amounts to four to five billion U.S. dollars per year. This is evidence of the weight family solidarity has reached in recent years. The importance of remittances for economic problems in a family, and the undeniable contribution this income represents for the economy of a country with a tenth of its population abroad, has gradually transformed the way emigration is seen, loosing the political connotations it had in the early decades of the Revolution. Emigration is understood now as a result of the economic situation. Although not necessarily a positive action, migrating for economic causes is accepted as natural, a neutral decision from the political point of view, something personal having to do with deciding where more favorable conditions are to be found, an option depending on individual and family possibilities and projects.

CONCLUDING COMMENTS

Situations as described in this chapter are not to be over generalized, although they can be considered individual responses to a crisis. This crisis, however, does not reach the extreme of having children quit school in order to work. School boards and parents maintain a strict monitoring system to prevent it. Most children hanging out in the tourist areas during school time, in school uniforms and asking for gifts from tourists, are not barefoot nor show signs of violence or neglect, nor are undernourished or suffer evident health problems. This reflects difference between the Cuban social and economic system and those in many other countries in the hemisphere and explains the standing of the Cuban socialist project in spite of its problems.

Other topics such as the decline in population growth, the increase in the average age for marriage, the refusal to procreate in the case of the women with higher educational levels, the frequent teenage pregnancies, the indiscriminate abortion practices and their use instead of other birth control that may temporarily be hard to get, the increase in the number of extended families, and the aging of the population are some of the issues influencing family life. It is impossible to analyze in detail all aspects or factors influencing families in this one chapter.

In the contributors' opinion, what is actually important is not whether couples marry or not, but that the decision to share their lives is taken with a full awareness of the responsibility they are taking on. This responsibility—and not marriage as such—should be permanent. It should be permanent regardless of decisions on how to best organize their lives, including the freedom to undo couple relationships and obsolete commitments when they no longer fit with the requirements of personal development. However, what was built during the relationship should not be destroyed and, especially, maintaining close ties with their offspring in the case of separation is important.

What happens in Cuba as far as the stability of couples is concerned is not too different from the situation in the rest of the world. Frequent problems between couples do not afflict Cuban society exclusively; what should be a source of concern are disagreements among relatives for spurious reasons that are disturbing the roots of family life. The problems pointed out are not exhaustive, but offer enough for debate and concern. Not only Catholics but also other Christians express concern about social and family instability, preach the value of marital fidelity and marriage, and organize activities that are well received and attended to in the community.

Specialists in social and religious studies speak about a religious revival when referring to the increase in attendance at the services by various religious persuasions in the last decade. However, the analysis of religious initiatives on the family environment and the constructive counterbalance of state institutions in this area has not been systematically approached (Ramírez Calzadilla, 2003). It should be kept in mind that cultural patterns transmitted by the family secure the continuity of every civilization and that social changes bear the stamp of strategies implemented for the transformation of the family (Fromm, Horkheimer, & Parsons, 1970).

A generation ago urban women often had three or four children, and in small towns or the countryside, women had even more. Today only a few courageous women are willing to give birth to more than one child and when they have more, they often are from different fathers. Couples forty years of age and older are more stable and, when the couple is functional, the man holds by consensus the main role. Otherwise, his public image would be damaged, which does not benefit either the wife or the children. Adult women without a partner are common because men of their age are often attracted to younger women. When fathers leave after younger and more attractive lovers, abandoned women usually retaliate by fostering bad relations with their children.

Smith and Padula (1996) argue that Cuban women have become more independent of men and families as they have come to control more resources. This has allowed them to risk divorce and become more assertive in their familial interactions. The classic role of family has been diminished due to women's income and state services.

Basic education is still free and compulsory. The free primary health care network of family doctors' offices, though not without its problems, covers fundamental necessities (e.g., routine checkups for children, elderly, expectant mothers, newborns, and works as a bridge to more specialized treatments and hospitals). This offers a basis to guarantee a life at the level of elemental requirements, complimented with a fixed monthly amount of groceries and a ration of consumer goods distributed according to a ration card.

Other services subsidized by the State include electricity, water, telephones, and public transportation. Although not sufficient, their price is in agreement with salary levels but the increased cost of consumer goods such as food, clothes, and shoes, as well as house repairs and electric appliances, has increased greatly above salary levels and have to be bought in CUC.

Contemporary challenges for Cuban families include the inadequate quality and quantity of housing, which is partly the product of the relative inadequacy of salaries, the dearth of leisure time options that might help to calm daily tensions, and inadequate remedies (legal and other) to conflict owing to a shortage of college trained professionals who can provide systematic treatment of complex family situations.

There are also macrosocial factors including priorities that demand permanent attention from the State: political and financial external pressures, problems having to do with consumption, and aging processes that in the short run will affect the availability of labor force and demand larger investments in health care for those in the third age. There are also permanent problems with basic service facilities and an inadequate number of houses to satisfy accumulated requirements.

These are some of the most pressing needs of Cuban families today for which the families themselves have been finding provisional solutions. A more detailed analysis as to the diversity of family organization from a gender point of view or from those of skin color, social, economic and cultural differences, geographic regions, or local specificity is impossible at this time due to the lack of appropriate research. Research tends to offer general results contributing to the drawing of policies for specific problems, and does not deepen too much into differences, although awareness of the importance of highlighting diversity seems to be emerging in academic circles and political levels. Given the lack of more specific research results, it is not feasible to offer now more accurate conclusions on the "typical" family model and it's regional, social, or cultural variations implying a systematic evaluation of its traditional elements and the speed and complexity of social and family changes reality imperceptibly imposes.

To conclude, the contributors would like to recall Humboldt (1998) when he wrote about "that place, celebrated by travelers of all nations." Cuba arouses today, among those that know or think they know it, great passions and fidelity or a visceral rejection that is not really justified by an in-depth analysis of the process of successful effort to maintain political independence and negotiate conditions for trade exchange not implying the elimination of the fundamental achievements of socialism. Notwithstanding tastes and preferences, what is truly important for all is that Cuba continues to be loyal to itself and has not lost its character as a paradise for many who see it as the only potential hope for economically dependent countries.

NOTES

1. The Revolutionary Government was organized by Fidel Castro and his partisans in January 1959 after the fight against President Fulgencio Batista. In April 1961, this government became socialist. This period is also referred to as the Revolution.

2. In the Hispanic world, everyone usually has a double surname, the first being the father's and the second one the mother's. They are not hyphenated. Listings are by the first surname, thus García Márquez, Gabriel, and not Márquez, Gabriel G., which would be normally the case in the English-speaking world.

EMERGING TRENDS

Chapter 19

Emerging Trends
for Family Scholarship Across Societies

Stephan M. Wilson
Charles B. Hennon

This book presents information about families within their socio-cultural contexts. Trends and conditions are of importance as family structuring and functioning are shaped by demographic, environmental, religious, political, and economic factors. These conditions all contribute in defining parameters within which families subsist. This includes the very nature of families, for example, how roles are defined, the size and composition of the family, job opportunities available, health conditions, and incidence of marriage and divorce. Likewise, how families are organized and act influence their social and physical environments. There is a nexus of interrelated events as real families reproduce and produce culture and social organization.

Chapter contributors often speak of these conditions and trends. For example, how religion influences family life in Iran, Italy, and the Philippines; how political conditions influence family life in China, Cuba, Romania, and Sweden; or how economic factors including conditions of employment affect families such as in Brazil, Germany, Kenya, and Mexico.

Some of the global changes affecting families include:

1) women's average age at first marriage and childbirth has risen, delaying the formation of new families; 2) families and households have gotten smaller; 3) the burden on working-age

parents of supporting younger and older dependents has increased; 4) the proportion of female-headed households has increased; and 5) women's participation in the formal labor market has increased at the same time that men's has declined, shifting the balance of economic responsibility in families. (Bruce, Lloyd, & Leopard, 1995, p. 5)

Some "universals" or worldwide changes recently noted include "movement toward individual partner choice, more divorces, lower fertility, and greater opportunities for women" (Adams, 2004, p. 1076). Among the family life patterns discussed in this book are

1. household types, family forms, and residency patterns;
2. age at first marriage, mate selection patterns, and changes in the meaning, incidence, and timing of premarital sex;
3. divorce;
4. fertility issues;
5. gender-related life chances and changing gender norms;
6. religion and ethnic traditions and their influence on family life;
7. diversity in family life in the form of social class, socioeconomic status, and caste;
8. families and stress;
9. aging and caregiving;
10. social policy.

Contributors in this book note many of the same changes indicated by Adams and Bruce and colleagues. However, when considering families across societies or cultures, while some similarities prevail and there is movement toward even greater homogeneity, a great variety in family composition, organization, and functioning is also readily apparent. So, while families everywhere face many of the same general challenges (e.g., finding a partner, earning a living, raising children, managing stress, or caring for the elderly), there remains much diversity in how these are accomplished.

By examining how different cultures and societies approach the challenges of family life, readers hopefully have developed a better understanding of, and appreciation for, cultures and societies differing from their own. This understanding can help readers to consider possibilities for the future of their own and others' societies.

THE FUTURE

Obviously, one cannot actually predict the future for families. However, a few social circumstances appear likely and warrant subsequent understanding by family scholars and others who are interested in families around the globe. Among these trends are

1. movements toward peace or war and social unrest;
2. changes in political and religious ideologies;
3. globalization;
4. increased access to communication and other technology (including the mass media);
5. population growth;
6. population movement.

How these trends could sway family life are worth considering.

Peace, War, and Social Unrest

Families benefit from peace and suffer from war. War can wreck havoc on families as members go off to war, perhaps suffering casualties. Families also face threats of death and destruction as invasions occur, bombs drop, and their communities become war zones. Families often flee and become refugees, sometimes living for years in refugee camps or resettling in other countries. Landmines worldwide pose a continuing threat to people, including children. Civil wars have been and are still occurring in many locations. In some places there are ethnic or religious conflicts (often mingled with political issues) leading to bloodshed. Ethnic cleansing destroys families. Terrorism makes families cautious.

While the cold war might be over, regional hot spots and terrorism continue. Civil unrest including ethnic or religious violence and civil war continues in some nations. In the 1990s, over two million children died (and three times this number were seriously injured or disabled) from armed conflicts; at any given time, around the globe there are about three dozen nations in some phase of major armed conflict (Worldpress, 2007). Examples include Algeria, Sudan (where slavery exists), Somalia and several other African nations, Haiti, Columbia, Cyprus, Russia, Indonesia, Iraq, and elsewhere. Some of the countries reviewed in this book have families recently or currently suffering from the effects of war and civil strife (i.e., Iran, Sierra Leone, South Africa, and Turkey). India has sporadic armed hostilities with Pakistan, and conflicts between Muslim and Hindu families in Kashmir have resulted in many deaths.

Worldwide, the disabilities and death to family members are real, tragic, and the effects long lasting. Forced migration or fleeing to avoid conflict disrupts families. The stress of war and terrorism takes its toll on emotional and economic health as well. As peaceful solutions are found, families can benefit. As war breaks out or continues, families literally die. It is safe to say that peace, war, and social unrest offer different challenges and choices to families. As conditions change, for better or worse, families will respond.

Changes in Political and Religious Ideologies

War and other civil disturbances are not the only features of the political milieu affecting families. Future changes in political as well as religious ideologies will have an influence on families throughout the world. Families form and function within the context of the political and religious orientations that dominate a region. Hence, marital dynamics, family formation, employment opportunities, gender issues, family stress, aging, and other family issues must be considered within a political and religious context.

Several illustrations can be gleaned from this book. For example, decrees from the government influence family size in China. The changes in Romania since 1989 are profound; families have had to make considerable adjustments. The reunification of Germany has placed many families under new federal regulations. Political changes in South Africa are influencing families. Cuba has been a socialist state for several decades, a fact that permeates all aspects of family living.

As governments change in type or in their focus on families, the implications for families can be extreme in "positive" or "negative" ways. For example, as welfare and other social safety net programs are changed, families often suffer. Poverty, economic conditions, poor health, crime, and other problems challenge many families in both more and less developed nations (United Nations, 2005c; United

Nations Development Programme [UNDP], 2001, 2004, 2006; United Nations Population Fund [UNPF], 2001). Policy sensitive to and supportive of families will continue to be on the policy agendas in many nations.

Norms and mores concerning family/gender roles, divorce, number of spouses, abortion, fertility, and sexual activity, for instance, often derive from religious doctrines and beliefs. Examples of such norms and resulting behaviors can be found in the chapters on families in Iran, Italy, Mexico, the Philippines, Turkey, and many others. Another example, but not from this book, is the return to polygamy in the Republic of Ingushetia. While the Soviets were in power, polygamy was illegal although apparently still practiced. With the president's decree, the Ingush can now follow their Islamic traditions in ways recognized by society and secular law ("Polygamy's Back," 1999). As another example, concerns have been expressed about the treatment of women and girls in more "fundamentalist Islamic" nations such as Afghanistan or Iraq. Likewise, the debate continues about the "circumcision" or "female genital mutilation" of girls and women in parts of Africa and the Middle East.

As religious contexts change, families are affected (Houseknecht & Pankhurst, 2000; Norris & Inglehart, 2004).[1] In general, the more fundamentalist the religious orientation, the more traditional patterns of gender and family are emphasized. In the future, as countries move toward or away from fundamentalist or stricter religious doctrines, the context within which families form and function will be altered. Likewise, as families become more or less religious, or seek "existential security," in secular societies, this will influence family functioning (Smith, 2006). As a case in point, Islam is one of the fast growing religions in the United States albeit not the fundamentalist version of Islam found in several other countries. Muslim families can have notions about modesty, family size, and gender roles adding to the diversity of "American" families. Mormons (Church of Jesus Christ of Latter Day Saints) are also increasing in numbers, not only in the United States but elsewhere (Jarvis, 2000). Family is integral to followers of this faith and many aspects of Mormon family life distinguish it from other family lifestyles. Many families, including Hispanic and other immigrants to the United States are becoming fundamentalist Christians (or Pentecostal) (also true in developing nations) (Kosmin,

Mayer, & Keyser, 2001). The use of birth control, child rearing practices including the use of spanking, gender roles, marital power, and perhaps the home schooling of children might distinguish such families. The Promise Keepers (and other such groups; Promise Keepers, 2007) and the roles of men in families, and efforts to stop abortion, are two movements that have been influencing family life in the United States (and elsewhere such as Portugal). There is diversity of religions as well as in religiosity, and thus in family life, everywhere. As religious diversity increases or decreases, so will family life. Religious diversity is one consequence of globalization, and globalization can help religious families "repair certain stresses and tears in the social fabric of their lives brought about by a rapidly changing world" (Jarvis, 2000, p. 238; see also A.T. Kearney, 2004).

Globalization

Globalization is resulting in what Robertson (1992, p. 6) termed "the compression of the world into a single space." Understanding families around the world not only requires sensitivity to political and religious changes, but to changing regional and global economic and other conditions as well. For instance, what the future might hold for families in less industrialized or less economically stable nations (e.g., Cuba, Philippines, Romania, and Sierra Leone) as the effects of globalization and economic development efforts materialize (A.T. Kearney, 2004).

Internal economic conditions are not insulated from global economic trends. Families have suffered due to the economic conditions in Argentina and many left for Europe and elsewhere. However, it is argued that in Brazil, not only are there better employment opportunities, but families benefit through less political corruption and higher quality consumer goods. These benefits for families derive from the country's desired participation in the global economy (Amaral, 2001). In various countries, globalization of the economy and multinational corporations are related to increased standards of living for both skilled and unskilled labors. In some cases, the gap between the poorest and the wealthiest families has decreased (A.T. Kearney, 2004; Rodas-Martini, 2001; UNDP, 2001, 2006). Other potential benefits to families from globalization include increased access to education and health care, social mobility, better conditions for women, and longer life expectancy. Reductions in fertility might also be beneficial to some families.

Globalization has increased global wealth and stimulated economic growth (A.T. Kearney, 2004; "Rich man, poor man," 2007; UNDP, 2001). At the same time, in certain areas it has also increased income inequality and environmental degradation (cf. Pratarelli, 2005). Flexible labor markets are associated with poverty and unemployment and related family and social problems (Briar-Lawson, Lawson, Hennon, & Jones, 2001; Frankman, 1995). Poverty is causing many families to increase their pressure on fragile natural resources to survive (UNDP, 2006; UNPF, 2001). Migration also results from globalization and associated economic opportunities and constraints (Briar-Lawson et al., 2001; Skinner, 1999; Wong, 1997).

Many changes to family functioning in less industrialized or non-Western nations can possibly result from the nature of global economic interdependency. For example, in addition to the ones mentioned, the concept of time and how families make use of time could change. Western ideas about "being on time" and employment versus family time might influence families as members are employed by multinational corporations or companies involved in international trade.

The changing nature of employment and the interconnected world economy also influences family life in more industrialized nations. Many high-tech jobs have been created and many families have accumulated wealth (Islam, 2000). At the same time, more employment is now found in the service sector, often at lower wages and with poorer working conditions and benefits. Families suffer from job insecurity as well as un- and underemployment. Economic recession means families, both poor and rich, need to make adjustments. People worldwide create their own employment, sometimes as petty commodity producers or micro entrepreneurs (Eversole, 2003; Hennon, Jones, Roth, & Popescu, 1998). Families often have multiple members (including children) employed, and some members have multiple jobs (Briar-Lawson et al., 2001; Hennon, Loker, & Walker, 2000). Multiple workers and jobs mean even more complications in balancing employment and family, and can increase stress. Both rural and urban families are being affected by globalization (Hennon & Hildenbrand, 2005; Phillips & Ilcan, 2003). Globalization, no doubt, is influencing families in myriad ways (Ritzer, 2003; UNDP, 2001). Globalization is multifaceted and does not mean just interconnected economies or multinational corporations (Hermans & Kempen, 1998):

> Processes of globalization are drawing people from different cultural origins into close relationships, as can be seen, for example, in the unprecedented expansion of tourism, the flourishing of multinational corporations, the emergence of new geographical unities (e.g., the European Community, the Association of Southeast Asian Nations, and the new unification of South American countries: Mercosur), the dissemination of pop culture, the increasing flow of migrations, the growth of diasporas, the emergence of Internet communities, and the establishment of global institutions (e.g., the International Monetary Fund and the United Nations). (p. 1111)

As globalization intensifies, there are reasons for believing that family diversity would be reduced. That is, families everywhere will become more similar in many ways. At the same time, there are reasons for believing that globalization can reduce cultural homogeneity and lead to more divergence in family patterns within societies. This idea can be captured in two concepts, hybridization and glocalization.

Hybridization is a result of cultural connection such as when cultures are not internally homogenous and externally distinctive (Hermans & Kempen, 1998). Hybrid family phenomena result when people transform existing family (i.e., cultural) practices into new practices. Interconnections among cultures and resulting hybridization make for family practices being localized. That is, ideas are fit to local conditions. While families might change, they can do so in a manner consistent with local customs and values, or at least in ways that are continuations rather than discontinuations with previous family patterns. As Hermans and Kempen argued, the greater the connection is across cultures, the more these cultures begin to interweave, resulting in complex mixtures and new genres of family structures and practices being created. In this manner, culture changes, but not necessarily in ways indicating less diversity across societies.

Rather than considering globalization as a process overriding locality, Robertson (1992) pointed to the global in its local manifestations.

His concept for this is *glocalization*. The process of glocalization helps in making "sense of two seemingly opposing trends: homogenization and heterogenization. These trends can be depicted as not only simultaneous but also complementary and interpenetrative" (Hermans & Kempen, 1998, p. 1114). With globalization, in which the global and the local interpenetrate, cultures develop as interconnected parts of a "world system." The idea of glocalization helps in remembering that the influences of diverse cultures are often modified in local applications. Families can be seen as adopting aspects of the global and re-working them in ways to fit with the local.

Along with changes in political, economic, health, and other institutions associated with globalization to which families must adapt, families are also exposed to "foreign" influences in other ways. These various factors and influences are all part of the context in which families live and function. Opportunities for borrowing coexist with choices to craft family life in ways reflecting homogenous cultural norms or in ways somewhat alien to the local culture as known. The result is families sometimes changing and being "alternative" to local sensibilities, sometimes hybridizing local with global, and sometimes rejecting the global and reflecting the local.

Technology, Communication, and Mass Media

Technology is another contributor to the context within which families function. This is true for technology as a manifestation of globalization as well as its realization in local infrastructure.

The rapid expansion of communication networks (e.g., World Wide Web, e-mail, cell phones, and facsimile transmissions) provides families with an array of opportunities for interaction and development. For example, some families are communicating through e-mail on a regular basis. People can communicate with relatives living in the same or in other countries. This enables families to interact regularly with relatives not in close proximity (e.g., children away at college, older persons and children in distant locations, relatives who have migrated, or noncustodial parents and their children after divorce). Besides cases found in countries like Australia, Germany, Sweden (including facilitating LAT relationships), or other industrialized nations, such communication technology enables families to "interact" with members who have migrated, such as from Cuba, Mexico, the Philippines, or Turkey. As these technologies become ingrained in family life, the very meaning of "being and living as family" can change. Coresidence might not be required. Kin in distant locations can be easily consulted about family matters. Moving away does not necessarily mean "moving out" or losing contact.[2]

This technology also permits access to a massive stock of information enabling families to gain knowledge about a variety of issues. Some families learn about resources and "self-help" by browsing the World Wide Web. Job opportunities can be found. Help is available for educating and raising children. Health care information is more readily accessible. Religious, economic, and political information is at one's fingertips.

With advances in technology, family patterns can change, becoming more "modern" or at least different. More education, more information, and more experiences can lead to changing family dynamics. Without such access to information or experiences, one only knows the local culture (Derné, 1994; UNDP, 2001). With such access or experiences, other possibilities can become part of a family's worldview. Technology has the potential for enabling families to learn about different ways of functioning, which might be contrary to the dominant cultural, political, and religious orientations in which they are living (e.g., reports of the Chinese government restricting access of citizens to the World Wide Web). Cultural norms are not fully shared. They are often contested by individuals and families. Hence, it is likely that the greater the distribution of the technology associated with worldwide communication networks, the greater the potential for variance in family patterns.

Mass media (including satellite television) and Westernization are powerful. Many contributors in this book indicate the influences these have been having on family life. People are being exposed to new ideas about sexuality, gender roles, love, parenting, and marriage. Young people, in particular, are often influenced in ways that create tension with their parents and older family members. As the forces of Westernization invade non-Western and less industrialized countries, changes in family functioning are likely to result. Examples of such change are found worldwide, such as in Romania, Turkey, and Iran. However, mass media and global communication can also lead to changes in family life in Western and more industrialized nations. Increased interest in Eastern and alternative health care by Western families is but one example. Using aspects of Eastern religions to help manage the stress of modern day living would be another. Entertainment choices, information about world events, demand for consumer goods, and culinary tastes are other examples. Globalization does not have to mean Westernization (Hermans & Kempen, 1998; Jisi, 2000; Ritzer, 2003).[3]

Technology can empower people. Harnessing technology can expand the choices open to families. In India, Internet connectivity in rural villages allows accessing and sharing of meteorological, crop, health, and other information. Families are better informed and thus can make better decisions. Technology also means employment and economic growth. A critical mass of entrepreneurial activities can generate sustainable momentum for socioeconomic development that can be of benefit to families. One representation of this is India that is experiencing a growth in regional, information technology-based, economic clusters. The skills needed for high-tech start-ups as well as supplying the skilled workers for established businesses has been driving the opening of new universities and the expansion of ancillary services (UNDP, 2001). The effects of globalization and technology-led growth can change the determinants of social mobility.

Communication and other technology can benefit families of all economic strata. There is now "unprecedented networking and knowledge-sharing opportunities brought about by the falling costs of communications. However, it is also a time of growing public controversy . . ." on a wide range of issues from pornography, to infusion of "foreign" values and ideas, privacy, how to decide about transgenic crops, or availability of lifesaving drugs for those in need (UNDP, 2001, p. iii). However, it is important to remember that the majority of people have never been on the Internet nor made an international telephone call.

Poor families everywhere face needs that technology can address. Examples include combating disease, growing and transporting food, or distance education. In some countries, concerns are voiced about the gap between poor and other families relative to the availability of computers and Internet accessibility. This gap potentially influences the educational achievements of children and thus the long-term conditions of family life. Research focused on the needs of poor families shows technology can be a critical tool for achieving success, not just one of the rewards for being successful. Technology in conjunction with other development tools can transform the lives of poor families while allowing sustainable economic development opportunities for poor countries (UNDP, 2001).

Families are regarded as the foundation for economic development (Cass & Cappo, 1995; Hennon et al., 1998; Zeitlin et al., 1995). Families create and provide human, social, and cultural capital for producing and reproducing a skilled labor force. Many families engage in entrepreneurial activities that create jobs for themselves and others (Hennon et al., 2000). Access to appropriate technology can be an asset for strengthening families as well as in families strengthening economies and societies. There is potential for improved quality of life for families, communities, nations, regions, and the world as knowledge creation and capacity building are directed toward basic needs and valued goals. With diversity in families, societies, economies, and governments, a diversity of strategic plans is required. Constraints must be considered and priorities must be established for resource allocation and the type of society, population, and families desired.

Population Growth

In general, the world's population is aging as people live longer and healthier lives with developing countries converging on the average life expectancy found in more developed countries (United Nations, 2005b; UNDP, 2006). In developing countries, life expectancy has increased by an average of nine years over the past three decades, compared with seven years in "richer" nations. The exception is sub-Saharan Africa where life expectancy is now lower than thirty years ago; in some cases by thirteen to twenty years.

Even with this "convergence," there are great disparities in life expectancy across nations. In 2001, twenty-two nations had life expectancy less than fifteen years. Over twenty nations experienced declines in average life expectancy between 1985 and 2000, in seven nations by more than seven years of life. Some of the decline in life expectancy is due to HIV/AIDS. There are about forty million people living with HIV/AIDS; 95 percent of these people live in developing countries and 70 percent in sub-Saharan Africa (United Nations, 2005b, 2005d; UNDP, 2004, 2006). In some nations, the life expectancy for women is now lower than for men, reflecting the "feminization" of HIV/ AIDS (UNDP, 2006). The shifting roles of women as nurturers and providers, comforters and protectors, and as traditional passive recipients to emerging decision makers is mirrored by shifting roles for men who may be called upon increasingly to parent, nurture, and to provide for the needs of dependents in what were once thought of as female patterns. This has many ramifications for family life.

Around 190 nations have Information, Education, and Communication (IEC) programs to increase public awareness and to change risky sexual behavior, and many nations have programs to promote condom use. However, supplies of condoms are short and poor quality remains an issue. In more developed regions of the world, around 13 percent of couples use condoms. In less developed regions the rate is 3 percent, and it is 1 percent in Africa (United Nations, 2005d).

In some areas the infant and maternal mortality rates are still high. Famine takes its toll. Health conditions including infectious diseases kill. Wars and violence cut short the lives of many people. The rate of population growth or decline has repercussions for families.

China is the world's most populous country; India could take over this distinction in the coming decades. The population of the world is increasing. In 2006 it was about 6.5 billion and is projected to reach 7.9 billion by 2025 (United Nations, 2005e). The current population is double of what it was in 1960. Fertility rates vary widely and remain high in many regions. The projected population growth will mostly take place in today's developing countries, especially in Africa and Asia, while some developed countries are projected to experience significant population decline. The forty-nine least-developed countries, who are already straining to provide basic social services to the people living there, will nearly triple in size from 668 million to 1.86 billion people. Whether world population reaches a higher projection of 10.9 billion, a lower projection of 7.9 billion, or the medium projection of 9.3 billion by 2040, likely depends on success in ensuring women's right to education and health, including reproductive health, and in ending absolute poverty stressing families (UNPF, 2001). Families are the arenas in which fertility behavior is played out.

As the population grows, there are demands on natural and social resources. Land becomes scarce, food production and distribution cannot always keep up, population density increases, and there are concerns about clean water and adequate fuel.[4] Population and the environment are closely related, but the connections between them are complex and varied. These connections depend on specific circumstances found within countries and regions. Understanding the connections requires considering the interaction among political structures, the family as an institution, affluence, consumption, technology, and population growth.[5] It also requires considering family dynamics, gender relations, and social change at all levels of society (Briar-Lawson et al., 2001; Henderson & Hoggart, 2003; Phillips & Ilcan, 2003; UNDP, 2006; UNPF, 2001).

Equal status between men and women and guaranteeing rights to reproductive health, including more control over the size and spacing of the family, will help to slow population growth. This will reduce the future size of the world's population and help relieve environmental and social stress. If women have only the number of children they want and can support, families will be smaller and population growth slower. This will allow time for crucial decisions to be made concerning the environment, food production and distribution, social services, and the standard of living and the quality of life of families everywhere (UNPF, 2001).

Resolutions to the concerns mentioned in previous text will affect families. Inadequate supplies of food, clean water, and housing, as well as fuel shortages, will have negative impacts. Electricity and other utility subsidies favor urban elites while poor people often spend long hours gathering fuel while also paying higher unit prices for energy. Rapid population growth influences economic growth, as there are more demands for limited resources, including money for education, health, and social security, and welfare programs. Population density influences housing cost and family functioning.

Simultaneous to world population growth, some countries (particularly in Europe) are decreasing in population and have below population replacement fertility rates. These countries are "dying" in a sense. In such countries, care for the elderly as well as having enough productive laborers are becoming concerns. Social security and other programs can suffer, as there are fewer workers per aged population, and the dependency ratio changes. In some cases, the social contract of the young caring for the old, and the social solidarity intrinsic to societies, is in jeopardy. Worldwide, families are confronting novel conditions relative to caregiving.

Population Movement

Populations also move. Urbanization is a common phenomenon and another challenge. One-half of the world's population is estimated to live in urban areas in 2007 and the number of large urban agglomerations is increasing. However, about one-half of all urban-dwellers live in settlements with fewer than 500,000 inhabitants (United Nations, 2005e). Cities in many parts of the developing world are growing at twice the rate of overall population growth, placing hard-to-meet demands on overburdened social services. Every day about 160,000 people move from rural areas to cities (UNPF, 2001). Families thus must adapt to novel social conditions and devise new lifestyles.

Unplanned urban development often makes things worse. In developing countries, many cities face serious environmental health challenges and worsening conditions due to rapid growth, lack of proper infrastructure to meet increasing needs, contaminated water and air, and more garbage than they can handle (UNDP, 2006; UNPF, 2001). Up to one-half the population of many urban areas live in squatter settlements or shantytowns, such as the *gecekondu* in Turkey, the squatter shanties of urban Nairobi (e.g., Kibera), and the *favelas* of Brazil. Families living here are vulnerable to catastrophic events like floods, storms, or earthquakes.

High fertility and large families are features of rural life. This is due, in part, because women lack choice in the matter. With fewer opportunities in rural areas, many men migrate, increasing women's family burdens and responsibilities. Urbanization offers women opportunities and risks. Pregnancy and childbirth are generally safer because health care is more accessible. City life also offers broader choices for education, employment, and marriage. At the same time, cities heighten the risk of sexual violence, abuse, and exploitation (UNPF, 2001).

People move due to social unrest and war. Families are on the move as refugees and in some cases to escape famine and disease. People also move in pursuit of employment and better life chances, but they do not always find it (Acosta, 2003, 2004; Jelloun, 2000; Radina, Wilson, & Hennon, in press; Skinner, 1999; Thomas, 1995; Weiner, 1995). People migrate to other countries as "labor migrants," "economic migrants," "economic refugees," or "guest workers." This sometimes leads to social unrest while enabling countries to fulfill labor needs and help fill pension coffers (especially in Europe with many countries experiencing declining populations) and spur economic development (Islam, 2000; United Nations, 2005a). Ireland, as one example, has recently experienced a population gain from its diaspora returning, as well as immigrants from Europe and Asia moving there due to economic growth and opportunities. Germany and Australia, as well as Belgium, host many Turkish people. African and Filipino immigrants work in Italy (Valentini, 1998). Many Filipinos work abroad, as the Philippines is a major exporter of labor as is Turkey. People from many different countries move to Israel. Sweden is experiencing an increase in families from countries different from traditional immigration patterns (Davishpour, 1999). Canada is now home to people from quite dissimilar cultures (Wong, 1997). The United States is the destination of choice for many families; the migration from Mexico to the United States is one of the largest sustained population movements in the world (Hennon, Peterson, Polzin, & Radina, 2006).

Migration often happens in stages, with some family members staying behind and joining the others later. Sometimes families are disrupted instead, creating other problems (Acosta, 2003, 2004; Jelloun, 2000; Radina et al., in press). Some contributors have sounded an alarm about the crisis arising due to migration because of political, economic, and social conditions, both for host countries and the countries of origin (Weiner, 1995). Among other concerns is the "brain drain" from countries that could use the skills and creativity of people moving elsewhere for better opportunities.

Families are agents of population growth and movement. Individual families make choices about fertility and moving or staying put. In many cases, families will feel they have little control and little choice. Individual acts accumulate into major demographic patterns. Families also suffer or benefit from the consequences of population growth and movement. Population pressures can negatively affect the life chances of families worldwide. Environmental degradation can lead to food shortages and health problems. Migration can disrupt families, or create opportunities for a better quality of life. Migration can offer better access to employment, health care, education, and in many cases, a safer environment can enhance the capacities of families to meet the needs of their members. Fertility choices might differ after migration, allowing more caregiving and nurturing for each individual member of the family. In the future, as populations grow faster or slower, as urbanization spreads or stabilizes, as migration increases or decreases, families will be both the causes as well as the recipients of the positive and negative consequences.

CONCLUDING COMMENTS

Given the anticipated social conditions—differing conditions of peace and war; the varied political, economic, and religious contexts; the influences of globalization; the expansion of worldwide communications networks and diffusion of ideas via mass media; and population dynamics—an increase in the heterogeneity of families can be expected. The contributors believe this will be true both within countries as well as among countries. Families both within and across nations face disparate economic and other conditions. When faced with challenges and choices, families can respond differently. Demographic and lifestyle changes reflect and shape socioeconomic and political change. Variations in loving, parenting, and aging will continue. The pushes and pulls of family obligations and privileges will shift in some ways but remain in others. Families will continue to discover and use a range of ways to address similar issues. Diversity will prevail.

This forecast is offered while at the same time realizing that there is some movement toward less heterogeneity and toward more homogeneity under the hegemonic influence of improved communications, mass media, Westernization, globalization, migration, and tourism. It is likely to continue. However, there will never be just one family type, or just one position on gender roles, or just one way to raise children within a country or throughout the world. The lessening of boundaries between various countries around the world continually heightens the potential for family variance within countries at the same time that there can be movement toward less family heterogeneity among countries.

NOTES

1. It has been argued that all nations privilege (by laws and policy) at least one religion, and what is or is not (i.e., defined as a cult or excluded) a religion is determined in regard to the hegemonic religion (Beyer, 2003). In some nations there is little separation between government and religion. *Harry Potter and the Sorcerer's Stone* (among other books) was banned from school libraries in The United Arab Emirates because it contravenes Islamic values (see, e.g., Kazemipur & Rezaei, 2003). Some nations have an official religion (this might be called "civil religions"; see Beyer, 2003). As an illustration, in some countries the dominant religion such as Roman Catholicism or another form of Christianity, often "dictates" much about family life. Examples could include Malta, Ireland, Poland, Mexico, and Greece. China formally allows freedom of worship (Eckholm, 2002). However, worship must be in regulated churches that belong to the Communist Party-sponsored patriotic association. Up to fifteen million Protestants belong to the legal Protestant body; millions more attend "house" churches and refuse to pledge allegiance to the atheist Communist Party. The government has been cracking down on unauthorized worship such as that in the South China Church, the banned Falun Gong spiritual movement, and some Buddhist groups, often classified as cults. Some members of these worship groups have received death sentences in court. See Beyer (2003), Houseknecht and Pankhurst (2000), and Norris and Inglehart (2004) for more information on the influence of religions and which (such as Christianity, Islam, Judaism, Buddhism, Hinduism, Daoism, and Sikhism) are considered core in various societies.

2. On the other hand, mobile phones, computers, portable music devices, televisions, and the like can also divide families, as members become engrossed in the communication and entertainment technologies. Family members can be "psychologically absent" while being physically in the same space, as each (or some) attends to searching the Web, instant messaging, telephone conversations, text messaging, a private world of music enabled by headphones, or to other technology. A question might be the extent to which newer technologies have both strengthened families and encouraged communication (e.g., children having mobile phones so parents feel more secure about their safety) while at the same time altered communication patterns such that face-to-face conversation is less developed or important.

3. Islamic youth with largely Westernized ways of life take part in radical anti-Western activities. China has achieved an economic and technological surge amidst globalization. Many U.S. based multinational corporations are controlled by foreigners who are not Westerners (Jisi, 2000). Some scholars "object to the idea that cultural experiences, past or present, are moving toward cultural uniformity or standardization, as for example, is expressed in views that emphasize the unidirectional cultural influences of the West on the rest of the world. This idea of uniformity overlooks . . . the pervasive influence of counter-currents that derives from the local reception of Western culture" (Hermans & Kempen, 1998, p. 1113).

4. Two billion people currently lack sufficient food. Water use has increased sixfold over the past seventy years. Unclean water and poor sanitation kill over twelve

million people each year while air pollution kills nearly three million more. Nearly 60 percent of the 4.4 billion people in developing countries lack basic sanitation while 33 percent do not have access to clean water. Twenty-five percent lack adequate housing, 20 percent do not have access to modern health services, and 20 percent of children do not attend school through grade 5. By 2050, 4.2 billion people could be living in countries where their basic needs cannot be met. Poverty and rapid population growth are a deadly combination. Poor people depend more directly on natural resources (available land, water, wood) and suffer most directly from environmental degradation. The increasing degradation of the environment results not only from population growth, but also from rising affluence and unsustainable consumption patterns. One-half the world's population lives on the equivalent of US$2 per day or less; about one-quarter of the population tries to survive on less than US$1 per day. While many people practice wasteful consumption, many others cannot consume enough to survive (UNDP, 2004, 2006; UNPF, 2001).

5. There exists a huge consumption gap between industrialized and developing countries. The world's richest countries (20 percent of global population) account for 86 percent of total private consumption. The poorest 20 percent account for just over 1 percent. The news conference announcing the publication of *Footprints and Milestones: Population and Environmental Change* indicated that over his or her lifetime, a child born in an industrialized country will add more to consumption and pollution than thirty to fifty children born in developing countries. The ecological "footprint" of the more affluent is far deeper than that of the poor. In many cases, it exceeds the regenerative capacity of the earth (UNPF, 2001).

References

A. T. Kearney/Foreign Policy Globalization Index. (2004). *Measuring globalization: Economic reversals, forward momentum.* Available at www.foreignpolicy.com/story/cms.php?story_id=2493.

Abbasi-Shavazi, M. J. (2002, March). *Recent changes and the future of fertility in Iran* (UN/POP/CFT/2002/CP/8). Paper presented at Expert Group Meeting on Continuing the Fertility Transition, New York, NY.

Abbasi-Shavazi, M. J., McDonald, P., & Hosseini-Chavoshi, M. (2003, April). *Changes in family, fertility behavior and attitudes in Iran.* Paper presented at the Conference on Institutions, Ideologies and Agencies: Family change in the Arab Middle East and Diaspora, Chapel Hill, NC.

Abd Al-ati, H. (1995). *The family structure in Islam.* Plainfield, IN: American Trust.

Åberg, M. (1996). *Män är så lata—de bara jobbar* [Men are so lazy—they only work]. Uppsala: Sociologiska institutionen.

Abraham, L. (2002). Bhai-behen, true love, time pass: Friendships and sexual partnerships among youth in an Indian metropolis. *Culture, Health and Sexuality, 4,* 337-353.

Abrahamian, E. (1982). *Iran between two revolutions.* Princeton, NJ: Princeton University Press.

Abreu, A., Jorge, A. F., & Sorj, B. (1994). Desigualdade de gênero e raça. O informal no Brasil em 1990 [Gender and race inequality. The informal in the Brazil of 1990]. *Revista de Estudos Feministas,* número especial, 2o semestre de 1994, 153-178.

Abu-Odeh, L. (1996). Crimes of honor and the construction of gender in Arab societies. In M. Yamani (Ed.), *Feminism and Islam: Legal and literary perspectives* (pp. 141-194). Berkshire: Garnet.

Acar, F. (1995). Women and Islam in Turkey. In S. Tekeli (Ed.), *Women in modern Turkish society: A reader* (pp. 46-65). London: Zed Books.

Acosta, A. R., & Vitale, M. A. (2003). *Família: Redes, Laços e Políticas Públicas* [Family: Webs, bonds and public policies]. São Paulo: Pontific Catholic University of São Paulo.

Acosta, D. (2001, February 28). *Habitat—Cuba: Housing, a real headache.* Available at domino.ips.org/ips%5Ceng.nsf/vwWebMainView/6BB5624B241BA74280256A07005F7431/?OpenDocument.

Acosta, D. (2002, December 6). *Health—Cuba: Sex education needed to fight overuse of abortion.* Available at domino.ips.org/ips%5Ceng.nsf/vwWebMainView/29FFB33AA474F31D80256C8700793C63/?OpenDocument.

Acosta, D. (2003a, May 7). *Cuba: Emigrants lose their homes, their country—'And we lose them.'* Available at domino.ips.org/ips%5Ceng.nsf/vwWebMainView/ AAC4C73347771CBCC1256D2000332127/?OpenDocument.

Acosta, D. (2003b, October 21). *Population: Cuba's ageing 'baby-boomer' generation presents challenges.* Available at domino.ips.org/ips%5Ceng.nsf/vwWeb MainView/14B844EFE29E8525C1256DC6006BDFE3/?OpenDocument.

Acosta, D. (2004, May 19). *Population: For Cubans, emigration is 'forever.'* Available at domino.ips.org/ips%5Ceng.nsf/vwWebMainView/5D50CDC227C1DB 34C1256E9900825770/?OpenDocument.

Adamchak, D. J. (1996). Population ageing: Gender, family support and the economic condition of the older Africans. *Southern African Journal of Gerontology, 5*(2), 3-8.

Adamesteanu, G. (1998). Statutul femeilor in Romania [Status of women in Romania]. *22—Social Dialogue Review, 6,* 9.

Adams, B. N. (2004). Families and family study in international perspective. *Journal of Marriage and Family, 66,* 1076-1088.

Adams, B. N., & Trost, J. (Eds.). (2005). *Handbook of world families.* Thousand Oaks, CA: Sage.

Adams, H. C. (2004). Fighting an uphill battle: Race, politics, power, and institutionalization in Cuba. *Latin American Research Review, 39,* 168-182.

Adamson, D., & Jones, S. (1996). *The South Wales valleys: Continuity and change.* University of Glamorgan, Occasional Papers in the Regional Research Programme.

Adelson, P., Frommer, M., & Weisberg, E. (1995). A survey of women seeking termination of pregnancy in New South Wales. *Medical Journal of Australia, 163,* 419-122.

Adeokun, L. (1987). Creole and Yoruba households and family size. In C. Oppong (Ed.), *Sex roles, population and development in West Africa: Policy-related studies on work and demographic issues* (pp. 91-100). Portsmouth, NH: Heinemann.

Adoption among Hindus. (2003). Available at www.helplinelaw.com.

Afkhami, M., & Friedl, E. (1994). *In the eye of the storm: Women in postrevolutionary Iran.* New York: I. B. Tauris.

Afonso, M. L. M. (1995). Gênero e processo de socialização em creches comunitárias [Gender and process of socialization in community child-care centers]. *Cadernos de Pesquisa, 93,* 12-21.

Afonso, M. L. M. (2001). *A Polêmica sobre adolescência e sexualidade* [The polemics about adolescence and sexuality]. Belo Horizonte: Edições do Campo Social.

Afonso, M. L. M., & Filgueiras, C. A. C. (1996). Maternidade e vínculo social [Motherhood and social bond]. *Revista de Estudos Feministas, 4,* 319-337.

Africa, G., & Disangcopan, A. (2004). *An exploratory study of selected civil cases on annulment.* Paper submitted as requirement for Sociology 113, University of the Philippines, Department of Sociology, Quezon City.

Aganon, M. E. (1995). Migrant labor and the Filipino family. In A. E. Perez (Ed.), *The Filipino family, a spectrum of views and issues* (pp. 79-96). Quezon City: University of the Philippines Office of Research Coordination and University of the Philippines Press.

Aghajanian, A. (1983). Ethnic inequality in Iran: An overview. *International Journal of Middle East Studies, 15*, 211-224.

Aghajanian, A. (1985). Living arrangement of widows in Shiraz, Iran. *Journal of Marriage and the Family, 47*, 781-785.

Aghajanian, A. (1986a). Economic activity of children in two Iranian villages. *Journal of South Asian and Middle Eastern Studies, 10*, 67-77.

Aghajanian, A. (1986b). Some notes on divorce in Iran. *Journal of Marriage and the Family, 48*, 749-755.

Aghajanian, A. (1988a). Husband-wife conflict among two-worker families in Shiraz, Iran. *International Journal of Sociology of the Family, 18*, 15-20.

Aghajanian, A. (1988b). The value of children in rural and urban Iran. *Journal of Comparative Family Studies, 19*, 85-97.

Aghajanian, A. (1990). War and migrant families in Iran: An overview of a social disaster. *International Journal of Sociology of the Family, 20*, 97-107.

Aghajanian, A. (1991). Population change in Iran, 1966-86: A stalled demographic transition? *Population and Development Review, 17*, 703-715.

Aghajanian, A. (1993, October). *Infant mortality trends and differentials in Iran.* Paper presented at the Annual Meeting of the Southern Demographic Association, Charleston, SC.

Aghajanian, A. (1994). The status of women and female children in Iran: Update from the 1986 Census. In M. Afkhami & E. Fiedl (Eds.), *In the eye of the storm: Women in post-revolutionary Iran* (pp. 44-60). New York: I. B. Tauris.

Aghajanian, A. (1995). A new direction in population policy and family planning in the Islamic Republic of Iran. *Asian-Pacific Population Journal, 10*, 3-21.

Aghajanian, A. (1999). Fertility transition in the Islamic Republic of Iran. *Asian-Pacific Population Journal, 14*, 21-42.

Aghajanian, A., Agha, H., & Gross, A. (1996). Cumulative fertility in Iran. *Journal of Comparative Family Studies, 27*, 59-72.

Aghajanian, A., Gross, A. B., & Lewis, S. M. (1993). *Evaluation of Iran fertility survey* (Working Paper 93-2). University of Washington, Center for Studies in Demography and Ecology.

Aghajanian, A., & Moghadas, A. (1998). Correlates and consequences of divorce in an Iranian city. *Journal of Divorce and Remarriage, 28*(3/4), 53-71.

Aghajanian, A., Tashakkori, A., & Mehryar, H. A. (1996, March-April). *Attitudes toward marriage, fertility, and labor market participation among adolescents in Iran.* Paper presented at the Annual Meeting of the Population Association of America, New Orleans, LA.

Agoncillo, T. A., & Guerrero, M. C. (1977). *History of the Filipino People* (5th ed.). Quezon City: Malaya Books.

Aguayo, V. M., Scott, S., & Ross, J. (2003). Sierra Leone—Investing in nutrition to reduce poverty: A call for action. *Public Health Nutrition, 6*, 653-657.

Ahmad, I. (2003). Between the ideal and the real: Gender relations within the Indian joint family. In M. Pernau, I. Ahmad, & H. Reifeld (Eds.), *Family and gender: Changing values in Germany and India* (pp. 36-63). New Delhi: Sage.

Ahmadnia, S., & Mehryar, H. A. (2004). *Attitudes of adolescents in Tehran toward marriage, fertility and family planning* (in Farsi). Working Paper, Center for Population Studies, Tehran: Ministry of Science and Technology.

Ahuja, R. (1999). *Society in India: Concepts, theories, and changing trends.* Jaipur: Rawat.

Aja Díaz, A. (2001). La emigración cubana entre dos siglos [Cuban emigration between the two centuries]. *Temas, 26,* 60-70.

Akman, N., & Yirmibesoglu, O. (1999, January 3). Cinayet Islemeyi Ozendiren Yargi [The judgment that advocates committing murder], *Sabah Turkish Daily Newspaper.* p. 3.

Akunga, A. B. (2004). *Community participation in the care of children orphaned by HIV/AIDS: A case study of Kibera Division, Nairobi, Kenya.* Unpublished manuscript, Kenyatta University, Nairobi, Kenya.

Alcantara, A. M. (1994). Gender roles, fertility, and the status of married Filipino men and women. *Philippine Sociological Review, 42,* 94-109.

Alfonso, J. C. (2003). La fecundidad y el envejecimiento en Cuba al inicio del siglo XXI (Fertility and aging in Cuba at the beginning of the 21st century). In *Información para estudios en población y desarrollo con enfoque de género* [Information for a gender-focused population and development studies]. Havana: Oficina Nacional de Estadísticas. (CD edition).

Alfonso, J. C. (2005, January). Lecture at the Centro de Investigación de la Cultura Cubana Juan Marinello.

Allen, W. R. (1979). Class, culture, and family organisation: The effects of class and race on family structure in urban America. *Journal of Comparative Family Studies, 10,* 301-313.

Amaral, L. H. (2001, October). Brazil on the road to change. *World Press Review, 48,* 15.

Amarteifio, J. O., & Davies, C. B. (1995). Women in the informal sector in Sierra Leone. *Development, 3,* 36-39.

Amato, P. R. (1994). The impact of divorce on men and women in India and the U.S. *Journal of Comparative Family Studies, 25,* 207-222.

Amirahmadi, H. (1990). *Revolution and economic transition.* New York: State University of New York Press.

Amnesty International. (2004, June 16). *Day of the African child: The unending plight of child soldiers.* Available at www.reliefweb.int/w/rwb.nsf/ByCountry/Sierra+Leone.

Amoateng, A. Y. (1997). The structure of urban black households: New survey evidence from a coloured and an African Community on the Cape Flats in the Western Cape of South Africa. *African Sociological Review, 1*(2), 22-40.

Amowitz, L. L., Reis, C., Lyons, K. H., Vann, B., Mansaray, B., Akinsulure-Smith, A. M., et al. (2002). Prevalence of war-related sexual violence and other human rights abuses among internally displaced persons in Sierra Leone. *Journal of the American Medical Association, 287,* 513-521.

Andenæs, A. (1989). Identitet og sosial endring [Identity and social change]. *Tidsskrift for Norsk Psykologforening, 26,* 603-615.

Anderson, S. (2003). Why dowry payments declined with modernization in Europe but are rising in India. *Journal of Political Economy, 111,* 269-310.

Anderson, S. A., & Sabatelli, R. M. (2007). *Family interaction: A multigenerational developmental perspective* (4th ed.). Boston: Allyn and Bacon.

Aparicio, R. (2002). Transición demográfica y vulnerabilidad durante la vejez [Demographic transition and vulnerability during aging]. In Consejo Nacional de Población (Ed.), *La situación demográfica en México 2002* (pp. 155-168). México D. F.: Consejo Nacional de Población.

Ardington, E., & Lund, F. (1995). *Pensions and development: How the social security system can complement programmes of reconstruction and development* (Development Paper 61). Midrand: Development Bank of Southern Africa.

Arés, P. (2004). Familia, ética y valores en la realidad cubana actual [Family, ethics and values in the present Cuban reality]. In *Concepción y metodología de la educación popular /Selección de lecturas/* (pp. 419-442). Havana: Editorial Caminos.

Arnold, F., Kishor, S., & Roy, T. K. (2002). Sex selective abortions in India. *Population and Development Review, 28,* 759-785.

Arranged marriages. (2004, June 8). Available at www.incestboard.com/Forum/Forum1/HTML/002289.html.

Ascroft, J. (1998). Catre o strategie nationala de informare—educatie—planificare [Toward a national strategy of information—education—planning]. *22—Social Dialogue Review, 61,* (PLUS—free supplement), vi.

Ashton, S. (1994). The farmer needs a wife: Farm women in Wales. In J. Aaron, T. Rees, S. Betts, & M. Vincentelli (Eds.), *Our sisters' land: The changing identities of women in Wales* (pp. 122-139). Cardiff: University of Wales Press.

Assis, S. G. (1994). *Crescer sem violência—um desafio para educadores* [Growing up without violence—A challenge to educators]. Rio de Janeiro: Fundação Oswaldo Cruz.

Australian Bureau of Statistics. (1993). *Child care, Australia* (Catalogue No. 4401.0). Canberra: Author.

Australian Bureau of Statistics. (1994a). *Births, Australia, 1994* (Catalogue No. 3301.0). Canberra: Author.

Australian Bureau of Statistics. (1994b). *Focus on families: Demographics and family formation* (Catalogue No. 4420.0). Canberra: Author.

Australian Bureau of Statistics. (1996). *Persons employed at home, September 1995* (Catalogue No. 6275.0). Canberra: Author.

Australian Bureau of Statistics. (1998a). *Family characteristics, Australia, 1997* (Catalogue No. 4442.0). Canberra: Author.

Australian Bureau of Statistics. (1998b). *How Australians use their time, 1997* (Catalogue No. 4153.0). Canberra: Author.

Australian Bureau of Statistics. (1999a). *Australian social trends, 1999* (Catalogue No. 4102.0). Canberra: Author.

Australian Bureau of Statistics. (1999b). *Births, Australia, 1998* (Catalogue No. 3301.0). Canberra: Author.

Australian Bureau of Statistics. (1999c). *Marriages and divorces, Australia, 1998* (Catalogue No. 3310.0). Canberra: Author.

Australian Bureau of Statistics. (2000a). *Caring in the community, Australia, 1998* (Catalogue No 4436.0). Canberra: Author.

Australian Bureau of Statistics. (2000b). *Labour force, Australia, July 2000* (Catalogue No. 6203.0). Canberra: Author.

Australian Bureau of Statistics. (2000c). *Marriages and divorces, Australia, 1999* (Catalogue No. 3310.0). Canberra: Author.

Australian Bureau of Statistics. (2001a). *Australian social trends 2001* (Catalogue No. 4102.0). Canberra: Author.

Australian Bureau of Statistics. (2001b). *Population of census and housing, 2001* [Customized data cube]. Canberra: Author.

Australian Bureau of Statistics. (2002a). *Labour force survey of families, 2002* [Data cube FA2.srd]. Canberra: Author.

Australian Bureau of Statistics. (2002b). *Marriages and divorces, Australia, 2001* (Catalogue No. 3310.0). Canberra: Author.

Australian Bureau of Statistics. (2002c). *Selected social and housing characteristics, Australia, 2001* (Catalogue No 2015.0). Canberra: Author.

Australian Bureau of Statistics. (2003a). *Ageing in Australia, 2001* (Catalogue No. 2048.0). Canberra: Author.

Australian Bureau of Statistics. (2003b). *Births, Australia, 2002* (Catalogue No. 3301.0). Canberra: Author.

Australian Bureau of Statistics. (2003c). *Child care, Australia, 2002* (Catalogue No. 4402.0). Canberra: Author.

Australian Bureau of Statistics. (2003d). *Expanded community profile* (Catalogue No. 2005.0) Canberra: Author.

Australian Bureau of Statistics. (2003e). *Labour force, Australia, December 2002* (Catalogue No. 6202.0). Canberra: Author.

Australian Bureau of Statistics. (2003f). *Marriages and divorces, Australia, 2002* (Catalogue No. 3310.0). Canberra: Author.

Australian Bureau of Statistics. (2004). *Labour force, Australia, February 2004* (Catalogue No. 6202.0). Canberra: AGPS.

Australian Institute of Family Studies. (1997). *Australian life course study, 1996* [Computer file]. Melbourne: Author.

Australian Institute of Health and Welfare. (2003). *Australia's mothers and babies, 2000* (AIHW Catalogue. No. PER 21). Sydney: AIHW National Perinatal Statistics Unit.

Aykan, H., & Wolf, D. A. (2000). Traditionality, modernity, and household composition: Parent-child coresidence in contemporary Turkey. *Research on Aging, 22,* 396-421.

Aytaç, I. A. (1998). Intergenerational living arrangements in Turkey. *Journal of Cross-Cultural Gerontology, 13,* 241-264.

Azadarmaki, T., & Bahar, M. (2006). Families in Iran: Changes, challenges and future. *Journal of Comparative Family Studies, 37,* 589-608.

Baban, A., & David, H. P. (1995). *Voci ale femeilor din Romania. Aspecte ale sexualitatii, comportamentului de reproducere si ale relatiilor de cuplu în epoca Ceausescu* [Women's voices in Romania: Aspects of sexuality, reproductive behavior and couple relations in Ceusescu's period]. Bucharest: UNICEF.

Babu, N. P., Nidhi, & Verma, R. K. (1998). Abortion in India: What does the National Family Health Survey tell us? *The Journal of Family Welfare, 44*(4), 45-54.

Badsha, N., & Kotecha, P. (1994). University access: The gender factor. *Agenda, 21,* 47-54.

Bagley, C., Madrid, S., & Bolitho, F. (1997). Stress factors and mental health adjustment of Filipino domestic workers in Hong Kong. *International Social Work, 40,* 373-382.

Bagley, F. R. C. (1971). The Iranian family protection law. In C. E. Bosworkth (Ed.), *Iran and Islam* (pp. 47-64). Edinburgh: Edinburgh University Press.

Bah, A. M. S. (2000). Exploring the dynamics of the Sierra Leone conflict. *Peace-keeping & International Relations, 29*(1), 1-4.

Baiju, S. (2003). Counseling in family planning. *The Journal of Family Welfare, 49*(2), 18-21.

Balasa, A., Halus, R., Jula, D., Vasile, P., & Marius, P. (1999). *Revision of the achievements of the country* [Human development report 1999]. Available at www.undp.org/hdro/HDI.html.

Banani, A. (1961). *The modernization of Iran.* Stanford, CA: Stanford University Press.

Banerjee, N. (2003). The marginal families. In M. Pernau, I. Ahmad, & H. Reifeld (Eds.), *Family and gender: Changing values in Germany and India* (pp. 278-295). New Delhi: Sage.

Barbagli, M. (1998). *La storia della famiglia in Italia* [History of the Italian family]. Bologna: Il Mulino.

Barbagli, M., & Saraceno, C. (1997). *Separarsi in Italia* [To separate in Italy]. Bologna: Il Mulino.

Barbosa, R. M., & Villela, W. V. (1996). A trajetória feminina da AIDS [The feminine trajectory of AIDS]. In R. Parker & J. Galvão (Eds.), *Quebrando o silêncio: Mulheres e AIDS no Brasil* (pp. 17-32). Rio de Janeiro, Brazil: Relume-Dumará; Associação Brasileira Interdisciplinar de Estudos sobre AIDS, Instituto de Medicina Social, Universidade Estadual do Rio de Janeiro.

Bardisa Ezcurra, L. (2003). Anticoncepción de emergencia ¿la píldora del día después? [Emergency contraception, the pill of the day after?]. *Sexología y sociedad, 22,* 21-26.

Barros, M. L. de. (1987). *Autoridade e afeto—avós, filhos e netos na família brasileira* [Authority and affection—Grandparents, children, and grandchildren in Brazilian family]. Rio de Janeiro: Jorge Zahar.

Basu, S., Kapoor, A. K., & Basu, S. K. (2004). Knowledge, attitude and practice of family planning among tribals. *The Journal of Family Welfare, 50*(1), 24-30.

Bauereiß, R., Bayer, H., & Bien, W. (1997). *Familien-Atlas II: Lebenslagen und Regionen in Deutschland* [Family atlas II: Life issues and areas in Germany]. Opladen: Leske und Budrich.

Bautista, V., & Roldan, A. (1995). Dissolution of marriage. In A. E. Perez (Ed.), *The Filipino family: A spectrum of views and issues* (pp. 40-56). Quezon City: University of the Philippine Office of Research Coordination and University of the Philippines Press.

Baxter, J., & Western, M. (1996). Satisfaction with housework: Explaining the paradox. In *5th Australian Family Research Conference.* Brisbane, Australia.

Beck, U. (1986). *Risikogesellschaft—Auf dem Weg in eine andere Moderne* [Risk society—Heading for a different modernity]. Frankfurt am Main: Suhrkamp.

Beck, U., & Beck-Gernsheim, E. (1990). *Das ganz normale Chaos der Liebe* [The very usual chaos of love]. Frankfurt am Main: Suhrkamp.

Beck, U., Giddens, A., & Lash, S. (1994). *Reflexive modernisation: Politics, tradition and aesthetics in the modern social order.* Cambridge: Polity Press.

Beckwith, C., & Saitoti, O. T. (1980). *Maasai.* New York: Abrams.

Behnam, D., & Amani, M. (1974). *La Population de L'Iran* [The population of Iran]. Paris: CICRED.

Bell, L., & Bell, D. (2000). Similarity and traditionalism in Japanese and U.S. marriage experiences. *Journal of Comparative Family Studies, 31,* 309-319.

Beltrán, U., Castaños, F., Flores, J., Meyenberg, Y., & del Pozo, B. E. (1996). *Los mexicanos en los noventa* [Mexicans in the nineties]. México D. F.: Instituto de Investigaciones Sociales, Universidad Nacional Autónoma de México.

Bengelsdorf, C. (1985). On the problem of studying women in Cuba. *Race and Class, 27,* 35-50.

Berik, G. (1995). Towards an understanding of gender Hierarchy in Turkey: A comparative analysis of carpet-weaving villages. In S. Tekeli (Ed.), *Women in modern Turkish society: A reader* (pp. 112-130). London: Zed Books.

Berja, C. L., & Ogena, N. B. (2004). Profile of the Filipino youth. In C. M. Raymundo & G. T. Cruz (Eds.), *Youth, sex, and risk behaviors in the Philippines* (pp. 14-26). Quezon City: Demographic Research and Development Foundation Inc. and University of the Philippines Population Institute.

Bernardo, A. A. (1990). *An exploratory study of selected civil court cases on annulment, legal separation, and support.* Unpublished A. B. thesis, Department of Sociology, University of the Philippines, Quezon City.

Berquó, E. (1989). A família no seculo XXI [The family in the XXI century]. *Ciência Hoje, 10*(58), 59-65.

Bertera, E. M. (2003). Social services for the aged in Cuba. *International Social Work, 46,* 313-321.

Berthin, G. D. (2002). *A decade later: Understanding the transition process in Romania* (National human development report—Romania 2001-2002). Bucharest: United Nations Development Programme—Romania.

Berthoud, R., McKay, S., & Rowlingson, K. (1999). Becoming a single mother. In S. McKrae (Ed.), *Changing Britain: Families and households in the 1990s* (pp. 354-376). Oxford: Oxford University Press.

Bertram, H., Bayer, H., & Bauereiß, R. (1993). *Familien-Atlas: Lebenslagen und Regionen in Deutschland* [Family atlas: Life issues and areas in Germany]. Opladen: Leske und Budrich.

Betts, S. (Ed.). (1996). *Our daughters' land: Past and present.* Cardiff: University of Wales Press.

Beyer, P. (2003). Constitutional privilege and constituting pluralism: Religious freedom in national, global, and legal context. *Journal for the Scientific Study of Religion, 42,* 333-339.

Bharadwaj, A. (2003). Why adoption is not an option in India: The visibility of infertility, the secrecy of donor insemination, and other cultural complexities. *Social Science & Medicine, 56,* 1867-1880.

Bharat, S. (1997). *Intellectual and psycho-social development of adopted children* (project report). Mumbai: Tata Institute of Social Sciences.

Bhatti, R. S. (2003). Enhancing marital and family relationships: A model. *Indian Journal of Social Work, 64*(2), 151-158.

Bill, J. (1988). *The eagle and the lion.* New Haven, CT: Yale University Press.

Billimoria, H. M. (1984). *Child adoption: A study of Indian experience.* Bombay: Himalaya.

Birth matters. (2001). Available at www.mariestopes.org.uk/birth_matters.html.

Bittman, M., & Lovejoy, F. (1993). Domestic power: Negotiating an unequal division of labour within a framework of equality. *Australian and New Zealand Journal of Sociology, 29,* 302-321.

Blankenhorn, D. (1995). *Fatherless America: Confronting our most urgent social problem.* New York: Basic Books.

Bledsoe, C. H. (1990). Transformation in sub-Saharan African marriage and fertility. *Annals of the American Association of Political and Social Science, 510,* 115-125.

Bledsoe, C. H., Banja, F., & Hill, A. G. (1998). Reproductive mishaps and western contraception: An African challenge to fertility theory. *Population and Development Review, 24*(1), 15-57.

Bodley, J. H. (1997). *Cultural anthropology: Tribes, states, and the global system* (2nd ed.). Mountain View, CA: Mayfield.

Boff, A. de M. (1995). *O namoro está no ar . . . Na onda do outro: Um olhar sobre os afetos em grupos populares* [Analysis of a radio program where couples meet: Affective relations among low-class groups]. Unpublished master's thesis, Social Anthropology, Federal University of Rio Grande do Sul, Brazil.

Bohler, K. F., & Hildenbrand, B. (1990). Farm families between tradition and modernity. *Sociologia Ruralis, 30,* 18-33.

Bohler, K. F., & Hildenbrand, B. (1997). *Bauernfamilien in der Krise* [Farm families in crisis]. Münster: LIT-Verlag.

Bonifazi, C., Menniti, A., & Palomba, R. (1996). *Bambini, anziani e immigrati* [Children, migrants and the elderly]. Florence: Nuova Italia.

Bose, S., & South, S. J. (2003). Sex composition of children and marital disruption in India. *Journal of Marriage & Family, 65,* 996-1006.

Bowman, H. L. (1998). Introduction. In H. L. Bodman & N. Tohidi (Eds.), *Women in Muslim societies: Diversity within unity* (pp. 1-18). Boulder, CO: Lynne Rienner.

Bradburd, D. (1984). The rules and the game: The practice of marriage among the Komachi. *American Ethnologist, 11,* 738-753.

Bradford, K. P., Barber, B. K., Olsen, J. A., Maughan, S. L., Erickson, L. D., Ward, D., et al. (2004). A multi-national study of interparental conflict, parenting, and adolescent functioning: South Africa, Bangladesh, China, India, Bosnia, Germany, Palestine, Colombia, and the United States. *Marriage and Family Review, 35,* 107-137.

Briar-Lawson, K., Lawson, H. A., Hennon, C. B., & Jones, A. R. (2001). *Family-centered policies & practices: International implications.* New York: Columbia University Press.

Brody, E. (1990). *Women in the middle: Their parent care years.* New York: Springer.

Bruce, J., Lloyd, C. B., & Leonard, A. (1995). *Families in focus: New perspectives on mothers, fathers, and children.* New York: Population Council.

Bruschini, C. (1994). O trabalho da mulher brasileira nas décadas recentes [The Brazilian women's labor in the recent decades]. *Revista de Estudos Feministas,* número especial, 2o. semestre de 1994, 179-199.

Budlender, D. (1998). *Women and men in South Africa.* Pretoria: Central Statistical Services.

Buijs, G., & Atherfold, G. (1995). *Savings and money-lending schemes: How rotating credit associations help poor families.* Pretoria: Co-operative Research Programme on Marriage and Family Life, Human Sciences Research Council.

Bundesministerium für Familie und Senioren. (Ed.). (1994). *Familien und Familienpolitik im geeinten Deutschland—Zukunft des Humanvermögens. 5. Familienbericht* [Families and family policy in unified Germany—The future of human assets. 5th Family Report]. Bonn: Author.

Burkart, G. (1993). Individualisierung und Elternschaft—Das Beispiel USA [Individualization and parenthood—The example of the USA]. *Zeitschrift für Soziologie, 22,* 159-177.

Burkart, G., & Kohli, M. (1992). *Liebe—Ehe—Elternschaft: Die Zukunft der Familie* [Love—marriage—parenthood: The future of the family]. München: Piper.

Buvinic, M., & Gupta, G. R. (1994). *Targeting poor woman-headed households and woman-maintained families in developing countries: Views on a policy dilemma.* New York: The Population Council.

Buzatu, S. (1978). *Conditia femeii—dimensiune a progresului contemporan* [Condition of women—Dimensions of contemporary progress]. Bucharest: Editura Politica.

Cabatit, A. J. (1998, August 4). When the wife earns more. *The Philippine Star,* p. 23.

Cabigon, J. V. (1999, May). *Idle, tired and retired elderly—a myth.* Paper presented at the National Press Conference on the Filipino Elderly, Galleria Suites, Mandaluyong City.

Cabigon, J. V. (2001, October). *Demographic profile of the Filipino family.* Updated paper previously presented during the First Family Health Forum organized by the Department of Health in collaboration with the Philippine NGO Council on Population, Health, and Welfare to celebrate Family Week, City State Tower Hotel, Manila.

Caldwell, J. C., & Caldwell, P. (1993). The South African fertility decline. *Population and Development Review, 19*(2), 225-262.

Caldwell, J. C., Orubuloye, I. O., & Caldwell, P. (1992). Fertility decline in Africa: A new type of transition? *Population and Development Review, 18*(2), 211-242.

Campbell, C. (1990). The township family and women's struggles. *Agenda, 4,* 1-22.

Campbell, E. K. (1994). Fertility, family size preferences and future fertility prospects of men in the Western Area of Sierra Leone. *Journal of Biosocial Science, 26*, 273-277.

Campos, M. C. S. de Souza (2006). Families in the third world countries [Special issue]. *Journal of Comparative Family Studies, 4*(4).

Campos, R. C. P. (1996). *AIDS e relações de gênero—A trajetória de mulheres parceiras de indivíduos soropositivos, em Belo Horizonte* [AIDS and gender relations—The trajectory of female partners of soropositives, in Belo Horizonte]. Unpublished master's thesis, Psychology, Universidade Federal de Minas Gerais, Belo Horizonte, Brazil.

Cardiff Women's Aid. (1990). *How we began.* Cardiff: Author.

Carmichael, G., Webster, A., & McDonald, P. (1997). Divorce Australian style: A demographic analysis. *Journal of Divorce and Remarriage, 26*(2/3), 3-37.

Carranza Valdés, J. (2002). La economía cubana: balance breve de una década crítica [Cuban economy: Brief balance of a critical decade]. *Temas, 30*, 30-41.

Carrasco, P. (1975). La transformación de la cultura indígena durante la colonia [The transformation of indigenous culture during the colonial period]. *Historia Mexicana, 25*(2), 175-203.

Carrasco, P. (1993). La familia conjunta en el México antiguo: El caso de Molotla [Joint family in the antique Mexico: The case of Molotla]. In P. Gonzalbo (Comp.), *Historia de la familia* (pp. 106-125). México D. F.: Instituto Mora/ Universidad Autónoma Metropolitana.

Carvalho, M. do C. B. de. (1994). A priorização da família na agenda da política social [The priority of the family in the social policy agenda]. In S. M. Kaloustian (Ed.), *Família Brasileira—A base de tudo* (pp. 93-108). São Paulo: Cortez Publisher; Brasília: United Nations Children's Fund (UNICEF).

Cass, B., & Cappo, D. (1995). *Families: Agents and beneficiaries of socioeconomic development* (Discussion paper). United Nations Interregional Meeting of National Coordinators/Focal Points for the International Year of the Family, Bratislava, Slovakia.

Castillo, G. T. (1979). *Beyond Manila: Philippine rural problems in perspective.* Ottawa, Canada: International Development Research Centre.

Castillo, G. T. (1993). *Where food and population meet: The Filipino household among other households* (Assessment on the State of the Nation). University of the Philippines Center for Integrative and Development Studies and University of the Philippines Press.

Catasús, S. (1999). *La nupcialidad cubana en el siglo XX* [Cuban nupciality in the 20th Century]. Havana: Editorial Ciencias Sociales.

Cavalleiro, E. (2000). *Do silêncio do lar ao silêncio escolar—racismo, preconceito e discriminação na educação infantil* [From silence at home to silence at school—racism, prejudice and discrimination in child education]. São Paulo: Contexto.

Center for Reproductive Rights. (2004). *Women of the world: South Asia—India.* Available at www.reproductiverights.org/pdf/pdf_wowsa_india.pdf.

Centro de Estudios en Población y Desarrollo, Fondo de Población de Naciones Unidas and Oficina Nacional de Estadísticas. (2003). *Informe Salud, bienestar y envejecimiento de las Américas, Resumen ejecutivo* [Report on health, welfare and aging in the Americas: Executive summary]. Havana: Author.

Chan, A., Scott, J., Nguyen, A., & Keane, R. (1999). *Pregnancy outcome in South Australia 1999.* Adelaide: Pregnancy Outcome Unit, Epidemiology Branch, Department of Human Services.

Charles, N. (1991). *Funding women's aid services to the community in Wales.* Cardiff: Welsh Office.

Chevannes, B. (1994). Presiones y tensiones. Análisis de la situación de la familia en el Caribe [Pressures and tensions. Situation analysis of the family in the Caribbean]. In *Familia y futuro. Un programa regional en América Latina y el Caribe.* Santiago de Chile: Naciones Unidas, Comisión Económica para América Latina y el Caribe.

Choice on termination of pregnancy act, No. 1891. (1996, November 22). Pretoria: South African Government.

Chou, L. P., & Zheng, C. (1987). Shilun woguo chengshi jiating de laoren shanyang [Discussion of aging supports of families in cities of China]. In Y. Liu & S. J. Xue (Eds.), *Zhongguo Hunyin Jiating Yanjiu* (pp. 354-368). Beijing: Shehui Kexue Wenxian Chubanshe.

Christensen, E. (1982). Når det første barn blir født [When the first child is born]. In E. Christensen (Ed.), *Fra to til tre. En bok om å bli foreldre* (pp. 194-202). København: Nytt nordisk forlag.

Chubin, S. (1988). *Iran and Iraq at war.* London: I. B. Tauris.

Chwarae Teg. (2002). *The role of women in the Welsh workforce.* Cardiff: Author.

Cindoglu, D. (1997). Virginity tests and artificial virginity in modern Turkish medicine. *Women's Studies International Forum, 20*(12), 253-261.

Cindoglu, D., & Sirkeci, B. (2001). Variables in explaining pre-natal care in Turkey: Social class, education and ethnicity re-visited. *Journal of Biosocial Science, 33,* 1-10.

Cliquet, R. L. (1991). The second demographic transition: Fact or fiction? *Population Studies* (No. 23). Strasbourg: Council of Europe.

Coale, A. J., & Chen, S. L. (1987). *Basic data on fertility in the provinces of China, 1940-82.* Hawaii: East-West Population Institute.

Código de la familia, Ley 1289 de febrero de 1975 [Code of the Family, Law 1289 of February, 1975]. (1979, February 15). *Gaceta Oficial,* 15 febrero de 1975 (1979). Havana: Editorial Orbe.

Codul familiei. Legea 4/1954 [Code of family. Law 4/1954]. (1954). *Buletinul official.* Bucharest: Monitorul Oficial.

Coelho, S. V. (1996). *Relações de gênero na comunicação do casal* [Gender relations in the couple communication]. Unpublished master's thesis, Psychology, Universidade Federal de Minas Gerais, Belo Horizonte, Brazil.

Cohen, B. (1998). The emerging fertility transition in sub-Saharan Africa. *World Development, 26,* 1431-1461.

Cohn, A., & Fonseca, A. (2004). O Bolsa-Família e a questão social [The family-income program and the social problem]. *Teoria e Debate, 57*(March/April), 10-15.

Comisia Antisaracie si Promovarea Incluziunii Sociale. (2002). *Planul national antisaracie èi promovare a incluziunii sociale* [National plan against poverty and for social inclusion]. Bucharest: Guvernul Romaniei.

Comisia Antisaracie si Promovarea Incluziunii Sociale. (2004). *Dinamica s1r1ciei èi a s1r1ciei severe în perioada 1995-2003* [Dynamics of poverty and severe poverty in the period 1995-2003]. Bucharest: Guvernul Romaniei.

Comisia Nationala pentru Statistica. (1996). *Anuarul statistic al Romaniei 1995* [Romanian statistical yearbook 1995]. Bucharest: Author.

Comisia Nationala pentru Statistica. (1999a). *Aspecte privind calitatea vietii populatiei in anul 1998* [On the population quality of life in 1998]. Bucharest: Author.

Comisia Nationala pentru Statistica. (1999b). *CESTAT—Buletin statistic* (Nr. 4) [CESTAT—Statistical bulletin (No. 4)]. Bucharest: Author.

Comisia Nationala pentru Statistica. (2000). *Informatii statistice operative* (Nr. 2/2000) [Operative statistical information (No. 2/2000)]. Bucharest: Author.

Comisia Nationala pentru Statistica & United Nations Development Program. (2000). *Femeile si barbatii* [Women and men]. Bucharest: Author.

Comissão Interministerial para a Formulação da Política Nacional da Família. (1994). *A política nacional da família—Documento final* [The national policy of the family—Final document]. Ministério do Bem-Estar Social, Secretaria da Promoção Humana, Brasília.

Conciliation Resources. (nd). *Gender and conflict in Sierra Leone.* Available at www.c-r.org/pubs/occ_papers/briefing5.shtml.

Consejo Nacional de Población. (1998). *La situación demográfica en México 1998* [The demographic situation in Mexico 1998]. México D. F.: Author.

Consejo Nacional de Población. (1999). *La situación demográfica en México 1999* [The demographic situation in Mexico 1999]. México D. F.: Author.

Consejo Nacional de Población. (2002). *La situación demográfica en Mexico 2002* [The demographic situation in Mexico 2002]. México D. F.: Author.

Cooper, D. (1972). *The death of the family.* Harmondsworth: Penguin.

Cortés, F. (1995). El ingreso de los hogares en contextos de crisis, ajuste y estabilización: Un análisis de su distribución en México, 1977-1992 [Household income in crisis, adjustment and stabilization contexts: An analysis of their distribution in Mexico, 1977-1992]. *Estudios Sociológicos, 13*(37), 91-108.

Cortés, F. (2000). *La distribución del ingreso en México en épocas de estabilización y reforma económica* [Income distribution in Mexico in stabilization and economic reform periods]. México D. F.: Centro de Investigaciones y Estudios Superiores en Antropología Social/Miguel Angel Porrúa.

Cortés, F., Hernández, D., Hernández, E., Székely, M., & Vera, H. (2002). Evolución y características de la pobreza en México en la última década del siglo XX [Evolution and characteristics of poverty in Mexico in the last decade of the XX century]. In Consejo Nacional de Población (Ed.), *La situación demográfica en México 2002* (pp. 121-140). México D. F.: Consejo Nacional de Población.

Cortés, F., & Rubalcava, R. (1995). *El ingreso de los hogares* [Household income]. México D. F.: Instituto Nacional de Estadística, Geografía e Informática/El

Colegio de México/Instituto de Investigaciones Sociales, Universidad Nacional Autónoma de México.

Costa, A. C. G. (1990). Infância, juventude e política social no Brasil [Childhood, youth, and social policy in Brazil]. In A. C. G. Costa, A. F. do A. Silva, D. Rivera, E. S. Moraes, & M. Cury (Eds.), *Brasil Criança Urgente: A Lei 8069/90* (pp. 69-105). São Paulo: Columbus Cultural.

Costa-Foru, X. C. (1945). *Cercetarea monografica a familiei* [Monographical research of family]. Bucharest: Fundatia Regelui Mihai.

Costello, M. A. (1994). The elderly in Filipino households: Current status and future prospects. *Philippine Sociological Review, 42*(1-4), 53-77.

Council of Europe. (1996). *Recent demographic developments in Europe.* Strasbourg: Council of Europe.

Cruz, G. T. (1999, May). *Who are the Filipino elderly?* Paper presented at the National Press Conference on the Filipino Elderly, Galleria Suites, Mandaluyong City.

Culture matters. (nd). Available at www.peacecorps.gov.wws/culturematters/index.html.

Cupitt, M., & Stockbridge, S. (1996). *Families and electronic entertainment.* Sydney: Australian Broadcasting Authority.

Currie, I. (1994). The future of customary law: Lessons from the lobolo debate. In C. Murray (Ed.), *Gender and the new South African legal order* (pp. 146-168). Kenwyn: Juta.

Dai, K. J. (1992). Tradition, social policy and change in marriage and family in China. In *Proceedings of Asia-Pacific Regional Conference on Future Family* (pp. 4-12). Beijing: China Social Science Documentation Publishing House.

Daichman, E. (1998). *Health professionals' perception of and responses to elder abuse.* Thousand Oaks, CA: Sage Publications.

Dalisay, G. A. (1983). *Fathers as parents: An exploratory study.* Unpublished master's thesis, Department of Psychology, University of the Philippines, Quezon City.

Dasgupta, S., Hennessey, S., & Mukhopadhyay, R. (1999). Caste, class and family structure in West Bengal villages. *Journal of Comparative Family Studies, 30,* 561-577.

David, F. P. (1994). The roles of husbands and wives in household decision-making. *Philippine Sociological Review, 42,* 73-93.

Davies, J. B., & Zhang, J. (1995). Gender bias, investments in children, and bequests. *International Economics Review, 36,* 795-818.

Davies, V. A. B. (2000). Sierra Leone: Ironic tragedy. *Journal of African Economies, 9,* 349-369.

Davishpour, M. (1999). Intensified gender conflicts within Iranian families in Sweden. *Nordic Journal of Women's Studies, 71,* 21-34.

Day, A. (1989). Kinship networks and informal support in later years. In E. Grebenik, C. Hohn, & R. Mackeusen (Eds.), *Later phases of the family life cycle: Demographic aspects* (pp. 112-132). Oxford: Oxford University Press.

Day, G. (2002). *Making sense of Wales.* Cardiff: University of Wales Press.

Dayan, N. (1994, August). *Psychological profile of petitioners for marriage nullification.* Paper presented at the 31st Annual Conference of the Psychological Association of the Philippines, Diliman, Quezon City.

D'Cruz, P., & Bharat, S. (2001). Beyond joint and nuclear: The Indian family revised. *Journal of Comparative Family Studies, 32,* 167-194.

Debert, G. G. (1994). Gênero e envelhecimento [Gender and aging]. In *Revista de Estudos Feministas, 2*(3), 33-51.

de Guzman, E. A. (1999, May). *Living arrangement of the Filipino elderly.* Paper presented at the National Press Conference on the Filipino Elderly, Galleria Suites, Mandaluyong City.

de Guzman, E. A., & Diaz, G. S. A. (1995). Dating opens doors for intimate behavior among the youth. *Young Adult Fertility and Sexuality Study II* (News Features on Survey Findings, Second of a Series). Quezon City: University of the Philippines Population Institute.

DeLey, W. (1986). Physical punishment of children: Sweden and the USA. *Journal of Comparative Family Studies, 19,* 419-431.

Dempsey, K. (1992). *A man's town: Inequality between women and men in rural Australia.* Melbourne: Oxford University Press.

Dempsey, K. (1997). *Inequalities in marriage: Australia and beyond.* Melbourne: Oxford University Press.

Dempsey, K., & de Vaus, D. A. (2004). Who cohabits in 2001? *Journal of Sociology, 40*(2), 157-178.

Dennis, N., & Erdos, G. (1992). *Families without fatherhood.* London: IEA Health and Welfare Unit.

De Oliveira, O., Ariza, M., & Eternod, M. (2001). La fuerza de trabajo en México: Un siglo de cambios [The workforce in Mexico: A century of changes]. In J. Gómez de León & C. Rabell (Eds.), *La población de México. Tendencias y perspectivas sociodemográficas hacia el siglo XXI* (pp. 873-923). México D. F.: Fondo de Cultura Económica/Consejo Nacional de Población.

Derné, S. (1994). Violating the Hindu norm of husband-wife avoidance. *Journal of Comparative Family Studies, 25,* 249-267.

De Sandre, P., Ongaro, F., Rettaroli, R., & Salvini, S. (1997). *Matrimonio e figli tra rinvio e rinuncia* [Marriage and children between postponement and renounce]. Bologna: Il Mulino.

de Vaus, D. A. (1995). *Australian Family Values Survey* [Computer file]. Bundoora: La Trobe University.

de Vaus, D. A. (1996). Children's responsibilities to elderly parents. *Family Matters, 45,* 16-21.

de Vaus, D. A. (1997a). Family values in the nineties: Gender gap or generation gap? *Family Matters, 48,* 4-10.

de Vaus, D. A. (1997b). Marriage. In D. A. de Vaus & I. Wolcott (Eds.), *Australian family profiles: Social and demographic patterns* (pp. 11-24). Melbourne: Australian Institute of Family Studies.

de Vaus, D. A. (2002). Marriage, births and fertility. *Family Matters, 63,* 36-39.

de Vaus, D. A. (2004). *Diversity and change in Australian families: A statistical profile.* Melbourne: Australian Institute of Family Studies.

de Vaus, D. A., & Gray, M. (2003). Family transitions among Australia's children. *Family Matters, 65,* 10-17.

de Vaus, D. A., Gray, M., & Stanton, D. (2003). *Measuring the value of unpaid household, caring and voluntary work of older Australians* (AIFS Research Paper 34). Melbourne, Australian Institute of Family Studies. Available at www.aifs .gov.au/institute/pubs/respaper/RP34.pdf.

de Vaus, D. A., & Millward, C. (1997). Work related self care of young Australian children. *International Journal of Sociology of the Family, 27,* 1-16.

de Vaus, D. A., & Qu, L. (1998). Intergenerational transfers across the life course. *UN Bulletin on Ageing, 2*(3), 12-20.

de Vaus, D. A., Qu, L., & Weston, R. (2003). Premarital cohabitation and subsequent marital stability. *Family Matters, 65,* 34-39.

de Vaus, D. A., Wise, S., & Soriano, G. (1997). Fertility. In D. A. de Vaus & I. Wolcott (Eds.), *Australian family profiles: Social and demographic patterns* (pp. 45-58). Melbourne: Australian Institute of Family Studies.

Dex, S., Lissenhurgh, S., & Taylor, M. (1994). *Women and low pay: Identifying the issues.* Manchester: Equal Opportunities Commission.

Dhruvarajan, V. (1988). Religious ideology and interpersonal relationships within the family. *Journal of Comparative Family Studies, 19,* 273-285.

Díaz Canals, T. (2004). *Ver claro en lo oscuro /El laberinto poético del civismo en Cuba/* [Clearly seeing in the darkness / Poetical labyrinth of civic-mindedness in Cuba]. Havana: Editorial Acuario, Centro Félix Varela.

Divorce. (2001). *Encyclopedia electronica.* Available at http://www.etronica.com/ xweb.exe/excite/article.html?recno=7385.

Domestic violence act, No. 116. (1998). Pretoria: South African Government.

Domingo, L. J., & Asis, M. B. (1995). Living arrangements and the flow of support between generations in the Philippines. *Journal of Cross-Cultural Gerontology, 10,* 21-25.

Dorjahn, V. R. (1989). Where do the old folks live? The residence of the elderly among the Temne of Sierra Leone. *Journal of Cross-Cultural Gerontology, 4,* 257-278.

Dorsey, D. (1982). *Design and intent in African literature.* Washington, DC: Three Continents Press.

Dorward, D. (2001). The tragedy of Sierra Leone: Diamonds and warlords. *The Australasian Review of African Studies, 23,* 38-48.

Drew, P. E. (2006). Iran (Jomhoori-Islam-Iran). *The International Encyclopedia of Sexuality.* Available at www2.hu-berlin.de/sexology/IES/iran.html#0.

Du, Y. (801, republished in 1987). *Tongdian* [Complete codes]. Beijing: Zhonghua Shuju.

Durán Gondar, A., Díaz Tenorio, M., Jiménez, Y. V., Córdova, A. G., & Hernández, A. C. (2003). *"Convivir en Familias sin Violencia." Una metodología para la intervención y prevención de la violencia intrafamiliar* [Living together in families without violence. A methodology for intervention and prevention of family violence]. Department of Family Studies, Psychological and Sociological Research Center, Havana. (With the collaboration of Save the Children Foundation UK.)

Echevarría, D. (2003, November). *Influencia de la condición de género en mujeres del sector empresarial* [Influence of gender in the entrepreneurial sector]. Paper presented at the Taller científico Impacto de las transformaciones económicas en las mujeres cubanas, Cátedra de la Mujer, University of Havana.

Eckholm, E. (2002, February 13). Furor over death sentences of 5 China church group. *The New York Times,* p. A10.

Eisenstein, H. (1984). *Contemporary feminist thought.* London: Unwin Paperbacks.

Elliot, F. R. (1996). *Gender, family and society.* London: Macmillan.

Employment equity act, No. 55. (1998). Pretoria: South African Government.

Encyclopaedia Iranica. (1995). Costa Mesa, CA: Mazda Publications.

Engfer, A. (1993). Kindesmißhandlung und sexueller Mißbranch [Child assault and sexual abuse of children]. In M. Markefka & B. Nauck (Eds.), *Handbuch der Kindheitsforschung* (pp. 617-629). Neuwied, Kriftel, Berlin: Luchterhand.

Engstler, H. (1999). *Die Familie im Spiegel der amtlichen Statistik* [The family in the mirror of official statistics]. Bonn: Bundesministerium für Familie, Senioren, Frauen und Jugend.

Engstler, H., & Menning, S. (2003). *Die Familie im Spiegel der amtlichen Statistik* [The family in the mirror of official statistics]. Bonn: Bundesministerium für Familie, Senioren, Frauen und Jugend. Available at www.bmfsfj.de/Redaktion BMFSFJ/ Broschuerenstelle/Pdf-Anlagen/PRM-24184-Gesamtbericht-Familie-im-Spieg, property=pdf.pdf.

Equal Opportunities Commission. (2003). *Facts about women and men in Wales 2003.* Cardiff: Author.

Eraydin, A. (1999). The role of female labour in industrial restructuring: New production processes and labour market relations in the Istanbul clothing industry. *Gender, Place and Culture, 6,* 259-272.

Ergöçman, B., Hanciog´lu, A., & Ünalan, T. (1995). *Trends in fertility, family planning and childhood mortality in Turkey.* Ankara/Calveron: Ministry of Health and Hacettepe University/Macro International.

Erman, T. (1997). The meaning of city living for rural migrant women and their role in migration: The case of Turkey. *Women's Studies International Forum, 20,* 263-273.

Esim, S. (2000). Solidarity in isolation: Urban informal sector women's economic organizations in Turkey. *Middle Eastern Studies, 36,* 140-152.

Esteinou, R. (1996). *Familias de Sectores Medios: Perfiles organizativos y socioculturales* [Middle class families: Organizational and sociocultural profiles]. México D. F.: Centro de Investigaciones y Estudios Superiores en Antropología Social.

Esteinou, R. (1999a). Familia y diferenciación simbólica [Family and symbolic differentiation]. *Nueva Antropología, 35,* 9-26.

Esteinou, R. (1999b). Fragilidad y recomposición de las relaciones familiares [Fragility and recomposition of family relations]. *Desacatos, 2,* 11-25.

Esteinou, R. (2005). Parenting in Mexican society. *Marriage and Family Review, 36*(3/4), 7-29.

Ethangatta, L. K. (1995). Nutritional status of low income elderly women in Nairobi, Kenya. In J. K. Gitobu & E. C. Murray (Eds.), *Home economics research in Kenya* (pp. 19-33). Nairobi, Kenya: Kenyatta University.

Evans, M. (1996). Care of the elderly. *Worldwide Attitudes, 8,* 1-7.

Everatt, D., & Orkin, M. (1993, March). *'Growing up tough' A national survey of South African youth.* Paper presented at the National Youth Development Conference, Broederstroom.

Everatt, D., & Orkin, M. (1994). "Families should stay together": Intergenerational attitudes among South African youth. *Southern African Journal of Gerontology, 3*(2), 43-48.

Eversole, R. (2003). My business pays me: Labourers and entrepreneurs among the self-employed poor in Latin America. *Bulletin of Latin American research, 22,* 102-116.

Facultad Latino Americana de Ciencias Sociales. (1993). *Mulheres LatinoAmericanas em Dados—Brasil* [Data on Latin American women—Brazil]. Madrid: Instituto de la Mujer, Spain.

Family Aging Supports and Social Services Research Group of Beijing Gerontology Society. (1996a). Shichang jingji tiaojian xia de jiating yanglao yu shehuihuai fuwu [Family supports and social service under the market economy]. *Laoling Wenti Yanjiu, 10,* 9-16.

Family Aging Supports and Social Services Research Group of Beijing Gerontology Society. (1996b). Shichang jingji tiaojian xia de jiating yanglao yu shehuihuai fuwu [Family supports and social services under the market economy]. *Laoling Wenti Yanjiu, 8,* 16-22.

Family code of the Philippines. (1987). Philippines (Republic) laws, statutes, etc. (Executive Order No. 209 as amended by Executive Order no. 277). Manila: Office of the President, Malacañang.

Family law provisions of the civil code of the Islamic Republic of Iran: Book 7 on marriage and divorce. (nd). Available at www.international-divorce.com/iran_divorce.htm.

Family values. (2003, Winter). *Middle East Quarterly, 10,* 14.

Faulkner, F. (2001). Kindergarten killers: Morality, murder and the child soldier problem. *Third World Quarterly, 22,* 491-504.

Fei, X. T. (1933). *Peasant life in China.* London: Routledge & Kegan Paul Ltd.

Fei, X. T. (1947). *Earthbound China.* Beijing: Life, Reading and New Knowledge Bookstore.

Feldman, K. D. (1994). Socioeconomic structures and mate selection among urban populations in developing regions. *Journal of Comparative Family Studies, 25,* 329-343.

Feliciano, M. S. (1994). Law, gender, and the family in the Philippines. *Law & Society Review, 28,* 547-559.

Ferme, M. C. (2001). *The underneath of things: Violence, history, and the everyday in Sierra Leone.* Berkeley: University of California Press.

Fernández Suárez, J. C. (2003). Balance demográfico de Cuba [Demographic balance of Cuba]. *Información para estudios en población y desarrollo con enfoque de género*. Havana: Centro de Estudios de Población, Oficina Nacional de Estadísticas.

Ferreira, M., Gillis, L. S., & Møller, V. (1989). Ageing in South Africa. *Social Research Papers*. Pretoria: Human Sciences Research Council.

Ferreira, M., Prinsloo, F. R., & Gillis, L. S. (1992). *Multidimensional survey of elderly South Africans, 1990-91: Key findings*. Cape Town: Human Sciences Research Council/University of Cape Town Centre for Gerontology.

Ferriol, A. (2003). Acercamiento al estudio de la pobreza en Cuba [An approach to the study of poverty in Cuba]. *Cuba. Investigación económica, 9*(1/2), 27-65.

Ferriol, A., Quintana, D., & Pérez Izquierdo, V. (1999). Política social en el ajuste y su adecuación a las nuevas condiciones [Social politics and their adjustment to the new situation]. *Cuba. Investigación económica, 1*, January-March [Electronic edition, 1995-2002].

Fieseler, G., & Herborth, R. (1989). *Recht der Familie und Jugendhilfe* [Family law and law of youth welfare]. Heidelberg: R. v. Deckert & C. F. Müller.

Figueira, S. (1987). *Uma nova família? O moderno e o arcaico na família de classe média Brasileira* [A new family? The modern and the archaic in the Brazilian middle-class family]. Rio de Janeiro: Zahar.

Figueiredo, L. (1993). *O avesso da memória: Cotidiano e trabalho da mulher em Minas Gerais no século XVIII* [The reverse of memory: Women's labor and daily life in Minas Gerais of the XVIII century]. Rio de Janeiro: José Olympio Editora; Brasília: Editora da Universidade de Brasília.

Filgueiras, C. A. C., Afonso, M. L. M., Carvalho, A. M. S., & Ladeira, C. B. (1995). *Famílias de crianças e adolescentes: Diversidade e movimento* [Families with children and adolescents: Diversity and movement.]. Belo Horizonte: Associação Municipal de Assistência Social.

Filipino women, issues and trends. (1995). Manila: National Commission on the Role of Filipino Women and Asian Development Bank.

Finney, A. (2006). *Domestic violence, sexual assault and stalking: Findings from the 2004/05. British Crime Survey* (Home Office Online Report 12/06). Available at www.homeoffice.gov.uk/rds/pdfs06/rdsolr1206.pdf.

Flanigan, S. (2000). *Arranged marriages, matchmakers, and dowries in the India*. Available at www.english.emory.edu/Bahri/Arr.html.

Fletcher, R. (1993). *The family and marriage in Britain*. Harmondsworth: Penguin.

Folha de São Paulo/Datafolha. (1998). *Racismo Cordial* [Cordial racism]. São Paulo: Editora Ática.

Fonseca, C. (1995). *Caminhos da Adoção* [Paths to adoption]. São Paulo: Cortez.

Fonseca, M. T. N. M. (2002). *Famílias e políticas sociais: subsídios teóricos e metodológicos para a formulação e gestão de políticas com e para famílias* [Theoretical and methodological guidelines for the elaboration and administration of policies with and for families]. Fundação João Pinheiro, Minas Gerais, Brasil.

Foucault, M. (1980). *História da sexualidade: A vontade de saber* [History of sexuality: The will to know]. Rio de Janeiro: Editora Graal.

Fouladi, M. (1996). La Transition de la Fecondite en Iran [Fertility transition in Iran]. *Population, 51*, 1101-1128.

Franco, D. (2000). *Italy: A never-ending pension reform.* Available at www.nber
.org/confer/2000/pension00/franco.pdf.

Franco, V. (1995). Conflicto de normas en las relaciones parentales en las culturas indígenas [Norm conflict in parental relations in indigenous cultures]. In V. Chenaut & M. T. Sierra (Eds.), *Pueblos indígenas ante el derecho* (pp. 125-140). México: Centro de Investigaciones y Estudios Superiores en Antropología Social/Centro de Estudios de México y Centro América.

Frank, M. W., Bauer, H. M., Arican, N., Fincanci, S. K., & Iacopino, V. (1999). Virginity examinations in Turkey: Role of forensic physicians in controlling female sexuality. *Journal of the American Medical Association, 282,* 485-490.

Frankman, M. J. (1995). Catching the bus for global development: Gerschenkron revisited. *Canadian Journal of Development Studies, 16,* 419-431.

Frederick, B. (2000). Popular culture, gender relations and the democratization of everyday life in Kenya. *Journal of Southern African Studies, 26*(2), 209-222.

Frederiks, M. (2002). The Krio in The Gambia and the concept of inculturation. *Exchange, 31,* 219-229.

Friedl, E. (1985). Parents and children in a village in Iran. In A. Fathi (Ed.), *Women and the family in Iran* (pp. 195-211). Leiden, Netherlands: E. J. Brill.

Fromm, E., Horkheimer, M., & Parsons, T. (1970). *La familia* [The family]. Barcelona: Eds. Península.

Fundatia pentru o societate deschisa. (2000). *Barometrul de gen* [Gender barometer] Bucharest: OSF. Available at www.gender.ro/gender_bar.htm.

Funder, K. (1996). *Remaking families: Adaptation of children and parents to divorce.* Melbourne: Australian Institute of Family Studies.

Furstenberg, F. F., & Cherlin, A. J. (1991). *Divided families: What happens to children when parents part.* Cambridge, MA: Harvard University Press.

Gao, Q. (1995). Woguo Laolian baozhang de jiben duice [The fundamental countermove of the senior social supports of our country]. *Shehui Gongzuo Yanjiu, 5,* 33-35.

García, B., & De Oliveira, O. (1994). *Trabajo femenino y vida familiar en México* [Female work and family life in Mexico]. México: El Colegio de México.

García, B., & De Oliveira, O. (2006). Mujeres jefas de hogar y su dinámica familiar [Women headed households and their family dynamic]. In R. Esteinou (Ed.), *Fortalezas y desafíos de las familias en dos contextos: Estados Unidos de América y México* (pp. 437-484). México, D. F.: Centro de Investigaciones y Estudios Superiores en Antropología Social (CIESAS) y Sistema Nacional para el Desarrollo Integral de la Familia (DIF).

García, B., & Rojas, O. (2002). Los hogares latinoamericanos durante la segunda mitad del siglo XX: Una perspectiva sociodemográfica [Latin American households during the second half of the 20th Century: A sociodemographic perspective]. *Estudios Demográficos y Urbanos, 17,* 261-288.

Garcia, M., & Aguilera, G. (2004). *Vivienda y familia. Evolución histórico-legislativa. Actuales conflictos* [Housing and family. Historical and legislative evolution. Present conflicts]. Unpublished report, University of Havana.

García Méndez, S. (1998). *Violencia conyugal: el hombre maltratador* [Marital violence and male abusers]. Havana: Centro de Investigaciones Jurídicas.

Garg, S. P. (1998). Law and religion: The divorce systems of India. *Tulsa Journal of Comparative & International Law, 6*(1), 1-20.

Gberrie, L. (1997, May 24). *Sierra Leone women: Circumcision divides a nation.* IPS—Inter Press Service. Available at www.ips.org.

Geißler, R. (1996). *Die Sozialstruktur Deutschlands* [Germany's social structure]. Opladen: Westdeutscher Verlag.

Genofre, R. M. (1995). Família: uma leitura jurídica [Family: A juridical approach]. In M. do C. B. de Carvalho (Ed.), *A família contemporânea em debate* (pp. 97-104). São Paulo: Cortez.

Geoghegan, A. (2004, June 17). Sierra Leone scarred by civil war. Australian Broadcasting Corporation, TV Program Transcript. Available at www.abc.net .au/7.30/content/2004/s1134493.htm.

Geohive. (2005). *Current world population (ranked).* Available at www.geohive. com/charts/pop_now.php.

Gerhard, U. (1995). Frauenbewegung und Ehekritik—der Beitrag der Frauenbewegung zu sozialem Wandel [Women's liberation and marriage criticism—the contribution of the emancipation movement to social change]. In B. Nauck & C. Onnen-Isemann (Eds.), *Familie im Brennpunkt von Wissenschaft und Forschung* (pp. 59-71). Neuwied, Kriftel, Berlin: Luchterhand.

Gershuny, J., Miles, I., Jones, S., Mullings, C., Thomas, G., & Wyatt, S. (1986). Time budgets: Preliminary analyses of a national survey. *Quarterly Journal of Social Affairs, 2*(1), 13-39.

Gibson, R., Wilson, S., Denemark, D., Meagher, G., & Western, M. (2004). *Australian Social Attitudes Survey, 2003* [Computer file]. Australian Social Science Data Archive: Australian National University.

Gill, I. K., Sharma, D., & Verma, S. (2003). Adolescents in single parent families. *The Journal of Family Welfare, 49*(1), 10-20.

Gitahi, C. (2002, May 13-15). Using bride price as an excuse for violence. *East African Standard* [on line]. Available at www.eastandard.net/issue/issue 13052002006.htm.

Given, B. P., & Hirschman, C. (1994). Modernization and consanguineous marriage in Iran. *Journal of Marriage and Family, 56,* 820-834.

Glezer, H. (1991). Cohabitation. *Family Matters, 30,* 24-27.

Gluvacov, A. (1975). *Afirmarea femeii in viata sociala* [Achievement of women in the life of the society]. Bucharest: Editura Politica.

Goldani, A. M. (1993). As famílias no Brasil contemporâneo e o mito da desestruturação [Families in contemporary Brazil and the myth of their lack of structure]. *Cadernos Pagú, 1,* 67-110.

Goldani, A. M. (1994). Retratos de famílias em tempos de crise [Pictures of families in period of crisis]. *Revista de Estudos Feministas,* número especial, 2o. semestre de 1994, 303-335.

Gómez de León, J. (1998). Fenómenos sociales y familiares emergentes [Emerging social and family phenomena]. In DIF (Sistema Nacional para el Desarrollo Integral de la Familia) (Ed.), *La familia mexicana en el tercer milenio* (pp. 10-27). México D. F.: Sistema Nacional para el Desarrollo Integral de la Familia.

Gómez de León, J. (2001). Los cambios en la nupcialidad y la formación de familias: Algunos factores explicativos [Changes in nuptiality and family formation: Some explaining factors]. In J. Gómez de León & C. Rabell (Eds.), *La población de México. Tendencias y perspectivas sociodemográficas hacia el siglo XXI* (pp. 207-241). México D. F.: Fondo de Cultura Económica/Consejo Nacional de Población.

Gómez de León, J., & Parker, S. (2000). Bienestar y jefatura femenina en los hogares mexicanos [Welfare and female headed household in Mexican households]. In M. P. López & V. Salles (Eds.), *Familia, género y pobreza* (pp. 11-45). México D. F.: Miguel Angel Porrúa Grupo Editorial.

Gonzalbo, P. (1998). *Familia y orden colonial* [Family and colonial order]. México D. F.: El Colegio de México.

González, S. (1996). Novias pedidas, novias robadas, polígamos y madres solteras. Un estudio de caso en el México rural [Petitioned brides, stolen brides, polygamous and single mothers. A case study in rural Mexico]. In M. P. López (Ed.), Hogares, familias: Desigualdad, conflicto, redes solidarias y parentales (pp. 29-38). México D. F.: Sociedad Mexicana de Demografía.

González Pagés, J. C. (2003). *En busca de un espacio: Historia de mujeres en Cuba* [In search of a space: History of women in Cuba]. Havana: Editorial Ciencias Sociales.

Gordon, S. (2002). Desarrollo social y derechos de ciudadanía [Social development and citizenship rights]. In C. Sojo (Ed.), *Desarrollo Social en América Latina* (pp. 151-214). México D. F.: Facultad Latinoamericana de Ciencias Sociales/Banco Mundial.

Gray, M., Qu, L., Renda, J., & de Vaus, D. (2003). Changes in the labour force status of lone and couple Australian mothers, 1983-2002 (AIFS Research Paper 34). Melbourne: Australian Institute of Family Studies. Available at aifs.gov.au/institute/pubs/respaper/RP33.pdf.

Greenwell, K. F. (2003). *The effects of child welfare reform on the levels of child abandonment and deinstitutionalization in Romania, 1987-2000.* Unpublished doctoral dissertation, The University of Texas, Austin.

Grossi, M. (1994). Novas/velhas violências contra a mulher no Brasil [New/old violence against women in Brazil]. *Revista de Estudos Feministas,* número especial, 2o. semestre de 1994, 473-483.

Groza, V., & Kalyanvala, R. (2004). Indian families adopting Indian children. *Indian Journal of Social Work, 64,* 93-113.

Gu, B. C., & Li, Y. P. (1996). Sex ratio at birth and son preference in China. In *Sex preference for children and gender discrimination in Asia* (pp. 43-89). Research Monograph 96-02. Seoul: KIHASA.

Gu, B. C., & Roy, K. (1996). Zhongguodalu, Zhongguo Taiwan Sheng he Hanguo chusheng yinger xingbiebi shitiao de bijiaofenxi [A comparative analysis of the abnormal sex ratio at birth in Mainland China, the Taiwan Province of China, and the Republic of Korea]. *Renko Yanjiu, 20*(5), 1-16.

Guanche, J. (1996). *Componentes étnicos de la nación cubana* [Ethnical components of the Cuban nation]. Havana: Fundación Fernando Ortiz.

Gubrium, J. F., & Holstein, J. A. (1990). *What is family?* Mountain View, CA: Mayfield.

Güneri, O., Sümer, Z., & Yildirim, A. (1999). Sources of self-identity among Turkish adolescents. *Adolescence, 34*, 535-546.

Guvernul Romaniei & UNICEF. (1997). *Situatia copilului si a familiei in Romania* [Situation of child and family in Romania]. Bucharest: Author.

Habermas, J. (1984). *Mudança estrutural da esfera pública: Investigações quanto a uma categoria da sociedade burguesa* [Structural change of public sphere: Investigations about a category of the bourgeois society]. (Translation of Strukturwandel der Öffentlichkeit.) Rio de Janeiro: Tempo Brasileiro.

Haeri, S. (1994). Temporary marriage: An Islamic discourse on female sexuality in Iran. In M. Afkhami & E. Fiedl (Eds.), *In the eye of the storm: Women in postrevolutionary Iran* (pp. 98-114). New York: I. B. Tauris.

Harrell-Bond, B. (1975). Some influential attitudes about family limitation in Sierra Leone. In J. C. Caldwell (Ed.), *Population growth and socioeconomic change in West Africa* (pp. 473-489). New York: Columbia University Press.

Harrell-Bond, B. (1977). The influence of the family caseworker on the structure of the family: The Sierra Leone case. *Social-Research, 44*, 193-215.

Hartley, R. (1993). Under the same roof: Young unmarried sexual relationships in parents' homes. *Family Matters, 36*, 40-43.

Haskey, J., & Kiernan, K. E. (1989). Cohabitation in Great Britain—Characteristics and estimated numbers of cohabiting partners. In *Population trends No. 58* (pp. 15-20). London: Her Majesty's Stationary Office.

Hatti, N., Sekher, T. V., & Larsen, M. (2004). *Lives at risk: Declining child sex ratios in India.* Lund Papers in Economic History (No. 93, 2004). Lund University, Population Economics, Department of Economic History, Lund, Sweden.

Haviland, W. A. (1996). *Cultural anthropology* (8th ed.). Forth Worth, TX: Harcourt.

Health Watch UP. (2004). *Abortion Assessment Project—India: State level dissemination meeting.* Lucknow: Kriti Resource Centre.

Hegland, M. E. (1990). Women and the Iranian revolution: A village case study. *Dialectical Anthropology, 15*, 183-192.

Heilborn, M. L. (1992). *Dois é par: Conjugalidade, gênero e identidade sexual em contexto igualitário* [Two is a couple: Conjugality, gender, and sexual identity in egalitarian context]. Unpublished doctoral dissertation, National Museum of Social Anthropology, Federal University of Rio de Janeiro, Brazil.

Heinze, B., Nadai, E., Fischer, R., & Ummel, H. (1997). *Ungleich unter Gleichen—Studien zur geschlechtsspezifischen Segregation des Arbeitsmarktes* [Unequal among equals—Studies on gender specific segregation of the labor market]. Frankfurt am Main: Campus.

HelpAge International. (1999a). *Addressing violations of the rights of older men and women.* London, UK: HelpAge International Publications.

HelpAge International. (1999b). *Older people in disasters and humanitarian crisis: Guidelines for best practice.* London, UK: HelpAge International Publications.

HelpAge International. (2001). *United Nations principles for older persons.* London, UK: HelpAge International Publications.

Henderson, S., & Hoggart, K. (2003). Ruralities and gender divisions of labour in Eastern England. *Sociologia Ruralis, 43,* 349-378.

Hennon, C. B., & Hildenbrand, B. (Eds.). (2005). Farm family responses to changing agricultural conditions: The actors' point of view [Special issue]. *Journal of Comparative Family Studies, 36*(3).

Hennon, C. B., Jones, A., Roth, M., & Popescu, L. (1998). Family-enterprise initiatives as a response to socioeconomic and political change in Eastern and Central Europe. *Journal of Family and Economic Issues, 19,* 235-253.

Hennon, C. B., Loker, S., & Walker, R. (2000). *Gender and home-based employment.* Westport, CT: Auburn House.

Hennon, C. B., & Medina, A. V. A. (1993, February). *Economic contributions of Portuguese women in Colonial Brazil.* Paper presented at the V Congreso Internacional e Interdisciplinario de la Mujer, Universidad de Costa Rica, San Pedro, Costa Rica.

Hennon, C. B., Peterson, G. W., Polzin, L., & Radina, M. E. (2006). Familias de ascendencia mexicana residentes en Estados Unidos: recursos para el manejo del estrés parental [Resident families of Mexican ancestry in United States: Resources for the handling of parental stress]. In R. Esteinou (Ed.), *Fortalezas y desafíos de las familias en dos contextos: Estados Unidos de América y México* (pp. 225-282). México, D. F.: Centro de Investigaciones y Estudios Superiores en Antropología Social (CIESAS) y Sistema Nacional para el Desarrollo Integral de la Familia (DIF).

Herlth, A., Brunner, E. J., Tyrell, H., & Kriz, J. (1994). *Abschied von der Normalfamilie? Partnerschaft kontra Elternschaft* [Farewell of the standard family? Partnership versus parenthood]. Berlin: Springer.

Hermans, H. J. M., & Kempen, H. J. G. (1998). Moving cultures: The perilous problems of cultural dichotomies in a globalizing society. *American Psychologist, 53,* 1111-1120.

Hernández, J. (1973). *Estudio sobre el divorcio* [Study on divorce]. University of Havana.

Herrera-Valdés, R., & Almaguer-López, M. (2005). Strategies for national health care systems and centers in the emerging world: Central America and the Caribbean—The case of Cuba. *Kidney International, 68*(Suppl. 98), S66-S68.

Higgins, P. (1985). Women in the Islamic Republic of Iran: Legal, social, and ideological changes. *Journal of Women in Culture and Society, 10,* 487-495.

Highest education attained by sex (2000 Census). (2000). Available at www.census .gov.ph/data/quickstat/qsgender.html.

Hildenbrand, B., & Lanfranchi, A. (1996). Kinder im "seelischen Grenzgängertum": Das Wandern zwischen den Welten beim Verlust transitorischer Räume [Children in "mental no-man's-land:" Swaying between different worlds after losing transitory spaces]. In P. Dillig & H. Schilling (Eds.), *Erziehungsberatung in der Postmoderne* (pp. 59-70). Mainz: Matthias-Grünewald-Verlag.

Hirsch, J. L. (2001). *Sierra Leone: Diamonds and the struggle for democracy.* London: Lynne Rienner.

Historisk statistik för Sverige [Historical statistics of Sweden]. (1969). Stockholm: Allmänna förlaget.

Hochschild, A. R. (1989). *The second shift: Working parents and the revolution at home.* New York: Viking.

Hoffer, C. P. (1972). Mende and Sherbro women in high office. *Canadian Journal of African Studies, 6,* 151-164.

Hoffmann-Riem, C. (1989). Elternschaft ohne Verwandtschaft. Adoption, Stiefbeziehung und heterologe Insemination [Parenthood without blood relationship. Adoption, steprelationship and in vitro fertilization]. In R. Nave-Herz & M. Markefka (Eds.), *Handbuch der Familien und Jugendforschung Band I* (pp. 389-412). Neuwied und Frankfurt am Main: Luchterhand.

Holland, J., Ramazanoglu, C., Sharpe, S., & Thomson, R. (1998). *The male in the head: Young people, heterosexuality and power.* London: Tufnell.

Hollander, D. (2004). Indian women who have daughters but no sons face an increased risk of marital dissolution. *International Family Planning Perspectives, 30*(1), 48-49.

Hollis, A. C. (1979). *The Maasai: Their language and folklore.* Westport, CT: Negro Universities Press.

Hoogland, E. (1995, July/August). The pulse of Iran. *Middle East Insight Magazine, 11,* 1-5.

Hortaçsu, N. (1989a). Targets of communication during adolescence. *Journal of Adolescence, 12,* 253-263.

Hortaçsu, N. (1989b). Turkish students' self-concepts and reflected appraisals of significant others. *International Journal of Psychology, 24,* 451-463.

Hortaçsu, N. (1995). Parents' educational level, parents' beliefs, and child outcomes. *Journal of Genetic Psychology, 156,* 373-383.

Hortaçsu, N. (1997). Family- and couple-initiated marriages in Turkey. *Genetic, Social, & General Psychology Monographs, 123,* 325-342.

Hortaçsu, N. (1999). The first year of family- and couple-initiated marriages of a Turkish sample: A longitudinal investigation. *International Journal of Psychology, 34,* 29-41.

Hortaçsu, N., Ertem, L., Kurtoglu, H., & Uzer, B. (1990). Family background and individual measures as predictors of Turkish primary school children's academic achievement. *The Journal of Psychology, 124,* 535-544.

Hortaçsu, N., Oral, A., & Yasak-Gültekin, Y. (1991). Factors affecting relationships of Turkish adolescents with parents and same-sex friends. *Journal of Social Psychology, 13,* 413-426.

Houseknecht, S. K., & Pankhurst, J. G. (Eds.). (2000). *Family, religion, and social change in diverse societies.* New York: Oxford University Press.

Huang, C. Y., & Tao, Y. (1987). Chengshi jiating de yanglao gongneng jiqi bianhua [Functions and changes of aging supports in city families]. In Y. Liu & S. J. Xue (Eds.), *Zhongguo Hunyin Jiating Yanjiu* (pp. 369-379). Beijing: Shehui Kexue Wenxian Chubanshe.

Humboldt, A. de. (1998). *Ensayo político sobre la Isla de Cuba* [Political essay on the Island of Cuba]. Havana: Fundación Fernando Ortiz.

Hunt, C. L., Pal, A. P., Coller, R. W., Espiritu, S. C., de Young, J. E., & Corpus, S. F. (1963). *Sociology in the Philippine setting* (Rev. ed.). Quezon City: Phoenix.

Hunt, C. L., Quisumbing, L., Espiritu, S., Costello, M., & Lacar, L. (1987). *Sociology in the Philippine setting: A modular approach.* Quezon City: Phoenix.

Ilkkaracan, P., & Women for Women's Human Rights. (1998). Exploring the context of women's sexuality in Eastern Turkey. *Reproductive Health Matters, 6*(12), 66-75.

Illo, J. F. I. (1989). Who heads the household? Women in households in the Philippines. In A. T. Torres (Ed.), *The Filipino women in focus* (pp. 168-189). Bangkok: UNESCO.

Index Mundi. (2005). *Cuba.* Available at www.indexmundi.com/cuba/.

India has approximately 7 million abortions annually. (2001, March 9). French Press Agency. Available at www.euthanasia.com/india2001.html.

Indian Child. (2004). *Dowry in India.* Available at www.indianchild.com/dowry_in_india.htm.

Informationszentrum Sozialwissenschaften 2000. (2000). Available at www.gesis.org/en/iz/index.htm.

Informe Central al VII Congreso de la FMC, La Habana, marzo del 2000 [Central Report to the 7th Congress of the Federation of Cuban Women]. (2000, March). Havana.

Ingersoll-Dayton, B., & Saengtienchai, C. (1999). Respect for the elderly in Asia: Stability and change. *International Journal of Aging and Human Development, 48,* 113-130.

Inglehart, R. (2000). *World Values Surveys and European Values Surveys, 1981-84, 1990-93 and 1995-1997* [Computer file]. Ann Arbor, MI: Institute for Social Research, ICPSR.

Institute of Applied Manpower Research. (2000). *Manpower profile Indian yearbook 2000.* New Delhi: Author.

Instituto Brasileiro de Geografia e Estatística. (2001). *Síntese de indicadores sociais 2000* [Synthesis of social parameters 2000]. Rio de Janeiro: Author.

Instituto Brasileiro de Geografia e Estatística. (2002). *Síntese de indicadores sociais 2001* [Synthesis of social parameters 2001]. Rio de Janeiro: Author.

Instituto de Historia de Cuba. (1993). *La colonia, Evolución socioeconómica y formacion nacional [de los orígenes a 1867]* [The colony, social and economic evolution and national formation (from its origins to 1867)]. Havana: Editora Política.

Instituto de Historia de Cuba. (1998). *Historia de Cuba.III La neocolonia, organización y crisis /desde 1899 hasta 1940/* [History of Cuba III. The neocolony, organization and crisis (from 1899 to 1940)]. Havana: Editora Política.

Instituto de Investigaciones Estadísticas. (1988). *Los censos en la población y vivienda en Cuba, estimaciones, empadronamiento y censos de la época colonial* [Censuses of population and housing in Cuba, estimations, inscription and censuses in Colonial Times), Vol. 1. Havana: Author.

Instituto Nacional de Estadística, Geografía e Informática. (1997). *Estadísticas de matrimonios y divorcios, 1996* [Marriage and divorce statistics, 1996]. México D. F.: Author.

Instituto Nacional de Estadística, Geografía e Informática. (2000a). *Indicadores de hogares y familias por entidad federativa* [Households and families: Indicators by state]. México, D. F.: Author.

Instituto Nacional de Estadística, Geografía e Informática. (2000b). *Los hogares con jefatura femenina* [Households with female heads]. México D. F.: Author.

Instituto Nacional de Estadística, Geografía e Informática. (2001). *Estadísticas de trabajo doméstico y extradoméstico en México. 1995-1999* [Statistics of domestic and extradomestic work in Mexico. 1995-1999]. México D. F.: Author.

Instituto Nacional de Estadística, Geografía e Informática. (2002a). *Estadísticas de matrimonios y divorcios* [Statistics of marriages and divorces]. México D. F.: Author.

Instituto Nacional de Estadística, Geografía e Informática. (2002b). *Uso del tiempo y aportaciones en los hogares mexicanos* [Use of time and contributions in Mexican households]. México D. F.: Author.

Instituto Nacional de Estadística, Geografía e Informática. (2003a). *La evolución de los hogares unipersonales* [The evolution of unipersonal households]. México D. F.: Author.

Instituto Nacional de Estadística, Geografía e Informática & Secretaría de Trabajo y Previsión Social. (2003b). *Encuesta Nacional de Empleo, 2003. Segundo Trimestre* [National Employment Survey, 2003. Second trimester]. México D. F.: Author.

Instituto Nacional de Estadística, Geografía e Informática, Instituto Nacional de las Mujeres. (2004). *Mujeres y hombres en México* [Women and men in Mexico]. México D. F.: Author.

Institutul National de Statistica. (2001). *Analize demografice* [Demographic analysis]. Bucharest: Author.

Institutul National de Statistica. (2002). *Anuarul statistic 2002* [Statistical yearbook 2002]. Bucharest: Author.

Institutul National de Statistica. (2003). *Recensamantul populatiei si al locuintelor la 18-27 martie 2002* [General results: Census of population and dwellings: 18-27 March 2002]. Bucharest: Author. Available at insse.ro/rpl2002revgen/rg2002 .htm.

Institutul National de Statistica. (2005). *Indicatori statistici* [Statistical indicators]. Available at www.insse.ro/portalindic.htm/.

International Monetary Fund. (2004, August 10). *IMF concludes 2004 Article IV Consultation with Turkey,* Public information notice (PIN) No:04/87. Available at http://www.imf.org/external/np/sec/pn/2004/pn0487.htm.

International Planned Parenthood Federation. (nd). *Romania.* Available at ippfnet. ippf.org/pub/IPPF_Regions/IPPF_CountryProfile.asp?ISOCode=RO.

International Planned Parenthood Federation. (2002). *Sierra Leone.* Available at Ippfnet.ippf.org/pub/IPPF_Regions/IPPF_CountryProfile.asp?ISOCode=SL.

Ionescu, A., Muresan, M., Costin, N. M., & Ursa, V. (1975). *Familia si rolul ei in societatea socialista* [Family and its role in the socialist society]. Cluj-Napoca: Editura Dacia.

Iran-Iraq War 1980-1988. (nd). Available at www.iranchamber.com/history/iran_ iraq_war/iran_iraq_war1.php.

Iran Statistical Center. (1996). *Report of the 1993 population sample survey.* Tehran: Author.

Iran Statistical Center. (1997). *Selective comparison of the censuses: 1986-1996.* Tehran: Author.

Iran Statistical Center. (1998). *Statistical yearbook of Iran, 1996.* Tehran: Author.
Iran Statistical Center. (2002). *Statistical yearbook of Iran, 2000.* Tehran: Author.
Iran Statistical Center. (2003). *Report on results from 2002 socioeconomic survey of Iran.* Tehran: Author.
Iran Statistical Center. (2004). *2003 labor force survey of households.* Tehran: Author.
Ironmonger, D., & Richardson, E. (1991). *Leisure: An input-output approach.* Melbourne: University of Melbourne, Centre for Applied Research on the Future.
Irvine, J. M. (1995). *Sexuality education across cultures.* San Francisco: Jossey-Bass.
Is this what John Redwood meant by family values? (2003, July 30). *Guardian Newspapers.* Available at http//www.buzzle.com/editorials/7-30-2003-43628.asp.
Isaac, R., & Shah, A. (2004). Sex roles and marital adjustment in Indian couples. *International Journal of Social Psychiatry, 50,* 129-141.
Islam, F. (2000, September). Let them in—It'll pay. *World Press Review, 47,* 19-20.
Istituto Nazionale di Statistica. (1993). L'evoluzione della fecondità nelle regioni italiane. Indicatori di periodo e di generazione [Trends in fertility in the Italian regions. Period and cohort indicators], *Notiziario, 4*(41), XIV.
Istituto Nazionale di Statistica. (1996a). *Famiglia, abitazioni e servizi di pubblica utilità* [Households, housing, and public services]. Rome: Author.
Istituto Nazionale di Statistica. (1996b). *Stili di vita e condizioni di salute* [Lifestyle and health conditions]. Rome: Author.
Istituto Nazionale di Statistica. (2000a). *La vita di coppia* [Living in couple]. Informazioni: 37. Rome: Author.
Istituto Nazionale di Statistica. (2000b). *Le strutture familiari* [Families and households]. Informazioni: 17. Rome: Author.
Istituto Nazionale di Statistica. (2003). *Annuario statistico italiano* [Italian statistical yearbook]. Rome: Author.
Istituto Ricerche sulla Popolazione. (1999). *Italia: Facts and trends in population.* Rome: Author.
Istituto Superiore di Sanità. (1993). *L'interruzione volontaria di gravidanza in Italia, 1989-1990* [Voluntary abortion in Italy, 1989-1990]. Rome: STISAN 93/94.
Italy by numbers. (2001). *Staying at home.* Available at http://zoomata.com/?p=449.
Iyer, S. (2003). Religion, reproduction and development in contemporary India. *Development, 46*(4), 50-56.
Jamshedji-Neogi, A., & Sharma, M. L. (2003). Coping with sexuality during adolescence. *The Journal of Family Welfare, 49*(2), 30-37.
Jamuna, D. (2003). Issues of elder care and elder abuse in the Indian context. *Journal of Aging & Social Policy, 15*(2/3), 125-142.
Japa, D. P. (1999, March 26). Crisis and the Filipino women: Carpe diem. *Philippine Daily Inquirer,* C1-C2.
Jarvis, J. (2000). Mormonism in France: The family as a universal value in a globalizing religion. In S. K. Houseknecht & J. G. Pankhurst (Eds.), *Family, religion, and social change in diverse societies* (pp. 237-266). New York: Oxford University Press.

Jelloun, T. B. (2000, September). Immigration tears people apart. *World Press Review, 47,* 18-19.

Jiang, D., Teng, G., Wang, A., & Qian, M. (1991). *Jiating Xili.* Beijing: Popular Science Press.

Jiang, M. (1997, January). Zhongguo jiaoyu jingfer touru de "bawu" huigu yu "jiuwu" zhan wang [Review of educational budgets in the "eight fifth" and focus in the "ninth fifth"]. *Zhongxiaoxue Guanli, 75,* 18-26.

Jigau, M. (2002). Disparities between rural and urban areas. In Ministry of Education and Research, Institute for Educational Sciences (coord. M. Jigau). *Rural education in Romania. Conditions, challenges and strategies of development* (2nd ed.) (pp. 9-33). Bucharest: Marlink.

Jisi, W. (2000, August). Does globalization mean Westernization? *World Press Review, 47,* 30.

Jocano, F. L. (1972). The cultural impediment to population control—small family norm for Filipino. *Solidarity, 7*(1), 24-29.

Jones, A. (2002). *Case study: Maternal mortality.* Available at www.gendercide .org/case_maternal.html.

Jones, S. (1998, January). *Enacted marriage and fatherhood without jural paternity: Signs of bilateral kinship among Xhosa in an Eastern Cape Township.* Paper presented at the annual conference of the Association for Anthropology in Southern Africa, Stellenbosch, University of Stellenbosch.

Joseph, S. (1998). Emergency contraception: An option for women's empowerment. *The Journal of Family Welfare, 44*(2), 54-58.

Kabaria, J. (2003). *Cohabitation among university students in Kenya.* Unpublished manuscript, Kenyatta University, Nairobi.

Kamara, A. I. (1983, September). *The changing family in the Sierra Leone context.* Paper presented at a UNESCO Conference in Maseru, Lesotho.

Kandiyoti, D. (1995). Patterns of patriarchy: Notes for an analysis of male dominance in Turkish society. In S. Tekeli (Ed.), *Women in modern Turkish society: A reader* (pp. 306-318). London: Zed Books.

Kapadia, S. (1999). Self, women and empowerment: A conceptual inquiry. In T. S. Saraswati (Ed.), *Culture, socialization and human development: Theory, research and application in India* (pp. 255-277). New Delhi: Sage.

Kazemipur, A. & Rezaei, A. (2003). Religious life under theocracy: The case of Iran. *Journal for the Scientific Study of Religion, 42,* 347-361.

Kelley, J. (2001). Attitudes towards homosexuality in 29 nations. *Australian Social Monitor, 4*(1), 15-22.

Kelley, J., Bean, C., & Evans, M. (1993). *National Social Science Survey, 1989-90: Family and Changing Sex Roles* [Computer file]. Canberra: Australian National University Social Science Data Archives.

KENGO. (1994). *Towards a comprehensive population policy: A review of population policies in Kenya.* Nairobi, Kenya: Author.

Kenkel, W. F. (1977). *The family in perspective* (4th ed.). Santa Monica, CA: Goodyear.

Kenyatta, J. (1953). *Facing Mount Kenya: The tribal life of the Gikuyu.* London: Secker and Warburg.

Kenyaweb. (2003). *AIDS awareness.* Available at www.kenyaweb.com/health/aids/impact.html.

Kesziharmat, S., & Kesziharmat, V. (1977). A Kalotaszegi egykezesrol [One kid in Kalotaszeg]. *Korunk, 12,* 19-27.

Kiernan, K., & Estaugh, V. (1993). *Cohabitation: Extra-marital childbearing and social policy.* London: Family Policy Studies Centre.

Kiminyo, D. M., & Ngige, L. W. (2000). *Baseline survey of early childhood education and care in Kwale, Migori and Kisumu, Kenya.* Nairobi: UNICEF.

King, E. M., & Domingo, L. J. (1986). The changing status of Filipino women across family generations. *Philippine Population Journal, 2*(1-4), 1-31.

Kinsella, K., & Ferreira, M. (1997, August). *Aging trends: South Africa* (International Brief (IB/97-2)). Washington, DC: U.S. Bureau of the Census.

Klemm, K., Böttcher, W., & Weegen, M. (1992). *Bildungsplanung in den neuen Bundesländern. Entwicklungstrends, Perspektiven und Vergleiche* [Education planning in the New Federal States. Trends of development, perspectives, and comparisons]. Weinheim/München: Juventa.

Kligman, G. (1998a). *Nunta mortului: Ritual, poetica si cultura populara in Transilvania* [The wedding of the dead: Ritual, poetics, and popular culture in Transylvania]. Iasi: Polirom.

Kligman, G. (1998b). *Politics of duplicity: Controlling reproduction in Ceusescu's Romania.* Berkeley: University of California Press.

Kosmin, B. A., Mayer, E., & Keyser, A. (2001). *American religious identification survey.* New York: The Graduate Center of the University of New York.

Krähenbühl, V. (1986). *Stieffamilien. Struktur—Entwicklung—Therapie* [Stepfamilies. Structure—development—therapy]. Freiburg: Lambertus.

Krishna Mohan, P. V. T., Khan, A. G., & Sureender, S. (2003). Two-child family norm: Women's attitude in Uttar Pradesh. *The Journal of Family Welfare, 49*(1), 21-31.

Kusum. (2001). The Indian Divorce (Amendment) Act 2001: A critique. *Journal of the Indian Law Institute, 43,* 550-558.

Laing, R. D., & Esterson, A. (1970). *Sanity, madness and the family: Families of schizophrenics.* Harmondsworth: Penguin.

Lambert, S., Petridis, R., & Galea, J. (1995). Occupational segregation in full-time and part-time employment. *Australian Bulletin of Labour, 22,* 212-225.

Landwehr, R., & Wolf, R. (1993). The Federal Republic of Germany. In B. Munday (Ed.), *European social services* (pp. 155-199). Canterbury: European Institute of Social Services.

Lane, T. (2004). In India, son preference declines with ideal family size, but remains strong. *International Family Planning Perspectives, 30,* 100-101.

Lange, A., & Lauterbach, W. (1997). "Wie nahe wohnen Enkel bei ihren Großeltern?" Aspekte der Mehrgenerationenfamilie heute [How close do grandchildren live to their grandparents? Aspects of multigenerational families today]. *Arbeitspapier Nr. 24 des Forschungsschwerpunkts "Gesellschaft und Familie" an der Sozialwissenschaftlichen Fakultät der Universität Konstanz.*

Laodong He Shehui Baozhang Bu, & Guojia Tongji Ju. (2003, April, 12). *2001 Niandu Laodong He Shehui Baozhang Shiye Fazhan Tongji Gongbao* [Annual statistics: Review on labor and social security development for 2001]. Available at http://www.cpirc.org.cn/tjsj/tjsj_gb_detail.asp?id=2076.

Lapidus, I. M. (1988). *A history of Islamic societies.* New York: Cambridge University Press.

Largest Muslim populations in the world. (nd). Available at www.aneki.com/muslim.html.

Larson, R., Verma, S., & Dworkin, J. (2001). Men's work and family lives in India: The daily organization of time and emotion. *Journal of Family Psychology, 15,* 206-224.

Larson, R., Verma, S., & Dworkin, J. (2003). Adolescence without family disengagement: The daily family lives of Indian middle class teenagers. In T. S. Saraswathi (Ed.), *Cross-cultural perspectives in human development* (pp. 258-286). New Delhi: Sage.

Lasch, C. (1977). *Haven in a heartless world—The family besieged.* New York: Basic Books.

Lavrín, A. (1991). Introducción: El escenario, los actores y el problema [Introduction: The setting, the actors and the problem]. In A. Lavrín (Ed.), *Sexualidad y matrimonio en la América Hispánica. Siglos XVI-XVII* (pp. 13-52). México D. F.: Consejo Nacional para la Cultura y las Artes/Grijalbo.

Leach, E. R. (1968). *A runaway world?* London: Oxford University Press.

Lee, K., Lush, L., Walt, G., & Cleland, J. (1998). Family planning policies and programmes in eight low-income countries: A comparative policy analysis. *Social Science and Medicine, 47,* 949-959.

Leeder, E. (2004). *Families in global perspective. A gendered journey.* Thousand Oaks, CA: Sage.

Legal Service India. (2005). *Helpline: An insight on Indian family laws.* Available at www.legalserviceindia.com/helpline/helpline_HOME.htm.

Levels and trends of contraceptive use as assessed in 1998. (1998). Available at www.un.org/popin/wdtrends/contraceptives1998.htm.

Levin, I., & Trost, J. (1992). Understanding the concept of family. *Family Relations, 41,* 348-351.

Levin, I., & Trost, J. (1999). Living apart together. *Community, Work and Family, 3,* 279-294.

LeVine, R. A., LeVine, S., Leiderman, P. H., Dixon, T. B., Richman, A., & Keefer, C. H. (1994). *Child care and culture: Lessons from Africa.* New York: Cambridge University Press.

Li, D. S., & Shen, C. L. (1991). *Zhongguo Chengshi Jiating—Wuchengshi Jiating Diaocha Shuangbianliang he Sanbianliang Ziliao Huibian* [Chinese city family— Summarized survey data collected from five Chinese cities]. Beijing: Shehui Kexue Wenxian Chubanshe.

Li, Q. Y. (1997, November). Guanche luoshi 15 da jingshen peiyang gaosuzhi laodongli [Put the spirit of 15th Conference into effect and train highly qualified labors]. *ZhongGuo PeiXun, 56,* 4-566.

Li, Y. P. (1993). Yinger chusheng xingbiebi jiqi he shehui jingji bianliang de guanxi: Pucha de jieguo he suofanying de xianshi [Sex ratio at birth and its relationship with social economic variables: Results of the survey and the facts reflected by the survey]. *Renko yu Jingji, 79*(4), 3-13.

Liang, J. M. (1990). Zhongguo de jihua shengyu [Birth control in China]. *Zhongguo Renko Kexue, 19*(4), 29-32.

Liang, Z. T., & Zhai, S. M. (1996). Shilun laonianren de quanyi baozhang wenti [Discussion of the safeguard of senior rights and interests]. *Zhongguo Renko Kexue, 4*, 46-49.

Liebig, P. S. (2003). Old-age homes and services: Old and new approaches to aged care. *Journal of Aging & Social Policy, 15*(2/3), 159-178.

Lin, Z. L. (1995). Tan laonianren shehui baozhang wenti [Discussion of the problem of the senior social supports]. *Fazhan Yanjiu, 6*, 23-24, 27.

Lindy, W., & Domingo, L. J. (1993). The social status of elderly women and men in the Filipino family. *Journal of Marriage and the Family, 55*, 415-426.

Lisk, F., & Stevens, Y. (1987). Government policy and rural women's work in Sierra Leone. In C. Oppong (Ed.), *Sex roles, population and development in West Africa: Policy-related studies on work and demographic issues* (pp. 183-202). Portsmouth, NH: Heinemann.

Lisk, I., & Williams, B. (1995). Marriage and divorce regulations in Sierra Leone. *Family Law Quarterly, 29*, 655-674.

Little, K. (1967). *The Mende of Sierra Leone: A West African people in transition.* London: Routledge and Kegan Paul.

Liu, Y. (1987). Zhongguo chengshi de fazhan yu bianhua—Wuchengshi jiating diaocha chuxi [Family developments and changes in Chinese cities—Preliminary analysis on the survey to families in five cities]. In Y. Liu & S. J. Xue (Eds.), *Zhongguo Hunyin Jiating Yanjiu* (pp. 81-99). Beijing: Shehui Kexue Wenxian Chubanshe.

Liwag, E. C. D., dela Cruz, A. S., & Macapagal, E. J. (1999). *A UNICEF and Ateneo study: How we raise our daughters and sons; child-rearing and gender socialization in the Philippines.* UN Children's Fund and Ateneo Wellness Center.

López, M. P. (1998). Género y familia [Gender and family]. In Sistema Nacional para el Desarrollo Integral de la Familia (Ed.), *La Familia Mexicana en el Tercer Milenio* (pp. 28-40). México D. F.: Sistema Nacional para el Desarrollo Integral de la Familia.

López, M. P., Salles, V., & Tuirán, R. (2001). Familias y hogares: Pervivencias y transformaciones en un horizonte de largo plazo [Families and households: Continuities and transformations]. In J. Gómez de León & C. Rabell (Eds.), *La Población de México. Tendencias y perspectivas sociodemográficas hacia el siglo XXI* (pp. 635-693). México D. F.: Fondo de Cultura Económica/Consejo Nacional de Población.

Loutfi, M. (2001). *Women, gender and work. What is equality and how do we get there?* Geneva: International Labour Office.

Lozano, A. (1997, May 29). O perfil das crianças que freqüentam as ruas de São Paulo [Characteristics of the children who live and work in the streets of São Paulo]. *Jornal Folha de São Paulo,* Caderno *3*, 7.

Lu, S. H. (1997). Huyinguan de toji yu bianqian yianjiu [Statistical analysis and study of changes about the concepts of marriage]. *Shehuixue Yianjiu, 68*(2), 37-47.

Lu, Z. (2000). Chinese husbands' participation in household labor. *Journal of Comparative Family Studies, 31*(2), 191-215.

Lüscher, K. (1993). Generationenbeziehungen—neue Zugänge zu einem alten Thema [Relationships between the generations—New approaches to an old subject]. In K. Lüscher & F. Schultheis (Eds.), *Generationenbeziehungen in "postmodernen" Gesellschaften* (pp. 17-47). Konstanz: Universitätsverlag.

Lutz, B. (1984). *Der kurze Traum der immerwährenden Prosperität* [The short dream of ever-lasting prosperity]. Frankfurt am Main: Campus.

Ma, X. (1982). Nongcun jiating jiegou de bianqian [Family structure changes in rural China]. *Renko Tansuo, 12*(2), 15-24.

Ma, X. (1984). Jiating guimo he jiegou de fazhan bianhua [Developments and changes in family size and structure]. In D. X. Xu (Ed.), *Dangdai Zhongguo Renko* (pp. 343-374). Beijing: Shehui Kexue Wenxian Chubanshe.

Ma, X. (1988). Jiating guimo he jiegou de fazhan bianhua [The changes and the developments of the family size and structure]. In D. X. Xu (Series Ed.) & X. Ma (Vol. Ed.), *Dangdai ZhongGuo de renko* (Vol. 4., pp. 343-374). Beijing: Chinese Social Science Press.

Ma, Y. C., Liu, Y., Sheng, X. W., & Meng, C. (1992). *Funui jiuye yu jiating: Zhongri bijiaoyianjiu diaochabaogao* [Women's employment and family: A comparative research of Chinese and Japanese families]. Beijing: Shehui Kexue Wenxian Chubanshe.

Ma, Y. C., & Shen, C. L. (1987). Woguo chengshi jiating jiegou leixing bianqian chutan [Preliminary exploration on the changes of city family structures and types in our country]. In Y. Liu & S. J. Xue (Eds.), *Zhongguo Hunyin Jiating Yanjiu* (pp. 158-182). Beijing: Shehui Kexue Wenxian Chubanshe.

MacCormack, C. P. (1975). Sande women and political power in Sierra Leone. *The West African Journal of Sociology and Political Science, 1,* 42-50.

MacIntyre, A., Aning, E. K., & Addo, P. N. N. (2002). Politics, war and youth culture in Sierra Leone: An alternative interpretation. *African Security Review, 11*(3), 7-15.

Maconachie, M. (1992). The allocation of domestic tasks by white married couples. *South African Journal of Sociology, 23,* 1-22.

Maqsood, R. W. (2005). *Payments to and from the bride in Islamic law and tradition.* Available at http://www.islamawareness.net/Marriage/Dowry/dowry_article 001.html.

Marginean, I. (Ed.). (2004). *Cauze sociale ale excluziunii copilului* [Social causes of child exclusion]. Romanian Academy, National Institute for Economic Research, Research Institute for the Quality of Life.

Marquetti Nodarse, H. (1997). La economía del dólar: Balance y perspectivas [The USD economy, summary and perspectives]. *Temas, 11,* 51-62.

Marriage. (nd). Available at countrystudies.us/india/86.htm.

Marsh, S., & McKay, S. (1993, August). Families, work and the use of childcare. *Employment Gazette.* London: Her Majesty's Stationary Office.

Martín, C., & Guadalupe, P. (1998). *Familia, emigración y vida cotidiana en Cuba* [Family, migration and daily life in Cuba]. Havana: Editora Política.

Martineau, R. (1998). Science and technology: Where are the women? *Agenda, 38,* 12-18.

Martinez, I. L. (2002). The elder in the Cuban American family: Making sense of the real and ideal. *Journal of Comparative Family Studies, 33,* 359-375.

Martínez, M., Morejón, B., Aja, A., and others. (1996). *Los balseros cubanos* [The Cuban ferrymen]. Havana: Editorial de Ciencias Sociales.

Mason, K. O., & Smith, H. L. (2000). Husbands' versus wives' fertility goals and the use of contraception: The influence of gender context in five Asian countries. *Demography, 37,* 299-311.

Mastura, M. O. (1994). Legal pluralism in the Philippines. *Law and Society Review, 28,* 461-475.

McCaa, R. (1996). Tratos nupciales: La constitución de uniones formales e informales en México y España, 1500-1900 [Marriage ways: The constitution of formal and informal unions in Mexico and Spain, 1500-1900]. In P. Gonzalbo & C. Rabell (Eds.), *Familia y vida privada en la historia de Iberoamérica* (pp. 21-58). México D. F.: El Colegio de México/Instituto de Investigaciones Sociales, Universidad Nacional Autónoma de México.

McCulloch, M. (1964). *Peoples of Sierra Leone.* London: International African Institute.

McKenry, P. C., & Price, S. J. (1995). Divorce: A comparative perspective. In B. B. Ingoldsby & S. Smith (Eds.), *Families in multicultural perspective* (pp. 187-213). New York: Guilford.

Medina, A. M. (2001). *Family violence in relation with gender. Perception of a group of teenagers.* Unpublished thesis, National Center for Sexual Education, Havana, Cuba.

Medina, B. T. G. (2001). *The Filipino family* (2nd ed.). Quezon City: University of the Philippines Press.

Medina, B. T. G., de Guzman, E. A., Roldan, A. A., & Bautista, R. M. J. (1996). *The Filipino family: Emerging structures and arrangements* (ORC Monograph Series I). Quezon City: University of the Philippines Office of Research Coordination.

Medindia. (2005). *Average age at marriage—India.* Available at www.medindia .net/health_statistics/general/marriageage.asp.

Mehta, S. (2001, August). A cure for multiple ills. *World Press Review, 48,* 43.

Menashri, D. (1992). *Education and the making of modern Iran.* Ithaca, NY: Cornell University Press.

Mendez, P. P., Jocano, F. L., Rolda, R. S., & Matela, S. B. (1984). *The Filipino family in transition: A study in culture and education.* Mendiola, Manila: Centro Escolar University Research and Development Center.

Menniti, A. (1997, October). Demotrends in Italy. *Demotrends, 1,* 4-5.

Menniti, A. (2004). Famiglia e politiche familiari [Family and family policies]. In E. Pugliese (Ed.), *Lo stato sociale in Italia* (pp. 77-105). Rome: Donzelli.

Menniti, A., & Palomba, R. (1994). Trends in marital instability in Italy. *Labour, 8*(2), 303-315.

Menniti, A., & Palomba, R. (1997). Attitudes of Italians. *Demotrends, 1,* 7.

Menniti, A., & Terracina, S. (1997). Le famiglie ricostituite [Reconstituted families]. In M. Barbagli & C. Saraceno (Eds.), *Lo stato delle famiglie in Italia* (pp. 272-281). Bologna: Il Mulino.

Men's traditional culture. (1996, August 10). *The Economist, 341,* 34.

Mercado, A. (1990, January 10). The '80s Filipino family, a survivor still. *The Manila Chronicle,* 35.

Meyer, T. (1996). Familienformen im Wandel [Changing ways of family]. In R. Geibler (Ed.), *Die Sozialstruktur Deutschlands* (pp. 306-332). Opladen: Westdeutscher Verlag.

Mier y Terán, M., & Partida V. (2001). Niveles, tendencias y diferenciales de la fecundidad en México [Levels, tendencies and differentials of fertility in Mexico]. In J. Gómez de León & C. Rabell (Eds.), *La Población de México. Tendencias y perspectivas sociodemográficas hacia el siglo XXI* (pp. 168-203). México D. F.: Consejo Nacional de Población/Fondo de Cultura Económica.

Migeod, F. W. H. (1970). *A view of Sierra Leone.* New York: Negro Universities Press.

Millward, C. (1997). Divorce and family relations in later life. *Family Matters, 48,* 30-33.

Millward, C., & de Vaus, D. A. (1997). Extended families. In D. A. de Vaus & I. Wolcott (Eds.), *Australian family profiles: Social and demographic patterns* (pp. 37-44). Melbourne: Australian Institute of Family Studies.

Millward, C., & Matches, G. (1995). *Work related childcare for urban families with preschool aged children.* Melbourne: Australian Institute of Family Studies.

Millward, C., Wolcott, I., de Vaus, D. A., & Soriano, G. (1997). Family care. In D. A. de Vaus & I. Wolcott (Eds.), *Australian family profiles: Social and demographic patterns* (pp. 107-118). Melbourne: Australian Institute of Family Studies.

Ministry for Welfare and Population Development. (1997a, August). *Draft white paper on population policy.* Pretoria: Government Printers.

Ministry for Welfare and Population Development. (1997b, August). *White paper for social welfare.* Available at www.polity.org.za/govdocs/white_ papers/social971.html.

Ministry of Health and Medical Education. (2003). *Preliminary report of Iran 2000 Demographic and Health Survey.* Tehran: Iran Ministry of Health and Medical Education.

Miralao, V. A., & Dongail, J. S. (1984, September). *Women's status in Philippine lowland and tribal communities.* Paper prepared for the Workshop on Ethnic Identity and the Status of Women, International Centre for Ethnic Studies, Colombo, Sri Lanka.

Mitrofan, I. (1989). *Cuplul conjugal, armonie si dizarmonie* [Married couple, harmony and disharmony]. Bucharest: Editura Stiintifica si Enciclopedica.

Mizsei, K., Slay, B., Mihailov, D., O'Higgins, N., & Ivanov, A. (2003). *Avoiding the dependency trap: The Roma human development report.* Available at roma.undp.sk.

Moezi, A. (1967). Marital characteristics in Iran. In *Proceedings of the International Union for the Scientific Study of Population, Sydney Conference* (pp. 976-982). Paris: International Union for the Scientific Study of Population.

Moghadam, F. (1994). Commoditization of sexuality and female labor force partici-
   pation in Islam: Implication for Iran, 1960-90. In M. Afkhami & E. Fiedl (Eds.),
   In the eye of the storm: Women in post-revolutionary Iran (pp. 80-97). New York:
   I. B. Tauris.
Moghadam, V. (1988). Women, work, and ideology in the Islamic Republic. *Inter-
   national Journal of Middle East Studies, 20,* 221-243.
Moghadam, V. M. (1993). *Modernizing women: Gender and social change in the
   Middle East.* Boulder, CO: L. Rienner.
The Mohamedan Marriage (Amendment) Act, 1988. (1988). *Annual Review of
   Population Law, 15,* 88.
Mohammadi, M. R., Mohammad, K., Farahani, F. K. A., Alikhani, S., Zare, M.,
   Tehrani, F. R., et al. (2006). Reproductive knowledge, attitudes and behavior
   among adolescent males in Tehran, Iran. *International Family Planning Per-
   spectives, 32,* 35-44.
Molina, V., & Sánchez, K. (1999). El fin de la ilusión: Movilidad social en la ciudad
   de México [The end of illusion: Social mobility Mexico City]. *Nueva Antropología,
   16*(55), 43-56.
Møller, V., & Sotshongaye, A. (1996). "My family eat this money too": Pension
   sharing and self-respect among Zulu grandmothers. *Southern African Journal of
   Gerontology, 5*(2), 9-19.
Momeni, J. (1972). Difficulties of changing age at marriage in Iran. *Journal of
   Marriage and the Family, 34,* 545-551.
Momeni, J. (1975). Polygyny in Iran. *Journal of Marriage and the Family, 37,*
   453-456.
Momsen, J. H. (2001). Backlash: Or how to snatch failure from the jaws of success
   in gender and development. *Progress in Development Studies, 1,* 51-56.
Monitorul Oficial al Romaniei (No. 120) [Romanian official monitor]. (1997).
   Bucharest: Regia Autonoma "Monitorul Oficial."
Monteiro, M. F. G. (1994). Saúde reprodutiva [Reproductive health]. In S. M.
   Kaloustian (Ed.), *Família Brasileira—A base de tudo* [Brazilian family—The
   basis for all] (pp. 172-183). São Paulo: Cortez Publisher; Brasília: United
   Nations Children's Fund.
Montes de Oca, V. (2001). Desigualdad estructural entre la población anciana en
   México. Factores que han condicionado el apoyo institucional entre la población
   con 60 años y más en México [Structural inequality among aging population in
   Mexico. Factors that have conditioned the institutional support among the popula-
   tion aged 60 or more in Mexico]. *Estudios Demográficos y Urbanos, 48,* 585-613.
Moore, S., & Rosenthal, D. (1993). *Sexuality in adolescence.* London: Routledge.
Moors, H., & Palomba, R. (Eds.). (1995). *Population, family and welfare.* Oxford:
   Clarendon Press.
Moroianu-Zlatescu, I. (1997). Familia contemporana [Contemporary family]. In
   Drepturile femeii; egalitate si parteneriat (pp. 33-38). Bucharest: Institutul
   Romanpentru Drepturile Omului.
Morris, L. (1990). *The workings of the household.* Cambridge: Polity.

Moss, P. M., Owen, C., Statham, J., Bull, J., Cameron, C., & Candappa, M. (1995). *Survey of day care providers in England and Wales.* London University, Thomas Coram Research Unit.

Moukachar, M. B. (1996). *Arca de brinquedos—Representações da infância em três gerações* [Social representations of childhood in three generations]. Unpublished master's thesis, Psychology, Universidade Federal de Minas Gerais, Belo Horizonte, Brazil.

Mukhopadhyay, C. C., & Seymour, S. C. (Eds.). (1994). *Women, education, and family structure in India.* Boulder, CO: Westview.

Mullatti, L. (1995). Families in India: Beliefs and realities. *Journal of Comparative Family Studies, 26,* 11-26.

Mummert, G. (1996). Cambios en la estructura y organización familiares en un contexto de emigración masculina y trabajo asalariado femenino: Estudio de caso en un valle agrícola de Michoacán [Changes in structure and family organization in an emigration male context and female salaried work: A case study in an agricultural valley of Michoacan]. In M. P. López (Ed.), *Hogares, familias: desigualdad, conflicto, redes solidarias y parentales* (pp. 39-46). México D. F.: Sociedad Mexicana de Demografía.

Muresan, C. (1996). L'evolution demographique en Roumanie: Tendances passés (1948-1994) et perspectives d'avenir (1995-2030) [Romanian demographic evolution: Past trends (1948-1994) and future perspectives (1995-2030)]. *Population, 4-5,* 813-844.

Myslik, W. D., Freeman, A., & Slawski, J. (1997). Implications of AIDS for the South African population age profile. *Southern African Journal of Gerontology, 6*(2), 3-8.

Naik, R. D. (1996). *A study of dowry practices.* Pune: Dastane Ramchandra.

Nassehy, V. (1991). Female role and divorce in Iran. *International Journal of Sociology of the Family, 21,* 53-65.

National AIDS Control Council. (2000). *The Kenya National HIV/AIDS strategic plan 2000-2005.* Nairobi: Office of the President, Republic of Kenya.

National AIDS Control Council. (2001). *AIDS in Kenya: Background, projections, impact, interventions and policy.* Nairobi: Office of the President, Republic of Kenya.

National Assembly for Wales. (nd). *Croeso / Welcome.* Available at www.wales.gov.uk/index.htm.

National Assembly of Wales. (1999). *Equal opportunities study for inclusion in European Structural Fund Program documents 2000-2006.* C. Williams, G. Day, T. Rees, & M. Standing (Eds.). Cardiff: Author.

National Assembly of Wales. (2001). *Children first newsletter.* Cardiff: Author.

National Assembly of Wales. (2002a). *A statistical focus on children in Wales.* Cardiff: Author.

National Assembly of Wales. (2002b). *Key health statistics for Wales 2002.* Cardiff: Author. Available at www.wales.gov.uk/keypubstatisticsforwalesfigures/content/health.

National Assembly of Wales. (2003). *Digest of Welsh statistics.* Cardiff: Author.

National Authority for Protection of Rights of Children and Adoption. (2004). Available at www.copii.ro.

National Commission on Higher Education. (1996). *NCHE Report, 1996*. Pretoria: Human Sciences Research Council Publishers.

National Statistics Office. (2002, October 16). *2000 Census of Population and Housing press release*. Manila: Author.

National Statistics Office. (2003, February 18). *2000 Census of Population and Housing press release*. Manila: Author.

Natividad, J. N., & Marquez, M. P. N. (2004). Sexual risk behaviors. In C. M. Raymundo & G. T. Cruz (Eds.), *Youth, sex, and risk behaviors in the Philippines* (pp. 70-94). Quezon City: Demographic Research and Development Foundation Inc., University of the Philippines Population Institute.

Natrajan, R., & Thomas, V. (2002). Need for family therapy services for middle-class families in India. *Contemporary Family Therapy, 24*, 483-504.

Nave-Herz, R. (1994). *Familie heute—Wandel der Familienstrukturen und Folgen für die Erziehung* [Family today—Changes in family structures and effects on bringing up children]. Darmstadt: Wissenschaftliche Buchgesellschaft.

Nave-Herz, R., Daum-Jaballah, M., Hauser, S., Matthias, H., & Scheller, G. (1990). *Scheidungsursachen im Wandel. Eine zeitgeschichtliche Analyse des Anstiegs der Ehescheidungen in der Bundesrepublik Deutschland* [Changing causes for divorce. A historical analysis of the rise in the rate of divorces in Germany]. Bielefeld: Kleine.

Ndambuki, G. (2000). Foreword to the report on poverty in Kenya. In Republic of Kenya (Ed.), *Poverty in Kenya* (p. 5). Nairobi: Central Bureau of Statistics.

Newman, D. M. (1999). *Sociology of families*. Thousand Oaks, CA: Pine Forge.

Ngige, L. W. (1993). *Intra-household resource allocation, decision making and child nutritional status in rural Thika, Kenya*. Unpublished doctoral dissertation, Michigan State University, East Lansing.

Ngige, L. W. (1995). Intra-household resource allocation, decision making and child nutritional status in rural Thika, Kenya. In J. K. Gitobu & E. C. Murray (Eds.), *Home economics research in Kenya* (pp. 7-18). Nairobi, Kenya: Kenyatta University.

Ngige, L. W. (2004). *Monograph on Kenyan family transformations*. Nairobi: Kenyatta University Publications.

Ngige, L. W., Mburugu, E., & Nyamu, F. (2004). *Continental plan of action for the family in Africa*. Nairobi: Centre for African Family Studies.

Nicolaci-da-Costa, A. M. (1985). Mal estar na família: Descontinuidade e conflito entre sistemas simbólicos [Discontent in the family: Discontinuity and conflict between symbolic systems]. In S. Figueira (Ed.), *Cultura da psicanálise* (pp. 147-168). São Paulo: Brasiliense.

Niranjan, S., Nair, S., & Roy, T. K. (2005). A socio-demographic analysis of the size and structure of the family in India. *Journal of Comparative Family Studies, 36*, 623-651.

No more weddings for young Pinoys. (2002, December 13). Young Adult Fertility Survey III press release. Quezon City: University of the Philippines Population Institute.

Noble, A. G., & Dutt, A. K. (Eds.). (1982). *India: Cultural patterns and processes.* Boulder, CO: Westview.

Norris, P., & Inglehart, R. (Eds.). (2004). *Sacred and secular: Religion and politics worldwide.* Cambridge: Cambridge University Press.

Nunes, M. J. F. R. (1994). De mulheres, sexo e igreja: Uma pesquisa e muitas interrogações [Women, sex and church: A research and many questions]. In A. de O Costa & T. Amado (Eds.), *Alternativas escassas—Saúde, sexualidade e reprodução na América Latina* (pp. 175-203). São Paulo: Programa de Direitos Reprodutivos/Fundação Carlos Chagas; Rio de Janeiro: Editora 34.

Oakley, R. L. (1998). Local effects of new social-welfare policy on ageing in South Africa. *Southern African Journal of Gerontology, 7*(1), 15-20.

Ochola, S., Wagah, M., & Omalla, J. N. K. (2000). *An assessment of the nutritional status and socioeconomic contributions of the elderly in Nairobi and Machakos Districts.* Nairobi: HelpAge International, Africa Regional Development Centre.

Office of National Statistics. (2001). *Census 2001, national report for England and Wales.* Available at www.statistics.gov.uk.

Office of National Statistics. (2002a). *Labour force survey spring 2002.* London: Author.

Office of National Statistics. (2002b). *New earnings survey 2002.* London: Author.

Office of Population Censuses and Surveys. (1987). *Marriage and divorce.* London: Her Majesty's Stationary Office.

Office of the Registrar General. (2001). *Provisional population totals: India.* Available at www.censusindia.net/results/resultsmain.html.

Office of the Registrar General. (2002). *Census of India 2001* (T 00-003: Population by sex and sex ratio). Available at www.censusindia.net/t_00_003.html.

Oficina Nacional de Estadisticas. (2000). *Anuarioe Estadístico de Cuba.* Available at www.camaracuba.cu/TPHabana/Estadisticas2000/estadisticas2000.htm.

Ofreneo, R. P. (1999). Confronting the crisis: Women in the informal sector. In J. F. Illo & R. P. Ofreneo (Eds.), *Carrying the burden of the world.* Quezon City: University of the Philippines Center for Integrative Studies.

Ojeda, N., & González R. (1992). Niveles y tendencias del divorcio y la separación en el norte de México [Levels and tendencies of divorce and separation in northern Mexico]. *Frontera Norte, 4*(7), 157-177.

Oliveira, M. C. (1996). A família Brasileira no limiar do ano 2000 [The Brazilian family near the year 2000]. *Revista de Estudos Feministas, 4*(1), 55-63.

Ominde, S. H. (1987). *The Luo girl: From infancy to marriage.* Nairobi, Kenya: Kenya Literature Bureau.

Ondigi, A. N. (2003). *Factors influencing prenatal health status among pregnant women attending prenatal clinics in selected low income areas of Nairobi, Kenya.* Unpublished doctoral dissertation, Kenyatta University, Nairobi, Kenya.

Oppong, C. (Ed.). (1987). *Sex roles, population and development in West Africa: Policy-related studies on work and demographic issues.* Portsmouth, NH: Heinemann.

Ordonez, L. G. (1988, August 29). Innovative curriculum reverses role models. *Manila Standard, 2*(201), 9.

Osanloo, A. (2006). Islamico-civil "rights talk": Women, subjectivity, and law in Iranian family court. *American Ethnologist, 33,* 191-209.

Osmond. J. (1988). *The divided kingdom.* London: Constable.

Pache, V. (1998). Marriage fairs among Maheshwaris: A new matrimonial system. *Economic and Political Weekly, 33,* 970-975.

Pacheco, M. de P. T. (1986). *Família e identidade racial—os limites da cor nas relações e representações de um grupo de baixa renda* [Family and racial identity—The limits of color in relations and representations of a low-income group]. Unpublished master's thesis, Anthropology, Universidade Federal do Rio de Janeiro, Rio de Janeiro, Brazil.

Pakzad, S. (1994). The legal status of women in the family in Iran. In M. Afkhami & E. Fiedl (Eds.), *In the eye of the storm: Women in post-revolutionary Iran* (pp. 169-187). New York: I. B. Tauris.

Palomba, R. (Ed.). (1987). *Vita di coppia e figli* [Children and couple's life]. Florence: Nuova Italia.

Palomba, R. (1995a). Italy: The invisible change. In H. Moors & R. Palomba (Eds.), *Population, family and welfare* (pp. 158-176). Oxford: Clarendon Press.

Palomba, R. (1995b). New fathers: Changes in the families and emerging policy issues. In M. C. P. van Dogen, G. A. B. Frinking, & M. J. G. Jacobs (Eds.), *Changing fatherhood* (pp. 183-196). Amsterdam: Thesis Publishers.

Palomba, R., Menniti, A., & Caruso, M. G. (1997, October). *Demographic changes, values and attitudes of young Italians.* Paper presented at International Scientific Union for Population Studies General Conference, Session 42, Beijing, China.

Palomba, R., & Sabbadini, L. L. (1994). *Different times* (English edn.). Rome: Commissione Pari Opportunità.

Pan American Health Organization. (2000). *Figure 1. Population structure, by age and sex, Cuba, 2000.* Available at www.paho.org/English/DD/AIS/cuba_graf_eng.pdf.

Pan American Health Organization. (2002). *Cuba.* Available at www.paho.org/English/DD/AIS/cp_192.htm.

Pan American Health Organization/World Health Organization, Ministry of Public Health. (2003). *Resumen Ejecutivo Año 2000* [Executive summary, Year 2000]. Havana: Author.

Pan, Y. K. (1992). Chinese family network and the development of science and technology. In *Proceedings of Asia-Pacific Regional Conference on Future Family* (pp. 53-59). Beijing: China Social Science Documentation Publishing House.

Parliament approves new civil code. (2001, November 2). Available at www.ntvmsnbc.com/news/116630.asp?cp1=1.

Parker, R. (1991). *Corpos, prazeres e paixões—A cultura sexual no Brasil contemporâneo* [Bodies, pleasures and passions—Sexual culture in contemporary Brazil]. São Paulo: Best Seller.

Parsons, T. (1943). The kinship system in the contemporary United States. *American Anthropologist, 45,* 22-38.

Peñano-Ho, L. (1999). A woman's stress: Society's burden or a matter of choice? In S. H. Guerrero (Ed.), *Gender-sensitive and feminist methodologies* (pp. 311-317). Diliman, Quezon City: University Center for Women's Studies.

Perez, A. E. (1999, May). *Strong family bonds sustain the Filipino elderly.* Paper presented at the National Press Conference on the Filipino Elderly, Galleria Suites, Mandaluyong City.

Pérez González, E. (2003). Homicidio y género [Gender and homicide]. *Sexología y sociedad, 23,* 12-16.

Pérez Izquierdo, V. (2000). Ajuste económico e impactos sociales. Los retos de la educación y la salud pública en Cuba [Economic adjustment and social impacts. Challenges in education and public health in Cuba] [Electronic edn., 1995-2002]. *Cuba. Investigación económica.*

Petre, Z. (1997). Tranzitia: un substantiv feminin [Transition: A feminine noun], *22—Social Dialogue Review, 59,* iii.

Petrucelli, J. L. (1994). Nupcialidade [Marriage rate]. In S. M. Kaloustian (Ed.), *Família Brasileira—A base de tudo* (pp. 159-171). São Paulo: Cortez Publisher; Brasília; United Nations Children's Fund.

Peuckert, R. (1991). *Familienformen im sozialen Wandel* [Ways of family and social change]. Opladen: Leske und Budrich.

Philippine Overseas Employment Administration. (2002). *Deployment of newly hired OFWs by skills category.* Available at poea.gov.ph/docs/deployed.

Philippine statistical yearbook. (2002). Manila: National Statistical Coordinating Board.

Phillips, L., & Ilcan, S. (2003). "A world free of hunger": Global imagination and governance in the age of scientific management. *Sociologia Ruralis, 43,* 434-453.

Phillips, M. (1996). *All must have prizes.* London: Little Brown and Company.

Piggot, J. (1874). *Persia: Ancient and modern.* London: Henry S. King.

Pilcher, J. (1994). Who should do the dishes? Three generations of Welsh women talking about men and housework. In J. Aaron, T. Rees, S. Betts, & M. Vincentelli (Eds.), *Our sisters' land: The changing identities of women in Wales* (pp. 31-47). Cardiff: University of Wales Press.

Pilcher, J., Delamont, S., Powell, G., & Rees, T. (1989). Challenging occupational stereotypes: Women's Training Roadshows and guidance at school level. *British Journal of Guidance and Counselling, 17*(1), 59-67.

Pilcher, J., Delamont, S., Powell, G., Rees, T., & Read, M. (1990). *An evaluative study of Cardiff Women's Training Roadshow.* Cardiff: Welsh Office.

Pimentel, S., & Pierro, M. I. V. (1993). Proposta de lei contra a violência familiar [A project of law against domestic violence]. *Revista de Estudos Feministas, 1*(1), 169-175.

Planck, U. (1964). *Der bäuerliche Familienbetrieb zwischen Patriarchat und Partnerschaft* [Farm families between patriarchal and partnership]. Stuttgart: Enke.

Polygamy's back. (1999, November). *World Press Review, 46,* 36.

Pop, L., & Voicu, B. (2002). School performance. In Ministry of Education and Research, Institute for Educational Sciences (coord. M. Jigau). *Rural education in Romania. Conditions, challenges and strategies of development* (2nd ed., pp. 149-166). Bucharest: Marlink.

Popenoe, D. (1988). *Disturbing the nest: Family change and decline in modern societies.* New York: Aldine.

Popenoe, D. (1993). American family in decline, 1960-1990: A review and appraisal. *Journal of Marriage and the Family, 55,* 527-542.

Popescu, L. (2003). Romania. In L. Walter (Ed.), *Encyclopedia of women's issues worldwide. Europe* (pp. 529-545). London: Greenwood.

Popescu, L. (2004). *Politicile sociale est-europene între paternalism de stat i responsabilitate individual* [East Europeans' social policies between state paternalism and individual responsibility]. Cluj: Presa Universitara.

Popescu, R. (2003). Familia tanara in societatea romaneasca [Young family in Romania]. *Calitatea vietii, 14,* 1-21.

Population Council—Americas. (2006). *Mexico.* Available at www.popcouncil.org/americas/mexico.html.

Population Council—Asia. (2006). *India.* Available at www.popcouncil.org/asia/india.html.

Povoledo, E. (2003, August 7). In Italy, summertime is for divorce. *International Herald Tribune.*

Pratarelli, M. E. (2005). Whence a theory of the "Commons": Modern implications for globalization and the global community. *Globalization, 5.*

Prefeitura Municipal de Belo Horizonte/Secretaria Municipal de Desenvolvimento Social. (2000). *Seminário de Políticas Sociais para Crianças de 0-6 anos* [Seminar for social policies for children 0-6 years old]. Belo Horizonte, Brazil.

Price, M. (2001). *Iranian marriage ceremony, its history & symbolism.* Available at www.iranchamber.com/culture/articles/iranian_marriage_ceremony.php.

Promise Keepers. (2007). Available at www.promisekeepers.org.

Qiao, X. C. (1994, July). *Zhongguo Shengyulu Xiajiang Houguo Yanjiu: Lilun Jiashe yu Yanjiu Silu* [Study of the results of the birth rate decrease in China: Theoretical assumption and the direction of the studies]. Paper presented at the Conference of New Population Problems and Coping Strategies During the Process of the Birth Rates Decreases in China, Bei Dai He, China.

Qiao, X. C. (1995). You Zhongguo 12 yi renko yenchu de jidian sikao [Several thoughts from the 12 million people in China]. *Renko Yanjiu, 19*(2), 1-9.

Quilodrán, J. (1996). El matrimonio y sus transformaciones [Marriage and its transformations]. In M. P. López (Ed.), *Hogares, familias: desigualdad, conflicto, redes solidarias y parentales* (pp. 59-69). México D. F.: Sociedad Mexicana de Demografía.

Quilodrán, J. (2001). Un siglo de matrimonio en México [A century of marriage in Mexico]. In J. Gómez de León & C. Rabell (Eds.), *La población de México. Tendencias y perspectivas sociodemográficas hacia el siglo XXI* (pp. 242-270). México D. F.: Fondo de Cultura Económica/Consejo Nacional de Población.

Radina, M. E., Wilson, S. M., & Hennon, C. B. (in press). Parental stress among U.S. Mexican heritage parents: Implications for culturally relevant family life education. In R. L. Dalla, J. Defrain, J. Johnson, & D. Abbott (Eds.), *Strengths and challenges of new immigrant families: Implications for research, policy, education, and service.* Lanham, MD: Lexington Books.

Raftery, A. E., Lewis, S. M., & Aghajanian, A. (1995). Demand or ideation? Evidence from the Iranian marital fertility decline. *Demography, 32,* 159-182.

Raikar-Mhatre, S. (1997). *Divorce & Christian marriages in India.* Available at www.indnet.org/res/marriages.html.
Raman, V. (2003). The diverse life-worlds of Indian childhood. In M. Pernau, I. Ahmad, & H. Reifeld (Eds.), *Family and gender: Changing values in Germany and India* (pp. 84-110). New Delhi: Sage.
Ramírez Calzadilla, J. (1995). Religión y cultura: las investigaciones sociorreligiosas [Religion and culture in religious social research]. *Temas, 1,* 57-68.
Ramírez Calzadilla, J. (2003). Cultura y reavivamiento religioso en Cuba [Culture and religious revival in Cuba]. *Temas, 35,* 31-43.
Ramos, C. (in press). Cambio jurídico y jerarquía familiar en el México decimonónico. Género y generación en el control de la patria potestad [Legal change and family hierarchy in 19th Century in Mexico: Gender and generation in the control of custody]. In M. Barros & R. Esteinou (Eds.), *Análisis del cambio sociocultural.* México D. F.: Centro de Investigaciones y Estudios Superiores en Antropología Social.
Ramu, G. N. (1991). Changing family structure and fertility patterns: An Indian case. *Journal of Asian and African Studies, 26,* 189-206.
Rao, A. B. S. V. R., & Sekhar, K. (2002). Divorce: Process and correlates. A cross-cultural study. *Journal of Comparative Family Studies, 33,* 541-563.
Ravindran, R. S. (2001, March 2). *The untold truth behind statistics.* Available at www.tamil.net/list/2001-03/msg00019.html.
Ravindran, T. K. S. (1999). Female autonomy in Tamil Nadu: Unravelling the complexities. *Economic and Political Weekly, 34*(16/17), WS 34-WS 44.
Raymundo, C. M. (1984). *Young adult fertility in the Philippines (First Report).* Quezon City: University of the Philippines Population Institute and Population Center Foundation.
Raymundo, C. M., Kabamalan, M. M., Berja, C. L., & Laguna, E. P. (2004). The social institutions surrounding the adolescents. In C. M. Raymundo & G. T. Cruz (Eds.), *Youth, sex, and risk behaviors in the Philippines* (pp. 27-49). Quezon City: Demographic Research and Development Foundation Inc., University of the Philippines Population Institute.
Recognition of customary marriages act, No. 120. (1998). Pretoria: South African Government.
Reddy, P. H. (1991). Family structure and age at marriage: Evidence from a south Indian village. *Journal of Asian and African Studies, 26,* 253-266.
Rees, A. D. (1950). *Life in a Welsh countryside.* Cardiff: University of Wales Press.
Rees, T. (1992). *Women and the labour market.* London: Routledge.
Rees, T. (1997). *Women in the Welsh workforce: 21 years of equality legislation.* Cardiff: Chwarae Teg.
Renda Changweihui. (1994a). Zhonghua Renmin Gongheguo Hunyin Fa (1980) [Marriage Law of P. R. China (1980)]. In G. Zhang (Ed.), *Quanguo Lushi Zige Kaoshi Bidu Falu Huibian* (pp. 558-562). Beijing: Zhongguo Falu Daxue Chubanshe.
Renda Changweihui. (1994b). Zhonghua Renmin Gongheguo Funu Quanyi Baozhangfa [Protection Law to women's rights and interests of P. R China

(1992)]. In G. Zhang (Ed.), *Quanguo Lushi Zige Kaoshi Bidu Falu Huibian* (p. 590). Beijing: Zhongguo Falu Daxue Chubanshe.

Renda, J. (2003). Polarisation of families according to work status. *Family Matters, 64,* 16-21.

Republic of Kenya. (1999). *Kenya demographic and health survey: 1998.* Calverton, MD: Macro International.

Republic of Kenya. (2000). *Poverty in Kenya.* Nairobi: Central Bureau of Statistics.

Republic of Kenya. (2001a). *The Republic of Kenya: 1999 Population and Housing Census.* Nairobi: Central Bureau of Statistics.

Republic of Kenya. (2001b). *The Republic of Kenya National Development Plan.* Nairobi: Government Printers.

Republic of Kenya. (2002a). *The Republic of Kenya: 1999 Population and Housing Census Vol. I: Population distribution by administrative areas and urban centres.* Nairobi: Central Bureau of Statistics.

Republic of Kenya. (2002b). *The Republic of Kenya: 1999 Population and Housing Census Vol. II: Social-economic profile of the population.* Nairobi: Central Bureau of Statistics.

Republic of Kenya. (2002c). *The Republic of Kenya: 1999 Population and Housing Census. Vol. III. Analytical report on population dynamics.* Nairobi: Central Bureau of Statistics.

Republic of Kenya. (2002d). *The Republic of Kenya: 1999 Population and Housing Census. The Popular Report.* Nairobi: Central Bureau of Statistics.

Republic of Kenya. (2002e). *The Republic of Kenya: 1999 Population and Housing Census. Vol. IV: Analytical report on fertility and nuptiality.* Nairobi: Central Bureau of Statistics.

Republic of Kenya. (2002f). *The Republic of Kenya: 1999 Population and Housing Census. Vol. V: Analytical report on mortality.* Nairobi: Central Bureau of Statistics.

Republic of Kenya. (2002g). *The Republic of Kenya: 1999 Population and Housing Census. Vol. VI: Analytical report on migration and urbanization.* Nairobi: Central Bureau of Statistics.

Republic of Kenya. (2002h). *The Republic of Kenya: 1999 Population and Housing Census. Vol. VII: Analytical report on population projections.* Nairobi: Central Bureau of Statistics.

Republic of Kenya. (2002i). *The Republic of Kenya: 1999 Population and Housing Census. Vol. VIII: Analytical report on education.* Nairobi: Central Bureau of Statistics.

Republic of Kenya. (2002j). *The Republic of Kenya: 1999 Population and Housing Census. Vol. IX: Analytical report on labour force.* Nairobi: Central Bureau of Statistics.

Republic of Kenya. (2002k). *The Republic of Kenya: 1999 Population and Housing Census. Vol. XI: Analytical report on gender dimensions.* Nairobi: Central Bureau of Statistics.

Republic of Kenya. (2003). *Kenya Demographic and Health Survey: 2003.* Calverton, MD: Macro International.

Rezac, S. J. (1994). Role of parental divorce in American patterns of intergenerational helping. *Family Matters, 39,* 14-17.

Rezac, S. J. (1998). *Intergenerational assistance in American and Australian families: The role of parental family structure.* Unpublished doctoral dissertation, University of Nebraska, Lincoln.

Ribeiro, I., & Ribeiro, A. C. T. (1994). *Família e desafios na sociedade Brasileira: Valores como um ângulo de análise* [Family and challenges in Brazilian society: Values as an angle of analysis]. São Paulo: Loyola e Centro João XXIII.

Rich man, poor man. (2007, January 20). *The Economist, 382,* 15-16.

Rissel, C., Richters, J., Grulich, A., de Visser, R., & Smith, A. (2003). Sex in Australia: First experiences of vaginal intercourse and oral sex among a representative sample of Australian adults. *Australian and New Zealand Journal of Public Health, 27*(2), 131-138.

Ritzer, G. (2003). Rethinking globalization: Glocalization/grobalization and something/nothing. *Sociological Theory, 21,* 193-209.

Roberts, C. (1993). Black women, recreation and organized sport. *Agenda, 17,* 8-17.

Robertson, R. (1992). *Globalization: Social theory and global culture.* London: Sage.

Robichaux, D. (1997). Las uniones consensuales y la nupcialidad en Tlaxcala rural y México: Un ensayo de interpretación cultural [Consensual unions and nuptiality in rural Tlaxcala and Mexico: An essay of cultural interpretation]. *Espiral, 4*(10), 101-141.

Robichaux, D. (Ed.). (2003). *El matrimonio en Mesoamérica ayer y hoy. Unas miradas antropológicas* [Marriage in Mesoamerica yesterday and today. Some anthropological views]. México D. F.: Universidad Iberoamericana.

Robles, L. (2001). El fenómeno de las cuidadoras: Un fenómeno invisible del envejecimiento [The caregivers phenomenon: An invisible phenomenon of aging]. *Estudios Demográficos y Urbanos, 48,* 561-584.

Rodas-Martini, P. (2001). *Has income distribution really worsened in developing countries? And has income distribution really worsened between the North and the South?* (Background paper for the *Human Development Report 2001*). Available at www.undp.org/hdro/Rioforum.html.

Rodríguez, P., Cañet, T., & Estévez, C. (2004, September). *Matrimonio y familia en la marginalidad* [Marriage and family in conditions of marginality]. Paper presented at the workshop Diálogo con el Seminario Permanente, Centro de Investigación y Desarrollo de la Cultura Cubana Juan Marinello.

Romero, F. R. P. (1978). Women's status in Philippine society. In *Fookien Times Philippine Yearbook.* Metro Manila: Fookien Times Yearbook.

Ross, F. C. (1996). Diffusing domesticity: Domestic fluidity in Die Bos. *Social Dynamics, 22*(1), 55-71.

Ross, J. A., & Frankenberg, E. (1993). *Findings from two decades of family planning research.* New York: The Population Council.

Rosser, C., & Harris, C. C. (1995). *The family and social change.* London: Routledge.

Roth, M. (1979). A hazastarsak pszichologiai osszeferhetosege [The psychological compatibility of spouses]. *Korunk, 3,* 163-165.

Roth, M. (1999). *Protectia copilului. Concepte, metode si dileme* [Child protection: Concepts, methods and dilemmas]. Cluj: Presa Universitara Clujeana.

Roth, M. (2000). Child welfare in Romania. In D. S. Iatridis (Ed.), *Social justice and the welfare state in Central and Eastern Europe: The Impact of privatization* (pp. 220-232). Westport, CT: Praeger.

Roth, M. (2003). Protecœia copilului între sentimentalism âi profesionalism [Sentimentalism and professionalism in child protection], *Revista de Asistenį1 sociall, 2,* 3-15.

Roth, M., & Bumbulut, S. (2003). Sexually abused children in Romania. In C. May-Chachal & M. Herczog (Eds.), *Child sexual abuse in Europe* (pp. 59-78). Strasbourg: Council of Europe Publishing.

Rowe, N. (2002). A comparative study of perceived caregiver burden in India and the United States. *The Gerontologist, 42*(Suppl. 1, abstract of paper), 108.

Rowland, D. (1998). *Cross-national trends in childlessness.* Canberra: Australian National University Research School of Social Sciences.

Ruback, R. B., & Pandey, J. (1991). Crowding, perceived control, and relative power: An analysis of households in India. *Journal of Applied Social Psychology, 21,* 315-344.

Sabbadini, L. L. (1995, April). *La famiglia nelle statistiche ufficiali* [The family in official statistics]. Paper presented at conference, Società Italiana di Statistica on Continuità e discontinuità demografiche [Demographic continuity and discontinuity]. Arcacavata Rende, Italy.

Sabbadini, L. L. (1999). Modelli di formazione e organizzazione delle famiglie [Models of family formation and organization]. In Proceedings of the conference on *Le famiglie interrogano le politiche sociali* [Families and social policies] (pp. 19-54). Rome: Prime Minister Office.

Sagner, A. (1997). Urbanization, ageing and migration: Some evidence from African settlements in Cape Town. *Southern African Journal of Gerontology, 6*(2), 13-19.

Salas, C. (1999). Empleo y tercera edad: Dinamismo y tendencias [Employment and the third age: Dynamics and tendencies]. In Comisión de Población y Desarrollo, Consejo Nacional de Población & Cámara de Diputados (Ed.), *Envejecimiento demográfico de México: Retos y perspectivas* (pp. 111-124). México D. F.: Comisión de Población y Desarrollo/Consejo Nacional de Población/Cámara de Diputados.

Samb, R. (1986, July). The "Bundo" secret society in Sierra Leone. *Inter-African Committee on Traditional Practices Affecting the Health of Women and Children Newsletter, 2,* 12-14.

Samuel, O. (1996). Cambios en la nupcialidad en México: El caso de Morelos [Changes in nuptiality in Mexico: The case of Morelos]. In M. P. López (Ed.), *Hogares, Familias: Desigualdad, Conflicto, Redes Solidarias y Parentales* (pp. 51-57). México D. F.: Sociedad Mexicana de Demografía.

Sanchez, L. (1994). Material resources, family structure resources, and husbands' housework participation: A cross-national comparison. *Journal of Family Issues, 15,* 379-402.

Sandi, A. M. (1996). Conditia femeilor care lucreaza in agricultura [Condition of women working in agriculture]. *22—Social Dialogue Review, 23*(Suppl.), vi.

Sandstrom, K. L., Martin, D. D., & Fine, G. A. (2003). *Symbols, selves, and social reality.* Los Angeles, CA: Roxbury.

Sankan, S. S. (1995). *The Maasai.* Nairobi, Kenya: Kenya Literature Bureau.

Santos, N. J. S., & Munhoz, R. (1996). A AIDS entre as mulheres: Reflexões sobre seus depoimentos [The AIDS among women: Reflections on their reports]. In R. Parker & J. Galvão (Eds.), *Quebrando o silêncio: mulheres e AIDS no Brasil* (pp. 115-135). Rio de Janeiro: Relume-Dumará; Associação Brasileira de Estudos Interdisciplinares da AIDS, Instituto de Medicina Social, Universidade Estadual do Rio de Janeiro, Brazil.

Saraswati, T. S. (1999). Adult-child continuity in India: Is adolescence a myth or an emerging reality? In T. S. Saraswati (Ed.), *Culture, socialization and human development: Theory, research and application in India* (pp. 213-232). New Delhi: Sage.

Sarti, C. A. (1995). Família e individualidade: Um problema moderno [Family and individuality: A modern problem]. In M. do C. B. Carvalho (Ed.), *A família contemporânea em debate* (pp. 39-50). São Paulo: Cortez.

Sarti, C. (1996). *A família como espelho—um estudo sobre a moral dos pobres* [The family as a mirror—A study about morals among the poor]. Campinas: São Paulo State University; São Paulo: Autores Associados.

Sastry, J. (1999). Household structure, satisfaction and distress in India and the United States: A comparative cultural examination. *Journal of Comparative Family Studies, 30,* 135-152.

Sauciuc, V. (1997). Avort, infanticid, abandon [Abortion, infanticide, abandonment]. *Viata Medicala, 38,* 5.

Sawhney, M. (2003). The role of non-governmental organizations for the welfare of the elderly: The case of Help Age India. *Journal of Aging & Social Policy, 15*(2/3), 179-191.

Scavone, L., Brétin, H., & Thébaud-Mony, A. (1994). Contracepção, controle demográfico e desigualdades sociais: Análise comparativa franco-brasileira [Contraception, demographic control, and social inequality: Comparative analysis between Brazil and France]. *Revista de Estudos Feministas, 2,* 357-372.

Schafer, R. (1997). Variations in traditional marriage and family forms: Responses to the changing pattern of family-based social security systems in Sierra Leone and Kenya. *The History of the Family, 2,* 197-209.

Schlesinger, B., & Raphael, D. (1993). The woman in the middle: The sandwich generation. *International Journal of Sociology of the Family, 23,* 77-87.

Schmidt, H.-D. (1996). Erziehungsbedingungen in der DDR: Offizielle Programme, individuelle Praxis und die Rolle der Pädagogischen Psychologie und Entwicklungspsychologie [Conditions of rearing children in the GDR: Official programs, personal practice and the role of pedagogical and developmental psychology]. In G. Trommsdorff (Ed.), *Sozialisation und Entwicklung von Kindern vor und nach der Vereinigung* (pp. 15-171). Opladen: Leske und Budrich.

Schneewind, K. A. (1997). Ehe ja, Kinder nein—eine Lebensform mit Zukunft? [Marriage yes, children no—A way of life with a future?] *System Familie, 10,* 160-165.

Schrage-Dijkstra, M. (1994). The changing family and aging. In G. J. Stolnitz (Ed.), *Social aspects and country reviews of population aging* (pp. 37-54). New York and Geneva: United Nations.

Schütze, Y., & Wagner, M. (1995). Familiale Solidarität in den späten Phasen des Familienverlaufs [Solidarity in the late phases of the familial trajectory]. In B. Nauck & C. Onnen-Isemann (Eds.), *Familie im Brennpunkt von Wissenschaft und Forschung* (pp. 307-327). Neuwied, Kriftel, Berlin: Luchterhand.

Scourfield, J., & Drakeford, M. (1999). Boys from nowhere: Finding Welsh men and putting them in their place. *Contemporary Wales, 12,* 3-17.

Secretaría de Educación Pública/Instituto Mexicano de la Juventud. (2000). *Encuesta Nacional de Juventud. Resultados Generales* [National Youth Survey. General results]. México D. F.: Author.

Semo, M. (2000, November 28). Romanians no longer believe. *Libération.* Reprinted in *World Press Review,* February 2001, 34.

Serbanescu, F., & Morris, L. (1994). *Reproductive Health Survey, Romania 1993. Preliminary report.* Ministry of Health, Institute of Mother and Child Care, Bucharest and Center for Disease Control and Prevention, Division of Reproductive Health, Atlanta.

Seymour, S. C. (2001). Child care in India: An examination of the "household size/infant indulgence" hypothesis. *Cross-Cultural Research, 35,* 3-22.

Shaditalab, J. (2005). Iran women: Rising expectations. *Critique: Critical Middle Eastern Studies, 14,* 35-55.

Sharma, A. (2003). Male involvement in reproductive health: Women's perspective. *The Journal of Family Welfare, 49*(1), 1-9.

Sharman, M. (1979). *Kenya's people: The people of the plains.* London: Evans Brothers.

Shavarini, M. K. (2005). The feminisation of Iranian higher education. *Review of Education, 51,* 329-347.

Shavarini, M. K. (2006). The role of higher education in the life of a young Iranian women. *Women's Studies International Forum, 29,* 42-53.

Shen, C. L., & Ma, Y. C. (1987). Shilun hunyin de "mendang hudui" wenti [Discussion of "well-matched social and economical status" in marriage]. In Y. Liu & S. J. Xue (Eds.), *Zhongguo Hunyin Jiating Yanjiu* (pp. 10-29). Beijing: Shehui Kexue Wenxian Chubanshe.

Sheng, X. W. (1992). Population aging and the traditional pattern of supporting the aged. In *Proceedings of Asia-Pacific Regional Conference on Future Family* (pp. 66-71). Beijing: China Social Science Documentation Publishing House.

Sheykhi, M. T. (2006). The elderly and family change in Asia with a focus in Iran: A sociological assessment. *Journal of Comparative Family Studies, 37,* 583-588.

Shiites. (2001). Available at mb-soft.com/believe/txo/shiites.htm.

Shorter, E. (1971). Illegitimacy, sexual revolution and social change in modern Europe. *Journal of Interdisciplinary History, 2,* 237-272.

Sierra Leone Research. (nd). Available at URL www.nsu.edu/resources/woods/sleone.htm.

Sillah, M.-B. (1994). Islam in Sierra Leone: The Colonial reaction and the emergence of national identity. *Journal of Muslim Minority Affairs, 15,* 121-143.

Simkins, C. (1986). Household composition and structure in South Africa. In S. Burman & P. Reynolds (Eds.), *Growing up in a divided society* (pp. 16-42). Johannesburg: Ravan.

Simon, R. J., & Altstein, H. (2003). *Global perspectives on social issues: Marriage and divorce.* Lanham, MD: Rowman & Littlefield.

Singh, M. (1996). Divorce in a rural north Indian area: Evidence from Himachali villages. *Man in India, 76,* 215-228.

Singh, R., Nath, R., & Nichols, W. C. (Eds.). (2005). Treating Indian families: In India and around the world [Special issue]. *Contemporary Family Therapy, 27*(3).

Sinha, D., & Tripathi, R. C. (2003). Individualism in a collectivist culture: A case of coexistence of opposites. In T. S. Saraswathi (Ed.), *Cross-cultural perspectives in human development: Theory, research and applications* (pp. 192-210). New Delhi: Sage.

Siqwana-Ndulo, N. (1998). Rural African family structure in the Eastern Cape Province, South Africa. *Journal of Comparative Family Studies, 29,* 407-417.

Sirjamski, J. (1964). The institutional approach. In H. T. Christensen (Ed.), *Handbook of marriage and the family* (pp. 33-50). Chicago: Rand McNally.

Sistema Nacional para el Desarrollo Integral de la Familia. (1998). *Una propuesta para continuar el cambio* [A proposal to continue the change]. México D. F.: Author.

Skinner, J. (1999). Review article: Globalization and the age of migration. *The Sociological Review, 64,* 603-608.

Smith, C. (2006). Review of the book *Sacred and secular: Religion and politics worldwide. Journal for the Scientific Study of Religion, 45,* 623-624.

Smith, D. (1993). The standard North American family. *Journal of Family Issues, 14,* 50-65.

Smith, L. M., & Padula, A. (1996). *Sex and revolution. Women in socialist Cuba.* New York: Oxford University Press.

Snell, G. S. (1986). *Nandi customary law.* Nairobi: Kenya Literature Bureau.

Solís, P. (2001). La población en edades avanzadas [The population in advanced ages]. In J. Gómez de León & C. Rabell (Eds.), *La población en México. Tendencias y perspectivas sociodemográficas Hacia el Siglo XXI* (pp. 835-869). México D. F.: Fondo de Cultura Económica/Consejo Nacional de Población.

South African Institute of Race Relations. (1996). *South African survey 1995\6.* Johannesburg: Author.

South African Institute of Race Relations. (1997). *South African survey 1996\7.* Johannesburg: Author.

South African Institute of Race Relations. (1998). *South African survey 1997\8.* Johannesburg: Author.

South African Institute of Race Relations. (1999a, January). *Fast facts* (No 1\99). Braamfontein: Author.

South African Institute of Race Relations. (1999b). *South African survey 1999\2000* (Millennium edn.). Johannesburg: Author.

Spencer-Walters, T. (2006). Creolization and Kriodom: (Re)visioning the "Sierra Leone experiment." In M. Dixon-Fyle & G. Cole (Eds.), *New perspectives on the Sierra Leone Krio* (pp. 223-255). New York: Peter Lang.

Spiegel, A., Watson, V., & Wilkinson, P. (1996). Domestic diversity and fluidity among some African households in Greater Cape Town. *Social Dynamics, 22*(1), 7-30.

Spitzer, L. (1974). *The Creoles of Sierra Leone: Responses to colonialism, 1870-1945*. Madison: University of Wisconsin Press.

Standing Committee of the National People's Congress (2004). *Zhong hua Renmin Gzonghegore Hunyinfa* [Marriage law of the People's Republic of China]. Beijing: Law Press.

State Institute of Statistics. (1995). *The population of Turkey: 1923-1994 demographic structure and development* (Publication No. 1716). Ankara: Author.

State Institute of Statistics. (2001). *Genel Nufus Sayimi 2000* [Census of Population 2000]. Ankara: T. C. Basbakanlik Devlet Istatistik Enstitutusu.

State Statistical Bureau. (1954). *Zhongguo Renko Tongji Nianjian 1954* [Annual reports of Chinese population, 1954]. Beijing: Zhongguo Tongji Chubanshe.

State Statistical Bureau. (1964). *Zhongguo Renko Tongji Nianjian 1964* [Annual reports of Chinese population, 1964]. Beijing: Zhongguo Tongji Chubanshe.

State Statistical Bureau. (1969). *Zhongguo Renko Tongji Nianjian 1969* [Annual reports of Chinese population, 1969]. Beijing: Zhongguo Tongji Chubanshe.

State Statistical Bureau. (1980). *Zhongguo Renko Tongji Nianjian 1980* [Annual reports of Chinese population, 1980]. Beijing: Zhongguo Tongji Chubanshe.

State Statistical Bureau. (1982). *Zhongguo Renko Tongji Nianjian 1982* [Annual reports of Chinese population, 1982]. Beijing: Zhongguo Tongji Chubanshe.

State Statistical Bureau. (1991). *Zhongguo 1990 Nian Renko Pucha 10% chouyang Ziliao* [Data collected from 10% of Chinese Population in 1990]. Beijing: Zhongguo Tongji Chubanshe.

State Statistical Bureau. (2003). *Zhongguo Renko Tongji Nianjian 2003* [Annual reports of Chinese population, 2003]. Beijing: Zhongguo Tongji Chubanshe.

Statham, J., Holtermann, S., & Stone, M. (1996). *Childcare in Wales: The 1996 audit.* Cardiff: Chwarae Teg.

Statistics South Africa. (1999). *The People of South Africa—Population Census 1996.* Pretoria: Author.

Statistisches Bundesamt. (2004a). *Bevölkerung* [Population]. Available at www.destatis.de/basis/d/bevoe/bevoetab1.php.

Statistisches Bundesamt. (2004b). *Einkommensverteilung und Armut* [Income distribution and poverty]. Available at www.destatis.de/download/veroe/2 17.pdf.

Statistiska Centralbyrån. (1968). *Befolkningsförändringar* [Population changes]. Stockholm: Author.

Statistiska Centralbyrån. (1990-1991). *Löner i Sverige* [Salaries in Sweden]. Stockholm: Author.

Statistiska Centralbyrån. (1992). *Folk-och bostadsräkningen 1990* [The 1990 Census]. Stockholm: Author.

Statistiska Centralbyrån. (1995a). *Aborter i Sverige* [Abortions in Sweden]. Stockholm: Author.

Statistiska Centralbyrån. (1995b). *Lönestatistisk årsbok* [Statistical yearbook about salaries]. Stockholm: Author.

Statistiska Centralbyrån. (2000). *Befolkningsstatistik 1998* [Population statistics]. Stockholm: Author.

Statistiska Centralbyrån. (2003). *Befolkningsstatistik 2002* [Population statistics]. Stockholm: Author.

Steinmetz, S. (2004). Parental versus government guided policies: A comparison of youth outcomes in Cuba and the United States. *Marriage and Family Review, 36*(3/4), 201-228.

Stengel, M. (2003). *Obsceno é falar de amor? Relações afetivas entre adolescentes* [Is it obscene to talk about love? Affection relations among teenagers]. Editora da Pontificial Catholic University of Minas Gerais, Belo Horizonte, Brazil.

Stevenson, H. W., Lee, S., & Stigler, J. W. (1986). Mathematics achievement of Chinese, Japanese, and American children. *Science, 231,* 693-699.

Steyn, A. (1995). Urban household structures in the Republic of South Africa. In C. C. Yi (Ed.), *Family formation and dissolution: Perspectives from East and West* (pp. 169-204). Taipei, Taiwan: Sun Yat-Sen Institute for Social Sciences and Philosophy, Academia Sinica.

Stone, L., & James, C. (1995). Dowry, bride-burning, and female power in India. *Women's Studies International Forum, 18,* 125-134.

Stonner L. (1991). *From the houses to the streets: The Cuban women's movement for legal reform 1898-1940.* Durham, NC: Duke University Press.

Suárez, M. A., Reyes, I. R., Casañ, P. P., & Castañeda Marrero, A. V. (nd). *Condition of childhood, adolescence, woman and family in Cuba.* New York: UNICEF, Center for Studies on Woman.

Sullivan, L., Maley, B., & Warby, M. (1997). *State of the nation: Statistical indicators of Australia's well being.* Melbourne: The Centre for Independent Studies.

Suppal, P., & Roopnarine, J. L. (1999). Paternal involvement in child care as a function of maternal employment in nuclear and extended families in India. *Sex Roles, 40,* 731-744.

Sutton, M., Hutson, S., & Thomas, J. (1996). The boys have taken over the playground. In S. Betts (Ed.), *Our daughters' land: Past and present* (pp. 223-240). Cardiff: University of Wales Press.

Tan, E. A. (1997). Economic development and well-being of women. In *Philippine human development report* (pp. 65-85). Philippines: Human Development Network and UN Development Programme.

Tan, L., & Li, J. X. (1997). Xinshiqi Zhongguo de jiating yu renko wenti: "Zhongguo de jiating yu renko wenti" xueshu yantaohui zongshu [Family and population issues in China at the present time period]. *Zhongguo Renko Kexue, 58*(1), 24, 62-64.

Tang, Z. X. (1995). Jianli xinxing de Zhongguo laonianren gongyang tixi [Construction of the new aging support systems in China]. *Jianhai Xuekan, 6,* 42-47.

Tang, Z. X., & Yie, N. K. (1994). Zhongguo yanglao fangshi bianqian jiqi duice [The changes of senior supports of China and the countermoves]. *Xuehai, 6,* 46-49.

Tapales, P. D. (1997). Women and governance: An update. In *Philippine human development report* (pp. 145-152). Philippines: Human Development Network and UN Development Programme.

Tapper, R. (1979). *Pasture and politics*. London: Academic.

Tekeli, S. (1995). *Women in modern Turkish society: A reader.* London: Zed Books.

Terwey, M. (1993). Sind Kirche und Religion auf der Verliererstrasse? Vergleichende Analysen mit ALLBUS- und ISSP-Daten [Are church and religion the losers? Comparative analyses with data from ALLBUS and ISSP]. In *ZA-Information No. 32* (pp. 95-112). Köln: Zentralarchiv für empirische Sozialforschung an der Universität zu Köln.

Tesliuc, E., Pop, L., & Panduru, F. (2003). Poverty in Romania: Profiles and trends during 1995-2002. In World Bank (Ed.), *Romania: Report on poverty, volume 2* (Report no. 26169-R0) (pp. 5-62). Bucharest: World Bank.

Theory Department of Chinese Employment Committee. (1998, January). Redian zhong de zhongdian—Qiye xiagang zhigong peixun qingkuang de diaoyan baogao [The key point in hot issues—The investigate report of unemployment training]. *ZhongGuo PeiXun, 58,* 8-11.

Thomas, T. N. (1995). Acculturative stress in the adjustment of immigrant families. *Journal of Social Distress and the Homeless, 42,* 131-142.

Thornton, A., & Fricke, T. (1987). Social change and the family: Comparative perspectives from the West, China, and South Asia. *Sociological Forum, 2,* 746-779.

Tiefenthaler, J. (1994). A multisector model of female labor force participation: Empirical evidence from Cebu Island, Philippines. *Economic Development and Cultural Change, 42,* 719-742.

Tinio, V. L. (1994). *A preliminary study of civil annulment in Metro Manila.* Seminar paper submitted as requirement in Sociology 213, Department of Sociology, University of the Philippines, Quezon City.

Tiwari, V. K., & Kumar, A. (2004). Premarital sexuality and unmet need of contraception among youth—Evidence from two cities of India. *The Journal of Family Welfare, 50*(2), 62-72.

Toktas, S. (1997). *Gender awareness: A study of women teachers and academicians who are graduates of girls' institutes 1960-1970.* Unpublished master's thesis, Middle East Technical University, Ankara.

Tornstam, L. (1994). *Åldrandets socialpsykologi* [The social psychology of aging]. Stockholm: Rabén Prisma.

Trigo, M. H. B. (1989). Amor e casamento no século XX [Love and marriage in the 20th century]. In M. A. DíIncao (Ed.), *Amor e família no Brasil* (pp. 88-94). São Paulo: Contexto.

Troisi, J. (2003, September). *The elderly and the changing role of the family.* Paper for the International Short Training Program in Demographic Aspects of Population Ageing and Its Implications for Socio-economic Development Policies and Plans, sponsored by the International Institute on Ageing, United Nations—Malta in collaboration with United Nations Population Fund, Malta and the University of Malta.

Trost, J. (in press). The Swedish marriage boom. *Journal of Family History.*

Trost, J. (1979). *Unmarried cohabitation.* Västerås: International Library.

Trost, J. (1981). Cohabitation in the Nordic countries: From deviant phenomenon to social institution. *Alternative Lifestyles, 4,* 401-427.

Trost, J. (1983). Mäns åsikter om ledighet från arbetet [Men's views on leave of absence]. *Family Reports, 3,* 1-20.

Trost, J. (1990). Fertility and the process of decision making. *Family Reports, 16,* 1-55.

Trost, J. (1993). *Familjen i Sverige* [Family in Sweden]. Stockholm: Liber.

Trost, J. (1995). Ehen und andere dyadische Beziehungen [Marriage and other dyadic relationships]. In B. Nauck & C. Onnen-Isemann (Eds.), *Familie im Brennpunkt von Wissenschaft und Forschung* (pp. 343-356). Berlin: Luchterhand.

Tuirán, R. (1993). Estructura familiar: Continuidad y cambio [Family structure: Continuity and change]. *Demos, 6,* 20-22.

Tuirán, R. (1999). Desafíos del envejecimiento demográfico en México [Challenges of demographic aging in Mexico]. In Comisión de Población y Desarrollo, Consejo Nacional de Población & Cámara de Diputados (Ed.), *Envejecimiento demográfico de México: Retos y perspectivas* (pp. 15-22). México D. F.: Comisión de Población y Desarrollo/Consejo Nacional de Población/Cámara de Diputados.

Tuirán, R. (2002). Migración, remesas y desarrollo [Migration, remmittances and development]. In Consejo Nacional de Población (Ed.), *La situación demográfica de México 2002* (pp. 77-87). México D. F.: Consejo Nacional de Población.

Tully, J. J. (1994). The place of Islamic law in Sierra Leone. *The Muslim World, 84,* 300-316.

Turkish demographic and health survey 1998. (1999). Ankara: Hacettepe University Institute of Population Studies.

Türkiye'de Nufus ve Saglik Arastirmasi, 2003, on rapor [Turkish demographic and health survey, preliminary results]. (2004). Ankara: Hacettepe University Institute of Population Studies.

Tyler, S. A. (1986). *India: An anthropological perspective.* Prospect Heights, IL: Waveland.

UN High Commissioner for Refugees. (2004a, June 7). *A rough but happy journey home for Sierra Leonean refugees.* Available at www.reliefweb.int/w/rwb.nsf/ByCountry/Sierra+Leone.

UN High Commissioner for Refugees. (2004b, July 26). *A Sierra Leonean family comes home.* Available at www.reliefweb.int/w/rwb.nsf/ByCountry/Sierra+Leone.

UN High Commissioner for Refugees. (2004c, July 21). *Last convoys leave for Sierra Leone as assisted repatriation ends.* Available at www.reliefweb.int/w/rwb.nsf/ByCountry/Sierra+Leone.

UNICEF. (nd). *At a glance: Romania.* Available at www.unicef.org/infobycountry/romania_statistics.html#5.

UNICEF. (1993). *Central and Eastern Europe in transition. Public policy and social conditions* (Regional Monitoring Report, 1). Florence: ICDC.

UNICEF. (1996a). *Progress of nations.* Available at www.unicef.org/pon96/atats36.htm.

UNICEF. (1996b). *The state of the world's children 1996.* Available at www.unicef.org/sowc96.

UNICEF. (1998). *Situation of AIDS orphans and vulnerable children in Kenya.* Nairobi: Author.

UNICEF. (2000a). *Progress of nations.* New York: United Nations Children Fund.

UNICEF. (2000b). *UNICEF Executive Director targets violence against women.* Available at www.unicef.org/newsline/00pr17.htm.

UNICEF. (2001). *Situation of AIDS orphans and vulnerable children in Kenya.* Nairobi: Author.

UNICEF. (2005). *At a glace: Cuba.* Available at www.unicef.org/infobycountry/cuba_statistics.html.

United Nations. (2000). *World marriage patterns.* New York: United Nations, Population Division, Department of Economic and Social Affairs.

United Nations. (2002). *Abortion policies: A global review.* New York: United Nations, Population Division, Department of Economic and Social Affairs. Available at www.un.org/esa/population/publications/abortion.

United Nations. (2003). *Partnership and reproductive behaviour in low-fertility countries.* New York: United Nations, Population Division, Department of Economic and Social Affairs. Available at www.un.org/esa/population/publications/publications.htm.

United Nations. (2005a, August 8). *International migration and development.* Available at www.un.org/esa/population/publications/ittmigreport/Int_Migration_Report.pdf.

United Nations. (2005b). *Population and HIV/AIDS 2005.* New York: United Nations, Department of Economic and Social Affairs, Population Division. Available at www.un.org/esa/population/publications/POP_HIVAIDS2005/HIV_AIDS chart_2005.pdf.

United Nations. (2005c). *Population challenges and development goals.* New York: United Nations, Department of Economic and Social Affairs, Population Division. Available at www.un.org/esa/population/publications/pop_challenges/Population_Challenges.pdf.

United Nations. (2005d, May 16). *Responses to HIV/AIDS epidemic remain insufficient* (press release). New York: United Nations, Department of Economic and Social Affairs, Population Division. Available at www.un.org/esa/population/publications/POP_HIVAIDS2005/Press_English.pdf.

United Nations. (2005e). *World population prospects: The 2004 revision.* New York: United Nations, Department of Economic and Social Affairs, Population Division. Available at URL www.un.org/esa/population/publications/WPP2004/2004Highlights_finalrevised.pdf.

United Nations Development Programme. (1996a). *Human development under transition 1996* (Summaries of national human development reports 1995: Europe and CIS (Romania)). Available at www.undp.org/rbes/nhdr/1996/summary/romania.htm.

United Nations Development Programme. (1996b). *Human settlements and eradication of poverty* (Human development report 1996). New York: Author.

United Nations Development Programme. (1996c). *The importance of habitat* (Romanian human development report 1996). Bucharest: Editura Expert.

United Nations Development Programme. (1998). *The role of the state* (National human development report 1998). Bucharest: Editura Expert.

United Nations Development Programme. (1999). *National policy building and advocacy for sustainable human development.* New York: Author.

United Nations Development Programme. (2000). *Transformation for human development* (South Africa human development report 2000). Available at hdr .undp.org/reports/detail_reports.cfm?view=576.

United Nations Development Programme. (2001). *Making new technologies work for human development* (Human development report 2001). Available at www .undp.org/hdr2001/.

United Nations Development Programme. (2002). *Deepening democracy in a fragmented world* (Human development report 2002). Available at hdr.undp.org/ reports/global/2002/en/.

United Nations Development Programme. (2003). *Millennium development goals: A compact among nations to end human poverty* (Human development report 2003) [Electronic version]. New York: Oxford University Press.

United Nations Development Programme. (2004). *Cultural liberty in today's world* (Human development report 2004). Available at hdr.undp.org/2004.

United Nations Development Programme. (2005). *International cooperation at a crossroads: Aid, trade and security in an unequal world* (Human development report 2005) [Electronic version]. New York: Author.

United Nations Development Programme. (2006). *Beyond scarcity: Power, poverty and the global water crisis* (Human development report 2006) [Electronic version]. New York: Author.

United Nations Development Programme Sierra Leone. (nd). *Challenges ahead.* Available at www.undpsalone.org.

United Nations Office for the Coordination of Humanitarian Affairs. (nd). Available at www.reliefweb.int/w/rwb.nsf/ByCountry/Sierra+Leone?OpenDocument&Start Key=Sierra+Leone&Expandview.

United Nations Population Division. (2002). *Abortion policies: A global review.* New York: United Nations Population Division, Department of Economic and Social Affairs.

United Nations Population Fund. (2001). *Footprints and milestones: Population and environmental change* (The state of the world population 2001). New York: Author.

Unsafe abortion. (2001). Available at www.mariestopes.org.uk/unsafe_abortion. html.

USAID. (2000). *Romanian country profile.* Available at www.usaid.gov/countries/ ro/rom.htm.

USAID Sierra Leone. (2004a, June 10). *The importance of keeping the peace in Kailahun District.* Available at www.usaid.gov/gn/sierraleone/sl_democracy/ news/040608_radio_moa/keepingthepeace.htm.

USAID Sierra Leone. (2004b). *The democracy and good governance strategic objective.* Available at www.usaid.gov/gn/sierraleone/sl_democracy/news/030613_ condomlaunch/index.htm.

USAID Sierra Leone. (2004c). *The reconstruction and reintegration strategic objective.* Available at www.usaid.gov/gn/sierraleone/sl_reintegration/index.htm.

Valentini van der Berg, S. (1998). Ageing, public finance and social security in South Africa. *Southern African Journal of Gerontology, 7*(1), 3-9.

Van de Kaa, D. (1987). Europe's second demographic transition. *Population Bulletin, 42*(1), 1-57.

Van der Waal, C. S. (1996). Rural children and residential instability in the Northern Province of South Africa. *Social Dynamics, 22*(1), 31-54.

Van Zyl Slabbert, F., Malan, C., Marais, H., Olivier, J., & Riordan, R. (Eds.). (1994). *Youth in the new South Africa: Towards policy formulation* (Main Report of the Co-operative Research Programme: South African Youth). Pretoria: Human Sciences Research Council.

Vancio, J. A. (1980). Realities of marriage of urban Filipino women. *Philippine Studies, 28,* 5-20.

Ventura, E. R., & Cabigon, J. V. (2004). Sex-related views. In C. M. Raymundo & G. T. Cruz (Eds.), *Youth, sex, and risk behaviors in the Philippines* (pp. 121-132). Quezon City: Demographic Research and Development Foundation Inc. and University of the Philippines Population Institute.

Vera, A. (2002). Procesos familiares de Cuba en la historiografía del siglo XX [Family processes in Cuba in 20th Century historiography]. In C. Jiménez, A. Irigoyen López, E. de Mesquita Samara, & T. Lozano Armendares (Eds.), *Sin distancias. Familias y tendencias historiográficas en el siglo 20* (pp. 165-190). Murcia: Universidad de Murcia-Universidad Externado de Colombia.

Vera, A. (2004a). La familia cubana en perspectiva [View of the Cuban family]. In P. Rodríguez (Ed.), *La familia en Iberoamérica 1550-1980* (pp. 126-165). Bogotá: Universidad Externado de Colombia/Convenio Andrés Bello.

Vera, A. (2004b, September). *¿Modelos de familia? Reflexiones acerca de voluntad y factibilidad* [Family models? Reflections on will and feasibility]. Paper presented at the International Workshop, Diálogo Internacional con el Seminario Permanente de Familia, Centro de Investigación y Desarrollo de la Cultura Cubana Juan Marinello.

Vergin, N. (1985). Social change and the family in Turkey. *Current Anthropology, 26,* 571-574.

Verma, S., & Saraswathi, T. S. (2002). Adolescence in India: Street urchins or Silicon Valley millionaires. In R. B. Brown, R. W. Larson, & T. S. Saraswathi (Eds.), *The world's youth: Adolescence in eight regions of the globe* (pp. 105-140). Cambridge: Cambridge University Press.

Vicente, C. M. (1994). O direito à convivência familiar e comunitária: Uma política de manutenção do vínculo [The right to community and family conviviality: A policy for maintaining bonds]. In S. M. Kaloustian (Ed.), *Família Brasileira— A base de tudo* (pp. 47-59). São Paulo: Cortez Publisher; Brasília; United Nations Children's Fund.

Viljoen, S. (1994). *The strengths and weaknesses in the family life of Black South Africans.* Pretoria: Co-operative Programme on Marriage and Family Life, Human Sciences Research Council.

Villaméa, L., & Quintanilha, C. (1997, July 2). Velhos de rua [Elders of the street] *Revista Isto É, 82.*

Vinat, R. (2001). *Las cubanas en la posguerra (1898-1902)/Acercamiento a la reconstrucción de una etapa olvidada/* [Cuban women in the postwar period (1898-1902)/An approach to the reconstruction of forgotten times]. Havana: Editora Política.

Vindhya, U. (2003). Private crimes and public sanction: Violence against women in the family. In M. Pernau, I. Ahmad, & H. Reifeld (Eds.), *Family and gender: Changing values in Germany and India* (pp. 322-348). New Delhi: Sage.

Visaria, L. (2005). *Sex selection abortion in India: Empirical evidence from Gujarat and Haryana States.* Available at iussp2005.princeton.edu/download.aspx ?submissionId=51652.

Vitale, M. A. F. (1995). Socialização e família: uma análise intergeneracional [Family and socialization: An analysis among generations]. In M do C. B. Carvalho (Ed.), *A família contemporânea em debate* (pp. 89-96). São Paulo: Cortez.

Wang, A. (1989). *DuShengZiNu JiaoYu XinLiXue* [Educational psychology of the only child]. Beijing: Guangming Ribao Press.

Wang, L. (1993). *Determinants of fertility transition: A cross-national analysis of China and Japan.* Unpublished master's thesis, Miami University, Oxford, OH.

Wang, L. (2003, August 19). *Zhonghua Renmin Gongheguo Hunyin Fa* (2001) [Marriage Law of P. R. China (2001)]. Available at http://www.lhabc.com/ wz/list.asp?id=558.

Wang, S. B. (1992). The influence of the change of marital ideas upon rural marriage and the family. In *Proceedings of Asia-Pacific Regional Conference on Future Family* (pp. 79-84). Beijing: China Social Science Documentation Publishing House.

Wang, S. Y. (1996). Qiantan kongzhi renko zengzhang yu laonian shehui baozhang [Brief discussion on controlling the population increase and senior social supports]. *Fujian Renko, 3,* 28-30.

Wang, Y. W. (1996). Zhongguo laonianfuniu de shehuijiazhi yu shehuidiwei jianxi [A brief analysis on aging women's social value and social status in China]. *Renko Yanjiu, 20*(1), 62-65.

Wangmann, J. (1995). *Towards integration and quality assurance in children's services.* Melbourne: Australian Institute of Family Studies.

Warde, A., & Hetherington, K. (1993). A changing domestic division of labour? *Work, Employment and Society, 7*(1), 23-45.

Weber, C. (1996). Erziehungsbedingungen im frühen Kindesalter in Kinderskrippen vor und nach der Wende [Conditions of rearing young children in child-care centers before and after reunification]. In G. Trommsdorff (Ed.), *Sozialisation und Entwicklung von Kindern vor und nach der Vereinigung* (pp. 173-242). Opladen: Leske und Budrich.

Weeks, H. (1996). *Population: An introduction to concepts and issues.* New York: Wadsworth.

Wei, J. S. (1989). Zhongguo renko kongzhi shinian pinggu ji jinhu de duicei [Evaluation of the ten years population control in China and the future coping strategies]. *Zhongguo Renko Kexue, 12*(3), 8-18.

Wei, S. (554, republished in 1974). *Wei Shu—Wang Baoxing Zhuan* [Wei book—About Wang Baoxing]. Beijing: Zhonghua Shuju.

Wei, Z. L. (1992). The Chinese family as the main base for taking care of the elderly. In *Proceedings of Asia-Pacific Regional Conference on Future Family* (pp. 91-100). Beijing: China Social Science Documentation Publishing House.

Weiner, M. (1995). *The global migration crisis: Challenge to states and to human rights.* New York: Harper Collins.

Weiskopf-Bock, S. (1985). The working Iranian mother. In A. Fathi (Ed.), *Women and the family in Iran* (pp. 187-194). Leiden, Netherlands: E. J. Brill.

Welsh Assembly Government. (2007a). *Children first.* Available at new.wales. gov.uk/topics/childrenyoungpeople/childrenfirst/?lang=en.

Welsh Assembly Government. (2007b). *Education and skills.* Available at URL new.wales.gov.uk/topics/educationandskills/?lang=en.

Welsh Assembly Government. (2007c). *Wales at work.* Available at new.wales .gov.uk/campaigns/walesatwork/?lang=en.

Welsh Office. (1993). *Welsh social trends No. 9.* Cardiff: Her Majesty's Stationary Office.

Welsh Office. (1999). *Statistical focus on Wales.* Cardiff: Her Majesty's Stationery Office.

Welter-Enderlin, R. (1992). *Paare—Leidenschaft und lange Weile* [Couples—Passion and boredom]. München: Piper.

Wenger, G. C. (1994). Old women in rural Wales: Variations in adaptation. In J. Aaron, T. Rees, S. Betts, & M. Vincentelli (Eds.), *Our sisters' land: The changing identities of women in Wales* (pp. 61-85). Cardiff: University of Wales Press.

Wenger, G. C., & Robinson, C. (1996, April). *Community care for older people in Wales.* Paper presented to Institute of Welsh Affairs Conference, Cardiff.

Weston, R. (1997). Family wellbeing. In D. A. de Vaus & I. Wolcott (Eds.), *Australian family profiles: Social and demographic patterns* (pp. 131-134). Melbourne: Australian Institute of Family Studies.

Weston, R., & Funder, K. (1993). There is more to life than economics. In K. Funder, M. Harrison, & R. Weston (Eds.), *Settling down: Pathways of parents after divorce* (pp. 210-234). Melbourne: Australian Institute of Family Studies.

Wheelock, J. (1990). *Husbands at home.* London: Routledge.

Wilson, S. M., & Ngige, L. W. (2005). Marriages and families in Sub-Saharan Africa. In B. B. Ingoldsby & S. D. Smith (Eds.), *Families in global and multicultural perspective* (2nd ed.) (pp. 247-273). Thousand Oaks, CA: Sage.

Wilson, S. M., Ngige, L. W., & Trollinger, L. J. (2003). Connecting generations: Kamba and Maasai paths to marriage in Kenya. In R. R. Hamon & B. B. Ingoldsby (Eds.), *Mate selection across cultures* (pp. 95-118). Thousand Oaks, CA: Sage.

Wolcott, I. (1997). Work and family. In D. A. de Vaus & I. Wolcott (Eds.), *Australian family profiles: Social and demographic patterns* (pp. 81-90). Melbourne: Australian Institute of Family Studies.

Wolcott, I., & Glezer, H. (1995). *Work and family life: Achieving integration.* Melbourne: Australian Institute of Family Studies.

Wolcott, I., & Hughes, J. (1999). *Towards understanding the reasons for divorce.* Melbourne: Australian Institute of Family Studies.

Wolpert, S. (1989). *A new history of India* (3rd ed.). New York: Oxford University Press.

Women are back in business in Sierra Leone. (2003, June). Available at www .christian-aid.org.uk/world/where/wca/partners/0307ard.htm.

Wong, L. L. (1997). Globalization and transnational migration: A study of recent Chinese capitalist migration from the Asian Pacific to Canada. *International Sociology, 123,* 329-351.

Wong, R. (1999). Transferencias intrafamiliares e intergeneracionales en México [Intrafamiliar and intergenerational transfers in Mexico]. In Comisión de Población y Desarrollo, Consejo Nacional de Población & Cámara de Diputados (Ed.), *Envejecimiento demográfico de México: Retos y perspectivas* (pp. 145-170). México D. F.: Comisión de Población y Desarrollo/Consejo Nacional de Población/ Cámara de Diputados.

Woortmann, K. (1984). A família trabalhadora [The working family]. *Ciências sociais hoje 5,* 69-87.

World Bank. (2002). *GenderStats, Summary gender profile.* Available at Devdata. worldbank.org/genderRpt.asp?rpt=profile&cty=CUB,Cuba&hm=home.

World Bank. (2003). *Romania: Poverty assessment, volume 1: Main report* (Report no. 26169-R0). Bucharest: Author.

World Bank. (2004). *Number of marriages by age group and by previous marital status of the bride and groom, Philippines: 2000.* Available at devdata.world bank.org.

The world factbook. (1997). Available at odci.gov/cia/publications/factbook/.

The world factbook. (2000). Available at www.umsl.edu/services/govdocs/wofact 2000/index.html.

The world factbook. (2004). Available at www.umsl.edu/services/govdocs/wofact 2004/index.html.

The world factbook. (2005). Available at www.umsl.edu/services/govdocs/wofact 2005/index.html.

The world factbook. (2006). Available at www.cia.gov/cia/publications/factbook/ index.html.

The world factbook. (2007). Available at www.cia.gov/cia/publications/factbook/ index.html.

Worldpress.com. (2007, January). *Armed conflict around the world.* Available at www.worldpress.org/signup.cfm?promoType=wallmap.

Wu, B. X. (1987). Chengshi hunyin de jichu [Foundations of marriage in cities]. In Y. Liu & S. J. Xue (Eds.), *Zhongguo Hunyin Jiating Yanjiu* (pp. 1-9). Beijing: Shehui Kexue Wenxian Chubanshe.

Wu, Y. X. (2002, April 27). *Zhounian Pandian, Xin Hunyin Fa* [Annual review of the New Marriage Laws]. Yanzhao Dushi Bao. Available at http://www.yzdsb .com.cn/20020427/ca116438.htm.

Wuchengshi Hunyin yu Jiating Yanjiu Ketizu [Five City Marriage and Family Research Project Group—FCMFRPG]. (1985). *Zhongguo Chengshi Jiating* [Chinese urban families]. Jinan: Shandong Renmin Chubanshe.

Wulf, D. (2005). *Panorama general del aborto clandestino en América Latina* [An overview of clandestine abortion in Latin America]. Available at www .guttmacher.org/pubs/ib12.html.

Wyse, A. (1989). *The Krio of Sierra Leone: An interpretive history.* London: C. Hurst.

Xinhuawang. (2004, May 7). *2003 nian Woguo Jiehun Lihunlv Junyou Zengjia (Mingzhengbu)* [Increase in both marriage and divorce rates in China in year 2003 (Ministry of Civil Affairs)]. Available at http://news.xinhuanet.com/ newscenter/2004-05/07/content_1455267.htm.

Xiong, B. J., & Dong, Z. Y. (1996). Laolian shehui baozhang de kunjing yu chulu [Problems of senior social supports and the solutions]. *Jingjixue Dongtai, 7,* 42-44.

Xu, A. Q. (1992). The changes of women's role and status, and transformation of family. *Proceedings of Asia-Pacific Regional Conference on Future Family* (pp. 101-107). Beijing: China Social Science Documentation Publishing House.

Xu, Z., Wan, C., Mussen, P., Shen, J., Li, C., & Cao, Z. (1991). Family socialization and children's behavior and personality development in China. *The Journal of Genetic Psychology, 152,* 239-253.

Xu, Z., Wang, A., Wu, N., & Min, R. (1990). Guanyu 3-6 Sui Youer Kongzhi Ziji Xingwei Nengli de Yanjiu [Studies on self-control ability among 3 to 6 years old children]. In F. Liu (Ed.), *XInli Fazhan De Jinqi Yanjiu* (pp. 277-292). Beijing: Beijing Normal Institute Press.

Xue, S. Z. (1992). Changes of women's status and role and trends of family development in China. In *Proceedings of Asia-Pacific Regional Conference on Future Family* (pp. 108-114). Beijing: China Social Science Documentation Publishing House.

Yalçın-Heckman, L. (1993). Asiretli Kadın: Göçer ve Yarıgöçer Toplumlarda Cinsiyet Rolleri ve Kadın Stratejileri [Woman in tribe: The gender roles and strategies of women in nomadic and semi-nomadic societies]. In S. Tekeli (Ed.), *1980'ler Türkiye'sinde Kadin Bakis A çysindan Kadinlar* (pp. 277-290). Istanbul: Iletisim Yayynlary.

Yalçın-Heckman, L. (1995). Gender roles and female strategies among the nomadic and semi-nomadic Kurdish tribes of Turkey. In S. Tekeli (Ed.), *Women in modern Turkish society: A reader* (pp. 219-234). London: Zed Books.

Yang, F. (1997, December). Xiagang gongren wenti de zhengjie zai nali [Where is the key problem of the unemployment?]. *Zhongguo Peixun, 57,* 58.

Yang, X. Z. (1993). Traditional Mosuo child-bearing values. *Chinese Sociology and Anthropology, 25*(4), 39-46.

Yang, Z. C. (1997). Laolian shehui baozhang yu jiating yanglao cengci xing fenxi [The administrative analysis of the senior social supports and family supports]. *Laoling Wenti Yanjiu, 8,* 8-14.

Yewlett, H. (1996). Marriage, family and career aspirations of adolescent girls. In S. Betts (Ed.), *Our daughters' land: Past and present* (pp. 241-258). Cardiff: University of Wales Press.

Yi, C. C. (Ed.). (1995). *Family formation and dissolution: Perspectives from East and West.* Taipei: Sun Yat-Sen Institute for Social Sciences and Philosophy, Academia Sinica.

Yie, N. Z. (1993). Lun woguo xiaokang shehui de laonian baozhang tixi [Discussion of the aging support system of our country]. *Shehui Kexue Zhangxian, 1,* 138-142.

Yorburg, B. (2002). *Family realities: A global view.* Upper Saddle River, NJ: Prentice Hall.

Yuan, L., & Mitchell, S. (2000). Land of the walking marriage. *Natural History, 109*(9), 58-64.

Yue, Q. P. (1994). Jindai hunyin jiating de bian qian [The changes of the modern marriage and family]. *Wenshi Zhishi, 5,* 18-24.

Yuksel, S. (1995). A comparison of violent and non-violent families. In S. Tekeli (Ed.), *Women in modern Turkish society: A reader* (pp. 275-287). London: Zed Books.

Zahedi, A. (2006). State ideology and the status of Iranian war widows. *International Feminist Journal of Politics, 8,* 267-286.

Zamfir, C. (1995a). Politica sociala in Romania in tranzitie [The social policy in Romania during the transition]. In E. Zamfir & C. Zamfir (Eds.), *Politici sociale* (pp. 414-438). Bucharest: Editura Alternative.

Zamfir, C. (1995b). Politica de Protectie Sociala [Social protection policy]. *Cercetari Sociale, 1,* 156-172.

Zamfir, C. (coord.). (1997). *Pentru o societate centrata pe copil* [For a society centered on the child]. Bucharest: Editura Alternative.

Zamfir, E. (1995). Politica de protectie a copilului in Romania [Child protection policy in Romania]. In E. Zamfir & C. Zamfir (Eds.), *Politici sociale* (pp. 200-244). Bucharest: Editura Alternative.

Zamfir, E., & Zamfir, C. (Eds.). (1993). *Tiganii intre ignorare si ingrijorare* [Gypsies between ignorance and concern]. Bucharest: Editura Alternative.

Zavala, M. E. (2001). La transición de la fecundidad en México [Fertility transition in Mexico]. In J. Gómez de León & C. Rabell (Coords.), *La Población de México. Tendencias y perspectivas sociodemográficas hacia el siglo XXI* (pp. 147-167). México D. F.: Sociedad Mexicana de Demografía/Fondo de Cultura Económica.

Zeitlin, M. F., Megawangi, R., Kramer, E. M., Colletta, N. D., Babatunde, E. D., & Garman, D. (1995). *Strengthening the family—Implications for international development.* Tokyo: United Nations University Press.

Zeng, Y. (1995). *Zhongguo Bashiniandai Lihun Yanjiu.* [Study of divorce in China in the 1980s]. Beijing: Beijing Daxue Chubanshe.

Zeng, Y., Gu, B. C., Tu, P., Li, B. H., & Li, Y. P. (1993). Woguo jinnianlai chusheng xingbiebi shenggao yuanyin jiqi houguo fenxi [Analysis of the reasons and the consequences of the increase in the sex ratio in our country in recent years]. *Renko yu Jingji, 76*(1), 3-15.

Zhang, C. Z. (1997). Jihua shengyu dui hunyin jiating de yingxiang [The impacts of birth control on marriage and family]. *Renko Zhanxian, 2,* 24-26.

Zhang, D. Q. (1993). *Shanbin Zhongde Hunyin yu Jiating* [Marriage and family in change]. Lanzhou, Gansu: Lanzhou Daxue Chubanshe.

Zhang, D. Q. (1995). Shehui gaige yu jiating [Reform of the society and family]. *Lanzhou Xuekan, 1,* 41-43.

Zhang, M. J. (1995). Zhongwai jiating yanglao fangshi bijiao [Comparisons of the patterns of the family aging supports between our country and foreign countries]. *Shehui Xue, 1,* 36-41.

Zhang, P. (1992). The sex ratio imbalance and its impact on mate nuptiality in China. In *Proceedings of Asia-Pacific Regional Conference on Future Family* (pp. 125-129). Beijing: China Social Science Documentation Publishing House.

Zhang, Z. G. (1994). Zhongguo Shengyu xiajiang jiqi hongguan jingji houguo yanjiu [Study of the birth rates decrease and its macro social and economic consequences in China]. *Renko Yianjiu, 18*(5), 11-20.

Zhao, C. (1995). *Matrilineal social structure of Yongning Naxi (Mosuo) in China.* Unpublished manuscript, University of Nebraska-Lincoln.

Zheng, F., & Wang, Z. (2003, November 25). *Ruoshi Qunti Chengwei Beijing Lianghui Remen Cihui* [Minority group became hot issue for two conferences in Beijing]. Available at http://www.zfr.scnu.edu.cn/zm/zz/15.htm.

Zhong, W. X. (1974). *Wei shu* [Wei book]. Beijing: Zhonghua Shuju.

Ziehl, S. C. (1994a). Social class and household structure. *South African Journal of Sociology, 24*(5), 25-34.

Ziehl, S. C. (1994b). Single parent families—focus on men. In T. Sono (Ed.), *African family and marriage under stress* (pp. 33-53). Pretoria: Centre for Development Analysis.

Ziehl, S. C. (1995). Affirmative action—living with contradictions. *Comment, 19*(Spring), 11-19. Grahamstown: Rhodes University, Philosophy Department.

Ziehl, S. C. (1997a). *Family diversity—a South African perspective focusing on Whites in Grahamstown.* Unpublished doctoral thesis, Rhodes University, Grahamstown, South Africa.

Ziehl, S. C. (1997b). Law, family ideology and multiculturalism in South Africa. *African Sociological Review, 1*(2), 41-59.

Ziehl, S. C. (1999, July). *Marriage—A dying institution? Evidence from the 1996 census.* Paper presented at the annual conference of the Demographic Society of South Africa, Saldanha Bay, South Africa.

Zoeteman, K. (2000). Rating the sustainability of nations. *Ecosystem Health, 6,* 237-245.

Zuñiga, E., & Gomes, C. (2002). Pobreza, curso de vida y envejecimiento poblacional en México [Poverty, life course and population aging in Mexico]. In Consejo Nacional de Población (Ed.), *La situación demográfica en México 2002* (pp. 141-153). México D. F.: Consejo Nacional de Población.

Index